Supervision

Key Link to Productivity

Tenth Edition

Supervision

Key Link to Productivity

Tenth Edition

Leslie W. Rue

Professor Emeritus of Management
Robinson College of Business
Georgia State University

Lloyd L. Byars

Professor Emeritus of Management
College of Management
Georgia Institute of Technology

McGraw-Hill Irwin

McGraw-Hill
Irwin

SUPERVISION: KEY LINK TO PRODUCTIVITY

Published by McGraw-Hill/Irwin, a business unit of The McGraw-Hill Companies, Inc., 1221 Avenue of the Americas, New York, NY, 10020. Copyright © 2010, 2007, 2004, 2001, 1999, 1996, 1993, 1990, 1986, 1981 by The McGraw-Hill Companies, Inc. All rights reserved. No part of this publication may be reproduced or distributed in any form or by any means, or stored in a database or retrieval system, without the prior written consent of The McGraw-Hill Companies, Inc., including, but not limited to, in any network or other electronic storage or transmission, or broadcast for distance learning.

Some ancillaries, including electronic and print components, may not be available to customers outside the United States.

This book is printed on acid-free paper.

1 2 3 4 5 6 7 8 9 0 DOW/DOW 0 9

ISBN   978-0-07-338137-4
MHID   0-07-338137-3

Vice president and editor-in-chief: *Brent Gordon*
Publisher: *Paul Ducham*
Director of development: *Ann Torbert*
Managing development editor: *Laura Hurst Spell*
Editorial assistant: *Jane Beck*
Vice president and director of marketing: *Robin J. Zwettler*
Associate marketing manager: *Jaime Halteman*
Vice president of editing, design and production: *Sesha Bolisetty*
Project manager: *Dana M. Pauley*
Lead production supervisor: *Carol A. Bielski*
Design coordinator: *Joanne Mennemeier*
Media project manager: *Suresh Babu, Hurix Systems Pvt. Ltd.*
Cover design: *Joanne Mennemeier*
Typeface: *10/12 Times New Roman*
Compositor: *Aptara®, Inc.*
Printer: *R. R. Donnelley*

Library of Congress Cataloging-in-Publication Data

Rue, Leslie W.
    Supervision : key link to productivity / Leslie W. Rue, Lloyd L. Byars.—10th ed.
        p. cm.
    Includes index.
    ISBN-13: 978-0-07-338137-4 (alk. paper)
    ISBN-10: 0-07-338137-3 (alk. paper)
    1. Supervision of employees. I. Byars, Lloyd L. II. Title.
HF5549.12.R83 2010
658.3'02—dc22   2009034500

To our parents who are no longer with us:
Harriet W. Rue, William H. Rue, and Henry L. Byars

Brief Contents

Contents

Chapter 19
Improving Productivity 365

Chapter 20
Providing a Safe and Healthy Work
Environment 389

Preface

We are both very happy that this book continues to be successful and is going into its tenth edition. Since the beginning, we have received positive feedback about the clear writing style and the practical orientation of the text. Many professors tell us that their students—many of whom are already practicing supervisors—often keep *Supervision* as a handbook and reference.

Another enduring feature of *Supervision* is its emphasis on productivity. Since 1981, when the first edition was published, productivity has remained a major concern of today's managers and government leaders. Time, experience, and research have all shown that the supervisor can have a significant impact on an organization's productivity. This edition continues to emphasize all aspects of a supervisor's impact on productivity.

Since change confronts today's supervisors on an almost daily basis, we have continued to place emphasis on the supervisor's role in managing and dealing with change and innovation, as well as providing updated coverage of entrepreneurship and the challenges facing small businesses. We have also further enhanced the material dealing with work groups and teams and updated the coverage of ethical decision making and the legal environment, including the effects of the Sarbanes-Oxley Act.

As with earlier editions, we have emphasized real-world applications seen from the supervisor's viewpoint by using numerous and varied examples throughout the text and in the end-of-chapter materials. Each chapter begins with a Supervision Dilemma, which is a realistic example related to the chapter topic. The same example is revisited at the end of the chapter in the Solution to the Supervision Dilemma. Also in keeping with the practical nature of this text, we have several Supervision Illustrations in each chapter. These illustrations contain real-life incidents or news stories that further shape the chapter focus. The overwhelming majority of these illustrations are new to this edition. Each chapter includes review questions, as well as several Skill-Building Questions. In addition, a Skill-Building Applications section at the end of each chapter contains two incidents (Mini Cases) and at least two experiential exercises, several of which are new to this edition. We have also added a section listing Key Terms at the end of each chapter.

ORGANIZATION OF THE TENTH EDITION

As with the previous edition, this edition is a refinement of a proven successful text. We have continued to organize the materials based on the skills necessary to successfully supervise. We feel that this is a very practical and academically sound approach. This edition is arranged in six major sections:

Section One: Foundations of Supervision

Section Two: Contemporary Issues

Section Three: Planning and Organizing Skills

Section Four: Staffing Skills

Section Five: Leadership Skills

Section Six: Controlling Skills

Section One provides a foundation necessary to embark on the practice of supervision. The topics covered span all supervisory jobs. Specific topics include the supervisor's job, decision making, communication, and motivation.

Section Two focuses on the more contemporary aspects of managing in today's world. The topics of managing change and innovation and ethics and organizational politics are covered in depth.

Section Three stresses the planning and organizing skills that today's supervisors must possess to be successful. Chapters are devoted to supervisory planning, time management, organizing and delegating, and understanding work teams.

Section Four emphasizes the important role that all supervisors play in the staffing process. Obtaining and developing people, equal employment opportunity, and counseling employees are all explored in this section.

Section Five is devoted to exploring the multitude of leadership skills that are necessary for successful supervision. Leading, handling conflict and stress, appraising and rewarding performance, and labor relations are all discussed at length.

Section Six discusses the different controlling approaches that are available to help supervisors. Control concepts and quality, improving productivity, and fostering a safe and healthy work environment are topics that are presented in this section.

We have attempted to write this book considering the needs of teachers, students, aspiring supervisors, and practicing supervisors. We have tried to arrange the concepts and materials to appeal to each of these groups. Naturally, we welcome any ideas and suggestions that might improve the book.

ONLINE LEARNING CENTER www.mhhe.com/ruesupervision10e

A complete set of instructor supplements, including instructor's manual, PowerPoints, and test bank, as well as student study aids, are available online.

ACKNOWLEDGMENTS

We are indebted to our families, friends, colleagues, and students for the assistance we have received. Unfortunately, space limitations allow us to name only a few. We give special thanks to the following reviewers, who provided many helpful comments during the preparation of the tenth edition: Patricia Worsham—California State Polytechnic University/Riverside Community College; Dennis Brode—Sinclair Community College; Paula Garcia—University of Texas, Brownsville.

Special thanks are extended to managing developmental editor Laura Hurst Spell, developmental editor and project manager Carol Bleistine, and editorial coordinator Jane Beck. Sincere appreciation is extended to Charmelle Todd for her typing and editing support and to Michelle Graham for her administrative support.

Foundations of Supervision

SECTION OUTLINE

1   SUPERVISION IN A CHANGING WORKPLACE
2   MAKING SOUND AND CREATIVE DECISIONS
3   IMPROVING COMMUNICATION SKILLS
4   MOTIVATING TODAY'S EMPLOYEES

CHAPTER ONE

Supervision in a Changing Workplace

Learning objectives

After studying this chapter, you will be able to:

1. Define supervision.
2. Describe the work of a supervisor.
3. Present the types of skills necessary to perform the job of supervision.
4. State the key reasons for supervisory success.
5. Define diversity in the workplace.
6. Explain the glass ceiling.
7. Explain who is an entrepreneur.
8. Describe a small business.

Supervision Dilemma

Global Insurance is a worldwide company with several thousand employees. Jane Harris and John Lewis are employees in one of the company's claims-processing offices. Both have been with the company for approximately six years. This morning, their department head, Les Thomas, gave Jane and John a big shock. He asked both of them if they would like to become supervisors in the claims-processing office. Les explained that two of the supervisors in the department were being promoted and that he needed two new supervisors. Les also stated that he felt that Jane and John would make good supervisors because they knew the job and knew the people in the department. Les asked both of them to think it over and let him know their decisions the next day. Later, John saw Jane at lunch and they began discussing the possibilities of the new jobs. However, both of them agreed that they had never given much thought to being a supervisor. Both wondered just what that would entail.

What Is Supervision?

1 LEARNING OBJECTIVES

2 LEARNING OBJECTIVES

Supervision is the first level of management in an organization and is concerned with encouraging the members of a work unit to contribute positively toward accomplishing the organization's goals and objectives. This means that the supervisor does not do the operative work but sees that it is accomplished through the efforts of others.

Although the definition is simple, the job of supervision is quite complex. The supervisor must learn to make good decisions, communicate well with people, make proper work assignments, delegate, plan, train people, motivate people, appraise performance, and deal with various specialists in other departments. The varied work of the supervisor is extremely difficult to master. Yet mastery of supervision is vital to organizational success because supervisors are the management persons that most employees see and deal with every day.

Who Are Supervisors?

The need for supervision dates back to biblical times. When Moses was attempting to lead the people of Israel from Egypt to the Promised Land, his father-in-law, Jethro, advised him as follows:

> Find some capable, godly, honest men who hate bribes and appoint them as judges, 1 judge for each 1,000 people; he in turn will have 10 judges under him, each in charge of 100; and under each of them will be 2 judges, each responsible for the affairs of 50 people; and each of these will have 5 judges beneath him, each counseling 10 persons.

Figure 1.1 shows the form of organization suggested to Moses. It contains the three levels of management that exist in most organizations. The top management of business organizations usually includes the chairman of the board, the president, and the senior vice presidents. This level of management establishes the goals and objectives of the organization and the policies necessary to achieve them. Middle management includes all employees below the top-management level who manage other managers. A supervisor's boss is normally classified as a middle manager. Middle management develops the departmental objectives and procedures necessary to achieve the organizational goals and objectives.

The third level of management includes supervisors. Supervisors manage operative employees—those who physically produce an organization's goods and services.

FIGURE 1.1   **Partial Organization Chart from Exodus**

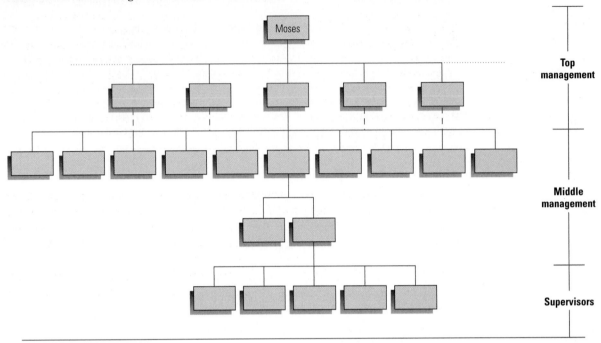

The three levels of management form a *hierarchy*. As can be seen in Figure 1.2, the management hierarchy is shaped like a pyramid, with very few senior managers at the top and many supervisors at the bottom.

Many names are used to describe the people who supervise. These names vary from industry to industry. Figure 1.3 lists some of the names given to supervisory jobs in different types of organizations. Regardless of the name, a supervisor is the manager who serves as the link between operative employees and all other managers.

The Fair Labor Standards Act (FLSA) and the Taft-Hartley Labor Act contain conditions that determine whether a person is considered to be a supervisor. The FLSA states

FIGURE 1.2
**The Management
Pyramid**

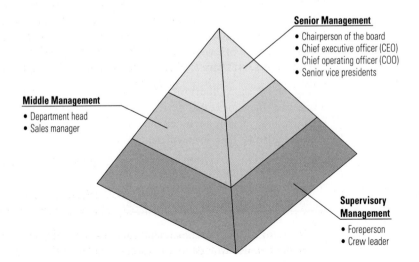

FIGURE 1.3
Supervisory Job Titles

Assistant cafeteria manager	Records and documents supervisor
Assistant credit supervisor	Records and materials supervisor
Crew leader	Shift supervisor
Employment supervisor	Supervisor for secretarial services
Head nurse	Supervisor of budget and cost control
Lead person	Supervisor of word processing
Meter routing supervisor	Training and safety supervisor
Office manager	Training supervisor
Powerhouse mechanic foreman	Utility foreman
Receiving and warehousing supervisor	Welding foreman

that a person is considered to be a member of management if the person is paid on a salary basis rather than an hourly basis and if the primary duties of the person are administrative, professional, or supervisory in nature. The Taft-Hartley Labor Act provides two guidelines in determining whether an employee is a member of management: (1) an employee is paid a specified base salary that is supposed to indicate managerial or professional status and (2) the duties or responsibilities of the job are associated with managerial or professional work. Generally, such duties require the employee to exercise judgment for a group of employees.

Sources of Supervisory Talent

The vast majority of new supervisors are promoted from the ranks of operative employees. Employees with good technical skills and good work records are the ones who are normally selected by management for supervisory jobs.

However, it should be noted that good technical skills and a good work record do not necessarily make a person a good supervisor. In fact, sometimes these attributes can act adversely to productive supervisory practices. As will be seen later in this chapter, other skills are also required to be an effective supervisor. Officers of labor unions are sometimes chosen for supervisory jobs. Because union officers are elected, it can be assumed that the voting employees view them as having some leadership abilities. Thus, they are a source of supervisory talent. Another source is new college graduates. Many organizations place such graduates in supervisory jobs after a brief training period.

Figure 1.4 shows a normal progression into supervision. A person who gets into supervision does not necessarily stop progressing. It is possible to rise from supervision to the top of the organization. In fact, developing the skills required for supervision prepares a person for higher levels of management.

The Activities of Supervision

Supervisors engage in five basic activities. These activities are planning, organizing, staffing, leading and controlling.

3 LEARNING OBJECTIVES

Planning involves determining the most effective means for achieving the work that is to be done by the work group. Generally, planning includes three steps:

Determining the present situation. Assess such things as the present condition of the equipment, the attitude of employees, and the availability of materials.

FIGURE 1.4
Progression of Jobs into Supervision

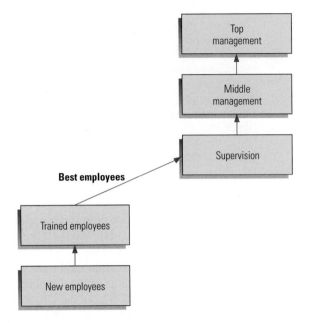

Determining the objectives. The objectives for a work unit are usually established by higher levels of management.

Determining the most effective way of attaining the objectives. Given the present situation, what actions are necessary to reach the objectives?

Everyone follows these three steps in making personal plans. However, the supervisor makes plans, not for a single person, but for a group of people. This complicates the entire process.

Organizing involves distributing the work among the employees in the work group and arranging the work so that it flows smoothly. The supervisor carries out the work of organizing through the general structure established by higher levels of management. Thus, the supervisor functions within a general structure and is usually given specific work assignments from higher levels of management. The supervisor then sees that the specific work assignments are done.

Staffing is concerned with obtaining and developing good people. Since supervisors accomplish their work through others, staffing is an extremely important function.

Leading involves directing and channeling employee behavior toward the accomplishment of work objectives and providing a workplace where people can be motivated to accomplish the work objectives.

Controlling determines how well the work is being done compared with what was planned. Basically, this involves measuring actual performance against planned performance and taking any necessary corrective action.

Supervisors spend the largest portions of their time on the leading and controlling activities. The other activities are not necessarily less important, but they usually take less of the supervisor's time. The supervisor must perform all of the activities in order to be successful. For instance, organizing is difficult without a plan. Good employees obtained through staffing will not continue to work in a poorly planned, poorly organized work environment. Furthermore, it is very difficult to lead people if planning, organizing, and staffing are not done properly. Thus, the five activities of supervision can be viewed as links in a chain. For the supervisor to be successful, each of these links must be strong.

FIGURE 1.5
The Chain of Supervisory Activities

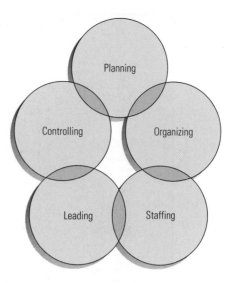

(See Figure 1.5.) It is also important to remember that the supervisory activities do not involve a sequential process, but generally occur simultaneously.

Skills of a Supervisor

The supervisor's work can also be examined in terms of the types of skills required. Three basic types of skills have been identified:

1. **Conceptual skills** are those that help supervisors understand how different parts of an organization relate to one another and to the organization as a whole. Decision making, planning, and organizing are activities that require conceptual skills.
2. **Human relations skills** are those that supervisors need to understand and work well with people. Interviewing job applicants, forming partnerships with other organizations, and resolving conflicts all require good human relations skills.
3. **Technical skills** are the specific abilities that employees use to perform their jobs. Operating a word processing program, designing a brochure, and training people to use a new budgeting system are all technical skills.

All levels of management require some combination of these skills. Different skills are more important at different levels of management, as Figure 1.6 shows. Conceptual skills are most important at the senior management level. Technical skills are most important for supervisors. Human relations skills are important at all levels of management.

Key Reasons for Supervisory Success

4 **LEARNING OBJECTIVES**

Supervisors are successful for many reasons. However, five characteristics are important keys to supervisory success:

1. *Ability and willingness to delegate.* Most supervisors are promoted from operative jobs and have been accustomed to doing the work themselves. An often difficult, and yet essential, skill that such supervisors must develop is the ability or willingness to delegate work to others.
2. *Proper use of authority.* Some supervisors let their newly acquired authority go to their heads. It is sometimes difficult to remember that the use of authority alone does not get the support and cooperation of employees. Learning when not to use authority is often as important as learning when to use it.
3. *Setting a good example.* Supervisors must always remember that the work group looks to them to set the example. Employees expect fair and equitable treatment from their

FIGURE 1.6
Mix of Skills Used at Different Levels of Management

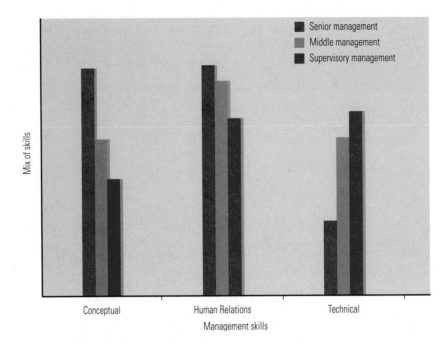

Senior management
Middle management
Supervisory management

Mix of skills

Conceptual   Human Relations   Technical
Management skills

supervisors. Too many supervisors play favorites and treat employees inconsistently. Government legislation has attempted to reduce this practice in some areas, but the problem is still common.

4. *Recognizing the change in role.* People who have been promoted into supervision must recognize that their role has changed and that they are no longer one of the gang. They must remember that being a supervisor may require unpopular decisions. Supervisors are the connecting link between the other levels of management and the operative employees and must learn to represent both groups.

5. *Desire for the job.* Many people who have no desire to be supervisors are promoted into supervision merely because of their technical skills. Regardless of one's technical skills, the desire to be a supervisor is necessary for success in supervision. That desire encourages a person to develop the other types of skills necessary in supervision—human relations, administrative, and decision-making skills.

The five characteristics discussed above are not the only ones necessary for supervisory success, but they are certainly some of the most important.

The Changing Nature of the Supervisor's Environment

Changes in Information Technology

Anyone who reads a newspaper recognizes that rapid changes are occurring in lifestyles, information technology, and the work environment. These changes influence the supervisor. This section reviews some of these changes and examines their impact on supervisors.

The phenomenal improvements in computer hardware have been accompanied by improvements in software and user compatibility. Modern computers are much more user friendly than those of the past. Supervisors today do not need to know sophisticated programming languages and computer jargon to use computers. The use of computers in the job of supervision is discussed throughout this book.

Because of the increasing sophistication of communication systems and the rapid increase in the use of computers, data and information are being provided at an accelerating rate. For example:

- Access to the Internet provides a wide array of information that previously was unavailable and/or difficult to obtain.
- Cell phones, e-mail, and teleconferencing enhance the opportunities for improved communications within businesses.

Rapid technological change requires supervisors to have increased technical skills. Furthermore, these changes require more skilled and trained employees. Higher levels of skill and training require new approaches to motivation and leadership. Thus, the supervisor needs more skill in the human relations area.

Changes in Outlook toward the Work Environment

Some forecasters predict that there will be more emphasis on the quality of work life in the future. The factors that can improve the quality of work life include:

1. Safe and healthy working conditions.
2. Opportunity to use and develop individual capabilities.
3. Opportunity for personal and professional growth.
4. Work schedules, career demands, and travel requirements that do not regularly take up family and leisure time.
5. The right to personal privacy, free speech, equitable treatment, and due process.

Because some of these factors fall within the scope of supervision, changes affecting them will have a direct impact on the manager's job.

Changes in Demographics

5   LEARNING OBJECTIVES

One of the more significant changes in today's environment is the increasing diversity of the American population. **Diversity** in the workforce means including people of different genders, races, religions, nationalities, ethnic groups, age groups, and physical abilities. The increasing diversity of the workplace represents a major social change in the United States. Supervision Illustration 1–1 describes the diversity efforts at American Airlines. The latest demographic data show that the United States is becoming more diverse. Figure 1.7 shows the projected population of the United States by race to the year 2050. It is interesting to note that as of today Hispanics have grown to be the largest ethnic group.

A multicultural workplace presents challenges for both employees and supervisors. For example, religious holidays, which are celebrated at different times throughout the year by Muslims, Christians, Jews, and other religious groups, have the potential to be a source of conflict among employees. Managers need to be sensitive to the needs of their employees when it comes to these holidays. On the other hand, employees should be responsible about arranging to take these days off.

What other challenges and contributions does the increasingly diverse workforce present? From an overall viewpoint, organizations must get away from the tradition of

FIGURE 1.7
Projected Population of the United States, by Demographic Group: 2010 to 2050

Source: U.S. Census Bureau, 2004, "U.S. Interim Projections by Age, Sex, Race, and Hispanic Origin," <http://www.census.gov/ipc/www/usinterimproj/>. Internet Release Date: March 18, 2004.

Demographic Group	Total % of Population					% Change from 2010 to 2050
	2010	2020	2030	2040	2050	
White alone	79.3	77.6	75.8	73.9	72.1	−9.08%
Black alone	13.1	13.5	13.9	14.3	14.6	+11.45%
Asian alone	4.6	5.4	6.2	7.1	8.0	+42.5%
Hispanic (of any race)	15.5	17.8	20.1	22.3	24.4	+57.42%
All other races*	3.0	3.5	4.1	4.7	5.3	+76.67%
Total	**100.0**	**100.0**	**100.0**	**100.0**	**100.0**	

*Includes American Indian and Alaska Native alone, Native Hawaiian and Other Pacific Islander alone, and two or more races.

SUPERVISION ILLUSTRATION 1–1

DIVERSITY AT AMERICAN AIRLINES

American Airlines has a long history of fostering equal employment opportunities for minority employees. In 1963, the airline hired the first African-American flight attendant to fly for a U.S. commercial airline. The first African-American pilot was hired in 1964 and its first female pilot was hired in 1973. Today, approximately 32 percent of American and American Eagle's domestic employees are minorities and about 40 percent of the two airlines' employees are female.

Equal Opportunity, the nation's first career magazine for minority college graduates, is read by more than 40,000 members of minority groups, representing students, entry-level workers and professional employees in many career disciplines. Readers of *Equal Opportunity* voted for companies they would most prefer to work for or that they believe are progressive in hiring members of minority groups. American

ranked number 25 on the Top 50 list, the only airline to make the prestigious group.

The top 50 ranking in *Equal Opportunity* magazine is the latest recognition of American's efforts to encourage diversity and inclusion across all facets of its business. Last year, American was named one of the "Top 60 Companies for Hispanics" by *Hispanic Business* magazine, one of just two airlines to make the list. American received that designation for the third consecutive year. In addition, for the seventh consecutive year, American received the highest possible score from the Human Rights Campaign, an organization dedicated to promoting and ensuring understanding of gay and lesbian issues through innovative education and communication strategies.

Source: Anonymous, "Diversity and Inclusion," *PR Newswire,* February 17, 2009, pp. 1–3.

---

fitting employees into a single corporate mold. Everyone will not look and act the same. Organizations must create new human resource policies to explicitly recognize and respond to the unique needs of individual employees.

Greater diversity will create certain specific challenges but also make some important contributions. Communication problems are certain to occur, including misunderstandings among employees and managers as well as the need to translate verbal and written materials into several languages. An increase in organizational factionalism will require that increasing amounts of time be dedicated to dealing with special-interest and advocacy groups.

In addition to creating the above challenges, greater diversity presents new opportunities. Diversity contributes to creating an organization culture that is more tolerant of different behavioral styles and wider views. This often leads to better business decisions.

6 LEARNING OBJECTIVES

Despite these changes, most senior managers in the United States are still white men. The problems women and minorities have had winning promotions to senior management positions gave rise to the term **glass ceiling**. This is the invisible barrier that prevents women and minorities from moving up in the organizational hierarchy.

Much emphasis is expected to be placed on breaking the glass ceiling. In fact, the election of Barack Obama as the first black person to the Office of President of the United States will open the door for women and minorities to move into the highest levels of management. Of course, the performance of Hillary Clinton as Secretary of State of the United States and Oprah Winfrey as CEO of Harpo should encourage other women in breaking the glass ceiling.

Role of Entrepreneurs in Business

Senior, middle, and supervisory managers are all **professional managers.** Professional managers are paid to perform management functions within a company. Like other employees, they receive salaries for the work they do. Professional managers work for businesses, but they do not own them.

SUPERVISION ILLUSTRATION 1–2

ENTREPRENEURSHIP IN UGANDA

Joseph Johnson, a retired banker and former port commissioner, is on a four-week adventure in Africa. He's acting as a scout—not seeking big game but helping to identify and groom the next generation of entrepreneurs in that part of the developing world, said Jerry Hildebrand, director of the Global Center for Social Entrepreneurship at University of the Pacific.

Johnson is teaching a workshop on how to write a business plan with detailed financial projections—the same sort of course he gives to master's candidates at Pacific—at St. Lawrence University in Uganda and the School of Finance and Banking in Rwanda.

The work is part of an effort by the Global Center and Pacific's School of International Studies to share educational and business resources between the two continents, Hildebrand said last week, one day before leaving Saturday with a delegation to Africa. That group of about a dozen includes people in finance, banking, real estate and business who have an interest in developing countries.

Anyone interested in more information about Johnson's ongoing African experience can visit his blog, and online journal, where he makes entries nearly every day—at http://uopafricatrip.blogspot.com/

Source: Adapted from Reed Fajii, *"Teaching Entrepreneurship in Africa: Retired Stockton Banker Offers Startup Lessons,"* McClatchy—Tribune Business News. October 29, 2008, Wire Feed.

7 LEARNING OBJECTIVES

Entrepreneurs are people who launch and run their own businesses. When they start out, they must perform many of the basic management functions that professional managers perform. As their companies grow, they sometimes hire professional managers. Many large companies, such as Google and Genentech, were started by entrepreneurs. Supervision Illustration 1–2 describes an entrepreneurship training course in Uganda.

Being an entrepreneur is much more risky than being a professional manager. Without the right skills and a lot of hard work, entrepreneurs can go out of business and lose all the money invested in their company. Starting and owning a company can be more rewarding than working for a company, however. Successful entrepreneurs can create prosperous businesses that provide large incomes and a feeling of personal accomplishment.

Entrepreneurs and professional managers often have different personal characteristics. Entrepreneurs tend to be more independent than managers, and they may have less formal education. Some entrepreneurs jump from job to job before starting their own businesses.

Entrepreneurs start with an idea for creating or modifying a product or service that they believe in. Entrepreneurs like the idea of making decisions and being their own bosses. They often find tremendous satisfaction in their work, and their financial rewards can be great. Being an entrepreneur means working long hours and making decisions about every aspect of a business. It also means taking risks. Unlike professional managers, entrepreneurs invest money in their businesses and risk losing all of it if their business does not succeed. Without entrepreneurs, there would be no new businesses and fewer exciting developments, or innovations, in business and industry.

Entrepreneurs own their businesses, but they can choose among several different types of ownership. Some entrepreneurs are *sole proprietors,* or people who run their businesses single-handedly. Certain types of work are particularly well suited to this form of ownership—medicine, dentistry, and accounting, for example. Many store owners are also sole proprietors. Other entrepreneurs may form partnerships, especially when a large sum of money is involved. One or more partners may supply the money while another runs the business. Two or more people may also run a business together. Still other small businesses may choose to *incorporate,* or become a corporation, to avoid being held personally liable for financial losses. Some entrepreneurs choose to own franchises.

Many large and medium-sized organizations have begun to encourage their managers to become more innovative and to take more risks. At Dell Computer, for example, CEO and founder Michael Dell encourages his employees to take risks by allowing them to work independently, make mistakes, and learn from the process. He sets hard-to-meet targets and encourages his employees to stretch themselves to meet them. His approach has helped Dell become one of the most successful companies in the country.

Businesses that want to encourage managers to think more like entrepreneurs must find ways to support and encourage people who develop new products and services. Like Michael Dell, they must be willing to accept failure and to encourage people even after a new idea fails. Entrepreneurship within a large or medium-sized company is sometimes called **intrapreneurship.**

Importance of Small Businesses

8 LEARNING OBJECTIVES

A **small business** is a company that is independently owned and operated. Some small businesses, such as neighborhood flower shops, restaurants, or dry-cleaning stores, serve local areas. Other small businesses, such as mail-order and Internet companies, serve customers all over the world. Owners of small businesses often perform all management tasks.

The Small Business Administration (SBA), the government agency that lends money to small businesses, considers a business small if it has fewer than 100 employees. According to this definition, more than 98 percent of the businesses in the United States are small businesses. These small businesses play an important role in the U.S. economy. They employ millions of American workers and sell billions of dollars of products and services.

Small businesses tend to produce more innovations than larger businesses. Many of the most important high-technology companies in the country, including Intel, Apple, and Microsoft, began as small businesses. Microsoft is one of the largest companies in the world, and its founder, Bill Gates, is one of the world's richest people. Some of today's small companies may eventually become corporate giants.

Supervision: Key Link to Productivity

Successful supervision requires the knowledge of, and ability to use, a multitude of skills. The primary measure used in determining a supervisor's success or failure is the productivity of the supervisor's work unit. This book is designed to provide the skills necessary for successful supervision. Practice in applying these skills can be gained by answering the discussion questions, studying the incidents described at the end of each chapter, and completing the exercises also provided at the end of each chapter. An important aid for the student is that the key terms used in a chapter are summarized at the end of each chapter.

This book is organized into six basic sections:

Section I	Foundations of Supervision
Section II	Contemporary Issues
Section III	Planning and Organizing Skills
Section IV	Staffing Skills
Section V	Leadership Skills
Section VI	Controlling Skills

Section I—Foundations of Supervision—fosters understanding the job of supervision in diverse workplaces, making sound and creative decisions, improving communication skills, and motivating today's employees. These should provide a necessary foundation for studying the skills of supervision.

Section II—Contemporary Issues—is concerned with managing change and innovation. This section also discusses ethics and organizational politics.

Section III—Planning and Organizing Skills—analyzes the supervisor's role in planning, organizing, and delegating work. Understanding the nature and importance of both formal and informal work groups is also discussed. The important issue of time management is also discussed in this section.

Section IV—Staffing Skills—examines the supervisor's role in obtaining and developing good employees. The topics of equal employment opportunity and counseling employees are discussed.

Section V—Leadership Skills—discusses human behavior and how a supervisor must have the ability to work well with people. Leading employees, handling conflict, appraising and rewarding performance, and labor relations are discussed in this section.

Section VI—Controlling Skills—describes the supervisor's role in determining how well the work is being done compared with what was planned. Topics such as supervisory control and quality; improving productivity through cost control; and providing a healthy and safe work environment are covered in detail.

Summary

The purpose of this chapter is to give the reader a clear understanding of what supervision involves. The chapter also discusses several reasons why supervisors are successful.

1. *Define supervision.* Supervision is defined in this book as the first level of management in the organization and is concerned with encouraging the members of a work unit to contribute positively toward accomplishing the organization's goals and objectives.

2. *Describe the work of a supervisor.* The work of a supervisor is often categorized into five areas: planning, organizing, staffing, leading, and controlling. Planning involves determining the most effective means for achieving the work of the unit. Organizing involves distributing the work among the employees in the work group and arranging the work so that it flows smoothly. Staffing is concerned with obtaining and developing good people. Leading involves directing and channeling employee behavior toward the accomplishment of work objectives. Controlling determines how well the work is being done compared with what was planned.

3. *Describe the three types of skills required of a supervisor.* Three basic types of skills have been identified. Technical skills refer to knowledge about such things as machines, processes, and methods of production. Human relations skills refer to knowledge about human behavior and the ability to work well with people. Conceptual skills help in understanding the relationship between different parts of an organization.

4. *State the key reasons for supervisory success.* Five key reasons for supervisory success are ability and willingness to delegate, the proper use of authority, setting a good example, recognizing the change in role, and desire for the job.

5. *Define diversity in the workplace.* Diversity means including people of different genders, races, religions, nationalities, ethic groups, age groups, and physical abilities in the workplace.

6. *Explain the glass ceiling.* The glass ceiling refers to a level within the organizational hierarchy beyond which very few women and minorities advance.

7. *Explain who is an entrepreneur.* Entrepreneurs are people who launch and run their own business.

8. *Describe a small business.* A small business is a company that is independently owned and operated.

Key Terms

Conceptual skills, 7
Controlling, 6
Diversity, 9
Entrepreneur, 11
Glass ceiling, 10

Human relations skills, 7
Intrapreneurship, 12
Leading, 6
Organizing, 6
Planning, 5

Professional manager, 10
Small business, 12
Staffing, 6
Supervision, 3
Technical skills, 7

Review Questions

1. What is supervision?
2. What are three general levels of management?
3. Give five names (or job titles) of supervisors.
4. Name three sources that organizations can use when seeking to fill supervisory positions.
5. What are the five activities that a supervisor performs?
6. Identify five characteristics that make supervisors successful.
7. What is the impact of the following changes on supervision?

    a. Changes in information technology.
    b. Changes in outlook toward the work environment.
    c. Changes in diversity.
8. Describe diversity.
9. Explain the glass ceiling.
10. Explain entrepreneurship.
11. Identify what a small business is.

Skill-Building Questions

1. "A good supervisor in a manufacturing plant could be a good supervisor in a bank." Discuss.
2. Do you think that supervision can be learned through books and study or only through experience? Why?
3. Do you think that the best worker also makes the best supervisor? Why or why not?
4. "A good supervisor should be able to do any job that he or she supervises better than any of the operative employees." Discuss your views on this statement.

Additional Readings

Buhler, Patricia, "Conducting Layoffs in an Uncertain Economy," *SuperVision,* March 2009, pp. 20–23.

Kaufman, Ron, "How to Harness the Power of Praise," *SuperVision,* March 2009, pp. 14–17.

Lindo, David K., "Can You Answer Their Questions?" *SuperVision,* January 2007, pp. 20–23.

Smith, Richard, "Dealing with Managers Who Do Not Take Supervision Seriously Enough," *Community Care,* September 4, 2008, p. 36.

Stanley, T. L., "Ethical Decision Making in Tough Times," *SuperVision,* March 2009, pp. 3–7.

SKILL-BUILDING APPLICATIONS

Incident 1–1

Promotion into Supervision

Roy Thomas has been with the Rebco Manufacturing Company for 15 years. He joined Rebco right after his high school graduation and has been with the company ever since.

Ten years ago, Rebco became unionized and Roy was one of the people primarily responsible for its unionization. He helped the organizer from the Teamsters Union plan the union election campaign. He helped get the local union established after the election and then served as its president for its first three years. After that, he continued to serve in various capacities with the local union. Two years ago, he was again elected for a three-year term as its president.

Over the years, Roy has developed a reputation for being firm but fair with the management of Rebco. He is well respected by both the members of the union and the management of Rebco.

Roy was quite shocked when he was recently called into the plant manager's office for the following discussion.

Bill Lindsay (Plant Manager): Good to see you, Roy.

Roy: Yeah, it's good to see you, Bill, especially when we're not arguing over a problem. I hope you didn't call me here for that.

Bill: No, Roy, I didn't. In fact, I called you here to talk about something else entirely. Some of our older supervisors are retiring shortly, as you know, and we would like you to consider becoming a supervisor.

Roy: A supervisor—you've got to be kidding! I've fussed and fought with you and the other managers around here for 10 years. Now you want me to join you. How would the employees react?

Bill: That's just it, Roy. We think they would be pleased. After all, they've elected you president of the local union twice already. You've got their respect. A good supervisor just needs to know how to handle people, and you sure know how to do that.

Roy: I just don't know, Bill. Give me a couple of days to think about it.

Questions (Explain your answers in writing.)

1. Do you think Roy would be a good supervisor?
2. What qualities does Roy possess that support your answer?
3. Do you agree with Bill Lindsay's statement that "a good supervisor just needs to know how to handle people"?
4. What do you think the reaction of the employees would be if Roy accepted the job?

Incident 1–2

Not Enough Time to Supervise

Len Massey is a supervisor in a large fire and casualty insurance company. He is in charge of a group of clerical workers who review policies and endorsements, calculate commissions, and maintain records. Before his promotion to supervisor, Len himself was a clerical worker in the department. It was largely due to his reputation as the best worker in the department that he was promoted. "If Len did the work," his co-workers said, "it is right."

This reputation has carried over into Len's supervisory practices. Everything coming out of his group is perfect. In fact, Len rechecks in detail all the work coming out of his group to ensure that it is accurate. It is not unusual for him to turn work back to one of his employees several times until it is perfect. Len's employees quickly recognized his eye for detail and his checking and rechecking of their work. One of them was recently overheard to say, "I don't really worry about accuracy in my work too much, because if I make an error, I know Len will catch it."

Last week, at Len's annual performance evaluation, his boss, Pam Levine, said that Len was spending too much time on detail work and not enough time on supervision. In fact, she said that he must start spending more time in supervision and less time in doing the work of others. Len's response to Pam was, "People in my unit don't seem to care about sloppy work, and since I'm responsible, I feel obligated to check it before it goes out."

Questions

1. Is Pam Levine right?
2. What does Len need to know about supervision?
3. What do you think of the reasons given for Len's promotion?

Exercise 1–1

Understanding the Job of a Supervisor

Exhibit 1.1 gives a job description for a maintenance supervisor in a manufacturing company. From this job description, classify the duties and responsibilities as to whether they are planning, organizing, staffing, leading, or controlling.

Also identify the specific skills of supervision—technical, human relations, administrative, and decision making—that are described in this job description.

Exercise 1–2

Required Attributes of a Supervisor

1. From the supervisory jobs listed on the next page, choose the one that is most attractive to you.
2. Form into groups of four or five with others who selected the same job as you.
3. Develop a group list of required and desirable skills for the job.
4. Present and defend your group's list before the entire class.

Exercise 1–3

The Supervisor's Personal Inventory

The following inventory has helped many supervisors determine to what extent their behaviors or practices

---

EXHIBIT 1.1
Position of Maintenance Supervisor

Source: Reprinted from *Job Descriptions in Manufacturing Industries* by John D. Ulery. Copyright © 1981 AMACOM. Used with the permission of the publisher, AMACOM, a division of American Management Association International, New York, NY. All rights reserved. http://www.amacombooks.org.

Basic Purpose

To supervise the maintenance activity through the implementation of a preventive maintenance program and an ongoing maintenance repair program for the facility, vehicles, production maintenance, and process equipment.

Duties and Responsibilities

1. Plans and implements effective procedures and policies for the maintenance department to ensure that all equipment, facilities, and utilities are in an acceptable state of repair.
2. Coordinates with vendors, suppliers, and contractors the installation of new equipment or equipment processes.
3. Establishes, with direction from the plant manager, priorities of all maintenance activities through a work order procedure.
4. Supervises all daily activities of the maintenance department through subordinates to ensure completion of assigned projects that will result in the least amount of machine downtime.
5. Monitors completion of maintenance projects to ensure that safety and quality standards are met.
6. Approves all requisitions relating to new and replacement parts, supplies, machinery, and equipment for the maintenance department.
7. Provides technical knowledge and expertise to solve problems of a mechanical, electrical, or hydraulic/pneumatic nature.
8. Develops and maintains responsible labor/management relations consistent with the labor agreement, including representing the company in certain grievances.
9. Schedules and assigns hourly personnel to maintain good housekeeping for the facility grounds and administrative offices.

Organizational Relationships

This position reports to the manager/engineering and maintenance and indirectly to the plant manager. Coordinates work with all service and production departments.

Position Specifications

Must possess 8 to 10 years' experience in maintenance, engineering, or related fields. Prefer minimum of 3–5 years' supervisory experience. Must be familiar with each of the following areas: boilers, air compressors, heating and air-conditioning, plumbing, welding, carpentry, electrical/electronic equipment, pneumatic hydraulics, and heavy manufacturing equipment.

SUPERVISOR
RIGHTS-OF-WAY AND LAND

ABC is a diversified energy company making important contributions in the pursuit of new energy resources around the world. A position of Supervisor—Rights-of-Way and Land is currently available at ABC's Houston location.

A college education is required, with a degree preferably in business, law, or engineering. Strong experience in pipeline right-of-way work is required with a minimum of three years of right-of-way field experience. Additional experience must include a minimum of five years of general right-of-way office experience, with a heavy supervisory background in right-of-way. The responsibilities will include supervising the acquisition of right-of-way and the settlement of claims; following litigations; and conducting and coordinating contact with the state and local authorities. The ability to negotiate and prepare amendatory, alteration, and relocation agreements is mandatory.

ABC offers competitive salaries, a comprehensive employee benefits program, and a variety of career challenges. If interested, send résumé and salary history to:

P.O. Box 000
An equal opportunity employer
Principals Only!

WEEKEND PRODUCTION SUPERVISOR

XYZ Corporation, a smoke-free environment and manufacturer of soft contact lenses and solution-related products, has an immediate opening for a Weekend Production Supervisor. This individual must be able to plan, organize, and control staffing, equipment, and facilities in an efficient manner within budgetary guidelines. This includes being held accountable for the quality and quantity of products produced, compliance with CGMP and OSHA standards, and guiding the department toward achieving departmental and company goals and objectives. BS/BA and one year production supervisory experience required. Solid background in highly technical production environment. Good written and oral communication skills. Must work weekends (11:00 PM to 11:00 AM), and a minimum of one additional day per week is required. We regret that we are unable to respond to all inquiries. We will only respond to those candidates selected for an interview.

Qualified applicants should forward résumé with salary requirements to:

XYZ
Corporation
P.O. Box 000

ACCOUNTING
A/R SUPERVISOR

Progressive company with high-volume receivables department is looking for a sharp individual with accounts receivable supervisory experience. Excellent starting salary and benefits. If you are a motivated self-starter, respond with salary history to Box 000.

SUPERVISING

Senior Auditor: Plan, direct, and conduct audits for client operations. Review and prepare corporate tax returns, develop budget forecast and analysis, and develop and improve accounting systems. Must have Bachelor's in Accounting for Business Administration with two years' experience in job or as Analyst or Accountant. Hours 9:00 AM–5:00 PM, Monday–Friday, overtime as needed. Those qualified, résumé to P.O. Box 000.

SUPERVISOR &
SALES MANAGER

French-owned, U.S.-based corporation seeks National Supervisor & Sales Engineer to supervise and coordinate the U.S. marketing and distribution efforts. Experience in the processes of importation of European products into the United States as well as fluency in written and spoken French are required. Applicants must have four years' experience in the stone products industry as well as six years' experience in construction supervision and sales of stone products. Send résumé to: P.O. Box 000.

contribute to difficulties for their employees. The items below represent important supervisor behaviors and practices that build positive work relationships. Rate yourself and your company on each item, giving yourself one (1) point if the item rarely applies, two (2) points if it sometimes applies, and three (3) points if it applies to you most of the time.

If you are not a supervisor, discuss how your current boss/supervisor behaves.

	Rating Scale		
	Applies Rarely 1	Applies Sometimes 2	Applies Most of Time 3
1. Know my job	•	•	•
2. Know my employees' jobs	•	•	•
3. Know my company's objectives and standard procedures	•	•	•
4. Convey my objectives and procedures to my employees	•	•	•
5. Define my objectives and procedures clearly	•	•	•
6. Try to resolve those objectives and procedures that are in conflict	•	•	•
7. Establish clear performance standards	•	•	•
8. Convey performance standards to my employees	•	•	•
9. Insist that performance standards are met	•	•	•
10. Try to improve substandard performance	•	•	•
11. Set standards for myself and follow them	•	•	•
12. My employees know what to expect from me	•	•	•
13. Avoid self-centeredness	•	•	•
14. Am employee-centered	•	•	•
15. Know my employees' strengths and weaknesses	•	•	•
16. Keep my employees well informed on matters affecting them	•	•	•
17. Keep channels of communication open	•	•	•
18. Actively lead, direct, and control employees when necessary	•	•	•
19. Allow my employees to lead and control themselves when they are able to	•	•	•
20. Avoid unjust criticism	•	•	•
21. Criticize employees in private	•	•	•
22. Give credit when it is earned	•	•	•
23. Commend employees publicly	•	•	•
24. Avoid taking credit for things my employees did	•	•	•
25. Show respect toward employees	•	•	•
26. Command respect from employees by my conduct	•	•	•
27. Discipline fairly	•	•	•
28. Discipline only when needed	•	•	•
29. Back employees to fullest when they are right	•	•	•
30. Refuse to back employees when they're wrong even though such refusal may lessen my popularity	•	•	•
31. Delegate as far down the line as possible	•	•	•
32. Value my employees' input	•	•	•
33. Provide opportunities to get employee input	•	•	•
34. Use the input I receive	•	•	•
35. Encourage employees to develop their sense of responsibility and initiative	•	•	•
36. Use my authority appropriately	•	•	•
37. My employees have pride in their accomplishments	•	•	•
38. Actively try to build esprit de corps	•	•	•
39. Practice what I preach	•	•	•

	Rating Scale		
	Applies Rarely **1**	**Applies Sometimes** **2**	**Applies Most of Time** **3**
40. Recognize my shortcomings	•	•	•
41. Compensate for my shortcomings	•	•	•
42. Retain my sense of humor in dealings with employees	•	•	•
43. Admit my errors when I'm wrong	•	•	•
44. Apply the same standards of conduct and performance to men and women	•	•	•
45. Continually strive to improve myself and my company	•	•	•

Scoring: Total all your points for the 45 items. If you scored 125 or above, your supervisory behaviors and company practices promote positive work relationships. If you scored between 100 and 124, some of your behaviors/practices may contribute to difficulties with employees, but no urgency for change is indicated unless one or more items scored very low. If you scored between 75 and 99, probably many of your behaviors/practices contribute to difficulties with employees, and you should ask yourself what you can do to improve the low scoring items. If you scored below 75, improving your overall supervisory behaviors/practices should be a high priority for you.

Regardless of your score, the awareness that comes from taking such an inventory is the prerequisite for self-improvement. Your inventory results can serve as the basis for eliminating managerial blind spots and creating a personal development plan to ensure that the impact of your behaviors and practices is a positive one.

Source: Adapted from "Eliminating Managerial Blind Spots," by Gary W. Hobson, *Supervision,* August 1990. Reprinted by permission of © National Research Bureau, P.O. Box 1, Burlington, IA 52601-0001.

Exercise 1–4

Understanding Diversity

As a part of communicating that an organization is truly committed to supporting a highly qualified and diverse workforce, supervisors should take every opportunity to demonstrate the use of nonsexist language.

A. In this vein, try and identify a nonsexist word to use in place of each of the following words that may carry a sexist connotation:

Man-hours	Waiter/Waitress
Girl Friday	Watchman
Layout man	Repairman
Salesman	Man-made
Foreman	Spokesman
Policeman	Draftsman

B. List additional words or terms that you think might carry a sexist connotation.

Selected Supervisory and Related Periodicals

This list provides the names of the more commonly referenced supervisory and related periodicals.

Academy of Management Review
Administrative Management
Arbitration Journal
Business Horizons
BusinessWeek
California Management Review
Forbes
Fortune
Harvard Business Review
Human Resource Management
Journal of Business
Management Review
Management Solutions
Management Today
Personnel Administrator
Personnel Journal
Supervision
Supervisory Management
Training and Development Journal
The Wall Street Journal (newspaper)

CHAPTER TWO

Making Sound and Creative Decisions

Learning objectives

After studying this chapter, you will be able to:

1. Differentiate between programmed and nonprogrammed decisions.
2. Discuss the importance of recognition and timeliness in decision making.
3. State the steps followed in the scientific method of decision making.
4. Name several potential advantages and disadvantages of group decision making.
5. List several traps that supervisors frequently fall into when making decisions.
6. Discuss the role that the supervisor plays in establishing a creative environment.
7. Describe several group-oriented techniques that can be employed by supervisors to encourage creativity.
8. Itemize some of the more frequently encountered barriers to organizational creativity.

Since the first day that Jane Harris accepted the supervisor's job, she has been concerned about the many tough decisions she has had to make. Just this morning, for example, Jerry Krzyzanowski, one of her employees, requested a change in the vacation schedule. Jerry had received a last-minute invitation to go on a Canadian hunting trip as his uncle's guest. Jerry considered this "the chance of a lifetime." The problem is that three other members of the department have already been approved for vacation during the same week that Jerry requested. Even with Jerry on hand, the department would be operating with a skeleton crew.

Jane has also been concerned about her apparent inability to come up with, and implement, new ideas. It seems to Jane that most of her employees are perfectly happy to do things the way they have been done for years. Last week, when she asked Jerry Krzyzanowski if he had considered reviewing the procedures for filing completed claims, Jerry replied, "Why change? It's worked well up to now."

One of the primary requirements of any manager's job is to make decisions and supervisors are no exception. Among the primary factors that distinguish supervisors from operative employees are the level and types of decisions that they must make. A supervisor must be concerned with how a decision might affect his or her employees and the organization. An operative employee, in contrast, is primarily concerned with how a decision affects him or her individually. People who don't like making decisions usually do not make good supervisors.

In fact, a supervisor's skill in making decisions is often a key factor in the kind of evaluation and rewards (promotion, money, assignments, etc.) that he or she receives. Moreover, a supervisor's decision-making ability will ultimately contribute to the success or failure of the organization.

As supervisors and managers move up through the different management levels of an organization, the complexity of the decisions required tends to increase. Figure 2.1 gives some examples of both expected and unexpected decisions that a supervisor might face. Although the supervisor generally has more time to deal with expected decisions than with unexpected decisions, this does not necessarily mean that expected decisions are easier to make or less critical. For example, a supervisor's recommendation to hire or not to hire a job applicant could have serious ramifications for a long time to come.

New technology has made information much more readily available to all levels of management, including supervisors. The proliferation of computers, the Internet, and intranets have all affected the information available to supervisors. However, the availability of information has not necessarily made decision making any easier or less important for supervisors.

FIGURE 2.1
Examples of Expected and Unexpected Decisions

Expected (Anticipated) Decisions

1. Recommendation concerning the hiring of a new job applicant.
2. Salary and promotion recommendations.
3. Approval of vacation requests.
4. Assignment of a new piece of equipment.

Unexpected (Unanticipated) Decisions

1. An employee requests next Friday off to attend a Shriners' convention.
2. An employee who doesn't seem to get along with others in the department requests a transfer.
3. A piece of major equipment is malfunctioning but still operable—should it be shut down until it is repaired?
4. An employee expresses fear of a new piece of equipment and refuses to use it.
5. Three employees call in sick today. What adjustments must be made to meet production schedules?

Decision Making versus Problem Solving

The terms *decision making* and *problem solving* are often confused and therefore need to be clarified. **Decision making,** in its narrowest sense, is the process of choosing from among various alternatives. A *problem* is any deviation from some standard or desired level of performance. **Problem solving,** then, is the process of determining the appropriate responses or actions necessary to alleviate a problem. Problem solving necessarily involves decision making, since all problems can be attacked in numerous ways and the problem solver must decide which way is best. On the other hand, not all decisions involve problems (such as a supervisor choosing whom to recommend for a promotion). However, from a practical perspective, most supervisory decisions do involve solving or at least avoiding problems.

 1 LEARNING OBJECTIVES

Decisions are often classified as programmed or nonprogrammed. **Programmed decisions** are reached by an established or systematic procedure. Normally, the decision maker is familiar with the situation in a programmable decision. Routine, repetitive decisions usually fall into this category. Supervisory decisions covered by organizational policies, procedures, and rules are programmed in that established guidelines must be followed in arriving at the decision.

Nonprogrammed decisions have little or no precedent. They are relatively unstructured and generally require a more creative approach by the decision maker; the decision maker must develop the procedure to be used. Generally, nonprogrammed decisions are more difficult to make than programmed decisions. Deciding on a new piece of equipment and next year's goals are examples of nonprogrammed decisions.

Recognition and Timeliness of the Decision

2 LEARNING OBJECTIVES

Recognizing the need to make a decision is a natural prerequisite to making a sound decision. Timeliness is also critical to a sound decision. Some supervisors always seem to make decisions on the spot, others tend to take forever in deciding even a simple matter, and still others just seem to ignore matters requiring decisions by acting as if the problems don't exist. The supervisor who takes pride in making quick decisions also runs the risk of making bad decisions. Failure to gather and evaluate available data, to consider employees' feelings, and to anticipate the impact of the decision can result in a very quick but poor decision. Just as risky, of course, is the other extreme—the supervisor who listens to the problem and promises to get back to the employee but never does. Nearly as bad is the supervisor who gets back to the employee—but only after an inordinate amount of time. There are other familiar types: The supervisor who never seems to have adequate information to make a decision, the supervisor who frets and worries over even the simplest decisions, and the supervisor who refers everything to the boss.

All of the types described above are either overconcerned or underconcerned about making a decision. They show little regard for the timing and quality of the decision. Especially when the situation involves some unpleasant matter (such as whether to lay off or dismiss an employee), it is common for the supervisor to make a quick decision and thus get rid of the problem or to ignore the problem and hope that it will go away. These are natural human reactions. Successful supervisors learn to resist such reactions and to make decisions with a proper concern for their timeliness.

Knowing when to make a decision is complicated by the fact that different decisions must be made within different time frames. For example, a supervisor would generally have much more time in deciding on promotion recommendations than in deciding what to do when three employees call in sick. Unfortunately, there is no magic formula that tells a supervisor when a decision should be made or how long it should take. The supervisor has to develop an awareness for the importance of properly timing decisions.

The supervisor should also understand the relationship between properly timing decisions and being decisive. Decisiveness is a necessary characteristic of a good supervisor. Avoiding a decision or putting off a decision can result in worse circumstances than making a questionable but timely decision. However, being decisive does not mean making a decision in the least amount of time. Being decisive means making a decision in a reasonable amount of time.

Steps in the Decision-Making Process

Once the supervisor has recognized the need to make a decision, there are things that he or she can do to affect the quality of the decision. Most successful supervisors use some type of systematic and logical approach to making decisions. The following steps, based on the scientific method, are recommended for making decisions:

3 LEARNING OBJECTIVES

1. Be alert to indications and symptoms of problems.
2. Tentatively define the problem.
3. Collect facts and redefine the problem if necessary.
4. Identify possible alternatives.
5. Gather and organize facts concerning identified alternatives.
6. Evaluate possible alternatives.
7. Choose and implement the best alternative.
8. Follow up.[1]

Each step is discussed in the following paragraphs. It should be noted that these steps are not always sequential. As new facts become available, for example, the decision maker might be required to loop back to Step 2 or Step 3.

Step 1: Be Alert to Indications and Symptoms of Problems

Being alert to indications and symptoms of problems is an integral part of recognizing the need to make a decision (which was discussed in the preceding section). All too often supervisors tend to brush off or ignore indicators and symptoms of problems. Supervisors should constantly be cognizant of any changes that might indicate a potential problem.

Step 2: Tentatively Define the Problem

Frequently, the hardest part of making a decision is defining just what the decision problem is. It is very difficult for a supervisor to make a sound decision about anything unless the exact nature of the problem is known. For example, suppose a certain sales employee is producing an unacceptably low number of sales. Is the problem due to the salesperson's abilities, the particular sales territory, new competition, the specific products being sold, or some other factor? Similarly, an employee complains about the workplace being too hot. Is the temperature set too high? Does the employee just prefer a cooler temperature? Is something wrong with the air conditioner? Or is the employee just a complainer?

Many supervisors find it difficult to distinguish between the symptoms of the problem and the problem itself. As a result, a supervisor may treat the symptoms and not the problem. Treating the symptoms is usually a short-term solution at best. For example, suppose your car has a faulty alternator, which in turn causes the battery to run down. If you treat the symptom and replace the battery, you will have solved the problem only for a very short time. At this stage, supervisors should do their best to define the problem based on the identified indicators and symptoms.

FIGURE 2.2
Factors to Aid in Defining the Problem

Symptoms:	What has alerted you to the problem?
	How did you recognize the problem?
	What is wrong?
	Have there been any obvious changes?
Location:	Where are the symptoms occurring?
Time:	When did you discover the symptoms?
	How long have they existed?
Extent:	How severe does the problem appear to be?

Step 3: Collect Facts and Redefine the Problem If Necessary

After the problem has been tentatively defined, based on the initial indicators and symptoms, a supervisor should then collect pertinent data and facts.

Figure 2.2 presents four factors that, when systematically addressed, can help define most problems. The responses to each of these factors should be recorded in writing to help the supervisor maintain objectivity. Figure 2.3 analyzes the factors of a problem concerning the poor quality of a particular product. By pinning down and identifying the symptoms, the location, the time, and the extent of the problem, the supervisor can usually get a much better grasp of what the problem really is. If a supervisor finds that he or she has several problems, then the problems should be prioritized and addressed in order.

Step 4: Identify Possible Alternatives

Once the problem has been clearly defined, possible alternatives can be identified. Obviously, any decision is only as good as the best of the alternatives that are considered. One common pitfall in identifying possible alternatives is considering only obvious alternatives or alternatives that have been used previously. With such an approach, many viable alternatives may not even be considered. As a general rule, the more alternatives generated, the better the final solution. There is a tendency among many supervisors to stop looking for alternatives once they have identified one or two that seem acceptable. A good rule of thumb is to try to generate at least four alternatives.

Asking for the opinions of others who may know something about the problem can be helpful in generating alternatives. The supervisor may become so involved in a particular problem that he or she overlooks alternatives obvious to a person who is not as close to the problem.

Suppose that in defining the reject problem explained in Figure 2.3, the supervisor suspects that the difficulty is a faulty machine. Possible alternatives might include:

1. Repair the machine.
2. Replace the machine with a reconditioned one.
3. Replace the machine with a new but identical model.
4. Replace the machine with a new, more modern model.

FIGURE 2.3
Defining the Problem

Symptoms:	Weekly reports show an inordinate number of low-quality units of a particular product being produced.
Location:	Machine 8, operated by E. B. Wilcox (shift 1); S. A. Lopez (shift 2); and N. A. Ibrahim (shift 3).
Time:	High number of poor-quality products began appearing on Wednesday, two weeks ago.
Extent:	Number of poor-quality units is running about three times the norm for that piece of equipment.

FIGURE 2.4
General Questions
for Gathering Facts
about Alternatives

- Does company (organization) policy have anything to say about the decision at hand?
- Has a similar situation occurred in the past? If so, what was done?
- What are the costs involved?
- How will this decision affect productivity? work procedures? employee morale?

Step 5: Gather and Organize Facts Concerning Identified Alternatives

After the problem and possible alternatives have been identified, the next step is to gather and organize facts that are relevant to the various alternatives. It is difficult, if not impossible, to make sound decisions without the pertinent facts. At the same time, however, a supervisor rarely has all of the facts that he or she would like. Of course, the timeliness of the decision has a major impact on how much data to gather and analyze. Successful supervisors learn to make decisions based on the available facts plus those that can be obtained within a reasonable amount of time and at a reasonable cost. Figure 2.4 lists some general questions that might be addressed in this phase.

It should be mentioned that today's supervisor can be faced with too much information. Computers and modern technology have made information overload a real problem for many supervisors. This occurs when the supervisor receives a huge number of irrelevant e-mails, computer printouts, and memos. For example, it is not unusual today for supervisors to receive several hundred e-mails a week. Similarly, it is not unusual for a simple and useful computer report to evolve into a large report with a lot of extraneous information. The problem facing the supervisor then is to sort out the relevant from the irrelevant information. Thus, organizing the available facts can be a difficult task.

Step 6: Evaluate Possible Alternatives

Once the facts have been gathered and organized, the next step is to evaluate each of the alternatives. Generally, this involves a comparison of their costs, the time required to implement them, their expected end results, and an evaluation of how the alternative would affect other areas of the business. Using the collected data, the supervisor should project what would happen if each of the alternatives were implemented. How long would this take? How much would it cost? What would be the favorable and unfavorable outcomes? It is usually helpful to develop a system for recording the evaluations in some written form. Table 2.1 shows a sample format. Such an approach provides much more objectivity than a simple mental evaluation of the alternatives. It permits all of the alternatives to be compared at the same time, and it uses the same categories of information in evaluating all those alternatives.

Step 7: Choose and Implement the Best Alternative

Choosing the best or most desirable alternative is not always as easy as it seems. Certainly, this step is made easier if the previous steps in the decision-making process were thorough. After the costs, time, and potential outcomes have been evaluated, the decision still requires some judgment and even willpower on the part of the supervisor. While some alternatives can usually be eliminated as soon as the data have been collected, others may require a closer look. In such situations, the supervisor draws on experience, intuition, and suggestions from others in making the final choice. Caution is necessary to prevent personal biases and prejudices from influencing the decision.

It is not unusual for the supervisor to select the best of the alternatives being considered even if none of them appears to be satisfactory. The tendency here is to select an alternative and thus get the decision out of the way. In essence, completing the decision becomes more important than the decision itself. In such situations, a viable alternative that should be considered is to do nothing. This alternative gives the supervisor time to go back and seek additional alternatives.

After the final decision has been made, the supervisor should take the necessary steps to implement it. These steps include assigning responsibilities, communicating the timetable

TABLE 2.1
Sample Format for Evaluating Alternatives

Alternative	Time Required to Implement (days)	Estimated Costs ($)	Favorable Points	Unfavorable Points
A. Repair machine	15	2,000	Employees are familiar with the machine; it has proved itself.	Might break down again soon; not as fast as new machine; takes longer to fix.
B. Replace with reconditioned machine	8	4,500	Same as old machine; no training necessary. Old machine has some salvage value.	Reconditioned machine may not last as long as new one; not as fast as some new models.
C. Replace with new but identical machine	5	6,800	Same as old machine; no training necessary; likely to last a long time.	Relatively expensive; not as fast as newer models.
D. Replace with new, more modern machine	5	8,000	Fastest machine available; additional production may be needed in the future; likely to last a long time.	Most expensive; operator will require some training.

to be followed, outlining the types of control to be used, and identifying potential problems. Experience has shown that employees (and people in general) are much less resistant to a decision when they understand the why, when, and what of the decision. When communicating the decision to the affected parties, the supervisor should explain why the decision was necessary, why the specific alternative was chosen, what actions are required, and what results are expected.

Step 8: The Follow-Up

The final phase of the decision-making process is to evaluate the outcomes of the decision. The basic questions to be answered are: Did the decision achieve the desired results? If not, what went wrong? Why? The answers to these questions can be of great help in a similar future situation. Unfortunately, many people have a tendency to stick with a decision even when it begins to be apparent that it is not going to work well. The key is to learn from the past and apply this knowledge to future decisions.

Group Decision Making

4 LEARNING OBJECTIVES

Two heads are better than one . . . or are they? Let's examine the pros and cons of this cliché. There are many advantages to involving employees in the decision process. The most obvious advantage is that with several people participating, there are more resources to call upon. This usually results in the generation of more and better alternatives. An equally important advantage is that the participation of employees in decisions results in their commitment to the decisions that are made. People more readily accept decisions in which they have participated than those that are forced upon them. If people participate in reaching a decision, they usually feel a commitment to make it work. The value of involving employees extends beyond the final decision. A more complete understanding of what alternatives were considered and how each was evaluated can be of enormous help in getting the group to accept change. This is especially true if those who must implement the change are the ones who participated in the decision.

Group decisions can be very advantageous in certain situations. However, group decisions have drawbacks that make individual decisions preferable in other situations. In general, groups that are not knowledgeable or organized will usually not make good decisions. And because group decisions almost always require more time, an individual decision is generally best when there is a critical time limitation. Another drawback to group decisions is the possibility that groupthink might occur. **Groupthink** occurs when the drive to achieve consensus among group members becomes so powerful that it overrides independent, realistic appraisals of alternative actions. In other words, the group becomes more interested in achieving consensus than in making the best decision. The underlying causes of groupthink can be pressure from management to reach a decision, limited resources, limited time, or merely pressure to conform. As a result of groupthink, criticism is suppressed and conflicting opinions are inadequately considered. A further potential problem with group decisions is the possibility that one person may dominate and control the group. It is also possible that pressure to conform may inhibit certain group members. Yet another possibility is that competition within the group may develop to such an extent that winning becomes more important than the issue itself. A final hazard of group decisions is the tendency of groups to accept the first potentially positive solution and give little attention to other alternatives. Rather than depending on a simple majority rule, effective groups go out and gather more information if the group is not convinced that they have reached a good solution.

In summary, group decisions are generally preferable where avoiding mistakes is of greater importance than speed and when implementation of the decision is primarily the responsibility of the group. Figure 2.5 summarizes the positive and negative aspects of group decision making. One way to enhance the effectiveness of group decision making is to provide preparatory training for employees concerning the process.

Group participation in decision making is not an all–or–nothing proposition. The degree of participation can vary widely from situation to situation. A common approach is for the supervisor to set certain limitations on the decision before turning it over to the group. Another approach is for the supervisor to reserve the right to modify or reject the group's decision. Still another approach is to have the group assist in the generation and evaluation of alternatives but not in the final selection of an alternative. Even when employees are not directly involved in the decision-making process, it is usually beneficial to keep them informed as to what is happening. Whatever approach is used, the supervisor must always be honest with the group and not mislead it as to what its role will be. The supervisor who

FIGURE 2.5
Positive and Negative Aspects of Group Decision Making

Positive Aspects of Group Decision Making

1. The sum total of the group's knowledge is greater.
2. The group generally develops a much wider range of alternatives.
3. Participation increases the acceptability of the decision to the group.
4. Group members better understand why a decision was made.

Negative Aspects of Group Decisions

1. Group decisions take more time.
2. The phenomenon of groupthink may occur.
3. One individual may dominate or control the group.
4. Pressures to conform may inhibit group members.
5. Competition may become overly intense among group members.
6. Groups have a tendency to accept the first potentially positive alternative.

SUPERVISION ILLUSTRATION 2–1

THE BENEFITS OF EXPLAINING DECISIONS

In a 2006 study, Phillip G. Clampitt, a consultant and communications professor at the University of Wisconsin, Green Bay found support for the notion that employees are more likely to support decisions when they are informed about the rationale behind the decisions. Mr. Clampitt's study surveyed approximately 300 managers and employees at more than 100 U.S. employers. Mr. Clampitt reported that employees of companies that explained decisions more fully were more than twice as likely to support those decisions as employees who got less information.

In 2004, a group of employees at Foremost Farms USA got a directive to make each block of American-style cheese weigh as close as possible to 640 pounds. Normally, the blocks varied by 30 to 40 pounds. The customer wanted precise weights so it could cut the blocks into smaller chunks for sale. Initially the directive went well. However, once the supervisors stopped checking, the employees went back to their old ways and the weights started fluctuating again. The company then developed a presentation to the employees explaining why the changes were necessary. Once the employees had been given the rationale for the necessary changes, the weights began to deviate much less.

Source: Phred Dvorak, "Theory & Practice: How Understanding the 'Why' of Decision Matters; Employees More Likely to Embrace Changes When Fully Informed," *The Wall Street Journal,* March 19, 2007, p. B.3.

asks for the group's input but never uses it is quickly recognized. Everyone is familiar with the supervisor who asks for the group's opinion and then does exactly what he or she wants to do anyway.

The Japanese have successfully used group decision making for years. Under the Japanese system, employees are involved through a form of collective decision making in which employees participate in decisions that affect them. Supervision Illustration 2–1 discusses how some supervisors and managers have been able to get their employees to better support their decisions.

Practical Traps to Avoid When Making Decisions

LEARNING OBJECTIVES

Many supervisors have a tendency to fall into one or more traps when making decisions. This section outlines some of these traps and offers some suggestions for avoiding them. It should be noted that these traps are not discussed in any order of importance.

Trap 1: Making All Decisions BIG Decisions

Everyone has run into the supervisor who treats every decision as if it were a life-and-death issue. Such a supervisor spends two hours deciding whether to order one or two boxes of rubber bands. This approach wastes much of the supervisor's time. It also keeps the employees confused; they have a hard time distinguishing between the important and not so important issues. As a result of this approach, the really important problems may not receive proper attention because the supervisor becomes bogged down in unimportant matters. This type of supervisor must learn to allocate an appropriate amount of time to each decision, based on its relative importance.

Trap 2: Creating Crisis Situations

Some supervisors seem to delight in turning all decision situations into crisis situations. A true crisis occurs when a decision must be made under extreme time constraints. In actuality, very few crises occur naturally. What usually happens is that the supervisor transforms a normal situation into a crisis situation. Even when a true crisis does occur, such as the breakdown of a major piece of equipment or an accident, the supervisor must learn to remain calm and think clearly. It is a good habit to always ask yourself, "How much time do I really have to make this decision?" It is easy and even natural to assume that you have less time than you actually do.

Trap 3: Failing to Consult with Others

The advantage of consulting others in the decision-making process was discussed earlier in this chapter. Yet some supervisors are reluctant to consult others. They fear that asking for advice will make them look incompetent. Many supervisors, especially new ones, are under the impression that they should know all the answers and that to ask someone else for advice would be admitting a weakness. These are natural tendencies and should be recognized as such. Successful supervisors learn to put good sense and their reasoning ability ahead of ego.

Trap 4: Never Admitting a Mistake

No one makes the best decision every time. If a supervisor makes a bad decision, it is best to admit this and do what is necessary to correct the mistake. The worst possible course is to try to force a bad decision into being a good decision. For example, suppose you buy a used car. After you have owned the car for a couple of months, it becomes apparent that the car is a lemon. It would probably be much better to admit the mistake and get rid of the car, even at a loss, than to pretend that the decision was a good one and continue to pour more money into the car. Again, the natural tendency is to not admit mistakes.

Trap 5: Constantly Regretting Decisions

Some supervisors may admit their mistakes but seem to be forever regretting their decisions—the good ones as well as the bad ones. These people always want to change the unchangeable. A typical sentence of theirs starts with the words "I sure wish I had . . ." Once a decision has been made and is final, don't brood over it. Remember, very few decisions are totally bad; some are just better than others. Often, a supervisor who spends time dreaming about "what ifs" will not have enough time to implement current decisions.

Trap 6: Failing to Utilize Precedents and Policies

Why reinvent the wheel? If a similar decision situation has occurred in the past, supervisors should draw on that experience. If a certain situation seems to be constantly recurring, it is often useful to implement a policy covering the situation. For example, it is wise to have a policy covering priorities for vacation time. Also, supervisors should keep abreast of current organizational policies. These can often help in decision situations.

Trap 7: Failing to Gather and Examine Available Data

Supervisors often ignore or fail to utilize available factual information. One common reason for this is that some degree of effort is normally required to gather and analyze data. In other words, it is easier to utilize only the data already on hand. A related problem is separating the facts from gossip and rumor. The general tendency is to believe only what one wants to believe and not to consider the facts.

Trap 8: Promising What Cannot Be Delivered

Supervisors sometimes make commitments when they don't have the necessary authority. Similarly some supervisors make promises that they know they can't keep. This is usually done to make the decision-making process easier for the supervisor. Also, supervisors may view such commitments and promises as ways of getting subordinates to go along with decisions. Such an approach almost always comes back to haunt the supervisor. The best approach is to promise no more than can be delivered.

Trap 9: Delaying Decisions Too Long[2]

As discussed in an earlier section of this chapter, many supervisors tend to put off making a decision "until we have more information." Timeliness is often critical and even good decisions can be ineffective if delayed too long. It is rare that any supervisor ever has all the information he or she would like. The key is for supervisors to know when they have adequate information.

Making Creative Decisions

Being creative does not necessarily mean coming up with revolutionary ideas. It does mean taking a fresh and uninhibited approach when making decisions and not being restricted by what has been done in the past. From a supervisory standpoint, being creative relates not only to the personal ideas of the supervisor but also to the climate that the supervisor establishes. Creative supervisors not only have new ideas but also elicit new ideas from their employees. The supervisor sets the creative tone; if he or she encourages creativity, the employees sense this and act accordingly.

The Creative Person

People tend to think of themselves and others as being creative or not creative. But being creative is not an all-or-nothing characteristic. Everyone can be creative to some extent. Creativity is not a mysterious power given to a select few. Typically, the person who believes "creativity is not my bag" has never tried to use his or her creative powers. Figure 2.6 lists some general characteristics of people who tend to excel in creativity.

Improving Personal Creativity

Unfortunately, most creativity is suppressed in the growing-up process. In fact, studies have shown that by the age of 40 the average adult retains only about 2 percent of the creativity that he or she possessed at age 5.[3] The key to improving personal creativity is unlocking the untapped creative potential that most people possess.

One aid to being creative is to concentrate. Think of only one problem or subject at a time, and strive to get as many different ideas as you can. Try and think "outside the box." Do not be limited by what seems to be practical. The initial step is to get a number of ideas. The evaluation of each idea takes place later. It is important that you use your subconscious brain. To do this, rest your conscious mind when you feel tired. The subconscious brain then takes over and reviews and relates thoughts that the conscious mind produced. This is commonly called "sleeping on the problem." In addition, be persistent. Keep trying. Useful ideas seldom result from the first attempts. You may well go over many ideas before you discover the one best suited to the situation. Finally, implement the idea. This can be a difficult step. It has been said that the most difficult task in the world is to drive an idea through the skull of a human being.

Establishing and Maintaining a Creative Climate

Every supervisor is responsible for the type of environment that he or she creates. Just how does the supervisor go about developing a creative environment? First and foremost, supervisors must demonstrate that they value creativity. All too often, supervisors pay lip service to creativity while rejecting any and all suggestions for doing things differently. Employees judge supervisors by what they do, not by what they say. Almost everyone has at one time or another approached the boss with a new idea only to be flatly rejected or ignored. This does not have to happen many times before employees "get the picture" and quit coming up with new ideas. On the other hand, the supervisor who reinforces creativity

6   LEARNING OBJECTIVES

FIGURE 2.6
Characteristics of Creative People

Source: Andrew J. DuBrin, *Human Relations: A Job-Oriented Approach,* 4th ed. (Englewood Cliffs, NJ: Prentice Hall, 1988), p. 105.

- Creative people tend to be bright rather than brilliant.
- Creative people have a youthful curiosity throughout their lives.
- Creative people are emotionally expressive and sensitive to the world around them and the feelings of others.
- Creative people tend to have a positive self-image; they feel good about themselves.
- Creative people have the ability to tolerate isolation.
- Creative people are nonconformists.
- Creative people often have thrill-seeking tendencies.
- Creative people are persistent.

SUPERVISION ILLUSTRATION   2–2

BRAINSTORMING ONLINE

Spinscape is a new tool that, according to its creators, introduces a completely new way of gathering and managing information. Previously, co-workers and individuals had to exchange information via a shared desktop, email or by phone calls. Spinscape enables individuals to collaborate and navigate over the internet.

The developers of Spinscape say they have anecdotal and hard data showing how globalization and an influx of information have complicated decision-making and information sharing. The goal of Spinscape is to yield better results by simplifying decision-making and information sharing. "Spinscape not only helps provide easy access to vast amounts of information exchanged by companies and individuals daily in disparate locations, but it gives people the ability to selectively share time sensitive and confidential data with select parties," says Marty Tibbitts, founder and chairman of BOSSdev, the developer of Spinscape. Spinscape gives users a new way to brainstorm and collaborate in a visual environment. For more information visit www.spinscape.com.

Source: "Spinscape Allows Users to Collaborate in a Visual Mind-Mapping Environment," *Business Wire,* April 23, 2008.

---

continues to get new ideas from employees. Group decision making, which was discussed earlier in this chapter, is one method of encouraging creativity among employees. Several other methods are discussed in the following sections.

Brainstorming

7 LEARNING OBJECTIVES

Brainstorming is an approach that involves presenting a problem to a group of people and then allowing the group to develop ideas for solutions. The basic approach is to encourage all participants to suggest any and all ideas that come to mind. The ideas may be wild and seemingly impractical, but they may lead to a creative solution. To encourage the free flow of ideas, no criticisms of suggested solutions are allowed at first. Only after all ideas have been presented and recorded does the group begin to evaluate them. Ideally, a brainstorming session should last from 45 minutes to an hour. The problem should not be discussed before the session. A small room and conference table should be used to encourage free communication. After the problem has been presented, a response should be sought from each participant. If an individual offers a suggestion, it is recorded. A person who does not have a suggestion merely says "pass." This process is repeated around the table a number of times until everyone passes. Such a procedure allows everyone an equal chance to participate and it prevents a few people from dominating the process.

Brainstorming is most applicable to simple decision problems requiring creative ideas. Naming a new product or service, coming up with a new use for a product, and identifying new ways to reduce wasted time are examples of situations where brainstorming might be effective. Supervision Illustration 2–2 describes a new software package designed to help companies and individuals brainstorm from disparate locations.

Brainwriting

Under **brainwriting,** group members are presented with a problem situation and then asked to jot down their ideas on paper without any discussion. The papers are not signed. The group members then exchange the papers with others, who build on the ideas and pass the papers on again until all have had an opportunity to participate.

Synectics

Synectics is a relatively new technique used in creative problem solving. Synectics uses metaphorical thinking to "make the familiar strange and the strange familiar." Analogies

SUPERVISION ILLUSTRATION 2–3

ENCOURAGING CREATIVITY

Just a few weeks after assuming leadership of the Tucson Unified School District, Superintendent Elizabeth Celania-Fagen introduced her executive team to the Walt Disney management model. Fagen believes that by exposing her staff to the Disney model, she can substantially improve staff creativity. Disney, who currently employs approximately 60,000 people, is well known for producing creative and loyal employees.

Fagen's initial plan is to send, over time, five different staff members to the Disney Institute for training. Each staff member will attend a different 3½ day seminar. Following the

Disney training experience, staff members will come back and, with the help of the district's professional development team, re-create their respective learning experiences for their peers. "We have to move this district forward and change the culture in fundamentally deep ways. We can't do it for free and we can't do it by doing what's already been done," says Fagen. Fagen hopes the business community will help fund the $3,500 cost for each 3½ day seminar attended.

Source: Rhonda Bodfield, "TUSD Staffers to Get Disney Training: Superintendent Says It Leads to Creativity, Top Customer Service," *McClatchy—Tribune Business News,* October 19. 2008.

are the best method for doing this. There appear to be several basic forms from which to springboard ideas:

- *Personal analogies.* Place yourself in the role of the object.
- *Direct analogies.* Make direct comparisons.
- *Symbolic analogies.* Look at the problem in terms of symbols.
- *Fantasy analogies.* Imagine the most perfect solution.

As an illustration of the fantasy analogy method, or "goal wishing," the participants fantasize about how a particular problem could be solved if there were no physical constraints. After developing a list of wishful solutions, the participants are encouraged to come up with the most absurd solutions they can imagine. Often at least one or two of these solutions can be refined into practical solutions. Supervision Illustration 2–3 describes how one school superintendent is trying to encourage creativity among her administrative staff.

Barriers to Organizational Creativity

Many organizations and supervisors have created numerous barriers that inhibit organizational creativity. Usually, but not always, these barriers have been established unintentionally, yet their effect is to discourage creativity among employees. Some of the more frequently encountered examples of organizational creativity barriers are:[4]

8 | LEARNING OBJECTIVES

Fear of failure. The simple fear of failure prevents many people from ever trying anything creative.

Premature criticism. Premature criticism and judgment of new ideas can quickly cause people to shy away from creative ideas.

The supervisor's shadow. Some supervisors create an environment that encourages employees to try to anticipate the way the boss is thinking. This discourages individual creativity.

Distractions and interruptions. Creative thinking is enhanced by quiet and uninterrupted periods of thinking time.

Protection of the status quo. Creative ideas often affect the status quo, and those who challenge the status quo often meet with criticism, lack of support, and threatened self-esteem.

Hierarchical idea filter. The more hierarchical levels an idea must pass through to be implemented, the greater the chances of its being distorted or lost.

Jane appears to have recognized the need to make decisions as a supervisor (pp. 22–23). If she is not already doing so, it would benefit her to get in the habit of using the scientific method to work through decisions. The major advantages of the scientific method are that it is systematic and objective (pp. 23–26).

As for coming up with and implementing better ways of doing things, Jane should try some of the approaches suggested in this chapter. First and foremost, she should concentrate on creating the proper climate to encourage new ideas (pp. 30–31). At a minimum, this means giving every suggestion a fair hearing. If a suggestion is workable, Jane should implement it and give the employee credit. If a suggestion is unworkable, she should take the time to explain why it won't work.

Next, Jane should utilize group decision making whenever possible. This might result in more creative solutions, and it would almost certainly increase the employees' acceptance of the decisions reached (pp. 26–28). Brainstorming, brainwriting, and synectics are all techniques that might be tried as appropriate opportunities present themselves (pp. 31–32).

Appropriated ideas. Some supervisors take credit for ideas that actually originated with one or more subordinates. This appropriation naturally discourages subordinates from generating new ideas.

Lack of support. Creative ideas are enhanced when they are supported by the supervisor and fellow employees.

Excessive togetherness. Excessive togetherness saps individuality and promotes consensus ideas that are rarely creative.

Summary

This chapter emphasizes the importance of decision making for successful supervision. It describes the scientific method for making decisions and discusses several traps to avoid when making decisions. The chapter also gives particular attention to establishing a climate that encourages creative decisions.

1. *Differentiate between programmed and nonprogrammed decisions.* Programmed decisions are reached by following an established or systematic procedure. Nonprogrammed decisions have little or no precedent and are relatively unstructured and generally require a more creative approach by the decision maker.

2. *Discuss the importance of recognition and timeliness in decision making.* Recognizing the need to make a decision is a natural prerequisite to making a sound decision. Timeliness is also critical to a sound decision. Good decision makers realize that different decisions must be made within different time frames.

3. *State the steps taken in the scientific method of decision making.* The scientific method of decision making is composed of the following steps: (1) be alert to indicators and symptoms of problems, (2) tentatively define the problem, (3) collect facts and redefine the problem if necessary, (4) identify possible alternatives, (5) gather and organize facts, (6) evaluate possible alternatives, (7) choose and implement the best alternative, and (8) follow up.

4. *Name several potential advantages and disadvantages of group decision making.* Potential advantages of group decision making include (1) the sum total of the group's knowledge is greater, (2) the group generally develops a much wider range of alternatives, (3) participation increases the acceptability of the decision to the group, and (4) group members better understand why a decision was made.

Potential disadvantages of group decision making include (1) it takes more time, (2) groupthink may occur, (3) one individual may dominate or control the group, (4) pressures to conform may inhibit group members, (5) competition may become overly intense among group members, and (6) groups have a tendency to accept the first potentially positive alternative.

5. *List several traps that supervisors frequently fall into when making decisions.* Among the traps that supervisors frequently fall into when making decisions are (1) making all decisions *big* decisions, (2) creating crisis situations, (3) failing to consult with others, (4) never admitting a mistake, (5) constantly regretting decisions, (6) failing to utilize precedents and policies, (7) failing to gather and examine available data, and (8) promising what cannot be delivered.

6. *Discuss the role that the supervisor plays in establishing a creative environment.* The supervisor sets the creative tone; if he or she encourages creativity, the employees sense this and act accordingly.

7. *Describe several group-oriented techniques that can be employed by supervisors to encourage creativity.* Brainstorming is an approach that involves presenting a problem and then allowing the group to develop ideas for solutions. Only after all ideas have been presented and recorded are any criticisms or evaluations of ideas allowed. In brainwriting, group members are asked to jot down on paper their ideas relating to a problem. Without discussion, the unsigned papers are then exchanged. The recipients build on the ideas and pass the papers until all have had an opportunity to participate. The input-output scheme first requires group members to describe the desired output of a problem. The next step is to list all possible combinations of inputs that could lead to the desired output. These possibilities are then evaluated until one emerges as the most preferred.

8. *Itemize some of the more frequently encountered barriers to organizational creativity.* The more frequently encountered barriers to organizational creativity include fear of failure, premature criticism, the supervisor's shadow, distractions and interruptions, protection of the status quo, hierarchical idea filter, appropriated ideas, lack of support, and excessive togetherness.

Key Terms

Brainstorming, 31
Brainwriting, 31
Decision making, 22
Expected decisions, 21

Groupthink, 27
Nonprogrammed decisions, 22
Problem solving, 22
Programmed decisions, 22

Synectics, 31
Unexpected decisions, 21

Review Questions

1. Give at least three examples of expected decisions and unexpected decisions that a supervisor might face.

2. Name the steps in the scientific approach to making decisions.

3. Why is it usually a good idea to generate several alternatives when making a decision?

4. Discuss both the positive and the negative aspects of group decision making.

5. Name and briefly discuss several traps that supervisors frequently fall into when making decisions.

6. List several characteristics of creative people.

7. Briefly describe the following techniques for encouraging creativity: brainstorming, brainwriting, synectics.

8. List several potential barriers to organizational creativity.

Skill-Building Questions

1. Do you think that the same general approach used in making organizational decisions should be used when making personal decisions? What are the differences and similarities?

2. Supervisor Bill Quane recently presented a decision situation to the members of his work group in order to get their input. Much to his dismay, he found considerable disagreement concerning the decision. At present, he is not sure what to do. What do you think he should do? Why?

3. As a supervisor faced with many decisions, how would you know which decisions should be made immediately and which should not be made immediately?

4. Identify a person whom you know that you consider to be highly creative. Does this person possess the characteristics shown in Figure 2.6?

References

1. These steps were delineated by Margene E. Sunderland, Fayetteville Technical Community College, Fayetteville, North Carolina.

2. Thanks to Elliott F. Porter of Los Angeles Trade Technical College for the inclusion of this trap.

3. Richard L. Bencin, "How to Keep Creative Juices Flowing," *International Management,* July 1983, p. 26.

4. This list of barriers is summarized from Bencin, "How to Keep Creative Juices Flowing," pp. 27–28.

Additional Readings

Burrows, Peter, "He Thinks Different," *BusinessWeek,* November 1, 2004, p. 20.

Forte, Jay, "Give Feedback, Get Performance," *Supervision,* February, 2009, pp. 3–4.

Link, Jonathan, "Creativity Without Borders," *Boards,* February, 2007, p. 40.

Thieman, LeAnn, "How to Overcome the 10 Biggest Mistakes in Decision Making," *Supervision,* June 2008, pp. 16–17.

SKILL-BUILDING APPLICATIONS

Incident 2–1

A Second Chance?

Word came down to the office supervisor, Jill Clark, that the Bright-Star Company had decided to upgrade its computerized billing, payroll, and inventory systems. The new system was substantially different from the existing one and had the long-term advantage of requiring two fewer people to operate it. One disadvantage was that the remaining employees would require extensive additional training.

The vendor providing the new system estimated that it would take about six weeks to fully implement the new system. After consulting with her boss, Jill decided that the fairest thing to do would be to survey each of the department's seven employees and see if anyone was interested in being transferred to another area. Jill was pleased that two employees said they would be happy to be transferred.

The Bright-Star Company had always demonstrated concern for its employees, and this instance was no exception. Jill was instructed to tell her employees that no one in the department would be laid off because of the new system.

The implementation period went very well, and the new system was successfully operating in just over six weeks. About six months later, however, and without much warning, sales for the company began to slow drastically. Jill soon received word to lay off five of the department's employees. None of the computer operators would be affected by the layoffs since the computer would continue to be used. Among those to be laid off by Jill was Barbara Peters. Barbara had been with Bright-Star seven years and was one of the employees who had volunteered for reassignment. Within a few minutes of receiving her layoff notice, Barbara went to Jill's desk.

Barbara: I've been here over seven years, and I need my job. You know my husband left me with three children to support.

Jill: I understand. Don't forget, I also have children.

Barbara: I hear that none of the computer system employees will be laid off. Let me have a shot at one of those jobs. After all, I have over seven years with the company.

Jill: Barbara, you know you are not qualified for that. After all, you volunteered for reassignment. I'm simply following company policy, which states—and I quote—"When it is necessary to reduce our labor force, seniority shall apply, providing performance and skill are equal."

Barbara: *Seniority* is the key word. You and I both know that I could learn to operate the new computer system in a few weeks. Originally, the idea scared me. But after seeing it in operation, I know I could catch on in no time. Jill, you owe me a second chance.

Questions

1. Do you think that the original decision regarding the selection of computer operators was fair? Justify your answer.

2. Do you think that Jill should reconsider her decision to lay off Barbara? Why or why not?

3. What alternatives are available to Jill, and which one would you choose?

Incident 2–2

Bad Times at Quality Shoe

Mack Moller was supervisor of the production department of the Quality Shoe Company. He received a call from the general manager informing him that production must be cut back 20 percent due to the current recession. Mack knew that this also meant that labor costs must be cut by approximately 20 percent. His problem was deciding where to make the cuts. Fortunately (as Mack saw it), Quality Shoe was not unionized. This gave him much more freedom to make decisions than he would have had if Quality were unionized. Some of the obvious alternatives were a layoff of employees based on seniority, a reduction of the hours worked by all employees, or a layoff of employees based on performance evaluations. Cutbacks were rare at Quality, and Mack knew that the current situation could cause a few waves if not properly handled.

Mack had recently attended a supervisory seminar on group and creative decision making and had been quite impressed. He decided that this would be an excellent opportunity to try out some of the ideas he had learned. He strolled out on the floor and stopped at Ralph Russell's workstation. Ralph had been at Quality almost 15 years, and Mack knew that he was well respected by all the production employees.

Mack: Ralph, we've got a problem. I just received word from the boss that production and labor must be cut by 20 percent.

Ralph: I've suspected that something like that might happen with the economy in a nosedive and everything else that is going on.

Mack: Ralph, I'd like you to get everybody in the department together [a total of 16 people] and discuss among yourselves how you think the cuts should be made. Once you reach agreement, let me know—but not later than the day after tomorrow! Try to come up with something creative.

Ralph: OK, Mack, but can't you give us some general guidelines to go by?

Mack: I guess I could, Ralph, but for starters I'd like to see what you come up with on your own.

Ralph: Just how much weight will our decision carry? We don't want to spend a lot of time on this if our ideas aren't going to count for anything.

Mack: As long as it's reasonable, I'll implement it in its entirety.

Questions

1. What do you think of Mack's approach to solving his problem?

2. How would you go about the task if you were Ralph?

3. What do you think Mack should do if he doesn't think that the group's decision is reasonable?

Exercise 2–1

Lost at Sea

This exercise is designed to demonstrate the value of group decision making. The exercise requires that you first make a set of decisions individually and then repeat the same decisions using a group format.

You are adrift on a private yacht in the South Pacific. Because of a fire of unknown origin, much of the yacht and its contents have been destroyed. The yacht is now slowly sinking. Your location is unclear because critical navigational equipment was destroyed and you and the crew were distracted trying to bring the fire under control. Your best estimate is that you are approximately 1,000 miles south-southwest of the nearest land.

Below is a list of 15 items that are intact and undamaged after the fire. In addition to these articles, you have a serviceable rubber life raft with oars large enough to carry yourself, the crew, and all the items listed below. The total contents of all survivors' pockets are a package of chewing gum, several books of matches, and five one-dollar bills.

Your task is to rank the 15 items below in terms of their importance to your survival. Place the number 1 by the most important item, the number 2 by the second most important, and so on through number 15, the least important.

—Sextant
—Shaving mirror
—Five-gallon can of water
—Mosquito netting
—One case of U.S. Army C rations
—Maps of the Pacific Ocean
—Seat cushion (flotation device approved by the Coast Guard)
—Two-gallon can of oil-gas mixture
—Small transistor radio
—Shark repellent
—20 square feet of opaque plastic
—One quart of 160-proof Puerto Rican rum
—15 feet of nylon rope
—Two boxes of chocolate bars
—Fishing kit

After everyone has completed the above rankings, your instructor will divide you into groups. Your group is to then rank the same items using a group consensus method. This means the ranking for each of the 15 survival items *must* be agreed upon by each group member before it becomes part of the group decision. Consensus is difficult to reach. Therefore, not every ranking will meet with everyone's complete approval. As a group, try to make each ranking one with which all group members can at least partially agree. Here are some guidelines to use in reaching consensus:

1. Avoid arguing for your own individual judgments. Approach the task on the basis of logic.

2. Avoid changing your mind if the change is only to reach agreement and to avoid conflict. Support

only solutions with which you are able to agree at least somewhat.

3. Avoid "conflict-reducing" techniques such as majority vote, averaging, or trading.

4. View differences of opinion as a help rather than a hindrance in decision making.

After you have completed your individual and group decisions, be prepared to discuss the following questions:

1. Were your group decisions better than your individual decisions? Why or why not?

2. Did any individual tend to dominate your group? If so, how could this situation have been better managed?

Source: Adapted from John E. Jones and J. William Pfeiffer, eds., *The 1975 Annual Handbook for Group Facilitators* (La Jolla, CA: University Associates, Inc., 1975).

Exercise 2–2

Assessing Your Creativity

Most of us believe we are more creative than we really are. Take a maximum of four minutes each on solving the following three problems.

1. Draw four straight lines connecting the dots in the diagram without lifting your pencil (or pen) off the paper. You are permitted to cross a line, but you cannot retrace any part of a line.

    •   •   •

    •   •   •

    •   •   •

2. What do the following words have in common (other than that they are all in the English language)?

calmness

canopy

deft

first

sighing

stun

3. Place 10 circles of the same size in five rows with four circles in each row.

After you have attempted each of the above problems, be prepared to discuss the following questions:

1. Why do you think these "simple" problems were difficult for you?

2. Do you think grade-school children tend to do better or worse than adults on problems such as these? Why?

Exercise 2–3

How Good a Boss Can You Be?

Below are five scenarios that could challenge even the most seasoned of managers. Choose what you think would be the most desirable—or the least damaging— option in each case. Be prepared to defend your choices.

1. Your previous boss now reports to you. When you worked under her, you believed she was a good boss and had been helpful in your advancement. Now, three years from retirement age, she seems indifferent to her work and often performs unsatisfactorily. You:

   a. Swallow your irritation and leave her alone for the remainder of her time with the company, possibly even reducing her responsibilities so that she doesn't impede the department's overall effectiveness.

   b. Tell her what she needs to improve in order to keep her job; then threaten to fire her if she doesn't improve.

   c. Try to persuade her to take early retirement.

2. You recently hired a woman who seemed exceptionally qualified to fill an important position in your company. She is doing a good job. But you now have evidence from a private source that she falsified her academic credentials. You:

   a. Terminate her immediately.

   b. Inform her that you know her credentials are false and that she is on probation—one slip and she's out.

   c. Quietly look for a replacement and then terminate her, thereby avoiding any disruptions in company operations.

3. As a new manager, you've turned in a poor-performance appraisal for a long-time employee. Your boss, who is fond of the employee, asks you to modify the evaluation to make it less severe. You:

   a. Quietly make adjustments; pleasing the boss is worth more than resisting a change no one will care much about anyway.

   b. Inform the employee you are making the change under pressure but will scrutinize his future work.

c. Refuse to make any changes on the grounds that you are compromising the quality of work this employee and your department are capable of.

4. You've been told confidentially by management that your branch office is to be closed. You will be transferred, but all 23 of your employees will be let go. So as not to disrupt productivity, you are forbidden to tell your people in advance. You:

a. Defy the order and let your people know exactly what's happening.

b. Plant a rumor and plan to deny responsibility for it.

c. Obey the order and worry about what explanations you'll make to distraught employees later.

5. A vice president in your division has asked you to form a task force charged with revamping the company's distribution system. You've negotiated successfully with various department managers for your task-force members—except for one highly regarded, independent-minded colleague. You need the special skills of one of her employees, but you have been unable to persuade her to let him join your task force. You:

a. Inform the vice president that she will not cooperate.

b. Suggest to her that word will get around she is not a team player like the other managers.

c. Prepare to negotiate with her, offering her special favors that you have not extended to the other managers.

Source: Thomas L. Quick, "How Good a Boss Can You Be?" *Working Woman*, November 1988, p. 139. Reprinted with permission from *Working Woman* magazine. Copyright © 1988 by WWJ Partnership.

CHAPTER THREE

Improving Communication Skills

Learning objectives

After studying this chapter, you will be able to:

1. Define communication.
2. Describe the interpersonal communication process and noise.
3. Describe problems that could arise from conflicting or inappropriate assumptions made in interpersonal communication.
4. Define semantics, and explain its role in interpersonal communication.
5. Define perception.
6. Explain how emotions may affect communication.
7. Explain active listening.
8. Explain the concept of feedback in communication.
9. Describe the grapevine.
10. Define and briefly discuss the e-mail process.
11. Define Internet and intranet.
12. Discuss two factors that complicate communications in international business activities.

Supervision Dilemma

John Lewis hadn't really thought about the importance of communication until after the conversation he had just completed with one of his best workers, Eva Sampson. John had given Eva an assignment and thought that he had clearly communicated the date when he wanted it completed. However, the assignment was not completed by that date because Eva thought she had more time than John had given her. What was the source of this communication failure, and how could it have been avoided?

LEARNING OBJECTIVES 1

Communication is the act of exchanging information. It can be used to inform, command, instruct, assess, influence, and persuade other people. Communication skills are important in all aspects of life, including business.

Supervisors use communication every day. In fact, they spend as much as three-fourths of their time communicating (see Figure 3.1). Good supervisors develop effective communication skills. They use these skills to absorb information, motivate employees, and deal effectively with customers and co-workers. Good communication can significantly affect a supervisor's success.

Communication as a Supervisory Skill

Communicating effectively is an important supervisory skill for several reasons:

- *Supervisors must give direction to the people who work for them.* Supervisors who fail to give clear guidance often find that employees perform their jobs poorly because they do not understand what is expected of them.

- *Supervisors must be able to motivate people.* Good supervisors use their ability to communicate to get other people excited about their jobs.

- *Supervisors must be able to absorb the ideas of others.* Supervisors interact with many people, including co-workers, customers, and suppliers. To be effective, they must be able to understand and accept other people's viewpoints.

- *Supervisors must be able to persuade other people.* Supervisors often have ideas that others oppose. To persuade other people to accept their ideas, supervisors must be able to communicate effectively.

FIGURE 3.1
Communicating in the Business World

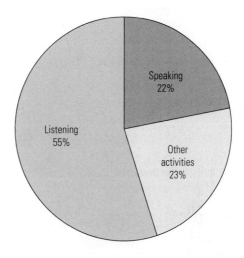

Speaking 22%

Listening 55%

Other activities 23%

Interpersonal Communication

Effective communication between individuals, especially between a supervisor and subordinates, is critical to achieving organizational objectives and, as a result, to managing people effectively. Estimates vary, but it is generally agreed that since supervisors spend much of their time with their subordinates, effective communication is critical to the wise and effective use of their time.

2 LEARNING OBJECTIVES

Interpersonal communication is an interactive process between individuals that involves sending and receiving verbal and nonverbal messages. The basic purpose of interpersonal communication is to transmit information so that the sender of a message is understood by the receiver of the message. Figure 3.2 presents a model of this dynamic and interactive process. An event or a condition generates information. The need to share the information, or inform another person about it, creates the need to communicate. The sender then creates a message (encodes) and communicates it verbally, nonverbally, or both. The receiver, in turn, perceives and interprets (decodes) the message and creates a reply message (feedback) as a response to it. This reply message may generate a response by the sender of the initial message, and the process continues in this fashion.

Often, however, many factors interfere and cause this process to fail. Some causes of communication failure are conflicting or inappropriate assumptions, different interpretations of the meanings of words (semantics), differences in perception, emotions either preceding or during communication, poor listening habits, inadequate communication skills, insufficient feedback, and differences in the interpretations of nonverbal communications. Noise is a term often used in the communication process. **Noise** refers to anything introduced into the message that is not included in the message. Supervision Illustration 3–1 describes a communication breakdown.

Conflicting or Inappropriate Assumptions

Have you ever thought you were being understood when you were really not? This is a common mistake made by most people. If one assumes that communication is flowing as intended, one tends to move on with the dialog without allowing feedback to indicate whether clarity of expression and communication has been achieved. Good supervisors

FIGURE 3.2
Model of the Interpersonal Communication Process

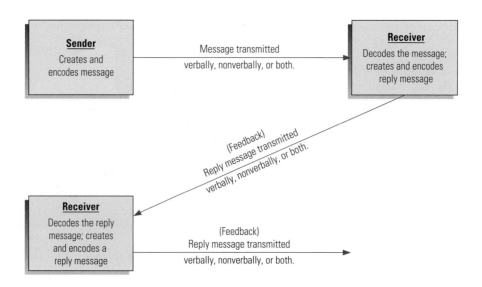

SUPERVISION ILLUSTRATION   3–1

COMMUNICATION BREAKDOWN

A communication error was blamed for a near collision at Los Angeles International Airport. The incident occurred when two airliners came within 800 feet of each other on a Los Angeles International Airport runway after an air traffic controller miscommunicated with the pilots, the FAA said.

The runway incursion on December 26 involved an American Airlines plane arriving from Mexico and a Mexicana Airlines plane preparing for takeoff. The arriving plane had just landed on the outer runway and was about to cross the inner runway where an Airbus A319 was about to take off for Morelia, Mexico.

The traffic controller told the American Airlines pilot to stop before crossing the inner runway. The pilot apparently misheard the direction and read back that he would go ahead and cross the runway. The controller did not catch the pilot's statement and cleared the Mexicana flight for takeoff before realizing that the American Airlines jetliner was about to roll onto the runway.

Source: Adapted from Jack Gillum, "TIA Tower-Plane Problems Cited," *Arizona Daily Star,* January 1, 2008.

3 LEARNING OBJECTIVES

always seek verbal or nonverbal feedback before continuing the communication process. Remember that interpretation of meaning can always be a problem when assumptions are involved. Messages such as "Stop," "Do this right now," and "Please don't" never seem to have the same meanings to employees that the supervisor intended. Sound communication usually flows from ensuring that the sender and the receiver see and understand assumptions in the same way.

Semantics

4 LEARNING OBJECTIVES

Semantics is the science or study of the meanings of words and symbols. Words themselves have no real meaning. They have meaning only in terms of people's reactions to them. A word may mean very different things to different people, depending on how it is used. In addition, a word may be interpreted differently based on the facial expressions, hand gestures, and voice inflections used.

The problems involved in semantics are of two general types. Some words and phrases invite multiple interpretations. For example, Figure 3.3 shows different interpretations of the word *fix.* Another problem is that groups of people in specific situations often develop their own technical language, which outsiders may or may not understand. For example,

---

FIGURE 3.3
Interpretations of the Word *Fix*

An Englishman visits America and is completely awed by the many ways we use the word *fix.* For example,

1. His host asks him how he'd like his drink fixed. He meant *mixed.*
2. As he prepares to leave, he discovers he has a flat tire and calls a repairperson, who says he'll fix it immediately. He means *repair.*
3. On the way home, he is given a ticket for speeding. He calls his host, who says, "Don't worry, I'll fix it." He means *nullify.*
4. At the office the next day, he comments on the cost of living in America, and one of his colleagues says, "It's hard to make ends meet on a fixed income." She means *steady* or *unchanging.*
5. He has an argument with a co-worker. The latter says, "I'll fix you." He means *seek revenge.*
6. A cohort remarks that she is in a fix. She means *condition* or *situation.*

physicians, government workers, and military employees are often guilty of using acronyms and abbreviations that only they understand.

Words are the most common form of interpersonal communication. Because of the real possibility of misinterpretation, words must be carefully chosen and clearly defined for effective communication.

Perception

Perception deals with the mental and sensory processes an individual uses in interpreting information she or he receives. Since each individual's perception is unique, people often perceive the same situation in different ways.

Perception begins when the sense organs receive a stimulus. The stimulus is the information received, whether it is conveyed verbally, nonverbally, or in another way. The sense organs respond to and organize the information received. When this information reaches the brain, it is further organized and interpreted, resulting in perception. Different people perceive the same information differently because no two people have the same personal experiences, memories, likes, and dislikes. In addition, the phenomenon of selective perception often distorts the intended message: People tend to listen to only part of the message, blocking out the rest for any number of reasons.

Examine Figure 3.4 below and answer the following questions:

1. In Figure 3.4(a), describe in writing the physical characteristics and age of the woman you see. After writing the physical characteristics and age, turn to page 54 and see how accurate you are.
2. In Figure 3.4(b), which shape is larger?
3. In Figure 3.4(c), which line—AX, CX, CB, or XD—is the longest?

Emotions Either Preceding or during Communication

Just as perception affects our cognitive processes during communication, emotions affect our disposition to send and receive the communication. Anger, joy, fear, sorrow, disgust, or panic (to mention only a few emotions) can all affect the way we send or receive messages. Emotional disposition is like the stage on which the communication piece plays its part: The stage can be perfectly prepared or in total disarray. The setting for the communication piece is obviously important. Communications during periods of high emotion usually have difficulty succeeding. Therefore, supervisors with good communication skills strive to manage the emotional as well as the physical communication environment.

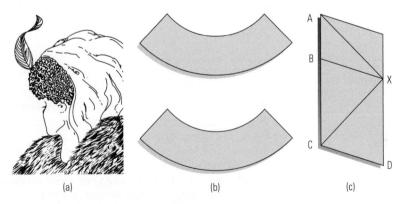

(a)   (b)   (c)

FIGURE 3.4   Illustrations of Perceptual Distortions

Sources: (a) Edwin G. Boring, "New Ambiguous Figure." *American Journal of Psychology,* July 1930, p. 444. Also see Robert Leeper, "A Study of a Neglected Portion of the Field of Learning—the Development of Sensory Organization," *Journal of Genetic Psychology,* March 1935, p. 62. Originally drawn by cartoonist W. E. Hill and published in *Puck,* November 8, 1915. (b) and (c) Gregory A. Kimble and Normal Gamezy, *General Psychology* (New York: Ronald Press, 1963), pp. 324–25.

Learning to Communicate

Supervisors communicate in writing and verbally. Before they can master either form of communication, they must be able to identify the audience, develop good listening skills, and understand the importance of feedback and nonverbal communication.

Understanding the Audience

Supervisors communicate with many different kinds of people. Hotel managers, for example, communicate with hotel guests, food and beverage managers, housekeepers, maintenance people, architects, travel agents, furniture salespeople, and many other types of people. Each of these groups of people represents a different audience.

To communicate effectively, supervisors need to determine their audience. Specifically, they need to be able to answer the following questions:

1. What does the audience already know?
2. What does it want to know?
3. What is its capacity for absorbing information?
4. What does it hope to gain by listening? Is it hoping to be motivated? Informed? Convinced?
5. Is the audience friendly or hostile?

Supervisors communicate with the hotel's housekeeping staff about complaints by guests. In doing so, they must inform the staff of the problem and motivate them to work harder to prevent complaints in the future. They would not need to provide background material on the nature of the housekeeper's role. The audience already understands what that role includes.

Developing Good Listening Skills

One of the most important skills a supervisor can develop is the ability to listen (see Figure 3.5). Good listening skills enable supervisors to absorb the information they need, recognize problems, and understand other people's viewpoints.

Supervisors need to learn to listen actively. **Active listening** involves absorbing what another person is saying and responding to the person's concerns (see Figure 3.6). Learning to listen actively is the key to becoming a good communicator.

Most people do not listen actively. Tests indicate that immediately after listening to a 10-minute oral presentation, the average listener has heard, comprehended, accurately evaluated, and retained about half of what was said. Within 48 hours, the effectiveness level drops to just 25 percent. By the end of a week, listeners recall only about 10 percent or less of what they heard.

Supervisors need to work at being active listeners. Many people daydream or think about an unrelated topic when someone else is talking. Some people become angry by a speaker's remarks and fail to fully absorb what the person is saying. Others become impatient and interrupt, preferring to talk rather than listen.

Learning to listen actively involves the following steps:

1. *Identify the speaker's purpose.* What is the speaker trying to achieve? Why is the speaker speaking?

7 | LEARNING OBJECTIVES

FIGURE 3.5
Are You a Good Listener?

- Are you open to what other people say to you, or do you make up your mind about things before you hear other people's views?
- Do you become bored when other people speak?
- Do you interrupt people when they are speaking?
- Do you daydream at meetings?
- Are you hesitant to ask clarifying questions?

FIGURE 3.6
Using Active Listening

> **1. Listening**
>
> Knowing how to listen is an important part of dealing with customers. Using active listening skills helps managers understand why customers are dissatisfied.
>
> **2. Responding**
>
> The way managers respond to complaints can be just as important as the way they solve the customer's problem. Businesspeople should always be courteous and friendly when dealing with customers. They should demonstrate interest in determining what went wrong and figuring out what they can do to solve the problem.
>
> **3. Making Sure the Customer Is Satisfied**
>
> Managers need to determine whether they have satisfied the customers' needs. To do so, they must interpret the feedback they receive from the customer.

2. *Identify the speaker's main ideas.* Which of the points are the key points? Which points need to be addressed by the listener?
3. *Note the speaker's tone as well as his or her body language.* Is the speaker angry? Nervous? Confident?
4. *Respond to the speaker with appropriate comments, questions, and body language.* Use facial expressions and body language to express the emotions you want to express. Establish eye contact, sit up straight, and lean toward the speaker to show interest. Ask a question or make a comment from time to time to show that you are listening attentively.

Feedback

Effective communication is a two-way process. Information must flow back and forth between sender and receiver. The flow from the receiver to the sender is called **feedback.** It informs the sender whether the receiver has received the correct message; it also lets the receiver know if he or she has received the correct message. For example, asking a person if she or he understands a message often puts the person on the defensive and can result in limited feedback. Instead of asking if a person understands a message, it is much better to request that the receiver explain what he or she has heard.

In an experiment designed to show the importance of feedback in the communication process, one person was asked to verbally describe to a group of people the layout of the rectangles shown in Figure 3.7. The group members were required to draw the layout based on the verbal description. The group received only a verbal description of the layout. The experiment was conducted in two ways. First, the group was not allowed to ask questions while the layout was being described, and the person describing the layout was hidden from view so the group could not see the person's facial expressions or other nonverbal communications. Thus, no feedback was present. In the second trial, the group was allowed to ask questions as the layout was being described, and the speaker was openly facing the

FIGURE 3.7
Rectangles in Communication Experiment

Source: From Harold J. Leavitt, *Managerial Psychology.* Copyright © 1972 The University of Chicago Press. Reprinted with permission.

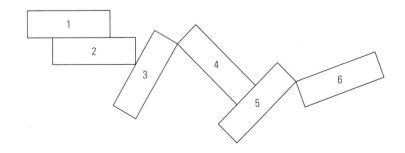

SUPERVISION ILLUSTRATION   3–2

KEEPING THE ATTENTION OF STUDENTS

Perhaps the most important part of a presentation is what the presenter doesn't say. Non-verbal communication speaks volumes. Verbal communication relays paragraphs. It's the way we say things that can make the most difference. An animated presenter who shows a lot of involvement and charisma can relay the exact same words as a monotone, motionless presenter but with a more powerful audience impact. The basis of non-verbal communication is recognizing that we are always sending and receiving messages. The instructor must embrace this notion and try to control the non-verbal communication atmosphere in order to positively affect learning.

The use of space and distance is an important element of non-verbal communication. In an instructional environment, you want students to be able to make eye contact with you at all times. If a question arises or you need to address the entire class, make way to the front of the room so all can see you easily. Avoid podiums if at all possible! A podium locks a presenter in a static position and masks body movement and gesturing. This solitary position tends to lose the audience.

There are two basic types of gestures; the emblem and the illustrative. An emblem is any gesture that has a common societal meaning; putting an index finger up to the mouth indicates a desire for silence. An illustrative gesture fills the gap for the emblems. These gestures add complementary meaning to a speech. Presenters often time throw their arms out or make broad arching sweeps as they try to reinforce a point.

Many people confuse tone and pitch with being a verbal element of communication. Instead, these elements are nonverbal cues used to accent the verbal message. The way something is said is perhaps more important than what is said.

Varying your pitch will put interest in your presentation. Control the volume of your voice—too soft or too loud will not be as effective as a mix. Vary your tempo as well. Slow down for people whose primary language is not English. Avoid speaking in a monotone voice at all costs. Implementing nonverbal actions like gesturing, movement and eye contact will help to make it easier to change tone.

Nothing breaks down barriers like making eye contact with members of the audience. This draws the students in and forces them out of a protective shell. A lack of eye contact can cause students to feel isolated and makes it easier to draw away from the presentation. Try to make eye contact with all audience members throughout the presentation so as to keep them engaged with the topic and aware of your presence. Don't stare. Eye contact should last only three to four seconds to have the desired impact. Anything shorter and no connection is made with the target. Anything longer will cause the person to feel uncomfortable and isolated.

Source: Adapted from Connie Moorhead, "Keeping the Student's Attention in the Classroom," *Security Dealer & Integrator,* December 2008, p. 22.

group. Thus, feedback was present. The results showed the layout was described more quickly to the group when no feedback was allowed. However, feedback greatly improved the accuracy and the group's degree of confidence in the accuracy of their drawings.

Understanding the Importance of Nonverbal Communication

People have a great capacity to convey meaning through nonverbal means of expression. One form of nonverbal communication, called **paralanguage,** includes the pitch, tempo, loudness, and hesitations in the verbal communication. People also use a variety of gestures in nonverbal communication. In America, for example, one can raise an eyebrow to indicate disapproval, interest, concern, or attention. In Japan, however, that raised eyebrow would be considered an obscene gesture.

People also communicate nonverbally by how close they stand to each other. Body posture and eye contact also communicate messages. For example, lack of eye contact can communicate indifference or shyness.

In summary, **nonverbal communication** is an important supplement to verbal communication and sometimes can even change the meaning of verbal communication. Nonverbal communication is an effective way to communicate emotions. When combined with verbal communication, it gives managers powerful tools for transmitting information to employees. Supervision Illustration 3–2 describes suggestions that can help keep the attention of you and your classmates.

SUPERVISION ILLUSTRATION 3–3

BUSINESS WRITING TIPS FOR NEW NURSES

In the clinical setting, writing is a critical skill for providing excellent nursing care and effective management. Clinical written communication includes documentation, orders, and notes related to care provided. New nurse managers, while possessing excellent clinical skills, often have little or no formal experience in writing business communications. Business communication studies show that, on average, nurse managers spend 31 to 40 percent of their working day writing. There are many excellent resources for nurse managers to help improve their written business communication skills. The new nurse manager may want to purchase a reference book for the office to use as new writing projects arise. Good writing skills can dramatically add credibility to the upcoming nurse leader. Nurse managers need not fear writing tasks by utilizing the writing process, following simple rules for different forms of written communication, and learning writing techniques from experts. As with clinical nursing skills, proficiency in writing comes with practice.

Source: Adapted from Jackie A. Smith and Helen Zsohar, "Business Writing Tips for the New Nurse Manager," *Nursing Management*, September 2008, p. 53.

Written Communication

Supervisors communicate in writing every day. They send e-mails, write letters, and draft reports. To communicate effectively, supervisors must be able to write clearly, concisely, and persuasively.

Before actually writing a business document, supervisors need to think about what they want to achieve. They must identify the purpose of the document, the audience, and the main point they want to convey. Using a form like that shown in Figure 3.8 can help them work through this stage of the writing process.

Principles of Good Writing

Many supervisors have difficulty writing well. To improve their writing, managers can apply several basic principles:

1. *Write as simply and clearly as possible.* Avoid writing in a way that is difficult to understand.
2. *Be sure that the content and tone of the document are appropriate for the audience.* Do not waste readers' time communicating information they already know. However, do not

FIGURE 3.8
Identifying the Purpose, Audience, and Main Point of a Document

Purpose
- Why am I writing this document?
- What action do I want the reader to take after reading it?

Audience
- Who will read this document?
- How much does the reader already know about the topic?
- How will the reader use the document?
- Are there any special sensitivities I should be aware of?

Main Message
- What is the main message I want to convey in this document?
- How will I support that message?

FIGURE 3.9
Suggestions for Improving Written Communication Skills

	Examples	
Tips	**Weak Writing**	**Strong Writing**
Use language that is easy to understand. Avoid using jargon or bureaucratic language.	Interfacing with foreign counterparts is likely to continue in the future at an accelerated pace.	We plan to work closely with foreign partners.
Use short, simple sentences.	After three years of declining sales, corporate management decided to adopt a quality-improvement program, which was instituted in all production units last month, with plans for expansion throughout the company by early April.	Sales fell for three consecutive years. In response, corporate management put a quality-improvement program in place in all production units. By April, it hopes to expand the program throughout the company.
Use restrained, moderate language that is not overly emotional.	Sales were terrible this year!	Sales were weaker than management had expected.
Avoid the passive voice in favor of the active voice.	The decision was made to create two new brochures.	The marketing department decided to create two new brochures.
Use gender-neutral language. Avoid sexist language.	Every man in this company does his best to increase company profits.	Everyone in our company does his or her best to increase company profits.

assume they are as familiar with the topic as you are. Always use a polite tone, especially when writing to customers.

3. *Proofread the document.* If you are using a computer, use the spell-check function. If you are not using a computer, use a dictionary to check the spelling of words you do not know. Always read the document for incorrect grammar or usage.

Figure 3.9 offers suggestions for improving written communication skills. Supervision Illustration 3–3 offers business writing tips for new nurses.

Oral Communication

Not all business communication is done in writing. In fact, most business communication is done orally.

Some oral communication is formal and takes place at meetings or interviews. Most oral communication is informal. It takes place in offices and hallways, next to the water fountain, in the cafeteria, and over the telephone.

The Importance of Oral Communication

Communicating well verbally is important for supervisors. Successful supervisors use their oral communication skills to give clear instructions, motivate their staffs, and persuade other people.

Being able to communicate effectively also is important because it can set the tone within a department or company. In some departments, managers say "good morning" to

FIGURE 3.10
Techniques for Speaking Effectively

Technique	Example
Enumeration (listing key points)	Our department is looking for people with excellent technical ability, outstanding communication skills, and the desire to contribute to a team.
Generalization followed by examples	We continue to demonstrate our commitment to staff education. Last year we sent almost half of our employees to seminars and training sessions. This year, we expect to include up to 75 percent of all employees in staff education.
Cause and effect	We increased our sales force by 25 percent in the North-east region in 2001. As a result, sales rose by more than $2 million.
Comparison and contrast	Our newest portable computer is as light as our competitors' and has as much computing power. It is $400 less expensive than our competitors' product, however.

as many co-workers as they can. They invite their employees to discuss problems with them. In other departments, supervisors isolate themselves from lower-level employees and make no effort to communicate. These small differences can have a big effect on employee morale.

Developing Oral Communication Skills

All businesspeople need to be able to speak effectively (see Figure 3.10). Whether they are talking to a colleague or presenting a keynote address before thousands of people, they need to follow the same rules of thumb:

1. *Make emotional contact with listeners by addressing them by name where possible.* When talking face-to-face, establish eye contact.
2. *Avoid speaking in a monotone.* Use your voice to emphasize important words within a sentence.
3. *Be enthusiastic and project a positive outlook.* Focus on what is going right, rather than what is going wrong.
4. *Avoid interrupting others.* Even if you know what the other person is going to say, avoid cutting other people off or finishing their sentences for them.
5. *Always be courteous.* Avoid getting angry when other people are talking, even if you disagree with what they are saying.
6. *Avoid empty sounds or words, such as "uh," "um," "like," and "you know."* Sprinkling your speech with empty fillers will make you sound unprofessional.

Choosing the Best Method of Communication

Supervisors need to master both written and verbal communication skills. They also need to understand when to use each kind of skill (see Figure 3.11). In general, verbal communication is most appropriate for sensitive communications, such as reprimanding or dismissing an employee. Written communication is most appropriate for communicating routine information, such as changes in company policies or staff. Choosing the best method of communication will help you relay information in an appropriate and professional manner.

FIGURE 3.11
Choosing the Best
Method of
Communication

Most Appropriate Method of Communication	Type of Situation
Oral communication alone	• Reprimanding employees • Resolving disputes within the company
Written communication alone	• Communicating information requiring future action • Communicating information of a general nature • Communicating information requiring immediate action • Communicating directives or orders
Oral communication followed by written communication	• Communicating information about an important policy change • Communicating with one's immediate superior about a work-related problem • Praising an employee for outstanding performance

Communicating within the Organization

In order to be an effective supervisor, the importance of the grapevine and e-mail must be understood.

The Grapevine

Many informal paths of communication also exist in organizations. These informal channels are generally referred to as the **grapevine.** During the Civil War, intelligence telegraph lines hung loosely from tree to tree and looked like grapevines. Messages sent over these lines were often garbled; thus, any rumor was said to be "from the grapevine." Grapevines develop within organizations when employees share common hobbies, hometowns, lunch breaks, family ties, and social relationships. The grapevine always exists within the formal organizational structure. However, it does not follow the organizational hierarchy; it may go from secretary to vice president or from engineer to clerk. The grapevine is not limited to nonmanagement personnel; it also operates among managers and professional personnel.

The grapevine generally has a poor reputation because it is regarded as the primary source of distorted messages and rumors. However, management must recognize that the grapevine is often accurate. Management must also recognize that information in the grapevine travels more rapidly than information in the formal channels of communication. Finally, management must recognize the resilience of the grapevine. No matter how much effort is spent improving the formal channels of communication, grapevines will always exist.

Because the grapevine is inevitable, management should use it to complement formal channels of communication. In utilizing the grapevine, honesty is always the best policy. Rumors and distorted messages will persist, but honest disclaimers by management will stop the spread of inaccurate information.

E-Mail

Especially valuable to communication in today's organizations is the use of electronic mail systems, or e-mail, provided by networked and online systems. The **e-mail** system provides for high-speed exchange of written messages through the use of computerized text processing and computer-oriented communication networks. The primary advantages of this system are that it saves time, eliminates wasted effort (such as unanswered or repeat phone calls), provides written records (if necessary) of communications without the formality of memos, and enables communication among individuals who might not communicate otherwise. Chapter 8 presents more discussion on e-mail.

SUPERVISION ILLUSTRATION 3–4

BUILDING BRANDS AT ENTERTAINMENT FUSION GROUP

Entertainment Fusion Group (EFG), a full service communications and marketing agency with headquarters in Los Angeles and New York City, has the ability to craft and deliver successful campaigns to build brands in the lifestyle, fashion, beauty, hospitality, film, television, music, and overall entertainment industry. (EFG) has announced the launch of a new division, Social Media 2.0. This sector of the company will focus on integrating social media in the public relations (PR) and marketing campaigns of all their clients. Utilizing the new trend in World Wide Web technologies, social media allows brands to garner more impressions and reach more consumers through social networking sites, blogs, video sharing, and other evolving web-culture communities. Social media is changing conventional methods of PR and marketing, thus maximizing a brand's exposure.

EFG has been pro-active in educating their clients in internet dynamics and urging them to take advantage of social media in order to make their communication more relationship-based. By utilizing social media press releases and online communities, i.e., Facebook, Twitter, MySpace, YouTube and blogs, brands are able to reach more consumers and media. Also, with the current state of the economy, people are more apt to browse the internet as opposed to buying publications as the same content is usually available online for free.

EFG's strategy to shift their PR and marketing plans toward online communications from traditional print and electronic media gives consumers more access to the brands. In today's business environment, accessibility is crucial to marketing and public relations practices. Consumers need to have a resource to receive information immediately and social media provides that. Brands need to have a presence online so that consumers can find information fast and easily through search engines.

Source: Adapted from Anonymous, "Entertainment Fusion Group," *Entertainment Newsweekly*, March 6, 2009, p. 70.

The Internet

11 LEARNING OBJECTIVES

The **Internet** is a global collection of independently operating, but interconnected, computers. Frequently referred to as the *information superhighway,* the Internet is actually a network of computer networks. Think of the Internet as analogous to the interstate highway system; just as the interstate system connects to different cities via many different routes, the Internet connects computers around the world via a number of different electronic pathways.

The real value of the Internet to supervisors is the information that it makes available. Through the Internet, supervisors can access massive amounts of information by accessing computers around the world that are linked together through the Internet. E-mail uses the Internet. Supervision Illustration 3–4 describes the use of new technology in communications.

Intranets

An **intranet** is a private, corporate, computer network that uses Internet products and technologies to provide multimedia applications within organizations. An intranet connects people to people and people to information and knowledge within the organization; it serves as an "information hub" for the entire organization. Most organizations set up intranets primarily for employees, but they can extend to business partners and even customers with appropriate security clearance.

Communication in International Business Activities

12 LEARNING OBJECTIVES

Communication in international business activities becomes more complicated in both the verbal and nonverbal communication processes. In verbal communication, the obvious problem of dealing with different languages exists. More than 3,000 languages are spoken, and about 100 of these are official languages of nations. English is the leading international language, and its leadership continues to grow. However, as anyone who has studied

Eva's misunderstanding of John's message illustrates a breakdown in the interpersonal communication process. Eva received John's message, interpreted it, and acted on it. However, the message that Eva received was not the message that John intended to send. This may have happened because of poor listening on Eva's part or because John did not get feedback from

Eva to ensure that the message he transmitted was the one she received. Several suggestions for improving listening skills are given on p. 45. John should be aware of the tips for receiving feedback on p. 46. He should also review the situations for using oral versus written communications on p. 51. Perhaps he should have put his instructions to Eva in writing.

a modern language knows, verbally communicating with a person in another language complicates the communication process.

The nonverbal communication process is even more complicated. Cultural differences play a significant role in nonverbal communication. For example, in the United States, people tend to place themselves about three feet apart when standing and talking. However, in the Middle East, individuals are likely to stand only a foot or so apart while conversing. This closeness obviously could intimidate an American manager.

There are no simple answers to the problems in communicating in international business activities. However, there are two things the manager should do: (1) learn the culture of the people with whom he or she communicates and (2) write and speak clearly and simply. Most people will have learned English in school and will not understand jargon or slang. As expansion into international business continues, these simple rules will become increasingly important.

Summary

1. *Define communication.* Communication is the act of transmitting information.

2. *Describe the interpersonal communication process and noise.* Interpersonal communication occurs between individuals. It is an interactive process that involves a person's effort to attain meaning and respond to it. It involves sending and receiving verbal and nonverbal messages. Noise refers to anything introduced into the message that is not included in the message.

3. *Describe problems that could arise from conflicting or inappropriate assumptions made in interpersonal communication.* Misunderstandings can occur when a speaker thinks he or she was being clear or was understood. Questions that go unanswered, points that are misunderstood, and meanings that are misinterpreted are examples of potential problems.

4. *Define semantics, and explain its role in interpersonal communication.* Semantics is the science or study of the meanings of words and symbols. Because of the possibility of misinterpretation, words must be carefully chosen and clearly defined to enable effective communication.

5. *Define perception.* Perception deals with the mental and sensory processes an individual uses in interpreting information received.

6. *Explain how emotions may affect communication.* Emotions affect one's disposition to send and receive communication. Anger, joy, fear, sorrow, disgust, or panic can all affect the way one sends and receives messages. Communications during periods of high emotion are often subject to distortion.

7. *Explain active listening.* Active listening involves absorbing what another person is saying and responding to the person's concerns.

8. *Explain the concept of feedback in communication.* Feedback is the flow of information from the receiver to the sender. For communication to be effective, information must flow back and forth between sender and receiver.

9. *Describe the grapevine.* The grapevine consists of the informal channels of communication that develop within the organization as a result of common hobbies, home towns, lunch breaks, family ties, and social relationships among employees.

10. *Define and briefly discuss the e-mail process.* The electronic mail, or e-mail, system provides for high-speed exchange of written messages through the use of computerized text processing and computer-oriented communication networks.

11. *Define Internet and intranet.* The Internet is a global collection of independently operating, but interconnected, computers. An intranet is a private, corporate, computer network that uses Internet products and technologies to provide multimedia applications within organizations.

12. *Discuss two factors that complicate communications in international business activities.* Communicating in a foreign language complicates the communications process. Cultural differences exhibited through nonverbal communications are also complicating factors.

Key Terms

Active listening, 45
Communication, 41
E-mail, 51
Feedback, 46
Grapevine, 51

Internet, 52
Interpersonal
   communication, 42
Intranet, 52
Noise, 42

Nonverbal communication, 47
Paralanguage, 47
Perception, 44
Semantics, 43

Solutions to Perception Questions for Figure 3.4

1. About 60 percent of the people viewing the picture in Figure 3.4(a) for the first time see a young, attractive, and apparently wealthy woman. About 40 percent see an old, ugly, and apparently poor woman. The figure below clarifies the profiles of the two women.

2. Shapes are same size.

3. AK, CK, CB, and XD are same length.

a. Profile of Young Woman
b. Profile of Old Woman

Source: Robert Leeper, "A Study of a Neglected Portion of the Field of Learning—the Development of Sensory Organization," *Journal of Genetic Psychology,* March 1935, p. 62.

(a)   (b)

Review Questions

1. What is communication?
2. Define interpersonal communication and noise.
3. Give an illustration of a conflicting assumption.
4. What is semantics?
5. What is perception, and what role does it play in communication?
6. How should one deal with emotions in communication?
7. What is feedback, and how does it affect the communication process?
8. What is active listening?
9. Explain the importance of nonverbal communication in interpersonal communication.
10. Describe the following organizational communication systems:
    a. E-mail communication system
    b. Grapevine
11. Describe two factors that complicate communications in international business.

Skill-Building Questions

1. Describe some ways the grapevine can be used effectively in organizations.
2. Explain why many managers frequently raise the following question: "Why didn't you do what I told you to do?"
3. Discuss the following statement: Meanings are in people, not words.
4. "Watch what we do, not what we say." Is this a good practice in organizations? Explain.
5. Poor communication of the organization's objectives is often given as the reason for low organizational performance. Do you think this is usually a valid explanation? Why or why not?

Additional Readings

Jooss, Ron and Jon Cook, "The Art of Listening," *Credit Union Management,* November 2008, p. 13.

Kowalski, Karren, "Tough Questions: Recognize and Resolve Communication Breakdown," *The Journal of Continuing Education in Nursing,* February 2008, p. 57.

Pearson, Samantha, "Crying Out for Communication," *Financial Times,* February 2009, p. 22.

Shafer, Shem, "Promoting Communication Skills in the Classroom," *The Education Digest,* February 2009, pp. 48–49.

Woodward, Greg, "I'm Listening," *Listen,* March 2009, p. 14.

SKILL-BUILDING APPLICATIONS

Incident 3–1

Who Calls the Shots?

The financial reports for the last quarter of operations for Brighton Cabinet Company were just received by the company's president, John Branner. After looking over the reports, John decided the purchasing department was paying too much for the company's raw materials, which include plywood, paneling, and flakeboard. He immediately called Joe Scott, vice president of manufacturing, and informed him of the decision. Exhibit 3.1 gives a partial organizational chart for Brighton Cabinet Company.

Joe called Bill Sloane, the supervisor of purchasing, and said, "Mr. Branner is upset over the cost figures for raw materials last quarter. You were well above budget. He wants them brought down this quarter!"

As Bill hung up the phone, he asked himself who figured out the budget for his department and if they realized plywood had gone up from $6.05 to $6.75 a sheet. Bill had been instructed to cut costs, and he was determined to do so. Two days later, Bill found a supplier who would sell Brighton plywood for $5.95 a sheet. He ordered a two-week supply.

On delivery, Bill's suspicions were confirmed. The plywood was of a poorer quality, but it would work. Bill decided to continue to buy the less expensive plywood.

A month later, Bill was approached by Ted Brown, supervisor of the assembly department, who asked, "Bill, what's with this plywood? All of a sudden, we've been having a lot of it split on us while trying to nail and staple the pieces together." Bill replied, "Well, Ted, Mr. Branner sent orders down for me to cut costs. I don't know how else to do it other than purchasing the lower-grade plywood. It was the only way out." Things were left as they were, and the quarter ended.

The financial reports for the quarter showed a drop in sales and profits. According to forecasts and trends of previous years, the profits and sales should have been higher. John Branner immediately called Mary Strickland, vice president of marketing, to his office and demanded an explanation. Mary explained,

> It seems that we have lost a couple of major builders as customers. They seem to think that our competitors have something better to offer. I have investigated the situation and have found that our cabinets are splitting more on installation because we are using a lower-grade plywood now. I talked to Joe Scott. He told me you had ordered him to cut costs, and the purchase of the lower grade was one of the few ways that costs could be reduced.

John immediately ordered Joe to begin purchasing plywood of the necessary quality. Joe then informed Bill. Later that day, Bill asked Joe what should be done with the three-week supply of the lower-grade plywood. "That's your problem," Joe snapped. Apparently, he had gotten a good chewing out from Branner.

After making several calls, Bill decided the only good offer for the plywood was made by the company that sold it to Brighton. But it would pay only 60 percent of what it cost Brighton. Bill agreed to the price, wanting to get rid of it to make room for the new supplies that would be coming in.

EXHIBIT 3.1
Partial Organization Chart for Brighton Cabinet Company

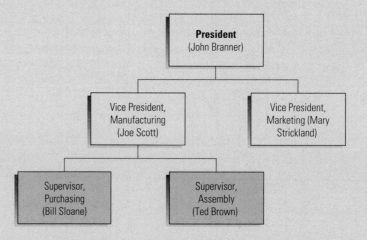

Three days later, Bill was called into Joe's office. Joe asked, "Bill, who gave you permission to sell that plywood at that price?" "No one," Bill replied. "It was my decision. It was the best deal I could find, and I needed to get it out to make room for the new supplies coming in."

"Well, Bill, with decisions like that, this company won't last very long," Joe commented. "You should have used up the other plywood a little at a time by mixing it with the higher-grade plywood. Don't let this happen again!"

Questions

1. How did this problem begin, and how could it have been avoided?
2. Describe the communication failures that occurred in this case.
3. Is Bill really responsible? Who else, if anyone, is responsible?
4. Comment on Joe Scott's talk with Bill at the end of the case.

Incident 3–2

"I Told You . . ."

Bruce Hobbs hung up the phone. The call had been from his boss, Judy Tinsley. She informed him that she had just received the weekly accounts payable report, which was prepared in his department, and that she had several problems with it.

Bruce immediately called John Logan, the employee in his department who was responsible for preparing the report. He asked John to come to his office immediately. The following conversation occurred:

Bruce: Judy just called and said there are several errors in the weekly accounts payable report.

John: I checked it carefully, and I'm certain I can explain . . .

Bruce [*interrupting John*]: I don't need an explanation. I told you no reports were to go out of here without my approval.

John: Well, I certainly haven't heard you say that.

Bruce: Maybe that's the problem—you just don't listen.

John: I do listen. You told us to check with you on any reports with which we had questions or concerns. I checked over the accounts

payable report, and there were some last-minute changes that caused some increases, but they can be explained.

Bruce: Didn't you feel you should check with me about those changes?

John: No, because I understood them.

Bruce: Well, let me make it clear. From now on, I want to see all reports before they leave this office.

Questions

1. What went wrong?
2. How could the situation been handled differently?
3. What do you think of Bruce's solution?

Exercise 3–1

Perception Test

Take a maximum of 10 minutes to complete the following test.

1. In 1963, if you went to bed at 8 o'clock P.M. and set the alarm to get up at 9 o'clock the next morning, how many hours of sleep would you get?
2. If you have only one match and enter a room in which there is a kerosene lamp, an oil stove, and a wood-burning stove, which would you light first?
3. Some months have 30 days; some have 31. How many have 28 days?
4. If a doctor gave you three pills and told you to take one every half-hour, how long would they last?
5. A man builds a house with four sides, and it is rectangular in shape. Each side has a southern exposure. A big bear comes wandering by. What color is the bear?
6. I have in my hand two U.S. coins that total 55 cents in value. One is not a nickel. Please bear that in mind. What are the two coins?
7. Divide 30 by ½ and add 10. What is the answer?
8. Take two apples from three apples, and what do you have?
9. An archaeologist found some gold coins dated 34 B.C. How old are they?
10. How many animals of each species did Moses take aboard the ark with him?

Exercise 3–2

Word Differences

We Americans supposedly speak the English language. However, anyone who has ever visited England knows that the English often use different words and phrases than we do. Can you identify what the English words or phrases in the left column below would be if spoken by an American?

chemist	a. elevator
phone engaged	b. mailbox
ring-up	c. orchestra seat
round up	d. line
wines and spirits	e. can
chipped potatoes	f. subway
give way	g. hood
to let	h. newsstand
ta!	i. taxes
it's mommy's go	j. suspenders
half five	k. aisle
mind your step	l. apartment
a bit dear	m. janitor
way out	n. hardware dealer
bonnet	o. truck
stall	p. exit
flat	q. drugstore
kiosk	r. busy
ironmonger	s. too expensive
pillar box	t. watch your step
porter	u. call
tin	v. go halfway around
lift	circle and straight up
queue	w. liquor store
lorry	x. french fries
rates	y. yield
braces	z. for rent
gangway	aa. bid adieu
underground	bb. it's mommy's turn
	cc. five-thirty

Exercise 3–3

What's Your Communication Style?

Carefully read each statement and its four endings. Grade these by assigning a 4 to the ending that most

describes you, a 3 to the next ending most like you, a 2 to the next ending most like you, and a 1 to the ending least like you. Once you have assigned a number, you may not use that number again in the set of four endings. For example, you may not assign a grade of 4 to both 1*a* and 1*b*.

1. I am most likely to impress my co-workers as
   a. Down to earth, practical, and to the point. *a* _____
   b. Emotional, sensitive to my own and others' feelings. *b* _____
   c. Cool, logical, patient. *c* _____
   d. Intellectual and somewhat aloof. *d* _____

2. When I am assigned a project, I am most concerned that the project will be
   a. Practical, with definite results that will justify my time and energy on it. *a* _____
   b. Stimulating, involving lively interaction with others. *b* _____
   c. Systematically or logically developed. *c* _____
   d. Breaking ground and advancing knowledge. *d* _____

3. In reacting to individuals whom I meet socially, I am likely to consider whether
   a. They are assertive and decisive. *a* _____
   b. They are caring. *b* _____
   c. They seem thorough and exact. *c* _____
   d. They seem highly intelligent. *d* _____

4. When confronted by others with a different opinion, I find it most useful to
   a. Pinpoint the key differences, and develop compromises so that speedy decisions can be made. *a* _____
   b. Put myself in the others' shoes, and try to understand their point of view. *b* _____
   c. Keep calm and present my material clearly, simply, and logically. *c* _____
   d. Create new proposals. *d* _____

5. Under pressure, I suspect I may come through to others as being
   a. Too concerned with wanting immediate action, and pushing for immediate decisions. *a* _____

TABLE 3.1
Some Traits Linked to Each Communication Style

Source: Reprinted with permission from *Medical Laboratory Observer*. Phyllis J. Kuhn, "Sharpening Your Communication Skills," 1987; 19(3), 53–56. Copyright 1987, Montvale, NJ, Medical Economics Company.

Positive	Negative
Intuitor	
Creative	Fantasy-bound
Idealistic	Impractical
Intellectual	Too theoretical
Feeler	
Caring	Wishy-washy
Conscientious	Guilt-ridden
Persuasive	Manipulative
Thinker	
Exact, precise	Nitpicker
Deliberate	Rigid
Weighs all alternatives	Indecisive
Senser	
Decisive	Impulsive
Assertive	Aggressive
Enjoys producing quick results	Lacks trust in others' ability
Technically skillful	Self-involved, status seeking

b. Too emotional and occasionally carried away by my feelings.   *b* _____

c. Highly unemotional, impersonal, too analytical and critical.   *c* _____

d. Snobbish, condescending, intellectually superior.   *d* _____

6. When lecturing to a group, I would like to leave the impression of being

    a. A practical and resourceful person who can show the audience how to, for example, streamline a procedure.   *a* _____

    b. A lively and persuasive individual who is in touch with the audience's emotions and moods.   *b* _____

    c. A systematic thinker who can analyze the group's problems.   *c* _____

    d. A highly innovative individual.   *d* _____

Now transcribe the numbers that you wrote beside each ending to the appropriate spaces below. Total the columns for questions 1–3 and for questions 4–6. The initials at the bottom of the columns—S, F, T, and I—stand for the different communication styles: senser, feeler, thinker, and intuitor. The column with the highest total for questions 1–3 is your communication style under relaxed conditions, and the column with the highest total for questions 4–6 is your style under stress conditions. Once you have defined your particular style,

check Table 3.1 above for the positive and negative traits associated with it. Note that you may have the positive traits without the negative ones or vice versa.

	a	*b*	*c*	*d*
1.	_____	_____	_____	_____
2.	_____	_____	_____	_____
3.	_____	_____	_____	_____
4.	_____	_____	_____	_____
5.	_____	_____	_____	_____
6.	_____	_____	_____	_____
Total	S	F	T	I

Source: From Phyllis Kuhn, "Sharpening Your Communication Skills," *Medical Laboratory Observer*, March 1987. Used with permission from Medical Laboratory Observer. Copyright © 1987 by Nelson Publishing, Inc. www.mlo-online.com.

Exercise 3–4

The Listening Quiz

Are you an effective listener? Ask a peer that you communicate with regularly and who you know will answer honestly to respond "yes" or "no" to these 10 questions. Do not answer the questions yourself. We often view ourselves as great listeners when, in fact, others know that we are not.

1. During the past two weeks, can you recall an incident where you thought I was not listening to you?

2. When you are talking to me, do you feel relaxed at least 90 percent of the time?

3. When you are talking to me, do I maintain eye contact with you most of the time?

4. Do I get defensive when you tell me things with which I disagree?

5. When talking to me, do I often ask questions to clarify what you are saying?

6. In a conversation, do I sometimes overreact to information?

7. Do I ever jump in and finish what you are saying?

8. Do I often change my opinion after talking something over with you?

9. When you are trying to communicate something to me, do I often do too much of the talking?

10. When you are talking to me, do I often play with a pen, pencil, my keys, or something else on my desk?

Use your peer's answers to grade your listening skills. If you received nine or 10 correct answers, you are an excellent listener; seven or eight correct answers indicates a good listener; five or six correct answers means you possess average listening skills; and less than five correct answers is reflective of a poor listener.

The answers most often given for effective listeners are: 1. no, 2. yes, 3. yes, 4. no, 5. yes, 6. no, 7. no, 8. yes, 9. no, 10. no.

Source: Adopted from Tom D. Lewis and Gerald Graham, "7 Tips for Effective Listening," *The Internal Audition,* August 2003, p. 23. Used with permission of the authors.

CHAPTER FOUR

Motivating Today's Employees

Learning objectives

After studying this chapter, you will be able to:

1. Define motivation.
2. Define the traditional approach to motivation.
3. Explain the hierarchy of needs.
4. Discuss the motivation-maintenance approach to motivation.
5. Discuss the preference-expectancy approach to motivation.
6. Explain the reinforcement approach to motivation.
7. State several things that the supervisor can do to affect employee motivation.

Supervision Dilemma

In recent weeks, Jane Harris has noticed that whenever she enters the office, several of her employees appear to be loafing or involved in gossipy conversations. In Jane's opinion, they just don't seem to be working very hard. A quick review of the human resources records verified another suspicion—absenteeism and tardiness have increased in recent months. Jane is baffled. Just two months ago, everyone received an 11 percent pay raise. In addition to this, the facilities of her department have been recently refurbished. What else could the employees possibly want?

"Nobody wants to work like they did when I was young." "Half the problems we have around here are due to a lack of personal motivation." "Our employees just don't seem to care." Such sentiments are often expressed by today's supervisors. However, motivating employees is not a new problem. Much of the pioneering work in the field of management was concerned with motivation. One can even find examples showing motivation problems existed back in biblical times.

What Is Motivation?

1 LEARNING OBJECTIVES

Numerous definitions can be found for the word *motivation*. Often included in these definitions are such words as *aim, desire, end, impulse, intention, objective,* and *purpose*. The word *motivation* actually comes from the Latin *movere,* which means "to move." In today's organizations, **motivation** means getting people to exert a high degree of effort on their job. A motivated employee is an employee who tries hard. The key to motivation, then, is getting employees to want to do a job. In this light, motivation is not something that the supervisor does *to* an employee. Rather, motivation is something that must come from within an employee. The supervisor can, however, create an environment that encourages motivation on the part of employees. This is the context in which the supervisor motivates employees.

Motivation can best be understood using the following sequence of events:

Needs → Drives or motives → Accomplishment of goals

In this sequence, needs produce motives, which lead to the accomplishment of goals. Needs are caused by deficiencies, which can be either physical or mental. For instance, a physical need exists when a person goes without sleep for a long period. A mental need exists when a person has no friends or no meaningful relationships with other people.

Motives produce action. Lack of sleep (the need) activates the physical changes of fatigue (the motive), which produce sleep (the accomplishment of the goal). The accomplishment of the goal satisfies the need and reduces the motive. When the goal is reached, balance is restored. Other needs soon arise, however, and the sequence repeats itself. Supervision Illustration 4–1 is an example of the use of incentives by CIGNA.

Understanding People

Every supervisor knows that some people are easier to motivate than others. Why is this true? Are some people simply born more motivated than others? No person is exactly like any other person. Each individual has a unique personality and makeup. Thus, because people are different, it stands to reason that different factors are required to

SUPERVISION ILLUSTRATION   4–1

INCENTIVES AT CIGNA

CIGNA, a global health service company, is dedicated to helping people improve their health, well-being and security. CIGNA Corporation's operating subsidiaries provide an integrated suite of medical, dental, behavioral health, pharmacy and vision care benefits, as well as group life, accident and disability insurance, to approximately 47 million people throughout the United States and around the world. People who are covered by a CIGNA health plan now have the opportunity to earn points that are redeemable for gift cards, merchandise and other rewards, such as travel packages, as part of the new CIGNA Incentive Points Program, which became available January 1 to CIGNA's employer customers who choose to offer it to their employees. Employees enrolled in the program can monitor the accumulation and redemption of their points through myCigna.com, much as they can monitor their accounts in airline, hotel and other rewards programs. The standard plan allows individuals to earn up to 200 points in a calendar year, but the employer has flexibility to set the cap.

They can earn points for participating in a variety of health-related activities, such as completing a health assessment or biometric screenings; reaching milestones in any of CIGNA's eight disease management programs, such as programs for diabetes, heart disease or depression; or actively participating in a lifestyle management program such as CIGNA's Quit TodaySM tobacco cessation program.

With a point equal to $1, employees enrolled in some health plans will also be able to convert their points to a cash contribution to a health reimbursement account or use them to defray health care premiums once the program is fully rolled out later this year.

Source: Adapted from Anonymous, "CIGNA; New CIGNA Incentive Points Program Rewards People for Making Healthy Choices," *Diabetes Week*, January 19, 2009, p. 153.

motivate different people. Yet many supervisors often expect all employees to react in a similar manner.

Not all employees expect or even want the same things from their jobs. People work for different reasons. Some people work because they have to work; they need money to pay their bills. Others work because they want something to occupy their time. Some people work for extra money—to buy something they would not otherwise be able to afford. Other people work so that they can have a career and its related satisfactions. In light of the many different reasons why people work, it is *not* logical to expect the same things to motivate everyone.

When attempting to understand the behavior of an employee, the supervisor should always remember that people do things for a reason. The reason may be imaginary, inaccurate, distorted, or unjustifiable, but it is real to the individual. The reason, whatever it may be, must be identified before the supervisor can understand the employee's behavior. All too often, the supervisor disregards an employee's reason for a certain behavior as being unrealistic or based on inaccurate information. Such a supervisor responds to the employee's reason by saying, "I don't care what he thinks—that is not the way it is!" Supervisors of this kind will probably never understand why employees behave as they do.

Yet another consideration in understanding the behavior of employees is the concept of the self-fulfilling prophecy, also known as the **Pygmalion effect.** This concept refers to the tendency of an employee to live up to the supervisor's expectations. In other words, if the supervisor expects an employee to succeed, the employee usually will succeed. Of course, the opposite is also true. If the supervisor expects an employee to fail, the employee will usually fail.

All in all, humans are very complex beings. Different things motivate different people. Today's supervisor must recognize these differences and learn to deal with them.

Basic Approaches to Motivation

2 LEARNING OBJECTIVES

Several basic approaches to motivation have been developed. The most widely recognized approaches are discussed below.

Traditional Approach

The **traditional approach** to motivation evolved from the work of Frederick W. Taylor and the scientific management movement in the early 1900s. Taylor's ideas were based on his belief that most reward systems were not designed to reward a person for high production. Taylor felt that the output of highly productive people would decrease when they discovered that they were receiving basically the same compensation as people who produced less. Taylor's solution was quite simple. He designed a system whereby individuals were compensated according to their production.

One of Taylor's problems was determining reasonable standards of performance. Taylor solved this problem by breaking jobs down into components and measuring the time necessary to accomplish each component. In this way, he was able to establish standards of performance "scientifically."

Under Taylor's reward system, one rate was paid for units produced up to the standard, but once the standard was reached, a significantly higher rate was paid not only for the units above the standard but for all of the units produced during the day. Thus under Taylor's system, employees could significantly increase their pay by exceeding the standard.

The traditional approach to motivation is based on the assumption that money is the primary motivator of people. Under this assumption, financial rewards are directly related to performance in the belief that employees will work harder and produce more if these rewards are great enough.

Need Hierarchy Approach

3 LEARNING OBJECTIVES

The **need hierarchy approach** to motivation is based on the assumption that employees are motivated to satisfy a number of needs and that money can satisfy, directly or indirectly, only some of these needs. The need hierarchy theory is based largely on the work of the psychologist Abraham Maslow.

Maslow felt that five levels of needs exist within individuals and that these need levels relate to one another in the form of the hierarchy shown in Figure 4.1.

The **physical needs** are basically the needs of the human body that must be satisfied in order to sustain life. These needs include food, sleep, water, exercise, clothing, shelter, and so forth. The **safety needs** are concerned with protection against danger, threat, or deprivation. Since all employees have, to some degree, a dependent relationship with the organization, the safety needs can be critically important. Favoritism, discrimination, and arbitrary

FIGURE 4.1
Maslow's Need Hierarchy

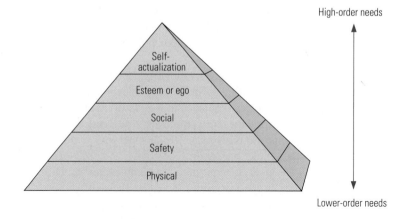

High-order needs

Self-actualization

Esteem or ego

Social

Safety

Physical

Lower-order needs

administration of organizational policies are actions that arouse uncertainty and therefore affect the safety needs.

The third level of needs is the social needs. The **social needs** include love, affection, and belonging. Such needs are concerned with establishing one's position relative to that of others. They are satisfied by the development of meaningful personal relations and by acceptance into meaningful groups of individuals. Belonging to organizations and identifying with work groups are ways of satisfying the social needs in organizations.

The fourth level of needs is the **esteem needs.** These needs include both self-esteem and the esteem of others. Maslow contended that all people have needs for the esteem of others and for a stable, firmly based, high evaluation of themselves. The esteem needs are concerned with the development of various kinds of relationships based on adequacy, independence, and the giving and receiving of indications of self-esteem and acceptance.

The highest-order needs in Maslow's hierarchy are **self-actualization** and **self-fulfillment:** the needs of people to reach their full potential in terms of their abilities and interests. Such needs are concerned with the will to operate at the optimum and thus receive the rewards that are the result of doing so. The rewards may not only be economic and social but also mental. The needs for self-actualization and self-fulfillment are never completely satisfied. One can always reach one step higher. Figure 4.2 lists several examples of each need level.

FIGURE 4.2
Examples of Needs and Workplace Examples to Satisfy Needs

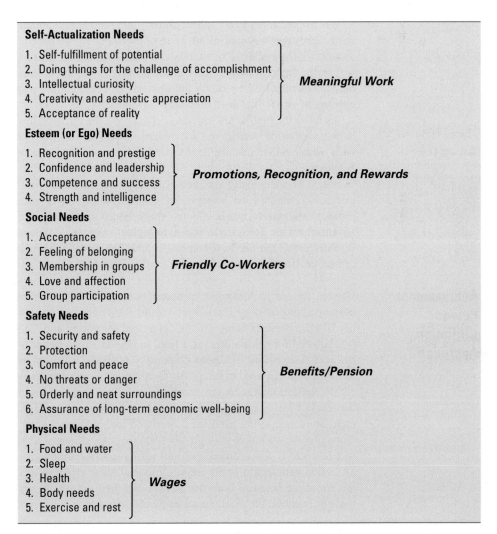

Self-Actualization Needs

1. Self-fulfillment of potential
2. Doing things for the challenge of accomplishment
3. Intellectual curiosity
4. Creativity and aesthetic appreciation
5. Acceptance of reality

Meaningful Work

Esteem (or Ego) Needs

1. Recognition and prestige
2. Confidence and leadership
3. Competence and success
4. Strength and intelligence

Promotions, Recognition, and Rewards

Social Needs

1. Acceptance
2. Feeling of belonging
3. Membership in groups
4. Love and affection
5. Group participation

Friendly Co-Workers

Safety Needs

1. Security and safety
2. Protection
3. Comfort and peace
4. No threats or danger
5. Orderly and neat surroundings
6. Assurance of long-term economic well-being

Benefits/Pension

Physical Needs

1. Food and water
2. Sleep
3. Health
4. Body needs
5. Exercise and rest

Wages

Maslow believed that at any given time only one need level serves as a person's primary motivation. He also believed that people start with the lower-order needs and move up the need hierarchy one level at a time as the lower-order needs become satisfied. Thus, until the physical needs have been substantially satisfied, they tend to dominate all other needs. Once the physical needs have been satisfied, the safety needs become dominant in the need structure. Different needs emerge as each of the respective need levels is satisfied.

In our society, the physical and safety needs are more easily and therefore more generally satisfied than the other levels of needs. In fact, Maslow estimated the percentage of persons satisfying the various need levels as follows: physical, 85 percent; safety, 70 percent; social, 50 percent; ego, 40 percent; and self-actualization, 10 percent. Many of the tangible rewards (pay and fringe benefits) given by today's organizations are used primarily to satisfy physical and safety needs.

Although the needs of the majority of people are arranged in the sequence shown in Figure 4.1, differences can occur, depending on an individual's learning experiences, culture, and social upbringing.

It is important to note that the strength of an individual's needs may shift back and forth under different situations. For instance, an individual's behavior might be dominated by the physical and safety needs in bad economic times and by the higher-order needs in good economic times.

It is not necessary to completely satisfy one need before another need emerges. Meeting some needs partially can result in an opportunity for another need to present itself. For instance, it is possible to be motivated by the social and esteem needs at the same time.

Finally, different individuals can use different methods to satisfy a particular need. Two individuals may have to satisfy the same social need, but the ways in which each of them chooses to satisfy that need may vary considerably.

As far as the motivation process is concerned, the thrust of the need hierarchy approach is that a satisfied need is not a motivator. Consider the basic physical need for oxygen. Only when individuals are deprived of oxygen can it have a motivating effect on their behaviors.

Many of today's organizations are applying the logic of the need hierarchy. For instance, compensation systems are generally designed to satisfy lower-order needs—physical and safety needs. On the other hand, interesting work and opportunities for advancement are designed to appeal to higher-order needs. Thus, the job of the supervisor is to determine the needs of employees and then provide the means by which those needs can be satisfied.

Achievement-Power-Affiliation Approach

Closely related to Maslow's approach is the **achievement-power-affiliation approach**, developed primarily by David McClelland. This approach holds that all people have three needs: (1) a need for achievement, (2) a need for power, and (3) a need for affiliation.

The need for achievement is a need to do something better or more efficiently than it has been done before. The need for power is basically a need to influence people. The need for affiliation is a need to be liked—to establish or maintain friendly relations with others.

McClelland maintains that most people have a degree of each of these needs but that the level of intensity varies. For example, a person may be high in the need for achievement, moderate in the need for power, and low in the need for affiliation. This person's motivation to work will vary greatly from that of a person who has a high need for power and low needs for achievement and affiliation. According to the achievement-power-affiliation approach it is the responsibility of supervisors to recognize the differences in the dominant needs of both themselves and their employees and to effectively integrate these differences. For example, an employee with a high need for affiliation would probably respond positively to demonstrations of warmth and support by the supervisor. An employee with a high need for achievement would probably respond positively to increased responsibility. Through self-analysis, supervisors can gain insight into how they tend to respond to employees. They may then want to alter their response to employees so that they can best fit the employee's needs.

Motivation-Maintenance Approach

4 LEARNING OBJECTIVES

Frederick Herzberg has developed an approach to motivation that has gained wide acceptance in management. His theory is referred to by several names: **motivation-maintenance** approach, dual-factor approach, and motivator-hygiene approach.

Herzberg's approach deals primarily with motivation through job design. The approach is based on the belief that the factors that demotivate or turn off employees are different from the factors that motivate or turn on employees. Herzberg maintains that the factors that tend to demotivate employees are usually associated with the work environment. These factors include such things as job status, interpersonal relations with supervisors and peers, the style of supervision that the person receives, company policy and administration, job security, working conditions, pay, and aspects of personal life that are affected by the work situation. Herzberg refers to these factors as **hygiene** or **maintenance factors.** He chose these terms because he perceived these factors as being *preventive* in nature. In other words, he believed that these factors would not produce motivation but could prevent motivation from occurring. Thus, proper attention to hygiene factors is a necessary but not sufficient condition for motivation. For example, Herzberg contends that pay will not motivate a person (at least for more than a short period of time) but that insufficient pay can certainly demotivate a person.

According to Herzberg, the factors that motivate people are factors related to the work itself as opposed to the work environment. These factors, which he calls **motivators,** include achievement, recognition, responsibility, advancement, and the challenges of the job. Herzberg maintains that true motivation occurs only when both the motivator factors and the hygiene factors are present. At best, proper attention to the hygiene factors will keep an individual from being dissatisfied but will not motivate the individual. Figure 4.3 lists some examples of hygiene and motivator factors.

As a solution to motivation problems, Herzberg developed an approach called **job enrichment.** Unlike job enlargement or job rotation, job enrichment involves upgrading the job by adding motivational factors such as increased responsibilities. **Job enlargement** merely involves giving an employee more of a similar type of operation to perform. **Job rotation** is the practice of periodically rotating job assignments. Designing jobs that provide for meaningful work, achievement, recognition, responsibility, advancement, and growth is the key to job enrichment. Herzberg's major contribution has been his emphasis on the relationship between the job content and the employee's feelings. Supervision Illustration 4–2 postulates that job enrichment does not work in all situations.

FIGURE 4.3
Hygiene and Motivator Factors

Hygiene Factors (relate to the environment)	Motivator Factors (relate to the job itself)
Policies and administration	Achievement
Style of supervision	Recognition
Working conditions	Challenging work
Interpersonal relations	Increased responsibility
Factors that affect employee's personal life	Advancement
Money, status, security	Personal growth

SUPERVISION ILLUSTRATION 4–2

JOB ENRICHMENT DOES NOT ALWAYS WORK

In his classic Harvard Business Review article, "One More Time, How Do You Motivate Employees," author Frederick Herzberg (1968) asserted that the way to motivate employees was to enrich their jobs. He wrote that they would perform better and do more if they were challenged intellectually, and they would get more psychological satisfaction from their work. But many managers have found that not all employees *want* to have their jobs enriched; many would prefer to do fairly routine and repetitive tasks, and intellectual challenges cause them stress. I have to admit that on some days, when problems are coming at me from every direction, my own job could use a little less enrichment. If I had a choice, for that little while I would escape from the office and mow the grass in the city's parks.

Experienced managers have found that a one-size-fits-all approach to employee motivation doesn't work. Challenges that motivate one person might actually discourage another. Some individuals seem to have a high need for praise and recognition, even when their work is mediocre; others don't seem to care about those things. Job enrichment *does* work for some people, in some situations. But how do we know when it will work, and what works for the other people and the other situations?

Source: Adapted from Scott Lazenby, "How to Motivate Employees: What Research Is Telling Us," *PM. Public Management*, September 2008, pp. 22–26.

Preference-Expectancy Approach

5 LEARNING OBJECTIVES

The **preference-expectancy approach** to motivation is based on the belief that people attempt to increase pleasure and decrease displeasure. According to this approach, employees are motivated to work if (1) they believe that their efforts will be rewarded and (2) they value the rewards that are being offered.

The belief that efforts will be rewarded can be broken down into two components: (*a*) the expectancy that increased effort will lead to increased performance and (*b*) the expectancy that increased performance will lead to increased rewards. These expectancies are developed largely from an individual's past experiences. For example, an employee may feel that working harder does not result in higher performance. Or an employee may believe that working harder does result in higher performance but that higher performance is not directly related to rewards. It should be pointed out that employee expectations are based on perceptions. These perceptions may or may not reflect reality—but whether or not they do, they represent reality to the employee.

The preference element of the preference-expectancy approach is concerned with the value that the employee places on the rewards that the organization offers. Historically, organizations have assumed that employees will value whatever rewards are provided. Even if this were true, certainly some rewards are less or more valued than others. In fact, certain rewards, such as a promotion that involves a transfer to another city, may be viewed negatively by some people. Figure 4.4 illustrates the preference-expectancy approach.

Supervisors can affect each of the components of the preference-expectancy approach. They can positively influence the expectancy that increased effort will lead to increased

FIGURE 4.4 **Preference-Expectancy Approach to Motivation**

$$\text{Motivation} = \left(\begin{array}{c} \text{Expectancy that increased} \\ \text{effort will lead to rewards} \end{array} \right) \times \left(\begin{array}{c} \text{Preference of the} \\ \text{individual for the rewards} \end{array} \right)$$

$$= \left[\left(\begin{array}{c} \text{Expectancy that} \\ \text{increased effort will} \\ \text{lead to increased} \\ \text{performance} \end{array} \right) \times \left(\begin{array}{c} \text{Expectancy that} \\ \text{increased performance} \\ \text{will lead to rewards} \end{array} \right) \right] \times \left(\begin{array}{c} \text{Preference of} \\ \text{the individual} \\ \text{for the rewards} \end{array} \right)$$

performance by providing proper selection and training and clear direction to employees. They can also affect the expectancy that increased performance will lead to rewards by linking rewards to performance. Of course, other factors such as the presence of a union can also affect how rewards are distributed. The employee's preference component, with regard to the rewards being offered, is often taken for granted by the supervisor. Supervisors should solicit feedback from their employees concerning the types of rewards they want. Since an organization is going to invest a certain amount of money in rewards (salary, fringe benefits, and so on), it should attempt to get the maximum return from this investment.

The development of the preference-expectancy approach is still in its infancy, and many questions remain to be answered. Some critics attack the theory on the grounds that it is overly rational, that humans often don't act as rationally as the approach assumes they act. Others say that the approach ignores impulsive and expressive behavior. Despite these criticisms, the preference-expectancy approach is one of the most popular approaches to motivation.

Reinforcement Approach

6 LEARNING OBJECTIVES

The **reinforcement approach** is closely related to the preference-expectancy approach. The general idea is that reinforced behavior is more likely to be repeated than behavior that is not reinforced. For instance, if employees are given a pay increase when their performance is high, then the employees are likely to continue to strive for high performance in hopes of getting another pay raise. Reinforcement assumes that the consequences of behavior determine an individual's level of motivation. Thus, an individual's motives are considered to be relatively minor in this approach.

Basically, four types of reinforcement exist: positive reinforcement, avoidance, extinction, and punishment. **Positive reinforcement** involves providing a positive consequence as a result of desired behavior. **Avoidance,** also called *negative reinforcement,* involves giving a person the opportunity to avoid a negative consequence by exhibiting a desired behavior. Both positive reinforcement and avoidance can be used to increase the frequency of desired behavior. **Extinction** involves providing no positive consequences or removing previously provided positive consequences as a result of undesirable behavior. In other words, behavior that no longer pays is less likely to be repeated. **Punishment** involves providing a negative consequence as a result of undesired behavior. Both extinction and punishment can be used to decrease the frequency of undesired behavior.

The current emphasis on the use of reinforcement in management practices is on positive reinforcement. Examples include increased pay for increased performance and praise and recognition when an employee does a good job. Supervisory Illustration 4–3 describes the use of positive reinforcement.

What Can the Supervisor Do?

7 LEARNING OBJECTIVES

In the light of the previously discussed approaches to motivation, a supervisor can do several things to affect employee motivation. Some of the most useful of these are to:

Make the work interesting.

Relate rewards to performance.

Provide valued rewards.

Treat employees as individuals.

Encourage participation and cooperation.

Provide accurate and timely feedback.

SUPERVISION ILLUSTRATION   4–3

POSITIVE REINFORCEMENT WITH WUMBLER PATCH

SCORE! Educational Centers, www.scorelearning.com, will begin integrating The Wumbler Patch's "Make The World A Better Place With Me" children's enrichment program into their monthly curriculum beginning March 14th. The launch will begin in Ridgewood, NJ, hometown to the original Wumbler Patch brick and mortar store (www.wumblers.com, www.wumblerpatch.com) and one of SCORE!'s most innovative centers nationwide.

SCORE! is a subsidiary of *Kaplan, Inc.,* the global education services provider, which is owned by *The Washington*

Post Company. SCORE! Educational Centers operates 80 centers throughout the United States providing children K through 9 with personal attention, positive reinforcement, and a customized curriculum to help children achieve their goals and reach their academic potential in math, reading, spelling, and writing. With The Wumbler Patch program on board, SCORE! will strengthen its teaching through fun activities that focus on educating children on their social, global, environmental, and humanitarian responsibilities.

Source: Adapted from Anonymous, "SCORE! Teams Up with the Wumbler Patch in Rounding Out Kids' Education," *PR Newswire*, March 2, 2009, Wire Feed.

Make the Work Interesting

Supervisors should carefully examine each job under their control. They should constantly ask, "Can this job be enriched to make it more challenging?" There is a limit to the extent that people can be expected to perform satisfactorily on very routine tasks. Doing the same simple task over and over again every minute of the workday can quickly lead to employee apathy and boredom.

The tendency of many supervisors is to say, "This job just can't be enriched." More often than not, however, jobs can be enriched without a total departmental reorganization. Take the example of an administrative assistant. How often is this person treated as being incapable of doing anything other than word processing and maybe a little filing? The usual result is that the administrative assistant becomes bored and demotivated. With a little planning and thought, however, the job can easily be enriched. He or she can be assigned such responsibilities as responding to certain correspondence, opening and sorting the mail, and making appointments. The key is to make the job challenging and interesting.

Relate Rewards to Performance

There are many reasons why supervisors are reluctant to relate rewards directly to performance. First and foremost, giving everyone an equal pay raise is much easier. Usually this approach requires very little justification and involves less hassle than relating rewards to performance. Second, union contracts generally require that everyone doing the same job be paid the same wage. Third, organizational policy may dictate that pay raises conform to guidelines that are unrelated to performance. Even in such instances, however, there are usually rewards other than pay that can be related to performance. These might include the assignment of preferred tasks or some type of formal recognition. The costs of failing to relate rewards to performance are great. The low performers are not motivated to do more, and the high performers are motivated to do less. Every supervisor should strive to relate rewards directly to performance.

Provide Valued Rewards

Most supervisors never stop to give any thought to what types of rewards are most valued by employees. Like all managers, supervisors usually tend to think of pay as the only reward at their disposal. Most supervisors truly believe that they have nothing to say about what rewards are offered. The common belief is that such decisions are made by upper management. However, employees may highly value many types of rewards other than pay.

For instance, they may highly value being assigned to work on a certain project or being assigned a new piece of equipment. Supervisors should know what rewards are at their disposal and what rewards the employees value.

Treat Employees as Individuals

As discussed earlier in the chapter, different employees have different needs. And different employees want different things from their jobs. Treating everyone the same ignores these differences. In today's highly impersonal world, there is an increasing tendency to treat employees as if they were computer numbers. However, most people want to receive special attention and be treated as individuals. This raises their self-esteem and makes them feel that they are a part of the organization. It also results in more frequent and candid interaction between supervisors and employees. In such a climate, employees naturally feel more like talking over their ideas with the supervisor.

Encourage Participation and Cooperation

Employees like to feel that they are a part of their surroundings and that they contribute to their surroundings. Employees also tend to be committed to decisions in which they have participated. The motivation benefits of true employee participation are undoubtedly high. Despite the potential benefits of participation, however, many supervisors do little to encourage it. Most supervisors do not intentionally discourage participation. They simply fail to *encourage* it. Take, for instance, the familiar suggestion box. As soon as employees discover that their suggestions are not taken seriously, it becomes a collection point for jokes! The employee who makes several worthwhile suggestions to no avail soon quits making suggestions. The point is that active participation does not just happen; it requires commitment from the supervisor. Employees must feel that their participation is genuinely valued.

Closely related to the need to encourage participation is the need to sufficiently explain the reasons for certain actions. Employees are more motivated to do something when they understand why it is being done.

Provide Accurate and Timely Feedback

No one likes to be in the dark about his or her performance. In fact, a negative performance review may be better than no review. An employee who receives such a review will at least know what must be done to improve. Lack of feedback usually produces frustration in employees and this frustration often has a negative impact on employee performance. Accurate and timely feedback involves more than just providing regularly scheduled performance appraisals (which are discussed in depth in Chapter 16). It also involves providing informal feedback on a regular basis.

It is easy for supervisors to fall into the trap of taking the performance of employees for granted. No one likes his or her work to be taken for granted. A simple verbal or written statement of appreciation can go a long way. A potential danger, however, is to become overly complimentary so that praise loses its impact.

Improperly used criticism can negatively affect motivation. Normally, criticisms should be communicated in private. There is often a strong urge to lash out verbally at a subordinate who does something wrong, but doing this very quickly turns the employee off. Feedback should include both the positive and negative happenings. All too often, supervisors focus only on the negative happenings. The goal is for the employee to know at all times exactly where he or she stands.

Job Satisfaction

Closely related to motivation is job satisfaction. In fact, many people view motivated employees as synonymous with satisfied employees. There are, however, important differences between motivated employees and satisfied employees.

FIGURE 4.5
**Determinants of
Satisfaction and
Dissatisfaction**

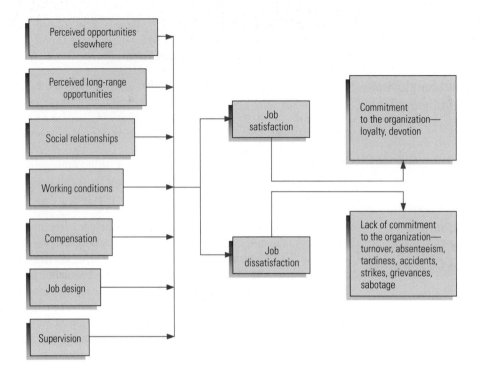

Job satisfaction refers to an employee's general attitude toward the job. It can be affected by such factors as working conditions, pay and benefits, the employee's attitudes toward the organization and supervision and toward the work itself, and the employee's health and age. Therefore, job satisfaction is a general attitude that results from specific attitudes and factors. It is an employee's mind-set with regard to the job. That mind-set may be positive or negative, depending on the employee's mind-set with regard to the major components of job satisfaction. Job satisfaction is not synonymous with organizational morale. Organizational morale refers to the employee's feeling of being accepted by, and belonging to, a group of employees through common goals, confidence in their desirability, and progress toward them. Morale is related to group attitudes, while job satisfaction is more of an employees attitude.

As mentioned earlier, a wide range of both internal and external factors affect an individual's level of satisfaction. The left portion of Figure 4.5 summarizes the major factors that determine an individual's level of satisfaction (or dissatisfaction). The right portion of the figure shows the organization behaviors generally associated with satisfaction and dissatisfaction. Individual satisfaction leads to organization commitment; individual dissatisfaction results in behaviors detrimental to the organization (turnover, absenteeism, tardiness, accidents, etc.). Employees who like their job design, supervision, and other job-related factors will probably be very loyal and devoted. But employees who strongly dislike their job design or any of the other job-related factors will probably be disgruntled and will often exhibit their disgruntlement by being late or absent or by taking other actions that disrupt the organization.

It must be remembered that satisfaction and motivation are not synonymous. Motivation is a drive to perform, while satisfaction reflects the employee's happiness with his situation. The factors that determine whether an employee is satisfied with the job differ from

Jane has learned that the motivation sequence is a continuous process that never ends. As one need is met, other needs arise that call for new actions by the supervisor. Several theories of motivation that should help Jane better understand her employees are discussed in this chapter. The need hierarchy theory (p. 64) should be of particular interest to Jane in understanding her problem. The motivation-maintenance theory (p. 67) should give her guidance in solving the problem. The account of what has been done for her employees (pay raises and the refurbishing of her department's facilities) indicates that the company has dealt with some of the maintenance factors of their jobs. However, Jane must remember that maintenance factors alone don't motivate employees. They can only prepare a condition in which motivation can happen. She must concentrate on the factors that motivate her employees. The suggestions offered on what a supervisor can do to affect employee motivation (pp. 69–71) should also be helpful to Jane.

those that determine whether an employee is motivated. *Satisfaction* is largely determined by the comfort offered by the environment and the situation. *Motivation,* on the other hand, is largely determined by the value of rewards and by their relationship to performance. The result of motivation is increased effort, which in turn increases performance if the employee has the necessary ability and if the effort is properly directed. The result of satisfaction is increased commitment to the organization, which may or may not result in increased performance. This increased commitment will, however, normally result in a decrease in such problems as absenteeism, tardiness, turnover, and strikes.

Summary

This chapter introduces the motivation process. It also presents and clarifies the relationships among the current theories of motivation. Several specific suggestions are presented to help the supervisor elicit high levels of motivation.

1. *Define motivation.* Motivation means getting people to exert a high degree of effort on their job.

2. *Define the traditional approach to motivation.* The traditional approach to motivation is based on the assumption that money is the primary motivator of people: If the monetary rewards are great enough, employees will work harder and produce more.

3. *Explain the hierarchy of needs.* The five levels of needs, in ascending order, are physical, safety, social, esteem, and self-actualization needs. The needs include food and water, sleep, exercise, clothing, and shelter. The physical safety needs are concerned with protection against danger, threat, or deprivation. Social needs are the need for love, affection, and belonging. The esteem needs include the need for both self-esteem and the esteem of others. The self-actualization needs are the needs of people to reach their full potential in applying their abilities and interests to functioning in their environment.

4. *Discuss the motivation-maintenance approach to motivation.* This approach postulates that all work-related factors can be grouped into two categories. The maintenance factors will not produce motivation but can prevent it. Factors in the other category, motivators, encourage motivation.

5. *Discuss the preference-expectancy approach to motivation.* This approach holds that motivation is based on a combination of the individual's expectancy that increased effort leads to increased performance, which leads to rewards, and of the degree of the individual's preference for the rewards being offered.

6. *Explain the reinforcement approach to motivation.* This approach to motivation is based on the idea that behavior that appears to lead to a positive consequence tends to be repeated, while behavior that appears to lead to a negative consequence tends not to be repeated.

7. *State several things that the supervisor can do to affect employee motivation.* Some of the most useful things that a supervisor can do to affect employee motivation are to make the work interesting, relate rewards to performance, provide valued rewards, treat employees as individuals, encourage participation and cooperation, and provide accurate and timely feedback.

Key Terms

Achievement-power-affiliation approach, 66
Avoidance, 69
Esteem needs, 65
Extinction, 69
Hygiene factors, 67
Job enlargement, 67
Job enrichment, 67
Job rotation, 67
Job satisfaction, 72

Maintenance factors, 67
Motivator factors, 67
Motivation, 62
Motivation-maintenance approach, 67
Need hierarchy approach, 64
Physical needs, 64
Positive reinforcement, 69
Preference-expectancy approach, 68
Punishment, 69

Pygmalion effect (self-fulfilling prophecy), 63
Reinforcement approach, 69
Safety needs, 64
Self-actualization, 65
Self-fulfillment, 65
Social needs, 65
Traditional approach, 64

Review Questions

1. What is motivation?

2. Are all employees motivated by the same things? Why or why not?

3. Describe the following approaches to motivation:

    a. Traditional.

    b. Need hierarchy.

    c. Achievement-power-affiliation.

    d. Motivation-maintenance.

    e. Preference-expectancy.

    f. Reinforcement.

4. Briefly discuss several specific actions that supervisors can take to improve employee motivation.

5. What is job satisfaction?

6. What are the differences between motivation and job satisfaction? What results are obtained from motivated employees? What results are obtained from satisfied employees?

Skill-Building Questions

1. "In the final analysis, money and benefits are all that employees are concerned about." Discuss your views on this statement.

2. Many supervisors believe that they can have little effect on employee motivation because so many rewards are of a fixed nature. For example, a union contract might set pay raises. How would you respond to these supervisors?

3. A seasoned supervisor recently made the following statement: "A satisfied employee is one that is not being pushed hard enough." Do you agree? Why or why not?

4. The LMN Company has decided to throw a party for all of its employees to show its appreciation for the highly successful year that has just concluded. It plans to hold the party at a fancy place with live entertainment and expensive food. The affair will be quite a bash. In fact, it is expected to cost over $100 per employee. What is your reaction to this idea?

Additional Readings

Flack, Jo-Anne, "MOTIVATION: It's Enough to Make You Scream," *Marketing Week,* February 12, 2009, p. 25.

Kaufman, Ron, "How to Harness the Power of Praise," *SuperVision,* March 2009, pp. 14–17.

Keefe, Linda, "Money Really Can Grow on Trees," *Nonprofit World,* Jan/Feb 2009, pp. 14–16.

McDonald, Tom, "Got Motivation," *Successful Meeting,* March 2008, p. 22.

Stanley, T. L., "A Motivated Workplace is a Marvelous Sight," *SuperVision,* March 2008, pp. 5–9.

Wormald, Karen, "Employee Incentives that Work," *Office Solutions*, January 2009, pp. 24–27.

SKILL-BUILDING APPLICATIONS

Incident 4–1

No Extra Effort

You are the supervisor of nurses in the pediatrics section of a 700-bed hospital in a metropolitan area. You have been in your job for six months, having moved from a similar position in a much smaller rural hospital.

You: I just can't seem to get my people to perform. They're all extremely competent, but they don't seem to be willing to put forth any extra effort. Take last Saturday evening. I thought Sue was going to have a fit when I asked her to help tidy up the nurses' station. She was quick to explain that that was the janitor's job.

Friend: Exactly what are the duties and responsibilities of your nurses?

You: They don't really have much responsibility. That always seems to fall on me. Their duties don't vary much from those of the average nurse—make sure medicines are taken on schedule, perform periodic checks on patients, and provide general assistance to doctors and patients. Of course, pediatrics does require a certain disposition to deal with children.

Friend: How do you evaluate their performance?

You: Mainly based on complaints and my general feeling about how they are doing. It's hard to evaluate the quality of their work since most of it is fairly routine. However, if I receive several complaints on a nurse, I can be pretty sure that the nurse is not doing the job.

Friend: Do you receive complaints very often?

You: That's just the problem. Recently, complaints have risen noticeably. The number of complaints is much higher here than at my former hospital. The worst part is that the nurses don't seem too concerned about it.

Friend: What financial rewards does the hospital offer?

You: They're all well paid—when I think that I started 30 years ago at $25 per week! Base pay is determined mainly on the basis of longevity. They also get paid vacations, insurance plans, and all the other usual goodies. I don't know of any complaints about compensation.

Friend: How about the promotion possibilities?

You: Well, all I know is that I was brought in from the outside. I really don't think many of the nurses aspire for promotions.

Friend: Have you considered firing any of them?

You: Haven't you read about the nationwide shortage of nurses? Who would I replace them with? I figure that half a nurse is better than no nurse.

Questions

1. Reconsider the situation. Why do you think the nurses are not motivated? List possible answers.
2. What could you do to improve the situation?

Incident 4–2

The Secure Employee

Archie Banks is 53 years old and has been with Allgo Products for 27 years. For the last seven years, he has been a top-paid machine operator. Archie is quite active in community affairs, and he takes an interest in most employee activities. He is very friendly and well liked by all the employees, especially the younger ones, who often come to him for advice. He is extremely helpful to these younger employees and never hesitates to help them when called upon. When talking with the younger employees, Archie never talks negatively about the company.

Archie's one shortcoming, as Tom Williams, his supervisor, sees it, is his tendency to spend too much time talking with other employees. This causes Archie's work to suffer, and perhaps more important, it hinders the output of others. Whenever Tom confronts Archie with the problem, Archie improves for a day or two and then he slips back into his old habit.

Tom considered trying to have Archie transferred to an area where he would have less opportunity to interrupt the work of other employees. However, Tom concluded that he needed Archie's experience, especially since he had no available replacement for Archie's job.

Archie is secure in his personal life. He owns a nice house and lives well. His wife is a librarian, and their two children are grown and married. Although he has never specifically said so, Archie feels that he is as high as he'll ever go in the company. This doesn't seem to bother him since he likes his present job and feels comfortable in it.

Questions

1. What would you do to motivate Archie if you were Tom Williams?
2. Suppose Archie liked his job so much that he didn't want to be promoted even if offered a higher job. What would you do to motivate Archie in this situation?

Exercise 4–1

Money as a Motivator

Your instructor will divide you into groups of three or four. Your group will be assigned one of the two following statements:

1. Money is the primary motivator of people.
2. Money is not the primary motivator of people.

Your assignment is to prepare for a debate with another group on the validity of the statement that your group has been assigned. You will be debating a group that has the opposing viewpoint.

At the end of the debate, prepare a brief statement summarizing the key points made by your opposing group.

Exercise 4–2

Motivation-Maintenance Approach

This exercise is designed to illustrate the motivation-maintenance approach to motivation.

1. Think of an instance in which you found a job highly motivating. The instance could have taken place yesterday or several years ago. Write a two-or three-sentence description of the situation. After you have completed the description, list the reasons that this situation had a motivational effect on you.
2. Repeat the same procedure, but this time describe an instance which you found highly *demotivating*.
3. Hand in the unsigned papers.
4. To determine if the experiences described support or refute the motivation-maintenance approach, have someone read each description aloud and decide whether the response fits into the maintenance or motivator categories.

Contemporary Issues

SECTION OUTLINE

CHAPTER FIVE

Managing Change and Innovation

Learning objectives

After studying this chapter, you will be able to:

1. Discuss the supervisor's role in introducing change.
2. Explain why employees tend to resist change.
3. Present several things that the supervisor can do to foster employee acceptance of change.
4. List six different strategies that may be used to implement a change.
5. Discuss three factors that affect the time it takes to successfully implement a change.
6. Describe Lewin's Force Field Analysis theory.
7. Briefly describe four essential principles that organizations must follow to manage innovation.
8. Explain what a learning organization is.

Things had just begun to settle down from the yearlong task of reorganizing the department into five-person work teams when John received word that a new computer would soon be installed. John remembered when the record keeping had been done primarily by hand. The transition to the first computer over 20 years ago had been traumatic, to say the least. Now everything would have to be put on a new computer for the third time. John wondered if this meant that he would have to reorganize again. Would the new computer replace some of his employees? John also wondered if the company would eventually replace him with a computer expert. As he remembered the resistance and the problems he experienced when they made the transition to the first and second computers, John wondered what he could do to make this transition go more smoothly. What could he do to enlist the support of his employees?

In today's world, change is an everyday occurrence. The following excerpt emphasizes the increased rate with which change has been occurring:

> Let us suppose that we can reduce to one year or 12 months the total duration of the known period of the history of man: some 30,000 years. In these 12 months that represent the life of all our ancestors from the Age of Stone until our days, it is toward the 18th of October that the Iron Age starts. It is the 8th of December that the Christian era begins.
>
> It is on the 29th of December when Louis XVI ascends the throne of France. What mechanical power does mankind possess at that epoch?
>
> Exactly the same as that which the caveman had possessed plus whatever he was able to derive from draft animals after the invention of the yoke.
>
> By the 30th of December, in the first 18 minutes of the morning, Watt invents the steam engine. On the same day, the 30th of December, at 4:00 P.M. the first railway begins to operate.
>
> And thus we reach the last day of the year. The 31st of December.
>
> At 5:31 A.M., Edison invents the first incandescent lamp. By afternoon, at 2:12 P.M. Blériot crosses the Channel. And not until 4:14 P.M. does World War I begin. At this date Western man disposes of 8/10 of a horsepower. This is notable and brutal progress because:
>
> During the whole year he has lived with only 1/10 of a horsepower. In one day he has multiplied it by 8, but only five hours suffice to bring this figure to 80.
>
> It is a fact that on the 31st of December at the 11th stroke of midnight Frenchmen dispose of 8 horsepower each. And at the same time, the Americans have 60 each, while the inhabitants of New York have 270 each.
>
> The following events take place during the last few minutes of the day: The first atomic bomb explodes, Neil Armstrong walks on the moon, and over 50 million computers are in use.[1]

Change affects all organizations, even the most successful. Managers at all levels are continually confronted with change. Consumers lose interest in some products and flock to new ones. Technological advances leave once-popular products obsolete. Prices of raw materials change, forcing manufacturers to adjust production processes or change prices. Organizations that fail to respond to change often find themselves out of business.

Change and the Supervisor

LEARNING OBJECTIVES

In his book *Thriving on Chaos,* Tom Peters stresses the importance of change to the modern organization: "To up the odds of survival, leaders at all levels must become obsessive about change." He adds, "Change must become the norm, not cause for alarm."[2] Similarly, Jack Welch, the well-known former CEO of GE, has been quoted as saying, "When the rate of change on the outside exceeds the rate of change on the inside, the end is in sight."[3] What does *change* mean from these perspectives? Simply put, it means that unless managers and supervisors have changed something, they have not earned their paychecks.

FIGURE 5.1
Types of Change Affecting the Supervisor

Technological	Environmental	Internal
Automation	Laws	Policies
Computers	Taxes	Procedures
Machines	Social trends	Methods
Equipment	Fashion trends	Rules
Processes	Political trends	Reorganization
New raw materials	Economic trends	Budget adjustments
Products	Interest rates	Job restructuring
Robots	Consumer trends	Human resources
	Suppliers	Management
	Population trends	Ownership
	International conflicts	Products/services sold

Most major changes in an organization are initiated at the upper levels of management. As these changes affect the overall organizations, they almost always work their way down to the supervisory level. All of the changes mentioned in the previous paragraph affect the supervisor's job. Some changes occur gradually; others occur suddenly. In either case, change can have serious repercussions for the supervisor. There are also many situations which warrant the supervisor to initiate change. For example, a supervisor may see a better method of doing a particular task. Change as it applies to supervision can be classified in three major categories: technological, environmental, and internal to the organization.

Technological change includes such things as new equipment, machinery, and processes. The technological advances since World War II have been dramatic. Automatically controlled machines and computers are common examples of technological advances that have greatly affected all of us.

Environmental change includes all of the nontechnological changes that occur external to the organization. New government regulations, new social trends, new political trends, and economic changes are examples of environmental change. Specific examples of such change include new tax rates, new laws, changes in interest rates, changes in fashions, and shifts in population. Ordinarily, changes of this kind have an indirect impact on the supervisor. However, there is very little that the supervisor can do to influence them.

Changes internal to the organization include such things as budget adjustments, methods changes, policy changes, reorganizations, and the hiring of new employees. These changes are the result of decisions made by the organization's management. It is not unusual for the supervisor to have an input into such decisions. Figure 5.1 summarizes the types of changes facing the supervisor.

The supervisor is often the focal point for implementing change. He or she is often the person responsible for introducing a change and seeing that it is successfully implemented. Thus, it is imperative that the supervisor know how to cope with change successfully.

Reactions to Change

How employees perceive a change greatly affects how they react to it. While many variations are possible, only four basic situations can occur:

1. If employees cannot foresee how the change will affect them, they will resist the change or be neutral, at best. Most people shy away from the unknown. An attitude often taken is that the change may make things worse.

SUPERVISION ILLUSTRATION 5–1

RESISTANCE TO CHANGE?

"The canal system of this country is being threatened by the spread of a new form of transportation known as 'railroads' and the federal government must preserve the canals. . . . If canal boats are supplanted by 'railroads,' serious unemployment will result. Captains, cooks, drivers, hostlers, repairmen, and lock tenders will be left without means of livelihood, not to mention the numerous farmers now employed growing hay for the horses. . . . As you may well know, Mr. President, 'railroad' carriages are pulled at the enormous speed of 15 miles per hour by 'engines' which, in addition to endangering life and limb of passengers, roar and snort their way through the countryside, setting fire to crops, scaring the livestock and frightening women and children. The Almighty certainly never intended that people should travel at such breakneck speed."

The above communication was from Martin Van Buren, then governor of New York, to President Andrew Jackson on January 21, 1829. In 1832 Van Buren was elected vice president of the United States under Andrew Jackson's second term. In 1836 Van Buren was elected president of the United States. It is also interesting that the first railroad into Washington, DC, was completed in time to bring visitors from Philadelphia and New York to Van Buren's inauguration.

Sources: Janet E. Lapp, "Ride the Horse in the Direction It's Going," *American Salesman,* October 1998, pp. 26–29; and *The World Book Encyclopedia,* Volume 20 (Chicago: World Book—Childcraft International, Inc.), 1979, p. 214.

2. If employees clearly see that the change is not compatible with their needs and aspirations, they will resist the change. In this situation, the employees are certain that the change will make things worse.

3. If employees see that the change is going to take place regardless of their objections, they may initially resist the change and then resignedly accept it. Their first reaction is to resist. Once the change appears inevitable, they often see no other choice than to go along with it.

4. If employees see that the change is in their best interests, they will be motivated to accept it.

Obviously, the key here is for employees to feel confident that the change will make things better. It is the supervisor's obligation to foster an accepting attitude. Note that three out of the four situations result in some form of resistance to the change. The manner in which employees resist change can vary dramatically. At one extreme, for example, an employee may mildly resist by showing no interest in the change; at the other extreme, an employee may resist by sabotaging the change.

Resistance to Change

 LEARNING OBJECTIVES

While most people profess to be open minded, they still resist change. This is especially true when the change affects their jobs. Resistance to change is a natural reaction. It is not a reaction common only to troublemakers. Supervision Illustration 5–1 provides a 150-year-old example of how even very influential and intelligent people often resist change.

Resistance to change may be explicit or very subtle. The employee who quits a job because of a change in company policy is resisting the change in an open and explicit manner. The employee who becomes very sullen because of the change but does not quit is resisting the change in a more passive manner.

There are many reasons why employees resist change. Some of the most frequently encountered reasons, called *barriers to change,* are discussed below.

Fear of the Unknown

It is natural for people to fear the unknown. The problem with many changes is that their outcome is not always foreseeable. And even if the outcome of a change is foreseeable, the results of the change are not often communicated to all of the affected employees. For example, employees may worry about and resist the installation of a new machine if they aren't sure what the impact of the machine will be on their jobs. Similarly, employees may resist a new supervisor simply because they don't know what to expect from him or her. Another related fear is the uncertainty that employees may feel about operating under a change. Thus, employees may fully understand a change, yet have serious doubts about whether they will be able to handle it. For example, employees may resist a new procedure because of a fear that they won't be able to master it.

Threat to Job or Income

Employees fear any change that they think threatens their job or income. The threat may be real or only imagined, but in either case the result is employee resistance. For example, a salesperson will resist a territory change if he or she believes that the change will result in less opportunity. Similarly, production workers will oppose new standards that they believe will be more difficult to achieve.

Fear That Skills and Expertise Will Lose Value

Everyone likes to feel valued by others, so anything that has the potential of reducing that value will be resisted. For example, an operations supervisor might resist implementation of a new, more modern piece of equipment for fear the change will make him or her less needed by the organization.

Threats to Power

Many people believe a change might diminish their power. For example, a supervisor may perceive a change to the organization's structure as weakening his or her power within the organization.

Inconvenience

Many changes result in personal inconveniences to the affected employees. If nothing else, change often forces employees to learn new ways. This may require additional training, schooling, or practice, any of which will probably inconvenience the employees. A common reaction of employees is that the change "isn't worth the extra effort required."

Threats to Interpersonal Relations

The social and interpersonal relationships among employees can be quite strong. For example, the opportunity to have lunch with a certain group of employees may be very important to the employees involved. These relationships may appear insignificant to everyone but those employees. When a change, such as a transfer, threatens the relationships, the affected employees often resist. Employees naturally feel more at ease working with people they know well. Also, a group may have worked out a routine for accomplishing its work based on the strengths and weaknesses of its members. Any changes in the group would naturally disrupt that routine.

Reducing Resistance to Change

LEARNING OBJECTIVES

The supervisor is also responsible for communicating the employees' feelings and reactions to middle management. Thus, the supervisor must represent the position of both management and the operative employees. In this process, the supervisor must cope with employees' anxieties and fears that are related to change. Regardless of where or how a change originated, the environment created by the supervisor can greatly affect employees' acceptance of the change. Several suggestions for creating a positive environment for change are presented in Figure 5.2 and discussed in the following paragraphs.

FIGURE 5.2
Suggestions for Reducing Resistance to Change

Build trust.
Discuss upcoming changes.
Involve the employees in the changes.
Make sure the changes are reasonable.
Avoid threats.
Follow a sensible time schedule.
Implement the changes in the most logical place.

Build Trust

If the employees trust and have confidence in the supervisor, they are much more likely to accept changes. Otherwise, they are likely to resist changes vigorously. Trust cannot be established overnight: it is built over a period of time. The supervisor's actions determine the degree of the employees' trust. If the employees perceive the supervisor as fair, honest, and forthright, they will trust him or her. If the employees feel that the supervisor is always trying to put something over on them, there will be no trust. Supervisors can go a long way toward building trust if they discuss upcoming changes with the employees and if they actively involve the employees in the change process.

Discuss Upcoming Changes

Fear of the unknown, one of the major barriers to change, can be greatly reduced by discussing any upcoming changes with the affected employees. During this discussion, the supervisor should be as open and honest as possible, explaining not only what the changes will be but why the changes are being made. The more background and detail the supervisor can give, the more likely it is that the employees will accept the changes. The supervisor should also outline the impact of the changes on each of the affected employees. People are primarily interested in how change will affect them as individuals. A critical requirement for success is that the supervisor allow the employees an opportunity to ask questions. This is the major advantage of an oral discussion over a written memo. Regardless of how thorough an explanation may be, employees will usually have questions. Supervisors should answer those questions to the fullest extent possible.

Involve the Employees

Another way to lower resistance to changes and build employee trust is to actively involve employees in the change process. Employee involvement in change can be extremely effective. It is only natural for employees to want to go along with changes that they have helped bring about. A good approach is to solicit employee ideas and inputs as early as possible in the change process. In other words, don't wait until the last minute to ask the employees what they think about a change. Ask them as soon as possible. When affected employees have been involved in a change from, or near, its inception, they will usually actively support the change. The psychology involved here is simple: No one wants to oppose something that he or she has helped develop.

Make Sure the Changes Are Reasonable

The supervisor should always do whatever is possible to ensure that any proposed changes are reasonable. Proposed changes that come down from upper levels are sometimes totally unreasonable. When this is the case, it is usually because upper management is not aware of certain circumstances. It is the supervisor's responsibility to intervene in such situations and communicate the problem to upper management. Figure 5.3 presents humorous examples of "unreasonable changes."

Avoid Threats

The supervisor who attempts to implement change through the use of threats is taking a negative approach likely to decrease employee trust. Also, most people resist being threatened into accepting something. A natural reaction is: "This must be bad news if it

FIGURE 5.3
Unreasonable
Changes?

CHANGE MEMO	
To: All personnel	
Subject: New sick leave policy	
Date: Today	
Sickness	No excuse! . . . we will no longer accept your doctor's statement as proof, as we believe that if you are able to go to the doctor you are able to come to work!
Death	(Other than your own) . . . this is no excuse . . . there is nothing you can do for them, and we feel sure that someone else with a lesser position can attend to the arrangements. However, if the funeral can be held in the late afternoon, we will be glad to let you off one hour early, provided that your share of the work is ahead enough to keep the business going in your absence.
Leave of absence	(For an operation) . . . we will no longer allow this practice. We wish to discourage any thoughts that you might need an operation, as we believe that, as long as you are an employee here, you will need all of whatever you have, and you should not consider having anything removed. We hired you as you are, and therefore anything removed would certainly make you less than we bargained for.
Death	(Your own) . . . This we will accept as an excuse. But we would like two weeks' notice, as we feel it is your duty to train someone else to do your job.

Also, we feel entirely too much time is being spent in the rest room. In the future, we will follow the practice of going in alphabetical order. For instance, those whose names begin with A will go from 8:00 to 8:15, B will go from 8:15 to 8:30, and so on. If you are unable to go at your time, then it will be necessary for you to wait until the next day when your turn comes again.

requires a threat." Even though threats may get results in the short run, they may be very damaging in the long run. They will usually have a negative impact on employee morale and attitude.

Follow a Sensible Time Schedule

As discussed previously, most changes are passed down to the supervisor for implementation. However, the supervisor can often influence the timing of changes. Some times are better than others for implementing certain changes. For example, the week before Christmas would ordinarily not be a good time to implement a major change. Similarly, a major change should ordinarily not be attempted during the height of the vacation season. The supervisor can often provide valuable insight regarding the proper timing of changes. If nothing else, the supervisor should always use common sense when recommending a time schedule for implementing a change.

Implement the Changes in the Most Logical Place

The supervisor often has some choice about *where* changes will take place. For example, the supervisor usually decides who will get a new piece of equipment. Common logic should be followed when making such decisions. Certain employees are naturally more adaptable and flexible than others. It makes good sense to introduce any changes through these employees. The supervisor who makes it a point to know his or her employees usually has a pretty good idea as to which of them are most likely or least likely to be flexible. Where possible, changes should be implemented in a way that minimizes their effect on interpersonal relationships. The supervisor should not attempt to disturb smooth-working groups.

The Five W's and an H

The preceding paragraphs suggest how to establish an environment that will readily accept change. Once a specific change has been singled out for implementation, the supervisor should always begin the implementation by explaining the **five W's and an H** to the employees—What the change is, Why the change is needed, Whom the change will affect, When the change will take place, Where the change will occur, and How the change will take place.

Strategies for Overcoming Resistance to Change

In addition to establishing a positive environment for change, there are certain strategies that can be used to help with the implementation of a specific change. Six such strategies are shown in Figure 5.4. It should be realized that these strategies are not mutually

Approach	Appropriate Situation	Advantages	Drawbacks
Education + communication	Where there is a lack of information or inaccurate information and analysis	Once persuaded, people will often help implement change	Can be very time-consuming if many people are involved
Participation + involvement	Where the initiators do not have all the information they need to design the change, and where others have considerable power to resist	People who participate will be committed to implementing change, and any relevant information they have will be integrated into the change plan	Can be time-consuming if participators design an inappropriate change
Facilitation + support	When people are resisting because of adjustment problems	No other approach works as well with adjustment problems	Can be time-consuming and expensive and still fail
Negotiation + agreement	Where someone or some group will clearly lose out in a change and where that group has considerable power to resist	Sometimes it is a relatively easy way to avoid major resistance	Can be too expensive; in many cases it alerts others to negotiate for compliance
Manipulation + co-optation	Where other tactics will not work or are too expensive	Relatively quick and inexpensive	Can lead to future problems if people feel manipulated
Explicit + implicit coercion	Where speed is essential and the change initiators possess considerable power	Speedy and can overcome any kind of resistance	Can be risky if it leaves people mad at the initiators

WORKING WITH CHARTS Before choosing a strategy for reducing resistance to change, managers must identify the source of resistance. *What strategy would you use to overcome resistance by employees who are confused about the implications of a proposed change?*

FIGURE 5.4 **Strategies for Overcoming Resistance to Change**

Source: John P. Kotter and Leonard A. Schlesinger, "Choosing Strategies for Change," *Harvard Business Review,* March–April 1979.

exclusive, but rather a combination of strategies may be used in a given situation. For example, suppose the ABC Company decided to reorganize its sales department by industry instead of by geographical region (as it had been). ABC's top management believes that this approach will allow the company to develop more expertise among its salespeople. Anticipating fierce opposition to the reorganization, the sales manager used a strategy of negotiation plus agreement. By recognizing that the reorganization would probably reduce salespeople's commissions in the short run, the sales manager got upper management to guarantee the salespeople's salaries for 12 months. Before industry assignments were made, the sales manager also met with all salespeople to find out what their industry preferences might be. Thus, the sales manager also used the participation plus involvement strategy.

Minimizing the Time to Implement a Change

5 LEARNING OBJECTIVES

Usually the longer it takes to implement a change, the greater the negative impact there is on productivity, performance, and morale. At least three factors specifically affect the time required to successfully implement a change.[4] The first is communication in the form of information about the change from both an organizational and personal perspective. The supervisor is usually the person responsible for communicating change to employees. Information should be accurate, timely, and delivered to the affected people. The second factor is engagement or the opportunity for people to become involved in the process and to have input into the decisions affecting the change. As discussed earlier in this chapter, employees become committed to successfully implementing a change when they are involved in the process. The third factor is the support provided to employees throughout the change process. If employees feel understood and supported by their supervisor, they are much more likely to endorse the change.

Lewin's Force Field Theory

6 LEARNING OBJECTIVES

In the late 1940s, psychologist Kurt Lewin contributed significantly to our understanding of the change process by developing his Force Field Analysis theory.[5] Essentially **Lewin's Force Field Analysis** theory states that there are two natural sets of forces that impact on any change—those forces that resist the change and those forces that encourage the change.

When managers and supervisors become familiar with Force Field Analysis, the question that often comes up is "Which is the best approach: to increase the driving forces for change or decrease the restraining forces?" Most managers and supervisors attempt to increase the driving forces because they have more direct control over them. Management expert and author Stephen Covey believes that it is usually better to spend energy reducing the restraining forces than increasing the driving forces. Covey uses the following analogy: "If I'm driving a car and see the emergency brake is partially on, should I release the brake or put on more gas?" Obviously releasing the brake would allow you to attain a higher speed more efficiently. Covey suggests that managers and supervisors spend about two-thirds of their energy on reducing restraining forces and one-third on increasing the driving forces.

Using the example of the reorganized sales force in the previous section, the sales manager (in trying to increase the driving forces) would attempt to convince the salespeople as to why the new reorganization is better. On the other hand, the sales manager might get a better response by attempting to reduce the restraining forces (concentrate

SUPERVISION ILLUSTRATION   5–4

INNOVATION INITIATIVES BY MICROSOFT

A recent study by New York-based Accenture found that 55 percent of management teams in large corporations prefer a commitment to innovation, but only 41 percent were satisfied with the frequency at which they bring innovative ideas to market. Furthermore, only 36 percent were satisfied with the time it takes to turn an idea into an actual product or service. These numbers prompted Microsoft to launch internal and external initiatives to foster innovation within itself and other companies. These initiatives involved the development of a formal process and the use of Microsoft technology. Specifically, Microsoft's innovation initiatives involved the following efforts:

- Creating IDEAGENCY, an internal organization that Microsoft employees can tap into to shepherd innovative ideas from initial concepts to final product or service.
- Working with software partners to develop solutions that support innovation processes in vertical industries.
- Developing an Innovation Process Management (IPM) initiative that emphasizes how Microsoft collaboration technology can support corporate innovation programs.

Source: Sidney Hill, Jr., "Managing Innovation: Microsoft Forum Showcases Tools, Processes for Successful Product Development," *Manufacturing Business Technology,* November 2008, p. 8.

4. An organization must work constantly on improving its climate for innovation. As used here, climate refers to the "feeling in the air" you get when you work for or visit an organization. Does the feeling in the air foster innovation and encourage employees to take risks? What happens when someone fails? Innovative climates expect a certain degree of failure, learn from failures, and share the learning throughout the organization. As the old saying goes, If you haven't failed, you haven't taken sufficient risks. Organizations with favorable climates for innovation provide the context for people to collaborate in groups, teams, divisions, and departments without boundaries of fear.

As the rate of change increases for today's organizations, the ability to innovate becomes more and more critical. By subscribing to the above principles, supervisors have a positive impact on an organization's ability to innovate and remain competitive. Supervision Illustration 5–4 describes several initiatives by Microsoft to foster innovation within itself and other companies.

The Learning Organization

8 LEARNING OBJECTIVES

If organizations are to encourage change and innovation, they must establish environments that support these actions. **Learning organizations** establish such an environment. A learning organization has been defined as an organization skilled at creating, acquiring, and transferring knowledge, and in modifying behavior to reflect the new knowledge.[7] Peter Senge, whose book *The Fifth Discipline* popularized the learning organization, has identified five principles for creating a learning organization:[8]

1. *Systems thinking.* Managers and supervisors must learn to see the big picture and not concentrate only on their part; they must learn to recognize the effects of one level of learning on another.

2. *Personal mastery.* Individual managers, supervisors, and employees must be empowered to experiment, innovate, and explore.

John is faced with implementing change in the form of a new computer system. In introducing the new system and related changes, John should first concentrate on creating a positive environment. He should discuss the upcoming changes with his employees and solicit their ideas (p. 83). At this time, John should explain the five W's and an H to them: What the change is, Why it is needed, Whom it will affect, When it will take place, Where it will take place, and How it will take place (p. 85). John should also make sure that the implementation schedule is realistic (p. 84). He should be aware that the natural reaction of many of his employees is to resist change (p. 81). John can overcome much of this resistance by carefully explaining what the new computer system will do and how it will affect each of his employees.

3. *Mental models*. Managers, supervisors, and employees should be encouraged to develop mental models as ways of stretching their minds to find new and better ways of doing things.

4. *Shared vision*. Managers and supervisors should develop and communicate a shared vision that can be used as a framework for addressing problems and opportunities.

5. *Team Learning*. Team learning is the process of aligning a team so as to avoid wasted energy and to get the desired results.

Honda, Corning, and General Electric are examples of companies that have become good learning organizations. In these organizations, learning, in whatever form, becomes an inescapable way of life for both managers and employees alike. These and other learning organizations are gaining the commitment of their employees at all levels by continually expanding their capacity to learn and change.

Summary

This chapter discusses the supervisor's role in introducing change in the organization. It offers several suggestions to help supervisors successfully deal with change. A three-step model for implementing change is presented. The nature and sources of job-related stress are explored.

1. *Discuss the supervisor's role in introducing change.* Although most changes are originated by middle or upper management, it is the supervisor who is usually responsible for implementing changes. To successfully implement changes, supervisors must constantly strive to create a positive environment for change.

2. *Explain why employees tend to resist change.* Some of the most frequently encountered reasons why employees resist change are (1) fear of the unknown, (2) threats to job or income, (3) fear that skills and expertise will lose value, (4) threats to power, (5) inconvenience, and (6) threats to interpersonal relations.

3. *Present several things that the supervisor can do to foster employee acceptance of change.* To foster employee acceptance of change, supervisors should build trust, discuss upcoming changes, involve employees in the changes, make sure the changes are reasonable, avoid threats, follow a sensible time schedule, and implement the changes in the most logical place. As the first step in implementing a change, supervisors should explain the five W's and an H—what, why, whom, when, where, and how—to affected employees.

4. *List six different strategies that may be used to implement a change.* Six strategies that may be used to implement a change are (1) education plus communication, (2) participation plus involvement, (3) facilitation plus support, (4) negotiation plus agreement, (5) manipulation plus co-optation, and (6) explicit plus implicit coercion.

5. *Discuss three factors that affect the time it takes to successfully implement a change.* Three factors that affect the time it takes to successfully implement a change are (1) communication—information about the change from both an organizational and personal perspective, (2) engagement—the opportunity for people to become involved, and (3) the support provided to employees throughout the change process.

6. *Describe Lewin's Force Field Analysis theory.* Lewin's Force Field Analysis theory states that there are two natu-

ral "forces" that affect change—those that resist it and those that encourage it.

7. *Briefly describe four essential principles that organizations must follow to manage innovation.* Essential principles for successfully innovating are (1) have a comprehensive approach; (2) include a systematic, organized, and continued search for new opportunities; (3) involve everyone in the innovation process; and (4) work constantly on improving the organization's climate for innovation.

8. *Explain what a learning organization is.* A learning organization is an organization skilled at creating, acquiring, and transferring knowledge, and in modifying behavior to reflect the new knowledge.

Key Terms

Creativity, 88
Environmental change, 80
Five W's and an H, 85

Innovation, 88
Internal changes, 80
Learning organization, 89

Lewin's Force Field Analysis, 86
Technological change, 80

Review Questions

1. Name the three major categories of change that are of concern to supervision.

2. Describe the four basic reactions of employees to change.

3. Name six common barriers to change (reasons for resistance to change).

4. Discuss several methods or approaches for reducing resistance to change.

5. List three factors that specifically can affect the time it takes to successfully implement a change.

6. Briefly outline six different strategies that can be used to implement change.

7. Discuss Lewin's Force Field Analysis theory.

8. Describe a model that summarizes the change process.

9. Define innovation and briefly discuss how organizations can successfully foster innovation.

10. How is innovation viewed in a learning organization?

Skill-Building Questions

1. Suppose that as a supervisor you received an order to implement a change that you personally opposed. What would you do?

2. Because of a recent OSHA (Occupational Safety and Health Administration) visit, you have been instructed to implement several changes relating to safety. You know that you employees are going to regard some of these changes as ridiculous. What might you do to get the employees to accept the changes?

3. Regarding Lewin's Force Field Analysis theory, do you believe that when implementing a change, most people tend to emphasize those forces that encourage a change or those forces that resist the change? Give an example to support your position.

4. Based on your personal experiences, do you think that most organizations do a good job of encouraging innovation? Why or why not?

References

1. Adapted from Rolf Nordling, "Social Responsibilities of Today's Industrial Leader," *Advanced Management Journal,* April 1957, pp. 19–20.

2. Tom Peters, *Thriving on Chaos* (New York: Alfred A. Knopf, 1987), p. 464.

3. Lon Matejczyk, "Commentary: Everyone for Ensuring Change," *The Colorado Springs Business Journal,* October 21, 2005, p. 1.

4. Jacqui Tizard, "Managing Change," *New Zealand Management,* March 2002, p. 64.

5. Much of this section is drawn from Stephen Covey, "Work It Out Together," *Incentive,* April 1997, p. 26.

6. Much of this section is drawn from Robert B. Tucker, "Innovation Discipline," *Executive Excellence,* September 2001, pp. 3–4; and Robert B. Tucker, "Innovation: The New Core Competency," *Strategy and Leadership,* January–February 2001, pp. 11–14.

7. David Garvin, "Building a Learning Organization," *Harvard Business Review,* July 1993, p. 78.

8. Peter M. Senge, *The Fifth Discipline: The Art and Practice of the Learning Organization* (New York: Doubleday, 1990); and Peter M. Senge, "Learning Organizations," *Executive Excellence,* September 1991, pp. 7–8.

Additional Readings

Cavaleri, Steven A., "Are Learning Organizations Pragmatic?" *The Learning Organization,* Vol. 15, Issue 6, 2008, p. 474.

D'Orleans, Jeanne, "Implementing, Managing Change is Everyone's Job," *Hotel and Motel Management,* June 2, 2008, p. 26.

Ramsey, Robert D., "How to Pitch a New Idea," *Supervision,* March 2004, pp. 8–9.

"U.S. Business Leaders Respond to Downturn by Ramping Up Internal Change," *PR Newswire,* May 29, 2008.

SKILL-BUILDING APPLICATIONS

Incident 5–1

A New Boss

Jane McBride has been an accounting supervisor for Boland's department store for over 15 years. The previous store manager, Whit Calhoun, was originally hired as a junior accountant by Jane. Jane has always believed that her job is to see that the work gets out. She believes that work is work. Sometimes it is pleasant and sometimes unpleasant. Any employee who doesn't like the work can adjust or quit. Jane believes that work is not a place for play.

As one might expect, Jane has a reputation for running things and not standing for any nonsense. Yet her turnover has historically been very low and almost all of her employees respect her. The employees also feel that Jane knows her business and will stand up for them.

Two months ago, Whit Calhoun retired and his replacement, Vincent Ball, took over as store manager. One of the first things Vincent did was call his supervisors together and present some major changes he hoped to make. These included (1) increasing employees' involvement in the decision-making process, (2) establishing a planning committee made up of three management representatives and three employees, (3) starting a suggestion system, (4) working out a new wage-incentive plan, and (5) installing an up-to-date performance appraisal system. Vincent stated that he would be active in the implementation of these changes.

Shortly after the meeting, Jane ran into Dan Driver, another supervisor who had been with Boland for many years.

Jane: It sure looks like Vincent is going to shake things up around here.

Dan: It sure does. Maybe it'll be for the good.

Jane: I can't see it if it is. He's going to stir things up that can only lead to trouble. We've got a good operation now. Why change it?

Dan: I agree we have a good operation, but it can still be improved. Maybe these changes will do just that. At any rate, I think we should support Vincent.

Jane: I'm not so sure things won't be worse.

Questions

1. Why do you think Jane is reluctant to accept Vincent's changes? Do you think Jane's reaction is unusual?
2. How would you suggest that Vincent go about implementing the desired changes?

Incident 5–2

A New Work Schedule

The Fit-Rite Shoe Company is located in a small town in a rural part of the state. John Azar, a mid-level manager, has just received notice that the company is going to a 40-hour, four-day workweek. This means that everyone will be required to work Monday through Thursday from 7 A.M. until 6 P.M. with an hour off for lunch. The memo announcing this change is accompanied by a detailed explanation of how much money this will save the company.

John knows that some of his employees will love the new schedule, but some of them are not going to like it at all. Of course everybody will like having Fridays off. However, the new schedule will definitely create problems for some employees. One problem is that many of the employees are women who have to get their children off to school, and the school bus doesn't pick them up until 7:30 A.M. Another reason is that many of the employees have extensive gardens in the summer. At present, they get home in plenty of time to work in their gardens, but getting off at 6 P.M. would not give them much time.

John wonders if top management is aware of these problems. He suspects that they were never considered since he can find no mention of them in documents accompanying the announcement.

Questions

1. Do you think John should voice the potential employee complaints to top management? If not, why? If so, how should John go about it?
2. Suppose John does approach management and the response is that the decision is final. If you were John, how would you attempt to implement the change?

Exercise 5–1

Preparing for Resistance to Change

One of the problems you face involves mistakes being made by employees who perform a particular operation. The same mistakes seem to occur in more than one department. You believe a training program for the people concerned will help reduce errors.

You are aware, however, that your supervisors may defend existing procedures simply because the introduction of training may imply criticism of the way they have been operating. You realize, too, that the supervisors may fear resistance by employees afraid of not doing well in the training program. All in all, you plan to approach the subject carefully.

You consider the following approaches for dealing with the situation:

1. Add to the agenda of your weekly staff meeting a recommendation that training be undertaken to help reduce errors.
2. Talk to all your supervisors individually and get their attitudes and ideas about what to do before bringing the subject up in the weekly staff meeting.
3. Ask the corporate training staff to come in, determine the training needs, and develop a program to meet those needs.
4. Since this training is in the best interests of the company, tell your supervisors they will be expected to implement and support it.
5. Appoint a team to study the matter thoroughly, develop recommendations, then bring it before the full staff meeting.

Other alternatives may be open to you, but assume these are the only ones you have considered. *Without discussion with anyone,* choose one of the approaches and be prepared to defend your choice.

Exercise 5–2

Change in the Airline Industry

Many organizations have had to change the way they do business since the tragic events of September 11, 2001. The airline industry has certainly been one of the most affected industries. Your instructor will divide the class into groups of four to six students per group. Once the groups have been formed, each group should respond to the following:

1. Identify what major changes have been implemented by or in the airline industry since September 11, 2001.
2. Does your group feel that these changes are positive or negative for the flying public? For airline employees?
3. Why does the group feel that these changes were not implemented before the tragic events took place?

After each group has answered the above questions, your instructor will ask each group to share their answers with the class.

Exercise 5–3

Generational Changes

Make a list of significant changes that have occurred in your generation, your parents' generation, and your grandparents' generation. After you have completed your list, your instructor will form you into groups of three or four. Once you are in your groups, discuss the changes that happened in each generation.

1. What changes had the most impact on society in general?
2. What changes had the most impact on you personally?
3. Do you think that the changes listed in (1) and (2) above were initially accepted or resisted by most people?

Exercise 5–4

Go to www.businessweek.com/innovators/ for the profiles of many of the great innovators of the past 75 years. Pick one of the persons listed. Research that person through the Internet or the library and be prepared to report to the class why you think the person was a successful innovator.

CHAPTER SIX

Ethics and Organization Politics

Learning objectives

After studying this chapter, you will be able to:

1. Define ethics and discuss what behaviors are considered unethical in the workplace.
2. Explain what a code of ethics is and describe what a code of ethics typically covers.
3. Discuss the role that supervisors play in setting the example of ethical conduct.
4. Identify the three areas that require ethical conduct by supervisors.
5. Summarize the requirements of SOX.
6. Define whistle-blowing.
7. Outline the steps the supervisor should follow when dealing with a dishonest subordinate.
8. Define the term *corporate culture* and explain how it can affect an organization's ethical standards.
9. Explain the concept of social responsibility.
10. Describe how a supervisor can positively increase his or her power base.
11. Define organization politics.
12. Discuss several guidelines that supervisors should follow when socializing with other members of the organization.

Supervision Dilemma

Jane Harris, a supervisor at Global Insurance Company, was caught off guard during lunch with a group of fellow supervisors. Some of them said they were able to slip away for a couple of hours each week to tend to personal business. Jane listened in a state of disbelief. How could these supervisors steal time from the company and not expect their subordinates to do the same?

What upset Jane was that they seemed to think nothing of it—to view it as accepted behavior. The real kicker came when one of the supervisors bragged that he had always been able to get a little extra money by padding his expense account. Jane left lunch wondering what the world had come to. Were ethics a thing of the past?

LEARNING OBJECTIVES

Ethics are standards or principles of conduct that govern the behavior of an individual or a group of individuals. Ethics are generally concerned with moral duties or with questions relating to what is right or wrong. The behaviors of supervisors, what goals they seek, and what actions they take are all affected by ethics. In any given situation, what a supervisor perceives as "right" naturally affects his or her actions and the actions of the employees.

Moral standards are the result of social forces and human experiences over hundreds of years. For example, society condemns cheating, lying, and stealing. However, the application of ethics is an individual consideration. Do you or do you not follow moral standards when dealing with others? Are you aware of a moral code and, if so, how do you interpret it?

Differences in awareness and interpretation of ethical standards create many problems. To illustrate, when does an action leave the sphere of honorable self-interest and become personal dishonesty? Does the fact that a person was not disciplined for a certain action make it acceptable?

All too often, actions are justified based on the means used or based on the ends accomplished. That is, do we hold an act to be morally right on the basis of the means used or on the basis of the end result? One might reason, for example, that the act of lying is acceptable if it achieves positive results. Conversely, one might consider any action that employs ethical means to be perfectly justifiable regardless of the outcome.

One problem in talking about business ethics is that there is no unanimity as to what is ethical and what is unethical. Little disagreement exists with regard to flagrant ethical violations such as embezzlement or stock fraud. Views become clouded, however, with regard to less obvious ethical questions, such as whether it is ethical to take longer than necessary to do a job or to engage in a few minutes of personal business on company time. Figure 6.1 lists several common practices that often involve questions of ethics in the workplace.

Content of Codes of Ethics

LEARNING OBJECTIVES

One concrete action that can be taken to encourage ethical standards is to establish a code of ethics. A **code of ethics** is a written statement of principles that should be followed in the conduct of business. Ideally, a code of ethics is comprehensive and addresses issues applicable to all areas of the organization. In general, codes of ethics are designed to serve three basic purposes: (1) to demonstrate a concern for ethics, (2) to transmit ethical values and standards to those working in the organization, and (3) to affect employee behavior by establishing behavioral expectations.

Some of the areas usually covered by a code of ethics include the following:

- Honesty
- Adherence to the law

FIGURE 6.1
Behaviors That Raise Ethical Questions in the Workplace

Using e-mail to harass co-workers.
Using company services (including the Internet) for personal use.
Padding an expense account.
Calling in sick to take a day off.
Authorizing a subordinate to violate company rules.
Pilfering company materials and supplies.
Accepting gifts/favors in exchange for preferential treatment.
Giving gifts/favors in exchange for preferential treatment.
Taking longer than necessary to do a job.
Divulging confidential information.
Doing personal business on company time.
Concealing mistakes.
Passing blame for errors to an innocent co-worker.
Claiming credit for someone else's work.
Falsifying time/quality/quantity reports.
Taking extra personal time (late arrivals, longer lunch hours and breaks, early departures).
Not reporting others' violations of company policies and rules.
Copying copyrighted computer software.
Hiring a key employee from a competitor.
Dating someone who works for you.
Abusive or intimidating behavior toward other employees.

- Product/service safety and quality
- Health and safety in the workplace
- Conflicts of interest
- Employment practices
- Selling and marketing practices
- Financial reporting
- Pricing, billing, and contracting
- Trading in securities/using confidential information
- Acquiring and using information about competitors
- Security
- Payments to obtain business
- Political activities
- Protection of the environment

If a code of ethics is to achieve its purposes and help mold the ethical environment of the organization, it must be communicated to all employees. The code can be communicated through company mailings, e-mails, bulletin board postings, employee handbooks, and general announcements. Many organizations require all new employees to sign a form confirming that they have read the company's code of ethics. Even more important than the method of communication is that the code be actively supported by all levels of management. Support for the code of ethics must start at the top of the organization and filter down through all levels. Employees must perceive that managers at all levels believe in and adhere to the code of ethics. If a comprehensive code of ethics does not exist, supervisors can clearly communicate their ethical expectations through their actions and personal behaviors. Supervision Illustration 6–1 presents the code of ethics of the Music Teachers National Association.

SUPERVISION ILLUSTRATION   6–1

CODE OF ETHICS OF THE MUSIC TEACHERS NATIONAL ASSOCIATION

Commitment to Students

- The teacher shall conduct the relationship with students and families in a professional manner.
- The teacher shall respect the personal integrity and privacy of students unless the law requires disclosure.
- The teacher shall clearly communicate the expectations of the studio.
- The teacher shall encourage, guide and develop the musical potential of each student.
- The teacher shall treat each student with dignity and respect, without discrimination of any kind.
- The teacher shall respect the student's right to obtain instruction from the teacher of his/her choice.

Commitment to Colleagues

- The teacher shall maintain a professional attitude and shall act with integrity in regard to colleagues in the profession.
- The teacher shall respect the reputation of colleagues and shall refrain from making false or malicious statements about colleagues.

- The teacher shall refrain from disclosing sensitive information about colleagues obtained in the course of professional service unless disclosure serves a compelling professional purpose or is required by law.
- The teacher shall respect the integrity of other teachers' studios and shall not actively recruit students from another studio.
- The teacher shall participate in the student's change of teachers with as much communication as possible between parties, while being sensitive to the privacy rights of the student and families.

Commitment to Society

- The teacher shall maintain the highest standard of professional conduct and personal integrity.
- The teacher shall accurately represent his/her professional qualifications.
- The teacher shall strive for continued growth in professional competencies.
- The teacher is encouraged to be a resource in the community.

Source: "Code of Ethics," *The American Music Teacher*, August/September 2004, p. 96.

Setting the Example

3   LEARNING OBJECTIVES

Although ethical behaviors of supervisors do not often make newspaper headlines, situations that test their ethics arise almost daily. Where it exists, a code of ethics provides the framework within which supervisors must act. However, numerous situations not specifically covered by a code of ethics often arise. In these situations, supervisors need to use individual judgment. It is often these judgments that most influence employee ethics. The supervisor must set the example. Subscribing to the theory of "Do what I say, not what I do" doesn't work. Employees are much more impressed by what supervisors do than by what they say. Employees' notions as to what is acceptable and not acceptable are largely based on the supervisor's actions. If employees perceive a supervisor as being slightly unethical or dishonest, they are likely to feel that similar behavior on their part is acceptable. For example, if the employees have reason to believe that the supervisor is "borrowing" things from the storeroom, they may not see anything wrong with their doing the same thing. On the other hand, some employees may still feel that doing this is wrong and thus lose respect for the supervisor.

Merely establishing a code of ethics does not prevent unethical behavior. To be effective, codes of ethics must be enforced. In fact, ethical codes that are not enforced probably do more harm than good. For this reason, it is important that companies discipline employees who violate their codes of ethics.

SUPERVISION ILLUSTRATION 6–2

DESTRUCTION OF STATE E-MAILS

A new lawsuit claims that two of the top aides of Matt Blunt, governor of Missouri, ordered all departments in the administration to regularly delete e-mails so potentially damaging messages wouldn't be available to the public.

The suit was filed by former Blunt lawyer Scott Eckersley. It says the governor's chief counsel at the time, Henry Herschel, called a meeting of staff attorneys and instructed them that "all e-mail should be deleted"—ignoring protests from some in the room that e-mails are public records. The suit also claims that the governor's chief of staff, Ed Martin, told staff members "to make sure they deleted their e-mails in both the inbox and trash files to ensure they did not have to be turned over to the press or public."

Eckersley, who was deputy counsel when he was fired, has claimed he was ousted after run-ins with Herschel,

Martin, and other Blunt aides about the handling of e-mails. He also has accused them of leading a smear campaign against him. His lawsuit says he peppered the aides with warnings that their orders violated state laws on how records should be retained and made available to the public. In an electronic age, e-mails sent on government computers or accounts are considered vital records.

The suit, filed in Jackson County Circuit Court, accuses the governor's office of defaming Eckersley and claims his firing violated state law protecting whistle-blowers. It asks for unspecified monetary damages.

Source: Adapted from Jo Mannies, "Suit Alleges Illegal Destruction of State E-mails," *McClatchy—Tribune Business News,* January 10, 2008, Wire Feed.

Making Ethical Decisions

Supervisors regularly make ethical decisions. These decisions have important consequences for both individuals and their companies. Behaving unethically can hurt, or even end, an individual's career. It can cause a company to lose millions of dollars or even go out of business altogether. Behaving ethically helps employees gain the trust of the people with whom they work. It can also help businesses gain the trust of customers, suppliers, and others.

Behaving Honestly

In many situations, the ethical course of action is clear-cut. Ethical employees never steal from their employers. They never lie about the hours they work. They never falsify documents. Supervision Illustration 6–2 describes an ethical issue involving e-mail.

Employee Theft

Employers trust their employees not to steal from them. Employees who behave ethically do not violate that trust.

Dishonest employees steal from their employers in a variety of ways. Some embezzle money or steal supplies or inventory from their employers. Some accept bribes from people who want to do business with their company. Others submit false expense accounts.

Lying about Hours Worked

Employees who behave ethically are honest about the hours they work. Employees who work at home, for example, accurately report how long they work. They do not take advantage of the fact that their managers cannot check to see if they are actually at their desks.

Ethical employees also show up at work unless they are ill or need to be away from their jobs for a legitimate reason. They do not pretend to be sick in order to stay home when they should be at work.

Falsifying Records

One of the worst ethical lapses an employee can commit is falsifying records. This can cause very grave damage to a company's reputation. It can even cause people to become ill or die. A manager at a pharmaceutical company, for example, who falsifies records documenting the side effects of the drugs the company produces can cause people who take the drug to die. A production supervisor who falsifies documents to indicate that computer parts were checked can cause his company to sell defective products. Years of excellent corporate performance can be wiped out by these kinds of unethical actions.

Areas Requiring Ethical Conduct by Supervisors

 4 LEARNING OBJECTIVES

Many areas of supervision require ethical conduct (some were listed in Figure 6.1). Most of these areas can be grouped into three general categories: (1) loyalty, (2) human relations, and (3) overt personal actions.

Loyalty

The category of loyalty has to do with where a supervisor's loyalties lie. Does the supervisor place personal interests ahead of everything else, or is he or she dedicated to the goals and needs of the employees, the organization, the family, or others? Regardless of the supervisor's leadership qualities, communication skills, or general knowledge, his or her personal influence will not be effective unless the employees view the stated objectives positively. Supervisors who are perceived as being interested only in themselves and their futures will have difficulty in getting the full cooperation of employees. Employees may ask themselves, "Would this supervisor destroy another person's career in order to advance?"

Human Relations

This category centers on a supervisor's concept of fairness. It is concerned with how the supervisor treats other people, especially subordinates. Ethics play a major role in determining how a supervisor treats subordinates. Is the supervisor consistent in the way that he or she deals with different subordinates, or does the supervisor play favorites? Are all of the supervisor's interpersonal dealings honest, or does he or she have a tendency to "talk behind people's backs"? Does the supervisor deceive his or her peers in order to make them look bad? Is the supervisor genuinely interested in the careers of subordinates?

Overt Personal Actions

The category of overt personal actions includes all of the other actions taken by a supervisor that may reflect his or her ethics. Those actions may be internal or external to the organization. Behavior inside the company would include such things as not circumventing organizational policy. External actions would include such things as how supervisors handle themselves in the community.

Figure 6.2 gives several examples under each category of the ethical conduct required of supervisors.

FIGURE 6.2
Examples of Ethical Conduct Required of Supervisors

Loyalty	Human Relations	Overt Personal Actions
Has concern for employee welfare.	Deals honestly with employees.	Doesn't cut corners to save time.
Has concern for company welfare.	Shows empathy when appropriate.	Is concerned with employee safety.
Has concern for employee families.	Objectively evaluates employees.	Never tries to cheat the company out of something.
Takes credit only when deserved.	Fairly disciplines employees.	Is well thought of in the community.

Laws Relating to Ethics in Business

Over the years, various laws have been enacted that directly relate to the issue of ethics in business. These laws apply to competitive behavior, corporate governance, consumer protection, and environmental protection.

Since the late nineteenth century the federal government has regulated companies to make sure that they do not engage in anticompetitive behavior. All companies operating in the United States must abide by these laws. Enforcement of these laws is handled by the Antitrust Division of the Justice Department and by the Federal Trade Commission.

Several laws protect consumers in the United States against unethical and unsafe business practices. These laws cover food and drugs, other manufactured products, and loans. A series of laws protects U.S. consumers against unfair lending practices. Under the Truth in Lending Act of 1968, creditors are required to let consumers know how much they are paying in finance charges and interest. The Equal Credit Opportunity Act of 1975 prohibits creditors from making credit decisions on the basis of discriminatory practices.

Since the late 1960s, environmental protection has been an important social and economic issue in the United States. This concern has been reflected in the many laws designed to protect the environment.

In the area of corporate governance, an important piece of legislation was passed in 2002. The Public Company Accounting Reform and Investor Protection Act **(Sarbanes-Oxley Act)** is also called SOX.

SOX includes requirements for auditor independence, restriction on firms engaging accounting firms for both auditing and consulting services, independence of firms' board committees, management's assessment of internal controls, and personal certification of financial reports by firms' CEOs and CFOs. Retaliation for whistle-blowing and altering or destroying documents to impede a federal investigation is generally illegal. Under SOX, employees can file complaints with the Occupational Safety and Health Administration (OSHA) if they have been retaliated against by their employer for reporting suspected corporate fraud or other activities related to fraud against shareholders. Supervision Illustration 6–3 describes a financial settlement under the Sarbanes-Oxley Act. Figure 6.3 summarizes the major points of the Sarbanes-Oxley Act.

Whistle-Blowing

In situations where supervisors and/or employees are not supported by their bosses regarding ethical or wrongdoing concerns, they must sometimes resort to whistle-blowing. **Whistle-blowing** is an attempt by an employee or former employee of an organization to disclose what he or she believes to be wrongdoings in or by the organization. One problem with whistle-blowing is that the whistle-blower places himself or herself at some risk should management react negatively or defensively to the information provided. There are many cases where employees have been fired or received other negative repercussions from whistle-blowing. Fortunately, over two-thirds of states have passed legislation to protect whistle-blowers from retaliation. At the federal level, the Organizational Sentencing Guidelines penalize companies for not allowing for internal policing (such as whistle-blowing) and reward companies that do allow for such procedures.

Dealing with Dishonest Employees

How does the supervisor deal with dishonest employees? Because the relationships involved differ, situations with dishonest subordinates are sometimes handled differently from those dealing with peers and other managers.

SUPERVISION ILLUSTRATION   6-3

BACKDATING OF STOCK OPTIONS

William McGuire ascended to the helm of what was then a regional health care company in 1989. Through a series of acquisitions, he turned UnitedHealth Group into a managed-care leader. Today the company serves more than 71 million people nationwide through traditional health plans, as well as Medicare and Medicaid programs, and health-related financial products.

In December 2006, McGuire left, along with two other UnitedHealth executives after an investigation commissioned by the company's board concluded that he had received stock option grants that were "likely backdated" to allow insiders to maximize financial gains.

The controversy was touched off by a *Wall Street Journal* report last year that questioned whether UnitedHealth and other companies had dated executives' options—after they were granted—to when the prices of the shares dipped particularly low in order to maximize the recipients' gains. The newspaper reported that McGuire received options on the days UnitedHealth's share price hit annual lows

in 1997, 1999, and 2000—timing that was all but impossible by chance.

During McGuire's 17-year tenure, UnitedHealth's share price increased fiftyfold. At the same time, he amassed a potential fortune in unexercised stock options that became the focus of probes by U.S. and state regulators. His shares were valued at one point at $1.6 billion.

In the settlement, McGuire agreed to return over $320 million in options. He also is forgoing the full value of his fully vested Supplemental Executive Retirement Plan (SERP), which is worth nearly $92 million, and about $8.1 million of incentive compensation benefits in a deferred compensation plan, said his lawyer, David M. Brodsky. McGuire already has repaid $198 million by repricing options, bringing his total giveback to more than $600 million. McGuire's settlement is the first under the Sarbanes-Oxley Act.

Source: Adapted from *Lisa Girion,* "Compensation; Ex-CEO to Make Huge Repayment; UnitedHealth Group's McGuire Agrees to Give Back $468 Million in Backdating Settlement," *Los Angeles Times,* Los Angeles, California: December 7, 2007, p. C1.

FIGURE 6.3

Major Points of the Sarbanes-Oxley Act of 2002

Source: Reprinted by permission of CPE, Inc., 3700 Reed Road, Suite 227, Broomall, PA 19008, 800-514-1114, www.cpeonline.com.

The SEC will direct the NYSE and NASDAQ to prohibit listing any public company whose audit committee does not comply with a new list of requirements affecting auditor appointment, compensation, and oversight. The audit committee must consist solely of independent directors.

CEOs and CFOs must certify in each periodic report containing financial statements that the report fully complies with Sections 13(a) and 15(d) of the Securities Exchange Act of 1934 and that the information fairly presents the company's financial condition and results of operations.

Certifying officers will face penalties for false certification of $1,000,000 and/or up to 10 years' imprisonment for "knowing" violation and $5,000,000 and/or up to 20 years' imprisonment for "willing" violation.

No public company may make, extend, modify, or renew any personal loan to its executive officers or directors, with limited exceptions.

The act sets a deadline for insiders to report any trading in their companies' securities to within two business days after the execution date of the transaction.

Each company must disclose "on a rapid and current basis" additional information about the company's financial condition or operations as the SEC determines is necessary or useful to investors or in the public interest.

All annual reports filed with the SEC containing financial statements must include all material corrections identified by a public accounting firm.

The act creates several new crimes for securities violations, including

- Destroying, altering, or falsifying records with the intent to impede or influence any federal investigation or bankruptcy proceeding.
- Knowing and willful failure by an accountant to maintain all audit or workpapers for five years.
- Knowingly executing a scheme to defraud investors in connection with any security.

With regard to subordinates, the supervisor must first recognize the problem and then build a case. For various reasons, supervisors are often reluctant to admit to problems involving dishonest employees. Some supervisors believe that bringing such a problem into the open would be bad for morale. Others mask the problem by arguing that "everybody does it." The problem is compounded if the dishonest employee has been with the company a long time and has a good work record. Whatever the case, such an employee should be confronted and dealt with appropriately. The supervisor must gather proof of the employee's dishonesty. This does not mean taking the word of others; it means carefully documenting the available evidence. For example, if an employee is suspected of stealing from the supply cabinet, care should be taken to document what was missing, the times it was missed, and the employee's whereabouts at those times. Once the supervisor is confident of the facts, he or she should confront the employee and follow the disciplinary system. The keys here are (1) recognize the problem, get the facts, and document the case; (2) confront the employee; and (3) follow the established disciplinary system.

The general approach followed in dealing with dishonest peers and other managers is similar to the one followed in dealing with dishonest subordinates. Since the relationships involved are significantly different, however, some deviation from this approach may be necessary. Moreover, you may not be in a position to deal directly with the problem. For example, if you suspect that a supervisor in another area is dishonest, you may never be in a position to prove or disprove your suspicions. In this case, you should deal cautiously with that supervisor and alert your boss as to your suspicions. When dealing with dishonest peers and other managers, it is in most cases better to report your suspicions and findings to your boss and let him or her confront those involved.

Supervisors should be aware that the usual tendency in dealing with dishonest employees is to do nothing and hope that the problem will go away. Unfortunately, the problem rarely goes away; it usually gets worse. In this same light, it is helpful to remember that most situations involving employee dishonesty start out small and grow.

Corporate Culture and Ethics

8 LEARNING OBJECTIVES

Simply stated, **corporate culture** means "the way we do things around here." Culture in an organization compares to personality in a person. Humans have fairly enduring and stable traits that help them protect their attitudes and behaviors. So do organizations. In addition, certain groups of traits or personality types are known to consist of common elements. Organizations can be described in similar terms. They can be warm, aggressive, friendly, open, innovative, conservative, and so forth. An organization's culture is transmitted in many ways, including long-standing and often unwritten rules; shared standards regarding what is important; prejudices; standards for social etiquette and demeanor; established customs for relating to peers, subordinates, and superiors; and other traditions that clarify to employees what is and is not appropriate behavior. Thus, corporate culture communicates how people in the organization should behave by establishing a value system conveyed through rites, rituals, myths, legends, and actions. In this light, corporate culture can certainly have a major impact on an organization's ethical standards and the ethical behaviors of its members.

Social Responsibility and Ethics

9 LEARNING OBJECTIVES

Social responsibility is a term that is often linked to organizational ethics. **Social responsibility** refers to the obligation that individuals or businesses have to help solve social problems. Most organizations in the United States feel some sense of social responsibility.

Businesses' concept of their role in society has changed dramatically over the past century. Beginning in the 1960s, many people began to believe that corporations should use their influence and financial resources to address social problems. They believed corporations should help solve problems such as poverty, crime, environmental destruction, and illiteracy.

According to this view, businesses should be responsible corporate citizens, not just maximizers of profit. Businesses have obligations to all of the people affected by their actions, known as stakeholders. Stakeholders include a company's employees, customers, suppliers, and the community.

Since the 1960s, corporations have increasingly demonstrated their commitment to social change. One example of this commitment is the increased diversity in the workplace, which was discussed in Chapter 1.

Building a Supervisory Power Base

Power is the ability to get others to respond favorably to instructions and orders. Put another way, power is the ability to influence others to do what you ask. The use of or desire for power is often viewed negatively in our society because power is often linked with the capacity to punish. While there are some negative types of power, there are also several very positive types. Fortunately, not everybody seeks or enjoys equal degrees of power. However, every supervisor needs some amount of power. Supervisors who have built a broad power base can more readily get employees' attention and cooperation and are more likely to be respected by higher-level managers.

In this light, there are many positive things that supervisors can do to increase their power base in a positive manner.

Gain the Respect of Subordinates

Gaining the respect of subordinates goes a long way toward building a power base. If your subordinates respect you, they will stand up for you in a crisis—they will give you active support when you need it. Others in the organization will interpret the support as a sign of power. Being competent and doing your job well is one of the best ways to gain the respect of subordinates.

Help Employees Be Successful

Helping subordinates be successful in their jobs not only reflects positively on a supervisor's performance but also promotes loyalty to the supervisor. Employees who believe that their supervisors are supportive and that their supervisors want them to succeed will go to great lengths to please their supervisors.

Be "in Good" with Your Boss

A certain amount of power goes with being in good with your boss. Subordinates and peers treat you with a certain respect if they know you have a close relationship with your supervisor. A later section in this chapter discusses ways "to keep your boss happy."

Seek Responsibility

Responsibility is accountability for reaching objectives, using resources properly, and adhering to organizational policy. Supervisors can gain power by seeking and accepting responsibility. The key here is to aggressively seek out additional responsibility rather than waiting for it to come. Peers and subordinates will automatically bestow a certain degree of power on the supervisor who has considerable responsibility.

Power, especially as related to leadership, is discussed in greater depth in Chapter 14.

Organization Politics

11 LEARNING OBJECTIVES

Organization politics refer to the practice of using means other than merit or good performance for bettering your position or gaining favor in the organization. Organization politics include such things as trying to influence the boss, trying to gain power, and trying to gain a competitive edge over your peers. Many people often associate sneaky, devious, or unethical behavior with the phrase "organization politics." However, this is not necessarily the case. There are many forms of organization politics that are not sneaky, devious, or unethical. Only when an individual pursues self-interest to the detriment of others or the organization does the behavior become unethical. When viewed in this light, almost any approach to organization politics can be ethical or unethical, depending on how it is used. Because organization politics are a reality in organizations, supervisors should understand them and know how to use them in a positive and ethical manner.

How to Keep Your Boss Happy

Almost all employees want to keep their bosses happy—and supervisors are no exception. Supervisors want to keep their bosses happy for many understandable reasons. A very obvious reason is to keep from getting fired. Even if your boss doesn't fire you, life can become pretty miserable if he or she doesn't like you. Knowing that your relationship with your boss is not good will keep you in constant fear of being fired or, at least, of not being treated fairly. And you can be pretty sure that you won't be a prime candidate for promotion! A poor relationship with your boss also means that you will probably not receive much coaching and counseling. This in itself can greatly hinder your progress.

Know Your Boss

The first step in keeping your boss happy is to know him or her. It is hard to keep a person happy if you don't know something about what makes that person tick. Answering the following questions will give you a better insight into your boss. It can also help you anticipate his or her actions.

> To whom does your boss report?
> What are your boss's primary responsibilities?
> What are your boss's chief successes, and when did they take place?
> What are some recent failings that are bothering him or her?
> Who are your boss's enemies?
> Who are your boss's friends?
> What is the extent of your boss's authority?
> What responsibilities and authority has your boss delegated?
> What are your boss's major concerns?
> On what basis is your boss being evaluated?
> What does your boss regard as good performance?
> On what basis is your boss evaluating you?

Be Loyal

Loyalty is a trait that all bosses admire. You can demonstrate your loyalty to your boss in a variety of ways. One good way is to defend the boss when he or she is being criticized. You can do this, even if you don't agree with the boss 100 percent, by pointing out probable reasons why the boss did whatever he or she did. A sure way to demonstrate disloyalty is publicly criticizing your boss. Regardless of how careful you try to be, such comments always seem to get back to the boss. Seemingly insignificant things often influence a boss's interpretations of loyalty. These include attendance at company functions and parties, willingness to work overtime and on Saturdays, and general enthusiasm. For example, a good performer who genuinely cares for the company may be branded by a boss as disloyal simply because he never attends company parties.

Show Respect for Your Boss

This doesn't mean that you have to bow and scrape at your boss's feet. It does mean that you should use common sense in your dealings with your boss. Be on time for meetings and conferences, talk and listen in a respectful manner, and use respectful gestures when in the boss's presence. In addition, exhibit a general attitude of respect toward your boss and his or her position. If you have occasion to disagree, do so in a tactful and respectful manner.

Seize Opportunities to Make Your Boss Look Good

In the usual course of events, many opportunities arise for you to make your boss look good. Take full advantage of them. When appropriate, praise your boss to top management. Be prepared in meetings to explain things that your boss might be asked, especially when you may know more about the details. Another suggestion is to head off problems that may be brewing for your boss or your department.

Avoid Antagonizing Other Departments

Don't contribute to poor relations with other departments. This is especially necessary if your boss must interact with those departments. You want your boss to think of you as someone he or she can trust in dealings with other departments. Antagonizing other departments only makes things more difficult for both you and your boss. Learn to reconcile differences among departments; undertake positive actions to keep problems from growing.

Insist on Feedback

One easy way to get on the bad side of your boss is to make a mistake and not know it. When this happens, it is easy to innocently repeat the mistake. Don't depend solely on formal performance appraisals for feedback. Create an environment that encourages your boss to tell you how you're doing. Take advantage of opportunities for informal discussions with the boss. For example, when your supervisor visits your area, ask for his or her opinion on how you handled a recent situation. As a part of this process, you must know how to accept negative feedback. Don't get angry or huffy when you get it; be grateful for your boss's honest evaluation.

Help Take the Load off Your Boss

Actively look for ways in which you can help take some of the load off your boss. Don't make the boss have to ask you every time he or she wants something done. Ask what you can do! Volunteer solutions to problems. Strive to be viewed as a problem solver and not a problem creator. Don't continually talk about how bad things are. Talk about what has been accomplished.

Socializing with Other Members of the Organization

LEARNING OBJECTIVES

Questions related to socializing with other members of the organization are influenced by both organizational ethics and organizational politics. Should the supervisor socialize with subordinates? Should the supervisor socialize with superiors? What tack should be taken

It appears that Global Insurance Company (Jane's company) could benefit from establishing a code of ethics (pp. 96–97). Such a code should clearly address the issues that confronted Jane (co-workers' tending to personal business on company time and padding expense accounts). Once the code has been developed, it should be communicated to all of Global's employees. Jane should now have a much better understanding of what actions are generally considered unethical.

Jane's peers are committing clearly unethical actions and Jane has recognized this problem. She should gather her facts and document her case to whatever extent she can. If Jane feels comfortable, she should personally confront her peers about their ethical behavior. Otherwise, she should present the evidence to her boss, Joyce Logan, and let her confront them (pp. 99–100).

by the person who is promoted to supervisor over former peers with whom he or she has frequently socialized (as a member of the bowling team, a softball team, and so forth)? Such questions, sooner or later, confront almost every supervisor. There are no hard-and-fast answers. However, these general guidelines should be followed:

1. Don't be overly eager to socialize with subordinates or superiors. Let things take their normal course.
2. Use common sense. Don't do anything while socializing that will later cause problems (such as getting highly intoxicated at a party at your boss's house). The supervisor who does not use common sense when socializing with superiors or subordinates is surely courting trouble.
3. Be yourself. Don't try to put on a false front to impress your boss or other superiors.
4. Don't try to use your rank when socializing with subordinates.
5. Don't make any work-related promises to subordinates while socializing.
6. Don't date or become romantically involved with subordinates.

Summary

This chapter discusses the importance that ethics and organization politics play in the life of the supervisor. It offers numerous guidelines to assist supervisors in dealing with ethical questions and to enhance their understanding of organization politics.

1. *Define ethics and discuss what behaviors are considered unethical in the workplace.* Ethics are standards or principles of conduct that govern the behavior of an individual or a group of individuals. Ethics are generally concerned with moral duties or with questions relating to what is right or wrong. Blaming or taking advantage of an innocent co-worker, divulging confidential information, falsifying reports, claiming credit for someone else's work, padding an expense account, and pilfering company materials and supplies are generally considered unethical behaviors.

2. *Explain what a code of ethics is and describe what a code of ethics typically covers.* A code of ethics is a written statement of principles that should be followed in the conduct of business. A code of ethics typically addresses such topics as ethical standards, questionable payments, meals, gifts, purchasing policies, and employee involvement in political campaigns and noncorporate political activities.

3. *Discuss the role that supervisors play in setting the example of ethical conduct.* As the final link between management and operative employees, supervisors play a major role in setting the ethical tone of the organization. Employees look to their supervisors for cues as to what is considered ethical behavior and what is not.

4. *Identify the three areas that require ethical conduct by supervisors.* Most of the areas requiring ethical conduct by supervisors can be grouped into three general categories: (1) loyalty, (2) human relations, and (3) overt personal actions.

5. *Summarize the requirements of SOX.* SOX includes requirements for auditor independence, restriction on firms

engaging accounting firms for both auditing and consulting services, independence of firms' board committees, management's assessment of internal controls, and personal certification of financial reports by firms' CEOs and CFOs.

6. *Define whistle-blowing.* Whistle-blowing is an attempt by an employee or former employee of an organization to disclose what he or she believes to be wrongdoings in or by the organization.

7. *Outline the steps the supervisor should follow when dealing with a dishonest subordinate.* When dealing with a dishonest subordinate, the supervisor should (1) recognize the problem, get the facts, and document the case; (2) confront the employee; and (3) follow the established disciplinary system.

8. *Define the term corporate culture and explain how it can affect an organization's ethical standards.* Corporate culture can be defined as "the set of important understandings (often unstated) that members of a community share in common." Corporate culture communicates how people in an organization behave by establishing a value system conveyed through rites, rituals, myths, legends, and actions. These rites, rituals, myths, legends, and actions have a direct impact on the organization's ethical standards.

9. *Explain the concept of social responsibility.* Social responsibility refers to the obligation that individuals or businesses have to help solve social problems.

10. *Describe how a supervisor can positively increase his or her power base.* Things that a supervisor can do to increase his or her power base include (1) gain the respect of subordinates, (2) help employees be successful, (3) be "in good" with your boss, and (4) seek responsibility.

11. *Define organization politics.* The term organization politics refers to the practice of using means other than merit or good performance for bettering your position or gaining favor in the organization. Because organization politics are a reality in organizations, supervisors should understand them and know how to use them in a positive and ethical manner. Organization politics include such things as trying to influence the boss, trying to gain power, and trying to gain a competitive edge over your peers.

12. *Discuss several guidelines that supervisors should follow when socializing with other members of the organization.* While there are no absolute hard-and-fast rules in this area, the following guidelines should be followed: (1) Don't be overly eager to socialize with subordinates or superiors; (2) Use common sense. Don't do anything while socializing that will later cause problems; (3) Be yourself. Don't try to put on a false front to impress your boss or other superiors; (4) Don't try to use your rank when socializing with subordinates; (5) Don't make any work-related promises to subordinates while socializing; and (6) Don't date or become romantically involved with subordinates.

Key Terms

Code of ethics, 96
Corporate culture, 103
Ethics, 96

Organizational politics, 105
Power, 104
Responsibility, 104

Sarbanes-Oxley Act (SOX), 101
Social responsibility, 103
Whistle-blowing, 101

Review Questions

1. What are ethics?

2. Give several examples of behaviors that most people would consider unethical.

3. What are codes of ethics, and why are they desirable?

4. What are three major areas that require ethical conduct by supervisors?

5. Define the term corporate culture.

6. Define social responsibility.

7. Define whistle-blowing.

8. Define organization politics.

9. List several things that you can do to help keep your boss happy.

10. What are some tactics that are often used to gain a competitive edge on peers?

11. Outline the basic guidelines that the supervisor should follow when socializing with superiors and subordinates.

Skill-Building Questions

1. Do you think that most people consider their personal ethical standards to be higher than those of their peers? Explain.

2. At a recent retirement party, a supervisor with 30 years of service boasted, "I've never played politics in my job." Do you think this is possible, and even if it is, do you think it is desirable?

3. Suppose your boss asked you to do something that you considered unethical. Would you do it? If not, how would you handle the situation?

4. What are your personal views regarding socializing with superiors? With subordinates?

Additional Readings

Abrams, Jim, "House Fortifies Whistleblower Protections," *The Washington Post,* January 29, 2009, p. A-17.

Anonymous, "What, No Football Tickets?" *McClatchy-Tribune Business News,* March 3, 2009, Editorial.

Aydt, Bruce, "No Special Treatment for First Offer," *Realtor,* March 2009, p. 20.

Brown, Warren K., "Promoting Integrity," *Professional Safety,* February 2009, p. 7.

Hagerty, James A., "Lenders Get a New Code," *The Wall Street Journal (Eastern Edition),* December 24, 2008, p. C-4.

Steinbrook, Robert, "Physician-Industry Relations— Will Fewer Gifts Make a Difference?" *The New England Journal of Medicine,* February 5, 2009, p. 557.

SKILL-BUILDING APPLICATIONS

Incident 6–1

Additional Expenses?

Principals

   Steve Richards—resident accounts supervisor for United Electric Company in Midland. Steve is 26 years old and is considered to have a bright future at United. He has been a supervisor for two months.

   Susan Moore—district manager in Midland for United Electric. Susan is 41 and has been in her present job nine years. Her district, Midland, has strong political influence in the company since the current president of United Electric was raised in Midland. Susan is Steve's boss.

   Chester ("Chet") Orr—division manager for United. He is 61 years old and is located at company headquarters about 30 miles from Midland. Chet is Susan's boss and also a close personal friend of the president of United.

   At 8:30 A.M. on Monday morning, Steve Richards is preparing to leave Susan Moore's office after planning the week's activities.

Steve: Oh, I almost forgot. As soon as I have my monthly expense voucher typed, I'll send it to you for signature so it can be forwarded to accounting.

Susan: I'm glad you mentioned that. I've been meaning to talk to you about your voucher this month. I have about $100 worth of items I want you to include on your voucher. My voucher is really loaded this month, and it would look bad to submit an extremely high amount—especially in light of the recent emphasis on personal expenses. It's really no big deal. Anyway, I'm the only one who has to sign it. When you get your check back, you can give me the extra $100. Here's an itemized list of my expenses that should be added to your expense report. Also, don't forget that we're supposed to go to lunch with Chet Orr today at 12 o'clock sharp.

Steve leaves Susan's office with the itemized list in his hand. During the morning, Steve gives much thought to Susan's request. He doesn't like the idea, but Susan is the boss. At about 11 A.M., Susan calls Steve on the intercom and says she can't make the lunch with Chet because the local congressman is making an unscheduled visit to the Midland office. Susan asks Steve to take Chet to lunch and give him her regrets and to tell Chet that she will see them after lunch around 2 P.M. Chet shows up at noon, and he and Steve leave for lunch.

Questions

1. If you were Steve, would you say anything to Chet about Susan's request? Why or why not?

2. How would you handle the situation with Susan if you were Steve?

Incident 6–2

The Date: Jim's Perceptions

It's been almost six months since Jim came to work at the downtown branch as an assistant branch manager for the First National Bank. Over this time period Jim has become fed up with the whole place. In his college days and during the period when he served as a supervisory trainee, things were a lot better. He was meeting new people and learning new things. Also, he didn't have to take "orders" from anyone.

   However, since he worked at the downtown branch, things have gone downhill from Jim's perspective. Jim thinks that his branch manager, Louise, takes herself and her work too seriously. Jim also believes that she goes out of her way to pick on him and that she assigns him menial jobs from time to time.

   On several occasions when Louise has seen Jim having lunch with the tellers, she asked him "not to be too friendly toward them since you're now in supervision." She stated that Jim should be more "professional."

   A few minutes ago Louise asked Jim to meet with her at 1 o'clock. During lunch break, the head teller informed Jim that this morning Louise had overheard some of the tellers say that he was out on a date with Patty—the newest teller—the previous evening.

Louise's Perceptions

Ever since Jim arrived—about six months ago—Louise has been concerned about his attitude. Given his excellent academic record and his apparent intelligence, Louise is very surprised about his job performance. She can find no fault with the quantity or quality of

Jim's work, but does find fault with his entire attitude and professionalism. This morning, for example, Louise found out that Jim was out on a date last night with Patty, the newest teller.

It is now 1 o'clock and Jim is entering Louise's office.

Questions

1. What do you think Louise should say to Jim?
2. Do you think that it is unethical for Jim to date a teller? Why or why not?

Exercise 6–1

Where Do You Stand?

Read the following descriptions, and then decide how you would respond to each of the situations described. Be prepared to justify your position in a class discussion.

Situation 1: Family versus Ethics*

Joe, a 56-year-old supervisor with children in college, discovers that the owners of his company are cheating the government out of several thousand dollars a year in taxes. Joe is the only employee in a position to know this. Should Joe report the owners to the Internal Revenue Service at the risk of endangering his family's livelihood, or should he disregard the discovery in order to protect his family's livelihood?

Situation 2: The Roundabout Raise

When Mary asks for a raise, her boss praises her work but says that the company's rigid budget won't allow any further merit raises for the time being. Instead, her boss suggests that the company "won't look too closely at your expense accounts for a while." Should Mary take this as authorization to pad her expense account on the ground that she would simply be getting the money that she deserves through a different route, or should she ignore this opportunity to obtain a "roundabout raise"?

Situation 3: The Faked Degree

Bill has done a sound job for over a year, but his boss learns that he got the job by claiming to have a college degree, although he actually never graduated. Should the boss dismiss him for submitting a fraudulent résumé, or should the boss overlook the false claim since Bill has otherwise proved conscientious and honorable and since making an issue of the degree might ruin Bill's career?

*The first five of these situations are adapted from Roger Richles, "Executives Apply Stiffer Standards Than Public to Ethical Dilemmas," *The Wall Street Journal,* November 3, 1983, p. 33.

Situation 4: Sneaking Phone Calls

Helen discovers that a fellow employee regularly makes about $100 a month worth of personal long-distance telephone calls from an office telephone. Should Helen report the employee to the company or disregard the calls on the grounds that many people make personal calls at the office?

Situation 5: Cover-Up Temptation

Martha discovers that the chemical plant in which she works as supervisor is creating slightly more water pollution in a nearby lake than is legally permitted. Revealing the problem will bring considerable unfavorable publicity to the plant, hurt the lakeside town's resort business, and create a scare in the community. Solving the problem will cost Martha's company well over $100,000. Outsiders are unlikely to discover the problem. The violation poses no danger to people; at most, it will endanger a small number of fish. Should Martha reveal the problem despite the cost to her company, or should she view the problem as little more than a technicality and disregard it?

Situation 6: E-Mail Messages

Juan, a recent college graduate, spends about an hour a day writing e-mail messages to his college classmates. In spite of this practice, Juan's performance is at least average if not better than that of his collegues. Should Juan's boss, Ruth, confront Juan about his misuse of company time?

Exercise 6–2

Evaluate Your Ethics

How will you act in situations that test your honesty and acceptance of rules, regulations, and codes of behavior?

That depends on the values you use to frame your approach to life and to work, says Paul Mok, president of Training Associates, a consulting firm.

Mok, with a doctorate in psychology and 20 years' experience advising corporations, says that most of us operate from one or more of four basic value sets, which are especially apt to surface during stress. He contends the key to predicting how someone will react under ethical pressure is discovering what his or her dominant values are. Mok developed a test, called SPOT (Situational Perceptions–Observations Test), to help in that discovery. Here is a sample from that test.

To identify your dominant value set(s) assign the numbers 4, 3, 2, and 1 to each set of four phrases that are shown to complete the eight self-descriptive statements below. Use 4 for the response that best describes you; 3, next most like you; 2, next; and 1, least like you.

1. In relating to a boss, I may:
   a. Express a lack of concern if a lack of concern is expressed to me.(S)
   b. Convey impatience with ideas that involve departures from procedures.(R)
   c. Show little interest in thoughts and ideas that show little or no originality or understanding of the company.(I)
   d. Tend to get impatient with lengthy explanations and direct my attention to what needs to be done right now.(C)

2. When circumstances prevent me from doing what I want, I find it most useful to:
   a. Review any roadblocks and figure out how I can get around them.(C)
   b. Rethink all that has happened and develop a new idea, approach, or view of my job.(I)
   c. Keep in mind the basics, pinpoint the key obstacles, and modify my game plan accordingly.(R)
   d. Analyze the motivations of others and develop a new "feel" for those around me.(S)

3. If I must deal with an unpleasant customer, I would probably try to:
   a. Clarify the problem and explore the alternatives.(R)
   b. Highlight in plain language what I want, need, or expect the customer to do.(C)
   c. Explain the "big picture" and how the situation relates to it.(I)
   d. Express empathy by putting myself in his or her shoes.(S)

4. In terms of things like personal phone calls on the job, a company should probably:
   a. Be understanding of the employees if they don't overdo it.(S)
   b. Make the rules clear and see that employees follow them.(R)
   c. Do what is best for company profits.(C)
   d. Explore company policies that are consistent with personal needs.(I)

5. If a friend told me he was "padding" the expense account for $10, I would probably:
   a. Advise the person not to; that he or she is stealing and should not do it.(R)
   b. Figure this is common practice even if it isn't right.(I)
   c. Figure each person is trying to survive the best he can.(C)
   d. Try not to be judgmental and see if I could help.(S)

6. If I have done something that goes against company policy and procedures, I probably:
   a. Would have done so to help others in the company.(S)
   b. Would be upset and need to reexamine my actions.(R)
   c. Would have done so to get results in the most practical way.(C)
   d. Would consider how the policies and procedures could be modified in the future.(I)

7. When I start a new job, I feel it is preferable to:
   a. Learn what is expected—what the rules are—and follow them.(R)
   b. See where the company is and what its orientation really is.(I)
   c. Make a name for myself based on competitive results.(C)
   d. Make friends and show I am a "regular" person.(S)

8. When co-workers take shortcuts, my actions will probably depend on:
   a. Whether the co-workers are good friends or not.(S)
   b. Whether they knew the rules; if they didn't, I would explain them.(R)
   c. Whether their actions would hurt me and my department.(C)
   d. Whether such shortcuts would significantly affect results.(I)

After each statement is a letter—S, R, I, or C. Make a column for each of the four letters, place your numbers (1 to 4) for each statement in the appropriate column, and total the figures. The category in which you scored highest corresponds to your primary value set; the second highest score shows your backup system.

- **S:** Socially oriented values are characterized by deep concern for the welfare of others. Someone meeting this profile might not see a conflict in stealing company resources to help indigent people.

- **R:** Rational values center on commitment to rules and regulations. A rationalist might be indecisive in a crisis not covered by specific rules or procedures.
- **I:** Individualistic values are expressed in autonomous thinking and the belief that people should evaluate rules rather than obey them blindly. Under stress, an individualist may become rigid and dogmatic, ignoring others and putting his or her cause above the established codes.
- **C:** Competitive values are typical of someone motivated by the desire "to win the game." If this means bending the rules or cutting corners, so be it.

Source: Reprinted by permission, *Nation's Business,* August 1987. Copyright 1987. U.S. Chamber of Commerce.

Exercise 6–3

Rating Your Boss on Ethics

If you are currently employed, rate your current boss on each of the items listed in Figure 6.1, page 97. If you are not currently employed, think of the last boss you had even if it was in a part-time or temporary job. Rate each item from a low of 0 (almost never) to a high of 5 (frequently) for each item. The lower the total score for all items, the higher the ethics of your boss.

Exercise 6–4

Whistle-Blowers

One of the most interesting issues in the field of business ethics is whistle-blowing. In 1986 Congress passed amendments to the False Claims Act of 1863 which offer whistle-blowers financial rewards for disclosing fraud committed against the federal government. The Sarbanes-Oxley Act passed in 2002 provides new protections for whistle-blowers in business. The Securities and Exchange Commission has proposed regulations that would in certain cases require lawyers to blow the whistle on corporations they serve that engage in securities fraud. Employees who can prove that they have been terminated or otherwise penalized for whistle-blowing are entitled to reinstatement and up to two times the amount of back pay, plus interest.

Some whistle-blowers under the False Claims Act have reaped very large rewards. Chester Walsh, who blew the whistle against General Electric for defense contractor fraud, received a payout in excess of $13 million. Gwendolyn Cavanaugh and Virginia Lanford split $8.2 million as a reward for reporting Medicare fraud by their employer, Vencor, a health care company. For the period of 1997 to 2001, it is estimated that whistle-blowers received $680 million for their share of recoveries.

Read the material shown above. Divide the class into teams of four or five students per team. Have each team prepare a ten minute presentation on a whistle-blowing incident. It is suggested that the Internet be used to gather the material needed to prepare the presentation.

Source: Adapted from Thomas L. Carson, Mary Ellen Verdu, and Richard E. Wokutch, "Whistle-Blowing for Profit: An Ethical Analysis of the Federal False Claims Act," *Journal of Business Ethics,* pp. 362–376.

Planning and Organizing Skills

SECTION OUTLINE

CHAPTER SEVEN

Supervisory Planning

Learning objectives

After studying this chapter, you will be able to:

1. Describe how an organization plans.
2. Describe the supervisor's role in the overall planning system of the organization.
3. Discuss the steps involved in the supervisory planning process—with special emphasis on setting objectives.
4. Identify the SMART criteria for setting objectives.
5. Discuss the role of contingency plans.
6. Differentiate among organizational policies, procedures, and rules.
7. List several common supervisory planning activities.
8. Understand the basic elements of a management by objectives (MBO) system.

After Jane Harris had been in her new supervisory job for only a few months, she realized the importance of meeting deadlines. This first came home to her when she missed a promised deadline on a large batch of claims. Joyce Logan, her department head, had phoned her on a Friday and asked if she could expedite a large batch of claims for a preferred customer. With little forethought, Jane promised to get them out by the follow-ing Tuesday. Due to some unexpected problems with office equipment, she did not get the claims out until late the next Thursday. When a similar incident occurred only a few weeks later, Joyce called her in and discussed the importance of setting objectives and meeting agreed-upon deadlines. Jane decided that she had better learn how to plan her workload more effectively.

The supervisor must plan his or her work if it is to be done effectively, properly, and on time. The supervisor's failure to plan can result in lost time, wasted materials, poor use of equipment, and misuse of space. The supervisor must also understand how his or her plans fit into the overall planning scheme of the organization.

How the Organization Plans

1 LEARNING OBJECTIVES

Ideally, all levels of management within an organization develop plans. The difference in the planning of the different levels lies in the methods they employ and the extent to which they plan. Most planning is carried out on an informal or casual basis. This occurs when planners do not record their thoughts but carry them around in their heads. A **formal plan** is a written, documented plan developed through an identifiable process. The appropriate degree of sophistication depends on the needs of the individual managers and the organization itself. The environment, size, and type of business are factors that typically affect the planning needs of an organization. It should be noted that formal planning can be just as beneficial to small organizations as to large organizations.

Plans developed at higher levels of management involve many people and resources and may be very complex. Such plans frequently deal with long-range time spans. A plan orchestrated by the top management of an organization is usually called a **strategic** or **corporate plan.** Although top management has the primary responsibility for developing the strategic plan, many levels of managers, including supervisors, are involved in the development of the plan.

Once the strategic plan has been developed, specific plans for the different parts of the organization are derived from it. This is done by starting at the higher-level organization units and working down to the lower units. For most organizations, this means starting with the highest-level divisions or departments and then developing plans for successively lower levels of the organization. The key is for each lower-level plan to be based on the plan at the next-higher level. This does not mean that plans are developed by higher levels of management and forced on lower levels. It does mean that lower-level plans are developed by managers at their respective levels based on the plans of higher levels. As the planning process moves down to lower levels in the organization, it becomes narrower in scope and covers shorter time spans. Furthermore, as plans cascade downward through the organization, they become more specific and detailed in nature. At the supervisory level, most plans have relatively short time spans and are very application oriented. In fact, most supervisory planning deals with time periods of a month or less. Figure 7.1 illustrates how supervisory planning relates to other levels of planning.

117

FIGURE 7.1   **The Relationships among Corporate, Departmental, and Supervisory Plans**

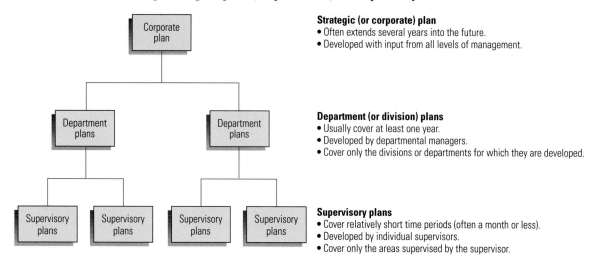

Strategic (or corporate) plan
- Often extends several years into the future.
- Developed with input from all levels of management.

Department (or division) plans
- Usually cover at least one year.
- Developed by departmental managers.
- Cover only the divisions or departments for which they are developed.

Supervisory plans
- Cover relatively short time periods (often a month or less).
- Developed by individual supervisors.
- Cover only the areas supervised by the supervisor.

The Supervisor and Strategic Planning

LEARNING OBJECTIVES

Strategic management is the process of developing strategic plans and keeping them current as changes occur internally and in the environment. It is through the strategic management process that top management determines the long-run direction and performance of an organization by ensuring careful formulation, proper implementation, and continuous evaluation of plans. Although orchestrated by top management, successful strategic management involves many different levels in the organization, including supervisors. For example, top management may solicit inputs from all levels of management when formulating top-level plans. Once top-level plans have been finalized, different organizational units may be asked to formulate plans for their respective areas. A proper strategic management process helps ensure that plans throughout the different levels of the organization are coordinated and mutually supportive.

Unfortunately, many managers think that strategic management is just for top managers and of little concern for supervisors.[1] As discussed in the preceding paragraph, *successful* strategic management necessarily involves managers at *all levels,* including supervisors. In addition to that necessity, there are additional benefits to supervisors. Engaging in the strategic management process allows supervisors to see the "big picture" by viewing the organization as an integrated whole. A positive outcome of this exposure is that supervisors develop more conceptual skills and better decision-making skills. Not only does this better prepare supervisors to make daily decisions, but it also prepares them to move up in the organization. An additional benefit of supervisors being involved in the strategic management process is that it fosters a long-range orientation. Because much of a supervisor's work focuses on the short range, this involvement can be a broadening and beneficial experience.

Gap analysis is a key part of strategic management that focuses on identifying areas needing improvement. Gap analysis consists of defining a desired state (such as level of sales or units produced), identifying the current situation, and comparing the two to identify obvious "gaps." Once the "gaps" have been clearly identified, plans can be formulated to reduce or eliminate the gaps. Gap analysis can be used by all levels of managers including supervisors.

The Supervisor's Role in Planning

3 LEARNING OBJECTIVES

Supervisory plans are derived from the plans of higher levels of management. Usually, the planning information that comes from upper management is general in nature. For example, upper management may establish production objectives. However, only rarely are these objectives accompanied by a detailed plan for reaching them. Such a plan must be developed by the supervisor. Developing a detailed plan involves answering the following questions: What must be done? Why must it be done? Where should it be done? Who should do it? How should it be done? In essence, supervisory plans operationalize the plans of higher management.

Successful planning for the entire organization involves gathering information from all levels. It is a common practice for the supervisor to provide information to upper-level managers for their use in planning. For example, supervisors are often asked by middle- and upper-level managers to contribute information about future human resource and equipment requirements. Such exchanges between supervisors and upper-level managers keep the supervisors informed and make plans more practical and workable. When gathering information for upper levels of management or for input into their own plans, supervisors often involve their employees in the process.

Figure 7.2 presents a model of the supervisory planning process. The different parts of the model are discussed in the following sections.

The What and How of Supervisory Planning

Planning is concerned not with future decisions but with the future impact of today's decisions. When planning, a supervisor should think about how today's decisions might affect future actions. **Planning** is the process of deciding what objectives to pursue during a future time period and what to do to achieve those objectives. As previously discussed, a supervisor's objectives are usually derived from the plans of higher levels of management. In fact, it is not unusual for a supervisor's objectives to be spelled out by higher levels of management. These objectives are usually broadly defined, however, and require further refinement by the supervisor.

Once the objectives have been established, the second phase of the planning process involves deciding what must be done to achieve them. Supervisory planning involves developing the details of how objectives are to be achieved.

Some people regard the objective-setting process as separate from the planning process. In their view, planning is determining *how* to achieve a given objective or set of objectives. Whether or not the objective-setting process is viewed as an integral part of the planning process, objectives must be established before the planning process can be completed. Obviously, it is not possible for a supervisor to formulate a course of action for reaching an objective if he or she does not know what the objective is.

Objectives versus Goals

An objective is a statement of a desired measurable result of what is to be achieved. When objectives are viewed in this way, the terms **objectives** and **goals** are interchangeable. Some authors and practitioners, however, distinguish between objectives and goals. These people usually view goals as broader, more encompassing, and longer range than objectives. They believe that objectives can be stated very concisely and in measurable terms. In this book, the terms *goals* and *objectives* will be used interchangeably. Instead of referring to objectives as

FIGURE 7.2
Supervisory Planning Process

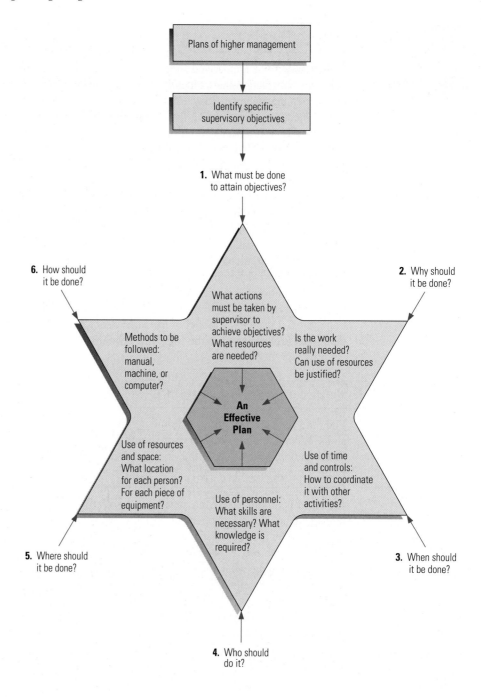

a subset of goals, we will refer to different levels of objectives. Figure 7.3 illustrates several levels of objectives.

Setting Objectives

Objectives enable the supervisor to focus directly on the targets to be reached within a given period. A supervisor's success depends largely on having a clear understanding of objectives. Similarly, a supervisor must be able to communicate these objectives to the employees who will actually perform the tasks necessary to achieve them.

FIGURE 7.3
Different Levels of Objectives

> **Corporate-Level Objective**
> To increase corporatewide sales by 20 percent for the current fiscal year.
> **International Division's Objective**
> To increase sales in the international division by 25 percent for the current fiscal year.
> **Production Department's Objective**
> To increase production of the department by 20 percent for the current fiscal year.
> **Production Supervisor's Objective**
> To produce 300 units of model B within the next 20 working days.

Objectives should be clear, concise, quantifiable, and measurable whenever possible. They should be detailed enough so that employees understand exactly what is expected. They should span all significant areas of the department. This usually means that several objectives must be set. The problem with a single objective is that it is often achieved at the expense of other desirable objectives. For example, a supervisor may go all out to achieve a production objective even if this means lowering quality.

At the supervisory level, objectives typically deal with quantity, quality, cost, personnel, and safety. For example, a supervisor may have the objective of increasing the department's production by 10 percent over the next 90 days. How objectives are set at the supervisory level and how they are stated can have a great deal to do with how successful a supervisor may be in reaching them.

How Objectives Are Set

Whenever feasible, supervisors should consult with and involve their employees in the objective-setting process. This does not mean that employees should actually set the objectives but that they should be given an opportunity to express their opinions and provide inputs. Most employees want to be asked for their opinions and suggestions. Objectives that are simply announced by the supervisor are less likely to be achieved than objectives that employees have helped formulate. Another good reason for involving employees is that they frequently have valuable information to contribute. Being near to, and actually performing, the work provides insight and practical experience that the supervisor may not have. However, it is not always possible to involve employees in the objective-setting process. For example, the supervisor's time frame may not allow for it. Involving employees is a practice that can be used in many circumstances and can be very beneficial to the supervisor and the organization. In those circumstances when it is not feasible to directly involve employees in the objective setting process, supervisors should keep the employees informed as to what is going on.

How Objectives Are Stated

4 LEARNING OBJECTIVES

Objectives that have the best chance for success follow the SMART criteria.[2] **SMART** stands for *specific, measurable, achievable, relevant,* and *time-based.* Each of these criteria is discussed below.

Specific. Specific in this context means that an observable action, behavior, or achievement is described *and* linked to a rate, number, percentage, or frequency. "Answer all written customer complains quickly" is a precise description of behavior, but it is not linked to a rate, number, percentage, or frequency. "Answer all written customer complaints within 48 hours" is specific and linked to a rate.

Measurable. A system, method, or procedure must exist that allows the tracking and recording of the specific action, behavior, or achievement upon which the objective is

FIGURE 7.4

Examples of How to Improve Work Objectives

Poor:	To maximize production.
Better:	To increase production by 10 percent within the next three months.
Poor:	To reduce absenteeism.
Better:	To average no more than three absent days per employee per year.
Poor:	To waste less raw material.
Better:	To waste no more than 2 percent of raw material.
Poor:	To improve the quality of service.
Better:	To receive no more than two written customer complaints per week for the next year.

focused. Using the previous example, a system must exist for measuring just how long it is taking to answer written customer complaints.

Achievable. Objectives should be set so that people are capable of achieving them. Some people think that objectives should be set just slightly higher than what can be attained. The thought here is to keep the employee stretching and to avoid the letdown that might occur once the objective has been reached. One problem with this approach is that it takes only a short time for employees to figure out that the objective is unattainable. This can quickly demotivate employees. On the other hand, most people are turned on, not off, when they reach a challenging goal. The key is for the objective to be challenging and realistic. Employees should be required to stretch, but the objective should be within their capabilities.

Relevant. Relevant in this context means the objective is viewed by affected employees as being important to the organization and as something that they can impact or change. If employees perceive an objective as unimportant or as something they can't impact or change, they are going to psychologically dismiss the objective.

Time-based. Somewhere in the stated objective there should be a specific date (day/month/year) or time frame for reaching or achieving the objective.

In addition to the above SMART characteristics, objectives should be regularly updated and assigned priorities. All too often, objectives are not regularly reviewed and updated. Pursuing outdated objectives wastes resources. Objectives should be reviewed periodically. Those that are no longer of value should be discarded. Others will need revising in light of recent changes. Because objectives are of differing importance, both the supervisor and employees should know an objective's relative importance. Everyone should know which objective is most important and which is least important. Then, if problems occur, everyone will be able to budget time accordingly. Prioritizing objectives does not involve deciding *how* the various objectives will be reached. It does involve establishing their relative importance. Deciding how the objectives will be achieved is part of action planning, which is discussed in the next section.

Figure 7.4 presents examples of how some poorly stated objectives might be better stated. Figure 7.5 shows some typical areas in which a supervisor might set objectives.

Action Planning

Once the objectives have been set and prioritized, the supervisor must decide how they will be achieved. This phase of the planning process is called **action planning.** When developing an action plan, a supervisor must answer the following questions:

1. What must be done? Precisely what actions must be taken to reach the stated objectives? Are there any viable alternatives? The supervisor must be sure that all of the actions taken contribute to the accomplishment of the objectives.

2. Why must it be done? This question serves as a check on question 1. Are the actions taken necessary? Can the use of resources be justified?

FIGURE 7.5
Typical Areas of Supervisory Objectives

1. Production or output:
   Usually expressed as number of units per time period.
   Example: Our objective is to average selling 20 units per week over the next year.
2. Quality:
   Usually expressed as number of rejects, number of customer complaints, amount of scrap.
   Example: Our objective is to receive fewer than 10 written customer complaints per month for the next six months.
3. Cost:
   Usually expressed as dollars per unit produced or dollars per unit of service offered.
   Example: Our objective is for the cost of each widget produced to average less than $5 over the next three months.
4. Human Resources:
   Usually expressed in terms of turnover, absenteeism, tardiness.
   Example: Our objective is to average for the current calendar year less than three days of absenteeism per employee.
5. Safety:
   Usually expressed in terms of days lost due to injury.
   Example: Our objective is to reduce the number of days lost due to injury this year by 10 percent.

3. When should it be done? The supervisor must decide how to coordinate the necessary actions with other activities. Dates and times should be selected and coordinated.
4. Who should do it? The supervisor must decide what skills and abilities are required. Once this has been accomplished, the appropriate human resources must be identified.
5. Where should it be done? This question is closely related to question 4. Where will the necessary people and equipment be located?
6. How should it be done? What methods and procedures will be used? Can existing procedures be used, or must new ones be developed?

By addressing each of these questions, the supervisor can work out the details of exactly how to proceed. This process can also help identify potential problems. Figure 7.6 provides an example of an abbreviated action plan. Supervision Illustration 7–1 describes an action plan developed to help a new jobholder succeed.

FIGURE 7.6
Abbreviated Action Plan

Supervisory Objective: To average 20 units per hour over the next year.

1. What must be done? Provide a complete rebuild of both milling machines.
2. Why must it be done? Both milling machines have been experiencing unplanned and costly downtime.
3. When should it be done? The rebuild on milling machine A should begin before the end of the month. The rebuild on milling machine B should begin as soon as the work on A has been completed.
4. Who should do it? Both machines should be rebuilt by our departmental maintenance team headed by Juan Perez.
5. Where should it be done? Both machines should be rebuilt by removing the necessary parts at their current locations.
6. How should it be done? The maintenance crew should remove those parts needing to be replaced or repaired. Replacement parts can be ordered from the manufacturer. Parts needing to be repaired can be either handled internally or sent to the manufacturer if necessary.

SUPERVISION ILLUSTRATION 7–1

AN ACTION PLAN FOR A NEW JOB

Andrew Davis was recently appointed the new director of the Worcester (Massachusetts) Regional Airport. Prior to this move, Mr. Davis had worked in numerous capacities for American Airlines for over twenty years. When asked why would he want to work for a struggling airport in Worcester, Mr. Davis cited both personal and professional reasons. He wanted to move back to his roots in New England and he wanted to stay in the aviation industry but not with an airline.

In preparation for his new job, Mr. Davis developed a thoughtfully crafted, comprehensive action plan. The plan involves prudent cost control, a build-up of general aviation and ground-based services, vigorous promotion, infrastructure improvements and exploring short-term revenue-generating opportunities while making a concerted effort to "stay ahead of the airline economic cycle and monitor and pursue opportunities in the rapidly changing airline industry." Specifically, the plan includes a step-by-step script of what to do, when to do it, and who to engage while doing it.

While this detailed action plan does not guarantee Mr. Davis' success, it should certainly help!

Source: Robert Z. Nemeth, "A New Boss at the Airport," *Telegram & Gazette,* January 11, 2009, p. A.11.

Contingency Plans

5 LEARNING OBJECTIVES

Regardless of how thorough the supervisor's plans are, there will always be things that go wrong or not as expected. What goes wrong is often beyond the control of the supervisor. For example, a machine may break down or the arrival of a new piece of equipment may be delayed. When such things happen, the supervisor must be prepared with a backup, or contingency, plan. **Contingency plans** address the "what-ifs" of the supervisor's job. Contingency planning gets the supervisor in the habit of being prepared and knowing what to do if something does not go as expected. Naturally, contingency plans cannot be prepared for all possibilities. What the supervisor should do is identify the most critical assumptions of the current plan and then develop contingencies for problems that have a reasonable chance of occurring. A good approach is to examine the current plan from the point of view of what could go wrong. Ideally you can identify a set of indicators to look for so as to know when you should initiate the contingency plan. The supervisor should discuss contingency plans with subordinates and other supervisors who would be affected by them. Supervision Illustration 7–2 discusses how a contingency plan recently "saved the day" at the Oklahoma City National Memorial and Museum.

Policies, Procedures, and Rules

6 LEARNING OBJECTIVES

Whenever supervisors engage in planning, they must take into account existing policies, procedures, and rules. Policies, procedures, and rules are designed to aid managers at all levels in carrying out their day-to-day activities.

Policies

Policies are broad, general guidelines to action. Policies usually do not dictate exactly how something should be done, but they do set the boundaries within which it must be done. A major purpose of policies is to ensure consistency in the decisions and actions taken throughout the organization.

SUPERVISION ILLUSTRATION 7–2

CONTINGENCY PLAN SAVES THE DAY

After sustaining substantial damage in the 1995 Oklahoma City bombing, the Journal Record Building was renovated as a museum and opened in 2000. Fortunately for the building and the museum, a contingency plan, called the Critical Incident Management Plan, was established shortly after the renovation.

On January 16, 2009, a museum volunteer reported water seeping into a stairwell. Employee Kari Watkins realized that the museum staff and volunteers would have to act fast to assess the situation, identify the source of the water, and make sure the contents of the museum were kept safe. According to Watkins, the Critical Incident Management Plan was activated

in about four or five minutes. "As water was flooding many areas of the building, the staff and volunteers began to secure the archives; water also began to flow through the vents and spill out throughout the museum. As water filled the third floor and seeped down, volunteers moved 94 boxes of archives and 25 rolled quilts to a dry area of the building." Watkins said that about 10,000 square feet of the building was flooded but the entire collection came away unscathed.

There is little doubt that having a viable contingency plan saved the day at the restored Journal Record Building.

Source: Kelley Chambers, "Archives Saved; Oklahoma City Memorial Officials Use Action Plan During Flooding," *Journal Record,* March 9, 2009.

Policies exist at all levels of an organization. A typical organization has some policies that relate to the entire organization and some policies that relate only to certain parts of the organization. For example, "This company will always try to fill vacancies at all levels by promoting present employees" is a policy that relates to the entire organization. On the other hand, "The public relations department will respond to all customer complaints in writing" is a policy that relates only to a single department.

Policies define the limits within which supervisors must operate. A company policy of trying to fill vacancies by promoting present employees does not dictate who should be promoted, but it does require that present employees be given preference. A supervisor charged with making a recommendation for filling a vacancy must abide by this policy. It is the supervisor's responsibility to make sure that his or her employees are aware of and understand the policies that relate to them.

Procedures

A **procedure** is a series of related steps or tasks performed in sequential order to achieve a specific purpose. In other words, procedures define in step-by-step fashion how a recurring activity should be accomplished. Well-established and formalized procedures are often known as **standard operating procedures (SOPs).**

Major advantages of procedures are that they achieve a degree of uniformity in how things are done and lessen the need for decisions. Figure 7.7 presents sample procedures that have been developed to support a company policy of responding to all customer complaints in writing.

FIGURE 7.7
One Company's Procedure for Responding to a Written Customer Complaint

Step 1:	All written customer complaints will be forwarded to the customer relations department within 24 hours of receipt.
Step 2:	Upon receipt of a written complaint, the customer relations department will respond in writing to the customer within 48 hours.
Step 3:	One copy of the response will be forwarded to any individuals directly affected by the complaint or response.
Step 4:	One copy of the complaint and response will be filed in the customer relations department and maintained for five years.

Rules

Rules require that specific and definite actions be taken or not taken with respect to given situations. For example, "No smoking in the building" is a rule. Rules leave little room for interpretation of what is to be done or not done. Unlike policies, they permit no flexibility or deviation. Unlike procedures, rules do not necessarily specify sequence. Also, rules usually involve a single action or lack of action whereas procedures involve a sequence of actions.

Common Supervisory Planning Activities

The previous sections examined the overall framework of supervisory planning. Within this framework, supervisors regularly engage in certain specific planning activities. Some of the most common planning activities performed by supervisors are considered next.

Providing Information for High-Level Planning

As discussed earlier in this chapter, upper-level management planners often ask supervisors for certain information. For example, supervisors are often called upon to provide estimates of their human resource and equipment needs.

Developing a Budget

A **budget** is a statement of expected results or requirements expressed in financial or numerical terms. While the monitoring and administration of a budget is part of the control function, the preparation of a budget is a planning activity.

Ideally, a supervisor plays a very active part in developing the budget for his or her area of responsibility. A common approach is to have the supervisor propose the initial budget for the department and then discuss it with the manager at the next higher level. Naturally, the supervisor must be able to justify the proposal and be willing to consider modifications suggested by upper management. This approach has the advantage of producing a realistic final budget that is thoroughly understood by the supervisor. A very important outcome of this approach is that supervisors are committed to the budgets because they had a role in their formulation. Once a budget has been prepared, it can be used very effectively as a control device (this is discussed further in Chapter 18).

Improvement Programs

Improvement programs that often involve supervisors include cost-reduction programs and programs aimed at improving safety, quality, methods, and housekeeping. Maintenance programs can be viewed as a type of improvement program. Successful improvement programs do not just happen; they must be carefully planned. Several types of improvement programs are discussed in detail in later chapters.

Human Resource Needs

Projecting and providing for the human resource needs of the department require careful planning. Included in this planning activity is the determination not only of staffing needs but also of things such as vacation scheduling and leaves of absence. In many instances, supervisors plan for unexpected absences by maintaining an auxiliary list of part-time employees who can be called in on short notice.

Production Planning

Production planning primarily involves determining the necessary materials, facilities, and human resources. The production plan is the crucial link between the demand for a company's products or services and its ability to supply those products or services at the right time for a reasonable cost. Resource allocation, routing, and scheduling are three of the most common production planning activities performed by supervisors.

SUPERVISION ILLUSTRATION   7–3

ROUTING AND SCHEDULING SOFTWARE INCREASES EFFICIENCY OF DELIVERY TRUCKS

Greggs is an English bakery company that has a fleet of 250 vehicles to deliver its various products to over 1100 of its stores in the U.K. Greggs recently implemented new routing and scheduling software from software firm Paragon at its Manchester bakeries. The Manchester operation operates 12 central bakeries, each of which supplies approximately 100 shops, with everything distributed overnight. The software from Paragon has enabled Greggs to develop a more cost-effective distribution strategy. Just in the Manchester

operation alone, Greggs was able to reduce its fleet size by eight vehicles, which it estimates will save it £200,000 (about $300,000 U.S.) a year.

The improvements to the Manchester operation were also assisted by utilizing some of Paragon's training courses, described by Paul Duggan, Greggs' national logistics project manager, as "not cheap but very beneficial."

Source: "Piece of Cake," *Motor Transport,* June 5, 2008, p. 6 and "Efficiency Gains Saves Baker's Dough," *Service Management,* July/August 2008, p. 8.

Resource Allocation

Resource allocation refers to the efficient allocation of people, materials, and equipment so as to successfully meet the objectives that have been established. Resource allocation determines what work will be performed by what person and/or machine and under what conditions. The materials needed must be determined and ordered. The work must be distributed to the different workstations. Human resource requirements must be determined and time requirements established for each stage of the production process.

Routing

Routing involves determining the best sequence of operations. Its purpose is to make optimum use of the existing equipment and human resources through careful assignment of resources. However, the desired level of output and the available mix of equipment and human resources place constraints on the sequence of operations. Although a route may appear to be fixed because of certain physical limitations, it should always be carefully analyzed. Flowcharts and other graphic devices are often used to help detect and eliminate inefficiencies in routes.

Scheduling

Scheduling develops the precise timetable that is to be followed in producing products or services. It involves determining not how long a job will take but when the work will be performed. The purpose of scheduling is to help ensure that the work is synchronized and completed within certain time limits. Scheduling is of course much easier if a thorough job has been done in analyzing the product or service route. Also, when scheduling it is sometimes easier for a supervisor to work backward from a due date.

Determining and implementing priorities are a major part of scheduling. The supervisor may be told which items have high priorities and which have low priorities, or the supervisor may be required to develop this information.

Anticipating lost time is a requirement of scheduling. Many supervisors try to schedule every minute of every working day. Such overscheduling can cause problems if a machine breaks down or if an employee is absent. At the same time, underscheduling can lead to idle equipment and personnel. Successful supervisors must learn to anticipate and schedule for the unexpected. Supervision Illustration 7–3 describes how one company in England has implemented a new scheduling software package to increase the efficiency of its delivery trucks.

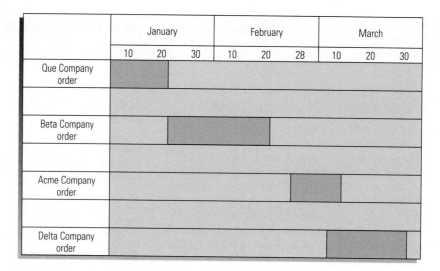

Figure 7.8 caption in margin: Gantt Chart for Scheduling Orders through an Assembly Department

	January			February			March		
	10	20	30	10	20	28	10	20	30
Que Company order									
Beta Company order									
Acme Company order									
Delta Company order									

Gantt Charts Numerous types of tools have been developed to help visualize and simplify scheduling. Most of these tools are adaptations of the **Gantt chart.** With a Gantt chart, the activities to be performed are usually shown vertically and the times required to perform them are usually shown horizontally. By plotting these activities and their respective times, the scheduler can visually determine when to schedule each activity. Figure 7.8 shows a Gantt chart for scheduling customer orders through an assembly department.

CPM and PERT The Gantt chart concept of identifying the work to be done and graphing it against time provided the foundation for more advanced scheduling methods known as networking methods. CPM (critical path method) and PERT (program evaluation and review technique) are two of the most popular of these methods. CPM and PERT are both discussed in more detail in the Appendix to this chapter.

Management by Objectives (MBO)

8 LEARNING OBJECTIVES

Management by objectives (MBO) is a style of supervising that has its roots in the planning function. MBO is a philosophy based on converting organizational objectives into personal objectives. MBO is also based on the premise that establishing personal objectives elicits employee commitment, which in turn leads to performance.

Once a supervisor's objectives have been set (as discussed earlier in this chapter), his or her attention is focused on establishing objectives for each employee. The idea is for the individual employee objectives to be derived from and relate directly to the supervisor's objectives. Under MBO, each employee has a part in determining work objectives and the means for achieving them. The supervisor and an employee jointly agree upon what the employee's work objectives will be and how they should be pursued. The key to success here is a genuine exchange of ideas between the supervisor and the employee. After the work objectives and the means for achieving them have been agreed upon, the employee is allowed considerable freedom in pursuing the work objectives. In effect, the employee is free to act within the constraints of what has been agreed upon. The emphasis is on the results that are achieved.

One of the most difficult aspects of an MBO system is deciding in what specific areas to set individual objectives. A helpful approach is for the individual to answer the following questions: How would I most like to be evaluated on my job? What things or areas should my boss look at to objectively evaluate my performance? The answers to these questions usually identify the areas in which objectives should be set. Difficulty in answering the

FIGURE 7.9
**Guidelines for
Setting Individual
Objectives**

Source: Adapted from Anthony
P. Raia, *Managing by
Objectives* (Glenview, IL:
Scott, Foresman, 1974), p. 67.

1. Adapt your objectives to the overall mission of the organization.
2. Quantify your objectives when possible.
3. Make your objectives challenging but realistic.
4. Establish reliable performance reports and milestones.
5. Put your objectives in writing, using clear and concise statements.
6. Limit your objectives to the most relevant key result areas.
7. Communicate your objectives to your employees.
8. Review your objectives with your superiors and employees to ensure consistency.
9. Modify your objectives as conditions and priorities change.
10. Do not continue to pursue objectives that become obsolete.

questions indicates that the individual may not thoroughly understand the job. Figure 7.9 provides some additional tips for setting individual objectives.

Periodic progress reviews are an essential ingredient of MBO. In these reviews, the employee is provided with direct feedback on actual performance as compared to planned performance (objectives). The manner in which such feedback is given is important. If the supervisor gives the feedback in a downgrading or hostile fashion, performance may be reduced. The important thing is to let the employee know how he or she is doing and to identify areas where the supervisor might provide help. The supervisor acts as a counselor and problem solver *with* the employee, not to the employee. Usually, it is recommended that feedback be provided formally at least two or three times each year. One major advantage of using MBO is that it makes the performance appraisal process more objective.

A final requirement of MBO is that the employees be rewarded on the basis of objective attainment. This means that employee rewards are directly linked to the results attained as measured by the agreed-upon objectives. MBO can work only when employees believe rewards are dependent on results.

Thus, for an MBO system to be successful, three minimum requirements must be met: (1) individual objectives must be jointly set by the supervisor and the employee; (2) employees must be periodically and regularly evaluated; and (3) employees must be rewarded based on objective attainment. Most MBO systems that have failed have fallen short on one or more of these requirements. For example, a supervisor might set objectives for employees and then ask the employees if they agree with the objectives. This is not *jointly* setting the objectives. Another example is the supervisor who does a good job of jointly setting the employees' objectives and periodically evaluating the employees but then gives everyone an equal across-the-board pay raise.

MBO is most effective when it is used at all levels of the organization. When this is done, the objectives at each level should contribute to achieving the objectives at the next-higher level. However, a supervisor can implement MBO in his or her department even if it doesn't exist at other levels. In either case, MBO will not succeed on its virtues alone. It must have the full attention of the supervisor and the employees; it must be thoroughly understood by everyone involved; and it must be given adequate time to succeed. It is not at all unusual for an MBO system to require up to a year for successful implementation. Figure 7.10 reiterates the basic elements of an MBO system.

FIGURE 7.10
**Basic Elements of
an MBO System**

1. Individual objectives are set jointly by the employee and the supervisor.
2. Individual employees are periodically evaluated and receive feedback from the supervisor concerning their performance.
3. Individual employees are evaluated and rewarded by the supervisor on the basis of objective attainment.

SUPERVISION ILLUSTRATION 7–4

SELLING EMPLOYEES IN THE BALANCED SCORECARD

Unilever Home & Personal Care—North America (HPC-NA) is a company composed of the former Chesebrough-Pond's, Helene Curtis, and Lever Brothers businesses. Some of their products include Q-Tips, Dove, Snuggle, and Wisk.

HPC-NA first began using a Balanced Scorecard (BSC) approach in 2000. At this time the board of directors began developing scorecards and eventually ended up with about a dozen key measures. During 2002, each business team and functional area developed customized scorecards directly tied to the board's scorecards. The next challenge was to bring the scorecard to life for the smaller organizational units and individual employees.

Bringing the BSC to the entire organization required a major communication effort involving three types of media: print, verbal, and electronic. Specifically, a brochure was developed, the monthly newsletter incorporated BSC information, regular meetings were held with employees to discuss BSC issues, and a BSC intranet Web site was developed. By putting a major emphasis on communicating with employees at all levels, HPC-NA was able to successfully implement its BSC system.

Source: Bridget Lyons and Andre Gumbus, "How Unilever HPC-NA Sold Its Employees on the Balanced Scorecard," *Strategic Finance*, April 2004, pp. 40–44, and "Can Unilever Create a Masterpiece?" *Strategic Direction*, May 2005, pp. 11–14.

Balanced Scorecard

Balanced scorecard (BSC) is a relatively new performance measurement system that is based on the MBO concept. Essentially BSC is a performance measurement framework through which organizations define strategic objectives at every level in the organization. BSC combines financial results with measurements of tasks that an organization must perform well to meet its objectives at all levels within the organization. The BSC strives to put equal emphasis on people, business processes, customer relationships, and financial performance. Under the BSC system, a cause-and-effect relationship between day-to-day business operations (quality control, training, customer service, etc.) and strategic objectives is established to determine if an organization is on track or not. Under BSC, operational managers and supervisors develop scorecards at every level in the organization so that each person can see how his or her job duties relate to and contribute to the higher-level objectives. The key is that the scorecards at one level are derived from the scorecards at the next level up. Once the scorecards have been developed, supervisors and employees use them to periodically assess how they are doing and what, if any, corrective actions should be taken. Supervision Illustration 7–4 describes how Unilever Home & Personal Care—North America was able to successfully implement a BSC system.

Summary

This chapter emphasizes the importance of planning to the supervisory process. The chapter contains a discussion of the basic steps in planning and a model of the supervisory planning process. Several of the most commonly encountered supervisory planning activities are discussed, with particular emphasis on management by objectives (MBO).

1. *Describe how an organization plans.* A strategic plan is developed by top management. Once the strategic plan

has been developed, specific plans for the different parts of the organization are derived from it. As the planning process moves down to subsequently lower levels in the organization, it becomes narrower in scope and covers shorter time spans.

2. *Describe the supervisor's role in the overall planning system of the organization.* Supervisory plans are derived from the plans of higher levels of management. Usually,

Jane has obviously had problems setting objectives and meeting deadlines in her new job as a supervisor. All indications are that she has a tendency to set or agree to deadlines with little thought as to what will be required to meet them. Jane should learn the importance of not being a "yes person." Before she arbitrarily accepts additional assignments, she should think through each individual request. Even where she has no choice but to agree to a deadline (for example, when her boss assigns one), there are helpful things she could do. She must realize that a deadline is a type of objective. In this light, she should make sure that the deadline meets the characteristics of a well-stated objective (pp. 121–122).

Jane's current method of planning her daily schedule does not allow for much flexibility, and consequently she has difficulty accommodating unexpected situations. Once a deadline has been agreed upon and clearly stated, Jane should develop an action plan for meeting it. This can be accomplished by addressing the questions listed on p. 122–123 and/or by following the model presented in Figure 7.6.

Possibly the most desirable approach of all would be for Jane and her supervisor, Joyce, to install a management-by-objectives system (pp. 128–129). This approach would ensure a clear understanding between them as to what is expected of Jane. It might also inhibit Joyce from "springing" unexpected deadlines on Jane.

the planning information that comes down to the supervisor is of a general nature, and the supervisor is charged with developing detailed action plans for reaching agreed-upon objectives.

3. *Discuss the steps involved in the supervisory planning process, with special emphasis on setting objectives.* Planning is the process of deciding what objectives to pursue during a future time period and what to do to achieve those objectives. Thus, the first step in the planning process is to establish objectives and the second step is to decide what must be done to achieve those objectives.

4. *Identify the SMART criteria for setting objectives.* SMART is an acronym for *specific, measurable, achievable, relevant,* and *time-based.*

5. *Discuss the role of contingency plans.* When things don't go exactly according to plan, supervisors must be prepared with a backup, or contingency, plan. Contingency plans address the "what-ifs" of the supervisor's job; they get the supervisor in the habit of being prepared if something does go wrong.

6. *Differentiate among organizational policies, procedures, and rules.* Policies are broad general guidelines to action. A procedure is a series of related steps or tasks performed in chronological order to achieve a specific purpose. Rules require that specific and definite actions be taken or not taken with respect to given situations.

7. *List several common supervisory planning activities.* Common supervisory planning activities include the following: providing information for high-level planning, developing a budget, implementing improvement programs, preparing paperwork and reports, projecting and providing for the human resource needs of the department, engaging in production planning, and implementing a management-by-objectives system.

8. *Understand the basic elements of a management by objectives (MBO) system.* The basic elements of an MBO system are that individual objectives are jointly set by the supervisor and the employee, employees are periodically and regularly evaluated, and employees are rewarded based on objective attainment.

Key Terms

Review Questions

1. Explain the strategic management process and the role that supervisors play in the process.

2. What time span do most supervisory plans cover?

3. Name and briefly discuss the SMART criteria for developing objectives.

4. What is action planning? What six questions should be addressed in action planning?

5. What is a contingency plan?

6. Define and distinguish among policies, procedures, and rules.

7. Name five specific planning activities in which supervisors commonly engage.

8. What are the differences between resource allocation and scheduling?

9. What is routing, and what does it do?

10. What is a Gantt chart?

11. What are the basic elements of an MBO system?

12. What is a balanced scorecard system?

Skill-Building Questions

1. Discuss the following statement: "Planning is something that supervisors should do when they don't have anything else to do."

2. Comment on the following: "Planning is concerned with the future implications of today's decisions and not with decisions to be made in the future."

3. Why do you think that supervisors often have a hard time determining how their plans and activities fit into the overall scheme of things for the organization? Would strategic management help with this problem? Why or why not?

4. Research has shown that more than half of the attempts to install MBO have failed. What do you think might be some reasons for this high failure rate?

References

1. Patricia Buhler, "Managing in the 90s," *Supervision,* March 1994, p. 7.

2. Much of this section is drawn from Gary Platt, "SMART Objectives: What They Mean and How to Set Them," *Training Journal,* August 2002, p. 23.

Additional Readings

Armitage, Howard, "Hands-On Scorecarding," *CMA Management,* October 2004, pp. 34–38.

Brockmann, Erich N., "Strategic Planning: A Guide for Supervisors," *SuperVision,* August 2008, pp. 3–9.

Ramsey, Robert D., "Why Deadlines and Quotas Don't Always Work," *SuperVision,* October 2008, pp. 3–5.

Stanley, T. L., "If You Don't Know Where You Are Going, You Can't Get There," *SuperVision,* December 2008, pp. 11–13.

SKILL-BUILDING APPLICATIONS

Incident 7–1

A Plan for Productivity Improvement

The management of the Kleetop Corporation had been concerned about the productivity of the engineering department for some time. During the past few years, it had tried numerous things in hopes of improving the situation. These included a study of work habits, implementation of flexible hours, and office improvements such as new lighting and painting. None of these things had any appreciable effect on productivity.

Last fall, Grady Cole became supervisor of the engineering department upon the retirement of Tom McCall. After he had been in his new job for a few weeks, he began working on a new plan for improving the productivity of the engineers. Grady's plan was to have each employee establish his or her own productivity goal for the next six months. That goal was then to be submitted to Grady for approval. Under this plan, Grady would have the final say concerning the goal. The plan called for Grady to meet once a month with each employee to discuss how the employee was progressing toward his or her goal. A major purpose of these meetings would be to identify problems and to devise methods for overcoming them. Furthermore, Grady's plan called for each employee to receive one honor point for each month that he or she reached the designated productivity goal. At the end of the six-month period, each employee would receive a $100 bonus for each point earned.

Grady's boss, Al Kowalski, was skeptical of the plan. After all, nothing that had been tried had worked. Also, Al suspected that everyone would try to set unacceptably low goals. Finally, after much pleading by Grady, Al agreed to let him try the plan for six months. Then the results of the plan would be evaluated and a decision about whether to continue it would be made. Grady was convinced that the plan would work.

Just before the plan was officially implemented, Grady held a series of meetings to explain it to his employees. Most of them thought it was a good idea. However, a few of the more senior employees questioned its value.

Questions

1. Do you think Grady's plan will work if it is implemented as described above? Why or why not?

2. Can you think of any ways in which Grady's plan might be improved?

3. What do you think are the chances that Grady's plan will enjoy initial successes and then slowly lose the group's interest as the newness wears off? Give reasons for your response.

Incident 7–2

What Should I Do Next?

Kim Allred is relatively new as a supervisor, having been promoted only two months ago. Before her promotion, she had worked for the company for seven years as a sales specialist in office equipment. There is no doubt that she is a whiz at selling office equipment. Because of her accepted expertise in the field, it was natural for her to be promoted when the supervisory opening in office equipment sales became available.

Yesterday, Kim received a memo from her boss, Ed Jackson, stating that all departmental plans for the next fiscal year were due by the end of the month, which was 10 days away. She immediately went into a panic. She had never prepared a formal plan, and she had no idea what was required. After worrying over the matter for a day, Kim decided that the best thing to do would be to ask Ed for some guidelines.

Kim: Ed, yesterday I received your memo regarding next year's plan. I've never prepared a formal plan, and frankly, I don't even know where to start.

Ed: Calm down, Kim. I apologize for forgetting that this is your first go-around in the planning process. What I am looking for is a plan for attaining the objectives that we agreed upon for your department last month. In other words, the ABCs of how you plan to accomplish each objective.

Kim: In other words, you want a written explanation of just how I expect to accomplish each objective. Just how detailed should this plan be, and what format are you looking for?

Questions

1. How would you answer Kim's questions if you were Ed Jackson?

2. How would you go about preparing this plan if you were Kim Allred? (Suggest a framework for Kim to follow.)
3. Do you think Kim's initial reaction to the planning process was unusual? Why or why not?

Exercise 7–1

Personal Objectives

Assume that you are scheduled to graduate from college or a vocational school in three months. Develop a list of personal objectives that you would like to achieve within one year after you graduate (try to come up with at least five). After you have established your objectives, prioritize them with regard to their importance to you. Then take your top two objectives and formulate a written action plan for achieving them. What do you think are the weakest parts of your plan?

Be prepared to discuss your plan with the class.

Exercise 7–2

Identifying Personal Goals

Please complete each of the assignments below as you come to them. (Do not read through the entire exercise and then begin filling in your answers.)

Assume you have just won $3 million (after taxes) in a state-sponsored lottery. List five things you would do or buy in the next six months.

1. _____
2. _____
3. _____
4. _____
5. _____

Assume you have just been told by your doctor you have six months to live, but you will feel relatively good until the end. List five things you would do or accomplish in the next six months.

1. _____
2. _____
3. _____
4. _____
5. _____

Now go back and circle any item on each list that has nothing to do with money or how long you will live. Which of these goals could you accomplish now, even without the lottery money or the fear of dying in six months? Could you accomplish some of these goals by some straightforward modification of your actual situation?

Exercise 7–3

How Well Do You Know Company Policies?

For your current job or, if you are not currently employed, for the last job you had, answer the following questions.

On the Job

1. Where and how should employees report they will be absent?
2. Does promotion depend on merit, seniority, or some combination of both?
3. How can an employee find out about job openings in other parts of the business?
4. How does your grievance procedure work? Exactly what should the employee do when he or she has a gripe?
5. Can you answer questions about your company's medical department? When is it open? Is a physician always in attendance?
6. How does your seniority system work? Is it companywide or departmental? What are an employee's rights under it?
7. What is the company's system of warnings and penalties when rules are broken?

Pay

8. What are the company's overtime policies? What does it pay for work over eight hours in one day? On holidays? On Saturdays? On Sundays? Is there a meal allowance? How much? Under what circumstances is it granted?
9. Is any sort of formal incentive system in operation? How does it work?
10. What is the policy on severance pay? What are the eligibility requirements?
11. Is an employee given time off to vote? How much?
12. Does the company pay employees who are called to jury duty?
13. What is the policy on military leave? If an employee serves in the National Guard, does the company pay him or her for the time spent in camp?
14. How is an employee paid for a holiday that occurs during his or her vacation period?

15. What is the company policy on pay increases? Are they automatic? Based on merit? If not, then what are they based on?

Benefits

16. Explain your firm's sick leave program. Is there paid sick leave in addition to sickness and accident insurance? If so, how long does it last?

17. What is the leave of absence policy?

18. When does an employee become eligible for pension benefits? Insurance? Hospitalization?

19. When does a new employee become eligible for a vacation? How long is it? How is the amount of vacation time determined? Can vacation time be carried over from one year to another? Is there any limit to how much vacation time can be accrued?

20. Are company loans available to employees? Is there a credit union?

21. Is there a company training program? Does the company sponsor any educational courses? If an employee wishes to take an outside course at an accredited college or technical school, will the company pay part or all of the cost?

22. Is there a stock buying plan for employees? If so, how does it work?

23. What is provided in the company pension plan? What are the eligibility requirements? Does an employee have vested rights in the pension fund?

24. Is retirement compulsory? If it is, at what age?

One final question: In those cases where you don't know the answer to a question, do you know whom to contact for a definitive response?

To calculate your score, count off 4 points for each question missed.

Source: Ted Pollock, "Mind Your Own Business," *Supervision,* February 1998, pp. 24–26.

Exercise 7–4

Setting SMART Objectives

Assess the objectives in Exhibit 7.1, then critique them. The purpose of the objective is described under the heading "Performance target." The person with whom the objective is being set is given in brackets. Review each of the objectives in Exhibit 7.1 against each of the SMART criteria, then make an entry in each box using the following key:

X = objective does not conform to this criteria
✔ = objective conforms to this criteria
? = difficult to tell if this conforms to this criteria

EXHIBIT 7.1
SMART Objectives

Source: Gary Platt, "SMART Objectives: What They Mean and How to Set Them," *Training Journal,* August 2002, p. 24.

	SPECIFIC	MEASURABLE	ACHIEVABLE	RELEVANT	TIME-BASED
Performance target: to improve profitability (department manager).					
1. Objective: to reduce overtime costs.					
Performance target: to improve customer care (receptionist).					
2. Objective: to ensure that 90 percent of items received (addressed to and for action by the receptionist) are replied to on day of receipt.					
Performance target: to improve leadership ability (team leader).					
3. Objective: to supervise the team better by 25 March 2010.					
4. Objective: to have agreed, set, and recorded three performance targets with each member of staff by the end of June 2010.					
Performance target: to reduce overall running costs (transport manager).					
5. Objective: to achieve a 500 percent reduction over previous year on transport costs (end of this week).					
6. Objective: to achieve a 5 percent reduction over previous year on transport costs.					
7. Objective: to achieve a 5 percent change over previous year on transport costs (by 2 March 2010).					
Performance target: to increase client base (marketing executive).					
8. Objective: to generate 15 new clients by 1 June 2010.					
9. Objective: to generate more clients.					
Performance target: to reduce waste and scrap output (production manager).					
10. Objective: by year-end (31 December 2010) to have reduced waste output by a reasonable amount.					
11. Objective: to adopt a just-in-time strategy for the stores.					

CPM and PERT

As introduced in this chapter, CPM (critical path method) and PERT (program evaluation and review technique) are two of the most popular networking methods. Both CPM and PERT were developed in the late 1950s. CPM and PERT result in a graphic network representation of the things to be done. The graphic network is composed of activities and events. An *activity* is the work necessary to complete a particular event; it usually consumes time. An *event* denotes a point in time; the occurrence of an event signifies the completion of all activities leading up to it. All activities originate and terminate at events. Activities are normally represented by arrows in a network; events are represented by circles. The dashed arrows, called *dummies,* show the dependent relationships among activities. They denote that the starting of an activity or a set of activities depends on the completion of another activity or set of activities.

Exhibit 7.2 shows the series of activities required to build a house as represented by a Gantt chart and by CPM and PERT. CPM and PERT methods have two distinct advantages over the Gantt chart: (1) They note explicitly the dependencies of the activities on each other (for example, the drywall in a house cannot be put up until all the electrical rough-in

EXHIBIT 7.2
Comparison of a Gantt Chart and CPM or PERT Chart for Building a House

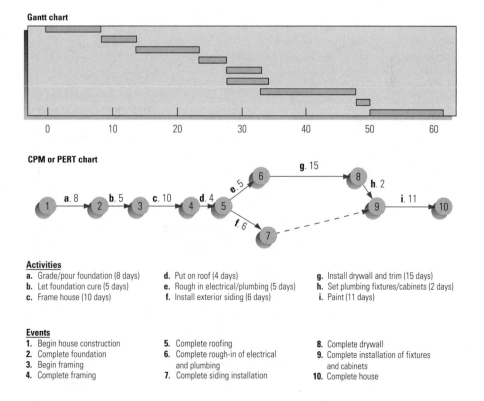

Activities
a. Grade/pour foundation (8 days)
b. Let foundation cure (5 days)
c. Frame house (10 days)
d. Put on roof (4 days)
e. Rough in electrical/plumbing (5 days)
f. Install exterior siding (6 days)
g. Install drywall and trim (15 days)
h. Set plumbing fixtures/cabinets (2 days)
i. Paint (11 days)

Events
1. Begin house construction
2. Complete foundation
3. Begin framing
4. Complete framing
5. Complete roofing
6. Complete rough-in of electrical and plumbing
7. Complete siding installation
8. Complete drywall
9. Complete installation of fixtures and cabinets
10. Complete house

has been completed); and (2) they show the activities in greater detail. Both of these advantages would help a supervisor in scheduling.

The path through the network that has the longest duration (based on a summation of estimated individual activity times) is referred to as the *critical path*. If any activity on the critical path lengthens, the entire sequence of events lengthens. Thus, the activities on the critical path should be watched most closely by the scheduler.

The major difference between CPM and PERT centers on the activity time estimates. CPM is used to schedule activities whose durations are known with some degree of certainty. PERT is used when the activity durations are more uncertain and variable.

Exercise

Drawing a CPM Logic Network

Based upon the following narrative description of a project, draw a CPM logic network that accurately shows the natural dependencies among the activities involved. Be prepared to share your network with the class.

The sheffield Manufacturing Company is considering the introduction of a new product. The first step in this project will be to design the new product. Once the product is designed, a prototype can be built and engineers can design the process by which the product will be produced on a continuous basis. When the prototype is completed, it will be tested. Upon completing the process design, an analysis will be made of the production cost per unit for the new product. When the prototype testing and the production cost analysis are both finished, the results will be submitted to an executive committee, which will make the final go-ahead decision on the product introduction and establish the price to be charged. Assuming that the committee's decision is positive, several steps can be taken immediately. The marketing department will begin designing sales literature. The production department will obtain the equipment to be used in the manufacture of the new product, hire the additional personnel needed to staff the process, and obtain an initial stock of raw materials. After sales literature has been designed, it will be printed. The new equipment obtained for the production process will have to be modified slightly. The production personnel will be trained as soon as the equipment modifications are complete, all necessary personnel have been hired, and the initial stock of materials has been obtained. When the printing of the sales literature is completed and the production personnel have been trained, the sales literature will be distributed to the salespersons and the product introduction will be considered complete.

Questions

1. What specific benefits do you think that a CPM network would provide on this project?

2. What information does the CPM network that you created provide that would not be provided by a Gantt chart of the same project?

CHAPTER EIGHT

Managing Your Time

Learning objectives

After studying this chapter, you will be able to:

1. Identify several common time wasters.
2. Analyze how you actually spend your time on the job.
3. Discuss how to plan your time.
4. Discuss how to optimize your work routine.
5. Identify several areas that typically have a high potential for better time utilization.
6. Discuss three alternative work schedules that can help employees better manage their time.

Although he has been in his supervisory job for only a relatively short time, John Lewis is beginning to feel that there are not enough hours in the day. Meetings, paperwork, unscheduled visitors, e-mail, and telephone calls seem to take up his entire day. Furthermore, rushing from one thing to another leaves John totally exhausted at the end of the day. He has also noticed that he is becoming much more irritable at home.

John recently observed one of his fellow supervisors preparing a "to do" list for the next day's activities. John wondered if he should be making a similar list and if there were any other techniques or tips that he should know about.

All of a supervisor's work is performed within time constraints. A supervisor may know the best way to handle a particular situation but may not have the time to do all that is necessary. No matter how knowledgeable and motivated supervisors are, their ability to manage time affects how successful they will be. The formal study of time management has been going on for almost 150 years. Supervision Illustration 8–1 describes some of the earliest works related to time management.

Typical Time Wasters

1 LEARNING OBJECTIVES

Time can be wasted in numerous ways. The following are some of the more common traps that can rob supervisors' time:

- Telephone interruptions.
- Reading and sending nonessential e-mails.
- Visitors dropping in without appointments.
- Meetings, both scheduled and unscheduled.
- Becoming obsessed with advanced communication technology such as the Internet.
- Crisis situations for which no plans were possible.
- Lack of objectives, priorities, deadlines.
- Cluttered desk and personal disorganization.
- Involvement in routine and detail that should be handled by others.
- Attempting too much at once and underestimating the time it takes to do it.
- Failure to set up clear lines of authority and responsibility.
- Inadequate, inaccurate, or delayed information from others.
- Indecision and procrastination.
- Lack of, or unclear, communication and instruction.
- Inability to say no.
- Lack of standards and progress reports that enable the supervisor to keep track of developments.
- Fatigue.

Obviously, not all of these time wasters can be eliminated. However, many of them can be either eliminated or reduced by applying sound supervisory practices. This chapter offers suggestions for eliminating some of these typical time wasters and for becoming a better manager of time.

SUPERVISION ILLUSTRATION   8–1

THE PIONEERS OF TIME MANAGEMENT

Englishman Samuel Smiles, the godfather of self-improvement, first sowed the seeds for the formal study of time management in 1859 when he published his phenomenal bestseller, *Self-Help*. *Self-Help*, which has never been out of print since its publication, emphasized that making maximum use of time is one of the keystone principles for a better, more productive life. In the Victorian age, the emphasis was on filling time with self-improvement (such as learning a foreign language or writing a memoir) rather than using it to do more.

In the very early 20th century, Arnold Bennett, another Englishman, published *How to Live on 24 Hours a Day*. In this book Bennett advises a typical family man how to carve out the equivalent of another day each week by better managing his time. Like his Victorian predecessors, Bennett advises his readers to use the gained time for self-improvement.

Around the same time that Bennett was publishing his book on time management, American Frederick W. Taylor was studying the "one best way" to perform manual tasks. Taylor's findings were published in a series of academic papers and books between 1895 and 1911. Taylor launched a management revolution that is still flourishing.

Taylor's contemporary disciples included two of the most colorful figures in U.S. industry, Frank and Lillian Gilbreth. This husband-and-wife team used early moving-picture technology to study the time it took to perform different jobs.

Source: Carol Kennedy, "A Brief History of Time," *Director*, November 2004, pp. 60–63.

Understanding Your Job

The ability to manage time makes any job easier, improves performance on the job, and reduces on-the-job stress. Higher levels of management often recognize this ability as a reason for advancement.

To manage time effectively, a supervisor must first have a thorough understanding of exactly what he or she is expected to do. Have you ever known a supervisor who spent an inordinate amount of time performing all the wrong tasks? As elementary as this may seem, a great many supervisors do not have a clear picture of what is expected of them. Numerous studies have shown that employees and their bosses often have a different understanding of the employee's job. Because of this, people often expend considerable time and effort performing a host of related and/or inconsequential tasks that are neither required nor appreciated by the boss. How much more effective it would be to channel that time and energy into accomplishing tasks that had been mutually determined by you and your boss. A good suggestion is for every supervisor and his or her boss periodically (at least once per year) to outline in writing what each perceives to be the major expectations of the supervisor's job. After each party has written down his or her expectations of the job, these lists should be exchanged and then discussed. Following this procedure should make it easier to reach a mutual agreement concerning the basic job expectations. The results of this process should then be reflected in the written job description of the supervisor's job.

Resolving any misunderstandings that surface here can reduce the possibility of conflict and can result in time savings. Once supervisors have a clear understanding of their job duties they should attempt to use time as efficiently as possible in carrying them out.

Analyzing Your Time

2 LEARNING OBJECTIVES

To manage time efficiently and effectively, supervisors must first have a clear understanding of exactly how their time is being spent. Then they can establish priorities for the various tasks and duties that make up their jobs, strive to improve their work habits, and eliminate needless effort.

FIGURE 8.1
Time Caddy

Time	Monday	Tuesday	Wednesday	Thursday	Friday
8:00–9:00					
9:00–10:00					
10:00–11:00					
11:00–12:00					
Lunch					
1:00–2:00					
2:00–3:00					
3:00–4:00					
4:00–5:00					

A **time inventory** is the same thing as a time budget. Analyzing the workday to see how time is being spent is as sensible as analyzing expenditures to see how money is being spent. In preparing a budget, one often discovers that money is being wasted on needless expenditures or low-priority items while important needs are being ignored. A similar discovery may be made when a time budget or inventory is prepared. Supervisors are often shocked to find that much of their time is being wasted or spent on low-priority items.

There are several ways to prepare a time inventory. One of the best ways is to keep a daily log. This log should briefly note each task you performed, the names of the other people who were directly involved in each task, and where the task was performed. It is best to make these log entries every few hours. If you wait until the end of the day, you may have trouble recalling everything that went on during the day. Figure 8.1 illustrates a very abbreviated example of a **time caddy** that can be used to prepare a time inventory. Feel free to design and use any form that captures the needed information. Do not attempt to analyze the data as you are recording them. The log should be kept over a period long enough to ensure that a representative sample of your use of time has been recorded. A two-week period is usually sufficient.

Naturally, you should try to pick a time period that you think will best reflect your normal duties. (For example, you would probably not want to use a period immediately following a vacation.) At the end of the recording period, you should carefully analyze the data to determine just how your time is being spent. A good approach is to divide the data into a manageable number of appropriate categories. Sample categories include telephone, meetings with subordinates, meetings with suppliers, office paperwork, time on the computer, and observing the work process. Almost always, supervisors are surprised at how much or how little time they are spending in certain areas. From this analysis, supervisors can identify changes they might want to make in allocating their time.

Planning Your Time

3 LEARNING OBJECTIVES

Many successful supervisors make a daily **"to do" list** of things to be accomplished. The key to preparing an effective "to do" list is to get in the habit of preparing it at the same time each day—usually at the end of the preceding or beginning of the current day. When composing your list, don't concern yourself with priorities because this may restrict your thinking. First, simply record everything that needs to be done as the thoughts come to you.

TABLE 8.1
Priority Setting of Work Activities

Ranking	Activity
2	Read interoffice mail.
2	Read e-mail.
4	Read brochures received through the mail.
2	Answer interoffice mail.
3	Read supervisory journal.
3	Lunch.
4	Personal telephone call.
2	Telephone call to human resource department to check on an employee's vacation days.
1	Schedule overtime for the weekend.
2	Safety meeting with all subordinates.
1	Grievance meeting in boss's office with grievant.
4	Return a telephone call from an office computer salesperson.
2	Prepare employee performance evaluation for an interview that is to be conducted in two weeks.

After you have exhausted this process, go back and prioritize the different tasks. The following scheme is useful for prioritizing different work activities:

Must do first	1
Must do	2
Desirable to do	3
Can wait	4

Table 8.1 gives an example of priority rankings. After you have inventoried your time and prioritized your work activities, you can then schedule your day. This involves more than simply superimposing your list on a time caddy or a personal planner. Among other things, consider your personal energy pattern and try to match your periods of peak effectiveness throughout the day with the degree of sensitivity or difficulty of the tasks to be performed. For example, your number-one priority may be a delicate negotiation requiring your peak mental abilities. If you are generally a slow starter in the mornings but build up momentum toward midday, you may want to arrange for that number-one priority negotiation at 10:00 or 11:00, rather than at 8:00 A.M. Schedule tasks with somewhat lower priorities that require less demanding mental concentration at the earlier time. Studies have shown that mid-morning tends to be the most productive time for most people and that late afternoon tends to be the least productive time.

In specifying more precisely *when* during the day you expect to perform each task, it is necessary to estimate the approximate amount of time required. This forces a degree of preliminary planning and organizing that helps overcome the inertia in getting a task started. Furthermore, the fact that a specific time has been assigned for each task throughout the day causes a supervisor to be more time conscious, and this seems to reinforce self-discipline.

Finally, a time caddy permits you to look a week ahead and reserve time for prior commitments. Thus, planning for each day's activities can take into account blocks of time previously committed, and thereby avoid future conflicts.

Many supervisors use a "follow-up" or "tickler" filing system to help manage their priorities. With such a system, issues are placed in a chronological file under the date that some future action needs to be taken. For example, if a certain letter needs to be sent out

SUPERVISION ILLUSTRATION 8-2

CAN PALM COME BACK?

Palm, based in Sunnyvale, California, was once the trendsetter in hand-held computers and it also helped pioneer the smartphone with its Treo device. However, Palm has since been left on the sidelines by Research in Motion Ltd.'s Blackberry and Apple Inc.'s iPhone. In mid 2007, the private equity group Elevation Partners took a 25 percent stake in Palm and hired Jon Rubinstein, a former Apple executive, as Palm's executive chairman.

At the 2009 Consumer Electronics Show, Palm emerged as an unlikely "star" with its new Palm Pre. The Palm Pre is built on a new operating system, called the Palm webOS, that the company says will make it easier for developers to create applications for Palm devices. "We think it is the first device that will automatically navigate the Web," said Rubinstein. Unlike previous Palm products, the Palm Pre can consolidate contact information from sources such as Microsoft's Outlook e-mail, the Facebook social networking site, and Google's Gmail e-mail program. Time will tell if the Palm Pre will put Palm back among the leaders in the smartphone industry.

Sources: Yukari Iwatani Kane, "Palm Phone Aims for Comeback," *The Wall Street Journal*, January 9, 2009, p. B.4 and Paul Taylor and Richard Waters, "Palm Pre Phone Grabs the Limelight," *Financial Times*, January 10, 2009, p. 10.

on the 15th of next month, a copy of the letter would be placed in a file that would be automatically reviewed on that date.

Electronic Organizers

Many electronic devices and software are available to help supervisors organize themselves and better utilize their time. Personal information managers and smartphones are discussed below.

Personal Information Managers

Software programs specifically designed to help manage individual time priorities and personal business are known as **personal information managers (PIMs)**. PIMs allow users to do most of their organizing right on the screen of their personal computer or on their handheld personal digital assistant (PDA). The basic features of most PIM programs include (1) a computerized Rolodex, date book, notepad, time sheet, and expense form; (2) electronic mail or messaging systems; and (3) tickler files to alert the user of meeting times and client follow-ups.

Initially, PIMs were tied to a computer at the office. Today PIMs are also available from service providers and can be accessed via a Web browser. These new cyber PIMs allow users to share their calendars over the World Wide Web with co-workers around the globe. Other features include to-do lists, auto-fill features to make data entry faster and easier, calling number identification support for instant contact information on incoming calls, and links to other electronic organizers. Stand-alone PIMs can range in price from less than $25 to over $5,000 depending on sophistication and power. Most online PIMs are free; all users have to do is register with the service.

Smartphones

The first mobile phone was created in 1973 but was not made publicly available until the early 1980's. The initial cost was around $3,500 and the phones were quite bulky. Since the birth of the mobile phone, it has gone through three upgrading stages: the color screen in 2002, the multimedia mobile phones during 2004–2006, and the smart phones.[1] **Smartphones** are converged telephone computer devices with full-blown embedded computer operating devices. Smartphones function as "mini laptops" with cell phone capabilities. Today's smartphones can provide full set business applications that can make a mobile employee more productive. Some of the possibilities are rich e-mail with attachment viewing, and sophisticated PIM. Supervision Illustration 8–2 describes a new smartphone from Palm.

Optimizing Your Work Routine

LEARNING OBJECTIVES

As you try to implement your work schedule, you may note a pattern of failures to meet the schedule. The pattern may provide a clue as to the source of the trouble or the disruption responsible for the failures. For example, John Doe blocks off an hour each morning from 10:00 to 11:00 for answering his e-mail and regular mail, but after numerous attempts to compose replies, he finds that he invariably ends up doing most of the task after everyone has gone home and the telephone quits ringing. By that time, however, his secretary has also left and he often can't find all the information he needs. In fact, it usually isn't until the next day that replies to the previous day's mail and e-mail are sent out. By then, John is running at least a day behind.

In studying his dilemma, John decides to carve out for himself a quiet hour each day—the time between 10:00 and 11:00 A.M. During this time, he asks not to be disturbed except for emergencies. He would never ask his secretary to lie by telling people he is not in, but simply instructs her to say, "I'm sorry but Mr. Doe is tied up right now. Can he call you back within the hour?" Most people, including the boss, will generally accept this response if John is conscientious and develops a reputation for returning those calls as promised. The secretary soon learns to arrange notices of telephone calls in the order of priority for return, not necessarily in chronological order of receipt. The boss, for example, may have been the last to call, but the secretary senses from the tone of his voice that he should be the first to be called back. During this quiet hour, John is virtually uninterrupted in composing replies to incoming correspondence; by 11:00 he has responded to his e-mails and has dictated other correspondence for his secretary. His secretary is then able to get the outgoing correspondence back to him for signature and in the mail before the close of business that day.

Similar situations may be obvious, as you periodically check to see whether you might combine compatible activities, such as those with similar physical locations or similar routines. In this way you can save time by working more wisely instead of just longer or harder.

Establishing Good Work Habits

LEARNING OBJECTIVES

When one stops to consider the paperwork, e-mails, telephone calls, meetings, and visitors that the average supervisor is faced with each day, it is not hard to see that he or she could spend the entire day on communication alone. Communication is an important part of the supervisor's job. Still, there are many ways in which a supervisor can manage the time spent on the communication process. This section discusses how supervisors can better manage their communication time by establishing good work habits.

Paperwork

It is rare when a supervisor is not swamped with paperwork. Most supervisors must write letters and memos; prepare or assist in preparing various reports; maintain and file certain records; and stay current by reading newsletters, magazines, and trade journals.

One suggestion for dealing with paperwork is to categorize it as you go through it. Basically, there are three classes of paperwork:

1. Requires action by the supervisor.
2. Needs reading, passing on to someone else, or filing.
3. Needs to be discarded.

Class 3 can be discarded and the paper can be recycled immediately. Classes 1 and 2 must be handled more carefully, but there are also effective means of dealing with such items.

A goal is to handle each piece of paper only once; do not set it aside until you have completed the necessary action. When it is not possible to complete the necessary action, such as with a very large task, at least take some action before putting the paper aside.

Letters and Memos

As suggested in the previous section, action should be taken on a letter without putting the letter down. Handwritten responses on the bottom of a letter are usually acceptable. Use form letters for responses whenever possible. Send copies of both letters and memos only to those with a definite need; resist the temptation to copy anyone who might possibly have a need. Consider responding by e-mail. Using e-mail may be much faster than using traditional correspondence. However, you must be certain that the other party checks his or her e-mail on a regular basis.

If you have an assistant or secretary, consider the use of a dictating machine. Giving dictation directly to your assistant or secretary wastes time because it ties up two people at the same time on the same letter or memo. Furthermore, many letters and memos can be answered directly by your assistant or secretary if he or she has enough information. Delegating the authority to answer certain letters and memos increases the assistant's or secretary's job scope and can be a source of motivation to them. Learn to view your assistant or secretary as your business partner and not as your servant! Finally, you can often use e-mail or the phone instead of sending a letter.

Report Writing

Many of the suggestions for handling letters and memos also apply to report writing. Plan the report completely before you start writing. Use a word processor or a dictating machine whenever possible. Keep the report as short as possible while covering the material that needs to be covered. Also, write the report for the reader. Big words and long sentences may impress the reader but may not get the message across.

Filing

Almost everyone has computer files or a filing cabinet full of material that will never be looked at again. Knowing what to save and what to throw away is not easy. When deciding whether something should be filed, answer the following questions:

1. Is this something that I should consider keeping?
2. How can I get this information if I ever need it and it isn't in my files?
3. How (exactly) am I going to use this piece of information within the next 12 months?[2]

After answering these questions, the supervisor can better decide whether to file something. If the information can easily be recaptured and the supervisor does not anticipate using the information in the intermediate future, it should ordinarily be discarded. Filing unneeded documents clutters up files and makes it harder to locate needed documents. One additional suggestion is to go through and clean out both hard files and computer files at least once a year. Get rid of material that you haven't used during the year.

Reading Material

We all have a stack of reading material that we intend to read "one of these days." Unfortunately, that day never comes, and the stack just gets higher and higher. One way to lessen this problem is to improve your reading skills. If your organization offers a seminar on reading skills, ask to attend it. Also, many local colleges and universities offer courses to help improve reading skills.

Another suggestion for handling reading materials is to scan the table of contents or the major headings. If either one of these looks interesting, you might read some or all of the material. Otherwise, you should probably throw it away.

E-Mail and Communication Technology

E-mail has the advantage of being extremely fast and inexpensive and being able to reach numerous people simultaneously. E-mails are also easier to handle and file as you read them when compared to regular mail and faxes. There are, however, problems associated with e-mail. One problem is that some people get hooked on e-mail and spend an inordinate amount of time sending and receiving messages. One recent survey by AOL found that nearly half (46 percent) of e-mail users said they were hooked on e-mail and 51 percent check their e-mail four or more times a day.[3] One in five said they check their e-mail more than 10 times a day. Another potential problem with e-mail is the tendency to send a message to everyone. As with letters and memos, send e-mail messages only to those with a definite need to know.

When using e-mail it is important to get to know the e-mail habits of your respondents. Be aware of how often they check their e-mail. Another concern when using e-mail is security. Do not rely on e-mail if you suspect that the other person has something to say that he or she prefers not to put in writing. Figure 8.2 summarizes some general guidelines for using e-mail.

There is no doubt that supervisors are relying more than ever on new communications technology to help them gather information and make decisions. Personal computers and the Internet can provide more information than one ever dreamed of, but they cannot create the time to retrieve the information. In fact, advanced technology tools can add to time management problems. For example, the idea that you can save time by doing everything on a personal computer can be deceptive. Certainly some tasks can be done more efficiently on a personal computer, but others cannot. Supervisors need to learn when to use advanced communications technology and when not to use it.

Meetings

Before a meeting is scheduled, a supervisor first needs to ask himself or herself the following question: "Is the meeting necessary or can another means of communication be used in place of the meeting?" If meetings are to be held, the effective handling of meetings is an important skill for the supervisor to develop. Most meetings should have a specific agenda that is closely followed. If the agenda of a meeting is given in advance to

FIGURE 8.2
Guidelines for Using E-Mail

Sources: Adapted from Lisa Aldisert, "Is E-Mail Holding You Hostage," *Bank Marketing,* June 2001, p. 46 and Scott Grabinger, "Tame the E-mail Beast! A Baker's Dozen," *Performance Improvement,* April 2008, pp. 5–6.

1. Don't e-mail a co-worker who sits around the corner, but rather go and have a conversation.
2. Think twice. Do you really need to send that e-mail? Many e-mails are useless or redundant.
3. Don't check your e-mail every 20 minutes. Cluster your send and receive activity to a few (two or three) times a day.
4. Don't assume everyone checks e-mail throughout the day and night. Let people know how often you check your e-mail.
5. Don't go to the Internet every time you check your e-mail.
6. When you reply to an e-mail, don't copy everybody—copy only those with a definite need to know.
7. Don't go back and forth with "thank you" or "OK" or "Good". Stop if you don't have anything of substance to say.
8. Keep it brief. If you find yourself writing a long message, it might be better to phone or visit in person.
9. There are a number of web-based tools available that enable colleagues to work as a group in ways that are more efficient than bouncing e-mails back and forth.
10. Read and respond only to e-mails that are pertinent to your day-to-day activities; delete others or save to read all at one time at the end of the day or some other appropriate time.

FIGURE 8.3
Guides for
Conducting Effective
Meetings

1. A specific agenda should be prepared and given in advance to each participant in the meeting. The agenda should specify which items require preparation by the participants. Prepared participants make for a more effective meeting, as time is more effectively used and the need for follow-up meetings is eliminated.
2. A specific time period should be established for the meeting.
3. The meeting should begin and end on time.
4. Each member should be encouraged to participate.
5. No member should be allowed to dominate the meeting.
6. The supervisor should actively participate but should not dominate the meeting.
7. Lengthy remarks should be politely curtailed.
8. Written summaries of the results of the meeting should be given to each participant as quickly as possible.

each of the participants, everyone can be prepared to discuss its items. Using e-mail is a good way to send out the agenda. A specific time period should be allocated for the meeting. All of these suggestions keep the meeting from unnecessarily dragging out. Each person at the meeting should be encouraged to participate, but the supervisor should not allow certain members to dominate the meeting. Lengthy remarks should be politely curtailed. The supervisor should lead the meeting and actively participate in the discussion but should be careful not to dominate the meeting. The meeting should begin and end at its scheduled time. Written summaries of the results of the meeting should be sent to each participant as quickly as possible. Figure 8.3 summarizes these key guides for conducting effective meetings.

Telephone and Fax

The telephone can either save or waste a lot of time. Too many supervisors allow the telephone to run their day. If you have a secretary, have the secretary hold your calls when you are attending an important meeting or working on an important problem. When you are on the phone for business reasons, realize that the time of two people is being tied up. Be polite, but make your point and get off the phone. Nothing is wrong with telling a caller in a polite manner that you have to get off the phone. Figure 8.4 lists these and several other tips to help you manage your telephone time.

The fax machine has many characteristics in common with e-mail. One advantage that the fax has over e-mail is that faxes are less likely to go unread for any length of time. Recent technology has made it possible to send faxes over the Internet and thus save costly long-distance phone calls.

Visitors

Supervisors often have expected and unexpected visitors. Salespeople are a common example. Visitors can monopolize precious time. One time saver here is to establish a policy of seeing only visitors who have made an appointment. Let the scheduled visitor

FIGURE 8.4
Tips for Better Time
Utilization with the
Telephone

1. Be available for outside calls only at certain times.
2. Bunch your outgoing calls to avoid interrupting yourself.
3. Place outgoing calls according to the other person's best times.
4. Develop an awareness of long-winded calls and learn to get off.
5. Have an agenda ready before making a call.
6. Hang up on hold calls for another party.
7. Where possible, have someone screen your calls.
8. Use conference calls when feasible.

FIGURE 8.5
**Tips for Handling
Visitor Interruptions**

1. Set time limits for visits and stick to them.
2. Set the agenda early in the conversation.
3. Meet visitors outside your door.
4. Confer while standing.
5. Do not place chairs in your office so that they are inviting to people passing by.
6. Do not place items such as candy dishes on your desk, as they invite visitors.
7. If a visitor becomes seated, get up from your seat to signal the end of the conversation.
8. Where feasible, have someone screen visitors.
9. Use the conference room or the other person's office so you can leave when you wish.
10. Reserve certain hours for visitors.

know how much time you have allowed for that visit. Then stick to that time. If visitors you don't want to see do get to you, don't let them seat themselves comfortably in your office. As soon as you see them coming, get up and meet them at your door or in the hall. Talk to them standing up. This communicates that you don't expect the visit to last long. Figure 8.5 summarizes several tips for managing visitor interruptions.

Procrastination

Two primary causes of procrastination by supervisors are complexity and fear. Supervisors are often overwhelmed by projects that seem complex, because they just don't know where to start. Fear causes procrastination when a supervisor must deal with an unpleasant task, such as disciplining an employee. All too often, supervisors think that a huge block of time must be available to them before they start work on a complex project. The key is to break the project down into smaller tasks and then to get started on one or more of these smaller tasks. When this occurs, most supervisors find that the project appears far less overwhelming.

Because valuable time and energy are often wasted by jumping from project to project, supervisors should use deadlines. These provide wanted and needed targets and assist in getting the work accomplished. Tasks such as work orders and reports carry their own deadlines, but others do not. Supervisors should assign dates for the completion of those that don't. This helps supervisors to schedule time better and to accomplish all projects on a timely basis.

The tendency is to hope that unpleasant tasks will go away. Unfortunately, they generally don't go away and they often get worse if you try to avoid them. It is usually much better to deal with an unpleasant task than to try to avoid it.

Delegating Work

Proper delegation is a major key to the supervisor's effective use of time. Doing work that a subordinate should handle is a most serious time waster of supervisors. Delegation frees a supervisor to perform the more important tasks of supervision. It also teaches subordinates to think for themselves, to make decisions, and to function effectively. Because of its importance, delegation is covered extensively in the next chapter (Chapter 9).

Managing Time through Alternative Work Schedules

6 LEARNING OBJECTIVES

In the last several years, organizations have increasingly departed from traditional work schedules in an attempt to better manage time and increase productivity. While changes in the work schedule do not generally alter work to be done, they can affect how the work is allocated. The most common alternative work schedules are flextime, telecommuting, and the compressed workweek.

Flextime

Flextime, or flexible working hours, allows employees to choose, within certain limits, when they start and end their workday. Usually the organization defines a core period

SUPERVISION ILLUSTRATION 8–3

TELECOMMUTING AT JETBLUE

From its inception in 2000, JetBlue Airways has used only at-home (telecommuting) agents in its reservation center in Salt Lake City. Most airlines have large call centers where employees come in or they use overseas outsourcing. All JetBlue agents, referred to as "crew members," live in the Salt Lake City area where the supervisors and managers work and where training takes place at the reservation center. No calls are received at the reservation center but employees do report monthly to meet with team supervisors, and report every other month for ongoing training.

JetBlue employs approximately 1,500 telecommuting reservation agents, seventy percent of whom are stay-at-home moms. Agents bid for six-to-eight hour shifts and can trade and give away shifts as their schedules require. Initial

training is five weeks with new hires spending the first two weeks in a classroom learning about the airline industry, the technology, and the company culture. The next three weeks are spent taking calls under supervision.

Attracting new at-home agents is far from a problem at JetBlue. The company opens the application process once a year for a 24-hour period and usually receives 1,200 to 1,400 applicants. According to company spokesperson Bryan Baldwin, "One of the great things about this system (telecommuting) is that when things get busy, like during a weather event, we can send an e-mail to all agents asking them to log in to help. The response is immediate—we don't have to wait for them to come in."

Source: Martha Frase-Blunt, "Call Centers Come Home," *HR Magazine,* January 2007, pp. 84–88.

(such as 10 A.M. to 3 P.M.) when all employees will be at work. It is then left to each employee to decide when to start and end the workday as long as the hours encompass the core period. Some flextime programs allow employees to vary the hours worked each day as long as they meet some specific total, which is usually 40 hours. Flextime has the advantage of allowing different employees to accommodate different lifestyles and schedules. Other potential advantages include avoiding rush hours and having less absenteeism and tardiness. From the employer's viewpoint, flextime can have the advantage of providing an edge in recruiting new employees, and also in retaining hard-to-find qualified employees. Also, organizations with flextime schedules have reported an increase in productivity and morale.[4] On the downside, flextime can create communication and coordination problems for supervisors. A recent nationwide survey conducted by the Families and Work Institute found that flextime was available in some form at 68 percent of the organizations polled.[5]

Telecommuting

Telecommuting is the practice of periodically or regularly working from home, from another remote location, or while traveling and being able to interact with the office and/or customers. Today's information technology (PCs, the Internet, smart phones, etc.) has made telecommuting a reality for many organizations. According to a survey sponsored by WorldatWork, 17.2 million Americans worked from home or remotely at least one day per month in 2008.[6] This represented a 74 percent increase from 2005. The U.S. Bureau of Labor Statistics estimated that just over 11 percent of Americans telecommuted at least one day per month in 2008.[7]

Advantages of telecommuting include less travel time, avoiding rush hour, avoiding distractions at the office, less environment pollution, and being able to work flexible hours. Potential disadvantages of telecommuting are insurance concerns relating to the health and safety of employees working at home. Another drawback is that some state and local laws restrict just what work can be done at home. Supervision Illustration 8–3 discusses how JetBlue has successfully used telecommuting with its reservation agents.

John, like most supervisors, is experiencing the frustrations that result from interruptions of a planned work schedule. Meetings, paperwork, uninvited visitors, and telephone calls can all disrupt a schedule. John should now have a heightened awareness of the requirements for time management, and this in itself should be helpful to him. As a start, he should analyze how he spends his work time by keeping a daily log for a couple of weeks (pp. 141–142). Then he should analyze the data he has gathered and determine the areas in which he is spending too much time and those in which he is not spending enough time. On this basis, he should make the necessary adjustments in his work schedule (pp. 142–144). He should also attempt to implement many of the time management tips discussed on pages 145–149.

Compressed Workweek

Under the **compressed workweek** (or condensed workweek), the number of hours worked per day is increased and the number of days in the workweek is decreased. Typically, this is done by having employees work 10 hours per day for four days per week (known as 4/40). Other variations of the condensed workweek include reducing the total number of hours worked to 36 or 38 hours. Advantages of the condensed workweek are lower absenteeism and tardiness, less start-up time, and more time available for employees to take care of personal business. One potential disadvantage is the fatigue that often accompanies longer hours. A 2008 nationwide survey by the Society for Human Resource Management reported that 37 percent of respondents offered some type of compressed workweek.[8]

Summary

This chapter introduces and discusses the topic of time management. It presents several tips for managing your time and improving your work habits.

1. *Identify several common time wasters.* The following are some of the more common ways in which time is wasted: telephone interruptions; visitors dropping in without appointments; unproductive meetings; reading nonessential e-mail; unnecessary crisis situations; lack of objectives, priorities, and deadlines; personal disorganization; overinvolvement in routine matters; attempting too much at once and underestimating the time it takes to do it; unclear lines of responsibility and authority; inadequate, inaccurate, or delayed information from others; indecision and procrastination; unclear communication; inability to say no; lack of standards and progress reports; and fatigue.

2. *Analyze how you actually spend your time on the job.* One of the best ways to analyze how you spend your time is to keep a daily log for two weeks. Every few hours, you should briefly note each task that you performed, the names of the people who were directly involved in the task, and where the task was performed. At the end of the data collection period, you should carefully analyze the data and compare your findings with the requirements of the job. You will probably discover that you are spending too much time in some areas and not enough in others.

3. *Discuss how to plan your time.* One key to preparing your time is to use a daily "to do" list. A daily "to do" list should be prepared at the same time each day, usually at the end or beginning of the day. When composing the list, don't be concerned with priorities, but record the activities as they come. After you have exhausted this process, go back and prioritize each activity. The next step is to superimpose your prioritized list on a time caddy. This step requires you to estimate how long each task will take and to specify when during the day you expect to perform each task.

4. *Discuss how to optimize your work routine.* A good way to improve your work routine is to notice any patterns of failure that might be regularly occurring (for example, you are continually late in getting your correspondence out). Once you become aware of these patterns, you can then look for ways to combine compatible activities and thus save time.

5. *Identify several areas that typically have a high potential for better time utilization.* The following areas typically have a high potential for better time management: (1) handling

paperwork; (2) writing letters, memos, and reports; (3) filing; (4) dealing with reading material; (5) handling meetings; (6) managing the telephone; (7) dealing with visitors; (8) overcoming the natural tendency to procrastinate; and (9) delegating work.

6. *Discuss three alternative work schedules that can help employees better manage their time.* The three most common alternative work schedules are flextime, telecommuting, and the compressed workweek. Flextime allows employees to choose, within certain limits, when they start and end their workday. Telecommuting is the practice of working at home or while traveling and being able to interact with the office. Under the compressed workweek, the number of hours worked per day is increased and the number of days in the workweek is decreased.

Key Terms

Compressed workweek, 151
Flextime, 149
Personal Information Manager (PIM), 144

Smartphones, 144
Telecommuting, 150
Time caddy, 142

Time inventory, 142
"To do" list, 142

Review Questions

1. Name several of the most frequently encountered time wasters.

2. What is a time inventory?

3. What factors should be covered in a daily time log?

4. What is a "to do" list?

5. Describe a scheme for prioritizing activities on a "to do" list.

6. What is a personal information manager (PIM)?

7. Identify three classes of paperwork.

8. What questions should be answered in determining whether to file a report or letter?

9. Give some guidelines for better time utilization of the telephone.

10. Give some general guidelines for using e-mail.

11. List several tips for handling visitor interruptions.

12. What are the three most common alternative work schedules?

Skill-Building Questions

1. "My boss determines how I spend my time, and I don't really have much control over it." Discuss how you feel about this.

2. "The problem with time management is that you never know when a crisis is going to occur." How would you respond to this statement?

3. Respond to the following statement: "If I could just get rid of my telephone and my e-mail, I would not have any problems managing my time.

4. Suppose that the most productive time of your boss's day is early morning and that this is your least productive time. What problems might this cause you? How might you deal with these problems? Can you think of any opportunities that this situation might present?

References

1. "Research and Markets: Global Smart Phone Markets & Industry Chain Report, 2008–2009," *Business Wire,* March 16, 2009.

2. Donna Niksch Douglass and Merrill E. Douglass, "Timely Techniques for Paperwork Mania," *Personnel Administrator,* September 1979, p. 21.

3. "AOL Email Survey: More Than Half of Users Admit They're 'Hooked' on Email," *Wireless News,* August 2, 2008.

4. Edward Prewitt, "Flextime and Telecommuting," *CIO,* April 15, 2002, p. 130.

5. "Work-Life Balance: Making Flextime Work for Your Firm," *IOMA's Report on Managing Benefits Plans,* December 2008, pp. 1–5.

6. "Telework Trendlines 2009, A Survey Brief by WorldatWork," accessed at www.workingfromanywhere.org/, March 19, 2009.

7. Ibid.

8. "Flexible Schedules Get a Boost from High Gas Prices," *HR Focus,* August 2008, pp. 10–11.

Additional Readings

Friel, Brian, "Stop Wasting Time," *Government Executive,* January 2009, p. 34.

Gleason, Matt, "Control Time and Plan Life," *McClatchy-Tribune Business News,* February 17, 2009.

Grabinger, R. Scott, "Tame the Email Beast! A Baker's Dozen," *Performance Improvement,* April 2008, pp. 5–6.

Gragg, Ellen, "Time Management Is On Your Side," *Office Solutions,* January/February 2005, pp. 16–19.

SKILL-BUILDING APPLICATIONS

Incident 8–1

Not Enough Time

Sara Lopez, supervisor of the information technology (IT) department, was involved in a minor car accident this morning and arrived 25 minutes late for work. As she entered her office, the telephone rang. It was Lewis Wiley, head of cost accounting, who said that there must have been some error in processing the last cost data since what he received yesterday afternoon makes no sense. He asked Sara to check into the matter and call him back.

While Sara was talking with Wiley, Bruce White, head of quality control, walked into her office. As soon as the telephone conversation ended, Bruce asked, "When am I going to get the quality reports for last week? I know you're busy, but the reports were due day before yesterday. I need them because we're having trouble in assembly." Sara said that the reports should be ready. She asked Bruce to wait a minute and walked out to the processing area, looking for her assistant, Clifford Sommer. Not seeing Cliff, she asked a another employee where Cliff was. "Haven't seen him, Ms. Lopez." Sara asked, "Have the quality reports for last week been finished?" The employee replied, "I don't know; Martha would know. I'll ask her for you." "Good, let me know right away. I'll be in my office." Several minutes later, Martha entered Sara's office and reported that the quality reports had not been processed yet. Sara then told Bruce that she would gather the data and process it right away. "I'll see that you get the reports this afternoon," she promised.

Sara started to prepare the data for running the quality reports. After spending nearly an hour searching through stacks of papers and cards, she located the necessary data. She was then interrupted by a telephone call from the receptionist: "A Mr. Elmer McCall from Eureka Computer Company is here to see you. He said he has an appointment at 12:00 noon for lunch." "An appointment with me at 12:00?" said Sara as she fingered her calendar but found no note of any such appointment. "Well, tell him I can't see him for 20 minutes or so." Sara returned to work on the quality reports, got them ready to process and then turned the job over to Cliff with instructions to process the reports that afternoon and deliver them in person to Bruce White.

The visit with McCall was social. McCall simply wanted to know if everything was working OK with the Eureka installation. Upon Sara's return to the office about 2:10 P.M., a telephone call reminded her that the production committee meeting was in process and asked whether she was coming right over to it. "Yes, I'm on the way now," replied Sara. Actually, she had forgotten about the meeting. It lasted till 4:00 P.M.; Sara was drowsy and thought it quite dull. On the way back to her office, Sara stopped to ask Bruce if he had received the quality reports. "Not yet," Bruce replied. Sara hurried back to her office to expedite work on the reports.

Questions

1. In your opinion, what is Sara's difficulty?
2. What suggestions do you feel are in order for Sara? Discuss.

Incident 8–2

A Hectic Day

Francis S. Russell is a supervisor for the Tri Cities Country Club. At the moment, this self-styled perfectionist is sitting up in bed, checking his TTD sheet for tomorrow. The TTD (Things to Do) itemizes his daily activities, placing them on an exact time schedule. Never one to browbeat subordinates, Russell had his own special way of reminding people that time is money. Ever since the days when he was the best waiter the club ever had, he had worked harder than the rest. It had paid off, too, because in only two years (when old Charlie retired), he was the heir apparent to the general manager of the club. As this thought crossed Russell's mind, his immediate pride was replaced with a nagging problem. Where was he going to find the time to do all the things his position required? He certainly couldn't afford to just maintain the status quo. Then his mind forced him to plan tomorrow's activities, so the problem was pushed into the background for future consideration. (Below is a portion of Russell's well-planned day.)

TTD—OCTOBER 16th

7:15   Breakfast with Johnson (the tennis pro) about information on his cataloging system for the club's tennis shop.

8:30   Meeting with Henry (assistant club manager). Tell him exactly how the annual meeting for the membership should be set up. Caution—he's shaky on questions.

9:15   Discuss progress on new office procedures manual with Charlie (general manager).

         [He's irritated because I've dragged my heels on this. Let him know I've got Newman working on the problem.]

9:45   Assign Pat Newman the job of collecting data and sample copies regarding office manuals in other clubs. Set up a system for him to use in analysis.

10:45   Call on Roger Bradshaw, a very influential board member, and solicit his support on the proposed budget.

         [As Russell jotted down some information on Bradshaw, he reflected that it was a shame no one else on his staff could really handle the big shots the way he could. This thought was pleasing and bothersome at the same time.]

12:00   Lunch with Roger Bradshaw at the club.

3:00   Meet with Frank Lentz, a new board member, and check his progress on the new membership campaign.

         [Russell thought about Lentz's usual wild ideas and hoped that he had followed the general theme and rough sketches he had prepared.]

7:30   Chamber of Commerce meeting. Look up Pierce Hansen—a friend and club member. He may be able to help secure Bradshaw's support on the budget.

Questions

1. Do you think Russell is highly motivated? Is he a good supervisor?
2. What problems do you see concerning Russell's effectiveness as a supervisor?
3. Assuming that you are Charlie, the general manager, what solutions would you recommend?

Exercise 8–1

Are You Using Your Time Effectively?

Take no more than 10 minutes to answer the following 10 questions. Answer each question carefully, and be prepared to argue in favor of your response. Your instructor will tell you how to score your responses.

	True	False
1. It's best to begin work with the task that worries you most.	___	___
2. A good way to accomplish more is to do two jobs at once (e.g., sign letters and take phone calls).	___	___
3. Answer correspondence by giving your ideas to your assistants. Let them write the letters.	___	___
4. Invite visitors to sit down in a chair on the opposite side of your desk.	___	___
5. The best way to handle "in-basket" material is to sort it so you can do the most important jobs first.	___	___
6. After delegating a job to a subordinate, check with him/her frequently on progress.	___	___
7. It's discourteous to refuse to take phone calls.	___	___
8. Don't review routine reports. Give this job to an assistant.	___	___
9. It's useless and time-consuming to write a plan for your day's activities.	___	___
10. Schedule regular staff meetings to discuss common business.	___	___

Source: Ted Pollock, "A Personal File of Stimulating Ideas and Problem Solvers," *Supervision,* May 1991, p. 24. Reprinted by permission of *Supervision,* The National Research Bureau, Inc., 424 North Third St., Burlington, Iowa 52601–5224.

Exercise 8–2

Time Trap Identification

Identify and list all those activities that you feel currently consume inordinate portions of your time. Consider primarily repetitive activities. You should be able to develop a list of at least five or more activities.

After identifying your time traps, *rank* them in the order of their significance to you.

Select the three most significant time traps and list them on a clean sheet of paper. Then indicate what specific actions you might take to overcome each of these traps. For each suggested action, list any problems that you think might be encountered. Why do you think that you have not previously implemented these actions?

Exercise 8–3

Time Management Assumptions

The following list contains 10 common assumptions concerning time management. Check whether you believe each statement is true or false. Be honest with yourself!

	True	False
1. If you really look, you can probably find many ways to save time.	____	____
2. Being busy and active is the best way to get the most done.	____	____
3. Time problems can usually be solved by working harder.	____	____
4. "If you want it done right, you'd better do it yourself" is still the best advice.	____	____

	True	False
5. Finding the problem is easy—it's finding the solution that is difficult.	____	____
6. Most of the ordinary day-to-day activities don't need to be planned—and you probably can't plan them anyway.	____	____
7. Managers who concentrate on doing things efficiently are also the most effective managers.	____	____
8. A good way to reduce time waste is to look for shortcuts in managerial functions.	____	____
9. Managing time better is essentially a matter of reducing the time it takes to accomplish various tasks.	____	____
10. No one ever has enough time.	____	____

Source: This exercise is adopted from Merrill E. Douglass, "Test Your Assumptions about Time Management," *Personnel Administrator,* November 1976, pp. 12–15. Reprinted with permission of the Society for Human Resource Management, Alexandria, Virginia.

CHAPTER NINE

Organizing and Delegating

Learning objectives

After studying this chapter, you will be able to:

1. Define departmentalization and describe several ways it is implemented in organizations.
2. Understand the difference between authority and responsibility and between line and staff personnel.
3. Explain the concept of centralized versus decentralized authority.
4. Define empowerment and explain what elements are necessary for it to thrive.
5. Identify and describe several principles of supervision based on authority.
6. Recount the basic steps in the delegation process.
7. Discuss why supervisors are often reluctant to delegate authority.
8. Describe some supervisory tasks that can't be delegated.
9. Describe several tips for making delegation more effective.

Supervision Dilemma

Prior to his promotion, John Lewis had often said and had heard other employees say, "We need to get organized around here." Now that he is a supervisor, John wants to do his best to ensure that his employees won't feel this way. He also remembers the many times when he had more than one supervisor telling him what to do. Since becoming a supervisor, John has discovered that getting things organized is not an easy job. For instance, the other day John asked one of his employees, Lou Berry, to get an order out to a preferred customer. When John checked on the order three days later, he found that nothing had been done. John wondered where he had gone wrong in delegating this task to Lou.

Organizing is the grouping of activities necessary to achieve common objectives. Organizing also involves the assignment of each grouping to a manager with the authority necessary to supervise the people performing the activities. Thus, delegation of authority is a major part of the organizing function. Both organizing and delegating are duties that a successful supervisor must master.

The Organization Structure

The **organization structure** results from the grouping of work activities and the assignment of each grouping to a manager. Generally, this structure is developed by upper levels of management. However, it is important that the supervisor know and understand the makeup of the total organization. The supervisor must be familiar with the job that the entire organization is meant to do and with the role that each part of the overall organization plays in doing that job. This familiarity helps the supervisor understand the job, work with other supervisors, and know what to delegate.

Organization Charts

An **organization chart** uses a series of boxes connected with one or more lines to graphically represent the organization's structure. Each box represents a position within the organization, and each line indicates the nature of the relationships between the different positions. The organization chart not only identifies specific relationships but also provides an overall picture of how the entire organization fits together. As organizations become larger and more complex, it becomes increasingly difficult to represent all of the relationships accurately.

Departmentalization

1 LEARNING OBJECTIVES

Departmentalization is the grouping of activities into related work units. Departmentalization is the method most often used to structure the organization. Departments can be formed on the basis of work function, product or service, geographic area, customer, or time. **Functional departmentalization** occurs when organization units are defined by the nature or function of the work. Although different terms may be used, most organizations have four basic functions: production, marketing, finance, and human resources. Production refers to the actual creation of something of value, either goods, services, or both. Marketing involves product or service planning, pricing the product or service with respect to demand, evaluating how to best distribute the good or service, and communicating information to the market through sales and advertising. Any organization, whether manufacturing or service, must provide the financial structure necessary for carrying out its activities. The human resources function is responsible for securing and developing the organization's people.

Each of these basic functions may be broken down as necessary. For instance, the production department may be split into engineering, manufacturing, quality control, and so on. The marketing department may be grouped into advertising, sales, and market research. Figure 9.1 charts a typical functional departmentalization.

FIGURE 9.1   **Functional Departmentalization**

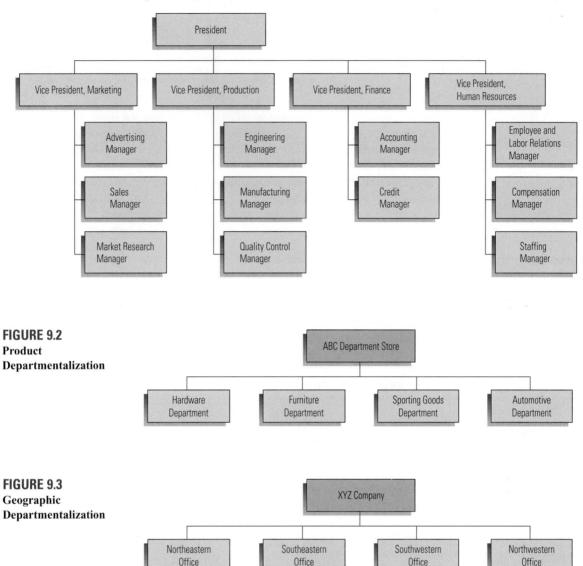

FIGURE 9.2
Product
Departmentalization

FIGURE 9.3
Geographic
Departmentalization

Under **departmentalization by product or service,** all the activities necessary to produce and market a product or service are under a single manager. Many retail stores are organized along these lines, having a hardware department, a furniture department, and so forth. Figure 9.2 illustrates how an organization might be structured using product departmentalization. **Geographic departmentalization** occurs most frequently in organizations with operations or offices that are physically separated from each other. A company with regional offices uses geographic departmentalization. Figure 9.3 shows how an organization using geographic departmentalization might look.

Departmentalization by customer is based on division by customers served. A common example is an organization that has one department to handle retail customers and one

FIGURE 9.4
Customer
Departmentalization

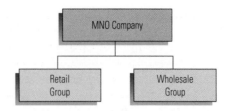

department to handle wholesale or industrial customers. Figure 9.4 shows a possible example of departmentalization by customer. **Departmentalization by process or equipment** occurs when organizational units are defined by the specific process of types of equipment being used. The painting department would be an example of departmentalization by process. **Departmentalization by time or shift** may be used by organizations that work more than one shift.

Most organizations do not use the same type of departmentalization at all levels. Figure 9.5 shows a sales organization that is departmentalized on a different basis at each level.

Authority and the Supervisor

Authority is the right to issue directives and expend resources. The lines of authority are established by the organization structure and link the various organization units together. The authority of supervisors is determined by upper levels of management and implemented through the organization structure. The amount of authority given to supervisors varies with the situation. Thus, some supervisors may be given much more authority than others. Almost all supervisors, however, have some authority to make work assignments. Additionally, supervisors often have the authority to organize the work unit within broad guidelines.

Line versus Staff* Authority

Within the organization structure are two major types of authority: line and staff. **Line authority** is based on the supervisor-employee relationship. With line authority, there is a direct line of authority from the top to the bottom of the organization structure. Line managers and line employees are directly involved in producing and marketing the organization's goods or services. For example, assembly-line supervisors are line managers in that they are directly involved in producing the organization's goods.

FIGURE 9.5 **Departmentalization of a Sales Organization**

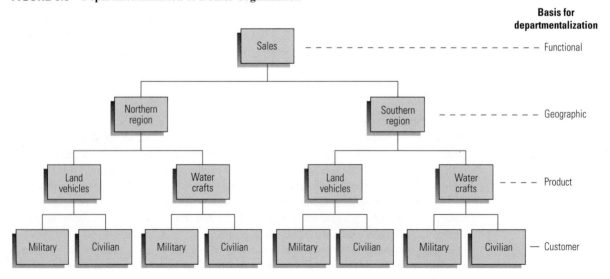

Staff authority is used to support, advise, and help line personnel. Staff employees are generally specialists in a particular field. For example, employees in the personnel department are normally considered to have staff authority since their authority is normally limited to making recommendations to line personnel. Safety and quality are examples of other areas that are usually considered to be staff functions.

Most organizations today have both line and staff. This means that they have both managers with line authority and managers with staff authority. The largest number of supervisors are usually line managers.

Line and Staff Conflict

The presence of both line managers and staff managers sometimes creates conflict. Some staff specialists resent the fact that they may be only advisers to line personnel and have no real authority over the line. At the same time, line managers, knowing they have final responsibility for the product or service, are often reluctant to listen to staff advice. Many staff specialists think they should not be in a position of having to sell their ideas to the line. They believe the line managers should openly listen to their ideas. If the staff specialist is persistent, the line manager often resents even more that the staff "always tries to interfere and run my department." The staff specialist who does not persist often becomes discouraged because "no one ever listens." In healthy organizations, line and staff respect each other and subsequently work well together.

Matrix Structure

The matrix (sometimes called *project*) form of organization is a way of forming project teams within the traditional line-staff organization. A project is "a combination of human and nonhuman resources pulled together in a temporary organization to achieve a specified purpose."[1] The marketing of a new product and the construction of a new building are examples of projects. Because projects have a temporary life, a method of managing and organizing them is sought so that the existing organization structure will not be totally disrupted and will maintain some efficiency.

Under the **matrix structure,** those working on a project are officially assigned to the project and to their original or base departments. A manager is given the authority and responsibility to meet the project objectives in terms of cost, quality, quantity, and time of completion. The project manager is then assigned the necessary personnel from the functional departments of the parent organization. Thus, a horizontal-line organization develops for the project within the parent vertical-line structure. Under such a system, the functional personnel are assigned to and evaluated by the project manager while they work on the project. When the project or their individual work on it is done, the functional personnel return to their departments or begin a new project, perhaps with a new project team.

Centralized versus Decentralized Authority

3 LEARNING OBJECTIVES

Limitations are placed on the authority of any position. **Centralization** and **decentralization** refer to the degree of authority delegated by top management. This is usually reflected in the numbers and kinds of decisions made by middle and supervisory management. The more decisions made by middle and supervisory management, the more decentralized the organization is said to be. Organizations are never totally centralized or totally decentralized but fall along a continuum ranging from highly centralized to highly decentralized. From the supervisor's perspective, the more freedom the supervisor has to make decisions, the more decentralized the organization tends to be. The trend in today's organizations is toward more decentralization. One impact of this trend is that

SUPERVISION ILLUSTRATION 9–1

TAMPA POLICE DECENTRALIZE

In early 2008, officials announced that the Tampa Police Department would decentralize its robbery squad. The belief is that decentralization of the robbery squad will reduce heists around the city. Tampa experienced nearly a 30 percent drop in reported stolen vehicles following a similar decentralization of the auto-theft detectives in the previous year.

Instead of having all nine robbery detectives operate out of the downtown headquarters, three robbery detectives will be assigned to each of the city's three police districts. The theory is that by being assigned to a specific district allows detectives to develop better contacts and tighter connections with the community. According to Craig Fraser, director of management services for the Police Executive Research Forum, "decentralization is a common element of community-oriented policing."

Source: Valerie Kalfrin, "Police Split Robbery Squad, Spread Detectives Out," *McClatchy-Tribune Business News,* March 14, 2008.

more authority is being given to supervisors. Supervision Illustration 9–1 describes how and why the Tampa Police Department recently decentralized its robbery squad.

Empowerment

4 LEARNING OBJECTIVES

Empowerment is a form of decentralization that involves giving employees substantial authority to make decisions. Under empowerment, supervisors express confidence in the ability of employees to perform at high levels. Employees are also encouraged to accept personal responsibility for their work. In situations where true empowerment takes place, employees gain confidence in their ability to perform their jobs and influence the organization's performance. One result of empowerment is that employees demonstrate more initiative and perseverance in pursuing organizational goals. In order for empowerment to thrive, the following four elements must be present:[2]

- *Participation.* Employees must be actively and willingly engaged in their respective jobs. They must want to improve their work processes and work relationship.
- *Innovation.* Employees must be given permission and encouragement to innovate and not do things the way they have always been done.
- *Access to information.* Employees at every level in the organization should make decisions about what kind of information they need to perform their job. This is different from traditional organizations where senior managers decide who gets what information.
- *Accountability.* Employees must be held accountable for their actions and the results achieved.

Accompanying the trend toward more decentralization in today's organizations is a trend toward increased empowerment of today's workforce. While some people believe that empowerment is praised loudly in public but seldom implemented, organizations have experienced very positive results from having empowered their employees. Supervision Illustration 9–2 discusses how empowering its employees has benefited one company.

Responsibility and the Supervisor

Responsibility is accountability for reaching objectives, using resources properly, and adhering to organizational policy. Once you accept responsibility, you become obligated to perform the assigned work, and you also become accountable to see that the work gets done. A certain degree of responsibility is inherent in every supervisory job. Put another way, it

EMPOWERMENT PAYS OFF AT THERMO FISHER

Employee empowerment is visible from the moment a visitor steps on the plant floor at Thermo Fisher Scientific, Inc. The company makes freezers used to store biological samples, microbiological incubators for applications such as in vitro fertilization and biological safety cabinets (BSC), which allow lab employees to safely handle contaminants. Employees lead plant tours and are eager to share the "ins and outs" of their jobs. It is obvious that employees are engaged in their work.

When new employees at the Marietta, Ohio plant have work-related questions, they can consult with a member of the plant's "Tree of Knowledge." The "tree" is a bulletin board that features pictures of employees who have worked at the plant for decades. Mark Zimmer, a welder at the facility, explains that he took a pay cut to hire on at Thermo Fisher 22 years ago. When asked why, he says that part of the reason is the sense of ownership the company provides for its employees. In 2007 alone, the plant saved $1.9 million from its employee-driven Practical Process Improvement (PPI) program. During this same time period, 227 PPI project teams participated in improvement projects, with more than 90 percent of full-time employees working on at least one event.

Source: Jonathan Katz, "Empowering the Workforce," *Industry Week,* January 2009, p. 43.

is almost impossible to hold a supervisory job and have no responsibility. Responsibility and supervision go hand in hand. The term *responsibility* as defined above should not be confused with the term *responsibilities* as used in defining job duties. When used to define job duties, responsibilities refer to the things that make up the supervisor's job. Figure 9.6 lists some typical supervisory responsibilities.

Power and the Supervisor

Many supervisors confuse power with authority. The terms are related, but they mean different things. As defined in Chapter 6, **power** is the ability to get others to respond favorably to instructions and orders. Power is personal in that it is a function of the person's ability to get others to act. As defined earlier, authority is the right to command and expend resources. Authority is positional in that it goes with a given position or title. A person holding a position automatically has the authority that goes with a position as long as he or she maintains that position.

Authority and power usually accompany each other. Thus, a supervisor who has a certain degree of authority usually has certain powers that go along with the authority. Almost all successful supervisors are able to get their employees to follow their lead.

FIGURE 9.6
Typical Supervisory Responsibilities

1. Assign specific duties to each employee.
2. Determine the amount of work to be accomplished by each employee.
3. Transfer employees within your department.
4. Authorize overtime.
5. Answer questions about time standards.
6. Make suggestions for improvements in work procedures.
7. Work with appropriate staff groups to develop and implement better work methods.
8. Counsel employees.
9. Process grievances.
10. Participate in drawing up departmental budgets.
11. Authorize repair and maintenance work.
12. Maintain production sales records.

Principles of Supervision Based on Authority

Because the proper use of authority is a key to successful supervision, numerous related principles have been developed. These five principles should be viewed as guides to assist the supervisor, not as laws to be followed without exception.

Parity Principle

The **parity principle** states that authority and responsibility must coincide. The supervisor must give employees the authority they need to do their jobs. At the same time, employees can be expected to accept responsibility only for those areas within their authority. In other words, if an employee is to assume certain responsibilities, then the supervisor must give the employee sufficient authority to meet those responsibilities. Delegation of authority does not come naturally to most supervisors; yet, it is critical to success. Delegation of authority is discussed at length later in this chapter.

Exception Principle

The **exception principle** (also known as *management by exception* and closely related to the parity principle) states that supervisors should concentrate their efforts on matters that deviate from the norm and let their employees handle routine matters. The idea is that supervisors should not become bogged down by insignificant and routine matters. The exception principle can be violated by insecure employees who refer everything to their supervisor because they are afraid to make decisions. It can also be violated by supervisors who continue to make decisions that have supposedly been delegated. The following example illustrates how the exception principle might be effectively used. Assume that it normally takes one week to replenish raw materials when they are ordered and that the company uses approximately 100 units of raw material per week. A supervisor might instruct an employee to reorder whenever the raw material inventory falls to a level of 300 units. Furthermore, the supervisor might instruct the subordinate to notify him or her if the raw material level ever reaches 100 units so that steps could be taken to avoid a stock-out. Thus, the supervisor would become involved only in those exceptional cases when the raw material inventory drops to 100 units.

Unity of Command Principle

The **unity of command principle** states that an employee should have one and only one immediate boss at a given time. In situations where employees are shared (such as in small companies), an employee should report to only one manager on any one task for which he or she is responsible. The same is true of employees assigned to a team or work group. Experts have speculated that violations of the unity of command principle account for almost one-third of the human relations problems in industry. Such a violation occurs when two or more supervisors tell an employee to do different things at the same time. This places the employee in a no-win situation. Regardless of what the employee does, one supervisor will be dissatisfied. Violation of the unity of command principle is usually caused by unclear lines of authority and poor communication.

Scalar Principle

The **scalar principle** states that authority flows one link at a time from the top of the organization to the bottom. The scalar principle is also referred to as the **chain of command**. Violations of the scalar principle occur when one or more links in the chain of command are bypassed. For example, suppose Jerry goes directly above his immediate boss, Ellen, to her boss, Charlie, for permission to take an early lunch break. Believing the request to be reasonable, Charlie approves it. Later, Charlie discovers that the other two people in Jerry's department had also rescheduled their lunch breaks, so that the department was unstaffed from 12:30 to 1:00 P.M. Had Ellen not been bypassed, this problem could have been avoided. The problem arose not because Charlie was incapable of making a good decision, but because he lacked the information needed to make such a decision.

FIGURE 9.7
Factors Affecting the Span of Control

Factor	Description	Relationship to Span of Control
Complexity	Job difficulty	Inverse*
Variety	Number of different types of jobs being managed	Inverse
Proximity	Physical closeness of jobs being supervised	Direct†
Quality of employees	General quality of employees being supervised	Direct
Ability of supervisor	Ability to perform supervisory duties	Direct

*As the factor of complexity (or variety) increases, the span of supervision decreases.
†As the factor of proximity (or equality or ability) increases, the span of supervision increases.

A common misconception is that every action must painfully progress through every link in the scalar chain. The key is to use common sense. A superior who has a need to know should be involved. On the other hand, purely informational requests can usually be met without going through a superior.

Span of Control Principle

The **span of control principle** (also called the *span of management*) refers to the number of employees a supervisor can effectively manage. For years, the span of control was thought to be five to seven. However, practitioners experienced many situations in which this was not the case. For example, a department of 50 claims processors all doing the same work would not require 8 to 10 supervisors. In modern times, the principle of the span of control has been revised to state that a supervisor's span depends on several factors: the complexity of the jobs, the variety of the jobs, the proximity of the jobs, the quality of the people filling the jobs, and the ability of the supervisor. *Complexity* refers to the difficulty of the jobs being supervised. Naturally, more complex jobs lower the span of control. *Variety* refers to the number of different types of jobs being managed; the more varied the jobs, the lower the span of control. *Proximity* has to do with the physical closeness of the jobs. If all the employees are working in one room, the span of control is greater than it would be if they were spread all over the building or city. *Quality of the employees* refers to the fact that some people require closer supervision than do others. The *ability of the supervisor* refers to the skill of the supervisor. Thus, in situations where employees are engaged in simple, repetitive operations in close proximity, the span of control can be very large. In situations involving highly diversified work, the span of control might be as low as three or four.

While much thought is given to ensuring that a supervisor's span is not too large, the opposite situation is often overlooked. It is easy for situations to develop in which too few employees are reporting to a supervisor. Such situations can lead to an inefficient organization. Figure 9.7 summarizes the factors affecting the span of control.

Delegating Authority and Responsibility

Failure to delegate is probably the most frequent reason that supervisors fail in their jobs. Delegation is an art. Unfortunately, it does not come naturally for many people. In its most common use, **delegation** refers to the delegation of authority. To delegate authority means to grant or confer authority from one person to another. Generally, authority is delegated to assist the receiving party in completing his or her assigned duties. For example, a supervisor may give employees the authority to organize their own work as long as they meet certain production requirements.

There is much debate about the delegation of responsibility. Some people say that you can delegate responsibility; others say that you can't. A close analysis of the issue generally reveals that the debate is more a communication problem than a misunderstanding of the concepts involved. Those who say that responsibility cannot be delegated contend that supervisors can never shed their job responsibilities by passing them on to their employees. Those who say that responsibility can be delegated point out that supervisors can certainly make their employees responsible for certain actions. Both parties are correct! Supervisors can delegate responsibility in the sense of making their employees responsible or accountable for certain actions. However, this delegation does not make supervisors any less responsible or accountable to their bosses. Thus, delegation of responsibility does not mean abdication of responsibility by the delegating party. Responsibility is *not* like an object than can be passed from individual to individual. Suppose a claims supervisor for a life insurance company decides to delegate to the claims investigators the responsibility for investigating all claims within a 60-day limit. The claims supervisor can certainly make the claims investigators responsible (accountable) for meeting this target. At the same time, however, the claims supervisor is no less responsible for the investigation of claims.

How to Delegate

6 LEARNING OBJECTIVES

Successful delegation involves three basic steps: (1) assigning work to the different employees in the work group, (2) creating an obligation (responsibility and accountability) on the part of each employee to perform the duties satisfactorily, and (3) granting permission (authority) to take the actions necessary to perform the duties. Thus, successful delegation involves the delegation of both authority and responsibility.

Assigning Work

The first step in assigning work is to identify what work should be delegated. A good way for a supervisor to identify which tasks should be delegated is to utilize a time log as discussed in Chapter 5. By recording and then analyzing a time log, a supervisor can often identify tasks that can and should be delegated. Once a supervisor has determined which tasks should be delegated, he or she must then decide which subordinates should handle each task. The supervisor should look upon this as a process of matching the available human resources with the task requirements. The key to success when assigning work is to make the best use of the skills and resources available. Therefore, supervisors must be well acquainted with the skills of their employees. Other factors that must be considered when making work assignments include:

1. The personal relationships involved.
2. The effect on others.
3. The attitudes of the affected parties.
4. Company policies that might be applicable.
5. Applicable provisions of a union contract (such as seniority).
6. Safety considerations.

Once the supervisor has decided how the work will be assigned, this information must be clearly communicated to the employees. It is important to note that the assignment of work involves telling employees *what* to do, not *how* to do it. Giving employees a certain amount of freedom as to how their job will be done creates an environment in which initiative and ideas are welcomed. Obviously, the degree of freedom allowed will vary with the specific work assignment. All too often, supervisors stifle employee creativity by demanding that everything be done exactly as prescribed by the supervisor. Most employees are all too happy to please, and thus any trace of creativity quickly disappears.

Creating an Obligation (Responsibility and Accountability)

Supervisors sometimes expect employees to seek and assume responsibility that they have not been asked to assume. Some supervisors engage in a game with their employees: "I know what I want Joe to do, but I'm not going to tell him." The reasoning here is that if Joe is ambitious enough, he will figure out exactly what the supervisor wants. In other words, the supervisor looks upon assignments as if they were tests to separate the more ambitious employees from the less ambitious employees. However, it makes a lot more sense and gets better results to simply tell an employee what is expected. Only after the employee has a clear understanding of what is expected can feelings of responsibility be created. These feelings of responsibility are influenced by the manner in which the supervisor arrives at and communicates expectations. For example, a supervisor who solicits the thoughts and ideas of employees is much more likely to foster feelings of responsibility. Unfortunately, many supervisors act like dictators when assigning work and then wonder why they don't evoke feelings of responsibility. Feelings of responsibility cannot be ordered by another person; they must come from within the individual.

Granting Permission (Authority)

Granting permission to take certain actions necessary to perform the assigned duties is often the most difficult part of delegating. Many supervisors think that once responsibility has been established, the employees should then ask for the necessary authority. This approach gives only the authority that is specifically sought by the employee. But why not empower employees so that they can better perform their jobs? As discussed earlier in this chapter, empowerment involves giving subordinates substantial authority to make decisions. The keys to successfully empowering employees are to express confidence in their abilities to perform at high levels, designing jobs so that employees have considerable freedom, setting meaningful and challenging goals, applauding good performance, and encouraging employees to take personal responsibility for their work.

Why People Are Reluctant to Delegate

LEARNING
OBJECTIVES

Many supervisors are promoted into their supervisory positions from the ranks of the operative employees. The move from operative employee to supervisor involves some differences that can affect the new supervisor's ability to delegate. An operative employee's performance is, for the most part, an individual function. In other words, an operative employee's performance is not normally dependent on anyone else. The performance of a supervisor, however, is almost totally dependent on the performance of others—namely his or her subordinates. Problems occur when the new supervisor does not fully realize this difference and, rather than concentrating on the functions of supervision, tries to do everyone else's job. The supervisor may think that the way to look good is to ensure that everyone's job is done right. This is a very natural trap to fall into. It is also the basis for most of the reasons why supervisors are reluctant to delegate.

If You Want Anything Done Right, Do It Yourself

Many supervisors subscribe to the old saying "If you want anything done right, do it yourself!" This attitude shows that the supervisor does not understand the supervisory process. It also indicates that the supervisor has done a poor job of selecting and training his or her employees. Supervisors who attempt to do it all themselves or to prove that they are superior operative workers spend a great deal of time on nonsupervisory tasks—and then they do not have time to perform their supervisory tasks.

The question is not whether the supervisor can do the job better but whether the employee can do it in an acceptable manner. If an employee can do the job satisfactorily, then the employee should be assigned the job and left alone to do it. It is sometimes helpful for the supervisor to look at the situation from a return on investment (ROI) standpoint. If the employee (who is paid less money per hour than the supervisor) can do the job in an acceptable manner, then the organization is getting more for its money than if the supervisor does it.

It Is Easier to Do It Myself

Supervisors often say that it is easier for them to do the job than to explain it to their employees. While this may be true in some cases, it usually represents a very shortsighted view. It may be easier for the supervisor to do the task the 1st time or even the 5th time around, but is it easier still on the 20th or the 50th time? In other words, although some investment of the supervisor's time may be required to train employees to do the job, this is usually the best approach. If a supervisor continually finds that an employee just can't seem to learn the task, the supervisor should carefully examine the hiring and training practices being used.

Fear of an Employee Looking Too Good

Some supervisors are inhibited from delegating by the fear that they might be replaced by an employee who looks too good. Such fears are totally unfounded for good supervisors. As mentioned previously, a supervisor's performance is, for the most part, a reflection of the employee's performance. If a supervisor's employees look good, the supervisor looks good. If the employees look bad, the supervisor looks bad. Experience has also shown that a truly outstanding employee will eventually move ahead regardless of the supervisor's actions. Under these circumstances, the supervisor might easily live to regret any actions taken to stifle that employee's work performance.

The Human Attraction for Power

Most people like the feel of power. Many supervisors get considerable satisfaction from having the power and authority to grant or not grant certain requests. A supervisor should realize that these feelings are natural and that it may take some conscientious effort to overcome them. The key is to learn to get satisfaction by accomplishing things through others.

More Confidence in Doing Detail Work

Some supervisors feel much more confident when doing detail and operative work than when performing their supervisory functions. Most people have some fear of the unknown and tend to shy away from it. Thus, it is understandable that a new supervisor would feel much more confident doing those things that he or she did successfully in the past. The behavior is likely to occur if the new supervisor has initial setbacks in performing the supervisory functions. Discouraged supervisors often attempt to immerse themselves in their old duties. Closely related to this problem is the supervisor who wants to do things because he or she has *always* done them. In either case, the end result is a failure to delegate.

Preconceived Ideas about Employees

Sometimes supervisors erroneously jump to conclusions about the capabilities of employees. For example, a supervisor might form a negative opinion about an employee's ability based on one occurrence. This occurrence may be very unrepresentative of the employee—or the supervisor may be unaware of the facts surrounding the circumstances. Yet another possibility is for supervisors to base an opinion of employees on secondhand information. Such information may come from other supervisors, employees, or personal acquaintances, and it

FIGURE 9.8
**Reasons Why
Supervisors Are
Reluctant to Delegate**

1. If you want anything done right, do it yourself.
2. It is easier to do it myself.
3. Fear of an employee looking too good.
4. The human attraction for power.
5. More confidence in doing the detail work.
6. Preconceived ideas about employees.
7. Desire to set the right example.

may be very inaccurate. Naturally, if a supervisor believes that an employee lacks ability, that supervisor will be reluctant to delegate to that employee.

Desire to Set the Right Example

Most supervisors want to set a good example for their employees. The problem, however, is to decide what a good example is. Some supervisors think that to set a good example they must be busy—or at least look busy—all the time. Such supervisors hoard work that should be delegated. A similar type of supervisor is the one who enjoys being a martyr. An example is the supervisor who thinks that he or she must always be the last one to leave the office or plant: "This place would fall apart if I didn't work here." Supervisors of this kind also tend to hoard work and not delegate. Figure 9.8 summarizes the reasons why supervisors are reluctant to delegate.

Why Employees Don't Want to Accept Delegation

While many employees not only accept but actively seek additional authority and responsibility, there are reasons why some employees try and avoid additional authority and responsibility.

It's Easier to Ask the Supervisor than to Make a Decision

This is especially prevalent when the supervisor is all too happy to provide solutions or answers in every situation. In these instances, employees become dependent on the supervisor and adopt the attitude of "why take a chance."

Fear of Criticism

If supervisors are overly critical of decisions made by subordinates, the subordinates will try and avoid putting themselves in a situation that may lead to being criticized.

Lack of Incentive

Employees may see no incentive or reason for accepting more authority and responsibility.

Some Feel That Certain Work Is Beneath Them

The supervisor sets the tone here. If supervisors act like certain tasks and responsibilities are beneath them, employees will often adopt the same attitude.

Some Figure the Supervisor Will Change It Anyway

In situations where the supervisor is never or rarely satisfied with decisions, other than his or her own decisions, employees learn to avoid making decisions.

Supervision Illustration 9–3 describes how one owner used delegation to help grow his business.

Tasks That Can't Be Delegated

While the problem of overdelegation is not common, it can occur. The quality and type of employees greatly affect what can be delegated. However, certain things normally should not be delegated.

SUPERVISION ILLUSTRATION 9–3

DELEGATE TO GROW

American Asphalt Company of W. Collingswood Heights, New Jersey has been in business for 106 years. Bob Brown purchased the company in 1986 and has since transformed the company from a small business with less than 10 employees to a company now employing over 100 people with $30 million in annual sales.

Brown believes that the best way to grow a business is to keep yourself out of the day-to-day operation; to work on the business instead of in the business. "Don't feel you have to do everything yourself. In order to grow you have to delegate responsibilities and trust other competent people. This allows you to step back a little bit and look at systems, customer relationships, and employee relationships and actually work on the business. Years ago, in order to grow, I would have worked harder and longer. Now, if I want to grow I'm going to look at who in the organization can handle more work load or if we need another person, equipment, or location."

Source: Kimberly Johnston, "Working "On" The Business," *Pavement,* January 2009, pp. 14–16.

Planning Activities

8	LEARNING OBJECTIVES

Planning activities (which were discussed in the last chapter) include deciding what objectives to pursue and how to achieve them. These activities also include the routing and scheduling of people and materials. While it is desirable to actively involve employees in planning activities, the supervisor should retain primary authority and responsibility for them. Although a supervisor may (and should) delegate certain parts of the planning process, he or she should retain authority for the coordination and finalization of plans.

Assigning Work

The assignment of work should also be controlled by the supervisor. As with planning activities, parts of this process may and probably should be delegated, but the supervisor should retain overall control.

Motivational Problems

Creating the proper work environment to enhance employee motivation is primarily the responsibility of the supervisor. This does not imply that employees do not play a significant part in their own motivation. However, it does imply that the supervisor will always have a strong influence on the work environment, which in turn affects employee motivation.

Counseling Employees

The supervisor normally should not delegate the counseling of employees regarding job-related issues. However, when an employee needs personal counseling or technical information that might better be supplied by a staff person, the supervisor should refer the employee to the proper source.

Resolving Conflict Situations

Whenever a conflict arises between two or more employees, the supervisor should assist in resolving the conflict. This does not mean that the supervisor should personally resolve the conflict, but that the supervisor should see that the involved parties resolve it.

Tasks Specifically Assigned to the Supervisor

It is generally not a good idea to delegate tasks or assignments that upper management expects the supervisor to do personally (such as serving on a committee).

Looking back at John's apparently unsuccessful delegation to Lou, let us see what John could have done differently. First, we must determine whether the task was one that should have been delegated. Based on the limited available information and reviewing the list of tasks that should not be delegated (pp. 169–170), we see no reason to believe that the task should not have been delegated. Having determined this, we must investigate the manner in which John attempted the delegation. Reviewing the basic steps in the delegation process (pp. 166–167), we find that John did assign the task to Lou; however, Lou may not have been the best person for this task. John was probably not successful in creating an obligation on Lou's part. In merely telling Lou what he wanted done, John did not go far enough. He should have clearly communicated his expectations to Lou and involved Lou in jointly establishing a due date for completion of the task. This would most likely have enlisted Lou's commitment to the task. John should also have clearly outlined the limits of Lou's authority.

Practical Tips for Effective Delegation

 9 LEARNING OBJECTIVES

Some specific things can be done to make it easier to delegate:

1. Know your employees' abilities. Become familiar with their major strengths and weaknesses by observing their work, discussing problems when they arise, and reviewing past performance appraisals.
2. Don't be afraid of overdelegating. Many supervisors don't delegate enough for fear of delegating too much.
3. Practice good communication skills when delegating. Give clear instructions and check that the employee understands what has been delegated.
4. Minimize overlap of authority. Establish clearly defined levels of authority. Avoid duplication of effort.
5. Give employees some freedom in deciding how to implement their authority. Delegate what to do, not how to do it.
6. Assign related areas of authority and responsibility to each individual. Try to make sure that the different assignments given to each individual are as closely related as possible.
7. Once you have delegated, let the employee take over. Don't rush in at the drop of a hat to straighten things out. Before giving assistance, make sure the employee has had a fair chance.
8. Don't expect perfection the first time. The question is not "Was the job done perfectly?" but "Was the job done in an acceptable manner?"

Summary

This chapter begins with a discussion of organization structure and of the role played by authority in establishing an organization structure. Five principles of supervision based on authority are discussed. The importance of delegation to the supervisory process is emphasized, and guidelines for successful delegation are presented.

1. *Define departmentalization and describe several ways it is implemented in organizations.* Departmentalization is the grouping of activities into related work units. Departmentalization can be implemented on the basis of work function, product or service, geographic area, customer, or time.

2. *Understand the difference between authority and responsibility and between line and staff personnel.* Authority is the right to issue directives and expend resources. Responsibility is accountability for reaching objectives, using resources properly, and adhering to organizational policy. Line personnel are directly involved in producing and marketing the organization's goods or services. Staff personnel support and advise line personnel.

3. *Explain the concept of centralized versus decentralized authority.* Centralization and decentralization refer to the degree of authority delegated by top management. The more decisions made by middle and supervisory

managers, the more decentralized the organization is said to be.

4. *Define empowerment and explain what elements are necessary for it to thrive.* Empowerment is a form of decentralization that involves giving subordinates substantial authority to make decisions. In order for empowerment to thrive, the following four elements must be present: (1) participation, (2) innovation, (3) access to information, and (4) accountability.

5. *Identify and describe several principles of supervision based on authority.* The parity principle states that authority and responsibility must coincide. The exception principle states that supervisors should concentrate their efforts on matters that deviate from the norm and let their employees handle routine matters. The unity of command principle states that an employee should have one and only one immediate boss. The scalar principle states that authority flows one link at a time from the top of the organization to the bottom. The span of control principle refers to the number of employees a supervisor can effectively manage and is dependent on several factors: the complexity, variety, and proximity of the jobs being supervised; the quality of the employees; and the ability of the supervisor.

6. *Recount the basic steps in the delegation process.* Successful delegation involves three basic steps: (1) assigning work to the different employees in the work group, (2) creating an obligation to perform the duties satisfactorily on the part of each employee, and (3) granting authority to take the actions necessary to perform the duties.

7. *Discuss why supervisors are often reluctant to delegate authority.* Supervisors may be reluctant to delegate for the following reasons: (1) fear that they are the only ones who can do the job right, (2) a belief that it is easier to do the job themselves, (3) fear of having an employee look too good, (4) their own attraction to power, (5) more confidence in doing their own detail work, (6) preconceived ideas about employees, and (7) a misconceived desire to set the right example.

8. *Describe some supervisory tasks that can't be delegated.* The quality and type of employees greatly affect what can be delegated. However, the following tasks should normally not be delegated: planning activities, assigning work, motivation work, counseling employees, resolving conflict situations, and tasks specifically assigned to the supervisor.

9. *Describe several tips for making delegation more effective.* These specific things can be done to make it easier to delegate: (1) know your employees' abilities; (2) don't be afraid of overdelegating; (3) practice good communication skills when delegating; (4) minimize overlap of authority; (5) give employees some freedom in deciding how to implement their authority; (6) assign related areas of authority and responsibility to each individual; (7) once you have delegated, let the employee take over; and (8) don't expect perfection the first time.

Key Terms

Authority, 160
Centralization, 161
Chain of command, 164
Decentralization, 161
Delegation, 165
Departmentalization, 158
Departmentalization by customer, 159
Departmentalization by process or equipment, 160
Departmentalization by product or service, 159

Departmentalization by time or shift, 160
Empowerment, 162
Exception principle, 164
Functional departmentalization, 158
Geographic departmentalization, 159
Line authority, 160
Matrix structure, 161
Organization chart, 158
Organization structure, 158

Organizing, 158
Parity principle, 164
Power, 163
Responsibility, 162
Scalar principle, 164
Span of control principle, 165
Staff authority, 161
Unity of command principle, 164

Review Questions

1. What is departmentalization? What are the different types of departmentalization?

2. Define authority. What is the difference between line authority and staff authority?

3. What is a matrix structure?

4. What is meant by centralized versus decentralized authority?

5. Define *empowerment*. What are some things a supervisor can do to foster an environment that encourages empowerment?

6. Define *responsibility*. Can authority and responsibility be delegated?

7. Define *power*. What is the difference between power and authority?

8. What is the parity principle?

9. What is the exception principle?

10. What is the unity of command principle?

11. What is the scalar principle?

12. What is the span of control principle?

13. What are three basic steps involved in delegation? Briefly discuss each.

14. State seven reasons why supervisors are reluctant to delegate authority.

15. List five reasons why employees are sometimes reluctant to accept delegation.

16. Name six general categories of things that should usually not be delegated.

17. Discuss several tips that can help a supervisor delegate.

Skill-Building Questions

1. If you were planning to give a 10-minute talk to your employees on the topic of delegation, what would you say? Give your answer in outline form.

2. Some supervisors contend that the art of delegation either comes naturally or never comes. Do you agree with this contention? Why or why not?

3. How does the concept of empowerment relate to delegation? Do you think that successful delegation depends on subordinates being empowered?

4. "The scalar principle creates so much red tape and slows down activity to such an extent that it creates more problems than it solves." Do you agree or disagree with this statement? Support your answer.

References

1. David Cleland and William King, *Systems Analysis and Project Management* (New York: McGraw-Hill, 1983), p. 187.

2. John H. Dobbs, "The Empowerment Environment," *Training and Development,* February 1993, pp. 53–55.

Additional Readings

Fenton, Traci. "Even Big Companies are Embracing a Democratic Style," *The Christian Science Monitor,* May 6, 2008, p. 9.

Froschheiser, Lee. "Unlock the Power and Potential of Your Team: 5 Secrets to Empower Your People and Become a Better Leader," *SuperVision,* June 2008, pp. 12–13.

Nefer, Barbara. "Don't Be Delegation-Phobic," *SuperVision,* December 2008, pp. 19–21.

Weiss, W. H. "Team Management," *SuperVision,* November 2004, pp. 19–21.

SKILL-BUILDING APPLICATIONS

Incident 9–1

Where Do You Start?

Carl was a hard-working supervisor. He had enough personnel in his organization to accomplish the workload, but in spite of this, his work was rarely done on time. One day, Carl excused himself from his boss's staff meeting, stating that he had to get back to the job. Roger, his boss, decided to spend the next morning with him.

When Roger arrived the next morning, Carl was talking on the phone and, at the same time, signing some forms. He interrupted the phone conversation and called to the secretary, "Mary, these forms are signed."

While still talking on the same phone call, Carl then thrust the signed forms toward Mary as she entered. His movement pushed the disorderly pile of papers off the corner of his desk. The papers were scattered on the floor by a breeze through an open window, and Mary began to pick them up. Carl shouted, "I'll think about it and call you back, Oliver." Then he said to Mary, "Don't pick them up, you'll just mix them worse." He scooped up a paper that was on the desk and handed it to the chief. "There is Don Pitt's idea of how to save about half the time we spend on processing. Wish we had time to try it out. What do you think of it?"

Mary came back in. "Bill Evans wants to know if he can start on the priority job right now," she said. "Tell him to wait," Carl replied. "I haven't time to finish training him, and I just can't trust him to start a job that important without checking it myself."

While Carl was picking up the fallen papers and sorting them, Mary brought in some forms. "You just signed those on the line for the president's signature, so I typed them over."

"Too much to do," muttered Carl, glancing at Roger as he signed. "If you're signing them now, I'll take them to the president right away," said Mary, reaching. "I'll take them," replied Carl, "the president might want to ask me about them."

Carl explained to Roger, "Don and Bob can't do a thing till I run these through. I'll be right back." He dashed off, but was back in a minute.

Questions

1. Do you think Carl is highly motivated? Is he a good supervisor?

2. What do you think are Carl's major problems?

3. What suggestions would you make to Carl?

Incident 9–2

Promotion Possible

Chang Kim has been the assistant supervisor of sales for the ABC Company for the past six months. As a result of poor sales over the past 18 months, his boss, the sales supervisor (the assistant's boss), has just been fired. The president of ABC then offers Chang his job, subject to the following stipulations:

- Chang cannot increase the advertising budget.
- Chang must continue to let Metro-Media, Inc., handle the advertising.
- Chang cannot make any personnel changes.
- Chang will accept full responsibility for the sales for this fiscal year (which started two months ago).

1. Do you think Chang should accept the job? Why or why not?

2. What organization principle has been violated?

3. If you were Chang, what would you tell the president of ABC?

Exercise 9–1

Minor Errors

Recently, you have noticed that one of the staff members on the same level as your boss has been giving you a hard time concerning reports that you submit to him. In reviewing your recent reports, you have discovered a few minor errors that you should have caught, but in your opinion they are not significant enough to warrant the kind of criticism you've been receiving.

Your boss and this particular manager have a history of bad relations, which may be one reason for the manager's criticism.

As you think about how to best handle the situation, you consider these alternatives:

Questions

1. Talk to the manager in private and ask him why he is being so critical.

2. Do nothing. This situation is probably temporary, and bringing undue attention to it will only make matters worse.

3. Since your boss may get involved, discuss the situation with him and ask for his advice on what to do.

4. Simply work harder to upgrade the reports. Make sure that there will be nothing to criticize in the future.

5. Discuss the situation with your boss, but minimize or "play down" the problem by letting him know that you feel that constructive criticism of this type is usually healthy.

Other alternatives may be open to you, but assume that these are the only ones you have considered.

Without discussion with anyone, decide which of these approaches you would take now. Be prepared to defend your choice.

Exercise 9–2

"In-Basket"

Imagine yourself in the role of supervisor of a shoe store. You have two assistant or shift managers, who also sell on the floor but have authority only when you are not present, and seven salesclerks, who work various schedules on the floor. The store is not unionized.

You have just arrived back from three days at the company headquarters and are faced with the following list of items in your in-basket:

1. Two applications for jobs (no positions open right now).

2. A note to call Mary (salesclerk) about vacation schedule.

3. A notice that the mall will be changing hours for the upcoming holiday and requesting notice of store plans.

4. A customer complaint regarding product quality.

5. Four shipping receipts indicating that about 130 pairs of shoes have been delivered and need to be stocked.

6. Bids from three companies responding to requests for bids on a cash register system (each store chooses its own).

7. A notice from the fire department of an impending inspection.

8. A note that the rest room is out of order.

9. Notice from the company headquarters that a holiday sale will begin soon.

10. Five advertisements and two catalogs from various vendors.

You should decide to "act on" or "delegate" each of the 10 items. After you have made these decisions, your instructor will assign you to a group with two or three other students. The group will then decide as a group which items should be "acted on" or "delegated."

Questions

These questions should be addressed both individually and by the group:

1. Which tasks are supervisory in nature and which are operational in nature?

2. How does each task compare to the list of tasks that can't be delegated on pages 169–170?

3. For those tasks that you chose not to delegate, were you influenced by any of the reasons listed in Figure 9.8?

Be prepared to discuss your answers with the class.

Exercise 9–3

Delegation Quiz I

This exercise is most applicable for students who are currently employed. If you are not currently employed, think of your most recent employment as you complete the quiz.

	Yes	No
1. Do you spend more time than you should doing detail work that others could do?	____	____
2. Do employees often interrupt you with questions and problems on their projects?	____	____
3. Are you still concerned with activities and problems on their projects?	____	____
4. Do you take work home regularly?	____	____
5. Do you work longer hours than your employees?	____	____
6. Are you making decisions that should be made at the level of your employees?	____	____
7. Do you feel you should be able to answer any question your boss asks you on any project in your shop?	____	____

8. Do you have trouble meeting deadlines? ＿＿ ＿＿

9. Do you have trouble establishing and maintaining priorities? ＿＿ ＿＿

10. Is your in-box often full? ＿＿ ＿＿

11. Are you expecting to call your office or to have them call you? ＿＿ ＿＿

If you answered yes to only one of these, chances are you're an excellent delegator. If you had two to four yes answers, you can improve. If you had five or more, you should place a high priority on improving your delegating.

Exercise 9–4

Delegation Quiz II

Like Delegation Quiz I this exercise is also most applicable for students who are currently employed. If you are not currently employed, think of your most recent employment as you complete the quiz. Upon completion of the quiz, your instructor will discuss the best answers with you.

1. What does delegation mean to you?
   a. Passing the buck to juniors
   b. Dumping responsibilities
   c. Tricking others into doing work that is rightfully yours
   d. None of the above

2. Are you nervous about delegating because
   a. you do not trust anyone else to do the work?
   b. you do not want to overburden someone else?
   c. you don't have time to train or prepare others?
   d. overwork is part of your job?

3. What word would you most associate with delegation?
   a. Risk
   b. Fear
   c. Guilt
   d. Trust

4. If you did delegate a task, or tasks, would they be
   a. the most boring ones?
   b. the least risky ones?
   c. the most risky ones?
   d. the ones that a subordinate could do just as well?

5. If you had to delegate an important job to a subordinate, would you
   a. issue it as an order?
   b. be very apologetic?
   c. leave it to someone else to convey?
   d. present it as an opportunity?

6. When delegating to someone, do you
   a. keep worrying that the job is not being done well?
   b. ask them to report back each time a decision is made?
   c. stipulate that if anything goes wrong it is their responsibility?
   d. tell them to come back to you only if there is a problem they cannot handle?

Source: This quiz is drawn from Mike Levy, "Good Delegator or Willing Martyr," *Director,* April 1999, p. 19.

Exercise 9–5

Hank Attempts to Delegate

Go to your university or college library, get online and look up the following article: W. Gale Cutler, "Hank Attempts to Delegate," *Research Technology Management,* March/April 2008, Vol. 51, Iss. 2, pp. 59–61.

1. Do you think Hank's criticism of Mike's decision is justified?

2. Which of the executives that reviewed the case do you most closely agree with? Why?

CHAPTER TEN

Understanding Work Groups and Teams

Learning objectives

After studying this chapter, you will be able to:

1. Describe formal and informal work groups.
2. Define group norms.
3. Explain group cohesiveness.
4. Define group conformity.
5. Define groupthink.
6. Understand the concept of team building.
7. Explain idiosyncrasy credit.
8. List the four phases in the life of teams.
9. Describe a quality circle.
10. Explain self-directed work teams.
11. Explain virtual work teams.

Prior to becoming a supervisor, Jane Harris ate lunch with the same group of people almost every day. Some of these people were from her own department and some were from other departments. The one thing they had in common was that they were all in a company-sponsored exercise program. Over lunch, they generally talked about what was happening in the company.

Jane realized that in her work unit there was also a small group of people who always seemed to be doing things together. However, something bothered Jane about this group. The group sometimes seemed to have a negative effect on the work of her unit.

All organizations depend on groups to achieve success. In organizations, a **group** is two or more people who interact to meet a shared goal, such as a group of students who meet to organize fund-raising or social events. A shared sense of purpose sets a group apart from just a gathering of people. In general, organizations have two types of groups: informal work groups and formal work groups (or teams).

Informal Work Groups

1 LEARNING OBJECTIVES

Informal work groups are formed voluntarily by employees of an organization. They develop from personal contacts and interactions among people. Groups of employees who lunch together regularly and office cliques are examples of informal work groups.

A special type of informal group is the *interest group*. Its members share a purpose or concern. For example, women managers might form a group to share ideas about issues that women in management face.

Work is a social experience. Employees interact while performing job duties in offices, factories, stores, and other workplaces. Friendships emerge naturally from these contacts. Informal groups formed around mutual interests fill important social needs. In earlier centuries, groups like extended families, churches, and small towns met these needs. Today people socialize mostly with people they meet at work.

Informal work groups affect productivity, the morale of other employees, and the success of supervisors. They can be the result of—and can help create—a shared sense of loyalty. This is especially prevalent in high-risk occupations, such as fire fighting and police work.

Informal work groups often develop in areas where employees work close together (such as offices with cubicles) and among employees in the same field (such as accounting or graphic design). Employees may band together to share fears or complaints. In such cases, informal groups work against organization goals.

Studies have identified the power of informal work groups in organizations. The Hawthorne studies discovered that groups may set their own productivity levels and pressure employees to meet them. In one group, employees who produced more or less than the acceptable levels met with name-calling, sarcasm, and ridicule. The Hawthorne studies concluded that informal organizations with their own social systems exist within formal organizations.[1] Supervision Illustration 10–1 shows the power of informal work groups.

In general, management does not formally recognize informal groups that revolve around friendships, interests, or shared working space and tasks. Yet an understanding of these groups can improve managers' work with formal groups. Employees join informal groups to meet a social need. They often gain great satisfaction from these groups. Supervisors should seek to duplicate this satisfaction in formal work groups.

SUPERVISION ILLUSTRATION   10–1

THE POWER OF TEAMS

Three Microsoft employees tossed out the corporate hierarchy and pulled together to complete the ultimate team-building exercises: a seven-day, 150-mile race last month across the Gobi Desert in remote Western China. The goal is to spread access to technology (and, eventually sales of Microsoft's products) to the "next billion" people in emerging markets around the world by 2015. The Gobi March, part of a series of extreme-endurance events called RacingThePlanet, pits teams and individuals against mountain passes as high as 10,000 feet, flat expanses of sun-baked desert, rocky riverbeds and deep gorges.

The racers were already used to spending extended stretches together away from the office because of a demanding international travel schedule. But they quickly realized that to be successful in the Gobi, they had to let go of the corporate structure that defined their work roles.

The team was composed of Orlando Ayala, a senior vice president, Fry Wilson, a senior director, who reports to Ayala, and William Calarese, a director, who reports to Wilson.

Across miles of hot, unforgiving desert, the elements took their toll. They watched other teams disintegrate as racers pushed too hard—or were pushed—to keep up. They finally broached an uncomfortable topic: What would they do if one person couldn't continue? "At that moment, we had to decide to be completely transparent and totally vulnerable to each other," Fry Wilson said, recalling the heated discussion. "To me, it was the turning point." "We all finish or nobody finishes," Ayala said.

On the final day the team awoke feeling good and decided to run to the finish, where they were greeted with cheers from the other racers and kids from a local school.

Source: Adapted from Benjamin Romano, "Golba March Teaches Microsoft Team about Potential," *McClatchy Tribune Business News,* July 21, 2008, Wire Feed.

Formal Work Groups

1 LEARNING OBJECTIVES

Management establishes **formal work groups** or work teams to carry out specific tasks. Formal groups may exist for a short or long period of time. A task force is an example of a formal group. These groups have a single goal, such as resolving a problem or designing a new product.

A different type of formal work group is the *command,* or *functional,* group. This group consists of a manager and all the employees he or she supervises. Unlike a task group, the command group's work is ongoing and not confined to one issue or product.

Group Norms

2 LEARNING OBJECTIVES

Group norms are the informal rules a group adopts to regulate the behavior of group members. They may be extremely simple—a group that lunches together may maintain a rigid seating order. They may include expectations that group members will remain loyal to each other under any circumstances. Whatever the norms, group members are expected to hold to them. Members who break the rules often are shut out.

Norms don't govern every action in a group, only those important for group survival. For instance, a working group's norms would affect its productivity levels, operating procedures, and other work-related activities. Norms may not be written down or even spoken. Rather, group members use their actions to show new members how to behave.

Group Behavior

Think about the informal groups of friends and classmates you have belonged to at school or in your neighborhood. However they develop, informal work groups share similar types of behaviors. They include cohesiveness, conformity, and groupthink.

Group Cohesiveness

Group cohesiveness is the degree of attraction among group members, or how tightly knit a group is. The more cohesive a group, the more likely members are to follow group norms. A number of factors affect the cohesiveness of informal work groups—size, success, status, outside pressures, stability of membership, communication, and physical isolation.

Size is a particularly important factor in group cohesiveness. The smaller the group, the more cohesive it is likely to be. A small group allows individual members to interact frequently. Members of large groups have fewer chances to interact; therefore, these groups tend to be less cohesive.

Think about how two close friends operate when they study together. Because they know each other well and talk easily, they have no trouble working together. Now imagine three new people in the study session. Everyone might not agree on the best way to cover material. It may be hard to work with different people. This might cause the study group to fall apart.

Success and status affect group cohesiveness. The more success a group experiences, the more cohesive it becomes. Several factors contribute to a group's status. For instance, highly skilled work groups tend to have more status than less skilled groups. Like groups that meet their goals, high-status groups tend to be more cohesive than other informal work groups. These relationships are reinforcing—success and status bring about cohesiveness, and cohesiveness brings about status and success.

Outside pressures, such as conflicts with management, can increase group cohesiveness. If a group sees management's requests as a demand or threat, it becomes more cohesive. In these situations, members may develop an "us against them" mentality.

A stable membership and easy lines of communication improve group cohesiveness. Long-standing members know each other well and are familiar with group norms. Employees who work in the same area socialize easily. In a production line, however, conversation is difficult and groups are less cohesive.

Finally, physical isolation from other employees may increase group cohesiveness. The isolation forces workers into close contact with each other and strengthens bonds.

Group Conformity

Group conformity is the degree to which group members accept and follow group norms. A group generally seeks to control members' behavior for two reasons. First, independent behavior can cause disagreements that threaten a group's survival. Second, consistent behavior creates an atmosphere of trust that allows members to work together and socialize comfortably. Members are able to predict how others in the group will behave.

Individual members tend to conform to group norms under certain conditions:

- When group norms are similar to personal attitudes, beliefs, and behavior.
- When they do not agree with the group's norms but feel pressure to accept them.
- When the rewards for complying are valued or the sanctions imposed for noncompliance are devalued.

Group Pressure and Conformity

Researchers have studied the influence of group pressure on individual members. One classical study of group conformity took place at a textile firm in Virginia.[2] A textile

FIGURE 10.1
Effect of Group Norms on a Member's Productivity

Source: Lester Coch and J. R. P. French, Jr., "Overcoming Resistance to Change," *Human Relations* (1948), pp. 519–20.

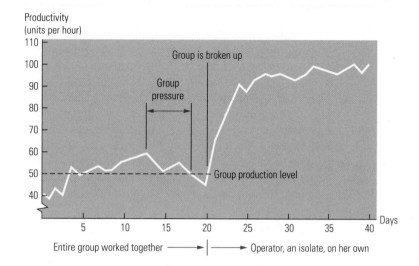

employee began to produce more than the group norm of 50 units per day. After two weeks, the group started to pressure this employee to produce less, and she quickly dropped to the group's level. After three weeks, all the members of the group were moved to other jobs except for this employee. Once again, her production quickly climbed to double the group norm (see Figure 10.1).

Groupthink

5   LEARNING OBJECTIVES

When group members lose their ability to think as individuals and conform at the expense of their good judgment, **groupthink** occurs. Members become unwilling to say anything against the group or any member, even if an action is wrong.

Keeping a group together under any circumstance is a goal in itself. Groups with this goal believe that the group is indestructible and always right. Group members justify any action, stereotype outsiders as enemies of the group, and pressure unwilling members to conform. In business, groupthink is disruptive because it affects employees' ability to make logical decisions.

One study of the influence of group pressures on individuals placed college students in groups of seven to nine people.[3] Group members were told they would be comparing lengths of lines on white cards. Figure 10.2 shows the cards and lines. The subjects in the study were then asked to pick the line on the second card that was identical in length to the line on the first card.

In the experiment, all but one member of each group were told to pick one of the two wrong lines on card 2. In addition, the uninformed member of the group was positioned to

FIGURE 10.2
Cards in Experiment

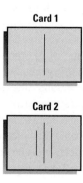

Card 1

Card 2

always be one of the last individuals to respond. Under ordinary circumstances, mistakes on the line selection occur less than 1 percent of the time. However, in this experiment, the uninformed member made the wrong selection in 36.8 percent of the trials.

An uninformed member confronted with only a single individual who contradicted the choice continued to answer correctly in almost all trials. When the opposition was increased by two, incorrect responses increased to 31.8 percent.

The experiment demonstrated that the group's behavior affected the behavior of the individual members; although some individuals remained independent in their judgments, others acquiesced on almost every judgment. Overall, group pressure caused individuals to make incorrect judgments in more than one-third of the cases. The experiment also showed that the more the members disagreed with the individual, the more likely the individual was to succumb to the judgment of the group.

The Importance of Teams

Teams play an important part in helping an organization meet its goals. Groups have more knowledge and information than individuals. They make communicating and solving problems easier. This creates a more efficient and effective company.

The importance of managing groups effectively is becoming recognized in the business world. Employees must work closely to improve production and maintain a competitive edge. Changes in the workforce are bringing men and women from different backgrounds together. Supervisors must work with groups to overcome cultural and gender differences. These, and other factors, make managing work groups one of management's most important tasks.

Influencing Work Groups

Studies at the Hawthorne plant, where researchers documented the existence of informal work groups, looked at the effects of various changes on employees' productivity. Researchers varied job factors, including the way employees were paid and supervised, lighting, the length of rest periods, and the number of hours worked. Productivity rose with each change.

This result led to the coining of the term **Hawthorne effect.** As you may remember from earlier in this chapter, the Hawthorne effect states that giving special attention to a group of employees changes the employees' behavior. The results of the studies show that when groups of employees are singled out for attention, they tend to work more efficiently.

Building Effective Teams

Members of informal work groups often develop a shared sense of values and group loyalty. Formal groups rarely share these qualities because members are assigned to them rather than volunteering for them. Managers are responsible for developing shared values and group loyalty in formal work groups.

The linking-pin concept is one way of describing management's role in work groups. The linking-pin concept holds that because managers are members of overlapping groups, they link formal work groups to the total organization. Managers improve communication and ensure that organizational and group goals are met. In other words, managers themselves are the linking pins (see Figure 10.3).

Building effective formal work groups often is called team building. **Team building** is the process of establishing a cohesive group that works together to achieve its goals. A team will be successful only if its members feel that working conditions are fair to all. A team can fail, even in a supportive organization, if a supervisor does not encourage fair play. Supervision Illustration 10–2 describes a team building activity at Kaiser Permanente.

6 LEARNING OBJECTIVES

TEAM BUILDING AT KAISER PERMANENTE

The idea to participate came about when leaders were planning a meeting for the national KP HealthConnect(TM) team. Searching for an unconventional way to build camaraderie among employees and find more effective ways of delivering services to their customers, Lisa Caplan, vice president of the KP HealthConnect(TM) Business Team, also hoped to produce something that could be returned to the community and provide aid to those in need.

In partnership with Odyssey Helping Hands, an organization devoted to facilitating philanthropic team building, a four-hour workshop was held in which Kaiser Permanente participants were challenged to assemble new, highly functional, prosthetic hands for distribution to children in developing nations who have lost limbs as a result of land mine explosions.

"It is an amazing experience to see the looks on peoples' faces when they realize that they are building something that will allow amputees to do things that we take for granted every day, such as writing, typing and even eating with standard utensils," said John Arntz, a facilitator of the workshop. "Participants can then apply the lessons learned to their personal work environments with a newfound appreciation of their support systems and the end result of their work."

More than 120 members of the national Kaiser Permanente HealthConnect(TM) team provided a helping hand to amputees with the donation of 60 prosthetic hands to victims of land mine accidents.

Source: Adapted from Anonymous, "Kaiser Permanente Team Builds Prosthetic Hands for Charity," *Health & Medicine Week,* March 24, 2008, p. 4934.

The success of a group or team can be measured in the same way as the success of organizations. Successful organizations and groups both meet their goals by using their resources well. Managers encourage teamwork by selecting group members carefully, creating a positive work environment, building trust, and increasing group cohesiveness. Figure 10.4 describes three steps to use in building productive teams.

Creating Groups

For a group to succeed, members must be able to perform the tasks assigned by management. Selecting the right individuals is key to the success of a group. The first step is to identify qualified people. Then management must make the group attractive to these individuals.

For most employees, a formal work group is attractive because it increases pay and offers some satisfaction. If employees see that joining a formal group can provide them

FIGURE 10.3   Linking-Pin Concept

Source: Rensis Likert, *New Patterns of Management* (New York: McGraw-Hill, 1961), p. 104.

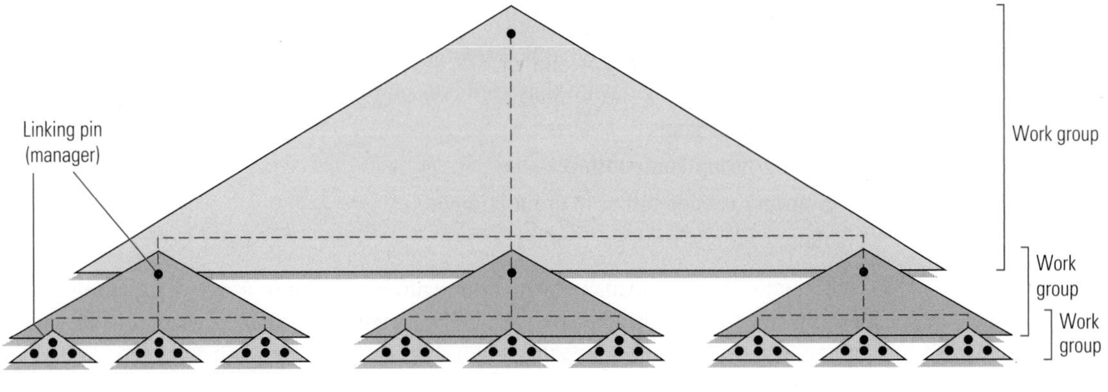

FIGURE 10.4
Steps for Building Productive Teams

1. **Selecting Individuals**

   The first step in building an effective team is finding the right people. Group members need to have the right skills and the right personality fit.

2. **Trust-Building**

   The second step is to build trust among group members and between the group and management.

3. **Encouraging Group Cohesiveness**

   The third step is to develop a cohesive group that conforms to group norms. Managers can improve group cohesiveness by keeping groups small, giving them clear goals, and rewarding them as a team.

with the same satisfaction that an informal group can, they are more likely to participate willingly.

Environment also can be important to the success of a group. An important requirement for meeting group goals is a suitable place to work. How the office is laid out and other physical factors will affect the group's ability to work together successfully.

Building Trust

Trust is essential among group members and between groups and management. A successful group effort means sharing responsibilities and making decisions together. Group members must feel that the entire group is willing and able to work together successfully to achieve goals. Without trust, groups can't set or stick to production norms.

Managers must have faith in their employees. They also must recognize the interests of the organization, the group, and the employees. Effective supervisors should become personally involved, take a real interest in group members, share information, and exhibit honesty.

Influencing a Team's Cohesiveness

Think about teams you have belonged to at school or summer camp. The successful teams are highly competitive and eager to succeed. Effective work groups share these characteristics. Both types of groups also draw their primary satisfaction from a sense of accomplishment, which comes from a job well done.

Supervisors can affect formal group performance levels by studying the degree of group conformity. Formal groups must be cohesive and dedicated to high performance norms in order to succeed. Supervisors can influence group cohesiveness by

- Keeping groups small.
- Selecting group members carefully.
- Finding a good personality fit between new and old employees.
- Developing an office layout that improves communication.
- Creating clear goals.
- Inspiring group competition.
- Rewarding groups rather than individuals.
- Isolating groups from each other.

High individual performance with poor team performance is not what winning is about, either in sports or in business. Individuals must surrender their egos so that the end result is bigger than the sum of its parts. When this happens, the team works together like fingers on a hand.

SUPERVISION ILLUSTRATION 10–3

QUALITY CIRCLES IN JAPAN

Toyota Motor Engineering & Manufacturing Inc wants to see a little more competitive spirit in its workforce. About 37 percent of the auto maker's assemblers participate in Toyota's global "Quality Circles" competition that pits worker against worker in a friendly competition to develop more efficient manufacturing methods. Quality Circles help Toyota maintain an edge over its competition, as technology becomes less of a differentiator among auto makers. Toyota has long touted its kaizen strategy of continuous improvement. In place since 1990, it encourages employees on the factory floor to submit new ideas to improve the manufacturing process.

Twice a year, Toyota holds a competition to identify the best ideas. A Silver Circle award is presented for the best

idea from one of every four quality circles. One of every four Silver Circles wins a Golden Circle award.

The winners of the Golden Circle then face off against each other in the Global Quality Circle competition, often held in Japan, Pat D'Eramo says. "There they participate with the rest of the world," he says. "It's very high pride for team members to participate, especially at the platinum level."

Toyota has long touted its kaizen strategy of continuous improvement. In place since 1990, it encourages employees on the factory floor to submit new ideas to improve the manufacturing process.

Source: Adapted from Byron Pope, "Toyota Says Quality Circles Still Paying Dividends," *Ward's Auto World,* June 2008, p. 20.

7 LEARNING OBJECTIVES

Some members of groups will always be permitted to depart from group norms. This phenomenon is known as the idiosyncrasy credit. The **idiosyncrasy credit** occurs when individuals who have played a significant role in a group are allowed some freedom within the group. People in this position have often helped develop a group's norms. Because the group's norms often are the same as their own, those who could use the idiosyncrasy credit often do not.

Phases in the Life of Teams

8 LEARNING OBJECTIVES

Effective work teams go through four phases of development—forming, norming, storming, and performing. Phase one (forming) occurs when the team members first come together. Uncertainty and anxiety are common feelings that members of the team experience. Therefore, the focus of the forming phase is for members of the team to get to know each other and have their questions answered. Phase two (norming) involves developing the informal rules that the team adopts to regulate the behavior of the team members. In phase three (storming), members of the team begin to question the leadership and direction of the group. In phase four (performing), the team becomes an effective and high performing team only if it has gone through the three previous phases.

Quality Circles

9 LEARNING OBJECTIVES

One type of formal work group is the quality circle. A **quality circle** is a group of employees, usually from 5 to 15 people, from a single work unit (such as a department) who share ideas on how to improve quality. The goal of a quality circle is to involve employees in decision making. Membership is almost always voluntary, and members share a common bond—they perform similar tasks.

Japan has used quality circles since the early 1960s. The idea arrived in the United States after executives from Lockheed Corporation visited Japan in the 1970s and saw the circles in action. Lockheed used quality circles to improve quality and save several million dollars.

Quality circles have benefits other than increasing employee participation. They encourage communication and trust among members and managers. They are an inexpensive way to provide employees with training while giving them a sense of control over their work lives. Most important, however, they may solve problems that have been around for years. Quality circles create strong lines of communication. "Me" becomes "us" in a good quality circle. Supervision Illustration 10–3 describes the importance of quality circles in Japan.

Self-Directed Work Teams

Another type of formal work group is the **self-directed work team (SDWT)**. SDWTs are empowered to control the work they do without a formal supervisor. Each SDWT has a leader who normally comes from the employees on the team. Most of these teams plan and schedule their work, make operational and personnel decisions, solve problems, set priorities, determine what employee does what work, and share leadership responsibilities.

Virtual Work Teams

A **virtual work team** is one in which team members work together across geographical or organizational boundaries by means of information technology. In a virtual work group, group members often do not see each other on a regular basis.

Groups and Leaders

When an informal group selects a leader, members choose the person most capable of satisfying the group's needs. The group gives this leader authority and can take this authority away at any time. This leader needs strong communication skills, especially in setting objectives for the group, giving directions, and summarizing information.

To see how informal groups choose leaders, imagine a group of people shipwrecked on an island. The group's first goal is to find food, water, and shelter. The individual best equipped to help the group survive would naturally become the leader. Later, the group's goal might change to getting off the island. The original leader may no longer be the best person to help meet this new goal, and a new leader could emerge. The process may continue through several leaders.

Gaining Acceptance

Supervisors assigned to formal work groups must work to gain acceptance as leaders. They generally do not have the same authority as leaders of informal groups. The formal authority granted by top management is no guarantee that a supervisor will effectively guide a group.

Think about how you respond to your teachers. You respect teachers who know their subject well, communicate information effectively, treat students with respect, and make fair judgments. Supervisors working with formal groups can use these same behaviors to gain the trust and respect of employees.

Supervisors must keep track of those changes within the organization that might affect the group. At times, they may have to modify group goals to meet new organizational goals. For example, an organization faced with strong competition may need to make decisions rapidly rather than rely on groups to come up with a solution. In these cases, supervisors must be ready to make immediate decisions for the group.

Encouraging Participation

Building an effective team requires a nontraditional managerial approach. In a traditional organizational structure, managers direct the employees who work for them. As part of a team, however, supervisors encourage participation and share responsibility, acting more like a coach than a supervisor.

One way of encouraging team spirit is to provide the group with a vision. People who organize groups to support social causes often use this approach. For example, one person may rally a community around a project such as reclaiming a vacant lot for a park. In the business world, supervisors can offer team members the possibility of designing a state-of-the-art product or service.

Supervisors lead by example. Their attitude and performance become the standard for group norms. A supervisor who believes that a group must listen to and support all members might create a group of top supervisors who share this feeling. Employees who see supervisors functioning within a cohesive group are more likely to work effectively in groups themselves.

Supervision and Informal Work Groups

Too many supervisors view informal work groups negatively. As mentioned earlier, however, such groups can have positive effects. Figure 10.5 summarizes some of the potential benefits from informal work groups. To realize those benefits, the supervisor must be aware of the impact of informal work groups on individuals.

Getting the Informal Work Group to Work with You instead of against You

As mentioned earlier in this chapter, the informal work group can have very positive benefits if its goals are compatible with the organization's goals. Obviously, some causes of negative work group behavior are outside the supervisor's control. However, a number of causes are within the supervisor's control. The purpose here is to summarize some of the factors that can encourage an informal work group to contribute positively. Some of these factors were also presented earlier as aids in developing a team spirit in the formal work group.

Communicate Openly

Most employees want to know what is happening in the organization—especially about things that will affect them. It is often said that informal work groups resist change. The statement is only partially true, however. Groups do resist changes that are going to affect them negatively. They are also likely to resist changes when they are not certain how the changes will affect them.

Keeping the members of the informal work group informed helps create the feeling that they are an accepted part of the organization and are needed. Keeping the lines of communication open also lets the supervisor quickly know about small problems before they develop into large problems. Moreover, since employees want to know what is going on, if the supervisor doesn't keep them informed, they will find out from others.

Encourage Group Participation in Decision Making

Allowing the group to participate in decisions that will affect it is very helpful in getting it to work positively with the supervisor. In Chapter 2, suggestions were offered on methods to use in getting group participation in decision making.

Respect the Informal Leader

Specific suggestions for dealing with the informal leader have already been made. These suggestions need to be followed if the supervisor is to get the support of the informal work group.

FIGURE 10.5
Potential Benefits from Informal Work Groups

1. Informal work groups blend with the formal organization to make a workable system for getting work done.
2. Informal work groups lighten the workload for the supervisor and fill in some of the gaps in that supervisor's abilities.
3. Informal work groups provide satisfaction and stability to the organization.
4. Informal work groups provide a useful channel of communication in the organization.

Jane has learned that informal work groups exist in all organizations and that effective supervisors must work with these groups. She has learned why informal work groups exist and what some of their characteristics are (p. 178). Informal work groups always attempt to get their individual members to conform to group norms. Jane has learned that informal work groups can have positive effects in an organization. She has also learned that she can get the informal work group in her department to work with her instead of against her by communicating openly, encouraging group participation in decision making, respecting the informal leader, removing production obstacles, practicing constructive discipline, being sensitive to individual needs, setting a good example and being consistent, attempting to provide group rewards, supporting the group when possible, and setting achievable goals for her work unit (pp. 187–189).

Remove Production Obstacles

The list of potential production obstacles is quite long. Among those obstacles are excess paperwork, improper maintenance, material shortages, ineffective policies and procedures, and poor working conditions. The best way to identify production obstacles is to ask the employees or the informal work group leader. Informal work groups appreciate a supervisor who is concerned and works toward removing performance obstacles. Even though the supervisor may not be able to remove all of the obstacles, he or she should keep the group informed about what is being done.

Practice Constructive Discipline

Chapter 17 will outline several suggestions for applying positive disciplinary procedures. If the informal work group feels that the supervisor is being unfair to one of its members, the supervisor will not get the support of the group.

Be Sensitive to Individual Needs

It is important to remember that groups in organizations are made up of individuals. These individuals have their own likes, dislikes, needs, and wants. The supervisor should attempt to develop an understanding of each individual's needs. Supervising people as individuals and attempting to help them satisfy their individual needs are steps toward winning over the group to which they belong.

Set a Good Example and Be Consistent

A supervisor must always remember that the members of the informal work group watch the supervisor's actions. The age-old saying "Actions speak louder than words" is very true for the supervisor. Supervisors whose behavior sets a poor example are very unlikely to get cooperation from the informal work group. Inconsistent behavior also contributes to negative behavior by the informal work group. For example, a supervisor who is demanding of one person in the group but lenient toward another person is unlikely to get support from the group.

Attempt to Provide Group Rewards

This suggestion may not be totally under the control of the supervisor. Some organizations have devised group incentive programs to help get group support. Praising the group when it deserves praise is an effective means of getting group support.

Support the Group When Possible

If the supervisor supports the informal work group in its legitimate claims to higher levels of management, the group is likely to give its support to the supervisor in return.

FIGURE 10.6
Guidelines to Promoting Positive Contributions from Informal Groups

1. Communicate openly.
2. Encourage group participation in decision making.
3. Respect the informal leader.
4. Remove production obstacles.
5. Practice constructive discipline.
6. Be sensitive to individual needs.
7. Set a good example and be consistent.
8. Attempt to provide group rewards.
9. Support the group when possible.
10. Set achievable goals for your work unit.

However, it is important not to develop a feeling among the employees that the supervisor is one of the gang and that "it is us against them." The supervisor is a member of the management team, and employees must know and respect this. Still, presenting and supporting legitimate employee concerns is a very effective way of getting support from the informal work group. The removal of performance obstacles is one area where the supervisor can effectively support employee concerns.

Set Achievable Goals for Your Work Unit

People are generally motivated to achieve a goal that they feel can be accomplished. On the other hand, if they feel they can't reach a goal, they generally can't and won't. Informal work groups behave in a similar fashion. They will not work toward unrealistic goals. Soliciting participation from the group when setting goals helps get its support in achieving goals.

Figure 10.6 summarizes these 10 guidelines for promoting positive contributions from informal work groups.

Summary

1. *Describe formal and informal work groups.* Formal work groups are established by the organizing function. Their structure and membership are established and recognized by management. Informal work groups result from personal contacts and interactions of people within the organization and are not formally recognized by the organization.

2. *Define group norms.* Group norms are the informal rules a group adopts to regulate and regularize group members' behavior.

3. *Explain group cohesiveness.* Group cohesiveness refers to the degree of attraction each member has for the group, or the stick-togetherness of the group.

4. *Define group conformity.* Group conformity is the degree to which the members of a group accept and abide by the norms of the group.

5. *Define groupthink.* Groupthink is a dysfunctional syndrome that cohesive groups experience that causes the group to lose its critical evaluative capabilities.

6. *Understand the concept of team building.* Team building is the process of establishing a cohesive group that works together to achieve its goals.

7. *Explain idiosyncrasy credit.* Idiosyncrasy credit refers to a phenomenon that occurs when certain members of a group who have made or are making significant contributions to the group's goals are allowed to take some liberties within the group.

8. *List the four phases in the life of teams.* The four phases are forming, norming, storming, and performing.

9. *Describe a quality circle.* A quality circle is composed of a group of employees (usually from 5 to 15 people) who are members of a single work unit, section, or department and whose basic purpose is to discuss quality problems and generate ideas to help improve quality.

10. *Explain self-directed work teams.* An SDWT is empowered to control the work they do without a formal supervisor.

11. *Explain virtual work teams.* A virtual work group is one in which team members work together across geographical or organizational boundaries by means of information technology.

Key Terms

Formal work groups, 179
Group, 178
Group cohesiveness, 180
Group conformity, 180
Group norms, 179

Groupthink, 181
Hawthorne effect, 182
Idiosyncrasy credit, 185
Informal work groups, 178
Quality circle, 185

Self-directed work team
    (SDWT) 186
Team building, 182
Virtual work team, 186

Review Questions

1. Describe a formal work group.
2. Describe an informal work group.
3. What is the Hawthorne effect?
4. What is a group norm?
5. What is group cohesiveness?
6. What is group conformity?
7. What are some suggestions for building group cohesiveness?
8. Outline the conditions under which individual members of a group tend to conform to group norms.
9. What is idiosyncrasy credit?
10. Explain the linking-pin concept.
11. What is team building?
12. What is a quality circle?
13. What is a self-directed work team?
14. What is a virtual work team?

Skill-Building Questions

1. Do you think it is possible to eliminate the need for informal work groups? Explain.
2. Discuss the following statement: The goals of informal work groups are never congruent with the goals of the formal organization.
3. Some employees are described as "marching to the beat of a different drummer." In light of the discussion in this chapter, what does this statement mean to you?
4. Cite one business example and one social example of what you perceive to be groupthink mentality.
5. Why do you think quality circles can be effective?

References

1. Elton Mayo, *The Human Problems of an Industrial Civilization* (Cambridge, MA: Harvard University Graduate School of Business Administration, 1946).
2. Lester Coch and John R. P. French, Jr., "Overcoming Resistance to Change," *Human Relations,* 1948, pp. 519–20.
3. Soloman Asch, "Opinions and Social Pressure," *Scientific American,* November 1955, pp. 31–34.

Additional Readings

Anonymous, "How to Get the Most out of Staff Team Building Days," *Recruiter,* November 26, 2008, p. 40.
Harmer, Janet, "Team-Building Exercises," *Caterer & Hotelkeeper,* May 7, 2008, pp. 56–57.
Leach, Linda Searle, Robert C. Myrtle, Fred A. Weaver, Sriram Dasu, "Assessing the Performance of Surgical Teams," *Care Management Review,* January–March 2009, p. 29.
Lin, Chad, Craig Standing, Ying-Chieh Liu, "A Model to Develop Effective Virtual Teams," *Decision Support Systems,* November 2008, p. 1031.
Proenca, Teresa, "Self-Managed Work Teams: a lean or an Autonomous Teamwork Model?," *International Journal of Human Resources Development and Management Review,* 2009, p. 59.

SKILL-BUILDING APPLICATIONS

Incident 10–1

One of the Gang?

Recently Ruth Brown was appointed as the supervisor of a group of employees in which she was formerly one of the rank-and-file employees. When she was selected for the job, the department head told her the former supervisor was being transferred because she could not get sufficient work out of the group. He also said the reason Ruth was selected was that she appeared to be a natural leader, she was close to the group, and she knew the tricks they were practicing to restrict output. He told Ruth he believed she could lick the problem and he would stand behind her.

He was right about Ruth knowing the tricks. When she was one of the gang, not only did she try to hamper the supervisor, but she was the ringleader in the group's efforts to make life miserable for her. None of them had anything personal against the supervisor; all of them considered it a game to pit their wits against hers. There was a set of signals to inform the employees the supervisor was coming so that everyone would appear to be working hard. As soon as she left the immediate vicinity, everyone would take it easy. Also, the employees would act dumb to get the supervisor to go into lengthy explanations and demonstrations while they stood around. They complained constantly, and without justification, about the materials and the equipment.

At lunchtime, the employees would ridicule the company, tell the latest fast one they had pulled on the supervisor, and plan new ways to harass her. All of this seemed to be a great joke. Ruth and the rest of the employees had a lot of fun at the expense of the supervisor and the company.

Now that Ruth is a supervisor, it is not so funny. She is determined to use her managerial position and knowledge to win the group over to working for the company instead of against it. She knows that if this can be done, she will have a top-notch group. The employees know their stuff, have a very good team spirit, and, if they would use their brains and efforts constructively, could turn out above-average production.

Ruth's former colleagues are rather cool to her now; but this seems natural, and she believes she can overcome it in a short time. What concerns her is that Joe James is taking over her old post as ringleader of the group, and the group is trying to play the same tricks on her that it did on the former supervisor.

Questions

1. Did the company make a good selection in Ruth? Explain.
2. What suggestions would you make to Ruth?
3. Are work groups necessarily opposed to working toward organizational goals? Explain.

Incident 10–2

Talkative Mike

Mike was an exceptionally friendly and talkative man—to the extent that he bothered his supervisor by frequently stopping the whole work crew to tell them a joke or a story. It didn't seem to bother Mike that it was during working hours or that somebody other than his crew might be watching. He just enjoyed telling stories and being the center of attention. The trouble was that the rest of the crew enjoyed him, too.

The supervisor had just recently taken over the department, and he was determined to straighten out the crew. He thought he would have no problem motivating such a friendly person as Mike. Because the crew was on a group incentive, the supervisor believed he could get them to see how much they were losing by standing around and talking. But there was no question about it: Mike was the informal leader of the crew, and they followed him just as surely as if he were the plant manager.

Mike's crew produced extremely well. When they worked—and that was most of the time—their output could not be equaled. But the frequent nonscheduled storytelling breaks did bother the supervisor. Not only could that nonproductive time be converted to badly needed production, but they also were setting a poor example for the other crews and the rest of the department.

The supervisor called Mike in to discuss the situation. His primary emphasis was on the fact that Mike's crew could make more money by better using their idle time. Mike's contention was, "What good is money if you can't enjoy it? You sweat your whole life away to rake in money, and then all you've got to show for it is a lot of miserable years and no way of knowing how to enjoy what's left. Life's too short to spend every minute trying to make more money." The discussion ended with Mike promising the group would quiet down; if their production didn't keep up, the supervisor would let him know.

Things did improve for a while; but within a week or so, the old pattern was right back where it had been. The supervisor then arranged to talk with the other members of the crew individually. Their reactions were the same as Mike's. As before, some improvements were noted at first; then the crew gradually reverted to the old habits.

Questions

1. Do you agree with Mike and his group?
2. Does the supervisor really have a complaint in light of the fact that Mike's group produces well above average?
3. If you were the supervisor, what would you do next?

Exercise 10–1

Characteristics of Effective Work Groups

You have been a member of many groups in your lifetime. Some of these groups include both formal and informal groups. Examples of such groups might include your Sunday school class, your neighborhood playmates when you were younger, your soccer or baseball team, and your co-workers at your summer job. Whether a formal or informal work group, all of us have been members of a group at some time. Some of the groups have been quite effective, and some have been quite ineffective.

Recall the most effective and the most ineffective groups of which you have been a member. Prepare a description of the characteristics of both groups. Be prepared to make a five-minute presentation of these characteristics in class.

Exercise 10–2

Crash Project

You are told that you and your work group have two weeks to implement a new program. You think two weeks are insufficient and you and your employees would have to work around the clock to complete it in that time. Morale has always been high in your group; yet you know some people just don't like overtime. As you think about how best to handle the situation, you consider these alternatives:

1. Tell your group the company is being pretty unreasonable about this: "I don't see what the big rush is. But it's got to be done, so let's all pitch in and help, shall we?"
2. Tell your group that you have told Bob Smith (your boss) you have a superb group of people: "If anyone in the company could get the job done, we could."
3. Tell the group your job is on the line: "If you want me around for a while, you will have to make a heroic effort."
4. Tell your group you don't want to hear any griping: "This is the nature of the job, and anyone who thinks he or she can't devote the extra time had better start looking for another job."
5. Tell the group the job must be done and ask them to make suggestions on how it can be completed within the deadline.

Other alternatives may be open to you, but assume these are the only ones you have considered.

Without discussion with anyone, decide which of these approaches you would take and be prepared to defend your choice.

Staffing Skills

SECTION OUTLINE

CHAPTER ELEVEN

Staffing and Training Skills

Learning objectives

After studying this chapter, you will be able to:

1. Describe the human resource planning process.
2. Define job analysis, job description, job specification, and skills inventory.
3. Describe the steps in the selection process.
4. Define tests, test validity, and test reliability.
5. Discuss the different types of employment interviews.
6. Discuss the supervisor's role in the orientation process.
7. Outline the steps in training employees in job skills.

Jane Harris knew when she took the supervisor's job that two of her employees would be leaving in approximately three months. One resigned to go back to school, and the other resigned because of a planned move to the West Coast. They were both good employees, and Jane wanted to be sure to replace them with equally qualified people. Because Jane wanted these replacements to get off to a good start once they were hired, she had recently started to think about how to train new employees. In fact, she felt that now might be a good time to give everyone in the department a short training program on claims processing.

One of the basic forms of work that a supervisor does is staffing. The **staffing function** of supervision is concerned with obtaining and developing qualified people. Since supervisors accomplish their work through the efforts of others, they find it very important to obtain good people. The major activities of the staffing function are recruiting, selecting, orienting, and training. **Recruiting** involves seeking and attracting qualified candidates for job vacancies. The purpose of **selection** is to choose the best person for the job from those candidates. **Orienting** is the process of introducing new employees to the organization, their work unit, and their jobs. **Training** involves the acquisition by employees of the skills, information, and attitudes necessary for improving their effectiveness. Supervisors may not be primarily responsible for all of the staffing activities, but they are usually involved in one or more of them. Thus, if supervisors are to be effective in the staffing function, they must understand each of these activities. The purpose of this chapter is to acquaint the supervisor with the activities and procedures of the staffing function. Supervision Illustration 11–1 describes one problem in the hiring process.

Human Resource Planning

1 LEARNING OBJECTIVES

Human resource planning (HRP) involves applying the basic planning process to the human resource needs of the organization. Once organizational plans are made and specific objectives set, the HRP process attempts to determine the human resource needs to meet the organization's objectives.

The first basic question addressed by the planning process is: Where are we now? Human resource planning frequently answers this question by using job analyses and skills inventories.

Job Analysis and Skills Inventory

2 LEARNING OBJECTIVES

Job analysis is the process of determining, through observation and study, the pertinent information relating to the nature of a specific job. Figure 11.1 is a partial job analysis form. The end products of a job analysis are a job description and a job specification. A **job description** is a written statement that identifies the tasks, duties, activities, and performance results required in a particular job. The job description should be used to develop fair and comprehensive compensation and reward systems. In addition, the accuracy of the job description can help or hinder recruiters in their efforts to attract qualified applicants for positions within the company. A **job specification** is a written statement that identifies the abilities, skills, traits, or attributes necessary for successful performance in a particular job. In general, a job specification identifies the qualifications of an individual who could perform the job. Job analyses are frequently conducted by specialists from the human resource department. However, managers should have input into the final job descriptions for the jobs they are managing. Figure 11.2 shows the relationship among job analysis, skills inventory, human resource planning, recruitment, and selection.

FIGURE 11.1
Partial Job Analysis Questionnaire

Source: From *Compensation Management,* by R. L. Henderson, pp. 148–49. © 1979. Reprinted by permission of Prentice-Hall, Inc., Upper Saddle River, NJ.

Job Analysis Information Format

Your job title _____ Code _____ Date _____

Class title _____ Department _____

Your name _____ Facility _____

Superior's title _____ Prepared by _____

Superior's name _____ Hours worked   A.M. _____   A.M. _____
                                                                                    to
                                                            P.M. _____   P.M. _____

1. What is the general purpose of your job?

2. What was your last job? If it was in another organization, please name it.

3. To what job would you normally expect to be promoted?

4. If you regularly supervise others, list them by name and job title.

5. If you supervise others, please check those activities that are part of your supervisory duties.

_____ Hiring	_____ Coaching	_____ Promoting
_____ Orienting	_____ Counseling	_____ Compensating
_____ Training	_____ Budgeting	_____ Disciplining
_____ Scheduling	_____ Directing	_____ Terminating
_____ Developing	_____ Measuring performance	_____ Other _____

6. How would you describe the successful completion and results of your work?

7. *Job Duties.* Please briefly describe WHAT you do and, if possible, HOW you do it. Indicate those duties you consider to be most important and/or most difficult.

   a. *Daily Duties*

   b. *Periodic Duties* (Please indicate whether weekly, monthly, quarterly, etc.)

   c. *Duties Performed at Irregular Intervals*

8. *Education.* Please check the blank that indicates the educational *requirements* for the job, not your *own* educational background.

   a. _____ No formal education required   e. _____ 4 year college degree
   b. _____ Less than high school diploma   f. _____ Education beyond under-
   c. _____ High school diploma or equivalent   graduate degree and/or
   d. _____ 2 year college certificate or   professional license
            equivalent

List advanced degrees or specific professional license or certificate required.

Please indicate the education you had when you were placed on this job.

Through conducting job analyses, an organization defines its current human resource needs on the basis of existing or newly created jobs. A **skills inventory** consolidates information about the organization's current human resources. The skills inventory contains basic information about each employee of the organization, giving a comprehensive picture of the individual. Through analyzing the skills inventory, the organization can assess the current quantity and quality of its human resources.

SUPERVISION ILLUSTRATION 11–1

INACCURATE RESUMES

The CEO of RadioShack was fired after it was discovered he didn't graduate from MIT. One of the chefs on a Food Network program never cooked for England's royal family. And it appears that Gazette publisher Steve Pope didn't actually help start a newspaper in Houston.

Some people lie about college degrees, others "embellish" job responsibilities and some lie about the length of time they worked at a certain place. Others inflate their former salaries, or lie about technical abilities or language fluency. And hiring experts say the tales are only growing taller—thanks in part to technology and executive profiles such as linkedin.com—and despite the increase of background checks.

"It's easier to find information to put on your resume," said John Challenger of Challenger, Gray and Christmas, a consulting firm. "And in these days of cost-cutting, companies are not doing the background checks. They think they need to cut somewhere, so they cut those."

Challenger agrees that misrepresentations can result in dismissal, and that might just be the tip of the iceberg. "Even if someone was doing a good job—when your boss finds out you've lied, it often doesn't matter," he said. "And then you have to lie at your next interview, and if they find out about that lie—it can be a vicious circle."

Source: Adapted from Amy Gillentine, "Keep Your Fingers Crossed If You Lie on Your Resume," *The Colorado Springs Business Journal*, March 6, 2009, p. 1.

Seven broad categories of information that may be included in a skills inventory are:

1. Personal data history: age, sex, marital status, etc.
2. Skills: education, job experience, training, etc.
3. Special qualifications: memberships in professional groups, special achievements, etc.
4. Salary and job history: present salary, past salary, dates of raises, various jobs held, etc.
5. Company data: benefit plan data, retirement information, seniority, etc.
6. Capacity of individual: scores on tests, health information, etc.
7. Special preferences of individual: location or job preferences, etc.

FIGURE 11.2
Relationship among Job Analysis, Human Resource Planning, Recruitment, and Selection

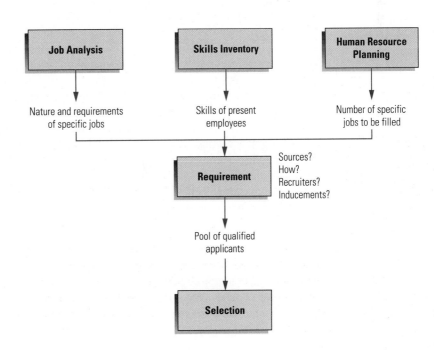

The primary advantage of a computerized skills inventory is that it offers a quick and accurate evaluation of the skills available within the organization. Combining the information provided by the job analysis and the skills inventory enables the organization to evaluate the present status of its human resources.

Specialized versions of the skills inventory can also be devised and maintained. One example would be the management inventory, which would separately evaluate the specific skills of managers such as strategy development, experiences (e.g., international experience or language skill), and successes or failures at administration or leadership.

In addition to appraising the current status of its human resources, the organization must consider anticipated changes in the current workforce due to retirements, deaths, discharges, promotions, transfers, and resignations. Certain changes in personnel can be estimated accurately and easily, whereas other changes are more difficult to forecast.

Forecasting

The second basic question the organization addresses in the planning process is: Where do we want to go? **Human resource forecasting** attempts to answer this question with regard to the organization's human resource needs. It is a process that attempts to determine the future human resource needs of the organization in light of the organization's objectives. Some of the many variables considered in forecasting human resource needs include sales projections, skills required in potential business ventures, composition of the present workforce, technological changes, and general economic conditions. Due to the critical role human resources play in attaining organizational objectives, all levels of management should be involved in the forecasting process.

Human resource forecasting is presently conducted largely on the basis of intuition; the experience and judgment of the manager are used to determine future human resource needs. This assumes all managers are aware of the future plans of the total organization. Unfortunately, this is not true in many cases.

Transition

In the final phase of human resource planning, the transition, the organization determines how it can obtain the quantity and quality of human resources it needs to meet its objectives as reflected by the human resource forecast. The human resource forecast results in a statement of what the organization's human resource needs are in light of its plans and objectives. The organization engages in several transitional activities to bring its current level of human resources in line with forecast requirements. These activities include recruiting and selecting new employees, developing current or new employees, promoting or transferring employees, laying off employees, and discharging employees. Given the current trend of downsizing in many organizations, some human resource departments now maintain a replacement chart for each employee. This confidential chart shows a diagram of each position in the management hierarchy and a list of candidates who would be qualified to replace a particular person should the need arise. Generally, the coordination of all the activities mentioned earlier is delegated to a human resource or personnel department within the organization. The staffing function is significantly influenced by government regulation, which is described in detail in Chapter 12.

Staffing from Internal and External Sources

An organization that has been doing an effective job of selecting employees has one of the best sources of supply for filling job openings: its own employees. Promotion from within is very popular with growing and dynamic organizations. If internal sources prove to be inadequate, external sources are always available. Though usually more costly and

FIGURE 11.3
Advantages and
Disadvantages of
Internal and
External Sources

Advantages	Disadvantages
Internal	
• Morale of promotee	• Inbreeding
• Better assessment of abilities	• Possible morale problems of those
• Lower cost for some jobs	not promoted
• Motivator for good performance	• Political infighting for promotions
• Causes a succession of promotions	• Need strong management-
• Have to hire only at entry level	development program
External	
• New blood bringing new perspectives	• May not select someone who will
• Cheaper and faster than training	fit the job or organization
professionals	• May cause morale problems for
• No group of political supporters in organi-	internal candidates not selected
zation already	• Longer adjustment or orientation time
• May bring industry insights	

time-consuming to pursue, external sources such as employment agencies, consulting firms, employee referrals, and employment advertisements can be valuable resources for an organization. Figure 11.3 summarizes the advantages and disadvantages of using internal and external sources for human resource needs.

With respect to internal promotions, one interesting proposition is the so-called Peter Principle. Proposed by Laurence J. Peter, the **Peter Principle** states that in a hierarchy such as a modern organization, individuals tend to rise to their levels of incompetence. In other words, people routinely get promoted in organizations and ultimately reach a level at which they are unable to perform. Organizations that maintain tight control in the human resource area, adhere to skills inventories, and conduct careful job analyses can minimize this effect.

Recruitment

Recruitment involves seeking and attracting a supply of people from which qualified candidates for job vacancies can be selected. The amount of recruitment an organization must do is determined by the difference between the forecasted human resource needs and the talent available within the organization. After the decision to recruit has been made, the sources of supply must be explored. Supervisory Illustration 11–2 describes recruitment at the University of Michigan.

Job Posting and Bidding

Job posting is the posting of notices of available jobs in central locations throughout the organization. This is done to make employees aware of job vacancies. Electronic mail (e-mail) systems and bulletin boards are used for job posting. In addition, many employers are now listing positions on the Internet. The posted notice normally gives the job title, the rate of pay for the job, and the qualifications necessary to perform the job. Interested employees contact the human resources department. After initial screening by the human resources department, qualified applicants are usually interviewed by the supervisor. In most circumstances, the final choice for the job is left up to the supervisor.

Job bidding is closely related to job posting. In **job bidding,** employees bid on a job based on seniority, job skills, or other qualifications. In unionized organizations, specific job bidding and job posting procedures are normally spelled out in the union contract.

SUPERVISION ILLUSTRATION 11–2

RECRUITMENT AT THE UNIVERSITY OF MICHIGAN

The warmth and informal vibe at times felt closer to a house party than a business conference this weekend at the annual conference sponsored by black business students at the University of Michigan—though anyone looking for a job came sharply dressed. In its 32nd year, the event came against the backdrop of race being out-lawed by voters in November 2006 as a consideration in school admission or hiring in the public sector. But the four-day conference and dozens of other events like it across the country show how committed corporations remain to diversity. The Black Business Students Association conference featured nearly two dozen

sponsors who invested thousands of dollars, plus numerous senior faculty and administrators, and some 300 current and prospective students.

While the federal government and some states including Michigan have scaled back race-specific measures aimed at leveling the playing field, corporations have plowed forward full force, partly because diversity is believed to make them more marketable and attractive to both customers and those in the workforce.

Source: Adapted from Alex P. Kellogg, "U-M. Students, Firms Come Together to Boost Diversity," the *Detroit Free Press.*

Advertising and the Internet

A widely used method of obtaining operative personnel is through the "Help Wanted" ads. The human resources department normally screens all applicants obtained from ads. Again, the supervisor interviews the most qualified applicants and normally makes the final hiring decision. Many companies now use the Internet to recruit new employees. The Internet allows a company to advertise job openings on a worldwide basis.

Employment Agencies

Some organizations recruit from state employment agencies. These agencies are operated in most cities with a population of 10,000 or more. Since individuals must register with the state employment service before receiving unemployment compensation, these agencies generally have up-to-date lists of unemployed persons. Contacts with state employment agencies are normally handled by an organization's human resources department.

Private employment agencies are sometimes used in hiring certain skilled personnel, such as computer operators and secretaries. Private agencies charge a fee for their service. Users of a private agency should know in advance the exact fees that are to be charged and how those fees are to be paid.

One advantage of using employment agencies is that the applicants may be already screened for the hiring organization. Many businesses now rely on agencies to provide temporary employees to meet seasonal demands. Businesses can thus preview the work of temporary employees and then decide if it would be beneficial to offer them a permanent position. At any rate, using temporaries enables a business to reduce labor costs because it reduces the number of full-time employees.

Colleges and Universities

Most colleges and universities have a placement office that solicits companies to come to the campus to interview students for jobs. This arrangement works well for both students and companies.

Internship and Co-Op Programs

Many firms use the Cooperative Education Departments of local colleges for recruitment of students. Under cooperative education, the student works for a business for a quarter/semester and then goes to school for a quarter/semester. Internship programs normally involve work for a student during the summer. Under both an internship and co-op program, the business can see the work of potential employees before they are hired permanently.

Employee Referrals

The present employees of an organization often become involved in the recruiting process. Recruiting through employees' referrals is normally informal and by word of mouth. For example, an employee might tell a neighbor about a job opening. One drawback to recruiting in this way is that it may lead to the formation of cliques, especially if employees recommend only their close friends and relatives.

Selecting Employees

The purpose of the selection process is to choose individuals who are most likely to succeed from those who have been recruited. Supervisors are normally directly involved in selecting employees for their departments.

Who Makes the Selection Decision?

In most large organizations, the human resources department does the initial screening of applicants, with the immediate supervisor making the final selection decision. This relieves the supervisor of the time-consuming responsibility of screening clearly unqualified applicants. It is not unusual for the supervisor to make the final selection, subject to the approval of higher levels of management.

The Selection Process

3 LEARNING OBJECTIVES

The steps used in the selection process vary from organization to organization. Figure 11.4 summarizes the general steps. These steps are not necessarily followed in full for each and every job.

Step 1: Screening from the Employment Application

A person who applies for an operative job usually completes an employment application form. Figure 11.5 shows a typical application form. Employment application forms are screened by the human resources department to eliminate unqualified people. Different forms are often used for clerical, technical, supervisory, and other major job groupings. Employment application forms should be designed so that they do not discriminate against certain groups. For example, questions about sex, age, race, religion, education, arrest record, and credit rating, which may not be job related, can result in charges of discrimination.

Step 2: Interview by Human Resources Department

After the initial screening of employment application forms, applicants are interviewed by a specialist from the human resources department. This interview is used to eliminate additional unsuitable and unqualified applicants. The interview is also used to fully

FIGURE 11.4 **Steps in the Selection Process**

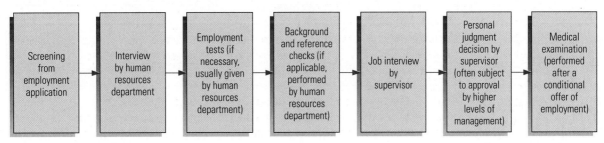

FIGURE 11.5 **A Typical Employment Application Form**

Employment application

Name	Last	First	Middle	Social security number

Local telephone		Business telephone	Other telephone

Present address		City	State	Zip code

Position desired		Are you legally eligible to work in the U.S.A.?	WPM typing	WPM shorthand

Minimum salary	Are you employed?	Notice required?	May we contact present employer?	Date available	

Education

School name	Complete address	Month/Year from	Month/Year to	Major area of study	Grade average	Graduation Date	Degree

Employment history (list current or most recent employment first)

Employer company name	Type of business	Street	Mailing address City State	Zip	From Mth/Yr	To Mth/Yr	Your position	Your supervisor	Salary	Reason for leaving

Work references

Name	Complete residence address	Business address	Telephone	Occupation	Years known

Name relatives and/or spouse employed by the XYZ company	Relationship	Where employed

Have you been convicted of a crime? (exclude minor traffic if fined $50 or less)	☐ Yes ☐ No If yes explain	Reason _____ Place _____ Date _____ Disposition _____

In case of emergency notify	Name	Phone	Address

Who referred you?	☐ Walk-in	☐ Employee referral	☐ Employment agency	☐ Newspaper ad	☐ Other

Describe additional skills, knowledge, or abilities relating to position sought

Interviewed by	I have read and understand the provisions on the reverse side of application. I certify all information given by me is correct.
	Signature _____ Date _____

XYZ Company is an equal employment opportunity organization and is an equal opportunity/affirmative action employer in compliance with TITLE VII and other civil rights laws.

explain the job and its requirements and to answer any questions that the applicant may have about the job.

Step 3: Employment Tests

Testing is a commonly used tool in medium and large organizations. It is one of the more controversial parts of the selection process because test scores are one of the most frequently used methods for predicting whether a person will perform well in a job. Of course, this prediction may or may not be correct. The law requires that there be a proven relationship between scoring high on the test and performing better on the job.

Many types of tests are used in the selection process. Among the more frequently used types are aptitude, psychomotor, job knowledge, proficiency, interest, and psychological tests. **Aptitude tests** measure a person's capacity or potential ability to learn and perform a job. **Psychomotor tests** measure a person's strength, dexterity, and coordination. **Job knowledge tests** measure the applicant's job-related knowledge. **Proficiency tests** measure how well the applicant can do a sample of the work that is to be performed. **Interest tests** are designed to determine how a person's interests compare with the interests of successful people in a specific job. **Psychological tests** measure personality characteristics.

Another type of test that can be used for screening job applicants is the polygraph test. The **polygraph,** popularly known as the lie detector, is a device that records physical changes in the body as the test subject answers a series of questions. The polygraph records fluctuations in blood pressure, respiration, and perspiration on a moving roll of graph paper. On the basis of the recorded fluctuations, the polygraph operator makes a judgment as to whether the subject's response was truthful or deceptive.

The use of a polygraph test rests on a series of cause-and-effect assumptions: stress causes certain physiological changes in the body; fear and guilt cause stress; lying causes fear and guilt. The use of a polygraph test assumes that a direct relationship exists between the subject's responses to questions and the physiological responses recorded on the polygraph. However, the polygraph itself does not detect lies; it only detects physiological changes. The operator must interpret the data that the polygraph records. Thus, the real lie detector is the operator, not the device.

Serious questions exist regarding the validity of polygraph tests. Difficulties arise if a person lies without guilt (a pathological liar) or lies believing the response to be true. Furthermore, it is hard to prove that the physiological responses recorded by the polygraph occur only because a lie has been told. In addition, some critics argue that the use of the polygraph violates fundamental principles of the Constitution: the right of privacy, the privilege against self-incrimination, and the presumption of innocence. As a result of these questions and criticisms, Congress passed the Employee Polygraph Protection Act of 1988 that severely restricts the commercial use of polygraph tests. Those exempt from this restrictive law are (1) all local, state, and federal employees (however, state laws can be passed to restrict the use of polygraphs); (2) industries with national defense or security contracts; (3) businesses with nuclear power–related contracts with the Department of Energy; and (4) businesses and consultants with access to highly classified information.

Private businesses are also allowed to use polygraphs under certain conditions: when hiring private security personnel; when hiring persons with access to drugs; and during investigations of economic injury or loss by the employer.

In the past few years there has also been a proliferation of drug-testing programs. Such programs have been instituted not only to screen job applicants but also to test current employees for drug use. It has been estimated that about 20 percent of the Fortune 500 companies have either instituted drug-testing programs or are contemplating their institution.

SUPERVISION ILLUSTRATION 11–3

BACKGROUND CHECK LEADS TO JAIL

A 28-year-old man who went to the sheriff's office in Allendale, South Carolina, for a routine job interview background check landed in jail this week when deputies found he did have a criminal history—he was wanted for an armed robbery in North Augusta, according to officials. Sherman Desheell Harley, 28, of Allendale, is charged with two driving violations and armed robbery with a deadly weapon. Allendale officials ran the background check Tuesday when Harley requested one. He was transported back to Aiken County and jailed the same day, according to investigators in North Augusta.

The 28-year-old was linked to a December 23, 2006, armed robbery at the Knox Avenue Tire Kingdom at which time two men, one armed with a handgun and the other with a shotgun, entered the store and ordered everyone to the ground, according to police documents. The incident reportedly occurred around 8 p.m. while there were several victims still in the store. The clerk told investigators at the time that one of the men ordered her to open the register and give him all the money. She said she complied with his demands, and the gunman then asked her where the rest of the money was kept. There wasn't any more money, she said, and the men left.

Source: Adapted from Karen Daily, "Routine Background Check for Job Puts Man in Jail; He's Wanted for Robbery," *Aiken Standard,* January 29, 2008.

Numerous lawsuits have been filed to contest the legality of such programs. Generally, a drug-testing program is on stronger legal ground if it is limited to job applicants. A probable cause for drug testing, such as a dramatic change in behavior or a sudden increase in accident rates, should be established before testing current employees. In addition, the results of drug testing should be protected to ensure confidentiality.

Generally, supervisors are not responsible for administering tests. These are normally administered by the human resources department. They should be used with other data on the applicant as an aid in the selection process and not as the sole deciding factor.

Step 4: Background and Reference Checks

Background and reference checks usually fall into three categories: personal, academic, and past employment. Contacting personal and academic references is generally of limited value, because few people will list someone as a reference unless they feel that that person will give them a positive recommendation. Previous employers are in the best position to supply the most objective information. However, the amount and type of information that a previous employer is willing to divulge varies. Normally, most previous employers will provide only the following information—yes or no to the question if this applicant worked there, what the employee's dates of employment were, and what position he or she held.

If a job applicant is rejected because of information in a credit report or another type of report from an outside reporting service, the applicant must be given the name and address of the organization that developed the report. The reporting service is *not* required by law to give the person a copy of his or her file, but it *must* inform the person of the nature and substance of the information. Supervision Illustration 11–3 describes the results of one background check.

Step 5: Job Interview by the Supervisor

The previous four steps in the selection process are generally conducted by the human resources department. In Step 5, the supervisor becomes actively involved in the selection process. The purpose of the job interview is to use all of the information obtained in the previous steps and determine the best person for the job.

LEARNING
OBJECTIVES

Interviews can be either structured or unstructured. In a **structured interview,** the supervisor knows in advance what questions are going to be asked, asks the questions, and records the results. Structured interviews have the advantages of providing the same information on all interviewees, ensuring that all questions are covered with all interviewees, and minimizing the personal biases of the supervisor.

Unstructured interviews have no definite checklist of questions or preplanned strategy. Such questions as "Tell me about your previous job" are asked. Much more participation by the interviewee is required in the unstructured interview.

Other types of interviewing techniques exist, but the supervisor will generally use a structured interview. The primary problem with interviews is that in an interview it is easy for the supervisor to become favorably or unfavorably impressed with the applicant for the wrong reasons.

Several common pitfalls are encountered in the interviewing process. One such pitfall is the evaluation of job applicants on the basis of personal biases. Supervisors, like all people, have such biases, but the supervisor should be careful not to let them play a role in the interviewing process. For example, the supervisor should not reject a qualified male applicant just because he has long hair.

Closely related to the pitfall of personal biases is the pitfall of the halo effect. The **halo effect** occurs when the supervisor allows a single, prominent characteristic of the interviewee to dominate judgment of all other characteristics. For instance, it is easy to ignore the other characteristics of a person who has a pleasant personality. However, merely having a pleasant personality does not necessarily mean that the person will be a good employee.

Overgeneralizing is another common pitfall. The supervisor should remember that the interviewee is under pressure during the interview and may become very nervous. Thus, the interviewee may not behave in exactly the same way on the job as during the interview.

Certain things can be done to overcome many of the pitfalls in interviewing. First, the supervisor should review all of the information that has been obtained in the previous steps of the selection process. Next, the supervisor should develop a plan for the interview. If a structured interview is to be used, the supervisor should write down all of the questions that are to be asked. The plan should include room arrangements. Privacy and some degree of comfort are important. If a private room is not available, the interview should be conducted in a place where other persons are not within hearing distance. The supervisor should also attempt to put the applicant at ease. The supervisor should *not* argue with the applicant or attempt to put the applicant on the spot. Engaging in a brief conversation about a general topic of broad interest or offering the applicant a cup of coffee can help ease the tension. The supervisor should always keep in mind, however, that the primary goal of the interview is to get information that will aid in the selection decision. Finally, notes should be taken to ensure that the facts obtained from the interview are not forgotten.

Employment interviewing is subject to legal considerations. Figure 11.6 gives a summary of some questions that can and cannot be asked in an employment review.

Step 6: Selection Decision by the Supervisor

At this point, all of the data from the previous steps in the selection process should be used. The supervisor should remember that in some cases none of the applicants may be satisfactory. The supervisor should not feel obligated to hire one of the applicants if none of them has the necessary qualifications. If this occurs, the job should be redesigned, more money should be offered to attract more qualified candidates, or some other action should be taken.

FIGURE 11.6   **Interviewing Guidelines**

Item	Prohibited Information (cannot be used to disqualify candidates)	Lawful Information (can be used to disqualify candidates)
Age	Age, birth certificate. Inquiries for the purpose of excluding persons 40 years of age and older. Inquiries as to date of graduation from college or high school to determine age.	Whether candidate meets minimum age requirements or is under 70. Requirement that candidate submit proof of age after hired. Whether candidate can meet the terms and conditions of the job in question.
Arrest record	Inquiries related to arrest.	None.
Conviction record	Inquiries regarding convictions that do not relate to performing the job under consideration.	Inquiries about actual convictions that relate reasonably to performing a particular job.
Credit rating	Inquiries concerning charge accounts, credit rating, etc., that do not relate to performing the job under consideration.	Inquiries about credit rating, charge accounts, etc., that relate reasonably to performing the job in question.
Education	Disqualification of candidate who does not have a particular degree unless employer has proven that the specific degree is the only way to measure the candidate's ability to perform the job in question.	Inquiries regarding degrees or equivalent experience. Information regarding courses relevant to a particular job.
Handicaps	General inquiries that would elicit information about handicaps or health conditions unrelated to job performance.	Whether candidate has any disabilities that would prevent him or her from performing the job. Whether there are any types of jobs for which candidate should not be considered because of a handicap or health condition.
Marital and family status	Child care problems, unwed motherhood, contraceptive practices, spouses' preferences regarding job conditions. Inquiries indicating marital status, number of children, pregnancy. Any question directly or indirectly resulting in limitation of job opportunity in any way.	Whether candidate can meet the work schedule of the job. Whether candidate has activities, responsibilities, or commitments that may hinder meeting attendance requirements. (Should be asked of candidates of both sexes.)
Military record	Discharge status, unless it is the result of a military conviction.	Type of experience and education in service as it relates to a particular job.
Name	Inquiries to determine national origin, ancestry, or prior marital status.	Whether candidate has ever worked under a different name.
National origin	Lineage, ancestry, descent, mother tongue, birthplace, citizenship. National origin of spouse or parents.	Whether candidate is legally eligible to work in the United States.
Organizations	Inquiries about membership to determine the race, color, religion, sex, national origin, or age of candidates.	Inquiries that do not elicit discriminatory information.
Race or color	Complexion, color of skin. Height or weight where it is not related to the job.	None.
Religion	Religious preference, affiliations, denomination.	Whether candidate can meet work schedules of the job with reasonable accommodation by employer if necessary.
Sex	Sex of applicant, where sex is not a bona fide occupational qualification (BFOQ).	Sex of applicant, where sex is a BFOQ (i.e., the physical characteristics of one sex are necessary to perform the job).
Work experience	None.	Candidate's previous job-related experience.

Source: Reprinted from *Boomerang II: A Management Training Program in Equal Employment Opportunity,* 1984. Used with permission from Leopold & Associates, Chicago, pp. 119–20.

Finally, the supervisor should remember that in most cases the decision to hire a person is subject to the approval of his or her own supervisor. Following the suggestions offered in this chapter should help ensure that the best person is selected and that his or her own supervisor will agree with the decision.

Step 7: Medical Examination

Many organizations require a person to take a medical examination. Medical examinations should take place after a conditional offer of employment. The medical exam is given not only to determine the person's eligibility for group life, health, and disability insurance but also to determine whether the person is physically capable of doing the job. Arrangements for the medical exam are usually handled by the human resources department.

Orienting the New Employee

 6   LEARNING OBJECTIVES

Orientation is concerned with introducing the new employee to the organization and the job. Orientation is not a one-time obligation, but an ongoing process. During the hiring process, most people learn the general aspects of the job and the organization. This usually includes such things as the job duties, working conditions, and pay.

Once the employee has been hired, the orientation program begins. Both the supervisor and the human resources department are involved in this program. In large organizations, the supervisor and the human resources department usually share the orientation responsibilities. If the organization has no human resources department, or has only a small one, the supervisor is generally responsible for conducting the orientation. Figure 11.7 summarizes the

FIGURE 11.7
Information to Be Covered in Orientation by the Supervisor If There Is No Human Resources Department

1. A welcome.
2. Objectives and philosophy of the organization.
3. An explanation of the organization's operations and levels of authority and of how these relate to each other.
4. A brief history of the organization.
5. What is expected of the new employee: attitude, reliability, initiative, emotional maturity, and personal appearance.
6. Job functions and responsibilities.
7. Introduction to the department and fellow workers.
8. General office practice and business etiquette.
9. Rules, regulations, policies, and procedures.
10. Why the organization needs the new employee.
11. City, state, and federal laws, if applicable.
12. Skill training.
13. Performance evaluation criteria.
14. Promotional opportunities.
15. Conditions of employment, punctuality, attendance, conduct, hours of work, overtime, termination.
16. Pay procedures.
17. Benefits, salary, job security, insurance, recreational facilities, employee activities, rest periods, holidays, vacation, sick leave, leave of absence, tuition refund, pension.
18. Safety and fire prevention.
19. Personnel policies.
20. Functions of management.
21. Techniques for learning.
22. Encouragement.

FIGURE 11.8
Information to Be Covered in Orientation by the Supervisor If There Is a Human Resources Department

1. Welcome the new employee.
2. Introduce the new employee to other employees in the work unit.
3. Familiarize the new employee with his or her job functions and responsibilities.
4. Explain the nature of the work and its relationship to the work of co-workers and that of the work unit as a whole.
5. Discuss policies on performance and conduct.
6. Familiarize the employee with the physical surroundings.
7. Discuss safety and fire prevention.
8. Review job performance criteria.

information that should be covered in the orientation program. Figure 11.8 shows what information is usually covered by the supervisor if a human resources department is involved.

Too many supervisors give little, if any, attention to the orientation process. A poor orientation program can quickly sour a new employee's attitude toward the job and the organization. Most people come to a new job with a positive attitude. However, if a new employee is made to feel unimportant by the lack of an orientation program, this attitude can quickly change. New employees will receive some type of orientation from either their fellow workers or the supervisor. Good, well-planned orientation programs reduce job learning time, improve attendance, and lead to better performance.

In summary, it is essential that the supervisor have a checklist of the items to be covered in the orientation. The supervisor should also provide an opportunity for questions from the new employee.

Training Employees

Training involves the acquisition of skills, concepts, rules, or attitudes by employees in order to increase their performance. The supervisor's primary role as a trainer falls in the area of **on-the-job training (OJT)** or in the area of job rotation. OJT is usually given by the supervisor or a senior employee. The employee is shown how the job is performed and then actually does it under the trainer's supervision. The major disadvantage of OJT is that the pressures of the workplace can cause the supervisor to either neglect the employee or give haphazard training. The major advantage of OJT is that the new employee is doing productive work and learning at the same time.

An old, yet still effective, system for giving OJT is the *job-instruction-training (JIT)* system. Figure 11.9 outlines the JIT system.

In **job rotation,** sometimes called **cross-training,** an employee learns several jobs and performs each job for a specific length of time. When cross-training has been given, the task of a person who is absent or leaves can be readily performed by others. Other benefits of job rotation include team building and individual skill development.

Regardless of the type of training used, there are several common pitfalls that the supervisor should avoid. Lack of reinforcement is a common error in training. An employee who is praised for doing a job correctly is likely to be motivated to do it correctly again. Too many supervisors only point out mistakes. Praise and recognition of a trainee can be a very effective means for reinforcing his or her learning. Too many supervisors tell people, "I'll let you know if you aren't doing the job right." However, people also want to know when they *are* doing the job right. Feedback about progress is critical to effective learning. Setting standards of performance for trainees and measuring their performance against the standards encourages learning.

FIGURE 11.9
Steps in the JIT System

Source: Adapted from War Manpower Commission, *The Training within Industry Report* (Washington, DC: Bureau of Training, 1945), p. 195.

Determining the Training Objectives and Preparing the Training Area

1. Decide what the trainee must be taught so that he or she can do the job efficiently, safely, economically, and intelligently.
2. Provide the right tools, equipment, supplies, and material.
3. Have the workplace properly arranged, just as the employee will be expected to keep it.

Presenting the Instruction

Step 1: Preparation of the trainee.
  A. Put the trainee at ease.
  B. Find out what the trainee already knows about the job.
  C. Get the trainee interested in and desirous of learning the job.
Step 2: Presentation of the operations and knowledge.
  A. Tell, show, illustrate, and question to put over the new knowledge and operations.
  B. Instruct slowly, clearly, completely, and patiently, one point at a time.
  C. Check, question, and repeat.
  D. Make sure the trainee understands.
Step 3: Performance tryout.
  A. Test the trainee by having him or her perform the job.
  B. Ask questions, beginning with why, how, when, or where.
  C. Observe performance, correct errors, and repeat instructions if necessary.
  D. Continue until the trainee is competent in the job.
Step 4: Follow-up.
  A. Put the trainee on his or her own.
  B. Check frequently to be sure the trainee follows instructions.
  C. Taper off extra supervision and close follow-up until the trainee is qualified to work with normal supervision.

"Practice makes perfect" definitely applies to the learning process. Too many supervisors try to explain the job quickly and then expect the trainee to do it perfectly the first time. Having trainees perform a particular job or explain how to perform a job maintains their concentration and facilitates learning. Repeating a job or task several times also helps. Learning is always helped by practice and repetition.

Frequently, supervisors have preconceived and inaccurate ideas about what certain people or groups of people can or can't do. A supervisor should realize that different people learn at different rates. Some learn rapidly and some learn slowly. The pace of the training should be adjusted to the trainee. A supervisor shouldn't expect everyone to pick the job up right away. Also, if a person is not a fast learner, this does not mean that the person will always be a poor performer. The supervisor should take the attitude that all people can learn and want to learn.

Several other methods are also used to train employees. These include vestibule training, apprenticeship training, classroom training, and programmed (or computer-assisted) instruction. Generally, the human resources department has the primary responsibility for conducting these types of training efforts. Supervisors may be asked to serve as trainers in any of these types of programs.

In **vestibule training,** the trainee uses procedures and equipment similar to those of the actual job, but located in a special area called a vestibule. Trainees are taught by skilled persons and are able to learn the job at their own speed without the pressures of production schedules. **Apprenticeship training** involves supervised training and testing for a minimum time period and until a minimum skill level has been reached. Formal **classroom training,** probably the most familiar type of training, involves lectures, movies, and exercises. Portions of orientation programs, some aspects of apprenticeship training, and safety programs are usually presented in a classroom setting. In **programmed instruction,** after material has been presented in text form, the trainee is required to read and answer questions relating to the text. A current extension of programmed instruction is **computer-assisted instruction (CAI).** Here a computer displays the material and processes the student's answers. In addition, Internet courses of instruction are available.

Steps in Training Employees in Job Skills

7 LEARNING OBJECTIVES

Supervisors are often required to train employees to perform the skills required in a particular job. Summarized next are five relatively simple steps that should be followed.

Get the Trainee Ready to Learn

The desire to learn comes from the trainee. The supervisor cannot force a person to want to learn. But the supervisor can show an interest in the person and point out why it is advantageous to learn to perform a particular job. Talk with the trainee. Find out something about her or his experience, ambitions, likes, and dislikes. Explain the importance of the job, why it will mean much to the person, and why it must be done correctly. Develop trainees' interest in wanting to learn; then they will be easy to teach.

Break Down the Work into Components and Identify the Key Points

This breakdown consists of determining the parts making up the total work. In each part, something is accomplished to advance the work toward completion. The operations breakdown can be viewed as a detailed road map that helps guide the trainee through the entire work cycle in a rational, easy-to-understand manner, without injury to the trainee or damage to the equipment.

A key point is any directive or information that helps a person perform a work component correctly, easily, and safely. Key points are the "tricks of the trade." Giving them to the trainee reduces the teaching time. Observing and mastering the key points help the trainee acquire the needed skill and perform the work effectively.

Work components and key points supply definite advantages. They clearly set forth the instruction pattern, they reduce the teaching time and simplify learning efforts, and they prevent costly errors. In addition, they foster technical improvements in the way the work is accomplished.

Demonstrate the Proper Way the Work Is to Be Done

Simply telling a person how to do a particular task is usually insufficient. You have to *tell and show.* How to perform work seems difficult when we merely hear it described—and some work is not easy to describe. Do a little at a time, pausing to point out the components and the key points. Let the trainee ask questions. Be reasonably certain that a component is fully understood before going on to the next step. However, no matter how carefully you demonstrate, the trainee may not be able to perform the work for these reasons: (1) if he was standing in front of you in order to see, he viewed the work done backwards (it is recommended that the instructor and the trainee be side by side and facing the same way); and (2) he has not physically gone through the steps.

Let the Trainee Perform the Work

The trainee is now ready to try doing the job under your guidance. At each component, let the trainee tell you what she is going to do. If she is correct, permit her to proceed. If not, correct her mistake and then permit her to proceed. Give the trainee encouragement when she is progressing correctly. Be firm in any corrective action that must take place. Be patient. Realize that mistakes will occur but that these are valuable because they reveal the

Jane has learned the steps in the job instruction training system (JIT) (p. 209). She has also learned that a supervisor should avoid several common pitfalls in order to make a new employee's training experience more meaningful. Lack of reinforcement is a common error in training. Praise and recognition can be very effective means for reinforcing a trainee's learning. Learning is always helped by practice and repetition. Finally, supervisors frequently have preconceived and inaccurate ideas about what certain people or groups of people can or can't do. Such ideas can either help or hinder a trainee's development. Jane has also learned the steps in training employees to perform job skills (pp. 210–211). She should incorporate these steps into all of the training she does.

trainee's learning difficulties and where the trainee hasn't learned. By letting the trainee perform the work, not only do you find out quickly what the trainee has learned and gain an insight into her ability to perform the work, but you also give the trainee some sense of satisfaction of accomplishment.

Put Trainees on Their Own Gradually

When you are reasonably sure that trainees can do the work, let them go ahead without you. But return periodically—perhaps four times the first day—to answer any questions and to see if all is going well. Above all, don't turn trainees loose and forget them. A trainee is going to have important questions, and he or she will feel better knowing that you are around to help and that you have an interest in the progress made.

Summary

This chapter describes the supervisor's role in recruiting, selecting, and training employees. It also presents specific information on orienting and training employees.

1. *Describe the human resource planning process.* Human resource planning (HRP) involves applying the basic planning process to the human resource needs of the organization, in order to determine the best way to meet the organization's objectives.

2. *Define job analysis, job description, job specification, and skills inventory.* Job analysis involves determining the pertinent information relating to the performance of a specific job. A job description is a written portrayal of a job and the types of work required by the job. A job specification gives the qualifications necessary to perform the job. A skills inventory consolidates information about the organization's current human resources.

3. *Describe the steps in the selection process.* Basically, there are seven steps in the selection process. These steps are not necessarily followed in full for each and every job. The seven steps are: screening from the employment application, interview by human resources department, employment tests, background and reference checks, job interview by the supervisor, selection decision by the supervisor, and a medical examination.

4. *Define tests, test validity, and test reliability.* Tests provide a sample of behavior used to draw inferences about the future behavior or performance of an individual. Test validity refers to the extent to which a test predicts a specific criterion. Test reliability refers to the consistency or reproducibility of the results of a test.

5. *Discuss the different types of employment interviews.* Interviews can be either structured or unstructured. In a structured interview, the supervisor knows what questions are going to be asked, asks the questions, and records the results. Unstructured interviews have no checklist of questions or preplanned strategy.

6. *Discuss the supervisor's role in the orientation process.* Orientation is concerned with introducing the new employee to the organization and the job. In large organizations, the supervisor and the human resources department usually share the orientation responsibilities. If the organization has no human resources department, or has only a small one, the supervisor is generally responsible for conducting the orientation.

7. *Outline the steps in training employees in job skills.* The five steps in training employees in physical skills are: get the trainees ready to learn, break down the work into components and identify the key points, demonstrate the proper way the work is to be done, let the trainees perform the work, and put the trainees on their own gradually.

Key Terms

Apprenticeship training, 209
Aptitude test, 203
Classroom training, 209
Computer-assisted instruction (CIA), 210
Cross-training, 208
Employment agencies, 200
Employment tests, 203
Halo effect, 205
Human resource forecasting, 198
Human resource planning (HRP), 195
Interest test, 203

Job analysis, 195
Job bidding, 199
Job description, 195
Job knowledge test, 203
Job posting, 199
Job rotation, 208
Job specification, 195
On-the-job training (OJT), 208
Orienting, 195
Orientation, 207
Peter Principle, 199
Polygraph, 203
Proficiency test, 203

Programmed instruction, 210
Psychological test, 203
Psychomotor test, 203
Recruiting, 195
Recruitment, 199
Reference checks, 204
Selection, 195
Skills inventory, 196
Staffing function, 195
Structured interviews, 205
Training, 195, 208
Unstructured interviews, 205
Vestibule training, 209

Review Questions

1. Define the following terms:
   a. Recruiting.
   b. Selection.
   c. Orienting.
   d. Training.
2. What is a job analysis? What role does it play in recruiting and selecting employees?
3. What are four methods of recruiting?
4. Who usually makes the final selection decision for operative employees?
5. What are the seven steps in the selection process?
6. Outline some of the information that should be covered in an employee orientation program.
7. Give several tips that can help a supervisor in training employees.

Skill-Building Questions

1. "The best way to train employees is to put them on the job immediately and let them learn from their mistakes." Discuss your views on this statement.
2. "A company should be able to hire whomever it wants, without government intervention." Discuss how you feel about this.
3. What are some questions you would ask a job applicant in a structured job interview?
4. "Some people just don't want to learn anything new." Discuss.

Additional Readings

Anonymous, "States Consider Drug Testing for Welfare Recipients," *Alcoholism & Drug Abuse Weekly,* February 23, 2009, p. 4.

Anonymous, "Validate Hiring Tests to Withstand EEO Scrutiny: DOT & EEOC Officials" *HR Focus,* May 2008, pp. 8–9.

Cohen, Steve M, "Reference Checking: How to Avoid Liability," *JCK,* May 2008, p. 330.

Davidson, Joe, "A Hiring Process in Need of Major Repair," *The Washington Post,* March 5, 2009, p. D-3.

Marino, Jennifer, "Baseball Blues," *Scholastic News (Edition 5/6)* March 9, 2009, p. 6.

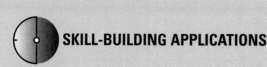

SKILL-BUILDING APPLICATIONS

Incident 11–1

Hiring a New Employee

John Arrington went to a meeting of all the supervisors in his company. The purpose of the meeting was to outline the company's new recruitment and selection program. John didn't pay much attention through most of the meeting because, as a supervisor, he had never really been involved in this process. The human resources department had always sent him his new employees.

However, about three-fourths of the way through the meeting, Tom Jackson, the human resources director, stated that one significant change in the new policy was that supervisors would now interview each job applicant. The human resources department would continue to screen applicants and would send five qualified people for any job opening in the supervisor's department. The supervisor would then interview each person in depth and make a recommendation to the human resources department. In fact, the supervisor would be required to rank the people from 1 to 5 (1 being the first choice for hiring and 5 being the last choice). Tom said that in most cases the human resources department would hire the supervisor's first choice. He explained that the change was being made because in the past supervisors had complained about not having enough input into who was hired in their departments.

John recognized what this change meant for him. He had two job openings in his department that needed filling immediately.

Questions

1. How can John prepare himself for his new responsibilities?
2. What do you think of the company's new procedure?
3. What problems might arise under the new procedure?

Incident 11–2

Lake Avionics

Sandra Hall is a new employee in the assembly department of Lake Avionics. On the day she started, Ken Williams, her supervisor, took her around and introduced her to all of the 28 employees in the department.

He then took her to his office and handed her the following documents: company policy and procedures manual, a booklet on company fringe benefits, a booklet describing the company's products, and a copy of the assembly department's work rules. He told Sandra to read over the documents and said that he would be back in two hours to answer any questions she might have.

When Ken came back, Sandra told him that she had no questions about the documents he had given her. Ken then took Sandra back to the assembly area and discussed her job with her. He explained that her job required her to perform about 20 different operations. His description lasted about 10 minutes. Ken then told Sandra that he would be tied up for the rest of the day and that Greg Larson, a 15-year employee, would go over the details of the job with her.

Greg assured Sandra that she could do the work and told her to just watch him for the rest of the morning. After lunch, Greg told Sandra to try her hand at doing the job. However, she became confused about how the parts were assembled and asked Greg to show her again. Greg said, "You'll just have to learn the hard way. That's the way I did it. Learn from your mistakes."

By the late afternoon Sandra was thoroughly demoralized. She just didn't seem to be getting the hang of the assembly operation. Shortly before quitting time, Greg came by and said, "Don't get down on yourself. Now you have learned the wrong way to do it. Tomorrow morning, I'll show you some short cuts that will make the job much easier."

Questions

1. What do you think of Sandra's training program?
2. How do you think Sandra feels about her new job?

Exercise 11–1

The Layoff

Two years ago, your organization experienced a sudden increase in its volume of work. At about the same time, it was threatened with an equal employment opportunity suit that resulted in an affirmative action plan. Under this plan, additional women and minority members have been recruited and hired.

Presently, the top level of management in your organization is anticipating a decrease in volume of work.

You have been asked to rank the clerical employees of your section in the event a layoff is necessary.

Below you will find biographical data for the seven clerical people in your section. Rank the seven people according to the order in which they should be laid off, that is, the person ranked first is to be laid off first, and so forth.

Burt Green: White male, age 45. Married, four children; five years with the organization. Reputed to be an alcoholic; poor work record.

Nan Nushka: White female, age 26. Married, no children, husband has a steady job; six months with the organization. Hired after the affirmative action plan went into effect; average work record to date. Saving to buy a house.

Johnny Jones: Black male, age 20. Unmarried; one year with organization. High performance ratings. Reputed to be shy—a "loner"; wants to start his own business some day.

Joe Jefferson: White male, age 24. Married, no children but wife is pregnant; three years with organization. Going to college at night; erratic performance attributed to work/study conflicts.

Livonia Long: Black female, age 49. Widow, three grown children; two years with the organization. Steady worker whose performance is average.

Ward Watt: White male, age 30. Recently divorced, one child; three years with the organization. Good worker.

Rosa Sanchez: Hispanic female, age 45. Six children, husband disabled one year ago; trying to help support her family; three months with the organization. No performance appraisal data available.

1. What criteria did you use for ranking the employees?
2. What implications does your ranking have in the area of affirmative action?

Exercise 11–2

OJT

Assume that you are the training supervisor of a large, local retail company. The company has seven department stores in your city. One of your biggest problems is adequately training new salesclerks. Because salesclerks represent your company to the public, the manner in which they conduct themselves is highly important. Especially critical aspects of their job include knowledge of the computerized cash register system, interaction with the customers, and knowledge of the particular products being sold.

1. Design a three-day orientation/training program for new salesclerks. Be sure to outline the specific topics (subjects) to be covered and the techniques to be used.
2. Specify what methods could be used to evaluate the success of the program.

CHAPTER TWELVE

Understanding Equal Employment Opportunity

Learning objectives

After studying this chapter, you will be able to:

1. Define protected groups.
2. Describe antidiscrimination laws that affect organizations.
3. Identify the major federal enforcement agencies for equal employment opportunity.
4. Define employment parity, occupational parity, and systemic discrimination.
5. Define affirmative action.
6. Define sexual harassment.

Supervision Dilemma

Jane Harris has just attended a brief orientation program given by the human resources department on her company's affirmative action program. Jane knew that this program had been the source of a great deal of controversy, especially among the senior employees. In fact, Jane had already been questioned about the program by some of her employees.

The orientation program made Jane much more aware of her responsibilities under the program. However, she felt that she needed additional information if she was going to give the program more than lip service.

A heightened awareness of equality issues and concerns has brought about sweeping antidiscrimination laws affecting organizations. All levels of management have been affected by these laws. The supervisor, however, probably has the greatest potential for violating them. Thus, it is crucial for supervisors to stay abreast of antidiscrimination laws. The supervisor is involved, directly or indirectly, in most of the decisions affected by antidiscrimination laws. These decisions concern hiring, job assignments, wages and salaries, performance evaluations, promotions, layoffs, recalls, discipline, and discharges. Laws prohibiting discrimination are not entirely new. The Civil Rights Acts of 1866 and 1870 and the Equal Protection Clause of the 14th Amendment were early laws that prohibited discrimination. However, enforcement of these and other antidiscrimination laws within organizations is much more recent. In addition, the laws are constantly changing, so it becomes more essential that the supervisor find ways to stay current.

What Are Protected Groups?

Usually, a discussion of discrimination assumes that women and African Americans are the groups that have been affected by discrimination. Although women and African Americans do constitute the two largest groups that discrimination has affected, they are by no means the only groups. Other, less obvious forms of discrimination have also occurred. Some supervisors have made decisions based on assumptions about such groups as short people, overweight people, singles, young married women of childbearing age, people without children, and people without cars. However, it is no longer legal to use most non-job-related factors for making decisions affecting people in organizations.

LEARNING OBJECTIVES

For the purposes of this chapter, race, color, sex, age, religion, national origin, and mental and physical handicaps identify the classifications of people that are called **protected groups.** A person's classification into a group by one of these characteristics means that he or she is protected from discrimination in organizations. For example, a supervisor cannot refuse to give an employee a particular job assignment just because the person happens to fall into one of these classifications. The assignment of jobs must be determined by ability to do or learn to do the job and must not be influenced by sex, race, or any other non-job-related factor.

Effects of Discrimination

Most people are aware of the effects of discrimination. Examining the make-up of employees of most large organizations generally shows the results of past discrimination. The jobs with authority are held primarily by white males. This is not the result of discrimination only; it is also the result of past inequalities in education.

The primary legislation controlling equal employment opportunity was enacted during the 1960s and early 1970s. That employment discrimination still exists is shown by statistics on unemployment, underemployment, and incomes. For example, women (who are the largest protected group) continue to be employed primarily in the same industries as they have been in the past: service industries, wholesale and retail trade, and the public service sector. The gap between the incomes of women and men who work full-time continues to be large—and it is widening. Furthermore, even though the situation has been changing, the percentage of African Americans and Hispanics in supervisory and management positions is still relatively small.

Antidiscrimination Laws That Affect Organizations

2 LEARNING OBJECTIVES

Many antidiscrimination laws affect organizations. The number of employees and the amount of business that the organization does with the federal government determine which of these laws affect the organization. The following paragraphs provide a brief description of the most important laws and court orders dealing with discrimination.

Title VII of the Civil Rights Act of 1964

Title VII of the Civil Rights Act of 1964, as amended by the Equal Employment Opportunity Act of 1972, has been the source of the greatest number of complaints concerning discrimination. This law prohibits discrimination based on race, color, religion, sex, or national origin in any term, condition, or privilege of employment. This law applies to all private employers of 15 or more people, all public and private educational institutions, all state and local governments, all public and private employment agencies, labor unions with 15 or more members, and joint labor-management committees for apprenticeships and training. This law established and gave the Equal Employment Opportunity Commission (EEOC) the power (1) to investigate job discrimination complaints, (2) to mediate an agreement between the parties to eliminate discrimination when such a complaint is found to be justified, and (3) to take court action to enforce the law when necessary.

Title VI

Title VI of the 1964 Civil Rights Act prohibits discrimination based on race, color, or national origin in all programs or activities that receive federal financial aid in order to provide employment. Although this law does not prohibit sex discrimination, some federal agencies prohibit sex discrimination by their own regulations.

Equal Pay Act

The **Equal Pay Act** was passed in 1963 and was later amended by Title IX of the Education Amendments Act of 1972. This law requires that all employers covered by the Fair Labor Standards Act (and others included in the 1972 extension) provide equal pay to men and women who perform work that is similar in skill, effort, and responsibility. In general, the Fair Labor Standards Act applies to individuals employed in interstate commerce or in organizations producing goods for interstate commerce and covers base pay as well as opportunities for overtime, raises, bonuses, commissions, and other benefits. The employer is also responsible for ensuring that all fringe benefits be equally available to all employees. Offering and paying higher wages to women and minorities in order to attract these groups are also illegal. Under this law, the only justification for paying a man more than a woman for doing the same job is differences in levels of seniority, responsibility, or skill.

Education Amendments Act

Title IX of the **Education Amendments Act** of 1972 extended coverage of the Equal Pay Act of 1963. Title IX prohibits gender discrimination against the employees or students of any educational institution receiving financial aid from the federal government.

SUPERVISION ILLUSTRATION   12–1

AGE DISCRIMINATION: YES OR NO?

Like many college students, Wanda Thomas dreams of finishing school and opening her own business. Because of her age, she'd like to get it done soon. The 68-year-old has been attending Wright College on the city's Northwest Side for several years and has almost completed her certificate in accounting. But the college's policy for senior citizens, she said, is holding her back.

Because of her age, the Chicagoan is eligible for six free hours of classes each semester at Wright. In the spring and summer semesters this year, Thomas used those six hours, then paid for additional classes to speed up her education. But when she tried to register for three classes in the fall, she was told her limit was six hours. Thomas said she asked Wright officials why she couldn't pay for additional classes,

as she had done in the past, and was told the college's policy did not allow it.

"Wright College administrators verify that Ms. Thomas, contrary to the above policy, was allowed to register for more than six hours and still receive the tuition waiver for the spring and summer 2008 semester," Dunn said. "This was an error on the part of the business service representative who apparently was not conversant with the academic policy." Dunn said the college correctly denied Thomas's request to take additional courses in the fall. But because Thomas was given conflicting information over the past year, Wright College administrators will allow her to register for additional classes in the spring.

Source: Adapted from Jon Yates, "Chicago Tribune What's Your Problem? Column: Promising Student Gets Held Back," *McClatchy—Tribune Business News,* December 23, 2008, Wire Feed.

Age Discrimination in Employment Act	The **Age Discrimination in Employment Act** was enacted in 1967 and amended in 1978. This law prohibits discrimination against people 40 years of age and older in any area of employment. This law applies to employers of 20 or more people. The law prohibits using age as a factor for making employment decisions. Supervision Illustration 12–1 describes an age discrimination case.
Affirmative Action	Executive Order 11246 was issued in 1965 and amended by Executive Order 11375 in 1967. The order requires federal contractors and subcontractors to have affirmative action programs. The purpose of these programs is to increase employment opportunities for women and minorities in all areas of employment. The order further requires that employers with federal contracts or subcontracts of $50,000 or more and 50 or more employees develop and implement written affirmative action programs. These programs are monitored by the **Office of Federal Contract Compliance (OFCC)** of the U.S. Department of Labor.
Veterans Readjustment Act	The Vietnam-Era **Veterans Readjustment Act** of 1974 requires that federal government contractors and subcontractors take affirmative action to hire and promote Vietnam veterans and disabled veterans. Such contractors and subcontractors with contracts of $10,000 or more must list all suitable job openings with state employment services. Such contractors and subcontractors with contracts of $50,000 or more and 50 or more employees are required to have written affirmative action programs for Vietnam veterans and disabled veterans.
Rehabilitation Act of 1973	The Rehabilitation Act of 1973, which was amended in 1977, prohibits employers from denying jobs to individuals merely because of a handicap. The law defines a handicapped person as one who has a physical or mental impairment that significantly limits one or more major life activities. This law applies to government contractors and subcontractors with contracts in excess of $2,500. The act requires contractors to make reasonable and necessary accommodations to enable qualified handicapped people to work as effectively as other employees.

Americans with Disabilities Act (ADA)

In May 1990, Congress approved the **Americans with Disabilities Act (ADA),** which gives the disabled sharply increased access to services and jobs. Under this law, employers may not:

- Discriminate in hiring and firing against persons qualified for a job.
- Inquire whether an applicant has a disability, but may ask about ability to perform a job.
- Limit advancement opportunity.
- Use tests or job requirements that tend to screen out the disabled.
- Participate in contractual arrangements that discriminate against the disabled.

The ADA obligates employers to provide *reasonable accommodation* to disabled employees as a means of enabling those employees to perform essential job duties. However, the ADA failed to define exactly what reasonable accommodation means. The ADA offers the following examples of what the terms may include:

Making existing facilities used by employees readily accessible to and usable by individuals with disabilities.

Acquisition of equipment and devices.

Reassignment to a vacant position.

Job restructuring, part-time or modified work schedules.

Appropriate adjustment or modifications of examinations, training materials, or policies.

Provision of qualified readers or interpreters.

Other similar accommodations for individuals with disabilities.

It is important to note that employers do not have to provide accommodations that impose an undue hardship in business operations. Thus, the application of ADA is strongly influenced by court decisions.

Civil Rights Act of 1991

The **Civil Rights Act of 1991** permits women, minorities, persons with disabilities, and persons belonging to religious minorities to have a jury trial and sue for punitive damages of up to $300,000 if they can prove that they are victims of intentional hiring or workplace discrimination. The law covers all employers with 15 or more employees. Prior to the passage of this law, jury trials and punitive damages were not permitted except in intentional discrimination lawsuits involving racial discrimination. The law places a cap on the amount of damages a victim of nonracial, intentional discrimination can collect. The cap is based on the size of the employer: $50,000 for companies with 15 to 100 employees; $100,000 for companies with 101 to 200 employees; $200,000 for companies with 201 to 500 employees; and $300,000 for companies with more than 500 employees.

A second aspect of this act was concerned with the burden of proof for companies with regard to intentional discrimination lawsuits. In a series of Supreme Court decisions beginning in 1989, the Court began to ease the burden-of-proof requirements on companies. Several of these decisions are described later in this chapter. This act, however, requires that companies must provide evidence that the business practice that led to the discrimination was not discriminatory but was job-related for the position in question and consistent with business necessity.

Family and Medical Leave Act (1993)

The **Family and Medical Leave Act (FMLA)** was enacted on February 5, 1993, to enable qualified employees to take prolonged unpaid leave for family- and health-related reasons without fear of losing their jobs. Under the law, employees can use this leave if they are seriously ill, if an immediate family member is ill, or in the event of the birth, adoption, or

SUPERVISION ILLUSTRATION 12–2

SEXUAL ORIENTATION DISCRIMINATION

Two hours south of San Francisco in the agricultural hub of Saunas, Calif., a Mexican immigrant worked as a foreman in a produce packing plant, supervising nearly 100 people for eight to 10 hours a day, sometimes seven days a week. In three years on the job, there were never any problems with coworkers or the boss—until the foreman began transitioning to be a woman. "After I started taking the hormones and dressing like a woman," Sandra says in Spanish via a translator, "I started being treated differently."

Her salaried pay was decreased to an hourly rate, and she suffered almost constant verbal abuse. Her boyfriend, who worked at the same plant, was beaten so viciously, he needed to take sick leave for three days. Yet instead of the attacker being fired, Sandra was demoted from her supervisory job. "I knew they were discriminating against me for who I was," she says. "And they continued to put pressure on

me that made my life very difficult." So Sandra fought back. She and her boyfriend found an attorney, sued their employer, and eventually won a settlement out of court.

Proyecto Poderoso, cosponsored by California Rural Legal Assistance (CRLA) and the National Center for Lesbian Rights, is one of the first outreach programs of its kind in the United States. Started in September 2007 with a grant from Pride Law Fund's Tom Steel Fellowship, the project was conceived after attorneys for CRLA noticed an increasing number of cases involving sexual orientation discrimination and harassment, particularly in Saunas, a magnet for Latino farmworkers. CRLA has 21 law offices throughout the state and provides free legal services to low-income people, many of whom are Spanish-speaking.

Source: Adapted from Patrick Range McDonald, "Field of Dreams," *The Advocate,* April 22, 2008, Wire Feed.

placement for foster care of a child. To qualify for the leave, employees must have been employed for at least a year and must have worked for no less than 1,250 hours within the previous 12-month period. FMLA took effect in August 1993 for companies without collective bargaining agreements. For companies with collective bargaining agreements, the law took effect on termination of the labor contract or on February 5, 1994, whichever came first.

Other Anti-discrimination Legislation

Discrimination in employment has also been prohibited by court rulings under the Civil Rights Acts of 1866 and 1870 and the Equal Protection Clause of the 14th Amendment. Discrimination because of race, religion, and national origin has also been found to violate rights guaranteed by the National Labor Relations Act. Many state and local government laws prohibit employment discrimination. Discrimination by an employer may lead to court action under any one or more of the laws and executive orders mentioned above. Supervision Illustration 12–2 shows one case that led to court action.

Figure 12.1 provides a summary of all significant equal employment opportunity laws and executive orders related to equal employment opportunity. Executive orders are issued by the president of the United States to give direction to governmental agencies.

Enforcement Agencies

 3 LEARNING OBJECTIVES

There are two major federal enforcement agencies for equal employment opportunity. These are the **Equal Employment Opportunity Commission (EEOC)** and the **Office of Federal Contract Compliance (OFCC)**. In the past, enforcement activities were conducted by many agencies. The trend has been toward consolidation of these activities. It is probable that more consolidation will occur in the future, perhaps with one agency performing all enforcement activities.

FIGURE 12.1 Summary of Equal Opportunity Laws and Executive Orders

Laws	Year	Intent	Coverage
Equal Pay Act	1963	Prohibits sex-based discrimination in rates of pay for men and women working in same or similar jobs.	Private employers engaged in commerce or in the production of goods for commerce and with two or more employees; labor organizations.
Title VII, Civil Rights Act (as amended in 1972)	1964	Prohibits discrimination based on race, sex, color, religion, or national origin.	Private employers with 15 or more employees for 20 or more weeks per year, educational institutions, state and local governments, employment agencies, labor unions, and joint labor-management committees.
Executive Order 11246	1965	Prohibits discrimination on the basis of race, sex, color, religion, or national origin; requires affirmative action regarding these factors.	Federal contractors and subcontractors with contracts in excess of $10,000. Employers with 50 or more employees.
Executive Order 11375	1967	Prohibits sex-based wage discrimination.	Government contractors and subcontractors.
Executive Order 11478	1967	Superseded Executive Order 11246 and modified some of the procedures under the previous orders and regulations.	
Age Discrimination in Employment Act (ADEA)	1967	Prohibits discrimination against individuals who are 40 years of age and older.	Private employers with 20 or more employees for 20 or more weeks per year, labor organizations, employment agencies, state and local governments, and federal agencies with some exceptions.
Rehabilitation Act, as amended	1973	Prohibits discrimination against the handicapped and requires affirmative action to provide employment opportunity for the handicapped.	Federal contractors and subcontractors with contracts in excess of $2,500, organizations receiving federal financial assistance, and federal agencies.
Vietnam-Era Veterans Readjustment Assistance Act	1974	Prohibits discrimination in hiring disabled veterans with 30 percent or more disability rating, veterans discharged or released for a service-connected disability, and veterans on active duty between August 4, 1964, and May 7, 1975. Also requires of certain employers written affirmative action plans.	Federal contractors and subcontractors with contracts in excess of $10,000. Employers with 50 or more employees and contracts in excess of $50,000 must have written affirmative action plans.
Pregnancy Discrimination Act (PDA)	1978	Requires employers to treat pregnancy like any other medical condition with regard to fringe benefits and leave policies.	
Immigration Reform and Control Act	1986	Prohibits hiring of illegal aliens.	Any individual or company.
Americans with Disabilities Act	1990	Increases access to services and jobs for disabled.	Private employers with 15 or more employees.
Civil Rights Act	1991	Reversed several Supreme Court decisions and allows juries to award punitive damages for job bias related to sex, religion, or disability.	Private employers with 15 or more employees; employees of U.S. Senate; employees of the White House; high-ranking state and local government employees.
Family and Medical Leave Act (FMLA)	1993	Enables qualified employees to take prolonged unpaid leave for family and health-related reasons without fear of losing their jobs	Private employers with 50 or more employees.
ADA Amendments Act	2008	Strengthened the ADEA	Same as ADEA

Interpretation and Application of Title VII and Affirmative Action

Knowing the laws and executive orders covering antidiscrimination helps avoid court actions. However, the intricacies of the laws and various interpretations by the courts may confuse even the best-intentioned person. It is impossible to discuss in this chapter all the details, interpretations, and exceptions affecting employers with regard to these laws. In fact, new interpretations are still emerging. However, some of the more important details are discussed in the following paragraphs.

Title VII of the Civil Rights Act of 1964

Title VII of the Civil Rights Act has probably been more fully interpreted by the courts than any of the other antidiscrimination laws. The courts have decided that whether the employer *intended* to discriminate is not an important factor. They have decided that employment practices denying opportunities to persons protected by Title VII are illegal no matter what the employer's intent. For instance, an employer who requires a college degree for a certain job may be required to show that the college degree is both job-related and an accurate predictor of success in the job. This is because requiring a college degree may have an adverse impact on certain groups (such as women and African Americans) protected by Title VII.

There are very few exceptions to Title VII. As has been discussed, nearly all organizations are covered to some degree by antidiscrimination laws. For years after the Civil Rights Act was passed, employers were still trying to get the courts to uphold traditional employment practices. One of the more notable cases was the airlines' demand that due to customer preference, flight attendants be female and fall within a certain weight range. The courts have not upheld these restrictions. As is apparent, there are now male flight attendants as well as less rigid weight requirements. Nearly every industry has been affected by Title VII and subsequent court rulings. Jobs have opened up to women and minorities and even to men that 20 years ago would have been off-limits.

The few exceptions to Title VII that do exist have been interpreted very narrowly by the courts. It is difficult to justify discrimination by business necessity, as allowed by the law. The employer must prove that the discrimination is essential to the safety, efficiency, and operation of the business and that no alternatives exist. State laws that may have contributed to discriminatory practices in the past have also been ruled by the courts to be superseded by Title VII. Title VII allows for sex discrimination only where sex is a bona fide occupational qualification (BFOQ). This exception has been very narrowly interpreted by the courts, which have limited its application to persons such as actors, models, rest room attendants, and security guards in a maximum-security prison. Title VII does not provide for the use of race or color as a BFOQ. Age may be considered a BFOQ where there is concrete evidence that it is a job-related factor and a business necessity. Age may be a BFOQ where public safety is involved, as with airline pilots or interstate bus drivers.

Another exception to Title VII is discrimination based on a bona fide seniority or merit system. Not all seniority and merit systems qualify under this exception. Seniority or merit systems that exclude protected groups from benefits are not valid exceptions. Seniority or merit systems that perpetuate past discriminatory practices are illegal. This is true even if there is no present discriminatory intent or practice.

Contractual agreements between the union and the employer are not legal or binding if they violate antidiscrimination laws. Clauses that limit certain jobs to one group or pay one group more for equal work are not binding. Contract negotiations must be opened as soon as this type of discrimination is discovered.

Two methods can be used by the EEOC to determine whether discrimination against a protected group has occurred. These methods are called (1) employment parity and (2) occupational parity. **Employment parity** exists when the proportion of protected employees employed by an organization equals the proportion in the organization's relevant labor market. **Occupational parity** exists when the proportion of protected employees employed in various occupations in the organization is equal to their proportion in the organization's relevant labor market. Large differences in either occupational or employment parity are called **systemic discrimination.** When systemic discrimination exists, the employer is usually required to engage in affirmative action.

History of Affirmative Action Programs

Of all the requirements concerned with discrimination, affirmative action programs are by far the most controversial. Affirmative action programs are required of certain federal contractors and subcontractors and may also be required of employers who have been found to have engaged in discriminatory hiring practices or systemic discrimination. Some employers and individuals mistakenly refer to equal employment opportunity as affirmative action. The elimination of hiring practices that have an adverse impact on protected groups is not affirmative action. **Affirmative action** refers to an employer's attempt to balance its workforce in all job categories with respect to sex and race in order to reflect the same proportions as those of its general labor market. Under an affirmative action plan, an employer prepares goals and timetables for the achievement of a balanced representation. When minorities and women achieve employment and occupational parity in organizations, affirmative action programs will no longer be necessary.

Affirmative action has resulted in several discrimination suits. The first real test case in this area was the Bakke case of 1978. Allan Bakke, a white male, brought suit against the medical school of the University of California at Davis. Bakke charged that he had been unconstitutionally discriminated against when he was denied admission to the medical school while some minority applicants with lower qualifications were accepted. The Supreme Court ruled in Bakke's favor but at the same time upheld the constitutionality of affirmative action programs.

In 1984, in a case involving Memphis, Tennessee, and its fire department, the Supreme Court ruled that the fire department could not insulate African Americans from layoffs and demotions under its affirmative action plan. The ruling indicated that when hard economic times hit and layoffs were necessary, employers could not be forced to scrap seniority plans favoring white men in order to protect "affirmative action" gains by minorities and women.

During the latter part of the 1980s, the Supreme Court rendered several decisions viewed by some advocates as being negative toward affirmative action programs. In *City of Richmond* v. *J. A. Crosan Company,* the Court ruled in 1989 that state and local governments must avoid racial quotas and must take affirmative action steps only to correct well-documented examples of past discrimination. Also, in 1989, the Court ruled in *Wards Cove* v. *Atonio* that employers can use evidence of a legitimate reason for a business practice as defense against statistics showing minorities were victims of discrimination. In *Martin* v. *Wilks,* the Court also ruled in 1989 that white employees could bring reverse-discrimination claims against court-approved affirmative action plans. It is interesting to note that the Civil Rights Act of 1991 reversed both of these Supreme Court decisions.

Most affirmative action programs concentrate on racial and ethnic minorities and women. Religious and national origin minorities have not benefited nearly as much from such programs. As more organizations representing these minorities press for changes, employers may be forced to develop affirmative action programs for these groups.

Quotas for hiring minorities and women are not required by law. However, written goals are required under affirmative action guidelines. Opponents of affirmative action programs feel that written numerical goals force inflexible, unreasonable demands on employers. They also feel that as a result of such goals, employers strive for a numerical result rather than the primary goal of equal employment opportunity. Proponents of affirmative action, however, argue that written affirmative action goals are like any other organizational goal to which quantitative measures are applied. Only when an employer consistently fails to reach its goals or when there is evidence that the employer has not acted in good faith will the enforcement agency step in to impose goals. By striving to eliminate discrimination within the organization, management can usually avoid court action and costly penalties.

It is important to note at this point that there is a significant difference between equal employment opportunity and affirmative action programs. Equal employment opportunity laws were enacted and remain in existence to prevent discrimination in the workplace. On the other hand, affirmative action's focus is to provide current opportunities to those members of groups who were previously denied access to employment and its concomitant training and development programs. Thus, equal employment opportunity laws are legal requirements and must be followed by a business organization. On the other hand, affirmative action programs can be voluntary or involuntary depending on the company's dealings with the federal government. In addition, recent trends in states such as California and Texas have been directed at stopping affirmative action programs in educational institutions.

Effect of Antidiscrimination Laws on the Supervisor

As mentioned earlier, antidiscrimination laws affect all levels of management. Developing policies to comply with these laws is imperative. Although these policies are formulated at the upper level of management, they are implemented at the middle and supervisory levels.

Hiring Practices

It is a well-known fact that the hiring policies and practices of employers may not discriminate against any person because of race, color, religion, national origin, sex, or age. Most government contractors and subcontractors are also legally required to provide equal employment opportunity to handicapped persons. Some supervisors are surprised to find how these requirements affect traditional hiring methods.

Obtaining information on a person prior to hiring has been affected by antidiscrimination laws. Certain questions have been explicitly prohibited by the courts. The burden of proof is on the employer to show that the information requested is being obtained for nondiscriminatory purposes, such as reports on affirmative action. As discussed earlier, non-job-related factors that have an adverse effect on the hiring of protected groups have been ruled illegal by the courts.

Employment application forms that solicit non-job-related information may result in charges of discrimination. The employer must then show that the data were not used to discriminate against a protected group. It is probably better in the long run for employers to remove questions concerning this type of information from their application forms.

Testing is another hiring practice that has received adverse attention. The courts have ruled that alternative hiring procedures are preferable to testing. Any test that adversely affects the employment opportunity of protected groups must be professionally validated.

Validation means that the results of the test are proved to be a significant predictor of an applicant's ability to perform job-related tasks. A good test is not only valid but also reliable. **Reliability** refers to the reproducibility of results with a predictor. For example, a test is reliable to the extent that the same person working under the same conditions produces approximately the same test results at different time periods. General intelligence and aptitude tests have been found invalid in many cases.

It is not suggested that all tests are unfair or result in discrimination. If a test provides an impartial way to identify qualified applicants, it reduces the use of more subjective judgments that can easily result in discrimination. For example, suppose it is determined that a particular computer-programming position requires knowledge of a certain computer language. It would be not only legal but also wise to test job applicants for knowledge in this language.

Interviews can also result in discrimination. It is imperative that the supervisor in any job interview be willing to evaluate an applicant on ability and potential. The supervisor must be aware of the actual job requirements and not use unrelated criteria as a basis for a decision. It is easy for the supervisor to overstep the legal bounds in questioning a job applicant. Therefore, questions relating to these topics should be carefully worded and used. Figure 11.6 in Chapter 11 provides some guidelines for questions that can be asked in a job interview. It is further suggested that the supervisor discuss with the boss or the human resources department the questions that he or she intends to ask a job applicant.

As has been implied, the best way to select an individual for a job is to use job-related factors. If supervisors are making the final selection decision, they should make certain that the decision is based on job-related factors. Making selection decisions on the basis of non-job-related factors excludes not only members of the protected groups but talented members of all groups. As can be seen, the supervisor can play a key role in making nondiscriminatory hiring decisions.

Job Assignments

Fairness in hiring does not by itself result in fairness on the job. Most jobs have pleasant and unpleasant tasks associated with them. For the supervisor to assign the more popular or pleasant tasks to one group of employees may result in charges of discrimination. For instance, asking female employees to perform more of the clerical tasks than are performed by the male employees in the same job may result in charges of discrimination. However, charges of reverse discrimination may also result when employers hire people from the protected groups for a job but do not require them to perform all the tasks of that job. For example, if a woman is hired as a packager and one of the job requirements is to lift 30-pound boxes, she should be required to do the lifting just like everyone else. If not, the male employees may charge the supervisor with reverse discrimination.

Performance Evaluation and Upward Mobility

Subjective performance evaluations can also result in discriminatory practices. Performance appraisals based on subjective criteria such as attitude, appearance, maturity, ambition, and personality are easily influenced by personal bias. Therefore, supervisors should always attempt to evaluate employees objectively.

Supervisors play an important part in the advancement opportunities of their employees. Traditionally, only certain groups of employees were thought to have advancement potential. This generally led to the promotion of white males; members of the protected groups were often not even considered for promotion. Employers today are sometimes required to evaluate their methods of promoting employees. They must look for objective, job-related factors in making promotion decisions. Supervisors may even be asked to recommend a certain percentage of women, minorities, or handicapped employees for promotion.

The supervisor must make an effort to consider all subordinates for advancement. The supervisor's evaluation must be objective and related to the job for which the employee is being considered. Even widely accepted policies such as promotion from within may be found to be discriminatory. If an organization is composed primarily of white males, promoting from within might have an adverse impact on the protected groups.

Disciplinary Action

Discipline must be based on objective considerations. Discipline for subjective considerations, such as appearance, should be avoided. Discipline must be thoroughly documented for all employees. Negligence in this area is often the reason for losing a discrimination case.

The standards for determining disciplinary action must be the same for all employees. As with hiring practices, seemingly neutral standards may have an adverse effect on a particular group. For example, a discharge due to an employee's arrest might be considered a violation of Title VII because it might be discriminating against one of the protected groups. Reverse discrimination charges may result when a woman or a member of a minority group is not discharged for an offense warranting discharge.

Disciplinary action against an employee for filing a Title VII complaint is illegal. In the case of a discharge, this type of discrimination will usually result in reinstatement with back pay. It is also illegal to threaten, pressure, or harass an employee into resigning, simply because the employee has filed a Title VII complaint. Management must encourage, rather than discourage, employees to voice their complaints within the organization. Encouraging an atmosphere of openness and maintaining a reputation of acting fairly on complaints reduce the possibility of charges.

A Positive Approach to Equal Employment Opportunity and Affirmative Action

The previous discussion consisted primarily of guidelines to help the supervisor avoid EEO complaints. The last part of this chapter discusses a positive approach for guiding the supervisor through equal employment opportunity and affirmative action programs.

Most people realize that a large number of people have not been utilized or have been underutilized in the past. The opportunity now exists for employing these people more fully. Organizations can benefit from this new reservoir of talent. In all of the protected groups, there are people who are not capable of doing the job. However, EEO and affirmative action do not require employers to hire unqualified employees. In fact, establishing and using job-related factors for employment decisions allows only the most qualified to be employed and to advance within the organization. This means that the persons hired and advanced should be the ones who are most capable of performing the job.

Equal employment opportunity will benefit not only the organization but also society. Past discrimination has prevented certain segments of society from finding employment, especially meaningful employment.

Managers of today's organizations must provide positive leadership toward the goal of equal employment opportunity just as they provide positive leadership in achieving all other goals. Supervisors have a major impact on the achievement of this goal. It is necessary for supervisors to be fully aware of EEO and affirmative action goals. Supervisors must communicate these goals in a positive way to their subordinates. As with any organizational goal, the supervisor's attitude is important to the achievement of these goals. A negative or passive attitude will most likely result in problems for the supervisor and the organization.

Finally, it cannot be stressed enough that EEO and affirmative action do not require an employer to hire unqualified employees. Their purpose is simply to give protected groups a fair and equal chance to obtain a position. The person must still be qualified and is expected to perform and produce on the job. EEO and affirmative action are not designed to protect unqualified applicants or poor performance by employees.

Preventing Sexual Harassment in the Workplace

In 1980, the EEOC published guidelines on **sexual harassment** in the workplace. The EEOC has taken the position that the Civil Rights Act prohibits such harassment, just as it prohibits harassment based on race, religion, and national origin.

Unwelcome sexual advances, requests for sexual favors, and other verbal or physical conduct of a sexual nature are considered sexual harassment under the following conditions:

1. Submission to such conduct is made either explicitly or implicitly a term or condition of an individual's employment.
2. Submission to or rejection of such conduct by an individual is used as the basis for employment decisions affecting that individual.
3. Such conduct has the purpose or effect of unreasonably interfering with an individual's work performance or creating an intimidating, hostile, or offensive work environment.

Organizations are considered responsible for the acts of their managers and supervisors regardless of whether the specific acts complained of were authorized or even forbidden by the employer and regardless of whether the employer knew or should have known of their occurrence. With respect to conduct between nonmanagerial employees, an employer is responsible for acts of sexual harassment where the employer knows or should have known of the conduct, unless the employer can show that it took immediate and appropriate corrective action.

Prevention is the best tool for the elimination of sexual harassment. The following suggestions are offered to assist the supervisor in preventing sexual harassment in the workplace:

1. Affirmatively raise the subject in employee meetings.
2. Express strong disapproval.
3. Describe the disciplinary actions that will be taken against employees guilty of sexual harassment.
4. Take appropriate disciplinary action when an act of sexual harassment occurs.
5. Inform employees of their right to raise sexual harassment claims.
6. Train employees in what constitutes sexual harassment.
7. Have a safe environment with confidential means where one can report violations.

Supervisors should not be reluctant to take action on sexual harassment claims. Normally, the human resources department is available to provide guidance and assistance on problems of this nature. However, it is important to remember that immediate and appropriate action must be taken by the supervisor. Supervision Illustration 12–3 describes a sexual harassment situation in Durham, NC.

SUPERVISION ILLUSTRATION 12–3

SEXUAL HARASSMENT

In a case that once again impugns the integrity of the Durham, NC, Justice system, Bob Brown Jr., the county's first public defender, admitted to the N.C. State Bar that he sexually harassed three women while they worked for him. In a consent order, signed Friday and posted Monday on the Bar's disciplinary notice site, Brown agreed to surrender his law license for five years. The order portrays Brown as a public defender who repeatedly made sexual advances toward women who worked for him, wrapping an arm around them, massaging their shoulders and stroking one's stomach. He questioned them about their sexual preferences, the order states, commented on their figures and asked their bra sizes.

The Bar's disciplinary hearing committee considered censure and reprimand as penalties but decided such disciplinary action "would not sufficiently protect the public because of the gravity of the harm" caused by Brown and "the risk that similar conduct would occur in the future." This was not the first time the Bar had heard such complaints against Brown. In 1996, he pleaded no contest to a misdemeanor assault charge. In that case, Brown was accused of grabbing a female client's buttocks. The State Bar reprimanded Brown and fined him. Under the disciplinary order filed this week, Brown could apply to get his license back in three years if he undergoes psychiatric evaluations and follows any treatment plans, pays all costs assessed by the Bar in connection with the disciplinary hearing and violates no state or federal laws.

The disciplinary action, effective March 8, comes nearly a year and a half after the Bar stripped former District Attorney Mike Nifong of his law license for prosecutorial misconduct during the Duke University lacrosse case.

Source: Adapted from Matt Welch, "Who's Harassed Now?" *Reason,* March 2009, p. 1.

Other Areas of Employment Discrimination

Numerous other issues have arisen in the areas of employment discrimination. This section briefly covers some of these additional issues.

Religion

Title VII, as originally enacted, prohibited discrimination based on religion but did not define the term. The 1972 amendments to Title VII added 701(j):

> The term religion includes all aspects of religious observance and practice, as well as belief, unless an employer demonstrates that he is unable to reasonably accommodate an employee's or prospective employee's religious observance or practice without undue hardship on the conduct of the employer's business.

The most frequent accommodation issue under Title VII's religious discrimination provisions arises from the conflict between religious practices and work schedules. The conflict normally occurs for people who observe their Sabbath from sundown on Friday to sundown on Saturday. The EEOC's 1980 *Guidelines on Religious Discrimination* proposes the following:

1. Arranging the voluntary substitutes with similar qualifications; promoting an atmosphere where such swaps are regarded favorably; and providing a central file, bulletin board, or other means of facilitating the matching of voluntary substitutes.
2. Flexible scheduling of arrival and departure times; floating or optional holidays; flexible work breaks; and using lunch time and other time to make up hours lost due to the observation of religious practices.
3. Lateral transfers or changes in job assignments.

First, Jane has learned the definition of protected groups. Next, Jane has obtained information on all of the significant antidiscrimination laws that affect organizations. These laws are Title VII and Title VI of the Civil Rights Act, the Equal Pay Act, the Age Discrimination in Employment Act, the Veterans Readjustment Act, the Rehabilitation Act, the Americans with Disabilities Act, and the Civil Rights Act of 1991. Jane now knows that the Equal Employment Opportunity Commission (EEOC) and the Office of Federal Contract Compliance (OFCC) enforce equal employment opportunity legislation. She also knows what affirmative action means (p. 223). Jane has learned that supervisors have a major impact on the implementation and achievement of equal employment opportunity goals and that they must communicate these goals to their subordinates in a positive way. Finally, Jane has learned what she can do to help prevent sexual harassment in the workplace (p. 227).

One significant case concerning religious discrimination is *TWA* v. *Hardison.* Larry G. Hardison, a TWA employee whose religion required him to observe his Sabbath on Saturday, was discharged when he refused to work on Saturdays. Hardison had previously held a job with TWA that allowed him to avoid Saturday work because of his seniority. However, he voluntarily transferred to another job in which he was near the bottom of the seniority list. Due to his low seniority, he was required to work on Saturdays. TWA refused to violate the seniority provisions of the union contract and also refused to allow him to work a four-day workweek. TWA did agree, however, to permit the union to seek a change of work assignments for Hardison, but the union also refused to violate the seniority provisions of the contract.

The Supreme Court upheld the discharge on the grounds that (1) the employer had made reasonable efforts to accommodate the religious needs of the employee, (2) the employer was not required to violate the seniority provisions of the contract, and (3) the alternative plans of allowing the employee to work a four-day workweek would have constituted an undue hardship for the employer.

The Supreme Court's ruling in this case was that an employer must reasonably accommodate religious preferences unless it creates an undue hardship for the employer. Undue hardship was defined as more than a *de minimus* cost; that is, the employer can prove it has reasonably accommodated a religious preference if it can show that the employee's request would result in more than a small (i.e., *de minimus*) cost to the employer.

Native Americans

Courts have found Native Americans to be protected by Title VII of the Civil Rights Act. In addition, Title VII benefits Native Americans by exempting them from coverage by the act, in that preferential treatment can be given to Native Americans in certain situations:

> Nothing contained in this title shall apply to any business or enterprise on or near an Indian reservation with respect to any publicly announced employment practice of such business or enterprise under which a preferential treatment is given to any individual because he is an Indian living on or near a reservation.

HIV-Positive

In addition, individuals who are diagnosed as HIV-positive, even if they haven't developed symptoms, are considered to be disabled and entitled to the protection of the Americans with Disabilities Act (ADA). In 1998, the U.S. Supreme Court (*Bragdon* v. *Abbott*) ruled that HIV is so immediately physically devastating that it's an impairment from the moment of infection. In this case, Sidney Abbott revealed her positive status to her dentist, Randon Bragdon, and he refused to fill her tooth cavity in his office but suggested that he do the procedure at a hospital with Abbott incurring the additional expense. Abbott refused and sued Bragdon under the ADA and state law. The Supreme Court ruled in Abbott's favor and held that HIV status is a disability under the ADA.

Sexual Orientation

The EEOC and the courts have uniformly held that Title VII does not prohibit employment discrimination against homosexuals. Courts have also held uniformly that adverse action against individuals who undergo or announce an intention to undergo sex-change surgery does not violate Title VII. Therefore, people who fall in those groups are protected only when a local or state statute is enacted to protect them. More court cases, however, must be decided before a clear picture can be gained concerning discrimination against people in these groups.

Summary

This chapter identifies the groups in organizations that have been most affected by discrimination. The effects of antidiscrimination legislation on the supervisor are discussed. A positive approach to equal employment opportunity and affirmative action is also presented.

1. *Define protected groups.* Race, color, sex, age, religion, national origin, and mental and physical handicaps identify the classifications of people that are called protected groups.

2. *Describe antidiscrimination laws that affect organizations.* Title VII of the Civil Rights Act prohibits discrimination based on race, color, religion, sex, or national origin. Title VI of the Civil Rights Act prohibits discrimination based on race, color, or national origin in all programs or activities that receive federal financial aid in order to provide employment. The Equal Pay Act requires employers to provide equal pay to men and women who perform work that is similar in skill, effort, and responsibility. The Age Discrimination in Employment Act prohibits discrimination against people over 40 years of age in any area of employment. The Veterans Readjustment Act requires that federal government contractors and subcontractors take affirmative action to hire and promote Vietnam veterans and disabled veterans. The Rehabilitation Act prohibits employers from denying jobs to individuals merely because of a handicap. The Americans with Disabilities Act gives the disabled sharply increased access to services and jobs. The Civil Rights Act of 1991 reversed several Supreme Court decisions, and allows juries to award employees punitive damages for discrimination based on sex, religion, or disability. The Family and Medical Leave Act (FMLA) enables qualified employees to take prolonged unpaid leave for family and health-related reasons without fear of losing their jobs.

3. *Identify the major federal enforcement agencies for equal employment opportunity.* The two major federal enforcement agencies are the Equal Employment Opportunity Commission (EEOC) and the Office of Federal Contract Compliance (OFCC).

4. *Define employment parity, occupational parity, and systemic discrimination.* Employment parity exists when the proportion of protected employees employed by an organization equals the proportion in the organization's relevant labor market. Occupational parity exists when the proportion of protected employees employed in various occupations in the organization is equal to their proportion in the organization's relevant labor market. Large differences in either occupational or employment parity are called systemic discrimination.

5. *Define affirmative action.* Affirmative action refers to an employer's attempt to balance its workforce in all job categories with respect to sex and race in order to reflect the same proportions as those of its general labor market.

6. *Define sexual harassment.* Unwelcome sexual advances, requests for sexual favors, and other verbal or physical conduct of a sexual nature are considered sexual harassment if submission to such conduct (1) is made either explicitly or implicitly a term or condition of employment, (2) is used as the basis for employment decisions affecting that individual, or (3) has the purpose or effect of measurably interfering with an individual's work performance or creating an intimidating, hostile, or offensive work environment.

Key Terms

Affirmative action, 223
Age Discrimination in
    Employment Act, 218
Americans with Disabilities
    Act (ADA), 219
Civil Rights Act of 1991, 219

Education Amendments
    Act, 217
Employment parity, 223
Equal Employment Opportunity
    Commission (EEOC), 220
Equal Pay Act, 217

Family and Medical Leave Act
    (FMLA), 219
Occupational parity, 223
Office of Federal Contract
    Compliance (OFCC), 218, 220
Protected groups, 216

Review Questions

1. Define the term *protected group.*
2. What determines which of the antidiscrimination laws affect a particular organization?
3. Describe the following antidiscrimination laws:
   a. Title VII of the Civil Rights Act.
   b. Title VI of the Civil Rights Act.
   c. Equal Pay Act of 1963.
   d. Title IX of the Education Amendments Act.
   e. Age Discrimination in Employment Act.
   f. Executive Order 11246 as amended by Executive Order 11375.
   g. Veterans Readjustment Act of 1974.
   h. Rehabilitation Act of 1973.
   i. Americans with Disabilities Act.
   j. Civil Rights Act of 1991.
   k. Family and Medical Leave Act (FMLA).
4. Define the term *BFOQ.*
5. What is systemic discrimination?
6. What does the term *affirmative action* mean?
7. Give some suggestions for creating a positive EEO and affirmative action environment.
8. What is sexual harassment?

Skill-Building Questions

1. Discuss the effects of discrimination on organization performance.
2. "The use of tests in hiring results in more objective evaluations of prospective employees." Discuss your view on this statement.
3. "The supervisor's primary objective should be to avoid making mistakes in employment decisions that can lead to EEO complaints." Discuss your view on this statement.
4. "Organizations should be allowed to hire anyone they choose." How do you feel about this statement? Discuss.

Additional Readings

Burns, Prue, and Jan Schapper, "The Ethical Case for Affirmative Action," *Journal of Business Ethics,* December 2008, pp. 369–380.

Macaulay, Alex, "Black, White & Olive Drab," *Southern Comfort,* Spring 2009, pp. 89–92.

Persky, Anna Stolley, "Free to Be," *ABA Journal,* February 2009, pp. 22–24.

Troyansky, David G, "Age Discrimination: An Historical and Contemporary Analysis," *Journal of Social History,* Winter 2008, pp. 541–555.

Wycliff, Don, "A New Day," *Commonweal,* February 13, 2009, p. 39.

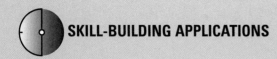

SKILL-BUILDING APPLICATIONS

Incident 12–1

This Is a Man's Job

Bill, Wally, and Jerry each have over 15 years' seniority in the maintenance department of the Elson Company. The maintenance department has 20 skilled employees—10 electricians, 5 plumbers, and 5 millwrights. Bill, Wally, and Jerry are electricians. They are all highly dependable and well-respected employees.

Several months ago, Angela Collins was hired as an electrician in the maintenance department. It became obvious rather quickly that Bill, Wally, and Jerry did not want her in the maintenance department. They told other people in the department, "Angela can't do the work and was only hired because she is a woman." The three of them conducted a campaign emphasizing Angela's shortcomings, getting into arguments with her, and urging other people to complain about her work to Ken Allen, supervisor of the maintenance department.

After several weeks of this, Bill, Wally, and Jerry asked for a meeting with Ken. At the meeting, they contended that Angela was not carrying her share of the load and that they were tired of doing her work. They said that if Angela didn't leave, they would. They told Ken that it was very easy for a skilled electrician to find a job.

Questions

1. How would you handle the situation? Be specific.
2. Do you feel that Angela has been given a fair chance?

Incident 12–2

Affirmative Action

Allen Russell is attending a supervisory development program offered by his company, Southeastern Gas Company. This is an honor for Allen because only a few supervisors are selected for the program each year. The program consists of two sessions, each lasting a week. The first session consists mostly of classroom training, with very little audience participation.

At the end of the first session, the human resources director of Southeastern, Larry Rankin, announces that each of the participants in the program will be required to make a 30-minute presentation to the group during the second session. He states that the presentation should be of interest to supervisors at Southeastern and that each person will be graded on his or her presentation. Larry asks that the participants each contact him with their topic within two days.

Allen knows that if he wants to move up at Southeastern, it is important that he do a good job in his presentation. After thinking it over, Allen decides to talk about Southeastern's affirmative action program and the supervisor's role in that program. When Allen gives Larry his topic, Larry is delighted. He tells Allen, "You know, the affirmative action program is very important, and I believe that most of our supervisors don't understand their role in it. I'll be looking forward to hearing your presentation."

Questions

1. Do you think that most supervisors understand their role in affirmative action programs? Explain.
2. If you were Allen, what points would you cover in the presentation? Develop an outline of your presentation.

Incident 12–3

Microsoft Helps—and Hires—Workers with Disabilities

Technology is taking employees to a brave new world of work, providing instant communication around the globe, automating tasks that once took hours to accomplish, and placing more information in workers' hands so that they can make smarter decisions. But beyond the new-routine business tools of word processors, databases, and spreadsheets are the so-called *assistive technologies,* which enable people with disabilities to function right alongside their able-bodied coworkers. These technologies often cost little to implement—half of them below $100—and help employers tap a new pool of knowledgeable and skilled workers.

Assistive technologies for personal computers range from customizable screen magnification options, specialized pointers that can attach to employees' foreheads or arms to replace the typical mouse, alternative keyboard controls, screen readers, Braille output displays, and speech-recognition and -synthesizing software. With its leadership in the PC market in general, it is not surprising that Microsoft Corporation is at the forefront of developing assistive technologies, But the company is also a leader in hiring and accommodating workers with disabilities. Mylene Padolina, a diversity consultant for Microsoft, says that prospective employees are asked whether they need any accommodations in their interviews. If a person with disabilities is hired, the company assesses and fulfills the worker's assistive technology needs. Typical disabilities within the Microsoft workforce are blindness, deafness, mobility impairment, and learning disabilities. Greg Smith, a lead software developer for Microsoft, who also is quadriplegic, uses a pointer attached to his right arm and a "sip and puff" headset to replace his mouse. Smith uses the PC throughout his workday to communicate, access and analyze information, surf the Internet, and write reports.

Questions

1. Microsoft has characterized its assistive technologies as "enabling the workplace" rather than the employee. Do you think most companies see the workplace as the problem instead of the disability? Why or why not?

2. Think of some assistive technologies, other than those mentioned here, that could help people with disabilities perform jobs. Surf the Web to find some ideas and prepare a list, along with the jobs that they could be used for.

Sources: Allan Hoffman, "Great Gadgets: Innovations for People with Disabilities in the Workplace," *Monster Career Center Special Report; Disabilities in the Workplace,* equalopportunity.monster.com, accessed October 9, 2002; "Enabling the Workplace," Microsoft Accessibility Web site, May 23, 2001, *www.microsoft.com;* Protection & Advocacy, Inc., "Microsoft Leads Push to Hire People with Disabilities," *PAI Newsletter,* Winter 1999/2000, p. 2.

Exercise 12–1

Affirmative Action Debate

Break the class into teams of four to five students. Each team should prepare to debate one of the following statements:

1. The federal government should not require affirmative action programs for private enterprise organizations that are federal contractors or subcontractors.

2. Affirmative action programs have been very helpful to minorities and women. Private enterprise organizations should be required to have affirmative action programs.

After the debate, the instructor should list on the board the points made by each team and discuss the issues involved.

Exercise 12–2

Legal Issues in Equal Employment Opportunity

Break the class into teams of two to three students. Each team should then be given the following assignment:

Go to the library and review several recent legal cases involving equal employment opportunity. Prepare a report for presentation in class concerning the facts, issues, and current status of the cases. Each team should make a 5- to 10-minute presentation of its findings.

Exercise 12–3

How Much Do You Know about Sexual Harassment?

A True or False Test for Employees	T	F
1. If I just ignore unwanted sexual attention, it will usually stop.	❏	❏
2. If I don't mean to sexually harass another employee, there's no way my behavior can be perceived by him or her as sexually harassing.	❏	❏
3. Some employees don't complain about unwanted sexual attention from another worker because they don't want to get that person in trouble.	❏	❏
4. If I make sexual comments to someone and that person doesn't ask me to stop, then I guess my behavior is welcome.	❏	❏
5. To avoid sexually harassing a woman who comes to work in a traditionally male workplace, the men simply should not haze her.	❏	❏
6. A sexual harasser may be told by a court to pay part of a judgment to the employee he or she harassed.	❏	❏
7. A sexually harassed man does not have the same legal rights as a woman who is sexually harassed.	❏	❏
8. About 90 percent of all sexual harassment in today's workplace is done by males to females.	❏	❏

9. Sexually suggestive pictures or objects in a workplace don't create a liability unless someone complains. ❏ ❏

10. Telling someone to stop his or her unwanted sexual behavior usually doesn't do any good. ❏ ❏

Answers: (1) False. (2) False. (3) True. (4) False. (5) False. (6) True. (7) False. (8) True. (9) False. (10) False.

A Test for Management Personnel　　　**T**　　**F**

1. An employer is not liable for the sexual harassment of one of its employees unless that employee loses specific job benefits or is fired. ❏ ❏

2. A court can require a sexual harasser to pay part of the judgment to the employee he or she has sexually harassed. ❏ ❏

3. A supervisor can be liable for sexual harassment committed by one of his or her employees against another. ❏ ❏

4. An employer can be liable for the sexually harassing behavior of management personnel even if it is unaware of that behavior and has a policy forbidding it. ❏ ❏

5. It is appropriate for a supervisor, when initially receiving a sexual-harassment complaint, to determine if the alleged recipient overreacted or misunderstood the alleged harasser. ❏ ❏

6. When a supervisor is talking with an employee about an allegation of sexual harassment against him or her, it is best to ease into the allegation instead of being direct. ❏ ❏

7. Sexually suggestive visuals or objects in a workplace don't create a liability unless an employee complains about them and management allows them to remain. ❏ ❏

8. The lack of sexual-harassment complaints is a good indication that sexual harassment is not occurring. ❏ ❏

9. It is appropriate for a supervisor to tell an employee to handle unwelcome sexual behavior if he or she thinks that the employee is misunderstanding the behavior. ❏ ❏

10. The intent behind employee A's sexual behavior is more important than the impact of that behavior on employee B when determining if sexual harassment has occurred. ❏ ❏

Answers: (1) False. (2) True. (3) True. (4) True. (5) False. (6) False. (7) False. (8) False. (9) False. (10) False.

Source: Adapted from Brian S. Moskal, "Sexual Harassment: An Update," *Industry Week*, November 18, 1991, p. 40.

CHAPTER THIRTEEN

Counseling and Supporting Employees

Learning objectives

After studying this chapter, you will be able to:

1. Determine when it is appropriate for the supervisor to counsel employees.
2. Differentiate between directive and nondirective counseling.
3. Present a general approach for counseling employees.
4. Define a "troubled employee."
5. Discuss ways to effectively supervise troubled employees.
6. Explain what employee assistance programs (EAPs) are.
7. Describe wellness programs.
8. Summarize the legal requirements for dealing with troubled employees.
9. Explain the difference between a "troubled" employee and a "problem" employee.
10. Explain the supervisor's role in career counseling.

Supervision Dilemma

Jane Harris thinks that one of her employees, Ken Hall, has a drinking problem. Jane is almost certain that she has smelled alcohol on Ken's breath several times. On at least two occasions during the past month, other employees have told Jane that Ken drinks on the job. However, Jane has never caught Ken drinking during working hours. In an effort to get additional information, Jane has examined Ken's personnel file. The file showed that Ken had taken a considerable amount of leave on Mondays. Jane has also reviewed Ken's performance appraisals over the past few years and has noticed that Ken's ratings have been declining. Jane has never faced a problem of this kind as a supervisor. She wonders what the best way is to handle the problem.

Supervisors, by the nature of their jobs, work with people. Not all employees can be supervised in the same manner. The supervisor may have some employees who are easy to supervise and some who are difficult to supervise. Some employees are well-adjusted, "normal" individuals, and other employees have personal problems that affect their work. Some employees need assurance that they are doing the right things. Some employees need some assistance in planning their careers. As a result of such situations, supervisors are required from time to time to counsel employees.

When and Why to Counsel

1 LEARNING OBJECTIVES

Numerous situations require the supervisor to act in a counseling role. In some situations, an employee may voluntarily seek the supervisor's counsel on certain matters. In other situations, a supervisor may find it necessary to approach the employee. Usually, this happens when a supervisor observes a decline in an employee's performance. A supervisor should never counsel an employee if the employee's problem appears to be beyond the supervisor's ability. This is usually the case with an employee who has a severe personal problem. In such cases, the supervisor should refer the employee to a person professionally trained to deal with that problem. If a supervisor attempts to counsel an employee in areas where the supervisor is not qualified, this may only add to the problem and further hinder the employee's performance. The overwhelming majority of situations appropriate for supervisory counseling involve employee performance issues, not employee personal problems.

Many positive effects may result from effective supervisory counseling. From the employee's viewpoint, the positive effects of counseling may include reassurance, release of emotional tensions, and clarification of his or her thinking. From the viewpoints of both parties, a positive effect of counseling may be improvement of the employee's performance. However, in order for supervisory counseling to be effective the supervisor must be properly trained.

Counseling Techniques

2 LEARNING OBJECTIVES

Above all else, the supervisor must establish the proper climate for counseling. Supervisors must communicate that they are there to help the employee and that they have a genuine concern for the employee. Whenever possible, the counseling interview should take place in a private and quiet setting.

Directive versus Nondirective Counseling

When counseling with employees, the supervisor may use either a directive or a nondirective approach. In **directive counseling,** the supervisor takes the initiative and asks the employee pointed questions about a problem. When the supervisor feels that he or she has a good grasp of what is causing the problem, he or she suggests several steps that the employee might take

236

to overcome it. In **nondirective counseling,** the employee assumes most of the initiative and the supervisor serves primarily as a listener. The employee is encouraged to discuss what he or she thinks is causing the problem and to develop solutions to it. Instead of asking pointed questions, the supervisor asks open-ended questions such as "Can you tell me more?" or "Would you elaborate on what you mean?" The nondirective approach is suggested for most situations because it tends to create an environment in which the employee is encouraged to come up with solutions and to focus on what he or she needs to change.

Steps in the Counseling Interview

Remember, most supervisory counseling involves employee performance issues. No one approach to counseling works best in all situations. The general approach outlined below for supervisors is a variation of the nondirective approach that should prove effective in most situations.[1]

Step 1. In a nonthreatening manner, describe what you have observed. Talk about actual performance and not about vague concepts such as attitude or motivation. Do not threaten or intimidate the employee.

Step 2. Ask the employee to comment on your observations. Encourage the employee to be open and honest. If you disagree with parts of the employee's response, do so in a gentle manner.

Step 3. If prior meetings have been held, briefly review what they accomplished.

Step 4. With the employee's input, identify the problem-solving techniques to be used. Do not attempt to solve the problem yourself, but guide the employee to resolve it alone. Be a good listener and let the employee talk.

Step 5. Once a solution has been agreed upon, restate the actions to be taken and reemphasize your concern about the problem.

Step 6. Always schedule a follow-up meeting, preferably in the near future.

Step 7. Document the meeting. While this is not always necessary, it is usually a good idea. The documenting should be done while the session is still fresh in your mind.

Supervising Troubled Employees

All employees have personal problems that from time to time influence their motivation to work. Health, family, legal, and financial problems are common types of personal problems that influence performance on the job. Employees normally solve these problems privately or with help and encouragement from someone else. Some employees, however, have lasting or recurrent personal problems that are too difficult to solve in these ways.

Some employees are able to keep their personal lives separate from their work. They may manage personal problems while remaining fully productive members of the workforce. But many employees with personal problems cannot keep those problems from affecting their job performance. When the job performance of an employee is affected by personal problems that normal counseling or disciplinary measures cannot correct, the employee is usually diagnosed as a troubled employee.

The types of problems already mentioned (health, family, legal, and financial problems) may be serious enough to cause significant work problems for the employee. Family problems can lead to mental or emotional problems, which in turn can lead to drug dependence, illness, and financial and legal problems. Alcoholism, mental or emotional instability, drug dependence, and other illnesses are some of the common causes that create troubled employees.

How the Troubled Employee Affects the Organization

The troubled employee affects productivity and the work environment in many ways. A primary result of bringing personal problems to the workplace is reduced productivity. Absenteeism and tardiness tend to increase, and efficiency is reduced. Bringing personal problems to the workplace also increases the costs of insurance programs, including sickness and accident benefits. Some industrial theft is due to the need of drug addicts to support their habits. Lower morale, increased friction among employees and between supervisors and employees, and more grievances also result from the presence of troubled employees. The permanent loss of trained employees due to disability, early retirement, and premature death is a problem associated with troubled employees. Difficult to measure, but a very real cost associated with troubled employees, is loss of business and damage to the public image of the organization.

Each year, American businesses face losses in the billions of dollars because of personal problems that accompany employees to work and have a negative effect on their attendance and job performance. The National Council on Alcoholism and Drug Dependence (NCADD) estimates that alcohol and drug abuse cost the American economy $276 billion per year in lost productivity, health care expenditures, crime, motor vehicle crashes, and other conditions.[2]

The NCADD also reported that:

- 6.6 percent of Americans employed in full-time jobs are heavy drinkers (five or more drinks a day on five or more days in the past 30 days).
- Forty percent of workplace fatalities and 47 percent of workplace injuries can be linked to alcohol consumption.
- Absenteeism among problem drinkers and alcoholics is approximately four to eight times greater than among other workers.[3]

The Substance Abuse and Mental Health Services Administration (SAMHSA) reported that as of 2007.[4]

- 8 percent of the total U.S. population aged 12 or older were current illicit drug users.
- Over 8 percent of full-time employed adults aged 18 and older were illicit drug users.
- Over 75 percent of all current illegal drug users over the age of 18 were employed either full or part time.

Substance abuse also results in reduced productivity, reduced work quality, damage to property and equipment, theft, lower morale, safety violations, and poor decision making. In addition to organizational costs, there are also personal and social costs. Studies have shown that alcohol abuse is related to increased suicide, homicide, accidents, and such ailments as heart disease and cirrhosis.

Similarly, there is a proven relationship between the use of illegal drugs and crime. The total cost to the families affected by the problems of troubled employees may never be known. Attempts to solve these problems are a service to the organization, the troubled employee, and society in general.

Help from the Organization

Until recent years, organizations attempted to avoid the employee's non-job-related problems. Although aware of the existence of these problems, organizations believed that they should not interfere with the employee's personal life. Instead, organizations tended to get rid of the troubled employees whose personal lives negatively affected their work. However, organizations have come to realize that it is often in their best interest to help rehabilitate troubled employees. At a minimum, salvaging the troubled employee saves the cost of hiring and training another employee. Most organizations have estimated the cost of hiring and training a new employee to be significantly greater than the cost of rehabilitating a troubled one. In addition, the increased productivity of an employee after treatment can be significant.

Today, many large organizations and a growing number of small organizations have implemented a variety of programs to help troubled employees. The supervisor plays a key role in these programs because it is the supervisor who is responsible for identifying and confronting the troubled employee. To handle this function, the supervisor must be properly trained.

Detecting the Troubled Employee

Personal problems do not necessarily make a person a troubled employee. Only when personal problems interfere with the employee's work performance should they become a concern to the supervisor. For a supervisor to hunt for personal problems and recommend help for all employees with such problems would be a violation of employees' right to privacy. Only when the problems affect the quality or quantity of work, when an employee becomes disruptive to the work environment, or when an employee asks for help should the organization concern itself with personal problems.

In some cases, employees with personal problems voluntarily seek help at work. This is much more likely to happen when the problems do not carry the stigma of social disapproval. Treating alcohol and drug dependency as illnesses rather than weaknesses should encourage employees to seek help voluntarily for these illnesses, as they would for any other physical illnesses.

Until recently, supervisors, along with family and friends, often attempted to help a troubled employee avoid detection. Rationalizing that the problem or the reasons for the problem will go away only prolongs treatment for the troubled employee. From the standpoint of both the troubled employee and the organization, overlooking rule violations and reduced productivity because the employee has personal problems may be the worst thing that the supervisor can do.

The supervisor must learn how to detect evidence of declining job performance. Through proper documentation, the supervisor can usually detect a deterioration in an employee's performance. The supervisor should make a habit of recording evidence of deteriorating relationships, unacceptable performance, and inability to follow rules.

Supervisors must be careful to be consistent in documenting performance problems. Noting inadequacies for one employee and not for others, just because the supervisor suspects that the employee has a serious personal problem, is unfair. Similarly, overlooking examples of poor performance because the employee gives a particularly sad or convincing excuse may only prolong the problem. Figure 13.1 provides a checklist to aid in detecting a troubled employee.

FIGURE 13.1
Detecting the Troubled Employee

1. Be alert to, and document, changes in personality that affect working relationships.
   a. Insubordination.
   b. Altercations with other employees or with the supervisor.

2. Be alert to, and document, changes in quality and quantity of work.
   a. Reduced output.
   b. Increased errors or defects.

3. Be alert to, and document, rule violations.
   a. Unexcused absences.
   b. Unexcused tardiness.
   c. Leaving workstation without permission.
   d. Dress code violations.
   e. Safety rules violations.
   f. Concealing or consuming drugs or alcohol on company premises.
   g. Involvement with law: garnishment of wages, drug traffic.

Confronting the Troubled Employee

Once a troubled employee has been identified, the supervisor must confront the employee. Most supervisors do not relish this responsibility. Sufficient documentation can greatly help the supervisor in this process. The confrontation between a supervisor and a troubled employee should consist primarily of three steps: (1) performance review, (2) referral to counseling and assistance, and (3) discussion of the consequences of the employee's actions.

Supervisors should first confront an employee with specific evidence of poor performance. Reviewing any available documentation with the employee is a good approach. It helps the employee realize that there is documented evidence of the poor performance. Be as specific as possible. For example, there is a big difference between "you have not been coming to work on time" and "you have been late to work 5 out of the past 12 workdays."

Supervisors should restrict criticism and discussion to job performance. Moralizing on the effects of drug abuse or other problems is not the supervisor's job. If the employee begins to talk about a problem, the supervisor should listen. However, it is not necessary for the supervisor to promote more discussion. The supervisor's advice to the employee should be limited to suggesting that the employee seek proper help. Supervisors should not try to act as a psychologist or medical doctor. They should not attempt to diagnose the cause of the employee's poor performance. They should make direct accusations only when there is specific evidence that the employee is breaking some policy or rule on the job. For example, a supervisor should not accuse an employee of using drugs without specific evidence.

The second step in the confrontation is referral of the troubled employee to professional counseling and assistance. At this point, an employee may become defensive or hostile. Supervisors should not be influenced by an employee's excuses or stories. Employees with personal problems have had plenty of practice convincing themselves and others that their problems are caused by external forces beyond their control. A supervisor may sympathize with the employee and may wish that the poor performance could be overlooked. But acting on this wish is detrimental to both the organization and the employee. The employee needs help. Postponing that help will not ease the problem. The employee may attempt to blame the supervisor for the problem. This is a common reaction of a troubled employee, and it should not be taken personally. A supervisor should be prepared for it and try to remain calm. Supervisors must remain firm but supportive at all times.

During this second step in the confrontation, supervisors should emphasize that the employee will not jeopardize his or her job by accepting assistance. Supervisors should point out that accepting assistance may, in fact, be the only way that the employee can continue employment with the organization. Supervisors should also emphasize that all aspects of the assistance program are confidential. Many organizations do not even record the assistance in the employee's personnel file.

Some organizations have company-based employee assistance programs, and some have insurance covering counseling and assistance programs. Other organizations use public assistance programs provided by the local, state, or federal government. Company-based programs, referred to as employee assistance programs (EAPs), are discussed later in this chapter. Supervisors should be aware of the options available for paying for this type of assistance and should communicate these options to the employee.

During the third step of the confrontation, supervisors should also discuss the need for performance improvement. If an employee accepts help, most organizations agree to work with him or her on a schedule of improvement. If an employee does not accept help, he or she should be informed of the consequences. Usually, if an employee refuses assistance and his or her performance does not improve, the employee is subject to dismissal. The

FIGURE 13.2
Confronting the
Troubled Employee

1. Performance review.
   a. Review documentation with employee.
   b. Restrict your criticism to job performance.
   c. Do not attempt to diagnose the cause of the poor performance.
   d. Do not attempt to counsel the employee concerning the nature of the problem.

2. Referral to counseling and assistance.
   a. Be firm and supportive.
   b. Be prepared for excuses and hostility.
   c. Explain that seeking help will not jeopardize the employee's job.
   d. Emphasize the confidentiality of the program.
   e. Know and discuss insurance coverage or other financial assistance.

3. Discussion of consequences of employee action.
   a. Discuss the need for improvement.
   b. Discuss the possible consequences of the employee's not accepting help.
   c. Discuss past successes of the program or similar programs.

employee should also be informed that to avoid discipline and dismissal he or she must maintain improved performance.

It is helpful at this point for supervisors to discuss the success of assistance programs in general. Once employees realize that the supervisor is aware of their poor performance and that assistance programs have a good chance of success, employees are much more likely to cooperate. Figure 13.2 outlines the necessary steps in the confrontation between a supervisor and a troubled employee.

Aiding and Evaluating Recovery

Troubled employees who have been referred for assistance are expected to be rehabilitated. The supervisor bears the primary responsibility for evaluating the extent of rehabilitation. That evaluation must be based on job performance. Other criteria, such as abstinence for drug and alcohol abusers, certification of recovery by the assisting agency, or continued participation in the assistance program, are less meaningful to the organization than improved job performance. The overriding objective of the supervisor and the organization should be that the employee not only recover but also begin to function satisfactorily on the job.

Employee Assistance Programs

LEARNING
OBJECTIVES

A 2007 survey by the Society for Human Resource Management (SHRM) found that 73 percent of responding companies offered an employee assistance program (EAP).[5] Experts estimate that as many as 90 percent of Fortune 500 companies offer employee assistance programs. Experts also estimate that EAPs are far less widespread among mid and small sized organizations. Originally, EAPs were primarily designed to deal with alcohol and drug problems. Today, EAPs are dealing with issues such as domestic violence, care for sick children and elderly parents, financial problems, depression, divorce, and the like. There are several types of EAPs. In the rarest type, diagnosis and treatment of the employee's problem are provided by the organization. In a second type, the organization hires a qualified person to diagnose the employee's problem. Then the employee is referred to the proper agency or clinic. In a third type, a coordinator evaluates the employee's problems only sufficiently to make a referral to the proper agency or clinic. Sometimes the coordinator is a consultant rather than a full-time employee of the organization. A final type of EAP occurs when the company contracts with a company that

TABLE 13.1
Ten Critical Elements of an EAP

Source: Adapted from F. Dickman and W. G. Emener, "Employee Assistance Programs: Basic Concepts, Attributes, and an Evaluation," *Personnel Administrator*, August 1982, p. 56. Reprinted with permission from the *Personnel Administrator*, published by the Society for Human Resource Management, Alexandria, VA.

Element	Significance
1. Management backing	Without this at the highest level, key ingredients and overall effect are seriously limited.
2. Labor union support (if a union is present)	The employee assistance program (EAP) cannot be meaningful if it is not backed by the employees' labor union.
3. Confidentiality	Anonymity and trust are crucial if employees are to use an EAP.
4. Easy access	For maximum use and benefit.
5. Supervisor training	Crucial to employees needing understanding and support during receipt of assistance.
6. Union steward training (if a union is present)	A critical variable is employees' contact with the union—the steward.
7. Insurance involvement	Occasionally, assistance alternatives are costly, and insurance support is a must.
8. Breadth of service components	Availability of assistance for a wide variety of problems (e.g., alcohol, family, personal, financial, grief, medical).
9. Professional leadership	A skilled professional with expertise in helping, who must have credibility in the eyes of the employees.
10. Follow-up and evaluation	To measure program effectiveness and overall improvement.

provides EAP services. In these type programs, employees go directly to the company providing the service.

Basically, there are three ways employees can end up using the services of an EAP:

1. *Self-referral.* The employee can confidentially refer himself or herself to the EAP.
2. *Recommended referral.* Their supervisor or another manager notices the employee seems to be having problems and encourages the employee to get assistance from the EAP.
3. *Mandatory referral.* Their supervisor or another manager identifies work-related behavior that needs to be addressed and believes that the EAP can assist in the process.[6]

For an EAP to be successful, it must first be accepted by the employees; they must not be afraid to use it. Experience has shown that certain elements are critical to the success of an EAP. Table 13.1 summarizes 10 of the most important characteristics of an EAP.

Studies have shown that company-based employee assistance programs can reduce absenteeism significantly. It has also been shown that EAPs help reduce on-the-job accidents and grievances. Workers' compensation premiums, sickness and accident benefits, and trips to the infirmary also tend to decrease when the organization institutes an EAP. The U.S. Department of Labor estimates that every $1 invested in an EAP saves employers from $5 to $16 in costs related to employee problems.[7] The national average annual cost for an EAP ranges from $12 to $20 per employee.[8] Supervision Illustration 13–1 describes how one EAP provider has carved out a niche.

As with many other areas, organizations are beginning to integrate the Internet into their EAP services. Some companies are using Internet-based services and tools to supplement more traditional face-to-face services. For example, employees who suffer from anxiety, depression, or substance abuse can be securely connected to a series of exercises that provide confidential, customized, and clinically sound feedback about their concerns. Supervision Illustration 13–2 describes how some EAPs are using the telephone to provide professional counseling services.

SUPERVISION ILLUSTRATION   13–1

EAP NICHE FOR NEW AVENUES

Thirty-year-old New Avenues, headquartered in South Bend, Indiana, provides employee assistance programs in 24 states utilizing 2,000 therapists and counselors. New Avenues has carved out a niche that allows companies to have one program for all its branch offices. "Our model grew out of the need to support employers that had multiple locations," says executive director Kathleen Ponko. "Usually the employer comes to us. We find the counselors available to support all their sites. We identify these counselors. We credential them. We contract with them to provide services on our behalf."

Currently New Avenues serves about 150,000 individuals under its various plans.

New Avenues goes to great efforts to find counselors in locations that are convenient to the employees being served. For example, New Avenues even finds counselors in hometowns of employees who commute to South Bend from such places as Valparaiso, Indiana, and Plymouth, Indiana. New Avenues' motto is "Maximizing Productivity and Well-Being."

Source: Gene Stowe, "New Avenues' Reach Extends to 24 States, 2,000 Therapists," *Tribune Business Weekly,* September 8, 2008, p. 9.

Wellness Programs

In addition to the EAPs discussed in the previous section, many companies have installed programs designed to prevent illness and enhance employee well-being. These programs are referred to as wellness or work/life programs and include such things as periodic medical exams, stop-smoking clinics, education on improved dietary practices, hypertension detection and control, weight control, exercise and fitness, stress management, accident-risk reduction, immunizations, and cardiopulmonary resuscitation (CPR) training. Some of the documented results of wellness programs include fewer sick days, reduced coronary heart disease, and lower major medical costs. Many also believe that employee productivity increases for employees who participate in exercise and fitness programs. Experts in the wellness field report that even small companies can offer wellness programs and that such programs do not have to be expensive.

A growing number of companies are integrating wellness programs and employee assistance programs (EAPs). The potential benefits are "one-stop" options for employees and reduced costs from running the programs separately. One classic example of the many organizations now adopting wellness programs is Adolph Coors Company. Coors claims that its 25,000-square-foot wellness facility, designed for employees and their spouses, has helped the company save over $2 million annually in medical claims and other health-related factors. The Coors program is designed around a six-step behavioral change model: awareness, education, incentives, programs, self-education, and follow-up and support. Chief among the elements that are critical for successful wellness programs are CEO support and direction, accessibility, inclusion of family, needs assessment, staffing with specialists, and establishment of a separate budget for wellness activities.[9] One survey taken in February 2009 reported that, in spite of the economic downturn, wellness programs were faring well in terms of funding and usage.[10] Supervision Illustration 13–3 describes how one company is offering incentives for participating in its wellness program.

Legal and Union Demands

Until the late 1970's organizations had the legal right to fire or refuse to hire employees who were drug or alcohol addicts. The Rehabilitation Act of 1973 was extended in 1977 to include alcohol and drug addicts. This act protects employable, qualified, handicapped

SUPERVISION ILLUSTRATION   13–2

COUNSELING OVER THE PHONE

For several years, many companies have used toll-free hotlines staffed around the clock to field employees calls about their problems. The people staffing these hotlines would refer the respective callers to the appropriate professionals for face-to-face help. Recently, some companies have advanced from using the telephone as a referral tool to integrating telephone therapy into their employee assistance programs. In what has been labeled teletherapy or telecounseling, professionals working in off-site call centers conduct counseling sessions with employees who phone in from home, the office, or the road. All but the most serious problems—such as severe addiction or depression—are being dealt with using teletherapy. Teletherapy may involve one-time or multiple, long-term phone sessions.

Proponents of teletherapy claim that it gives people faster access to help and that it is especially well suited for companies with employees in rural areas or employees who travel extensively. Opponents of teletherapy believe that it's much easier to misdiagnose a client without face-to-face interaction. Opponents also have reservations about confidentiality and licensing questions.

Recent studies provide support for telephone EAP consultation. In one study, approximately 90 percent of the respondents rated their overall satisfaction with telephone counseling as "good" or "better" and 87 percent rated their degree of problem resolution as "improved" or "greatly improved".

BPS Retail and Commercial Operations, a subsidiary of Bridgestone Americas, has had great success using teletherapy. After introducing teletherapy, EAP use at BPS jumped 70 percent; the percentage of people getting better increased from 30–50 percent to 92 percent; and the company's EAP costs dropped almost 30 percent.

Sources: Michelle V. Rafter, "EAP's Tout the Benefits of Dial-Up Counseling in Place of Face-to-Face," *Pensions & Investments*, November 2004, pp. 75–77, copyright Crain Communications, Inc.; and George E. Hargrave, Deirdre Hiatt, Rachael Alexander, Ian A. Shaffer, "Help Is On The Line," *Behavioral Healthcare*, November 2008, pp. 20–23.

---

employees (including alcohol and drug addicts) from discrimination in employment by federal contractors or subcontractors. It states that handicapped employees cannot be discriminated against in federally financed employment, education, and services. The Comprehensive Rehabilitation Service Amendments of 1978 state that the term *handicapped individual* does not include any individual who is an alcoholic or drug abuser whose current use of alcohol or drugs prevents the individual from performing his or her job duties or constitutes a direct threat to property or the safety of others.

Thus, a person may not be discriminated against with respect to employment *solely* because of alcoholism or drug addiction. However, an employer is not obligated to hire people whose use of alcohol or drugs prevents them from satisfactorily performing their job duties. In addition, an employer is not obligated to hire people whose use of alcohol or drugs results in a direct threat to the property or safety of others. Supervisors should realize that their organization can be held liable for injuries caused by a person who is under the influence of drugs or alcohol.

Organizations and unions are beginning to include employee assistance programs in their collective bargaining agreements. The supervisor may find that the contract restricts his or her actions in the handling of problem employees. Some unions have assistance programs. These differ from employer programs primarily in the way the employee enters the program. The union program is voluntary, whereas employer programs usually demand participation for certain employees who are not performing satisfactorily.

In a unionized organization, the supervisor has the added responsibility of informing the union steward of the employee's participation in an assistance program. Keeping the steward informed helps ensure the union's cooperation. The steward can be very helpful in getting the employee to accept assistance.

SUPERVISION ILLUSTRATION 13-3

INCENTIVES FOR WELLNESS

Dalbey Education employs 275 people and provides products and services focused on creating entrepreneurial success through mentor-based education and support. Since its inception in 1995, Dalbey Education has provided educational products and support to more than 500,000 students.

On January 6, 2009, Dalbey Education launched a new wellness program for its employees. Under this program, called Virgin HealthMiles, employees can earn an extra $500 a year. The program is provided through the health benefits company Humana Inc. The program incentivizes and rewards healthy goals such as exercising, lowering blood pressure, and losing weight. Employees set their own goals, track their activity and key health measurements using self-tracking tools such as GoZone® pedometers and HealthZone measurement stations. They also monitor their progress on their own personal online tracking center. As employees proceed through the program's "reward levels" and reach key milestones, they earn up to $500 in HealthCash in the form of a gift card to a national retailer, a personal check or to donate to a charity of their choice. In the first six weeks of the program, approximately 35 percent of employees were participating in the program.

Source: "Dalbey Education Launches Health and Wellness Program," *PR Newswire*, February 25, 2009.

Problem Employees

9 LEARNING OBJECTIVES

In addition to the troubled employees previously discussed, there are other categories of employees that can have a negative impact on the department's performance. The "flirter," the "evangelist," the "socializer," the "busybody," the "complainer," and "lovebirds" are all examples of employees who can cause problems. Such employees behave in a manner that disrupts normal operations. At the least, they set a poor example and distract others. If their behavior is not checked, they may negatively affect the climate of the entire department. When a problem employee of this type is detected, the supervisor should immediately counsel the employee, using the techniques described earlier in this chapter. If counseling is ineffective, the supervisor may be forced to invoke some type of disciplinary action. Discipline is discussed in Chapter 17.

Career Counseling

10 LEARNING OBJECTIVES

Every so often a supervisor is asked by employees for some type of career counseling. Just what is the supervisor's role in these situations? Many supervisors are reluctant to engage in any form of career counseling because they haven't been trained in this effort or they feel that it is not in the best interest of the organization. It is not necessary to be a trained psychologist to be successful in career counseling. Supervisors who follow the counseling guidelines discussed earlier in this chapter can be successful. As far as being in the best interest of the organization, career counseling is usually a win-win situation for both the employee and the organization. Even in situations that result in an employee leaving, the organization is usually better off in the long run. Employees who remain usually feel better about their job and are better equipped to help the organization. First and foremost, supervisors must realize that the primary responsibility for career planning rests with each individual employee. The supervisor's role is to assist the employee and to help the employee evaluate his or her ideas, not to plan or make decisions for the employee. It is of primary importance for supervisors to demonstrate a caring attitude

Since Jane has detected a decline in Ken Hall's performance and suspects a drinking problem, she should attempt to counsel Ken, following the guidelines suggested in this chapter (p. 237). Specifically, she should present her documentation in a non-threatening manner and ask Ken to comment on her suspicions. If Ken acknowledges the problem, Jane should ask him for ideas on how to help overcome the problem. If Ken denies the problem, Jane should make sure that she has presented all of her evidence, warn Ken that she will be looking for evidence of a drinking problem, and point out that Ken's performance must improve.

The next step is to wrap up the discussion and summarize what has been decided and what actions will be taken. Before dismissing Ken, Jane should set a time to follow up on the actions agreed upon. Immediately after Ken has gone, Jane should document what was decided.

Depending on what happens during her confrontation with Ken, Jane might suggest that Ken participate in the company's employee assistance program (pp. 241–242). In any case, Jane would want to be sure that Ken is aware of what the company's EAP can do for him.

---

toward employees and their careers. Being receptive to employee concerns and problems is another requirement. Some additional specific suggestions for helping supervisors become effective career counselors are:

1. *Recognize the limits of career counseling.* Remember that the supervisor serves as a catalyst in the career development process. The primary responsibility for developing a career plan lies with the individual employee.

2. *Respect confidentiality.* Career counseling is very personal and has basic requirements of ethics, confidentiality, and privacy.

3. *Establish a relationship.* Be honest, open, and sincere with the employee. Try to be empathetic and see things from the employee's point of view.

4. *Listen effectively.* Learn to be a sincere listener. A natural human tendency is to want to do most of the talking. It often takes a conscious effort to be a good listener.

5. *Consider alternatives.* An important goal in career counseling is to help employees realize that there are usually a number of available choices. Help the employees to expand their thinking and not necessarily be limited by past experience.

6. *Seek and share information.* Be sure the employee and the organization have assessed the employee's abilities, interests, and desires. Make sure that the organization's assessment has been clearly communicated to the employee and that the employee is aware of potential job openings within the organization.

7. *Assist with goal definition and planning.* Remember that the employees must make the final decisions. Supervisors should serve as "sounding boards" and help ensure that the individual's plans are valid.[11]

Summary

Numerous situations require supervisors to act in a counseling role. This chapter discusses many of these situations and presents guidelines for counseling employees. It also offers guidelines for detecting, confronting, and managing troubled employees. Employee assistance programs (EAPs) are singled out for special attention.

1. *Determine when it is appropriate for the supervisor to counsel employees.* If the supervisor feels competent to offer counsel, he or she should counsel employees who voluntarily seek counsel or employees whose performance has declined. If the supervisor does not feel competent to offer counsel, he or she should refer such employees to a professionally trained person.

2. *Differentiate between directive and nondirective counseling.* In directive counseling, the supervisor takes the initiative and asks the employee pointed questions about a

problem. When the supervisor feels that he or she has a good grasp of what is causing the problem, he or she suggests several steps that the employee might take to overcome it. In nondirective counseling, the employee assumes most of the initiative and the supervisor serves primarily as a listener. The employee is encouraged to discuss what he or she thinks is causing the problem and to develop solutions to it.

3. *Present a general approach for counseling employees.* A general approach for counseling employees consists of these seven steps: (1) In a nonthreatening manner, describe what you have observed. (2) Ask the employee to comment on your observations. (3) If prior meetings have been held, briefly review what they accomplished. (4) With the employee's input, identify the problem-solving techniques to be used. (5) Restate the actions to be taken. (6) Set a time for follow-up. (7) Document the meeting.

4. *Define a "troubled employee."* A troubled employee is one whose job performance is affected by personal problems that cannot be corrected by normal counseling or disciplinary measures.

5. *Discuss ways to effectively supervise troubled employees.* A supervisor can effectively supervise troubled employees first by learning to detect them. Once a troubled employee has been identified, the supervisor should confront the employee. A part of the confrontation is to refer the employee to counseling and assistance. After a troubled employee has been through the necessary counseling and assistance program, the supervisor bears responsibility for evaluating the extent of rehabilitation based on the employee's job performance.

6. *Explain what employee assistance programs (EAPs) are.* EAPs are designed to provide assistance to employees with personal problems. There are several types of EAPs. In the rarest type, diagnosis and treatment of the employee's problem are provided by the organization. In a second type, the organization hires a qualified person to diagnose the employee's problem. The employee is then referred to the proper agency or clinic. In the most common type, a coordinator evaluates the employee's problem only sufficiently to make a referral to the proper agency or clinic.

7. *Describe wellness programs.* A wellness program is a company-implemented program designed to prevent illness and enhance employee well-being.

8. *Summarize the legal requirements for dealing with troubled employees.* The Rehabilitation Act of 1973 and subsequent amendments protect employable, qualified, handicapped workers (including alcohol and drug addicts) from discrimination in employment by federal contractors or subcontractors. However, employers are not obligated to hire people whose use of alcohol or drugs prevents them from satisfactorily performing their job duties or presents a direct threat to property or the safety of others.

9. *Explain the difference between a "troubled" employee and a "problem" employee.* A "troubled" employee is one whose job performance is affected by personal problems that cannot be corrected by normal counseling or disciplinary measures. Alcohol and drug abusers are examples of troubled employees. A "problem" employee is one who has a negative impact on the organization's performance but whose problem can usually be corrected with counseling and/or discipline. "Flirters" and "socializers" are examples of "problem" employees.

10. *Explain the supervisor's role in career counseling.* The primary responsibility for career planning rests with each individual employee. The supervisor's role is to assist the employee and to help the employee evaluate his or her ideas, not to plan or make decisions for the employee.

Key Terms

Career counseling, 245
Directive counseling, 236
Employee assistance program (EAP), 241

Nondirective counseling, 237
Problem employee, 245

Troubled employee, 237
Wellness program, 243

Review Questions

1. What are the differences between directive and nondirective counseling?

2. Outline the seven steps in a counseling interview.

3. Outline several suggestions for helping supervisors become effective career counselors.

4. Define a "troubled employee."

5. How do troubled employees affect the workplace environment?

6. What are some rules that the supervisor should observe when identifying troubled employees?

7. What are the three steps in the confrontation between the supervisor and the troubled employee?

8. What points should the supervisor emphasize when referring an employee to professional help?

9. What are some rules that the supervisor should follow to aid the troubled employee in the rehabilitation process?

10. What is an employee assistance program (EAP)?

11. What are four general types of employee assistance programs?

12. Explain wellness programs.

13. How do the Rehabilitation Act of 1973 and its amendments affect the supervisor's relationships with alcohol and drug abusers?

14. In addition to troubled employees, what other kinds of employees can have a negative impact on the work unit's performance?

15. Why are some supervisors reluctant to engage in a form of career counseling?

Skill-Building Questions

1. "Employees with personal problems that affect their work performance are basically weak people." Discuss your views on this statement.

2. Should a supervisor try to give an employee advice on how to solve a personal problem? Why or why not?

3. "In order to help a troubled employee, the supervisor must get to the root of the employee's problem." Discuss your views on this statement.

4. Many supervisors believe that troubled employees deserve whatever they get. How do you feel about this?

References

1. Much of this section is adapted from Steve Buckman, "Finding Out Why a Good Performer Went Bad," *Supervisory Management,* August 1984, pp. 39–42.

2. The National Council on Alcoholism and Drug Dependence, "Alcohol and Drug Dependence Are America's Number One Health Problem," http://www.ncadd.org/facts/numberoneprob.html, accessed on March 31, 2009.

3. The National Council on Alcoholism and Drug Dependence, "Alcohol and Other Drugs in the Workplace," http://www.ncadd.org/facts/workplac.html, accessed on March 31, 2009.

4. http://oas.samhsa.gov/NSDUH/2k7NSDUH/2k7 results.cfm, accessed on March 31, 2009.

5. Stephen Miller, "Survey–Employees Undervalue Benefits," *HR Magazine,* August 2007, p. 30.

6. William Atkinson, "Investments, Not Costs," *Textile World,* May 2001, p. 42.

7. Sheila Livadas, "Employee Assistance Programs Evolve, Broader Scope," *Rochester Business Journal,* May 23, 2008, p. 28.

8. Ibid.

9. Shari Caudron and Michael Rozek, "The Wellness Payoff," *Personnel Journal,* July 1990, pp. 54–62; as described in John M. Ivancevich, *Human Resource Management* (Burr Ridge, IL: Richard D. Irwin, 1995), pp. 636–37.

10. "Buck Consultants: Workplace Wellness Programs Fare Well During Economic Downturn, Reveals Buck Consultants Survey," *Obesity, Fitness & Wellness Week,* April 4, 2009, p. 2771.

11. Adapted from N. T. Meckel, "The Manager as Career Counselor," *Training and Development Journal,* July 1981, pp. 65–69.

Additional Readings

Boen, Jennifer L., "Speaker: Wellness is an Economic Issue: Employers Should Offer Incentives for Healthy Behaviors to Help Control Health Care Costs, He Says at Conference," *McClatchy-Tribune Business News,* March 13, 2008.

Greenwald, Judy, "Joint EAP, Work/Life Programs Cut Costs," *Business Insurance,* March 29, 2004, pp. T3–5.

Shreve, Meg, "Intervention Key in Battle Against Drug Abuse," *Business Insurance,* August 16, 2004, p. 6.

Spath, Patrice L., "Counseling to Help Problem Employees," *OR Manager,* April 2005, pp. 23–24.

Stanley, T. L., "Character Counts," *Supervision,* April 2007, pp. 9–11.

SKILL-BUILDING APPLICATIONS

Incident 13–1

Changes in an Employee's Behavior

Jack Sampson, a clerk in the human resources department of the Franklin County Hospital, had been with the hospital for four years. Until the last several months, he had been an ideal employee. He had always been excellent at answering other employees' questions. Furthermore, he was active in both community and church activities. He was married and had two children.

However, Mel Dillon, director of human resources for Franklin County Hospital, had noticed some significant changes in Jack's behavior during the last three or four months. Jack's work had become sloppy, and he had been very irritable and snappish when answering questions from employees. He had been absent from work on five occasions during the past two months. Before that, he had never missed a day of work. In addition, he had been late to work three times during the past month. This had never happened before. One day, Jack missed the weekly staff meeting. Afterward, he explained his absence by saying that he had forgotten about it.

Mel decided to talk to Jack about the change in his behavior. Jack explained he hadn't been feeling well lately. Mel suggested that he see a doctor, but Jack said, "I'll be OK. Just bear with me for a little while."

After another three weeks, Jack's behavior and performance did not improve. In fact, they seemed to be getting worse. During that time, Mel noticed that Jack was staying away from his desk for long periods. Since Jack's job didn't require him to be away from his desk for long periods, Mel decided to find out where he was going. As Jack was leaving his desk the next day, Mel followed him at a respectable distance. Jack went into one of the hospital's storage rooms and stayed there about 10 minutes. This storage room was for hospital supplies; as far as Mel could determine, Jack had absolutely no reason for being in it. A short time later, Mel thought he smelled alcohol on Jack's breath.

Questions

1. What should Mel do at this time?
2. How should Mel handle the overall problem?

Incident 13–2

Smoking in the Stockroom

Boyd Coleman was hired as a stock clerk 18 months ago. Until recently, Elena Ramirez, supervisor of the stockroom, had been very pleased with his work. She even talked him into enrolling in evening courses at a community college for which the company paid his tuition.

About two months ago, Elena noticed that Boyd had become very careless in his work. Two weeks ago, she had to give him a written reprimand for taking unauthorized leaves from the stockroom. Boyd's behavior improved for a week, but Elena felt that his work then again deteriorated. She called him into her office, where the following discussion occurred:

Elena: Boyd, I just don't know what I'm going to do about you. You started out so well. What happened?

Boyd: Nothing happened. You're just picking on me.

Elena: Picking on you! You know I've tried to help you. Remember, I was the one who got you to start school. That reminds me of something. The school called yesterday and said that you hadn't been in class for three weeks. Why?

Boyd: I just decided that the classes were useless. I don't need that stuff anyhow.

Elena: Boyd, something is bothering you. I don't know what it is, but I would like to help.

Boyd: Nothing is bothering me, and I want you to stop meddling in my personal life.

Elena: I'm not meddling. I would just like to help. As your supervisor, however, I must say that your performance on the job is my business, and it must improve. Do you understand?

Boyd: Yeah, I guess so.

Shortly thereafter, while walking through the stockroom, Elena heard two voices coming from behind a large stack of boxes. One of the voices said, "Don't smoke it all; let me have some of it." Elena recognized this voice as Boyd's. Elena also noticed a strange, sweet odor coming from the same area.

Questions

1. Would you confront the two people right now?
2. Should Elena walk away and discuss the problem with her boss?
3. How well did Elena handle the situation with Boyd before this incident?

Exercise 13–1

What Is the Problem?

Lately, one of your subordinates has been unusually irritable with several people in your department. You have purposely refrained from taking action because you believe that the parties involved should work out such difficulties. This approach has worked well in similar situations in the past. This morning, however, your subordinate directed some unnecessary remarks to you, and now it is apparent that you must act. Before you have an opportunity to discuss the situation, you hear through the grapevine that the subordinate is having marital difficulties, which obviously could be the source of the problem.

In handling the situation, you feel your best approaches are the following:

1. Mention that you've heard about the marital difficulties and that, although sympathetic, you don't feel that personal problems should influence behavior toward co-workers or job performance.
2. Privately advise other staff members that your subordinate is having some personal problems, and ask for their understanding during this difficult period.
3. Approach the problem by using yourself as an example. Indicate that you sometimes have personal problems and irritations but that you try not to let them affect you on the job. Then suggest that the subordinate exert extra effort to be less abrasive with others.
4. Ask questions and attempt to get a thorough understanding of your subordinate's problem so that you can give appropriate advice.
5. Mention that you have noticed the subordinate's recent irritable behavior, and listen to what the subordinate has to say. Then, in an understanding way, indicate that personal problems should not be allowed to affect job performance.

Other alternatives may be open to you, but assume that these are the only ones you have considered. *Without discussion with anyone,* decide which of these approaches you would take. Be prepared to defend your choice.

Source: Adapted from P. R. Jones, B. Kaye, and H. R. Taylor, "You Want Me to Do What?" Reprinted from the *Training and Development Journal,* July 1981, p. 62. Copyright 1981, *Training & Development,* American Society for Training and Development. Reprinted with permission. All rights reserved.

Exercise 13–2

How Do You Rate as a Career Counselor?

This quiz helps supervisors to examine their knowledge of the career counseling function and to discover those areas in which some skill building may be necessary. Rate your knowledge, skill, and confidence as a career counselor by scoring yourself on a scale of 0 (low) to 10 (high) on each of the following statements:

____ 1. I am aware of how career orientations and life stages can influence a person's perspective and contribute to career planning problems.

____ 2. I understand my own career choices and changes and feel good enough about what I have done to be able to provide guidance to others.

____ 3. I am aware of my own biases about dual career paths and feel that I can avoid these biases in coaching others to make a decision on which way to go with their careers.

____ 4. I am aware of how my own values influence my point of view, and I recognize the importance of helping others to define their values and beliefs so they are congruent with career goals.

____ 5. I am aware of the pitfalls of "shooting behind the duck" and try to keep myself well informed about my organization, so I can show others how to "shoot ahead of the duck."

____ 6. I know the norms existing within my own department as well as those within other departments and parts of the organization, so I can help others deal with them effectively.

____ 7. I understand the organizational reward system (nonmonetary) well enough to help others make informed decisions about career goals, paths, and plans.

_____ 8. I have access to a variety of techniques I can use to help others articulate their skills, set goals, and develop action plans to realize their career decisions.

_____ 9. I am informed about the competencies required for career success in this organization in both the managerial and technical areas, so I can advise others on the particular skills they need to build on and how to go about developing that expertise.

_____10. I feel confident enough about my own skills as a career counselor that I can effectively help my people with their problems and plans and make mid-course corrections when necessary.

Scoring

Add up your score and rate yourself against the following scale:

  0–30 It might be a good idea if you found *yourself* a career counselor.

31–60 Some of your people are receiving help from you. . . . However, do you know how many and which ones are not?

61–80 You're a counselor! You may not be ready for the big league yet, but you are providing help for your people.

81–100 Others have a lot to learn from you. You understand the importance of career counseling, and you know how to provide it.

Exercise 13–3

Who Is Right?

Because of his short temper and stubborn attitude, George was assigned to various jobs during his five years with the ABC Company. When the quality of George's work declined along with his attitude, management began using progressive discipline. After getting suspended for insubordination, George was warned that another insubordination would result in discharge. At this same time, management urged George to seek counseling through the company's employee assistance program (EAP). George refused to seek the help of the EAP.

At one point, George's supervisor became so concerned about George's behavior that the supervisor temporarily removed him from his job. Management then offered George a "last chance" agreement, which required George to seek counseling through the company's EAP. George signed the agreement only to announce later that he couldn't live up to its terms. After management suspended George, he insisted that he be terminated instead. Management obliged George by terminating him.

At this point, George withdrew his termination request and filed a grievance seeking reinstatement. He said that he objected to the "last chance" agreement because it required him to participate in the EAP, which was supposed to be voluntary. George stated that if he participated in the EAP, he would be admitting that he had done something wrong. Management replied that his insubordination and poor performance were sufficient grounds for discharge and that they had gone beyond the call of duty by offering him another chance. Management further stated that George's consistent refusal to get help left no alternative but termination.

1. Does George fit the definition of a "troubled employee"?

2. Do you think George should have been offered the "last chance" agreement? Why or why not?

3. How would you have handled the situation if you had been George's supervisor?

Source: From "Troubled Employees," by William E. Lissy, *Supervision,* January 1996. Reprinted by permission of © National Research Bureau, P.O. Box 1, Burlington, IA 52601-0001.

Leadership Skills

SECTION OUTLINE

CHAPTER FOURTEEN

Developing Leadership Skills

Learning objectives

After studying this chapter, you will be able to:

1. Define leadership.
2. Describe three basic styles of leadership.
3. Define supportive and directive leaders.
4. Explain transactional and transformational leadership.
5. Explain servant leadership.
6. Define leadership characteristics.
7. Describe leader attitudes—Theory X and Theory Y.
8. Discuss the Managerial Grid®.
9. Explain the situational approach to leadership.

Supervision Dilemma

John Lewis has been a supervisor for over a year now, yet he still feels unsure of his ability to lead his employees. Oh, sure, he can order them around, but do they really follow his leadership? John can't help noticing Marlin O'Neal's group. Marlin has been a supervisor for over five years, and his group seems to operate like a well-oiled machine. Marlin's employees seem to trust him completely and never hesitate to follow his lead. On the other hand, John feels that he has to "sell his soul" to get his employees to follow his lead. He can't help wondering if Marlin knows something he doesn't.

Leadership is probably researched and discussed more than any other topic in the field of management. New suggestions, methods, and tips for improving leadership skills are offered each year. Everyone seems to acknowledge the importance of leadership to supervisory and organizational success. This chapter offers perspectives on leadership processes and styles.

Defining Leadership

LEARNING OBJECTIVES

Leadership is the ability to influence people to willingly follow one's guidance or adhere to one's decisions. Obtaining followers and influencing them in setting and achieving objectives makes a leader. Leadership and management are not necessarily the same. In practice, though, effective leadership and effective management must ultimately accompany one another. Supervision Illustration 14–1 gives one executive's opinion on the dimensions of leadership.

Formal versus Informal Leaders

Supervisors are formal leaders in the sense that they are formally appointed by the organization. Other types of leaders may emerge who are not formally appointed by the organization. These leaders, known as informal leaders, are chosen by the group itself. It is not unusual for a work team to have an informal leader in addition to the supervisor. Informal leaders generally emerge because they are viewed by the group as filling its needs. A group's informal leader may change as the group's needs change. The following simple example illustrates this point. Suppose a group of people are shipwrecked on a desolate island. The group's first need would probably be to find food, water, and shelter, so the group would select as its leader the person viewed by the group as the one who could best help it acquire these essentials. After this had been done, other needs would emerge. The need to escape from the island would probably emerge rather quickly. The person originally selected as the leader may not be the person perceived by the group as the most capable in achieving the newly emerging needs. In that case, the group might select a new leader. Furthermore, the group might continue to change its leaders depending on the changes in its needs.

If a group has an informal leader in addition to the supervisor, this does not necessarily indicate that the supervisor is not a good leader. The informal leader may be fulfilling group needs that shouldn't be met by the supervisor. For example, an informal leader may be chosen because of a knack for telling jokes and keeping things on the light side. On the other hand, informal leaders may also cause detrimental behavior. For example, an informal leader might convince the group to restrict output. Successful supervisors do not try to overpower or eliminate informal leaders. Rather, they recognize them and learn to work through them to everyone's benefit.

SUPERVISION ILLUSTRATION 14–1

FIVE DIMENSIONS OF LEADERSHIP

In our current economic environment, many are looking for companies helmed by great leaders. Tom Gardner, co-founder and CEO of The Motley Fool, recently discussed leadership with former Medtronic CEO Bill George, author of "True North" (Jossey-Bass, $30) and "Authentic Leadership" (Jossey-Bass, $20). George is worth hearing, as he led Medtronic to a 60-fold increase in its value during his 10-year tenure. He identifies five dimensions of an authentic leader:

First, leaders must have a purpose. They must know why they want to lead and where they're going.

They must practice and live their values every day—and not just the ones they articulate.

They must lead with their hearts, not just their heads. Obviously, intellect is necessary, but George believes that having the heart is key: "This means having the passion for the work, having a real understanding of compassion for the people you work with, having a real deep understanding and empathy for your customers, and having the courage to make difficult decisions.

"When you think about it, passion, compassion, courage and empathy are all matters of the heart, not of the head. There are so many leaders who have been brilliant leaders but have failed because they failed in that dimension."

George noted that many leaders have vast networks of superficial relationships, when they really need deeper networks, where there's "a sense of two-way commitment between the individuals."

His fifth dimension is "having the self-discipline to get results."

Source: Adapted Anonymous, "Great Leadership, by George," *McClatchy—Tribune Business News.* March 9, 2000, Wire Feed.

Basic Styles of Leadership

 LEARNING OBJECTIVES 2

While there are numerous variations, there are three basic styles of leadership—autocratic, democratic, and laissez-faire. The main differences among these styles concern how decisions are made and who makes them. Generally, the autocratic leader makes all decisions for the group. The **autocratic leader** centralizes power and enjoys giving orders. Under this style of leadership, followers contribute little, if anything, to the decision-making process. The **democratic leader** wants the followers to share in making decisions. This type of leader guides and encourages the group to participate in making decisions. Even though the decision making is shared, the leader still has the final say. The **laissez-faire leader** pretty much allows the group members to do as they please. Such a leader allows the members of the group to make all the decisions. In effect, the laissez-faire leader only provides information to the group and does not direct or guide the group. The laissez-faire leader is rarely seen in organizations. A more detailed description of each of the three leadership styles is given in Figure 14.1.

While one of these styles (or a variation of one) tends to dominate, a supervisor can learn to use various styles of leadership to fit different situations. Balancing the style of leadership to fit different situations is described later in this chapter.

Supportive or Directive Leadership?

In addition to the three basic styles of leadership, leaders can be categorized as being supportive or directive. **Supportive leaders** are genuinely interested in the well-being of group members. Such a leader is sensitive to the employees as human beings. This leader wants to build morale, avoid conflict, and help the employees gain personal satisfaction. The supportive leader is usually very concerned about maintaining a good personal relationship with the employees.

LEARNING OBJECTIVES 3

Directive leaders focus primarily on successfully performing the work. Such a leader spends considerable time directing the employees in solving production problems. The emphasis is on getting the job done. The directive leader spends very little time providing

FIGURE 14.1
Styles of Leadership

Autocratic Style

Leader
1. The leader is very conscious of his or her position.
2. The leader has little trust and faith in members of the work group.
3. This leader believes that pay is a reward for work and the only reward that will motivate employees.
4. Orders are issued to be carried out with no questions allowed and no explanations given.

Group members
1. No responsibility is assumed for performance, with employees merely doing what they are told.
2. Production is good when the supervisor is present, but poor in the supervisor's absence.

Laissez-Faire Style

Leader
1. The leader has no confidence in his or her leadership ability.
2. This leader does not set goals for the group.

Group members
1. Decisions are made by whoever in the group is willing to make them.
2. Generally, productivity is low and work is sloppy.
3. Employees have little interest in their work.
4. Morale and teamwork are generally low.

Democratic Style

Leader
1. Decision making is shared between the leader and the work group.
2. When the leader is required or forced to make a decision, his or her reasoning is explained to the group.
3. Criticism and praise are given objectively.

Group members
1. New ideas and change are welcomed.
2. A feeling of responsibility is developed within the work group.
3. Quality of work and productivity are generally high.
4. The group generally feels successful.

emotional support and reassurance for the employees. A directive leader is not necessarily harsh or rude, but one who simply gives priority to work accomplishment over human feelings.

Directive leaders generally employ an autocratic style of leadership. Supportive leaders generally employ a more democratic style of leadership. Most leaders are not all directive or all supportive. A large middle ground is occupied by some mix of these two extremes.

Transformational and Transactional Leaders

LEARNING OBJECTIVES

Another approach to the analysis of leadership has been based on how leaders and followers influence one another. Under this approach, leadership is viewed as either a transactional or transformational process. **Transactional leadership** takes the approach that leaders engage in a bargaining relationship with their followers. Under this approach, the leader (manager)

1. Tells employees what they need to do to obtain rewards.
2. Takes corrective action only when employees fail to meet performance objectives.

Transformational leadership involves cultivating employee acceptance of the group mission. The manager– employee relationship is one of mutual stimulation and is characterized by charisma on the part of the leader, inspiration by the leader, consideration by the leader of individual needs, and intellectual stimulation between the leader and followers.Transformational leaders go beyond transacting with their followers and transform not only the situation but also the followers.

Servant Leadership

5 LEARNING OBJECTIVES

Servant leadership, still another philosophy of leadership, is based on the belief that the leader exists to meet the needs of the people who he or she nominally leads. The servant leader takes the fulfillment of followers' needs as his or her primary aim. The servant leader believes that the business exists as much to provide meaningful work to employees as it does to provide a quality product or service to the customer.

Leadership Characteristics

6 LEARNING OBJECTIVES

The first studies ever done in the area of leadership focused on looking at personality traits and physical characteristics of successful leaders. These early researchers believed that leaders were different from ordinary people in terms of personality and physical characteristics. However, this approach has not produced any definitive findings. The end result has been that in over 50 years of study, no single set of personality traits or set of physical characteristics can be used to pinpoint a leader from a nonleader. At the same time, however, it is recognized that certain characteristics are desirable in most leadership situations.

Self-Confidence

Self-confidence stems from having precise knowledge and knowing how to use it. People with a high degree of self-confidence generally gain the confidence of those around them. Few employees want to follow a leader who appears not to know what he or she is doing.

Mental and Physical Endurance

Almost all leaders are subjected to situations that try their patience. The ability to control his or her temper and to be coolheaded can be very advantageous to the leader. Mental and emotional stress can be physically exhausting. Therefore, leaders should have enough physical endurance to withstand hardships and disappointments that might arise.

Enthusiasm

Enthusiasm is contagious! It is easy for group members to get excited about their work if the leader is excited about the work. On the other hand, no one wants to work for a dull and negative leader.

Sense of Responsibility

A leader should seek, not avoid, responsibility. Leaders who actively seek responsibility are admired by most followers. Followers like to feel that their leaders will stick up for them in difficult times. Leaders who attempt to avoid responsibility are quick to lose the admiration of their followers.

Empathy and Good Human Relations

Successful leaders are able to empathize with their followers. This means being able to see things from the followers' point of view. Because leadership involves working with others, good human relations skills are essential for leaders. A leader must be able to work with followers and understand their problems.

It should be stressed that possession of the characteristics described above does not guarantee success as a leader. Many other factors may affect a leader's success. However, possession of these characteristics is certainly desirable and it usually increases the chances of success.

Leader Attitudes and Expectations

7 LEARNING OBJECTIVES

Basically, supervisors can have two assumptions concerning the basic nature of people. These two divergent assumptions are termed *Theory X* and *Theory Y*.[1] **Theory X** maintains that the average employee dislikes work and will do whatever is possible to avoid it. **Theory Y** states that people like work and that it comes as naturally as rest and play. (Figure 14.2 defines Theory X and Theory Y in greater detail.) Many leaders basically subscribe to either Theory X or Theory Y and behave accordingly. Thus, it is likely that a supervisor subscribing to Theory X would use a more autocratic style of leadership than that used by a supervisor subscribing to Theory Y. An important point is that a supervisor's attitude toward human nature has a large influence on that person's behavior as a leader. It should also be realized that the Theory X/Theory Y issue is not always a matter of choice by the supervisor. For example, if a supervisor inherits a group of Theory X employees who have been supervised under a Theory X style, an immediate switch to Theory Y style could cause problems.

Others have also investigated the relationship between a leader's expectations and the performance of individuals within the group. Specifically, the relationship between a leader's expectations of an employee and the resulting performance achieved by the employee has received considerable attention.

Generally, it can be said that if the supervisor's expectations are high, the subordinates' productivity is likely to be high. On the other hand, if the supervisor's expectations are low, the subordinates' productivity is likely to be poor. This phenomenon is sometimes referred to as the **self-fulfilling prophecy**. Supervision Illustration 14–2 describes Theory X managers in India.

FIGURE 14.2
Assumptions about the Basic Nature of Employees

Theory X

1. The average employee has an inherent dislike of work and will avoid it whenever possible.
2. Because of this dislike of work, most employees must be coerced, controlled, directed, and threatened with punishment to get them to put forth adequate effort toward the achievement of organizational objectives.
3. The average employee prefers to be directed, wishes to avoid responsibility, has relatively little ambition, and wants security above all.

Theory Y

1. To the average employee, the expenditure of physical and mental effort in work is as natural as play or rest.
2. External control and the threat of punishment are not the only means for bringing about effort toward organizational objectives; employees will exercise self-direction and self-control in the service of objectives to which they are committed.
3. Commitment to objectives is a function of the rewards associated with their achievement.
4. The average employee learns, under proper conditions, not only to accept but to seek responsibility.
5. The capacity to exercise a relatively high degree of imagination, ingenuity, and creativity in the solution of organizational problems is widely, not narrowly, distributed in the workforce.
6. At work, the intellectual potentialities of the average employee are only partially utilized.

SUPERVISION ILLUSTRATION 14–2

THEORY X MANAGERS IN INDIA

While the West might benefit by sending out the so called "low-end" jobs to India, we will end up inheriting the problems of alienation. That is why I am convinced that it is time for a second QWL (quality of work life) movement and this time around, it has to be born in India!

While every leader will swear that he makes Theory Y assumptions about his people, his actions are mostly Theory X. Organizations love managers who run a tight ship, who micromanage, who are directive and quickly jump in when

things are going wrong. Things like the Blackberry only make this easier. When you demonstrate Theory X assumptions, your people will live up to the prophecy of being irresponsible or at best do what is asked of them. Theory X managers can never create ownership. Given the pressures of performance and the lack of preparation for leadership, I am afraid that India faces the grave danger of breeding more and more Theory X managers.

Source: Adapted from Ganesh Chella, "Poor Ownership the Result of Poor Leadership," *Businessline,* February 4, 2008, p. 1.

Managerial Grid®

8 LEARNING OBJECTIVES

The **Managerial Grid** uses a two-dimensional grid to identify and relate different styles of leadership. The vertical axis of the grid represents concern for people (supportive style). The horizontal axis represents concern for production (directive style). Figure 14.3 shows some of the more obvious styles that may be identified by means of the Managerial Grid.[2] The Managerial Grid is intended to serve as a framework that enables supervisors to learn what their leadership style is and to develop a plan for moving toward a team-management style of leadership (upper right-hand corner of the grid). This approach has been criticized for assuming that a team-management style works best in all situations.

When leadership styles are discussed, this question always surfaces: "Which style is best?" Some people feel that the team-management style works best in all situations. Others believe that the most appropriate style of leadership usually depends on the situation.

Choosing the Best Style

Implying that a supervisor should be supportive rather than directive (or vice versa) does not offer much guidance for daily leadership situations. All of us can think of situations in which a task-centered (autocratic) leader was very successful. We can also think of situations in

FIGURE 14.3
Managerial Grid®

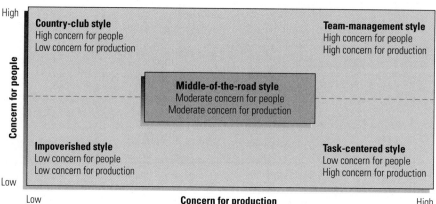

FIGURE 14.4   **Classification of Situations**

Situation	1	2	3	4	5	6	7	8
Leader-member relations	Good	Good	Good	Good	Poor	Poor	Poor	Poor
Task structure	Structured	Structured	Unstructured	Unstructured	Structured	Structured	Unstructured	Unstructured
Position power	Strong	Weak	Strong	Weak	Strong	Weak	Strong	Weak

Favorable for leader → *Unfavorable for leader*

Situational Approach to Leadership

9   LEARNING OBJECTIVES

which a supportive democratic leader was equally successful. Practice and research both have shown that *no one leadership style works best in all situations.*

The **situational approach to leadership** attempts to identify the particular styles of leadership that are appropriate for particular situations.[3] Three dimensions of the situation have an impact on the leader's effectiveness. These dimensions are (1) leader-member relations, (2) task structure, and (3) position power. *Leader-member relations* refer to the degree of the followers' trust and respect for the leader. *Task structure* is the extent to which the followers' tasks are structured—that is, routine and repetitive work versus unstructured work. *Position power* refers to the power and influence of the leader.

Using these three dimensions, different situations can be classified as to the favorableness for the leader. For example, the most favorable situation for the leader is one in which there are good leader-member relations, a structured task, and strong position of power. The least favorable situation for the leader has just the opposite features. Figure 14.4 shows the classification of situations. Using this scheme, the following relationships exist:

1. When the situation is either highly favorable or highly unfavorable to the leader, directive leadership tends to result in the most effective group performance.
2. When the situation is moderately favorable to the leader, supportive leadership tends to result in the most effective group performance.

Thus, the overriding conclusion is that the most effective style of leadership depends on the situation! So it seems if the situation is highly favorable or unfavorable to the leader, adopt a directive style. If the situation is moderately favorable, adopt a supportive style. The key to success lies in matching one's leadership style to the situation.

Leadership and Morale

In addition to its obvious impact on employee performance, the appropriateness of one's leadership style can have an impact on many areas of the organization. The group's morale or team spirit is greatly affected by the type of leadership style employed. Morale usually refers to the general attitude of the group and to the group's overall level of satisfaction. Morale can have a very significant impact on many variables, such as turnover, attendance, tardiness, and sabotage. Prolonged low morale can even contribute to poor mental health.

There are things that the leader can do to raise the morale of the group:

1. Be a good communicator. This involves good listening as well as clear directions.
2. Be considerate. Being considerate of the group members doesn't mean that production will slide.

SUPERVISION ILLUSTRATION   14–3

EMCOR GROUP, INC.

EMCOR Group, Inc., a Fortune 500(R) leader in mechanical and electrical construction, energy infrastructure and facilities services for a diverse range of businesses, is proud to announce that it has been named the 2009 World's Most Admired Company in the Engineering and Construction industry by FORTUNE magazine. EMCOR was named America's #1 Most Admired Company in the industry in the 2008 FORTUNE ranking.

FORTUNE's Most Admired list is the definitive report card on corporate reputations. The annual ranking was compiled starting with some 1,400 companies and, after sorting, surveying 689 companies, in 64 industries, from 28 countries. The Hay Group, FORTUNE's survey partner, asked 4,047 executives, directors, and analysts to rate companies in their industry on nine criteria, from investment value to social responsibility. A company's

score must rank in the top half of its industry survey. The full list of companies appears in the March 16, 2009 edition of FORTUNE, and is currently available at www.fortune.com.

EMCOR has also continued its "Touching Lives" corporate responsibility program, which includes the further expansion of its "Taking KidSafety to the Street(TM)" program, leveraging EMCOR's fleet of more than 6,000 service vehicles nationwide to display posters from the National Center for Missing and Exploited Children (NCMEC) of missing children. To date, EMCOR's efforts have aided in the recovery of 130 children since the inception of the program less than four years ago.

Source: Anonymous, "EMCOR Group, Inc. Named by FORTUNE Magazine World's #1 Most Admired Company in the Engineering and Construction Industry," *Business Wire,* March 10, 2009, Wire Feed.

3. Encourage employee input. Encourage the employees to take an interest and participate in what is going on.

4. Maintain a clean and safe environment. A sloppy and dangerous environment breeds low morale.

5. Keep your word. Don't say one thing and do another.

6. Be fair. Treat everyone equally, and don't play favorites.

7. Set a good example. Remember that the leader is constantly being watched.

Implications for Today's Supervisors

Can any general conclusions be drawn concerning leadership for today's supervisors? The following points can be made concerning effective leadership:

1. A combination of high-supportive and high-directive styles is often a successful leadership style.

2. Under emergency or high-pressure situations, emphasis on the work is desirable and often preferred by employees.

3. Since the supervisor is frequently the only information source for employees regarding their work, they often expect the supervisor to structure their behavior.

4. Higher management often has set preferences regarding the leadership styles employed by lower-level managers and supervisors.

5. Some leaders can adjust their behavior to fit the situation, while others appear to be fake and manipulative when they attempt to make such adjustments.

Supervision Illustration 14–3 describes the results of effective leadership.

John has learned that being a successful leader means getting employees to willingly follow him. He has learned that there are three basic leadership styles—autocratic, democratic, and laissez-faire (p. 256). He has also learned that the most effective leadership style depends on the situation and that the key to success lies in matching one's leadership style to the situation (pp. 260–261). He is now aware that his expectations play a big role in his employees' performance. If his expectations are high, the productivity of his employees is also likely to be high (p. 259).

Summary

This chapter defines leadership and shows its relationship to the supervisory process. Different approaches to leadership are presented, along with specific implications for today's supervisors.

1. *Define leadership.* Leadership is the ability to influence people to willingly follow one's guidance.

2. *Describe three basic styles of leadership.* The autocratic leader centralizes power and enjoys giving orders. The democratic leader wants the followers to share in making decisions. The laissez-faire leader allows the group members to do as they please.

3. *Define supportive and directive leaders.* Supportive leaders are genuinely interested in the well-being of the group members. Directive leaders focus primarily on the work being successfully performed.

4. *Explain transactional and transformational leadership.* Transactional leadership takes the approach that leaders engage in a bargaining relationship with their followers. Transformational leadership is concerned with leaders who have some charisma and possess the ability to inspire followers to subordinate their own interests for the good of the organization. Transformational leaders go beyond transacting with their followers and transform not only the situation but also the followers.

5. *Explain servant leadership.* Servant leadership is based on the belief that the leader exists to meet the needs of the people whom he or she nominally leads.

6. *Define leadership characteristics.* The basic leadership characteristics that are desirable for most supervisory situations include self-confidence, mental and physical endurance, enthusiasm, a sense of responsibility, empathy, and good human relations skills. Working to develop these characteristics will not guarantee success as a leader, but it will increase a supervisor's chances of obtaining success.

7. *Describe leader attitudes—Theory X and Theory Y.* Theory X maintains that the average employee dislikes work and will do whatever is possible to avoid it. Theory Y states that people like work and that it comes as naturally as rest and play.

8. *Discuss the Managerial Grid®.* The Managerial Grid uses a two-dimensional grid to identify and relate different styles of leadership. The vertical axis of the grid represents concern for people. The horizontal axis represents concern for production.

9. *Explain the situational approach to leadership.* The situational approach to leadership identifies the particular styles of leadership that are appropriate for particular situations. If the situation is highly favorable or highly unfavorable to the leader, adopt a directive style. If the situation is moderately favorable to the leader, adopt a supportive style.

Key Terms

Autocratic leader, 256
Democratic leader, 256
Directive leaders, 256
Laissez-faire leader, 256
Leadership, 255

Managerial Grid®, 260
Self-fulfilling prophecy, 259
Servant leadership, 258
Situational approach to leadership, 261

Supportive leaders, 256
Theory X, 259
Theory Y, 259
Transactional leadership, 257
Transformational leadership, 258

Review Questions

1. What is leadership?
2. Describe the following leadership styles.
   a. Autocratic.
   b. Democratic.
   c. Laissez-faire.
3. Compare and contrast a supportive leader with a directive leader.

4. Explain transactional and transformational leadership.
5. Explain servant leadership.
6. Describe Theory X and Theory Y.
7. What is the Managerial Grid®?
8. Describe the situational approach to leadership.
9. List seven things that a leader can do to improve group morale.

Skill-Building Questions

1. What do you think of the leader who says, "Do what I say, not what I do"?
2. Discuss the following statement: "Leaders are born, not developed."
3. How can you explain the fact that leaders who employ entirely different leadership styles may enjoy equal success? For example, two football coaches who use very different leadership styles may both be very successful.
4. Support or refute the following statement: "If a leader thinks that a certain follower is going to fail, then that follower will fail."

References

1. See Douglas McGregor, *The Human Side of Enterprise* (New York: McGraw-Hill, 1960).
2. See Robert Blake and Jane Mouton, "How to Choose a Leadership Style," *Training and Development Journal,* February 1982, pp. 38–45.
3. See Fred E. Fiedler, *A Theory of Leadership Effectiveness* (New York: McGraw-Hill, 1967).

Additional Readings

Anonymous, "Becoming a Better Leader: How to Use Self-Analysis and Self-Improvement to Boost Your Leadership Skills, *PR Newswire,* February 16, 2009, Wire Feed.

Kincaid, Sara, "Grads Want to Revive Leadership Program," *McClatchy-Tribune Business News,* March 4, 2009, Wire Feed.

Nealy, Michelle J., "Sharpening Leadership Skills, Connecting with Sisters," *Diverse Issues in Higher Education,* March 5, 2009, p. 7.

Preston, Suzanne, "Today's Students Preparing to be Tomorrow's Leaders," *McClatchy-Tribune Business News,* February 2, 2009, Wire Feed.

Vasil, Gary J., "Make It Happen Now," *Automotive Design and Production,* December 2009, p. 25.

SKILL-BUILDING APPLICATIONS

Incident 14–1

Jealousy at the Bank

You have recently been promoted to supervisor of teller operations at the downtown office of the Fourth National Bank. Prior to this assignment, you held a similar position at one of the branch offices. Some of your initial gratification over receiving the job was taken away when you heard through the grapevine that many of the downtown tellers were upset about your appointment. Rumor had it that these tellers were infuriated that the head teller, Janice Adams, did not get the job.

You: I don't know what to do. I feel as though I've never had a chance in this job. Everybody seems to hate me from the start because I got this job instead of Janice Adams.

Your Boss: What has happened since you've been here?

You: When I arrived, I was full of energy and was committed to being a good leader. The very first thing I did was hold a group meeting and tell all the tellers that I welcomed their input and that my door was always open. That was about four weeks ago, and not one teller has come into my office yet. The next thing I did was send out a memo soliciting suggestions for improving the department. I did receive some suggestions, but no two were the same. In fact, many were in direct conflict with one another. For example, one suggestion was to implement more detailed procedures. Another suggestion was to relax the "overly rigid" procedures.

Your Boss: What have you done since you got the suggestions?

You: To be honest, nothing. As I said before, no clear trends or ideas emerged. Some people seemed to even resent my original memo. One response said that good supervisors could come up with their own ideas. Naturally, with the situation being as it is, I am reluctant to implement anything for fear of making matters worse. At the same time, I know that the situation is deteriorating every day.

Your Boss: Didn't you just request a raise for several of your employees?

You: I sure did. That seemed like a good way to win them over. Anyway, several of them are definitely underpaid in comparison with the industry average. Of course, you know I don't have a lot of authority in this job. All I can do is make recommendations. At any rate, I'm frustrated by the situation and I don't know how long I can take it.

Questions

1. Do you think that giving the employees a pay raise will win them over?
2. How might you handle the situation now after learning about different styles of leadership?

Incident 14–2

Promises You Can't Keep

Roy Radcliff was hired four years ago as supervisor of the order processing section of the Golden Platter Recording Company. Golden Platter has enjoyed overwhelming success in its seven-year history. Sales this year increased 38 percent over last year's sales. Several people in the company, including Roy, believe that Golden Platter will soon be in the $50 million category.

Roy's optimism spilled over to his employees. He constantly reminded them of Golden Platter's tremendous potential. In fact, Roy had most of his employees convinced that promotions would come automatically if they just stayed with the company and did as they were told. "Just keep your nose clean" was one of his favorite counsels. Almost everyone took him at his word and thought that he was a great guy to work for.

To even Roy's surprise, he was offered a job as sales representative for the company in what he described as a fabulous territory. David Wong was chosen to replace him. David had established an excellent reputation as an assistant supervisor in the maintenance department. Soon after David took over the order processing section, he discovered that Roy had made impossible promises to many of his employees. Two employees had been promised promotions that were obviously beyond their capabilities. Several had been led to believe that unrealistically high pay raises would be forthcoming. To top it all off, Roy had told all employees in the order processing section that they could take a coffee break whenever they wanted to.

Questions

1. What do you think of Roy's leadership style?
2. Why do you think that someone might resort to Roy's style of leadership?
3. What would you do if you were David?

Incident 14–3

Does the Congregation Care?

You are talking with a young pastor of an independent church with 300 adult members. The pastor came directly to the church after graduating from a nondenominational theological school and has been in the job for eight months.

Pastor: I don't know what to do. I feel as if I've been treading water ever since the day I got here; and frankly, I'm not sure that I will be here much longer. If they don't fire me, I may leave on my own. Maybe I'm just not cut out for the ministry.

You: What has happened since you came to this church?

Pastor: When I arrived, I was really full of energy and wanted to see how much this church could accomplish. The very first thing I did was to conduct a questionnaire survey of the entire adult membership to see what types of goals they wanted to pursue. Unfortunately, I found that the members had such mixed (and perhaps apathetic) feelings about the goals that it was hard to draw any conclusions. There were also a few who strongly favored more emphasis on internal things, such as remodeling the sanctuary, developing our music program, and setting up a day care center for the use of the members. Most of the members, however, didn't voice any strong preferences. A lot of people didn't return the questionnaire, and a few even seemed to resent my conducting the survey.

You: What have you done since you took the survey?

Pastor: To be honest about it, I've kept a pretty low profile, concentrating mainly on routine duties. I haven't tried to implement or even push any major new programs. One problem is that I've gotten the impression, through various insinuations, that my being hired was by no means an overwhelmingly popular decision. Evidently, a fairly substantial segment of the congregation was skeptical of my lack of experience and felt that the decision to hire me was railroaded through by a few members of the Pastoral Search Committee. I guess I am just reluctant to assume a strong leadership role until some consensus has developed concerning the goals of the church and I've had more time to gain the confidence of the congregation. I don't know how long that will take, though; and I'm not sure I can tolerate the situation much longer.

Questions

1. Analyze and explain the situation using any of the theories of leadership discussed in this chapter.
2. What would you recommend the young pastor do?

Exercise 14–1

Insubordination?

Your company installed a new performance management system this year. You distributed the information and forms several weeks ago, and they were due to be completed two weeks ago. One manager reporting to you has not yet returned his forms. This morning, you ran into him in the parking lot and asked him about it. He reacted angrily. "I haven't had time to do it," he said. "I don't have enough time to get my job done as it is, much less take the time necessary to have my people write a bunch of meaningless information."

You ask him to stop by your office later to discuss the matter. As you think about how to handle the situation during the meeting, you consider several alternatives:

1. In view of his attitude and behavior, it is clearly appropriate to exercise your authority. Tell him in no uncertain terms that this task must be done if he expects to continue as a supervisor.

2. Tell him why this program is important, and use your best persuasion technique to sell him on carrying it out willingly.

3. Remind him that no salary increases, including his own, will be processed until the forms have been completed. Establish another deadline, and let him know that you expect the forms to be turned in by that date.

4. Explain to him that appraising employee performance is a part of every supervisor's job and that he is being evaluated on his performance in implementing this program.

5. Tell him that you understand the difficulties of his job and the shortage of time available to do it, but remind him that this is a mandatory program that has top management's backing.

Other alternatives may be open to you, but assume that these are the only ones you have considered. *Without discussion with anyone,* choose one of them. Be prepared to defend your choice.

Exercise 14–2

Situational Approach to Leadership

Under the situational approach to leadership, different situations call for different leadership styles. Assuming this approach is correct, outline specific situations in which you would employ an autocratic style of leadership. In addition, outline situations in which you would employ a participative style of leadership. Be very specific in describing the situation. Be prepared to present to the class your list of situations for both leadership styles.

Exercise 14–3

Test Your Leadership Style

Read both statements in each entry in the following list and circle either *a* or *b* to indicate which one best describes you—or is the least incorrect about you. You must answer every question to arrive at a proper score.

1. *a.* You are the person people most often turn to for help.
   b. You are aggressive and look after your best interests first.

2. *a.* You are more competent and better able to motivate others than most people.
   b. You strive to reach a position where you can exercise authority over large numbers of people and sums of money.

3. *a.* You try hard to influence the outcome of events.
   b. You quickly eliminate all obstacles that stand in the way of your goals.

4. *a.* There are few people you have as much confidence in as you have in yourself.
   b. You have no qualms about taking what you want in this world.

5. *a.* You have the ability to inspire others to follow your lead.
   b. You enjoy having people act on your commands and are not opposed to making threats if you must.

6. *a.* You do your best to influence the outcome of events.
   b. You make all the important decisions, expecting others to carry them out.

7. *a.* You have a special magnetism that attracts people to you.
   b. You enjoy dealing with situations requiring confrontation.

8. *a.* You would enjoy consulting on the complex issues and problems that face managers of companies.
   b. You would enjoy planning, directing, and controlling the staff of a department to ensure the highest profit margins.

9. *a.* You want to consult with business groups and companies to improve effectiveness.
   b. You want to make decisions about other people's lives and money.

10. *a.* You could deal with level upon level of bureaucratic red tape and pressure to improve performance.
    b. You could work where money and profits are more important than other people's emotional well-being.

11. *a.* You typically must start your day before sunrise and continue into the night six to seven days a week.
    b. You must fire unproductive employees regularly and expediently to achieve set targets.

12. *a.* You must be responsible for how well others do their work (and you will be judged on their achievement, not yours).
    b. You have a workaholic temperament that thrives on pressure to succeed.

268 Section Five *Leadership Skills*

13. *a.* You are a real self-starter and full of enthusiasm about everything you do.

    b. Whatever you do, you have to do it better than anyone else.

14. *a.* You are always striving to be the best, the top, the first at whatever you do.

    b. You have a driving, aggressive personality and fight hard and tough to gain anything worth having.

15. *a.* You have always been involved in competitive activities, including sports, and have won several awards for outstanding performance.

    b. Winning and succeeding are more important to you than playing just for enjoyment.

16. *a.* You will stick to a problem when you are getting nowhere.

    b. You quickly become bored with most things you undertake.

17. *a.* You are naturally carried along by some inner drive or mission to accomplish something that has never been done.

    b. Self-demanding and a perfectionist, you are always pressing yourself to perform to the limit.

18. *a.* You maintain a sense of purpose or direction that is larger than yourself.

    b. Being successful at work is the most important thing to you.

19. *a.* You would enjoy a job requiring hard and fast decisions.

    b. You are loyal to the concepts of profit, growth, and expansion.

20. *a.* You prefer independence and freedom at work to a high salary or job security.

    b. You are comfortable in a position of control, authority, and strong influence.

21. *a.* You firmly believe that those who take the most risks with their own savings should receive the greatest financial rewards.

    b. There are few people's judgment you would have as much confidence in as your own.

22. *a.* You are seen as courageous, energetic, and optimistic.

    b. Being ambitious, you are quick to take advantage of new opportunities.

23. *a.* You are good at praising others and you give credit readily when it's due.

    b. You like people, but have little confidence in their ability to do things the right way.

24. *a.* You usually give people the benefit of the doubt, rather than argue openly with them.

    b. Your style with people is direct, "tell it like it is" confrontation.

25. *a.* Although honest, you are capable of being ruthless if others are playing by devious rules.

    b. You grew up in an environment that stressed survival and required you to create your own rules.

Find Your Score

Count all the *a* responses you circled and multiply by 4 to get your percentage for leadership traits. Do the same with *b* answers to arrive at supervisor traits.

Leader (number of *a*'s)   ___ × 4 = ___ %
Supervisor (number of *b*'s)   ___ × 4 = ___ %

Interpret Your Score

Consider yourself a supervisor if you score more than 65 percent in the supervisor tally above; consider yourself a leader if you score more than 65 percent in the leader tally. If your scores cluster closer to a 50–50 split, you're a leader/supervisor.

The Leader

Your idea of fulfilling work is to motivate and guide co-workers to achieve their best and to reach common goals in their work by functioning in harmony. You are the sort of person who simply enjoys watching people grow and develop. You are commonly described as patient and encouraging in your dealings with people and a determined self-starter in your own motivation. Since you have a natural ability for inspiring top performances, there's usually little turnover among your employees, and staff relations are harmonious. At times, however, you may be too soft on people or overly patient when their performance lags. Where people are concerned, you may be too quick to let emotions get in the way of business judgments. Overall, you're the visionary type, not the day-to-day grinder.

The Supervisor

You are capable of getting good work out of people, but your style can be abrasive and provocative. You are especially competent at quickly taking charge, bulldozing through corporate red tape, or forcing others to meet tough work demands. Driven partly by a low threshold for boredom, you strive for more complexity in your work. But you love the "game" of power and the sense of having control over others. Also, your confidence in your own ideas is so strong that you may be frustrated by working as part of a team. Your tendency to see your progress as the battle of a great mind against mediocre ones is not the best premise for bringing out the best in others. Therefore, the further up the corporate ladder you go, the more heavily human-relations problems will weigh against you.

The Leader/Supervisor Mix

As a 50–50 type, you probably do not believe in the need to motivate others. Instead, you maintain that the staff should have a natural desire to work as hard as you do, without needing somebody to egg them on. You do your job well, and you expect the same from your subordinates. This means that while your own level of productivity is high, you are not always sure about how to motivate others to reach their full potential. Generally, however, you do have the ability to get others to do as you wish, without being abrasive or ruffling feathers. You may pride yourself on being surrounded by a very competent, professional staff that is self-motivated, requiring little of your own attention. But don't be too sure: Almost everyone performs better under the right sort of encouraging leadership.

CHAPTER FIFTEEN

Handling Conflict and Stress

Learning objectives

After studying this chapter, you will be able to:

1. Define conflict.
2. Outline the five stages of conflict.
3. Discuss the useful effects of conflict.
4. Explain the basic perspectives for analyzing conflict in organizations.
5. Describe five strategies for dealing with interpersonal conflict.
6. Discuss the nature and sources of job-related stress.
7. Define burnout and workaholism.
8. Suggest several guidelines for managing organizational and personal stress.

Supervision Dilemma

Jane Harris was in her office reflecting on a situation that had just occurred. She had just stopped an argument between two of her best employees. The argument had started with a discussion that the two employees were having about an upcoming political election. The discussion became rather heated, and Jane felt that the two employees were close to blows. Although this was an unusual situation, Jane felt that she was increasingly having to handle other types of conflict both in and out of her work unit. As Jane reflected on the situation, she felt that she was continually feeling stress created by situations such as this and by the demands of her job in general. Jane wondered if she could do a better job of handling conflicts and at the same time reduce the stress she experienced.

Some conflict is inevitable in organizations. Supervisors are routinely faced with conflict situations and must learn how to deal with them. Too many supervisors view conflict as something that should be avoided at all costs. However, conflict can have positive as well as negative results. Effective supervisors learn to curb the negative results of conflict and to guide conflict toward positive results. Because stress often accompanies conflict and because of the increasingly complex environment in which supervisors work, stress is something that supervisors must learn to manage.

What Is Conflict?

LEARNING OBJECTIVES

Conflict is a condition that exists when one party feels that some concern of that party has been frustrated or is about to be frustrated by a second party. The term *party* in the previous sentence refers to individuals, groups, or even organizations.

Conflict is a dynamic process that does not usually appear suddenly. In fact, conflict generally passes through several stages, or cycles. The usual stages of conflict are as follows:

LEARNING OBJECTIVES

1. **Latent conflict.** At this stage, the basic conditions for conflict exist but have not been recognized by the parties.
2. **Perceived conflict.** The basic conditions for conflict are recognized by one or both of the parties.
3. **Felt conflict.** Internal tensions begin to build in the involved parties, but the conflict is still not out in the open.
4. **Manifest conflict.** The conflict is out in the open, and the existence of the conflict becomes obvious to parties that are not involved.
5. **Conflict aftermath.** The conflict is stopped by some method. How the conflict is stopped establishes new conditions that lead either to a new conflict or to more effective co-operation between the involved parties.

A particular conflict situation does not necessarily pass through all of these stages. In addition, the parties involved in the conflict may not be at the same stage at the same time. For example, it is entirely possible for one party to be at the manifest stage and the other to be at the perceived stage.

Positive and Negative Aspects of Conflict

It has been estimated that managers spend at least 20 percent of their time dealing with conflict. Furthermore, it is safe to say that the manner in which a supervisor handles a conflict situation influences whether the conflict has a positive or negative impact.

The negative aspects of conflict are generally quite obvious. Most people can think of conflict situations in their organization that have diverted time, energy, and money away from the organization's goals. Moreover, it is entirely possible for such a situation to turn into continuous conflict and cause further harm to the organization. Conflict may cause one or more employees to leave the organization. It can adversely affect the health of the involved parties. Intense conflict can lead to sabotage, stealing, lying, distortion of information, and similar behaviors that can have a disastrous effect on the organization.

On the other hand, when properly managed, conflict can have certain very useful benefits:

1. Conflict often causes changes. Attempting to determine the cause of a conflict and developing a solution to the conflict cause changes to occur.
2. Conflict energizes people. It helps eliminate monotony and boredom in that it wakes people up and gets them moving.
3. Conflict is a form of communication. Recognizing a conflict may open up new and more effective channels of communication.
4. Conflict can be healthy in that it relieves pent-up emotions and feelings.
5. Conflict can be educational in that the participants often learn a great deal not only about themselves but also about the other people involved.
6. The aftermath of conflict can be a stronger and better work environment.

Types of Conflict in Organizations

Conflict can be either internal or external to the individual. Conflict *internal* to the individual is called **intrapersonal conflict.** Conflict *external* to the individual falls into one of three general categories—*interpersonal, structural,* or *political.*

Intrapersonal Conflict

Because intrapersonal conflict is internal to the individual, it is very difficult to analyze. Basically, intrapersonal conflict relates to the *need-drive-goal motivation sequence* (see Figure 15.1). In this sequence, needs produce motives leading to the achievement of goals. Needs are caused by deficiencies. These deficiencies can be either physical or mental. For example, a physical need exists when a person goes without food for 48 hours. Motives produce action. Lack of food (the need) causes the physical feelings of hunger (the motive), which produces eating (the action or goal). Achievement of the goal satisfies the need and reduces the motive.

Intrapersonal conflict can result when barriers exist between an individual's drives or motives and the achievement of his or her goals. For example, employees who feel that they have not received a promotion because of race or sex are very likely to experience intrapersonal conflict. This situation leads to frustration on their part. Intrapersonal conflict can also occur when goals have both positive and negative aspects and when competing or conflicting goals exist. Both of these types of intrapersonal conflict are discussed below.

Frustration

Frustration, which is one form of intrapersonal conflict, occurs when people feel that something is stopping them from achieving goals that they would like to achieve. The

FIGURE 15.1
The Motivation Sequence

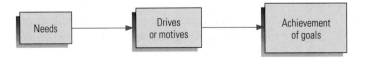

Needs → Drives or motives → Achievement of goals

results of frustration in an organization are numerous and varied. Among the possibilities are higher absenteeism, higher turnover, poorer health, and even sabotage.

Goal Conflict

Another form of intrapersonal conflict results from goal conflict. **Goal conflict** occurs when an individual's goal has both positive and negative aspects or when competing or conflicting goals exist. There are three forms of goal conflict:

1. *Conflicting positive goals.* This situation occurs when a person must choose between two or more positive goals. For example, say that a person is offered two equally attractive jobs. Suppose that a supervisor in Company A is approached by the personnel manager of Company B and offered a supervisory job in Company B. If the supervisor likes the present job but also thinks that the new job would be very good, he or she is faced with conflicting positive goals. This situation produces some intrapersonal conflict.

2. *Goals with both positive and negative aspects.* This situation occurs when a person is pursuing a goal that has both positive and negative aspects. A person who is offered a job in supervision may feel that the job has both positive and negative aspects. The positive aspects might include an increase in salary, more authority, and a higher status. The negative aspects might include having to manage other people and having to spend more time on the job.

3. *Goals that have only negative aspects.* This situation occurs when a person is confronted with two or more negative goals. For example, a person may be working at a job he or she dislikes but may consider quitting and looking for another job as equally undesirable.

Goal conflict can generally be resolved by making a decision and eliminating the source of the conflict. Supervisors can help deal with intrapersonal conflict only if they can identify when and why it is occurring. Therefore, supervisors must learn to identify intrapersonal conflict not only within employees but also within themselves.

Interpersonal Conflict

Interpersonal conflict, which is external to the individual, can result from many factors. It can occur between two supervisors, between two of a supervisor's employees, between the supervisor and the boss, or between the supervisor and an employee.

One cause of interpersonal conflict is opposing personalities. Sometimes people just seem to rub each other the wrong way. For example, if a person who is constantly playing practical jokes and a person who is quiet and reserved are in regular contact with each other, these two people might experience interpersonal conflict because of their differing personalities.

Prejudices based on such characteristics as personal background can also cause interpersonal conflict. Everyone is familiar with the potential that exists for conflict based on racial, sexual, or religious differences. More subtle prejudices can also cause interpersonal conflict. Conflict based on such prejudices can arise between the college graduate and the person without a college degree, between the married person and the divorced or single person, or between the experienced employee and the new hire.

Jealousy and envy are also sources of interpersonal conflict. Supervisors sometimes experience such conflict when they are first promoted. Before the promotion, the supervisor is one of the gang. After the promotion, conflict can develop between the supervisor and some (former) friends because of envy and jealousy.

Structural Conflict

Structural or intergroup conflict results from the nature of the organizational structure. Such conflict is independent of the personalities involved. For example, the marketing department naturally wants the production department to produce every size and color that the customer could possibly imagine. The production department, of course, wants to limit the number of sizes and colors of the product. This type of conflict is a natural by-product of the organization structure and the outlook of the various departments. Various types of structural conflict are discussed below.

Differing Goals

Each department of an organization has its own goals. Ideally, all of these goals should contribute to the overall success of the organization. Unfortunately, different department goals often result in conflict. An example is the previously described conflict between the production and marketing department. Another example is the conflict that occurs between the marketing and finance departments. Most marketing departments like to keep a large stock of finished goods inventory so that customer demands can be instantly met. On the other hand, most finance departments like to keep inventories low because of the carrying costs. The result is conflict between these departments.

Mutual Dependence of Departments

When two departments are dependent on each other, a potential for structural conflict exists. For example, marketing and production departments are often dependent on each other for their success. If marketing doesn't sell the product, production can't produce it. If production doesn't produce the product, marketing can't sell it. If either department fails to perform, the other is likely to experience negative repercussions.

Unequal Dependence of Departments

When one department is dependent on another department for its success, a potential for conflict exists. For example, staff departments such as the human resources department are generally dependent on the line departments. The human resources department must solicit the cooperation of the line departments, but the line departments don't have to accept the ideas of the human resources department. This can cause conflict.

Role Dissatisfaction

Certain departments or groups in organizations sometimes feel that they are not receiving enough recognition or status. When this occurs, they often generate conflicts with other departments or groups. For example, an internal auditing department may feel that it is not getting enough recognition. To show its importance and thus gain the recognition that it feels it deserves, this department may develop a conflict with other departments.

Ambiguities

When the credit or blame for the success or failure of a particular assignment cannot be determined, conflict between the persons or groups that may deserve the credit or blame is likely to result. For example, changes in production techniques require the efforts of both the engineering department and the production department. However, credit for the success or failure of the changes is difficult to assign, and thus conflict between these departments can result.

Competition

When two or more employees are competing against one another for a promotion or a preferred job assignment, conflict is likely to result. This conflict can be positive in that it may cause these employees to work harder and produce more. However, it must be supervised correctly to achieve positive results and avoid negative outcomes.

Dependence on Common Resources

When two departments share common but scarce resources, conflict often results. For example, conflict can result if two departments share the same copy machine and each department feels that its work should come first.

Communication Barriers

Conflict arising from communication barriers is often encountered in situations involving multiple locations or branch offices. The physical separation of branch offices from the home office has the potential for conflict. This form of conflict can also result from language and semantic differences. For example, conflict can arise between engineers and production people because the engineers use technical language to describe a production process, whereas the production people use less technical terms.

Organizational Conflict

Organizational conflict is conflict between employees and the organization itself. Organizational conflict pits employees or groups of employees against the organization. Changes in policies that negatively affect employees, such as a cutback in benefits offered, are one source of organizational conflict. Reorganizations, corporate downsizing, layoff of employees, and tightening of expenses are other examples of sources of organizational conflict.

Political Conflict

Intrapersonal, interpersonal, and structural conflicts are usually not planned by the parties involved. They generally just happen, due to circumstances. On the other hand, **political conflicts** (sometimes called *strategic conflicts*) are planned and often intentionally started. Generally, such conflicts result from the promotion of self-interest on the part of an individual or a group. The individual or group that starts the conflict intends to get an advantage over the other party. For example, when control of a new project is viewed as being very worthwhile, managers within the organization often engage in political conflict to gain control of the project.

The participants in political conflicts are not necessarily unethical or dishonest. The reward structure of many organizations often encourages political conflicts. If such conflicts are managed properly, they can have the positive effects described earlier in this chapter. Unfortunately, conflicts of this type can easily become unfair and result in severe negative outcomes.

Managing Conflict

As described earlier, conflict is an inherent part of any organization. Even though some conflict may be beneficial to an organization, unresolved conflict or conflict that is resolved poorly often results in negative consequences such as job withdrawal behaviors, quitting, low morale, and lower levels of goal attainment. Successful resolution of conflict among employees often depends on the employees' immediate supervisor. The objective of the supervisor is not to resolve the conflict but to act as a referee and counselor in helping the participant(s) reach an acceptable solution. Understanding the type of conflict—intrapersonal, interpersonal, intergroup, organizational, or political—and the stage of the conflict cycle will aid the supervisor.

Supervisors most frequently deal with intrapersonal and interpersonal conflict. Therefore, these two forms of conflict are discussed in more depth in this section. As was stated earlier, intrapersonal conflict is very difficult to analyze. Supervisors should not go around looking for intrapersonal conflict in every situation. However, when an employee asks to discuss a personal problem with the supervisor, the supervisor should look for signs of *intrapersonal conflict*. The supervisor should be very cautious in giving advice relating to intrapersonal problems. In fact, the supervisor should normally refer the employee to the company's employee assistance program in handling the problem (employee assistance programs were discussed in detail in Chapter 13). But if the intrapersonal conflict affects the employee's work performance, the supervisor must take action.

Supervisors can use the following strategies in dealing with *interpersonal conflicts:*

1. Compromise.
2. Smoothing over the conflict and pretending that it does not exist.
3. Withdrawing.
4. Forcing the conflict to a solution.
5. Confrontation.

Compromise

Compromise is effective in dealing with interpersonal conflict when it benefits both parties. It can be used when the issue in question is not very important. It can also be used to expedite solutions under time pressures or to obtain temporary solutions to complex problems. Unfortunately, compromise often leaves the real cause of the conflict unsolved and provides the groundwork for future conflict.

Smoothing Over or Pretending Conflict Does Not Exist

A second strategy is to smooth over the conflict and pretend that it does not exist. The supervisor using this approach pretends that "we are all one big happy family." This approach rarely leads to long-term solutions and generally results in more conflict.

Withdrawal

A third strategy is withdrawal. If the supervisor has two employees who are engaged in interpersonal conflict, one of them can be moved or transferred. If a supervisor is involved in a conflict with an employee, with the boss, or with another supervisor, he or she can say, "I don't want to talk about it." Again, however, withdrawal does not address the underlying cause of the conflict and usually provides the basis for future conflict.

Forcing a Solution

A fourth strategy is to force the conflict to a solution. For example, if two supervisors are engaged in an interpersonal conflict, their boss can say, "This is the way it is going to be, and that ends it." A supervisor can take the same approach to a conflict between two employees. Like the previous strategies, this one may only sow the seeds for future conflict.

Confrontation

The final strategy is confrontation between the participants. For this strategy to work, some basic guidelines must be followed:

1. Before the confrontation begins, review the past actions of the participants, and clarify the issues causing the conflict.
2. Encourage the participants to communicate freely. They should get their personal feelings out in the open and should not hold back grievances.
3. Don't try to place blame. This only polarizes the participants.
4. Don't surprise either party with confrontations for which either party is not prepared.
5. Don't attack sensitive areas of either party that have nothing to do with the specific conflict.

6. Don't argue aimlessly.
7. Identify areas of mutual agreement.
8. Emphasize mutual benefits to both parties.
9. Don't jump into specific solutions too quickly.
10. Encourage all of the participants to examine their own biases and feelings.

Confrontation has proven to be the most effective and lasting method for resolving conflict. On the other hand, forcing the conflict to a solution has been found to be the least effective means of resolving conflict. Therefore, supervisors should avoid that approach whenever possible.

Conflict and Diversity

Conflict can and does arise in the workplace when differences in thinking styles, speech patterns, lifestyles, national origins, ethnicity, religion, age, functional expertise, company experience, and a host of other variables are present. The key to using these differences to the organization's advantage is to properly manage the potential conflict. Supervisors can take either a reactive or proactive approach to manage the conflicts created by diversity in the workplace. Under the reactive or pacification approach, organizations do only the minimum required by law; diversity is viewed as a necessary evil to procure government contracts or to avoid litigation. The results produced by this approach are usually negative in the form of lawsuits, reduced competitiveness, turnover, and so on. With the proactive approach, employees work together toward mutually acceptable solutions, and differences among the organization's members are used to the organization's advantage. One of the primary tenets of the proactive approach is to encourage employee suggestions for improving organizational culture and policies.

Managing Stress

Just as conflict is a part of everyday organizational life, so is stress. **Stress** can be defined as an arousal of mind and body in response to real or perceived demands or threats. The increased blurring or merging of work and home life as a result of today's technology (i.e., beepers, cell phones, e-mail, Internet access) can also result in additional stress on supervisors.

Not all stress is bad. Managed or controlled stress can contribute positively to personal growth and development. Also, many positive events—such as marriage, moving to a new city, or taking a new job—are accompanied by stress. Excessive stress, however, is generally harmful. Among employees, stress of this kind manifests itself in increased absenteeism, job turnover, lower productivity, mistakes on the job, low levels of motivation, increased legal and insurance expenses, and higher workers' compensation payments. Excessive stress has been estimated to cost U.S. industry over $300 billion annually.[1] Numerous surveys confirm the job stress is far and away the leading source of stress for American adults and that job stress has steadily increased over the past few decades.[2] In addition to its previously mentioned job-related manifestations, excessive stress can manifest itself in such health problems as high blood pressure, tension headaches, ulcers, insomnia, heart attacks, and even death.

Stress arises in situations in which an individual is unable to respond or perform adequately. In other words, a person is likely to experience stress when an imbalance exists between perceived demands and one's capacity to meet those demands. For example, conflict and change in an organizational setting are often accompanied by increased stress.

SUPERVISION ILLUSTRATION 15–1

AVOIDING BURNOUT

More and more Americans are taking sabbaticals as a way of recharging themselves. Most sabbaticals allow the recipient to take time off with an appreciable pay cut while retaining benefits. The most common factor leading to the decision to take a sabbatical is burnout. Other factors include layoffs and the depressed economy. Given today's turbulent economic times, sabbaticals also offer employers an alternative to layoffs.

Accenture is a professional services consultancy that has 178,000 employees worldwide. In 2007, Accenture made available to all U.S. employees a self-funded sabbatical program called Future Leave. The program was in response to an employee survey which revealed that the most requested work/life program the company lacked was a sabbatical.

Although the sabbatical program is unpaid, employees can set money aside from each paycheck or each month, so when they do go on leave funds will be available. Under Future Leave employees can take up to three months off every three years to do whatever they want. According to Sharon Klun, Accenture's Phoenix-based Director of Work/Life Initiatives, the return on investment is "huge because you're keeping people you would normally lose."

Source: Sally Roberts, "Sabbatical Programs Aid Work/Life Balance," *Business Insurance,* January 19, 2009, pp. 11–12.

Types of Job-Related Stress

6 LEARNING OBJECTIVES

Stress can result from an imbalance of demand and capacity related to a person's job, physical condition, social environment, or personal problems. This section will deal specifically with job-related stress, which the supervisor's actions can directly affect. Some of the more frequently encountered sources of job-related stress are:

1. *Task stress.* The task or job is too difficult.
2. *Role stress.* The individual is not clear on exactly what he or she should be doing.
3. *Human environmental stress.* This condition is caused by overcrowding or understaffing.
4. *Physical environmental stress.* Poor physical conditions exist, such as extreme cold or heat or poor ventilation.
5. *Social stress.* Interpersonal conflict occurs among employees.
6. *Burnout.* Burnout occurs when an employee loses interest in and motivation for doing the job.

Because of its increasing prevalence in today's workplace, burnout is discussed further in the following section.

Burnout

7 LEARNING OBJECTIVES

Burnout is one potential result of excessive job-related stress over a long period of time. Burnout can be formally defined as a state of physical, emotional, and mental exhaustion caused by long-term involvement in situations that are emotionally demanding. It occurs when an employee loses interest in and motivation for doing the job. It generally takes place in three stages: (1) an increased feeling of emotional exhaustion, (2) a callous and dehumanized perception of others, and (3) a negative self-evaluation of one's effectiveness. A recent survey of 7,600 employees nationwide by CareerBuilder.com reported that 78 percent of the respondents said they were burned out.[3]

The consequences of burnout are serious. Naturally, an employee who has lost interest and motivation is not going to be a good performer. As one would suspect, burnout is frequently accompanied by absenteeism, frequent job turnover, and even an increase in the use of drugs and alcohol. Because burnout usually results from stress, the same guidelines that are offered below for managing stress should be followed to reduce the potential for burnout. Supervision Illustration 15–1 discusses one approach that some organizations are taking to help their employees avoid burnout.

SUPERVISION ILLUSTRATION 15–2

REDUCING STRESS AT CLARK NUBER

Clark Nuber is a regional accounting and consulting firm in Bellevue, Washington, with revenues of approximately $25 million and about 150 employees. In 2008 Clark Nuber was named one of the Best Small Companies to Work for in America for the second straight year.

While most accounting firms encourage hellacious hours, especially during the time period from January through April, Clark Nuber's leaders prefer that tax specialists limit peek-period hours to 55 hours per week—low by accountants' standards.

David E. Katri, president and chief executive officer, views the January–April time as an "opportunity season, a time to engage with clients, not crush season." Katri's philosophy is "people before clients."

"We're a professional services firm. Our people are what drive the business, and we need happy and excited people in the workplace to provide great results for our clients."

At Clark Nuber thank-yous are the norm. They range from a $10,000 bonus for bringing a new manager on board, to themed get-togethers in the snack room, to "Bob bucks" that employees hand one another for jobs well done. The "bucks" are named for founder Bob Nuber and convert to retail gift cards.

Source: Terence F. Shea, "Employee First," *HR Magazine*, July 2008, pp. 36–37.

Workaholism

Workaholism can be a cause of stress. Workaholism is working to the exclusion of everything else in one's life. It is an addiction that causes a person to become so obsessed with work that he or she is crippled emotionally and physically. Workaholics constantly think about work, work long hours, and often sacrifice sleep, food, exercise, family, and friends in favor of work.

One might think that having an organization full of workaholics would be desirable from the organization's viewpoint. However, a workaholic environment creates stress, burnout, and low morale. Also, workaholics are often not the most efficient employees because they frequently engage in doing unnecessary things.

Organizational Guidelines for Managing Stress

8 LEARNING OBJECTIVES

Many organizations have undertaken certain actions to reduce the amount of job-related stress experienced by their employees. Among these actions are:

- Shortening hours of direct contact with customers.
- Granting special leaves (sabbatical programs).
- Introducing early retirement programs.
- Installing on-site exercise facilities.
- Actively involving employees in the decision-making processes.
- Fulfilling the realistic expectations of employees.
- Clearly defining employee jobs.
- Introducing changes gradually.
- Requiring that everyone take a vacation.

Naturally, some of these actions are more appropriate in some situations than in others. For any of these actions to work, the organization must first have an awareness of its potential for dealing with stress-related problems. Supervision Illustration 15–2 discusses how one accounting firm has attempted to reduce job stress for its employees.

SUPERVISION ILLUSTRATION 15–3

YOGA TO REDUCE STRESS

Yoga is a combination of physical poses, breathing techniques, and guided meditation. In addition to reducing stress, yoga has been used to help people with insomnia, anxiety, depression, arthritis, heart disease, and fatigue. According to Rachel Permuth-Levine, a deputy director at the National Institutes of Health's Heart, Lung and Blood Institute in Bethesda, Maryland, yoga can also help with conditions typically associated with office work, such as eyestrain, carpel tunnel syndrome, and back pain.

Many employers offer some type of yoga program. For example, Sandia National Laboratories, a national security laboratory in New Mexico offers free yoga classes for its 8,300 employees at an on-site fitness center. According to Stephanie Holinka, a spokesperson for Sandia, one of the Sandia's main reasons for offering yoga is to help employees feel more relaxed and less stressed. "On the days I've gone, I feel so much clearer when I get back here. You end up coming back with a lot of energy, which is nice."

Source: Leah Carlson Shepherd, "Yoga Can Help Employees Stretch Away Stress, Anxiety, Burnout," *Employee Benefit News*, April 1, 2009, p. 36.

Personal Guidelines for Managing Stress

Fortunately, supervisors and employees can do many things both on and off the job to reduce stress for themselves. Some of these are summarized below:

1. Pay attention to the physical needs of exercise, diet, and rest. Exercise should be regular (at least three times per week). Avoid large amounts of junk food and get enough sleep.
2. Don't create artificial deadlines. When deadlines are necessary, make them realistic and base them on normal working conditions.
3. Pace yourself. Try not to personalize everything about your job. Learn to step back and keep things in perspective. Take a breather when you begin to feel irritable.
4. Inject a change into your routine. List the things you have to do, and organize them according to priority and urgency. Then, as you complete them, your stress will ease as your feeling of accomplishment grows.
5. Periodically perform an emotional audit. Identify the pressure points in your life, and recognize the times when you are most susceptible to stress.
6. Share persistent problems with others. Don't let problems build up inside. Learn to share problems with your spouse, friends, colleagues, or a professional. Sometimes talking it out is a way of working it out.
7. Learn to relax away from the job. Develop non-work-related hobbies, and build time into your schedule for engaging in these hobbies on a regular basis. Go to a movie; take time to read something appealing to you.
8. Get away for lunch. It doesn't have to be every day, but you should get away from the office or plan for lunch on a regular basis. Have lunch with a close friend. Having lunch with a close friend who deeply cares for you can lift your spirits.
9. Drink lots of water. Keep water at your workstation. Some people recommend drinking as many as eight glasses of water each day.
10. Utilize your mental and spiritual resources. Different forms of meditation and contemplation can help reduce stress.

Supervision Illustration 15–3 discusses how yoga can be used to reduce stress.

First, Jane has learned that conflict is inevitable in organizations. In addition, she has learned that conflict can have both positive and negative consequences (pp. 271–272). The conflict that Jane faced was a form of interpersonal conflict. Jane has learned that there are five strategies that a supervisor can use in dealing with interpersonal conflicts: compromise; smoothing the conflict over and pretending that it does not exist; withdrawing; forcing the conflict to a solution; and confrontation, or problem solving (pp. 276–277). Jane should probably use confrontation to resolve the conflict between her two employees. If she uses confrontation, suggestions that she should follow are offered on pages 276–277.

It is good that Jane has realized that she is experiencing significant levels of stress related to her job. She should first try and determine the type or types of stress she is experiencing (p. 278). Once Jane is aware of the types of stress she is most frequently experiencing, she should follow the appropriate guidelines on page 280 for personally managing her stress.

Summary

This chapter explores the causes of conflict in organizations. Several methods of resolving conflict are presented to aid the supervisor in resolving conflict in a constructive manner.

1. *Define conflict.* Conflict is a condition that results when one party feels that some concern of that party has been frustrated by a second party.

2. *Outline the five stages of conflict.* The five stages of conflict are latent conflict, perceived conflict, felt conflict, manifest conflict, and conflict aftermath.

3. *Discuss the useful effects of conflict.* Conflict has these potentially useful effects: it causes change, it energizes people, it is a form of communication, it often provides an outlet for pent-up emotions and feelings, it may be an educational experience, and it may result in a stronger and better work environment.

4. *Explain the basic perspectives for analyzing conflict in organizations.* Conflict in organizations can be analyzed from two basic perspectives. Conflict as a process internal to the individual is called intrapersonal conflict. Conflict can also be external to the individual—individual versus individual, individual versus group, group versus group, organization versus organization, or any combination of these. External conflict is of three general types: interpersonal, structural, or political.

5. *Describe five strategies for dealing with interpersonal conflict.* There are five general strategies for dealing with interpersonal conflict: (1) withdraw one or more of the participants, (2) smooth over the conflict and pretend that it does not exist, (3) compromise for the sake of ending the conflict, (4) force the conflict to a conclusion by third-party intervention, and (5) establish a confrontation between the participants in an effort to eliminate the underlying source of the conflict.

6. *Discuss the nature and sources of job-related stress.* Stress arises in situations in which an individual is unable to respond or perform adequately—that is, when an imbalance exists between perceived demands and one's capacity to meet those demands. Some of the more frequently encountered sources of job-related stress are excessively difficult tasks, lack of clarity about what should be done, overcrowding or understaffing, poor physical conditions, interpersonal conflict, and burnout.

7. *Define burnout and workaholism.* Burnout is a state of physical, emotional, and mental exhaustion caused by long-term involvement in situations that are emotionally demanding. Workaholism is working to the exclusion of everything else in one's life. It is an addiction that causes a person to become so obsessed with work that he or she is crippled emotionally and physically.

8. *Suggest several guidelines for managing organizational and personal stress.* Supervisors and employees can do many things to reduce their own stress. Some of them are paying attention to the physical needs of exercise, diet, and rest; not creating artificial deadlines; pacing yourself; changing routine; periodically performing an emotional audit; sharing persistent problems with others; learning to relax away from the job; getting away for lunch; drinking lots of water; and utilizing mental and spiritual resources.

Key Terms

Burnout, 278
Conflict, 271
Conflict aftermath, 271
Felt conflict, 271
Frustration, 272
Goal conflict, 273

Intrapersonal conflict, 272
Interpersonal conflict, 273
Latent conflict, 271
Manifest conflict, 271
Organizational conflict, 275
Perceived conflict, 271

Political conflict, 275
Stress, 277
Structural or intergroup
   conflict, 273
Workaholism, 279

Review Questions

1. Describe the five stages, or cycles, of conflict.
2. Describe some positive and negative outcomes of conflict.
3. Define four types of conflict in organizations.
4. Discuss some causes of interpersonal conflict.
5. Outline the causes of structural conflict.
6. Discuss the five strategies for solving interpersonal conflict.
7. What are some guidelines for using the confrontation approach to conflict?
8. Name and define six sources of job-related stress.
9. Identify the three stages that generally accompany burnout.
10. Define workaholism.
11. Describe several actions that an organization might take to reduce employee stress.
12. Name several ways that a supervisor might reduce stress.

Skill-Building Questions

1. "Supervisors should avoid conflict at all costs." Discuss.
2. "Supervisors should smooth over any conflict that they have with their boss." Discuss your views on this statement.
3. Comment on the following statement: "Stress is inherent in every job, and employees must learn to cope on their own."
4. Do you agree with the following statement? "Burnout is just a newfangled notion that gives lazy people an excuse not to work." Why or why not?

References

1. Rebecca Tonn, "Work Stressors Lead to Increased Costs, Decreased Productivity," *The Colorado Springs Business Journal,* March 6, 2009.
2. "Job Stress," http://www.stress.org/job.htm, accessed on April 7, 2009.
3. "Employee's Suffer from Burnout," *IOMA's Report on Salary Surveys,* August 2008, p. 9.

Additional Readings

Angelica, Marion Peters. "Eight Steps to Managing Conflict," *Nonprofit World,* July–August 2002, pp. 29–32.

Bacal, Robert. "Organizational Conflict—The Good, the Bad, and the Ugly," *Journal for Quality and Participation,* Summer 2004, pp. 21–22.

Brown, Duncan. "Time to Grow Up and Resolve Our Disputes," *Personnel Today,* October 26, 2004, p. 11.

Markiewicz, Dan. "No One is Bullet-Proof From Stress," *ISHN,* December 2008, pp. 22–23.

McCullum, Kenya. "Extinguishing Burnout," *OfficePro,* October 2008, pp. 18–20.

Stanley, T. L. "Control Your Job Stress," *SuperVision,* February 2008, pp. 3–5.

SKILL-BUILDING APPLICATIONS

Incident 15–1

Trouble in the Claims Department

Barbara Riley, supervisor of the claims section of the Reliance Insurance Company, really has a problem. She has been having trouble with two of her best employees. Ruth Gordon is 55 years old and has been with the company for 30 years. She started out as a secretary and has worked her way up to senior claims representative. She knows the claims procedures better than anyone, and she prides herself on the fact that many of the younger employees, most of whom are college graduates, come to her for help on their more difficult claims problems. She takes particular pride in the fact that she is of help to them even though she is not a college graduate.

Juan Perez is 24 years old and a recent business administration graduate from a large local university. Since joining the claims unit, he has made numerous suggestions for improving procedures. Just recently, he proposed an entirely new system for processing claims.

Barbara has decided to discuss the problem with her boss, Bill Rucker. The discussion goes as follows:

Barbara: I just don't know, Bill. Sometimes I feel like putting Juan and Ruth in a room and not letting them out until they agree to get along.

Bill: What do they argue about?

Barbara: Anything that comes up! You can count on it that if Juan proposes something, Ruth will be against it. Juan also contributes to the problem in that he acts like Ruth doesn't exist. If he would just ask for her advice every now and then, it would help.

Bill: How is it affecting everyone?

Barbara: For some time, most people sort of ignored it. Now, however, the arguments are getting out of hand and people are beginning to choose sides.

Questions

1. What is causing the conflict?
2. What method has Barbara been using in dealing with the conflict?
3. Recommend a solution to this conflict situation.

Incident 15–2

Getting Rid of Bart

Bart had been with the QTZ Company for almost 20 years. QTZ is a large firm in the Southwest that manufactures high-tech products. By age 54, Bart had attained a nice salary with good benefits and pension. He had a superior work record and consistently positive performance appraisals.

As a result of a recent downsizing, Bart's boss was replaced by a younger manager. The new manager made it explicitly clear to Bart, without explanation, that Bart's days were limited at QTZ and that Bart should start looking for new employment. Immediately afterward, Bart was moved into a smaller office with no windows. His assistant was assigned to someone else and his last seven years of expenses were audited. Bart's next two performance appraisals were all below average. The new boss also became abusive and purposely belittled Bart in front of his peers and threatened him in private.

After almost one year of harassment, Bart was summarily fired without severance pay and no notice. By this time Bart had used up his sick leave and vacation pay trying to recover from a bout with ulcers and a severe sleep disorder. In addition, Bart was depressed, anxious, and despondent.

Questions

1. Is Bart's stress understandable? What could he have done to avoid it?
2. What would you do at this point if you were Bart?
3. In general terms, discuss the potential costs of this situation to QTZ.

Source: Adapted from C. Brady Wilson, "U.S. Businesses Suffer from Workplace Trauma," *Personnel Journal,* July 1991, p. 48.

Exercise 15–1

Conflict over Quality

This morning, your department completed a large order and turned it over to quality control. The quality control supervisor has just come to tell you that she must tighten up on inspection standards because a number of complaints have been received from the field. She feels that the order must be reworked by your department to pass inspection. You try—but fail—to persuade her to impose the stricter standards only on future lots.

Reworking units will set you back a couple of days in your production schedule. You can explain this to your superiors. But the costs, which will be charged to your budget, will be much more difficult to explain.

As you reflect on what has happened, you are clearly annoyed. You decide that something must be done, and you see your alternatives as follows:

1. You can calm down, issue instructions to rework the units, and do the best you can with the budgeting and scheduling problems.

2. You can send the quality control supervisor a memo clearly outlining the cost considerations and ask her to help you find a solution.

3. You can call the quality control supervisor and ask her to meet with you to discuss the situation further at her earliest convenience.

4. You can go to the plant manager (to whom both you and the quality control supervisor report), point out the budget and scheduling difficulties, and request that the old standards be applied this one last time.

5. You can tell the quality control supervisor that if she does not go along with your suggestion to impose the stricter standards only on future production, you will no longer be able to lend her one of your operators for inspection work.

Other alternatives may be open to you, but assume that these are the only ones you have considered. *Without discussion with anyone,* choose one of the alternatives and be prepared to defend your choice.

Exercise 15–2

Truth and Misconceptions about Stress

Answer "True" or "False" to the following questions to see how much you know about stress and what you can and should do about it. Your instructor will discuss the answers with you after you have completed the quiz.

1. Stress is primarily an American disease.

2. Stress isn't always a negative condition; in fact, sometimes stress can be good for us.

3. The secret to escaping the damaging effects of stress is to avoid potentially stressful situations.

4. The more hours you work, the greater your stress.

5. A complex person suffers more from stress than one who has a simpler self-evaluation. Limit the facets of your personality and you'll improve your ability to cope with stress.

6. In the workforce, people in management positions with a great deal of responsibility feel the greatest amount of stress.

7. Putting aside time for leisure is one of the best ways to reduce the negative effects of stress; the harder you play, the better the results.

8. Don't put off solving your problems until tomorrow, even if you have to stay up half the night to work them out.

Source: A. Gaedeke, "The Truth and Misconceptions about Stress," *Manager's Magazine,* August 1989, pp. 29–30. Reprinted with permission of *Manager's Magazine,* a publication of LIMRA International, Inc., 300 Day Hill Road, Windsor, CT 06095.

Exercise 15–3

Are You a Workaholic?

The following questions may indicate if you have an obsession with work (or school). If you are currently working, answer the questions with regard to your job. If you are not currently working, answer the questions with regard to school.

Do you get more excited about work than anything else?

Do you regularly work through lunch or read work-related materials during meals?

Do you often work—or call work—during planned time off?

Do you have difficulty delegating work to others?

Do you work more than 55 hours a week?

Do you work far beyond what is reasonably expected to meet your job requirements?

Do you find it "necessary" to work late and on weekends, whether or not it is a busy time?

Do you appear exhausted or high-strung?

Do you seem to have a personal life? Do you talk about your family, friends, or weekend activities?

Do you seem physically rigid? Do you complain about back pain, headaches, ulcers, or other health problems?

Do you walk or talk very fast?

Do you regularly take work home?

Do you underestimate how long a project will take and then rush to complete it?

Answering "yes" to a few of the questions does not constitute workaholism, but the more "yes" answers you got, the more at risk you are.

Sources: Adapted from Kathryn Tyler, "Spinning Wheels," *HR Magazine,* September 1999, pp. 34–40; and Workaholics Anonymous World Service Organization.

Exercise 15–4

Measuring Your Level of Stress

The following quiz (Exhibit 15.1) will enable you to determine how vulnerable you are to stress, how much stress there is in your life, and how well you handle its effects. Please respond to each question honestly by checking the answer that most accurately describes your situation as it *actually is,* not as you would like it to appear or as you think it should be. The scoring instructions are provided at the end of the quiz.

EXHIBIT 15.1 **Stress Quiz**

Stress Experience	Times Experienced			
	Often	**Sometimes**	**Seldom**	**Never**
1. During the past three months, how often were you under considerable strain, stress, or pressure?	____	____	____	____
2. How often do you experience any of the following symptoms: heart palpitations or a racing heart, dizziness, painfully cold hands or feet, shallow or fast breathing, restless body or legs, insomnia, chronic fatigue?	____	____	____	____
3. Do you have headaches or digestive upsets?	____	____	____	____
4. How often do you experience pain in your neck, back, arms, or shoulders?	____	____	____	____
5. How often do you feel depressed?	____	____	____	____
6. Do you tend to worry excessively?	____	____	____	____
7. Do you ever feel anxiety or apprehension even though you don't know what has caused it?	____	____	____	____
8. Do you tend to be edgy or impatient with your peers or subordinates?	____	____	____	____
9. Do you ever feel overwhelmed with feelings of hopelessness?	____	____	____	____
10. Do you dwell on things you did but shouldn't have done?	____	____	____	____
11. Do you dwell on things you should have done but didn't do?	____	____	____	____
12. Do you have any problems concentrating on your work?	____	____	____	____
13. When you're criticized, do you tend to brood about it?	____	____	____	____
14. Do you tend to worry about what your colleagues think of you?	____	____	____	____
15. How often do you feel bored?	____	____	____	____
16. Do you find that you're unable to keep your objectivity under stress?	____	____	____	____
17. Of late, do you find yourself more irritable and argumentative than usual?	____	____	____	____
18. Are you as respected by your peers as you want to be?	____	____	____	____
19. Are you doing as well in your career as you'd like to?	____	____	____	____
20. Do you feel that you can live up to what top management expects from you?	____	____	____	____
21. Do you feel that your spouse understands your problems and is supportive of you?	____	____	____	____
22. Do you have trouble with any of your associates?	____	____	____	____

(continued)

EXHIBIT 15.1 **Stress Quiz** (continued)

Stress Experience	Times Experienced			
	Often	**Sometimes**	**Seldom**	**Never**
23. Do you sometimes worry that your associates might be turning against you?	_____	_____	_____	_____
24. Is your salary sufficient to cover your needs?	_____	_____	_____	_____
25. Have you noticed lately that you tend to eat, drink, or smoke more than you really should?	_____	_____	_____	_____
26. Do you tend to make strong demands on yourself?	_____	_____	_____	_____
27. Do you feel that the boundaries or limits placed on you by top management regarding what you may or may not do are fair?	_____	_____	_____	_____
28. Are you able to take problems in stride, knowing that you can deal with most situations?	_____	_____	_____	_____
29. Do you stay productive and seldom "lose your cool" under stress?	_____	_____	_____	_____
30. Do you feel neglected or left out in meetings?	_____	_____	_____	_____
31. Do you habitually tend to fall behind with your work?	_____	_____	_____	_____
32. During the last year, have you or anyone in your family suffered a severe illness or injury?	_____	_____	_____	_____
33. Have you recently moved to a new home or community?	_____	_____	_____	_____
34. During the last three months, have any of your pet ideas been rejected?	_____	_____	_____	_____
35. Is it difficult for you to say no to requests?	_____	_____	_____	_____
36. Do you generally work better under pressure?	_____	_____	_____	_____
37. Are you able to focus your concentration under pressure?	_____	_____	_____	_____
38. Are you able to return to your normal state of mind reasonably soon after a stressful situation?	_____	_____	_____	_____

Scoring: Add up your points based on the answer key below. See "What your score means" on p. 288.

	Often	**Sometimes**	**Seldom**	**Never**		**Yes**	**No**		**Yes**	**No**
1.	7	4	1	0	17.	4	0	28.	0	3
2.	7	4	1	0	18.	0	3	29.	0	3
3.	6	3	1	0	19.	0	4	30.	4	0
4.	4	2	0	0	20.	0	5	31.	3	0
5.	7	3	1	0	21.	0	5	32.	6	0
6.	6	3	1	0	22.	3	0	33.	3	0
7.	6	3	1	0	23.	4	0	34.	4	0
8.	5	2	0	0	24.	0	3	35.	3	0
9.	7	3	1	0	25.	5	0	36.	0	3
10.	4	2	0	0	26.	4	0	37.	0	3
11.	4	2	0	0	27.	0	3	38.	0	4
12.	4	2	0	0						
13.	4	2	0	0						
14.	4	2	0	0						
15.	4	2	0	0						
16.	6	4	1	0						

Source: This quiz was drawn from Eugene Raidsepp, "Overcoming Job-Related Stress," *Supervision*, August 1987, p. 307. Reprinted by permission of The National Research Bureau, P.O. Box 1, Burlington, IA 52601-0001.

What Your Score Means

90–167: A score in this range indicates not only that your troubles seem to outnumber your satisfactions but also that you are presently subjected to a high level of stress. You are, no doubt, already aware of your pressures, and you are rightfully concerned about your own psychological and physical well-being.

You should by all means do everything possible to avoid as many stressful situations as you can until you feel more in control of your life. It might be a good idea for you to go over the quiz to pinpoint the major sources of your present stress.

You might also need to develop more effective ways to manage how you respond to stressful situations. Your vulnerability to stressful events shows that you may be overreacting to problems or you may not be as willing to cope with adversities as you could be.

You might want to consider seeking professional help. Sometimes even a few hours of counseling can be of great help. You might also want to pay heed to the wise words of a cardiologist who offers the following three rules for combating stress:

Rule 1: Don't sweat the small stuff.

Rule 2: Everything is small stuff.

Rule 3: If you can't fight it, or flee from it, flow with it.

45–89: A score within this range indicates either that your stress seems to be moderate or that you are probably handling your frustrations quite well. You should, however, review various aspects of your daily life and try to relieve stress before it starts building up. Because you may have occasional difficulties in coping with the effects of stress, you might want to consider adding some new methods of dealing with disappointments.

Remember, we all have to face and live with occasional states of unwellness. We can ignore them, or we can turn situations of stress and pressure into an opportunity for further emotional growth. Life can either grind us down or polish us up—and the choice is largely our own.

0–44: A score in this range indicates that your stress is relatively low and that you probably are in great shape. In spite of minor worries and concerns, stress doesn't seem to be causing you any serious problem.

You have, no doubt, good adaptive powers, and you are able to deal quite well with situations that make you temporarily uptight. You seem to have been able to strike a good balance in your ability to cope with and control stress.

Exercise 15–5

Which of the following categories do you think would best describe your level of stress in your current job (if you are not currently employed, in the last job you had):

A. chilled out and relatively calm, Stress is not much of an issue.

B. Fairly low. Coping should be a breeze, but you probably have a tough day now and then.

C. Moderate Stress. Some things about your job are likely to be pretty stressful but probably not much more than most people experience.

D. Severe. You may still be able to cope, but life at work can sometimes be miserable.

E. Stress level is potentially dangerous.

After you have chosen the category that you think best describes your situation, go online to http://www.stress.org/2001Harris.pdf and complete the Workplace Stress Scale Quiz. Follow the instructions on the website, interpret your score and determine your actual stress category. Compare your actual stress category to your predicted category.

Exercise 15–6

Life Events Causing Stress

Research has shown that certain life events tend to be correlated with the onset of certain physical illnesses. In other words, people have a tendency to get sick (e.g., cold or flu) following certain events that require adjustment. Think back to the last time you were sick and determine which, if any, of the events shown in Exhibit 15.2 immediately preceded your illness. The mean values indicate the relative impact of each respective life event. Add up the mean values associated with each life event that you experienced. The higher the total value, the more these events probably contributed to your getting sick.

A total score of more than 300 is considered to be high, and in large group studies, high scores have been correlated with susceptibility to illness and accidents. The first step in managing stress is to become familiar with life events and be aware of the amount of change they require, including positive events that also require adaptive energy.*

*Adopted from Edward A. Charlesworth and Ronald G. Nathan, "How to Build Healthy Responses to Stress," *Advertising Age*, January 21, 1985, p. 38.

EXHIBIT 15.2
Social Adjustment Rating Scale

Source: "Social Readjustment Rating Scale" developed by Thomas Holmes and Richard Rahe. Both are with the University of Washington, School of Medicine.

Life Event	Mean Value
1. Death of spouse.	100
2. Divorce.	73
3. Marital separation.	65
4. Detention in jail or other institution.	63
5. Death of a close family member.	63
6. Major personal injury or illness.	53
7. Marriage.	50
8. Being fired at work.	47
9. Marital reconciliation with mate.	45
10. Retirement from work.	45
11. Major change in the health or behavior of a family member.	44
12. Pregnancy.	40
13. Sexual difficulties.	39
14. Gaining a new family member (e.g., through birth, adoption, relative moving in).	39
15. Major business readjustment (e.g., merger, reorganization, bankruptcy).	39
16. Major changes in financial state (e.g., a lot worse off or a lot better off than usual).	38
17. Death of a close friend.	37
18. Changing to a different line of work.	36
19. Major change in the number of arguments with spouse (e.g., either a lot more or a lot less than usual regarding child rearing or personal habits).	35
20. Taking on a mortgage greater than $100,000 (e.g., purchasing a home or a business).	31
21. Foreclosure on a mortgage or loan.	30
22. Major change in responsibilities at work (e.g., promotion, demotion, lateral transfer).	29
23. Son or daughter leaving home (e.g., marriage, attending college).	29
24. In-law troubles.	29
25. Outstanding personal achievement.	28
26. Spouse beginning or ceasing work outside the home.	26
27. Beginning or ceasing formal schooling.	26
28. Major change in living conditions (e.g., building a new home, remodeling, deterioration of home or neighborhood).	25
29. Revision of personal habits (e.g., dress, manners, associations).	24
30. Troubles with the boss.	23
31. Major change in working hours or conditions.	20
32. Change in residence.	20
33. Changing to a new school.	20
34. Major change in usual type and/or amount of recreation.	19
35. Major change in church activities (e.g., a lot more or a lot less than usual).	19
36. Major change in social activities (e.g., clubs, dancing, movies, visiting).	18
37. Taking on a mortgage or loan of less than $100,000 (e.g., purchasing a car or home improvement).	17
38. Major change in sleeping habits (a lot more or a lot less sleep, or change in part of day when asleep).	16
39. Major change in number of family get-togethers (e.g., a lot more or a lot less than usual).	15
40. Major change in eating habits (a lot more or a lot less food intake, or very different meal hours or surroundings).	15
41. Vacation.	13
42. Christmas.	12
43. Minor violations of the law (e.g., traffic tickets, jaywalking, disturbing the peace).	11

Note: The dollar figures used in this example have been adjusted for inflation.

CHAPTER SIXTEEN

Appraising and Rewarding Performance

Learning objectives

After studying this chapter, you will be able to:

1. Define performance appraisal.
2. Define performance.
3. Explain the determinants of performance.
4. Explain the contents of a job description.
5. Define job analysis.
6. List and describe the major performance appraisal methods.
7. Discuss common errors made in performance appraisals.
8. Suggest ways to make performance appraisal systems more legally acceptable.
9. Define compensation.

Supervision Dilemma

John Lewis has just been informed by the human resources department that it is time to conduct performance appraisals of his employees. Prior to becoming a supervisor, John had always felt uncomfortable during his performance appraisal. He had always felt that he was on the defensive. Now that he is a supervisor, he doesn't want his employees to feel the same way. However, John knows that some of his employees deserve an unfavorable appraisal. He certainly isn't looking forward to those sessions.

1 LEARNING OBJECTIVES

Appraising employee performance is one of the most difficult and important parts of the supervisor's job. **Performance appraisal** is a process that involves communicating to an employee how well he or she is performing the job and also, ideally, involves establishing a plan for improvement. All supervisors are constantly making judgments about the contributions and abilities of their employees. For example, supervisors may conclude that some employees show initiative, whereas others have a great deal of ability but must be constantly pushed.

Performance appraisals are handled in most organizations in one of two ways. Informal appraisals occur in all organizations, and many small businesses have informal appraisal systems. Under such a system, no formal procedures, methods, or times are established for conducting performance appraisals.

If a supervisor conducts appraisals informally, the employee will be given a general impression of how the supervisor feels about his or her performance. In all too many cases, such appraisals are conducted only when the employee has made a mistake. As a result, employees often develop negative feelings about this type of performance appraisal.

The other way of handling performance appraisals is to have a formal appraisal system. Under such a system, procedures, methods, and times are established for conducting appraisals. The basic purpose of this chapter is to describe formal performance appraisal systems.

It is important to note that formal appraisal systems contain an informal element. For example, general comments that a supervisor makes about an employee's performance are a type of informal performance appraisal. Supervisors must realize that any comment made by a supervisor about an employee's performance is viewed by the employee as a form of performance appraisal. Thus, the supervisor must use informal reviews to reinforce good performance and discourage poor performance. Supervision Illustration 16–1 describes the performance appraisal system at the Jelly Belly Candy Company.

What Is Performance?

2 LEARNING OBJECTIVES

3 LEARNING OBJECTIVES

Performance refers to how well an employee is fulfilling the requirements of the job. Basically, an employee's performance is determined by a combination of three factors—effort, ability, and direction. Effort refers to how hard a person works. **Ability** is concerned with the person's capability. **Direction** refers to how well the person understands what is expected on the job. Figure 16.1 illustrates these relationships. Performance is often confused with effort. Although a person's performance is somewhat dependent on effort, it should be measured in terms of the results achieved, not in terms of the effort expended.

An employee's performance can be influenced by conditions that are not under the employee's direct control. Such factors include inadequate work facilities and equipment, restrictive policies that affect the job, lack of cooperation from other people and departments, and even luck. One job of the supervisor is to work with other levels of

SUPERVISION ILLUSTRATION 16–1

JELLY BELLY CANDY COMPANY

Candy making is a fun business, and so it's no surprise that it's fun to work at the Jelly Belly Candy Company of Fairfield, California. But at this family-owned company, there's no fooling around when it comes to promoting employee performance and job satisfaction. So when Jelly Belly decided to overhaul and automate its antiquated employee performance management (EPM) process, it was looking for a serious solution to help give its employees across the United States fair, accurate appraisals.

The Jelly Belly Candy Company makes Jelly Belly brand jelly beans in 50 flavors, as well as candy corn and other treats. Introduced in 1976 and named by former U.S. president Ronald Reagan as his favorite candy, the company's jelly beans are exported worldwide. Herman Goelitz Candy was founded in 1869 by Albert and Gustav Goelitz, whose great-grandsons own and run Jelly Belly today.

A committee set up by the company selected Halogen eAppraisal™, a Web-based employee performance and talent management application from Halogen Software. "We liked the way it looked, and we really liked the user-friendliness of it. It's easy for the managers to use and it's customizable without overwhelming them," Margie Poulos said. After two days of training by Halogen staff, four members of Jelly Belly's HR team set out to train the company's supervisors on the new system. About 50 managers received a crash course in using Halogen eAppraisal, and then used it to complete annual evaluations in May. Jelly Belly's HR team is now customizing the software to include more relevant competencies and to respond to comments from managers and staff on the new system.

The new automated employee performance appraisal system has completely formalized and organized Jelly Belly's employee evaluation process. "It allows us to standardize competencies across job classifications, add signature and comment sections to make our process more interactive, and increase accessibility for remote managers," Brown said.

Under Jelly Belly's old system, employees conducting reviews started from scratch once a year with new performance journals. Halogen eAppraisal will let them log notes throughout the year and regularly update their on-line appraisals. Employees use one consistent form to add comments and to sign their appraisals.

management to eliminate environmental factors that can negatively affect the performance of employees.

To obtain an acceptable level of performance, all three of the factors that determine performance must be present to some extent. If an employee puts forth a great deal of effort, has above-average ability, but lacks a good understanding of the job, the probable result would be unsatisfactory performance. If an employee understands what is

FIGURE 16.1
Factors That Determine Level of Performance

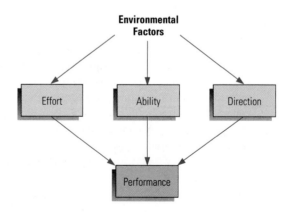

expected on the job, works very hard, but lacks the ability to do the job, his or her performance would probably also be poor. Finally, if an employee has good ability, understands the job, but is lazy and exerts little effort, his or her performance is also likely to be poor. It should be pointed out that an employee who is weak in one of the performance factors can compensate for that weakness by being strong in one or both of the other factors. For example, you may have known an employee who didn't have excessive ability but was a high performer because he or she knew the job well and worked extra hard.

The key to obtaining good performance, therefore, is to encourage effort by employees, to develop their ability, and to clearly communicate what they are expected to do on the job. A supervisor can use several means to ensure that employees are properly directed. Two of the best are carefully developed job descriptions and performance appraisal systems.

Job Descriptions and Job Specifications

A **job description** states the characteristics of a job and the types of work that are performed in the job. A **job specification** gives the qualifications necessary to perform a job. It states the experience, training, education, knowledge, skills, and abilities necessary to do the job.

A job description and job specification result from a **job analysis,** which is the process of determining, through observation and study, the pertinent information regarding a specific job. In most large organizations, job analyses, job descriptions, and job specifications are developed by the human resources department. However, the supervisor plays a key role in their development by providing much of the necessary information to the human resources department. In small organizations, supervisors may actually develop job descriptions and job specifications for the jobs under their authority. If called upon to develop job descriptions and job specifications, a supervisor should carefully study each job to ensure that it is described accurately. The supervisor should remember that the overriding purpose of a job description is to communicate to the employee what he or she is expected to do on the job. Thus, clearly communicating an accurate job description to the employee is the first step in the performance appraisal process.

Many organizations combine the job description and job specification into one document. Figure 16.2 shows such a combination in a posting for the position of academic adviser for a large university.

Performance Appraisal Defined

Performance appraisal is a process that involves communicating to an employee how well the employee is performing the job and also, ideally, involves establishing a plan for improvement. Performance appraisals are used for many purposes in organizations. Among these purposes are wage and salary administration, promotions or demotions, transfers, layoffs, discharges, counseling with employees, and human resources planning. Performance appraisal systems have three principal purposes: (1) to improve employee performance in the present job, (2) to prepare employees for future opportunities that may arise in the organization, and (3) to provide a record of employee performance that can be used as a basis for future management decisions. Many of the benefits that result from a sound performance appraisal system are outlined in Figure 16.3.

FIGURE 16.2   Job Description—Academic Adviser, XXX University

Position Summary

To perform a variety of complex administrative work involved in the coordination of the recruitment and admissions process for a specific school or college within the university.

Major Responsibilities

Perform any combination of the following duties according to specific departmental guidelines.
1. Advise students in all matters affecting academic progress.
2. Perform administrative duties for recruitment and admissions process to include readmission decisions, degree petitions, etc.
3. Serve as liaison with faculty, directors, student leaders and organizations, and other campus programs and departments.
4. Coordinate a team of faculty admissions advisers.
5. Administer international student affairs with student visas, admissions, and counseling.
6. Coordinate scholarship decision making and follow up with major corporations to increase financial opportunities for students.
7. Compile data for strategic planning and special projects.
8. Supervise clerical staff and student assistants. Activities and decisions are varied in nature, requiring the solving of both common and unusual problems.

Types of Contacts

Negotiates with or persuades students, individuals in other departments, academic/research faculty, potential students, other colleges/universities, alumni, and parents. Advises or interprets information for supervisors, advisory committees, and directors/chairpersons.

Major Knowledge and Skills

For this job, an advanced level of knowledge is typically required in conflict resolution, foreign cultures, quality assurance/control, quality management, project management, admissions/enrollment, academic counseling, career counseling, personal counseling, financial aid sources, program administration, student relations, and cataloging. A solid/working knowledge is necessary in mathematics, auditing, course development, data analysis, data compilation, data entry, database management, education law, regulations or laws, filing/shelving, loan administration, PC applications, PC operation, preparation of management reports, public relations, records management, recruiting, risk management, searching catalogs/databases, and word processing/typing. This job requires interpersonal communications such as advising, recommending, or counseling, directing or delegating, exchanging information, interviewing, negotiating, selling, persuading, or influencing, one-on-one job training, and troubleshooting; group communications such as participating in meetings; and preparing written communications such as documentation, memoranda, and letters. This job requires operating or maintaining standard office equipment. This job requires computer knowledge to search computer files, and/or generate standard reports, to input or edit information into spreadsheets or programs, to do word processing and/or desktop publishing, to design and/or program spreadsheets, databases, and/or custom reports.

Performance Appraisal Methods

Ideally, performance appraisals should be directly related to job success. However, locating or creating satisfactory measures of job success can be difficult. There are many jobs for which performance measures can be developed but with a greater degree of difficulty (for example, evaluating the job performance of a high school teacher or a staff specialist). In addition, job performance is often influenced by factors outside the employee's control. For example, the performance of a machine operator is partially influenced by the age and condition of the equipment. For these reasons and others, performance appraisals are often based on personal characteristics and other subjective factors. Among the personal characteristics that are frequently used in performance appraisal systems are integrity, dependability, attitude, initiative, and judgment.

FIGURE 16.3
Benefits of a Sound Performance Appraisal System to the Organization, the Supervisor, and the Employee

Benefits to the Organization

1. Provides an evaluation of the organization's human resources.
2. Gives the organization a basis for making future human resources decisions.
3. Increases the potential of the organization's present human resources for meeting the present and future needs of the organization.
4. Improves employee morale.

Benefits to the Supervisor

1. Provides the supervisor with a clearer picture of the employee's understanding of what is expected on the job.
2. Gives the supervisor input into each employee's development.
3. Improves the productivity and morale of the supervisor's employees.
4. Helps the supervisor identify capable replacements for higher-level jobs within the supervisor's work unit.
5. Helps to identify future training needs.

Benefits to the Employee

1. Allows the employee to present ideas for improvement.
2. Provides the employee with an opportunity to change his or her work behavior.
3. Lets the employee know how the supervisor feels about his or her performance.
4. Assures the employee of regular and systematic reviews of performance.
5. Gives the employee a chance to discuss problem areas and design mutual solutions.

Numerous problems exist in performance appraisal systems based on personal characteristics. One problem is that supervisors often resist such systems. The major reason for their resistance is that systems of this type place the supervisor in the position of being a judge with the employee being the defendant. Another problem is that such systems tempt the supervisor to favor close friends and associates. Because it is natural to see favorable characteristics in friends, the supervisor may never realize that favoritism is influencing his or her appraisals. Despite the problems, performance appraisal systems based on personal characteristics and subjective evaluations are still in widespread use.

The most frequently used performance appraisal methods are:

6 LEARNING OBJECTIVES

1. Graphic rating scale.
2. Essay appraisals.
3. Checklist.
4. Forced-choice rating.
5. Critical-incident appraisals.
6. Work-standards approach.
7. Ranking methods.
8. Management by objectives (MBO).
9. Multi-rater assessment (or 360-degree feedback).

Upper levels of management usually decide which type of performance appraisal system an organization will use. Ideally, the supervisor should have some input into that decision. However, the success or failure of any performance appraisal method is largely determined by the supervisor's use of the method. This section describes the various performance appraisal methods. The Appendix at the end of this chapter gives an example of a typical form used in a performance appraisal system.

FIGURE 16.4 Sample Items on a Graphic Rating Scale Evaluation Form

Quantity of work (the amount of work an employee does in a workday)

( )	( )	( )	( )	( )
Does not meet requirements.	Does just enough to get by.	Volume of work is satisfactory.	Very industrious, does more than is required.	Superior production record.

Dependability (the ability to do required jobs with a minimum of supervision)

( )	( )	( )	( )	( )
Requires close supervision, is unreliable.	Sometimes requires prompting.	Usually completes necessary tasks with reasonable promptness.	Requires little supervision; is reliable.	Requires absolute minimum of supervision.

Job knowledge (information that an employee should have on work duties for satisfactory job performance)

( )	( )	( )	( )	( )
Poorly informed about work duties.	Lacks knowledge of some phases of job.	Moderately informed; can answer most questions about the job.	Understands all phases of job.	Has complete mastery of all phase of job.

Attendance (faithfulness in coming to work daily and conforming to work hours)

( )	( )	( )	( )	( )
Often absent without good excuse, or frequently reports for work late, or both.	Lax in attendance or reporting for work on time, or both.	Usually present and on time.	Very prompt; regular in attendance.	Always regular and prompt; volunteers for overtime when needed.

Accuracy (the correctness of work duties performed)

( )	( )	( )	( )	( )
Makes frequent errors.	Careless; often makes errors.	Usually accurate; makes only average number of mistakes.	Requires little supervision; is exact and precise most of the time.	Requires absolute minimum of supervision; is almost always accurate.

Graphic Rating Scale

With the **graphic rating scale,** the supervisor is asked to evaluate an individual on such factors as initiative, dependability, cooperativeness, and quality of work. The graphic rating scale is one of the most widely used performance appraisal methods. One of the biggest problems with its use is that many supervisors have a tendency to evaluate everyone a little above average. However, this method does give the same information on all employees and it is relatively inexpensive to develop. Figure 16.4 gives some questions used on a graphic rating scale.

Essay Appraisals

Essay appraisals require the supervisor to write a series of statements about an employee's past performance, potential for promotion, and strengths and weaknesses. One problem with the essay appraisal is that the length and content of the written statements can vary considerably from supervisor to supervisor. In addition, this method depends on the writing skills of the supervisor. For these reasons, it is difficult to compare essay appraisals made by different supervisors.

Checklist

With the **checklist,** the supervisor does not actually evaluate but merely records performance. The supervisor checks yes or no responses on a series of questions concerning the

FIGURE 16.5
Sample Checklist
Questions

	Yes	No
1. Does the employee produce work that meets quality standards?	_____	_____
2. Does the employee have a thorough knowledge of the job?	_____	_____
3. Does the employee work without detailed instructions?	_____	_____
4. Does the employee assist others when his or her work has been completed?	_____	_____

employee's performance. Figure 16.5 gives some typical questions. The principal advantage of this method is that it is easy to use. The scoring key for the checklist is usually kept by the human resources department, which computes the relative rating of the employee. Individuals with high scores are rated as better employees than those with low scores.

Supervisors are generally not aware of the values associated with each question; but since they can figure out the positive and negative aspects of the questions, bias can be introduced into their answers. Furthermore, assembling the questions is a difficult job. Another drawback of this method is that a different set of questions must be assembled for most job categories.

Forced-Choice Rating

The **forced-choice rating** method requires the supervisor to choose which of two statements is either most (or least) applicable to the employee being reviewed. The supervisor is required to choose between both favorable and unfavorable statements. Figure 16.6 gives some examples of statements that might appear in a forced-choice rating method.

Under the forced-choice rating method, the supervisor is not given the weights or scores assigned to each statement. Due to the nature of the questions, the supervisor usually cannot determine which answer is best. The human resources department or a member of higher management applies the weights and develops a score. Again, employees with higher scores are rated as better than those with lower scores. The forced-choice rating method attempts to eliminate bias by forcing the supervisor to choose between statements that are not obviously distinguishable. The biggest drawback of this method is that it can frustrate supervisors. In addition, the cost of developing the form may be high. Supervision Illustration 16–2 describes the use of forced-choice rating at GE.

Critical-Incident Appraisals

With **critical-incident appraisals,** the supervisor keeps a written record of unusual incidents that show both positive and negative actions by an employee. The employee is then evaluated based on actual behavior. When this method is used, the employee being evaluated should always be given a chance to state his or her views on each incident. This also provides the employee with an opportunity to establish an understanding of the behavior that the supervisor is seeking.

FIGURE 16.6
Sample Questions for
a Forced-Choice
Rating Method

From each set of statements, choose the one statement that best describes the employee being evaluated.

1. Keeps work up-to-date.
2. Approaches problems with an open mind.

1. Uses sick leave to excess.
2. Takes little interest in the job.

1. Organizes work well.
2. Produces work that meets quality standards.

SUPERVISION ILLUSTRATION 16–2

FORCED CHOICE RANKING AT GE

Jack Welch, and General Electric brought forced ranking into the spotlight with the publication of GE's 2000 annual report where Welch "explained and extolled" the use of forced ranking at GE. Since then its popularity as a performance evaluation tool has continued to grow. By some estimates as many as one-fifth to one-third of all companies are using forced ranking in some form. A recent study by Novations Group Inc. found that a total of 54.8 percent of all responding companies used forced ranking. Still, the total number of firms using it may be understated because some firms are unwilling to admit publicly to using the practice. Along with its growth in popularity has been a fair share of criticism.

Forced ranking is a differentiation process where managers are required to evaluate an employee's performance, based on predetermined categories, against other employees in the department or peer group. These employee performance rankings are then applied to a bell curve. Those that rank at the bottom of the curve: usually the bottom 10 percent, are either put on probation, coached to improve performance, or terminated. Those at the head of the curve, usually the top 20 percent, are generously rewarded for their performance.

Source: Adapted from Beth Hazels and Craig M. Sasse, "Forced Ranking: A Review," S.A.M. Advanced *Management Journal*, Spring 2008, pp. 35–41.

For this method to be effective, the supervisor must record pertinent incidents as they occur. This can be time-consuming and burdensome. Another drawback is the strong tendency to record or stress primarily negative incidents.

Work-Standards Approach

With the **work-standards approach,** attempts are made to establish objective measures of an employee's work performance. An example of a work standard for production workers is the number of pieces produced per hour. A salesperson's quota is another type of work standard. Work standards for professional, staff, and clerical workers are much more difficult to define. Generally speaking, work standards should reflect the "normal output of a normal person." They attempt to answer the question "What is a fair day's work?" Thus, the work-standards approach is used more frequently for operative workers in production jobs than for other types of employees.

The major advantage of the work-standards approach is that it bases the performance appraisal on factors that are generally more objective than those used in other methods. To be effective, of course, the standards must be fair and the employees must view them as being fair.

Ranking Methods

The most commonly used ranking methods are alternation ranking, paired-comparison ranking, and forced-distribution ranking. Under **alternation ranking,** a supervisor's employees are listed down the left side of a sheet of paper. The supervisor then chooses the most valuable employee, crosses this name off the list, and places it at the *top* of the column on the right side. The supervisor then selects and crosses off the name of the least valuable employee and places it at the *bottom* of the right-hand column. The supervisor then repeats this process for all the names on the left side. The listing of names on the right side gives the supervisor a ranking of his or her employees from most valuable to least valuable.

Under **paired-comparison ranking,** the supervisor again lists his or her employees' names down the left side of a sheet of paper. The supervisor then evaluates the performance of the first employee on the list against the performance of the second employee on the list. If the supervisor feels that the performance of the first employee is better than that of the second employee, he or she places a check mark by the first employee's name. The first employee is then compared to each of the other employees. In this way, the first

FIGURE 16.7
Forced-Distribution Curve

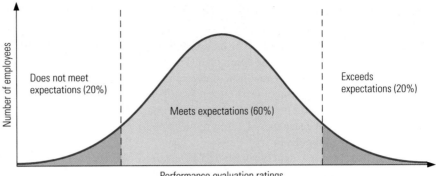

employee is compared with all the other employees on the list. The process is repeated for each of the other employees. The employee with the most check marks is evaluated to be the most valuable employee, and the employee with the least check marks is evaluated to be the least valuable. The major problem with the paired-comparison method is that it becomes unwieldy when a large number of employees are being compared.

Under **forced-distribution ranking,** the rater compares the performance of employees and places a certain percentage of employees at various performance levels. This method assumes that the performance level in a group of employees will be distributed according to a bell-shaped, or "normal," curve. Figure 16.7 illustrates how the method works. The rater is required to rate 60 percent of the employees as meeting expectations, 20 percent as exceeding expectations, and 20 percent as not meeting expectations.

One problem with forced-distribution ranking is that a bell-shaped distribution of performance may not be applicable to small groups of employees. With such groups, even if the distribution approximates a normal curve, it is probably not a perfect curve. This means that some employees will probably not be rated accurately if forced-distribution ranking is used. Also, this method is dramatically different from the other methods in that it makes each employee's performance evaluation a function of the performance of other employees in the job. In addition, none of the ranking methods explain or quantify the differences between employees. In fact, the difference between the top employee and the one at the bottom of the list may only be time and maturity factors.

Management by Objectives (MBO)

Management by objectives (MBO) was introduced and discussed as a means of planning in Chapter 7. MBO is also used as a performance appraisal method and is similar to the work-standards approach. With MBO, the supervisor and the employee jointly agree on what the employee's work objectives will be and how they will be accomplished. The employee is then allowed considerable freedom in accomplishing the work objectives. The employee's performance appraisal is based on the degree to which the work objectives are accomplished.

Multi-Rater Assessment (or 360-Degree Feedback)

One currently popular method of performance appraisal is called **multi-rater assessment,** or **360-degree feedback.** With this method, managers, peers, customers, suppliers, or colleagues are asked to complete questionnaires on the performance of the employee being evaluated. The person assessed also completes a questionnaire. The questionnaires are generally lengthy. Typical questions are: "Are you crisp, clear, and articulate? Abrasive? Spreading yourself too thin?" The human resources department provides the results to the employee, who in turn gets to see how his or her opinion differs from those of the group doing the assessment.

Frequency of Performance Appraisals

There seems to be no consensus on the question of how frequently performance appraisals should be conducted. The answer seems to be as frequently as is necessary to let employees know how they are doing. Many organizations require a formal performance appraisal at least once a year. However, most employees want to know how well they are doing more often than once a year. Therefore, it is recommended that the supervisor do at least two or three reviews each year in addition to the formal annual performance appraisal.

A supervisor should be aware of the necessity for more frequent appraisals for new employees or employees who are being retrained. These informal appraisals can be very effective in the development process of these employees.

Supervisor Biases in Performance Appraisals

7 LEARNING OBJECTIVES

Several common supervisor biases have been identified in performance appraisals. **Leniency** is the grouping of ratings at the positive end instead of spreading them throughout the performance scale. **Central tendency** is the rating of all or most employees in the middle of the scale. Leniency and central tendency errors make it difficult if not impossible to separate the good performers from the poor performers. In addition, such errors make it difficult to compare ratings from different raters. For example, it is possible for a good performer who is rated by a manager committing central tendency errors to receive a lower rating than that of a poor performer who is rated by a manager committing leniency errors. A recency error occurs when the supervisor recalls only the most recent events, either positive or negative, just prior to appraising the employee.

Another common bias in performance appraisals is the **halo effect.** This occurs when supervisors allow a single prominent characteristic of an employee to influence their judgment on each of the items in the performance appraisal. A frequent result is that the employee being evaluated receives approximately the same rating on every item.

Personal preferences and prejudices can also cause errors in performance appraisals. Supervisors with biases or prejudices tend to look for employee behaviors that conform to their biases. Appearance, social status, dress, race, and sex have influenced many performance appraisals. Supervisors have also allowed first impressions to influence later judgments of an employee. First impressions are only a sample of behavior; however, people tend to retain these impressions even when faced with contradictory evidence later. Supervision Illustration 16–3 describes how an employee had his performance appraisal lowered.

Overcoming Biases in Performance Appraisals

As can be seen from the above discussion, the potential for biases in performance appraisals is great. One approach to overcoming these biases is to make refinements in the design of appraisal methods. For example, it could be argued that the forced-distribution method of performance appraisal attempts to overcome the biases of leniency and central tendency. Unfortunately, because refined instruments frequently do not overcome all the obstacles, it appears unlikely that refining appraisal instruments will totally overcome errors in performance appraisals.

SUPERVISION ILLUSTRATION 16-3

LOWERING A PERFORMANCE APPRAISAL

The plaintiff seeks a preliminary injunction and restraining order against the Syracuse City Police enjoining its employees and police officers to "stay away from [the] plaintiff and his residence." The plaintiff was arrested in May for aggravated harassment. He filed a civil rights lawsuit alleging he was not read his Miranda rights and the detective would not let him put on his socks or notify his mother that he was leaving prior to his removal from his residence. The plaintiff now "fears for his safety and well being" and is "not sure why a police officer and an undercover agent" came to his residence after he filed his civil rights complaint.

The plaintiff is employed by the federal government at the Defense Finance and Accounting Service and is bringing action under the Privacy Act of 1974 and Title VII. A verbal eruption by the plaintiff directed at another employee prompted a complaint and investigation of the plaintiff. He claims the defendants violated his rights under the Privacy Act when his supervisor investigated a complaint against him without speaking to him and reviewing his side of the dispute. The plaintiff also claims his supervisor lowered his annual performance appraisal from "highly successful" to "fully successful" in retaliation for the plaintiff's prior equal employment opportunity activity.

Source: Adapted from *The Daily Record* Staff "Case Digests," *The Daily Record*, Rochester, NY, July 9, 2008, Wire Feed.

A more promising approach to overcoming biases in performance appraisals is to improve the skills of raters. Suggestions on the specific training that should be given to raters are often vague, but they normally emphasize that raters should be given training to observe behavior more accurately and judge it fairly. At a minimum, raters should receive training in (1) the performance appraisal method(s) used by the company, (2) rater biases and causes of those biases, (3) the importance of the rater's role in the total appraisal process, (4) the use of performance appraisal information, and (5) the communication skills necessary to provide feedback to the employee.

Conducting Performance Appraisal Interviews

Appraising the employee's performance is only half of the supervisor's job in performance appraisal systems. The other half is communicating the appraisal to the employee. The purposes of communicating the performance appraisal are to (1) provide the employee with a clear understanding of how the supervisor feels the employee is performing the job, (2) clear up any misunderstandings about what is expected, (3) establish a program of improvement, and (4) improve the working relationship between the supervisor and the employee.

Effective performance appraisal interviews are the result of good planning by the supervisor. Whatever form or method is used, considerable time and thought should be given to completing the form. The form should not be completed in the few minutes before the interview. When feasible, the employee should be given at least a week's notice of the upcoming appraisal.

A private room or office should be used, interruptions should be held to a minimum, and the confidential nature of the information should be explained to the employee. The performance appraisal interview is not the time to tell the employee off. You are trying to make the job easier for the employee and to help him or her become a happier and more productive employee. Figure 16.8 gives some questions that the supervisor should consider before discussing the performance appraisal with the employee.

FIGURE 16.8

Questions That the Supervisor Should Consider Prior to the Performance Appraisal Interview

1. What are the specific good points on which you will compliment the employee?
2. What are the specific improvement points you intend to discuss?
3. What reactions do you anticipate? How do you intend to handle these reactions?
4. Can you support your performance appraisal with adequate facts?
5. What specific help or corrective action do you anticipate offering?
6. What is your approach for gaining acceptance of your suggested corrective action?
7. What follow-up action do you have in mind?

General dos and don'ts of the performance appraisal process can help supervisors to not only prevent but reduce the errors that always seem to plague the process. The dos include the following:

1. Base performance appraisal on job performance only and not other factors unrelated to the job.
2. Use only those rating scales that are relevant to the job itself and are indicators of objective performance and attainment.
3. Sincerely work at the appraisal interview process.
4. Be problem solving oriented.

The don'ts include the following:

1. Don't criticize. Be proactive.
2. Carefully avoid the halo effect and leniency errors.
3. Dominate conversations about performance. Encourage employees to speak and to address issues in the evaluation process themselves.
4. Avoid general prescriptions to fix performance. Always present concrete and realizable objectives. Performance goals are the foundation of productivity.

In addition to the steps outlined above, most organizations require that the employee and supervisor sign the performance evaluation form, acknowledging that the appraisal interview has been conducted and that the employee has read the evaluation. Ideally, the employee should be given a copy of the evaluation.

When conducting performance evaluations, it is extremely important that the supervisor be specific so that people know exactly what they are doing well and what needs improvement. In addition, it should be remembered that the performance review should be a two-way learning experience. The supervisor should ask for feedback from the employee as to how the supervisor might improve his or her own performance. Figure 16.9 presents a suggested set of specific steps to be followed when conducting an employee performance review.

Preparing for Your Own Performance Appraisal Interview

Like your employees, you as supervisor also receive performance appraisals. You probably also have some of the same feelings that your employees have before the appraisal is conducted. Figure 16.10 offers some suggestions on how to prepare for your own performance appraisal session. You can also give these suggestions to your employees in advance of their performance appraisal so that they will be better prepared. Remember, regardless of which side of the fence you are on, a performance appraisal should be a learning, growing experience.

FIGURE 16.9
Steps in the Performance Appraisal Interview

Source: Adapted from "The Annual Performance Review Discussion—Making It Constructive," by Herbert H. Meyer, reprinted with permission of *Personnel Journal,* Costa Mesa, CA. All rights reserved. Copyright © October 1977.

Performance Review Discussion

Employee's name _____

Date of discussion _____

Introduction
- Put employee at ease.
- Purpose: Mutual discussion of how things are going.

Employee's view
- How does he/she view job and working climate?
- Any problems?
- Suggestions for changes, improvement?

Supervisor's view of employee's performance
- Summary statement only.
- Avoid comparisons with others.

Behavior desirable to continue
- Mention one or two items only.

Opportunities for improvement
- No more than one or two items.
- Do not present these opportunities as "shortcomings."
- Keep the suggestions work-related.

Performance improvement plan
- Plan should be employee's plan.
- Supervisor merely tries to help and counsel.

Future opportunities
- Advancement possibilities?
- Future pay increase possibilities?
- Warning for poor performer.

Feedback from employee on supervisor's suggestions for performance changes, improvements.
- Any problems?

Questions
- Any general concerns?
- Close on constructive, encouraging note.

FIGURE 16.10
Suggestions for the Supervisor Preparing for His or Her Own Performance Appraisal

1. Using whatever form or method is used by your boss, evaluate your own performance.
2. Outline the ways in which your boss can help you do your job better.
3. Determine any additional training that you feel you need in order to do your job better.
4. Suggest any changes (reports, procedures, etc.) that would make you more effective in your job.
5. Develop a program for your self-improvement and discuss it with your boss.
6. Outline your long-range plans. Where would you like to be? How are you preparing to get there?

FIGURE 16.11

How to Conduct a Performance Appraisal Interview with a Poor Performer

1. Attempt to create a setting in which the employee feels encouraged to share his or her views and listen to what you have to say.
2. Be firm but fair.
3. Let the employee know exactly where he or she is weak and how to make improvements.
4. Get the employee to participate in setting goals for the present job.
5. If a transfer seems in order, get the employee to participate in setting goals for the new job.
6. Reach an agreement on what is to be achieved and the deadline for achieving it.
7. Emphasize your availability for future talks, and encourage the employee to come to you if problems remain or develop.

Handling the Poor Performer

Supervisors are frequently faced with the common problem of what to do about the poor performer. There may be a number of causes for the employee's poor performance. Improper placement, poor training, poor communication, and lack of motivation are common causes of poor performance.

The supervisor's alternatives in dealing with the poor performer are: (1) improve the employee's performance to an acceptable level; (2) transfer the employee to a job that better fits his or her abilities; (3) demote the employee to a job that he or she can handle; or (4) if unable to accomplish any of these possibilities, attempt to terminate the employee. Of course, these alternatives are influenced by government regulations and by whether the organization is unionized. The supervisor should make careful preparation for any action that is to be taken, document all steps, and work closely with the human resources department.

A supervisor who has decided that an employee's performance is unacceptable should plan for an immediate interview with the employee. Putting off or delaying the interview is unfair to both the employee and the organization. Delaying the handling of the poor performer may also increase the chance of litigation when action is finally taken. Figure 16.11 outlines the main points that the supervisor should cover with a poor performer during this interview.

It is also important to note that an employee's poor performance may be caused by personal problems. Managing employees with personal problems was covered in depth in Chapter 13. You may wish to review that chapter for more information.

Performance Appraisal and the Law

Title VII of the Civil Rights Act permits the use of a bona fide performance appraisal system. Performance appraisal systems generally are not considered to be bona fide when their application results in adverse effects on minorities, women, or older employees.

A number of court cases have ruled that performance appraisal systems used by organizations were discriminatory and not job-related. In one case involving layoffs, *Brito et al.* v. *Zia Company*, Spanish-surnamed workers were reinstated with back pay because the company had used a performance appraisal system of unknown validity in an uncontrolled and unstandardized manner. In *Mistretta* v. *Sandia Corporation*, performance appraisals were used as the main basis of layoff decisions affecting a disproportionate number of older employees. The judge awarded the plaintiffs double damages plus all court costs.

In *Chamberlain* v. *Bissel, Inc.*, an evaluator expressed dissatisfaction with an employee's performance but did not inform the employee that his job was in jeopardy. On being terminated, the employee sued the company claiming he had never been warned that he might be dismissed. The Michigan state court ruled the company had been negligent in not informing the employee that he might be fired and awarded the employee $61,354 in damages.

In *PriceWaterhouse* v. *Hopkins,* the plaintiff, Ann Hopkins, charged she was denied a partnership at PriceWaterhouse because of sexual stereotyping. Although Hopkins had generated more new business and logged more billable hours than any other candidate for partner, she was denied partnership consideration because the partners concluded she lacked the proper interpersonal skills. The Court ruled that interpersonal skills were a legitimate performance evaluation measure, but it found that some of the evaluations of Hopkins were sexual stereotyping. For example, one member of the firm advised Hopkins to walk, talk, and dress in a more feminine fashion. In its decision, the Supreme Court found that PriceWaterhouse had violated Title VII of the Civil Rights Act and stated that evaluating employees by assuming or insisting that they match a stereotype was illegal.

8 LEARNING OBJECTIVES

Many suggestions have been offered for making performance appraisal systems more legally acceptable. Some of these include (1) deriving the content of the appraisal system from job analyses; (2) emphasizing work behaviors rather than personal traits; (3) ensuring that the results of appraisals are communicated to employees; (4) ensuring that employees are allowed to give feedback during the appraisal interview; (5) training managers in how to conduct proper evaluations; (6) ensuring that appraisals are written, documented, and retained; and (7) ensuring that personnel decisions are consistent with the performance appraisals.

Rewarding Performance

The previously described systems and methods of appraising employee performance are useful only if they are closely tied to the organization's reward system. Appraising performance without a system that ties the results of the appraisal to the organization's reward system creates an environment where employees are poorly motivated.

Organizational Reward System

The organizational reward system consists of the types of rewards the organization offers. **Organizational rewards** include all types of rewards, both intrinsic and extrinsic, that are received as a result of employment by the organization. **Intrinsic rewards** are internal to the individual and are normally derived from involvement in work activities. Job satisfaction and feelings of accomplishment are examples of intrinsic rewards. Most extrinsic rewards are directly controlled and distributed by the organization and are more tangible than intrinsic rewards. Figure 16.12 provides examples of both intrinsic and **extrinsic rewards.**

Though intrinsic and extrinsic rewards are different, they are also closely related. Often an extrinsic reward provides the recipient with intrinsic rewards. For example, an employee who receives an extrinsic reward in the form of a pay raise may also experience feelings of accomplishment (an intrinsic reward) by interpreting the pay raise as a sign of a job well done.

FIGURE 16.12
Intrinsic versus Extrinsic Rewards

Intrinsic Rewards	Extrinsic Rewards
Sense of achievement	Formal recognition
Feelings of accomplishment	Fringe benefits
Informal recognition	Incentive payments
Job satisfaction	Base wages
Personal growth	Promotion
Status	Social relationships

John has learned that the best thing a supervisor can do is to be well prepared. John is now better prepared to handle performance appraisals because he now knows more about the various kinds of performance appraisal methods (pp. 294–299). He also knows the potential errors that can occur in conducting performance appraisals—leniency, central tendency, and the halo effect (p. 300). His anxiety about conducting performance appraisals is understandable. Most supervisors experience some anxiety about doing this. When conducting performance appraisals, it is extremely important that John be specific so that his employees know exactly what they are doing well and what needs improvement. Finally, John has learned a number of ways to handle the poor performers in his work group (p. 304).

9 LEARNING OBJECTIVES

Relating Rewards to Performance

Compensation consists of the extrinsic rewards offered by the organization and includes the base wage or salary, any incentives or bonuses, and any benefits employees receive in exchange for their work. The base wage or salary is the hourly, weekly, or monthly pay employees receive for their work. Incentives are rewards offered in addition to the base wage or salary and are usually directly related to performance. Benefits are rewards employees receive because of their employment with the organization. Paid vacations, health insurance, and retirement plans are examples of benefits.

The free enterprise system is based on the premise that rewards should depend on performance. This performance–reward relationship is desirable not only at the corporate level but also at the individual employee level. The underlying idea is that employees will be motivated when they believe good performance will lead to rewards. Unfortunately, many extrinsic rewards provided by organizations do not lend themselves to being related to performance. For example, paid vacations, insurance plans, and paid holidays are usually determined by organizational membership and seniority rather than by performance.

Other rewards, such as promotion, can and should be related to performance. However, opportunities for promotion may occur only rarely. When available, the higher positions may be filled on the basis of seniority or by someone outside the organization.

A key organizational variable that can be used to reward individuals and reinforce performance is basing an employee's annual pay raise on his or her performance. This is often referred to as **merit pay**. Even though many U.S. companies have some type of merit pay program, most do a poor job of relating pay and performance. Surveys repeatedly show that neither top management nor rank-and-file employees have much confidence that a positive relationship exists between performance and pay.

If relating rewards to performance is desirable, why is it not more widespread? One answer is that it is not easy to do; it is much easier to give everybody the same thing, as evidenced by the ever-popular across-the-board pay increase. Relating rewards to performance requires that performance be accurately measured, and this is not easy. It also requires discipline to actually match rewards to performance. Another reason is that many union contracts require that certain rewards be based on totally objective variables, such as seniority. While no successful formula for implementing a merit pay program has been developed, a number of desirable preconditions have been identified and generally accepted.

1. *Trust in management.* If employees are skeptical of management, it is difficult to make a merit pay program work.
2. *Absence of performance constraints.* Because pay-for-performance programs are usually based on individual ability and effort, the job must be structured so that an employee's performance is not hampered by factors beyond his or her control.

3. *Trained managers.* Managers must be trained in setting and measuring performance standards.

4. *Good measurement systems.* Performance should be based on criteria that are job specific and focus on results achieved.

5. *Ability to pay.* The merit portion of the salary-increase budget must be large enough to get employees' attention.

6. *Clear distinction among cost of living, seniority, and merit pay.* In the absence of strong evidence to the contrary, employees will naturally assume a pay increase is an economic or a longevity increase.

7. *Well-communicated total pay policy.* Employees must have a clear understanding of how merit pay fits into the total pay picture.

8. *Flexible reward schedule.* It is easier to establish a credible pay-for-performance plan if all employees do not receive pay adjustments on the same date.

Summary

1. *Define performance appraisal.* Performance appraisal involves determining and communicating to an employee how he or she is performing the job and establishing a plan for improvement.

2. *Define performance.* Performance refers to the degree of accomplishment of the tasks that make up an employee's job.

3. *Explain the determinants of performance.* Job performance is the net effect of an employee's effort in terms of abilities, role perceptions, and results produced. This implies that performance in a given situation can be viewed as resulting from the interrelationships among effort, abilities, role perceptions, and results produced. Effort refers to the amount of energy an employee expends in performing a job. Abilities are personal characteristics used in performing a job. Role perception refers to the direction in which employees believe they should channel their efforts on their jobs.

4. *Explain the contents of a job description.* A job description should include the following: date written, job status, job title, supervision received, supervision exercised, job summary, detailed list of job responsibilities, principal contacts, competency or position requirements, required education or experience, and career mobility.

5. *Define job analysis.* Job analysis is a formal process of determining and reporting information related to the nature of a specific job.

6. *List and describe the major performance appraisal methods.*

   • The graphic rating scale method requires the manager to assess an individual on factors such as quantity of work, dependability, job knowledge, attendance, accuracy of work, and cooperativeness.

   • The essay appraisal method requires the manager to describe an employee's performance in written narrative form.

   • The checklist method requires the manager to answer yes or no to a series of questions concerning the employee's behavior.

   • The forced-choice rating method requires the manager to rank a set of statements describing how an employee carries out the duties and responsibilities of the job.

   • The critical-incident appraisal method requires the manager to keep a written record of incidents, as they occur, involving job behaviors that illustrate both satisfactory and unsatisfactory performance by the employee being rated.

   • The works standards approach involves setting a standard or expected level of output and then comparing each employee's performance to the standard.

   • Ranking methods (alternation, paired comparison, and forced distribution) require the manager to compare the performance of an employee to the performance of other employees.

   • Management by objectives involves using the objectives set in the management-by-objectives process as a basis for performance appraisal.

   • Multi-rater assessment requires that managers, peers, customers, suppliers, or colleagues are asked to complete questionnaires on the performance of the employee being evaluated.

7. *Discuss common errors made in performance appraisals.* Leniency is the grouping of ratings at the positive end of the performance scale instead of spreading them throughout the scale. Central tendency occurs when performance appraisal

statistics indicate that most employees are evaluated similarly as doing average or above-average work. Recency occurs when performance evaluations are based on work performed most recently. The halo effect occurs when managers allow a single prominent characteristic of an employee to influence their judgment on each separate item in the performance appraisal.

8. *Suggest ways to make performance appraisal systems more legally acceptable.* Some suggestions include deriving the content of the appraisal system from job analyses; emphasizing work behaviors rather than personal traits; ensuring that the results of the appraisals are communi-

cated to employees; ensuring that employees are allowed to give feedback during the appraisal interview; training managers in conducting proper evaluations; ensuring that appraisals are written, documented, and retained; and ensuring that personnel decisions are consistent with performance appraisals.

9. *Define compensation.* Compensation consists of the extrinsic rewards offered by the organization and includes the base wage or salary, any incentives or bonuses, and any benefits employees receive in exchange for their work.

Key Terms

Ability, 291
Alternation ranking, 298
Central tendency, 300
Checklist, 296
Compensation, 306
Critical-incident appraisal, 297
Direction, 291
Essay appraisal, 296
Extrinsic rewards, 305
Forced-choice rating, 297

Forced-distribution ranking, 299
Graphic rating scale appraisal, 296
Halo effect, 300
Intrinsic rewards, 305
Job analysis, 293
Job description, 293
Job specification, 293
Leniency, 300
Management by objectives (MBO), 299

Merit pay, 306
Multi-rater assessment or 360-degree feedback, 299
Organizational rewards, 305
Paired comparison ranking, 298
Performance, 291
Performance appraisals, 291
Ranking methods, 298
Work-standards approach, 298

Review Questions

1. Define performance appraisal.
2. What is performance? What factors influence an employee's level of performance?
3. Identify at least three uses of performance appraisal information.
4. Describe the following methods used in performance appraisal:
   a. Graphic rating scale
   b. Essay
   c. Checklist
   d. Forced-choice rating
   e. Critical incident
   f. Work standards
   g. Ranking methods
   h. Management by objectives
   i. Multi-rater assessment

5. Define the following types of performance appraisal errors:
   a. Leniency
   b. Central tendency
   c. Recency
   d. Halo effect
6. Outline some factors that influence the success or failure of performance appraisal interviews.
7. Describe some suggestions for making performance appraisal systems more legally acceptable.
8. Identify three basic components of compensation and give examples of each.
9. Outline some preconditions for implementing a merit pay program.

Skill-Building Questions

1. What are your thoughts on discussing salary raises and promotions during the performance appraisal interview?

2. Which method of performance appraisal do you think is the fairest? Why? (You may have to cite an example to explain your reason.) Under which method would you like to work? Why?

3. It has been said that incentive plans work for only a relatively short time. Do you agree or disagree? Why?

4. Why do you think management frequently uses across-the-board pay increases?

Additional Readings

Anonymous, "Performance Evaluations," *Partner's Report,* January 2009, pp. 4–5.

Bourne, Mike, "Performance Measurement: Learning from the Past and Projecting the Future," *Measuring Business Excellence,* 2008, p. 67.

Forte, Jay, "Give Feedback, Get Performance," *SuperVision,* February 2009, pp. 3–4.

Fox, Adrienne, "Curing What Ails Performance Reviews," *HRMagazine,* January 2009, pp. 52–57.

Gallagher, Tracy, "360-Degree Performance Reviews Offer Valuable Perspectives," *Financial Executive,* December 2008, p. 67.

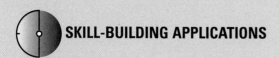

SKILL-BUILDING APPLICATIONS

Incident 16–1

Determining Pay Raises

About four months ago, Judy Holcomb was promoted to supervisor of the Claims Department for a large eastern insurance company. It is now time for all supervisors to make their annual salary increase recommendations. Judy doesn't feel comfortable in making these recommendations because she has been in her job only a short time. To further complicate the situation, the former supervisor has left the company and is unavailable for consultation.

There are no formal company restrictions on the kind of raises that can be given, but Judy's boss has said the total amount of money available to Judy for raises would be 8 percent of Judy's payroll for the past year. In other words, if the sum total of the salaries for all of Judy's employees was $200,000, then Judy would have $16,000 to allocate for raises. Judy is free to distribute the raises any way she wants, within reason.

Summarized below is the best information on her employees that Judy can find from the files of the former supervisor of the Claims Department. This information is supplemented by feelings Judy has developed during her short time as supervisor.

John Thompson: John has been with Judy's department for only five months. In fact, he was hired just before Judy was promoted into the supervisor's job. John is single and seems to be a carefree bachelor. His job performance, so far, has been above average, but Judy has received some negative comments about John from his co-workers. Present salary: $31,000.

Carole Wilson: Carole has been on the job for three years. Her previous performance appraisals have indicated superior performance. However, Judy does not believe the previous evaluations are accurate. She thinks Carole's performance is, at best, average. Carole appears to be well liked by all of her co-workers. Just last year, she became widowed and is presently the sole support for her five-year-old child. Present salary: $32,000.

Evelyn Roth: Evelyn has been on the job for four years. Her previous performance appraisals were all average. In addition, she had received below-average increases for the past two years. However, Evelyn recently approached Judy and told her she believes she was discriminated against in the past due to both her age and sex. Judy thinks Evelyn's work so far has been satisfactory but not superior. Most employees don't seem to sympathize with Evelyn's accusations of sex and age discrimination. Present salary: $30,000.

Jane Simmons: As far as Judy can tell, Jane is one of her best employees. Her previous performance appraisals also indicate she is a superior performer. Judy knows Jane badly needs a substantial salary increase because of some personal problems. She appears to be well respected by her co-workers. Present salary: $31,500.

Bob Tyson: Bob has been performing his present job for eight years. The job is very technical, and he would be difficult to replace. However, as far as Judy can discern, Bob is not a good worker. He is irritable and hard to work with. Despite this, Bob has received above-average pay increases for the past two years. Present salary: $27,000.

Questions

1. Indicate the size of the raise you would give each of these employees.
2. What criteria did you use in determining the size of the raise?
3. What do you think would be the feelings of the other people in the group if they should find out what raises you recommend?
4. Do you think the employees would eventually find out what raises others received? Would it matter?

Incident 16–2

Conducting a Performance Appraisal

Plant manager Paul Dorn wondered why his boss, Leonard Hech, had sent for him. Paul thought Leonard had been tough on him lately; he was slightly uneasy at being asked to come to Leonard's office at a time when such meetings were unusual. "Close the door and sit down, Paul," invited Leonard. "I've been wanting to talk to you." After preliminary conversation, Leonard said that because Paul's latest project had been finished, he would receive the raise he had been promised on its completion.

Leonard went on to say that since it was time for Paul's performance appraisal, they might as well do that now. Leonard explained that the performance appraisal was based on four criteria: (1) the amount of high-quality merchandise manufactured and shipped on time, (2) the quality of relationships with plant employees and peers, (3) progress in maintaining employee safety and health, and (4) reaction to demands of top management. The first criterion had a relative importance of 40 percent; the rest had a weight of 20 percent each.

On the first item, Paul received an excellent rating. Shipments were at an all-time high, quality was good, and few shipments had arrived late. On the second item, Paul also was rated excellent. Leonard said plant employees and peers related well to Paul, labor relations were excellent, and there had been no major grievances since Paul had become plant manager.

However, on attention to matters of employee safety and health, the evaluation was below average. His boss stated that no matter how much he bugged Paul about improving housekeeping in the plant, he never seemed to produce results. Leonard also rated Paul below average on meeting demands from top management. He explained that Paul always answered yes to any request and then disregarded it, going about his business as if nothing had happened.

Seemingly surprised at the comments, Paul agreed that perhaps Leonard was right and that he should do a better job on these matters. Smiling as he left, he thanked Leonard for the raise and the frank appraisal.

As weeks went by, Leonard noticed little change in Paul. He reviewed the situation with an associate:

> It's frustrating. In this time of rapid growth, we must make constant changes in work methods. Paul agrees but can't seem to make people break their habits and adopt more efficient ones. I find myself riding him very hard these days, but he just calmly takes it. He's well liked by everyone. But

somehow, he's got to care about safety and housekeeping in the plant. And when higher management makes demands he can't meet, he's got to say, "I can't do that and do all the other things you want, too." Now he has dozens of unfinished jobs because he refuses to say no.

As he talked, Leonard remembered something Paul had told him in confidence once. "I take Valium for a physical condition I have. When I don't take it, I get symptoms similar to a heart attack. But I only take half as much as the doctor prescribed." Now, Leonard thought, I'm really in a spot. If the Valium is what is making him so lackadaisical, I can't endanger his health by asking him to quit taking it. And I certainly can't fire him. Yet, as things stand, he really can't implement all the changes we need to fulfill our goals for the next two years.

Questions

1. Do you think a raise was justified in Paul's situation? Explain.

2. What could have been done differently in the performance appraisal session?

3. What can be done now to change the situation?

Exercise 16–1

Developing a Performance Appraisal System

A large public utility has been having difficulty with its performance evaluation program. The organization has an evaluation program in which all operating employees and clerical employees are evaluated semiannually by their supervisors. The form they have been using is given in Exhibit 16.1. It has been in use for 10 years.

EXHIBIT 16.1   **Performance Evaluation Form**

Performance Evaluation

Supervisors: When you are asked to do so by the personnel department, please complete this form on each of your employees. The supervisor who is responsible for 75 percent or more of an employee's work should complete this form on him or her. Please evaluate each facet of the employee separately.

Facet	Rating				Score
Quality of work	Excellent	Above average	Average	Below average	Poor
Quantity of work	Poor	Below average	Average	Above average	Excellent
Dependability at work	Excellent	Above average	Average	Below average	Poor
Initiative at work	Poor	Below average	Average	Above average	Excellent
Cooperativeness	Excellent	Above average	Average	Below average	Poor
Getting along with co-workers	Poor	Below average	Average	Above average	Excellent
					Total __

Supervisor's signature _____

Employee name _____

Employee number _____

The form is scored as follows: excellent = 5; above average = 4; average = 3; below average = 2; and poor = 1. The scores for each facet are entered in the right-hand column and are totaled for an overall evaluation score.

In the procedure used, each supervisor rates each employee on July 30 and January 30. The supervisor discusses the rating with the employee and then sends the rating to the personnel department. Each rating is placed in the employee's personnel file. If promotions come up, the cumulative ratings are considered at that time. The ratings are also supposed to be used as a check when raises are given.

The system was designed by Joanna Kyle, the personnel manager, who retired two years ago. Her replacement was Eugene Meyer. Meyer graduated 15 years ago with a degree in commerce from the University of Texas. Since then he's had a variety of experiences, mostly in utilities. For about five of these years, he did personnel work.

Eugene has been reviewing the evaluation system. Employees have a mixture of indifferent and negative feelings about it. An informal survey has shown that about 60 percent of the supervisors fill out the forms, give about three minutes to each form, and send them to personnel without discussing them with the employees. Another 30 percent do a little better. They spend more time completing the forms but communicate about them only briefly and superficially with their employees. Only about 10 percent of the supervisors seriously try to do what was intended.

Eugene also found that the forms were rarely used for promotion or pay-raise decisions. Because of this, most supervisors may have thought the evaluation program was a useless ritual. In his previous employment, Eugene had seen performance evaluation as a much more useful experience. It included giving positive feedback to employees, improving future employee performance, developing employee capabilities, and providing data for promotion and compensation.

Eugene has had little experience with design of performance evaluation systems. He believes he should seek advice on the topic.

Write a report summarizing your evaluation of the strengths and weaknesses of the present appraisal system. Recommend some specific improvements or data-gathering exercises to develop a better system for Eugene Meyer.

Exercise 16–2

Who Are "Normal" Employees?

Assume your company has just adopted the form shown in Exhibit 16.2 for its performance evaluation system. Assume further that your company has also instituted a policy that every manager's performance appraisals must conform to the accompanying bell-shaped curve. Using this curve, a manager who has 10 employees would have one that would be ranked as excellent, one that would be ranked above average, six that would be ranked average, one that would be ranked below average, and one that would be ranked unsatisfactory.

Prepare a 10-minute presentation summarizing the problems, advantages, and disadvantages of using such a system.

EXHIBIT 16.2

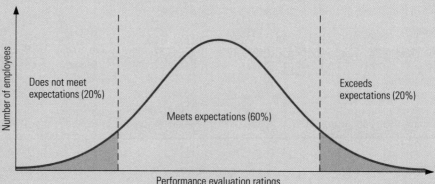

Exercise 16–3

Generally, at your college or university at the end of the semester or quarter you will be asked to complete a form to give your evaluation of the professor. Exhibit 16.3 gives an example of such a form.

1. Prepare a list of the pluses and minuses of such a system.

2. Suppose there are 60 students in the class and only 34 complete the form. Does this invalidate the evaluation?

3. What does performance mean in evaluating a professor? Be prepared to discuss your answers in class.

EXHIBIT 16.3

Item	(5) Strongly agree	(4) Agree	(3) Partly agree & partly disagree	(2) Disagree	(1) Strongly disagree	N/A	No of resp.	Interpolated median
1. Course seemed well planned and organized								
2. Good job covering course objectives/content								
3. Explained complex material clearly								
4. Was approachable and willing to assist								
5. Encouraged students to consult with him/her								
6. Class attendance important in promoting learning of material								
7. Number of assignments was reasonable								
8. Exams covered course content/objectives								
9. Exams were of appropriate difficulty								
10. Instructor was an effective teacher								

Student comments about the class or instructor _____
_____
_____

PERFORMANCE APPRAISAL RECORD FOR NON-SUPERVISORY EMPLOYEES*	
EMPLOYEE NAME:	**EMPLOYEE IDENTIFICATION #:**
JOB TITLE:	**UNIT:**
REVIEWED BY:	**DATE OF REVIEW**
REVIEW PERIOD: FROM:	TO:

*Used with permission of Georgia Institute of Technology.

Instructions

This form should be completed by the employee's immediate supervisor.

The appraisal process involves assessing the employee's work performance during the review period relative to specific indicators and an overall rating. The following rating categories are employed:

Highly Successful	Fully Successful	Needs Improvement

This scale is applied to the following performance indicators:

- Work Habits
- Job Knowledge
- Communications
- Attendance/Punctuality

- Teamwork
- Productivity
- Customer Service

The performance levels are defined for each indicator. Please note that the definitions included herein are intended to describe *in general* a given level of performance relative to the factor being rated. *They are not meant to be all-inclusive of conditions which must exist in order to legitimately rate an employee at a given level.* Rather the definitions are intended to convey, in broad terms, a "snapshot" description of conditions which typically exist at a performance level.

Assign a rating for each indicator and enter comments as appropriate in the space provided. *For any indicators rated as "Highly Successful" or "Needs Improvement," enter in the Comments section specifically what causes justify the rating.* Entries in the Comments section for "Fully Successful" ratings are optional. Add additional pages as necessary.

Additionally, space has been provided at the end of the form to enter performance indicators that are not included but that you feel are applicable to the employee's job and demonstrated performance during the review period.

Following the rating of each indicator, formulate an overall rating reflective of those individual ratings and enter on the final page of this form.

Space has been provided for the rater to note any development actions that will occur during the next review period and for the employee to record any comments regarding the evaluation and/or developmental actions planned.

The rater should sign the form in the space provided and obtain the signatures of the employee and the rater's immediate supervisor.

The completed form should be sent to the Office of Human Resources for further processing and filing.

Work Habits

How well does the employee organize and execute assignments? To what degree is ongoing supervision/monitoring required to ensure that work is properly completed? How well does the employee demonstrate self-discipline and reliability relative to work to be performed?

❏ Highly Successful	❏ Fully Successful	❏ Needs Improvement
Always performs assigned tasks as directed. Often completes tasks ahead of schedule and provides assistance to others. Understands and demonstrates the ability to effectively prioritize assignments to make the most efficient use of time and resources.	Consistently accepts responsibility for assigned work and performs tasks as directed. Ensures that results are complete and meet expectations prior to beginning a new assignment.	Work performed is often not acceptable and must be redone by employee and/or others. Employee is generally perceived as unreliable and requires more than normal supervisory monitoring of work in progress.

Job Knowledge

How well does the employee demonstrate sufficient skill and knowledge to perform all parts of the job effectively, efficiently, and safely?

❏ Highly Successful	❏ Fully Successful	❏ Needs Improvement
Possesses job knowledge that is well beyond normally acceptable as demonstrated by thorough understanding of how to perform regular work assignments as well as how those assignments relate to other areas. Serves as resource to others regarding work processes and procedures. Continuously strives to further improve job knowledge.	Demonstrates thorough understanding of all procedures and processes required to effectively perform all assignments. Very rarely needs help regarding how to execute a given assignment. When new procedures or processes are introduced, learns quickly and begins efficient application.	Often shows lack of understanding of how to perform assignments. Frequently requires assistance from supervisor or others in order to complete task due to lack of knowledge of applicable procedures and processes.

Communications

How well does the employee present ideas, concepts, and courses of action in a clear and concise manner? Does the employee listen well and ask appropriate questions?

❑ **Highly Successful**	❑ **Fully Successful**	❑ **Needs Improvement**
Demonstrates oral and/or written communications skills that result in very clear and concise messages and feedback. Very rarely is it necessary to ask employee to explain unclear or ambiguous communications. Exhibits the ability to explain or describe in a manner that is easily understood by most recipients.	Communicates with others effectively, speaking and/or in writing. Possesses and uses vocabulary required to successfully express thoughts, ideas, and explanations. Presents comprehensive feedback. Keeps supervisor and co-workers informed.	Often fails to make thoughts, ideas, and explanations clear to others, speaking and/or in writing. Feedback is typified by the need to reword or elaborate in order to obtain required level of understanding.

Attendance/Punctuality

To what degree does the employee consistently report for work on schedule and prepared?

❑ **Highly Successful**	❑ **Fully Successful**	❑ **Needs Improvement**
Consistently observes regular work schedule and makes self available to work both scheduled and unscheduled overtime. These actions are typified by volunteering to remain at work in emergencies or promptly responding to recalls received from home. Readily accepts scheduled overtime assignments. Volunteers to work overtime in areas outside normal work area when opportunities present themselves.	Consistently adheres to assigned work schedule by arriving, beginning work, stopping work, and departing as scheduled. During the work period, arrives to meetings, work sites, etc. on time or slightly before the scheduled time. Makes appropriate notification when delays to arriving to work on time are unavoidable. Is consistently regarded as a reliable employee.	Demonstrates a pattern of disregard for assigned work schedule by arriving late and/or leaving early. Is often late for appointments during the work day and may extend rest and meal periods beyond scheduled times.

Teamwork

How well does the employee work effectively with others and display an appropriate balance between individual and group efforts?

❑ **Highly Successful**	❑ **Fully Successful**	❑ **Needs Improvement**
Ideas for improvement contributed to group work effort are well received and normally result in process improvements and productivity. Consistently volunteers to help others within work group as work schedule permits. Contributes positively to resolution of conflict or problem encountered.	Contributes meaningfully to work group efforts by offering new ideas for improvement, sharing knowledge, and otherwise demonstrating a cooperative manner in dealing with supervisors and co-workers. Does his or her part toward group efforts.	Shows little or no interest in group efforts. Rarely demonstrates active participation in group interaction. Not perceived as a team player, preferring to work independently.

Productivity

To what degree do the employee's work efforts result in the desired outcomes to include quality, quantity, and timeliness?

❏ **Highly Successful**	❏ **Fully Successful**	❏ **Needs Improvement**
Assignments are always completed as scheduled and at the desired level of output. Often they are completed ahead of schedule and at a level of quality and/or quantity well beyond expectations. Ideas and suggestions to improve productivity are offered and frequently generate positive results.	Assignments are consistently completed on or at times ahead of schedule and at the desired level of output both in terms of quality and quantity. If conditions impacting productivity are outside the control of the employee, he or she notifies the supervisor in a timely manner.	Assignments are at times not completed as scheduled and/or the desired level of work output is not met. Work must often be redone by the employee or others, resulting in delays.

Customer Service

How effectively does the employee interact with customers in serving their needs? For purposes of this appraisal, "customer" is defined as anyone (either internal or external to the organization) requiring information or service related to the employee's job duties, knowledge, and experiences.

❏ **Highly Successful**	❏ **Fully Successful**	❏ **Needs Improvement**
Goes out of his or her way to ensure customer satisfaction. Processes both routine and nonroutine customer inquiries and concerns in ways that result in a high degree of customer satisfaction. Goes beyond basic inquiry to learn of and respond to relevant issues that may not necessarily be apparent initially.	Responds in a timely, courteous, and informed manner to customer inquiries and concerns. When an immediate response is not possible, provides necessary follow-up and keeps customer informed.	At times appears indifferent to customer concerns. Does bare minimum or less in the way of response to customers. While not necessarily discourteous, displays only the basics in the way of consideration for customer needs.

Additional Indicator: _____

Definition:_____

❏ **Highly Successful**	❏ **Fully Successful**	❏ **Needs Improvement**

COMMENTS ON RATINGS

```
_____
_____
_____
_____
_____
_____
_____
_____
```

Overall Rating

In considering your ratings of the individual performance indicators and the employee's accomplishments relative to job expectations over the entire review period, how well is he or she performing?

❏ Highly Successful	❏ Fully Successful	❏ Needs Improvement
The employee clearly goes beyond job requirements on a consistent basis. This is demonstrated not only by several indicator ratings being "Highly Successful" but is also reflected by the general impression of accomplishment well beyond expectations. These conditions exist on a continual rather than occasional basis.	The employee is fully successful in most if not all performance indicators. If improvement is needed, progress toward that need is being made at an acceptable or better rate. In most all cases job performance can be summarized as completing job assignments as expected and at times going well beyond expectations.	The employee has been rated as "Needs Improvement" in at least one indicator and the need for improvement in overall job performance is clearly evident. Regardless of the reason, the employee has demonstrated a lack of desired achievement during the review period. Need for further development or other actions are noticeably obvious.

DEVELOPMENTAL PLANS

```
_____
_____
_____
_____
```

EMPLOYEE COMMENTS

```
_____
_____
_____
_____
_____
_____
```

SIGNATURES

Employee & Date:	Supervisor & Date:	Next Level Supervision & Date:

CHAPTER SEVENTEEN

Employee and Labor Relations

Learning objectives

After studying this chapter, you will be able to:

1. Explain employment at will and employment arbitration.
2. Define discipline.
3. Explain the key features of the formal discipline process.
4. Define grievance, union steward, and arbitration.
5. Describe the differing philosophies of unions and management.
6. Discuss significant labor laws.
7. Describe four main types of union organizations.

While having lunch with her friend Bill Thomas, a supervisor in the underwriting department, Jane Harris learned that Bill just had a grievance filed against him by one of his employees. Bill had suspended the employee for coming in late to work. The employee had been late four times in the past five months, but Bill didn't say anything to him about it on the first two occasions. On the third occasion, Bill gave the employee a written reprimand. On the fourth, Bill suspended him.

The clerical employees of Global Insurance Company are unionized. The union contract has a disciplinary procedure that calls for an oral warning on the second occurrence of tardiness during a six-month period, a written warning on the third, and a suspension on the fourth. The grievance filed against Bill Thomas stated that he had not followed the proper disciplinary procedure.

Jane had been a member of the union prior to her promotion. She hadn't paid much attention then to the discipline and grievance procedures because they didn't affect her. Now, as a supervisor, Jane feels she needs to know more about the disciplinary process and unions.

When a member of management wants to take an action against an operative employee for violating an organizational rule, the organization's discipline procedure is used to resolve the problem. When an employee has a complaint against the organization or its management, the organization's grievance procedure is normally used to resolve the problem. Some organizations have very formal discipline and grievance procedures; others have less formal procedures; still others have no formalized procedures. The purpose of this chapter is to outline typical discipline and grievance procedures and to suggest ways of handling disciplinary actions and grievances positively. The latter part of this chapter discusses the role of unions in organizations.

Employment at Will and Employment Arbitration

LEARNING OBJECTIVES

Until recently, management decisions on discipline and discharge in nonunionized organizations have been relatively free of judicial review. Courts intervened only in those cases violating legislation concerning equal employment opportunity. Generally, the concept of **employment at will** has applied. Employment at will means that when an employer hires employees to work for an indefinite period of time and the employees do not have a contract limiting the circumstances under which they can be discharged, the employer can terminate the employees at any time.

However, a Supreme Court decision (*Circuit City Stores* v. *Adams,* 121 S. Ct. 1302 [2001]) held that employers may require employees to sign an arbitration agreement binding them to mandatory arbitration of disputes arising out of or relating to their employment. Thus, the Supreme Court held that employers may require employees to agree to resolve any such employment-related disputes through final and binding arbitration. This type of arbitration is referred to as employment arbitration as opposed to contract arbitration. This court decision means that nonunionized companies should not only develop appeal procedures for employment disputes but also ensure that supervisors within the company follow the guidelines discussed in this chapter.

A Positive Approach to Discipline

LEARNING OBJECTIVES

Discipline should be viewed as a condition within an organization whereby employees know what is expected of them in terms of the organization's rules, standards, and policies and what the consequences are of infractions. The basic purpose of discipline should be to teach about expected behaviors in a constructive manner.

A formal discipline procedure usually begins with an oral warning and progresses through a written warning, suspension, and ultimately discharge. Formal discipline procedures also outline the penalty for each successive offense and define time limits for maintaining records of each offense and penalty. For instance, tardiness records might be maintained for only a six-month period. Tardiness prior to the six months preceding the offense would not be considered in the disciplinary action. Less formal procedures generally specify the reasons for disciplinary action as being for just or proper cause.

Preventing discipline from progressing beyond the oral warning stage is obviously advantageous to both the employee and management. Discipline should be aimed at correction rather than punishment. If the behavior can be corrected by an open talk between the supervisor and the employee, there is less chance that the problem will become a source of bitterness. Formal oral or written warnings are less likely to cause animosity than a disciplinary suspension. It is obviously not in the supervisor's best interest to deprive employees of their income if their behavior can be corrected by an oral or written warning. A disciplinary suspension not only hurts the employee but also frequently deprives the supervisor and the organization of a needed employee. Of course, the most costly and least acceptable form of discipline is discharge. In most cases, supervisors should make every effort to avoid discharging an employee. Supervisors should view discipline as a means of encouraging employees to willingly abide by the rules and standards of the organization.

Maintaining Good Discipline

One of the most important ways of maintaining good discipline is communication. Employees cannot operate in an orderly and efficient manner unless they know the rules. The supervisor has the responsibility of informing employees of the organization's rules, regulations, and standards. The supervisor must also ensure, when necessary, that employees understand the purpose of the rules and regulations. It is also essential that the supervisor remind employees in a friendly manner when their adherence to the rules has become lax. It is important to note that employees also have an obligation to become familiar with company rules and regulations. The sole responsibility is not on the supervisor. The supervisor should foster the overall atmosphere that encourages employees to become informed.

Whenever possible, counseling should precede the use of disciplinary reprimands or stricter penalties. Through counseling, the supervisor can uncover problems affecting employee relations and productivity. Counseling also develops an environment of openness, understanding, and trust. This encourages employees to maintain self-discipline.

To maintain effective discipline, supervisors must always follow the rules that employees are expected to follow. There is no reason for supervisors to bend the rules for themselves or for a favored employee. Employees must realize that the rules are for everyone. It is a supervisor's responsibility to be fair toward all employees.

Applying the Discipline Procedure

Although most employees do follow the organization's rules and regulations, there are times when supervisors must use discipline. Figure 17.1 lists a number of reasons for using discipline. Supervisors must not be afraid to use the disciplinary procedure when it becomes necessary. Employees may interpret failure to act as meaning that a rule is not to be enforced. Supervisory decisions to discipline after a period of lax enforcement contribute to poor morale and reduced productivity. Failure to act can also frustrate employees who are abiding by the rules. Applying discipline properly can encourage borderline employees to improve their performance.

Source: Adapted from Frank Elkouri, and Edna Elkouri, How Arbitration Works, ed. by Alan M. Ruben, (Washington, DC: Bureau of National Affairs, 2003).

FIGURE 17.1
Reasons for Disciplining Employees

Absenteeism
Tardiness
Loafing
Absence from work
Leaving place of work (includes quitting early)
Sleeping on job
Assault and fighting among employees
Horseplay
Insubordination
Threat to or assault of management representative
Abusive language toward supervisor
Profane or abusive language (not toward supervisor)
Falsifying company records (including time records, production records)
Falsifying employment application
Dishonesty
Theft
Disloyalty to government (security risk)

Disloyalty to employer (includes competing with employer, conflict of interest)
Moonlighting
Negligence
Damage to or loss of machinery or materials
Incompetence (including low productivity)
Refusal to accept job assignment
Refusal to work overtime
Participation in prohibited strike
Misconduct during strike
Slowdown
Union activities
Possession or use of drugs
Possession or use of intoxicants
Obscene or immoral conduct
Gambling
Abusing customers
Attachment or garnishment of wages

Before supervisors use the discipline procedure, they must be aware of how far they can go without involving higher levels of management. They must also determine how much union participation is required. If the employee to be disciplined is a member of a union, the contract may specify the penalty that must be used. Other requirements may also be specified by the contract, such as who must be present during a disciplinary meeting and the length of time a record of the discipline can be kept on an employee's record. Figure 17.2 is an example of a union contract clause covering discipline.

Because a supervisor's decisions may be placed under critical review in the grievance process, supervisors must be careful when applying discipline. Even if there is no union agreement, most supervisors are subject to some review of their disciplinary actions. To avoid having a discipline decision rescinded by a higher level of management, it is important that supervisors follow the guidelines discussed below.

Guidelines for Effective Discipline

Every supervisor should become familiar with the law, union contract, and past practices of the organization as they affect disciplinary decisions. Supervisors should resolve with higher management and the human resources department any questions that they may have about their authority to discipline.

The importance of maintaining adequate records cannot be overemphasized. Not only is this important for good supervision but it can also prevent a disciplinary decision from being rescinded. Written records often have a significant influence on decisions to overturn or uphold a disciplinary action. Past rule infractions and the overall performance of employees should be recorded. A supervisor bears the burden of proof when his or her decision to discipline an employee is questioned. In cases where the charge is of a moral or criminal nature, the proof required is usually the same as that required by a court of law (proof beyond a reasonable doubt). Adequate records by the supervisor and witnesses are of utmost importance in cases of this type. Written records of good performance and

FIGURE 17.2
Typical Union
Contract Provision
Relating to Discipline

ARTICLE XXI

Discharge, suspension, or other disciplinary action

The EMPLOYER shall not discharge nor suspend any employee without just cause, but in respect to discharge or suspension shall give at least one warning notice of a complaint against such employee to the employee, in writing, and a copy of same to the UNION affected, excepting that no warning notice need be given to an employee before discharge if the cause of such discharge is unauthorized use of company vehicle, dishonesty, drinking of alcoholic beverages while on duty, use of narcotics (as described by the Pure Food and Drug Act), barbiturates, or amphetamines while on duty, or engaging in physical violence while on duty, to the employee who initiates such action, recklessness resulting in serious accident while on duty, the carrying of unauthorized passengers or failure to report a serious accident or one which the employee would normally be aware of flagrant disregard of reasonable instructions that do not conflict with the terms of this Agreement, willful destruction of EMPLOYER's or public property, becoming involved in a serious motor vehicle accident while driving the Company car as a result of negligence or recklessness. Discharge or suspension must be by proper written notice to the employee and the UNION affected. Warning notices shall have no force or effect after nine (9) months from the date thereof. Any employee may request an investigation as to his or her discharge or suspension. Should such investigation prove that an injustice has been done to an employee, he or she shall be reinstated. The terms and conditions of such reinstatement may provide for full, partial, or no compensation for time lost. Appeal from discharge must be taken within five (5) days by written notice to the EMPLOYER and a decision reached within ten (10) days from the date of discharge. If no decision is reached between the EMPLOYER and the UNION within ten (10) days, the parties shall immediately proceed to the steps as set out in the grievance procedure for a final disposition of the matter.

improvement can also be helpful, especially if the supervisor is defending himself or herself against a charge of inconsistency made by a disciplined employee.

Another key prediscipline responsibility of the supervisor is the investigation. This should take place before discipline is administered. The supervisor should not discipline and then look for evidence to support the decision. What appears obvious on the surface is sometimes completely discredited by investigation. Accusations against an employee must be supported by facts. Many decisions to discipline employees have been overturned due to an improper or less-than-thorough investigation. Supervisors must guard against taking hasty action when angry or when there has not been a thorough investigation. Before disciplinary action is taken, the employee's motives and reasons for the rule infraction should be investigated and considered. The employee's work record should also be a prediscipline consideration.

Furthermore, if the organization is unionized, the union should be kept informed on matters of discipline. Some organizations give unions advance notice of their intention to discipline an employee. Copies of warnings are often sent to the union.

Administering Formal Discipline

3 LEARNING OBJECTIVES

A supervisor is expected to use progressive, corrective discipline. As has been stated, it is to the supervisor's and the organization's advantage to correct the employee's behavior with a minimum of discipline. Sometimes, however, counseling and oral warnings are not sufficient and the employee must be formally reprimanded. A formal warning is less likely to be reviewed by higher management and less likely to produce resentment than a suspension or a discharge. Still, the supervisor should keep some key points in mind when issuing a formal warning.

The application of formal discipline should emphasize that discipline should be directed against the act rather than the person. Other key features of the formal disciplinary process are immediacy, advance warning, consistency, and impartiality.

Immediacy refers to the length of time between the misconduct and the discipline. For discipline to be most effective, it must be administered as soon as possible, but without making an emotional, irrational decision.

As has been discussed, discipline should be preceded by *advance warning*. The supervisor cannot begin to enforce previously unenforced rules by disciplining an employee as an example. The notation of rules infractions in an employee's record is not sufficient to support disciplinary action. An employee who is not advised of an infraction is not considered to have been given a warning. Noting that the employee was advised of the infraction and having the employee sign a discipline form are both good practices. Failure to warn an employee of the consequences of repeated violations of a rule is an often-cited reason for overturning a disciplinary action.

A key element in discipline is *consistency.* Inconsistency lowers morale, diminishes respect for the supervisor, and leads to grievances. Consistency does not mean that an absence of past infractions, long length of service, a good work record, and other mitigating factors should not be considered when applying discipline. However, an employee should feel that under essentially the same circumstances any other employee would have received the same penalty.

Supervisors should take steps to ensure *impartiality* when applying discipline. The employee should feel that the disciplinary action is a consequence of what he or she has done and is not a matter of personality or of relationship to the supervisor. The supervisor should avoid arguing with the employee and should administer discipline in a straightforward, calm manner. Administering discipline without anger or apology and then resuming a pleasant relationship aid in reducing the negative effects of discipline.

Ordinarily, the supervisor should administer discipline in private. Only in the case of gross insubordination or flagrant and serious rule violations would a public reprimand be desirable. A public reprimand helps the supervisor regain control of the situation. Even in such situations, however, the supervisor's objective should be to regain control, not to embarrass the employee. A good supervisor praises in public and reprimands in private.

Finally, the supervisor should warn the employee of the result of repeated violations. Sometimes suggestions to the employee concerning ways to correct his or her behavior are beneficial.

Supervisors should be very reluctant to impose disciplinary suspensions and discharges. Usually, discipline of this degree is reserved for higher levels of management. However, even though supervisors usually lack the power to administer disciplinary suspensions or discharges, they are nearly always the ones who must recommend such action to higher management. Since discipline of this kind is more likely to be reviewed, more costly to the organization, and more likely to affect overall morale and productivity than other kinds of discipline, it is very important for the supervisor to know when such discipline should be recommended.

The supervisor is expected to use corrective discipline whenever possible. Some offenses, however, may justify discharge. Among these offenses are stealing, striking a supervisor, and manifesting gross insubordination. The supervisor must be able to show, sometimes beyond a reasonable doubt, that the offense was committed. Attention to the points discussed in the prediscipline recommendations is especially important in supporting a decision to discharge an employee.

As with any lesser discipline, but even more essential in suspension and discharge, the employee has the right to a careful and impartial investigation. This involves allowing the employee to state his or her side of the case, to gather evidence supporting that side, and usually to question the accuser. If an employee's alleged offense is very serious, the supervisor may suspend the employee pending a full investigation. This may be necessary if an employee has been accused of a serious crime whose repetition would endanger others.

FIGURE 17.3
Supervisory Checklist for Applying Discipline

1. Be familiar with the law, union contract (if applicable), and past practices of the organization as they affect disciplinary decisions.
2. Maintain adequate records.
3. Investigate rule infractions and mitigating circumstances.
4. Keep the union informed (if applicable).
5. Administer discipline as soon as possible.
6. Precede formal discipline with a warning.
7. Be consistent among employees.
8. Relate the penalty to the offense rather than the person.
9. Administer discipline in private.
10. Warn the employee of the results of a future violation.

The suggestions outlined in the preceding paragraphs should help the supervisor maintain discipline in a positive manner and with minimal application of the harsher forms of discipline. When the supervisor needs to apply the discipline procedure, following these suggestions should reduce the chances of a grievance—or, if a grievance is filed, the chances of having the disciplinary action overruled. Figure 17.3 provides a checklist of rules that should be observed when applying discipline. Figure 17.4 outlines the formal discipline steps.

Minimizing Grievances

 4 LEARNING OBJECTIVES

Employees have not always had the right to complain, especially formally, against the organization. With the advent and growth of labor unions, employees have gained in power, and the grievance procedure is a significant part of that power. A **grievance** is a formal dispute between management and an employee or employees over some condition of employment. The grievance procedure is a formal method for resolving grievances. Through the grievance procedure, complaints are aired, ambiguities in the labor agreement are identified for settlement in future negotiations, and organizational policy is further defined. Many nonunionized organizations also have grievance procedures.

A grievance usually begins with an informal complaint by an employee. Often this complaint will be talked out between the employee and the supervisor before it becomes a formal grievance. The supervisor should not be afraid of complaints. A reasonable number of complaints usually indicates a healthy atmosphere. Proper handling of complaints by the supervisor is extremely important. Once a complaint enters the formal grievance procedure, additional time, people, and cost will be needed to reach a decision.

The grievance procedure varies among organizations. Small organizations tend to have a less formal procedure with fewer steps—usually one or two. Large organizations have a more formal procedure with more steps—typically three or four. The first step usually involves the complaining employee (called the **grievant**), the supervisor, and, if there is a union contract, the union steward. The **union steward** is an operative employee whom the union members select to work with them on handling their grievances. Subsequent steps involve higher levels of management and the union hierarchy. Arbitration is usually the final step in the grievance procedure. **Arbitration** is a process by which both the union and

FIGURE 17.4
Formal Discipline Steps

1. Oral warning
2. Written warning
3. Suspension
4. Discharge

SUPERVISION ILLUSTRATION   17–1

WORKING IN THE RAIN

A dispute arose between Southwestern Electric Power Company and International Brotherhood of Electrical Workers Local 738. Southwestern Electric Power Company is a regulated public utility company serving some 900,000 persons in northwest Louisiana, northeast Texas, and western Arkansas. The company is organized into four geographical operating divisions, three of which are unionized. All the union divisions are covered by the same collective bargaining agreement, which in one form or another has existed for over 50 years. The dispute arose on Sunday, when the crew headed by senior lineman Lenny Ray and supervised by foreman Kincy reported for work at 8:00 A.M. on a prearranged overtime job scheduled at the Merritt Tool Company plant in Kilgore, Texas. It was raining, and the crew objected to working in the rain. Kincy told them that he had been told that when prearranged overtime had been scheduled, it was to be worked, rain or shine. The crew told him they would do the work only under protest and would file a grievance, which they did.

Because the union and company were unable to resolve the grievance at the lower steps of the grievance procedure, it went to arbitration. The following union contract provisions were in effect at the time the grievance was filed:

Pertinent Contract Provisions

Article 14
GENERAL OPERATING RULES
Rule 10
INCLEMENT WEATHER

Only emergency line work shall be done out of doors by line crews when it is raining. For all the other Employees covered by this Agreement work in the rain shall be held to such minimum as is reasonably necessary for the protection and preservation of the property of the Company and for the rendition of safe, economical, and satisfactory services to the public. Employees on hourly rates of pay shall receive straight time on rainy days for such work as they perform, but in the event no work is performed, they shall be allowed one hour's pay for reporting to work at 8:00 A.M. and one hour's pay for reporting to work at 1:00 P.M.

All Employees required to work outside in rainy weather shall be furnished rain coats or rain suits, hats, and rubber boots.

Arbitrator's Award

1. The Company did violate the Agreement when it required linemen to perform work in the rain on Sunday.

2. The Company will compensate all the men involved by paying them four (4) hours pay at time and one-half in addition to pay already received.

Source: Labor Relations Reporter-Labor Arbitration Reports, 94 LA 443–447 (Washington, DC: Bureau of National Affairs).

management agree to abide by the decision of an outside party regarding the grievance. Supervision Illustration 17–1 describes an arbitration case. Figure 17.5 illustrates a typical grievance procedure.

Grievances arise for a wide variety of reasons. The most frequently grieved problems are disciplinary actions, promotions and layoffs, and distribution of work (including overtime). Some grievances are the result of failures to abide by the union contract, the law, or past practices of the organization. Other grievances result from failures of the union contract to address the unsure or the unclear nature of the contract and/or past practice concerning the issue. Regardless of the nature of the complaint, the grievance procedure provides a method for resolving the dispute.

There are many reasons for allowing the supervisor to settle a complaint before it enters the grievance procedure or at the lowest possible step of the grievance procedure. First, this saves time and money. Settling the grievance at the supervisory level saves the time of higher levels of management and the time of the union steward. Second, by achieving settlement before entering the formal grievance procedure or at the first level of the procedure, the supervisor develops the employee's confidence in the organization's ability to

FIGURE 17.5
Typical Grievance Procedure

ARTICLE XI

GRIEVANCE PROCEDURE

Section 1. It is the intent and purpose of this article to provide for the presentation and equitable adjustment of grievances. The parties agree that in the interest of proper disposition of grievances there will be certified by the Union, two (2) grievance committeemen, and stewards who will aid in the disposition of grievances.

Grievances shall be presented within ten (10) workdays after the occurrence is known.

Step 1. The Employee and the designated department steward of the employee's department will discuss the problem with the employee's immediate supervisor, and these parties will attempt to resolve the grievance no later than the end of the shift.

Step 2. If the grievance is not settled in Step 1, the grievance stating the nature of the controversy shall be reduced to writing and submitted within ten (10) workdays to the assistant Plant Manager. He shall meet and give his answer in writing within five (5) workdays thereafter.

Step 3. In order for the grievance to be considered further, the committee shall serve notice of appeal on the Employer within five (5) workdays following the disposition of the grievance in Step 2. Such grievance shall be discussed thereafter between the Union's Business Manager or his representative, the grievance committee, and the plant manager within three (3) workdays after the date of notice of appeals. A written answer to the grievance will be made within three (3) workdays after the date of meeting. Either party may produce at the meeting any persons familiar with the facts involved to aid in a solution of the problem.

Step 4. In the event of any dispute or controversy which cannot be settled by mutual agreement under the foregoing procedure, either party may have the right, within ten (10) workdays following Step 3, to go to arbitration.

Section 2. The failure of the aggrieved party or his representative to present the grievance within the prescribed time limits in Step 1, 2, or 3 shall be considered a waiver of the grievance.

Grievances that arise out of suspension or discharge cases will be introduced into Step 2 within five (5) workdays after the company has notified the Union of the termination. If the grievance is unresolved after being treated in Step 2, it will be deemed to be waived to Step 3 of the grievance procedure. A Step 3 meeting will be convened and a written answer given within five (5) workdays from the date that the grievance is waived to Step 3.

The time limits in this Article may be extended by mutual agreement by both parties.

Section 3. Employees serving as stewards or witnesses in processing grievances under Article XI above shall suffer no loss in pay while attending meetings with the Company.

make decisions and solve problems. Many times, an employee's attitude about the job and the organization is based on his or her relationship with the supervisor. Early settlement also develops the confidence of higher levels of management in the supervisor's ability and confidence between the management and the union in their ability to settle differences and avoid costly arbitration. Early settlement also prevents minor problems from becoming major disturbances that upset morale and disrupt the entire organization.

Stressing pregrievance or early settlement of a complaint at the supervisory level does not mean that the supervisor should settle every complaint. Very unusual cases or decisions that could affect many employees are best referred to higher levels of management or the human resources department. An organization may be just as accountable for its supervisor's decisions as for decisions made by the plant manager, the president, or the owner. Grievances that result in the interpretation of broad general policies and union contract clauses are generally not settled at the supervisory level.

Under no circumstances should the supervisor attempt to obstruct the grievance procedure. Many times that procedure acts as a safety valve, preventing more costly employee actions.

Differing Philosophies of Unions and Management

5 LEARNING OBJECTIVES

In a unionized organization, the supervisor is the primary link between the organization and the union members. The supervisor's first responsibility is to uphold the interests of management. At the same time, the supervisor must fulfill the contractual obligations of management and see that the union fulfills its obligations.

The legal requirements and restraints in unionized organizations are many and complex. Knowing how these requirements and restraints affect organizations is essential to good supervision. Understanding the purpose and structure of labor unions also helps the supervisor manage within a unionized organization.

Unions and management operate on two conflicting philosophies. Generally, the union philosophy is that the management has exploited labor in the past and continues to do so. Unions usually believe that management is more interested in making a profit than in furthering the welfare of its employees. Unions maintain that profits are produced by employees' work and that employees should be well compensated to reflect their input.

Management usually looks unfavorably on unions. It feels that unions are attempting to take over decisions that should be reserved for management. Management often feels that unions foster inefficiency and reduce profits. Management also feels that unions strive to gain power for themselves and to divide the employees' loyalty. Management usually maintains that its interests are identical with the interests of its employees. If employees are to prosper, then the organization must prosper.

Development of Labor Law

6 LEARNING OBJECTIVES

The first U.S. unions began as organizations of skilled workers as early as 1790. These unions sought to eliminate competition by banding together people in the same craft. Their members restricted competition by agreeing among themselves to keep the skills of their craft a secret except to a very few. The early unions were generally held to be illegal.

In 1842, the Supreme Court of Massachusetts ruled that it was not illegal to belong to a union but that strikes and boycotts by unions might be illegal. In the late 19th century and the early 20th century, two federal laws were passed that inhibited the formation of unions. The first of these laws, the **Sherman Antitrust Act of 1890,** made it illegal to restrain trade. This law was originally thought to apply to businesses only. However, the Supreme Court decided that a union applying a national boycott against a company's products was in restraint of trade. Thus, the Sherman Antitrust Act was applied against unions and restricted their growth. The *Clayton Act,* passed in 1914, was at first considered pro-union. It stated that labor unions were *not* to be considered in restraint of trade under the Sherman Antitrust Act. However, court interpretations of this law determined that a union engaged in a strike or boycott activity could be in restraint of trade. In addition, yellow-dog contracts and injunctions were used to restrict unions. A **yellow-dog contract** is an agreement between an employee and management that, as a condition of employment, the employee will not join a labor union. An **injunction** is a court order to prohibit certain actions. For example, management could obtain injunctions to prohibit unions from striking. Supervision Illustration 17–2 describes how union activity sometimes has resulted in violence.

During the 1920s and 1930s, public sentiment became more pro-union. As the Industrial Revolution progressed, employers had less need for skilled craft employees and more need for semiskilled or unskilled employees. Semiskilled and unskilled employees lacked the job security that the skilled employees had. They were much easier to replace and much more dependent on management. Because management was not always fair in

SUPERVISION ILLUSTRATION   17–2

STRIKE AT COLORADO FUEL AND IRON COMPANY (CFI)

The Colorado Fuel and Iron Company (CFI) owned about 300,000 acres of mineral-rich land in southern Colorado. This geographical insulation helped enable CFI to impose rather primitive conditions over its 30,000 workers. Most of the workers lived in company-owned camps located 10 to 30 miles from any big towns. Within the camps, unsanitary conditions led to 151 persons contracting typhoid in 1912 and 1913. Wages were paid in a currency valid only in company stores.

These conditions sparked union-organizing activity. The United Mine Workers (UMW) demanded an eight-hour day, enforcement of safety regulations, removal of armed guards, and abolition of company currency. The company refused to negotiate on these issues.

Thus, in September 1913, up to 10,000 workers at Colorado Fuel and Iron Company went on strike. After the strike began,

tensions rose quickly. CFI hired a large number of guards from outside the state, armed them, and paid their salaries.

Violence erupted almost immediately. First, a company detective and a union organizer were killed. A few days later, CFI troops broke up a strikers' mass meeting and killed three workers. Vengeful miners then killed four company men. Governor Ammons called out the National Guard to protect all property and those people who were still working.

On April 20, 1914, a major battle erupted between the strikers and the National Guardsmen. The fire that resulted led to the deaths of two women and 11 children. Several battles occurred over the next several days until, finally, on April 28, 1914, several regiments of federal troops were called in to end the war.

Source: Adapted from Graham Adams, Jr., *Age of Industrial Violence, 1910–1915* (New York: Columbia University Press, 1966), pp. 146–75. For more information about the United Mine Workers, visit its Web site at: www.umwa.org.

its treatment of these employees, they began to push for legislation to support their rights. The bad economic times that began during the early 1930s also stimulated pro-union laws.

The first of the pro-union laws was the *Norris-La Guardia Act of 1932*. This act made yellow-dog contracts illegal and made it more difficult for employers to obtain injunctions. It also gave all employees the right to organize and bargain with their employers. The act did not, however, make it mandatory for employers to bargain with unions.

In 1935, Congress passed the *National Labor Relations Act (Wagner Act)*. This act was considered to be the workers' Magna Carta. It *required* employers to bargain collectively with the union. It also created the **National Labor Relations Board (NLRB),** which is responsible for supervising union elections and investigating unfair labor practices. The National Labor Relations Act led to increased power and growth of unions.

As America moved from the depressed economy of the 1930s to a boom economy during World War II, unions realized that they could demand very high wages and benefits. Furthermore, there were no laws requiring unions to bargain in good faith with employers. Because of rapid inflation and the sometimes crippling effect of a union's refusal to bargain, the Labor-Management Relations Act **(Taft-Hartley Act)** was passed in 1947. This act upheld the right of employees to unionize, but it also broadened management's rights and prohibited unfair labor practices on the part of both unions and management. The act also prohibited **closed shops.** That is, it prohibited a union from requiring that a person be a member of the union before he or she could be hired by an employer. The act did allow union shops. In an **agency shop,** employees who don't belong to the union must pay the union a fee instead of union dues. In a **union shop,** the union can require an employee who has been working for a specified period of time to become a member. However, the act also allowed individual states to pass laws prohibiting union shops. Twenty-one states now have such laws. These laws are called **right-to-work laws** (RTW). RTW laws ensure that workers are not forced to join unions or pay union dues as a condition of employment. Figure 17.6 lists the states with RTW laws.

FIGURE 17.6
States That Have
Right-to-Work Laws

Alabama	Nevada
Arizona	North Carolina
Arkansas	North Dakota
Florida	South Carolina
Georgia	South Dakota
Idaho	Tennessee
Iowa	Texas
Kansas	Utah
Louisiana	Virginia
Mississippi	Wyoming
Nebraska	

The **Labor-Management Reporting and Disclosure Act (Landrum-Griffin Act)** was passed in 1959. This act is primarily concerned with the protection of the rights of individual union members. For example, it permits union members to sue their unions and it requires that any increase in union dues be approved by a majority of the members (on a secret ballot).

Other legislation concerning unions has primarily affected government employees. In 1962, *Executive Order 10988* was issued. This order recognized the rights of federal government employees to join unions and bargain collectively. However, it prohibited strikes and it prohibited making union membership a condition of employment. *Executive Order 11491,* issued in 1968, gave the U.S. secretary of labor the authority to supervise union elections and investigate unfair labor practices in the public sector. Figure 17.7 summarizes the major laws and executive orders that have affected unions and organizations.

The latest labor legislation which is quite controversial is the *Employee Fair Choice Act (EFCA).* The proposed Act replaces the current process used in voting in union organizing campaigns with a system called "card check." This new system allows a union to organize a company if a majority of employees simply sign a card. The system that is presently used has a federally-supervised secret ballot election when the employees are deciding whether to join a union.

FIGURE 17.7
Laws and Executive
Orders Affecting
Unions and
Organizations

Law	Year Enacted
Sherman Antitrust Act	1890
Clayton Act	1914
Norris-La Guardia Act	1932
National Labor Relations Act (Wagner Act)	1935
Labor-Management Relations Act (Taft-Hartley Act)	1947
Labor-Management Reporting and Disclosure Act (Landrum-Griffin Act)	1959
Executive Order 10988	1962
Executive Order 11491	1968

Structure of Labor Unions

7 LEARNING OBJECTIVES

The four main types of union organizations are (1) federations of local, national, and international unions; (2) national and international unions; (3) city or statewide federations of local unions; and (4) local unions. Figure 17.8 gives some historical dates in the formation of these types of union organizations.

FIGURE 17.8
Historical Dates in the Labor Movement

Year	Event
1792	First local union—Philadelphia Shoemaker's Union
1833	First city federation—New York, Philadelphia, Baltimore
1850	First national union—International Typographical Union
1869	Knights of Labor—first attempt to form a federation of unions
1886	Formation of American Federation of Labor (AFL)
1938	Formation of Congress of Industrial Organizations (CIO)
1955	Merger of the AFL and the CIO

The **AFL–CIO** (American Federation of Labor–Congress of Industrial Organizations) is a federation of local, national, and international unions that represents a majority of all union members in the United States. Its basic policies are set and its executive council is elected at a national convention that is held every two years. Each national and international union sends delegates to the national convention. The number of delegates from each union is determined by the size of its membership. Local unions that are directly affiliated with the AFL–CIO can send only one delegate.

In 2005, several unions decided to drop their affiliation with the AFL–CIO. One of these unions is the teamsters union. It is uncertain at the time of this writing what the impact of those changes will be.

Most national and international unions are organized similarly to the AFL–CIO. They have a periodic national convention at which each local union is represented in proportion to its membership. The convention elects an executive board, which is responsible for conducting the operations of the national or international union.

The city or statewide federations are composed of, and supported by, the local unions. These federations promote the interests of labor in the area they serve.

Most local unions operate under a national or international union. However, an independent local union can join the AFL–CIO without belonging to a national or international union. As a rule, the membership of a local union elects officers who carry on its activities. These officers normally conduct union business in addition to working at their regular jobs. They generally receive no pay from the union for their union activities. Larger local unions hire full-time paid personnel to carry out their activities. In most cases, the local union depends heavily on the staff of its national or international union for assistance in handling contract negotiations, strikes, and important grievances.

Reasons for Joining Unions

It should be recognized that people join unions even when management has been fair in dealing with its employees. Some of the more important reasons for joining unions are purely economic. These are (1) higher wages, (2) greater job security, (3) better fringe benefits, and (4) more clearly defined procedures for advancement (normally, seniority). People also join unions for many other reasons. These reasons include (1) better working conditions; (2) more meaningful work; (3) fairer rules and procedures for determining promotions, discipline, and so on; (4) opportunity to be recognized, respected, and heard on issues; (5) opportunity to complain formally; and (6) the wish to belong to an organization of people with similar needs and desires.

Most members of unions join them for positive reasons. Some employees, however, join unions because they must do so in order to continue their employment. Even in states having right-to-work laws, many employees feel pressured into joining the union. These employees would prefer not to join the union for various reasons; among them are (1) the employee wants to progress into management and therefore identifies more with management than with the union, (2) the employee feels that the union protects the mediocre worker and does not support the merit reward system, (3) the employee wants to avoid loss of income through union dues or strikes, and (4) the employee distrusts the union.

Union Organization Drive

The union organization drive is usually started by the employees of the organization. For one or more of the reasons previously discussed, a group of employees determines that a union is desirable. A representative of a national or international union is then asked by this group to visit the company and solicit members. The union must obtain signed authorization cards from at least 30 percent of the employees before a representation election can be called. Such an authorization card states that the employee desires representation by a specific union. When 30 percent of the employees sign authorization cards, the union may request a representation election through the National Labor Relations Board (NLRB).

The NLRB must first determine what the bargaining unit is (which employees the union will represent) and whether the authorization requirement has been fulfilled. If it has, a secret-ballot election is then conducted. If the union receives a simple majority of the votes cast, it becomes the exclusive bargaining representative of the employees within the bargaining unit. That is, the union represents all of the employees whose work classification places them within the unit that the union covers. The union must represent all of the employees within that unit, whether or not they are union members. It should be noted that the union does *not* have to receive a majority of the votes of all the employees in the bargaining unit. It only has to receive a majority of the votes cast. Figure 17.9 gives a flowchart for a union organizing campaign.

Supervisor's Responsibility to the Employer and the Union

In a unionized organization, the supervisor has a dual responsibility. The supervisor's first responsibility is, of course, to the employer. As a member of management, the supervisor must work toward achieving good productivity. As a member of management, the supervisor must also help uphold the commitments of management under the contract. The union holds the organization responsible for the supervisor's actions or lack of action in dealing with it and its members. The Labor-Management Relations Act, passed in 1947, outlines some unfair labor practices that the supervisor is legally required to avoid. These include (1) restraining employees from forming or joining a union, (2) trying to influence the labor organization, (3) discriminating against union members, and (4) discriminating against an employee for participating in a charge against the employer under the Labor-Management Relations Act.

A union can be either friendly or antagonistic toward management. This friend-or-foe relationship is partially determined by how well the supervisor does his or her job. The supervisor's relationship with the union begins during the union organization drive and continues during the negotiation and administration of the contract. The supervisor must fulfill his or her responsibilities during these phases of the union relationship.

FIGURE 17.9
Organizing Campaign

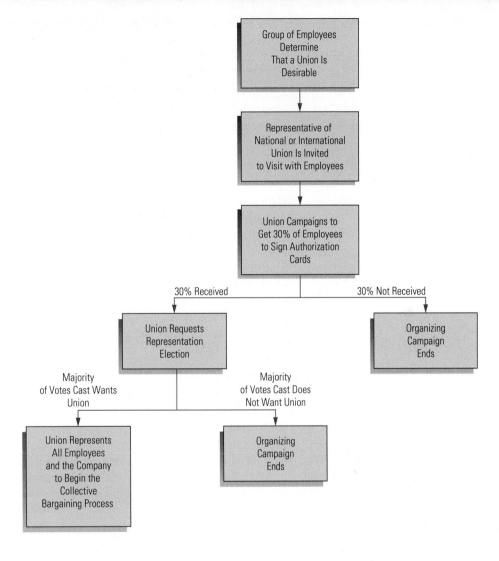

Supervisory Responsibilities and Unions

Most organizations feel that keeping the union out is best. Many organizations pride themselves on treating their employees so well that they do not need or desire union representation. However, if a union begins an organization drive, the supervisor is in an extremely precarious situation. In this situation, the supervisor's actions are restricted by law.

Supervisors are free to give their views, arguments, or opinions about unions. However, they are forbidden to use threats, reprisals, or promises of benefits to get employees to choose or not to choose union representation. Knowing what to say and what not to say can be tricky. There is often a fine line between whether a statement is legal and whether it is illegal. Figure 17.10 gives some examples of legal and illegal statements. It is important to remember that the organization's human resources department is available for assistance in resolving any questions that the supervisor may have in this area.

Jane has learned about the differing philosophies of unions and management and about the development of labor law (p. 328). She has also learned why people do or do not join labor unions (pp. 331–332). She now knows that union organization drives are usually started by the employees of an organization and that during such a drive her responsibilities are to consult with higher management before dealing with officials of the union, to avoid arguing with employees over unionization, not to threaten or bribe employees directly or indirectly with regard to joining the union, not to discriminate against any employee who is involved in the unionization attempt, and not to change wages or fringe benefits during that attempt (p. 334).

In summary, supervisors should observe the following guidelines during a union organization drive: (1) consult higher management before dealing with officials of the union, (2) avoid arguing with employees over unionization, (3) do not threaten or bribe an employee directly or indirectly with regard to joining the union, (4) be very careful not to discriminate against any employee who is involved in the unionization attempt, and (5) do not change wages or fringe benefits during the unionization attempt.

The supervisor should also be on the lookout for unfair labor practices by the union. The union cannot force employees to participate in its activities. Complaints against the union may be filed with the NLRB.

During an organization drive, supervisors frequently feel bewildered or hurt by the employees' attempt to unionize. Many supervisors see this attempt as a reflection on their leadership skills. But—as discussed previously—there are numerous other reasons why employees attempt to unionize.

If a union is successful in becoming the employees' representative, the supervisor must accept the situation. The supervisor must then learn to lead within the restraints set by the union. There is much more flexibility within those restraints if the union and the organization develop a good relationship. The supervisor's relationship with the union is established primarily through the employees and the union steward. A supervisor who deals openly and fairly with employees and the union steward promotes a good relationship with the union.

FIGURE 17.10

Legal and Illegal Statements by a Supervisor in a Union Organizing Campaign

Source: Adapted from F. L. Sullivan, "Union Organizing in the 1980s; A Guide to the Law in Union Organizing," *Supervisory Management*, August 1982, pp. 24–25.

Illegal:	If the union gets in, your hours will be cut.
Legal:	If we were under a contract similar to the one that this union has with our competitor, you would probably have your hours cut and layoffs would probably occur.
Illegal:	If the union is elected, your wages and benefits will be cut.
Legal:	The law requires the company to bargain in good faith with the union; but this means that the benefits you receive after the union gets in may be less than those you have now or that you may get the same benefits, arranged differently. If the benefits are rearranged, the new formula may favor employees other than those in your group.
Illegal:	You will lose your right to deal directly with management if the union gets in.
Legal:	This union negotiates contracts in which it is the sole spokesman for employees on grievance matters.

Summary

The purpose of this chapter is to outline typical discipline and grievance procedures and to present a positive approach to handling discipline and grievances. The chapter also examines the role of unions in organizations.

1. *Explain employment at will and employment arbitration.* Employment at will means that when an employer hires employees to work for an indefinite period of time and the employees do not have a contract limiting the circumstances under which they can be discharged, the employer can terminate the employees at any time. Employment arbitration occurs when a nonunionized employer requires employees to sign an arbitration agreement binding them to mandatory arbitration of disputes out of or relating to their employment.

2. *Define discipline.* Discipline refers to conditions within an organization whereby employees know what is expected of them in terms of the organization's rules, standards, or policies.

3. *Explain the key features of the formal discipline process?* The formal discipline system emphasizes that discipline should be directed against the act rather than the person. Other key features are immediacy, advance warning, consistency, and impartiality.

4. *Define grievance, union steward, and arbitration.* A grievance is a formal dispute between management and an employee or employees over some condition of employment. A union steward is an operative employee whom union members select to work with them on handling their grievances. Arbitration is a process by which both the union and management agree to abide by the decision of an outside party regarding a grievance.

5. *Describe the differing philosophies of unions and management.* The union philosophy is that management has exploited labor in the past and continues to do so. Unions usually believe that management is more interested in making a profit than in furthering the welfare of its employees. Management usually looks unfavorably on unions. It feels that unions are attempting to take over decisions that should be reserved for management.

6. *Discuss significant labor laws.* The Sherman Antitrust Act made it illegal to restrain trade, and the Supreme Court ruled that this act applied to unions. The Clayton Act stated that labor unions were not to be considered in restraint of trade. However, the Court ruled that a union engaged in a strike or boycott activity could be in restraint of trade. The Norris-La Guardia Act made yellow-dog contracts illegal and made it more difficult for employers to obtain injunctions. The National Labor Relations Act (Wagner Act) required employers to bargain collectively with unions and created the National Labor Relations Board (NLRB). The Labor-Management Relations Act (Taft-Hartley Act) upheld the right of employees to unionize, but it also broadened management's rights and prohibited unfair labor practices of both unions and management. The Labor-Management Reporting and Disclosure Act (Landrum-Griffin Act) is primarily concerned with the protection of the rights of individual union members. Executive Order 10988 recognized the rights of federal government employees to join unions and bargain collectively. Executive Order 11491 gave the U.S. secretary of labor the authority to supervise union elections and investigate unfair labor practices in the public sector.

7. *Describe four main types of union organizations.* The four main types of union organizations are (1) federations of local, national, and international unions; (2) national and international unions; (3) city or statewide federations of local unions; and (4) local unions.

Key Terms

AFL-CIO, 331
Agency shop, 329
Arbitration, 325
Closed shops, 329
Discipline, 320
Employment at will, 320
Grievance, 325

Grievant, 325
Injunction, 328
Labor-Management Reporting and Disclosure Act (Landrum-Griffin Act), 330
National Labor Relations Board (NLRB), 329

Right-to-work laws, 329
Sherman Antitrust Act of 1890, 328
Taft-Hartley Act, 329
Union shop, 329
Union steward, 325
Yellow-dog contract, 328

Review Questions

1. Explain employment at will.
2. Define employment arbitration.
3. What is discipline?
4. Give 10 reasons why an employee might be disciplined.
5. What are some actions that should be taken by the supervisor in the prediscipline stage?
6. What are the key features of formal discipline?
7. What is a grievance?
8. What is a union steward? arbitration?
9. What are yellow-dog contracts? What are injunctions?
10. Describe four laws that affect the union movement.
11. What are the four main types of union organizations?
12. Give four reasons for joining a union.

Skill-Building Questions

1. The union and management philosophies outlined in this chapter are in conflict. Which philosophy do you agree with, and why?
2. Can the supervisor single out employees who are less active in the union for preferred job assignments? Why or why not?
3. "Grievance procedures are only used by troublemakers and should be abolished." Discuss your views on this statement.
4. "A supervisor's disciplinary action against an employee should never be overturned." Discuss.

Additional Readings

Benton, Elizabeth, "No Union Committed to Concessions," *McClatchy-Tribune Business News,* February 15, 2009, Wire Feed.

Fuller, Bethany, "Business Owners Worried about Possible Labor Changes," *McClatchy-Tribune Business News,*" February 15, 2009, Wire Feed.

Gagliano, Grace, "Pro-Union Bill Stirs Workers Employers," *McClatchy-Tribune Business News,* March 5, 2009, Wire Feed.

O'Leary, Mary E., "Graduate Students again Try to Organize," *McClatchy-Tribune Business News,* March 5, 2009 Wire Feed.

Seaton, Douglas, and Emily L. Ruhsom, "The Employee Free Choice Act: No Choice for Employer or Employee," *Employee Relations Law Journal,* Spring 2009, pp. 3–16.

SKILL-BUILDING APPLICATIONS

Incident 17–1

Working with Trudy

Jane Eason is new in her job as supervisor of the word processing section at the city government of Monroe. Fifteen people work in Jane's unit, and all of them are members of the American Federation of Government Employees (AFGE).

Trudy Sullivan works for Jane and is also a union steward for the AFGE. In her capacity as union steward, Trudy often has to leave her job as a word processor operator and go to other departments to handle employee complaints and grievances.

Jane has gotten along well with Trudy in the short time she has known her and wants to maintain this relationship. Yesterday, however, an awkward situation came up. Trudy informed Jane that Sue Ellison, another word processor operator in Jane's section, had approached her about filing a grievance against Jane. Jane knew exactly what it was about. Just three days ago, Jane had give Sue a written warning about her tardiness. Sue had felt that the written warning was unfair.

Trudy and Jane discussed the situation. Jane had hoped that Trudy would agree with her and not file the grievance. Much to Jane's surprise, however, Trudy didn't agree with her and informed her that she would be receiving a formal grievance that day. Jane really felt strange about justifying her actions to Trudy. After all, Trudy also worked for her.

Questions

1. Do you feel that this situation is unusual in unionized organizations?
2. If you were Jane, how would you handle the situation?

Incident 17–2

Wildcat Strike

Frank Wozniak, supervisor of the maintenance department of Grayson Manufacturing, was facing a real problem. His employees were discussing walking out of the plant on a wildcat strike. They weren't upset with Frank; they were considering the action out of sympathy for the employees in another department. These employees had walked out about 30 minutes ago and

had sent word back into the plant asking Frank's people to join them.

The walkout had occurred because Albert Hanks, the supervisor of the other department, had fired an employee for supposedly drinking on the job. Frank's people said that the guy had really been fired because Albert disliked him, and that no bottle had been found. They also said that Albert was antiunion and had fired the guy right on the spot. Frank asked his men not to walk out until he could check out the story. They agreed to wait for 30 minutes.

Frank immediately called Linda Peterson, the human resources manager of Grayson. She confirmed Frank's worst fears. According to Linda, everything his employees had told him about Albert was true.

Questions

1. How should Albert handle the situation?
2. What should the company do?

Incident 17–3

You're Fired!

On September 30, 2005, James Arnold was hired as a mechanic by a large national automobile leasing firm in Austin, Texas. James, the only mechanic employed by the firm in Austin, was to do routine preventive maintenance on its cars. When he first began his job, he was scheduled to punch in on the time clock at 7 A.M. On October 30, 2005, James's supervisor, Russ Brown, called him to his office and said, "James, I've noticed that you've been late for work seven times during October. What can I do to help you get here on time?"

James replied, "It would be awfully nice if I could start work at 8 A.M., instead of 7 A.M."

Russ then stated, "James, I'm very pleased with your overall work performance, so it's OK with me if your workday begins at 8 A.M."

During the month of November 2005, James was late eight times. At the end of November, Russ and James had a conversation similar to the one that they had had at the end of October. As a result, James's starting time was changed to 9 A.M. On January 11, 2006, Russ Brown posted the following notice on the bulletin board: *"Any employee late for work more than two times in any pay period is subject to termination."* On January 20, 2006,

Russ called James into his office and gave him a letter that read, "During this pay period, you have been late for work more than two times. If this behavior continues, you are subject to termination." James signed the letter to acknowledge that he had received it.

James was late eight times during February 2006, and between March 1 and March 11 he was late five times. On March 11, 2006, Russ notified him that he had been terminated for his tardiness.

On March 12, 2006, James came to Russ with his union representative and demanded that he get his job back. James charged that another employee in the company, a woman, had been late as many times as or more times than he had been. James also charged that Russ had been punching the time clock for this woman because he had been having an affair with her. The union representative then stated that three other people in the company had agreed to testify to these charges under oath. The union representative then said, "Russ, rules are for everyone. You can't let one person break a rule and penalize someone else for breaking the same rule. Therefore, James should have his job back."

Questions

1. Should James be reinstated in his job?
2. Was an effective disciplinary procedure followed?
3. What would you do about the charges against Russ if you were his boss?

Incident 17–4

Keys to the Drug Cabinet

Marcus Brown, a 22-year-old African American, had been employed for only two and one-half weeks as a licensed practical nurse in the security section of a local hospital's alcohol and drug treatment center. He worked the 11 P.M. to 7 A.M. shift. Taking charge of the keys to the drug cabinet was one of his responsibilities.

One morning, at 1 A.M., he became ill and the night supervisor, Margaret Handley, gave him permission to go home. A short time later, she realized that Marcus had failed to leave the keys to the drug cabinet when he signed out. She immediately tried to reach him by telephoning his home.

More than a dozen attempts to reach Marcus proved futile; all Margaret got was busy signals. Finally, at 3 A.M., a man answered, but he refused to call Marcus to the phone, saying that Marcus was too ill to talk. Margaret became frantic and decided to ask the police to retrieve the keys.

The police arrived at Marcus's home at 6:30 A.M. They found Marcus preparing to leave for the hospital so that he could return the keys. The police took the keys and returned them to the hospital. At 11 P.M., Marcus reported to work on his assigned shift, apologized for having failed to leave the keys, and questioned the necessity of calling the police.

Two days later, however, the unit director, Adam Webb, informed Marcus that he had been terminated. The reason cited for the discharge was that he had failed to turn in the drug cabinet keys before leaving the hospital and that he had them in his possession from 1 A.M. to 7 A.M. the following day. Marcus learned that Margaret Handley had been verbally reprimanded for her handling of the case.

Marcus filed an appeal regarding his dismissal with the human resources director of the hospital. However, the unit director's recommendation was upheld.

Questions

1. What would your decision be if you were asked to decide this case?
2. Should a supervisor and an employee be disciplined equally?

Exercise 17–1

Mock Arbitration

Summarized below is a situation in which you are to conduct a mock arbitration. The class will be divided into teams, five to six students per team. Each team will be assigned to represent either the union or the company. Your team must decide on the witnesses that you want at the hearing. Your opposing team must be given the names and job titles of your witnesses. During class time, two teams will conduct the mock arbitration.

Background

General Telephone Company of the Southeast (Georgia), hereinafter referred to as "the company," provides local telephone service within certain areas of the state of Georgia. Its employees, as defined by Article 1 of the agreement, are represented by the Communications Workers of America, hereinafter referred to as "the union." The parties are operating under an agreement that became effective June 28, 2005.

The grievant, Cassandra Horne, was hired by the company as a service representative. On August 30, 1997, she was promoted to installer-repairer and was responsible for installing and repairing the equipment of residential and single-line business customers. The grievant's record is free of any disciplinary entries, and she is considered by her supervisor, Fred Carter, to be a satisfactory employee.

On May 19, 2004, the grievant suffered an on-the-job injury to her knee while attempting to disconnect a trailer from a company van. At some time after the injury, the grievant went on disability for approximately eight weeks. She then returned to work with a statement from the company physician allowing her to perform her normal work. After approximately three weeks, the grievant was still experiencing pain in her knee and was diagnosed by another physician as having a tear in the cartilage below her kneecap. She went back on disability and had surgery performed on October 19, 2004, to repair damage to the cartilage and ligament of her knee.

During the grievant's absence, her disability benefits expired and she agreed to take a six-month leave of absence beginning November 10, 2004. When the grievant's leave expired, on May 11, 2005, she was terminated from her employment with the company.

The company argued that according to the company physician the grievant could not perform installer-repairer work and that no other jobs were open that the grievant could perform. The union argued that the grievant had been cleared by her personal physician and that she felt she could do the work of installer-repairer. A grievance was filed at Step 1 on June 10, 2005, and was denied by the division human resources manager, Jerry L. Leynes. The grievance was submitted to arbitration, and it is now before the arbitrator for decision and award.

The company states that the issue before the arbitrator is as follows: Did the company violate the contract by terminating the grievant from her position as an installer-repairer, and, if so, what should the remedy be? The union states that the issue before the arbitrator is as follows: Is the discharge of the grievant for just or proper cause; if not, what should the remedy be?

Pertinent Provisions of the Agreement

Article 1, Recognition

The company recognizes the union as the whole and exclusive collective bargaining agency with respect to rates of pay, hours of employment, and other conditions of employment for all employees within the exchanges coming under the operating jurisdiction of the above-named company. All supervisory and professional employees and those performing confidential labor relations duties are excluded from the bargaining unit.

Article 4, Work Jurisdiction

1. The company recognizes the right of its employees to perform its work and will make every reasonable effort to plan its work and forces to accomplish this end.

2. The company agrees that in its employment of contract labor to assist in the carrying out of its programs of construction, installation, removal, maintenance, and/or repair of telephone plant, it will not lay off or part-time, nor continue on layoff or part-time status, any regular employee performing the same work as that which is being performed by contract labor.

Article 11, Absences from Duty

1. Leaves of absence, without pay, not to exceed six (6) months, will be granted by the company for good and compelling reason upon receipt of written request for such leave. Each such request will be approved or disapproved dependent upon the merit of the request. Such leaves may be extended for an additional period of not to exceed three (3) months.

   1.1 Working for another employer during leave shall constitute ground for termination of employment.

   1.2 Applying for unemployment compensation during leave may constitute grounds for termination of employment, except that this shall not be applicable where the employee has requested reinstatement in accordance with the provisions of this article and no work is available.

   1.3 A leave of absence shall not carry a guarantee of reemployment, but the employee concerned, desiring to return from leave, shall be given opportunity for reemployment before any new employees are hired, provided the returning employee is qualified to perform the work.

Article 12, Paid Absences

4. In cases of physical disability resulting from compensable accidental injury while on the job, the company will pay the difference, if any, between the amount paid to the employee workers' compensation and the employee's basic rate in accordance with the schedule set forth below. No waiting period will be required.

4.1 Up to five (5) years' accredited service, full pay not to exceed thirteen (13) weeks.

Article 23, Discharges, Suspensions, and Demotions

1. Requirement and limitations
   1.1 Any discharge, suspension, or demotion shall be only for proper cause and by proper action.
   1.2 Any employee who is discharged, suspended, or demoted shall, at the time of discharge, suspension, or demotion, be given a written statement setting forth the complete reasons for such action.

Exercise 17–2

Discipline in a Nonunionized Business

Assume that you are the office supervisor for a small business with 75 employees. You are not unionized. Lately, however, you have been receiving numerous complaints from employees about actions taken by some of the production supervisors. You feel that some system should be developed to handle these complaints.

Develop a formal procedure for handling complaints for your company. Be prepared to explain your system and answer questions regarding the advantages and the potential problems in implementing your system.

Exercise 17–3

Contract Negotiations

You will be put on a team of three to four students. Each team in the class will be required to negotiate a contract for a company or a union.

The company's wage scale, $5.80 per hour, compares favorably with most firms in its area but is about 8 percent below those firms that employ workers of equivalent skill. Wages have not increased in proportion to cost-of-living increases over the past three years.

At the last bargaining session, the company and union took the following positions:

1. *Hospital and medical plan*
   Past contract: Company paid one-fourth of cost, employee paid remaining three-fourths.
   Union: Demanded company pay full cost.
   Company: Refused to pay more than one-fourth.

Company	1/4	2/4	3/4	4/4	Union
	0	20,000	40,000	60,000	

Proportion of company payment
Increase in total dollar value per year

2. *Wages*
   Past contract: $5.80 per hour
   Union: Demanded an increase of 60 cents per hour.
   Company: Refused outright.

Company	0	10	20	30	40	50	60	Union
	0	31,200	62,400	93,600	124,800	156,000	187,200	

Cents increase per hour
Total dollar value per year

3. *Sliding pay scale to conform to cost of living*
   Past contract: Pay scale is fixed through the term of the contract.
   Union: Demanded pay increases in proportion to increases in the cost of living.
   Company: Rejected outright.

Company	No	Yes	Union
	0	120,000	

Total dollar value per year

4. *Vacation pay*
   Past contract: Two weeks' paid vacation for all workers with one year service.
   Union: Wants three weeks' paid vacation for workers with 10 years of service.
   Company: Rejected.

Company	2 weeks/ 1 year	3 weeks/ 20 years	3 weeks/ 15 years	3 weeks/ 10 years	Union
	0	10,000	20,000	30,000	

Total dollar value per year

Each week on strike (10 minutes of negotiations in the exercise) costs the company $40,000 in lost profits and the workers $40,000 in lost wages.

1. Negotiate the above contract issues with another team (as assigned by your instructor).
2. At the end of negotiations, your instructor will summarize the beginning, ending, and costs for each negotiation.

Source: *Supervision,* May 1991, p. 13. Courtesy of International and Domestic Negotiating Institute.

Exercise 17–4

How Do You Rate as a Business Negotiator?

"It's important for people to know how they feel about negotiating before they get involved in a business negotiation," says Dr. Eugene Mendonsa, director of the International and Domestic Negotiating Institute in Red Bluff, California.

To get a feeling for how you rate as a business nego-tiator, Mendonsa offers this short quiz. He cautions that people should answer the questions honestly to get a true profile. Give the questions a rating of 0, 1, 2, 3, 4, or 5. Zero means the statement is totally incorrect and five means the statement is totally correct.

1. I think luck has a lot to do with whether or not I get a good deal. _____

2. It's easy for me to get angry when disagreements arise in a business negotiation. _____

3. I feel uncomfortable negotiating with people of higher status. _____

4. I normally don't ask probing questions that might cause embarrassment. _____

5. Sometimes I have a problem thinking fast on my feet when the pressure gets intense. _____

6. I don't get too friendly with my opponents during a business negotiation. _____

7. I would feel uncomfortable making an extremely low offer for something that is probably worth much more. _____

8. It is important to me that most of my opponents like and accept me. _____

9. I'd rather deal with a general manager than a company president. _____

10. Helping my opponent to "save face" is not particularly important. _____

11. Where I happen to end up sitting at a business negotiation is not that important to me. _____

12. My business negotiating counterparts are usually honest and fair. _____

13. If I encounter rudeness or hostility, I wouldn't show my counterparts much courtesy. _____

14. I feel uncomfortable getting into a confrontation during a business negotiation. _____

15. I am more frank and open than tactful and discreet. _____

16. I would never negotiate prices in a department store. _____

17. I feel uncomfortable with long silences during a business negotiation. _____

18. I never get emotional or irritated in a business negotiation, not even when I am provoked. _____

19. I normally don't know much about my counterparts until the actual business negotiating starts. _____

20. I don't find it that beneficial to do a lot of advanced preparations for a normal business negotiation. _____

Add up your score:

0 to 15 = Superstar!
16 to 30 = Good business negotiator
31 to 45 = OK, but a lot to learn
46 plus = You shouldn't be negotiating business deals unless you get some proper training.

"Most business negotiations sour because of errors that are made in the process. People either don't know what to do, don't remember what to do, are afraid, or get angry. But with a little work and determination, most people can improve their business negotiation abilities dramatically," concludes Mendonsa.

Source: *Supervision*, May 1991, p. 13. Courtesy of International and Domestic Negotiating Institute.

Controlling Skills

SECTION OUTLINE

CHAPTER EIGHTEEN

Supervisory Control and Quality

Learning objectives

After studying this chapter, you will be able to:

1. Outline the three basic steps in the control process.
2. Identify tools and techniques most frequently used by supervisors to exercise control.
3. Define what quality means to a supervisor, and list several reasons for maintaining quality.
4. Differentiate between product quality control and process quality control.
5. Define the concept of quality assurance.
6. Discuss total quality management (TQM).
7. Define the following terms: continuous improvement, quality at the source, six sigma, and lean manufacturing.
8. Summarize the focus of ISO 9000/ISO 9001 and ISO 14000.
9. Explain the purpose of a zero-defects program.
10. Define a quality circle.
11. Cite several guidelines that supervisors can follow to help build quality job habits among employees.
12. Relate the overriding purpose of the Malcolm Baldrige National Quality Award.

Since taking over as supervisor of the claims section, John Lewis has discovered that things often don't get done as they should. John has missed deadlines. In addition, his department has mishandled claims and made basic processing errors. On top of this, John's department ran out of claim forms last week. Much to John's dismay, it took three days to get some replacements.

John does not expect everything to go perfectly, and he understands why certain things can go wrong. What he doesn't understand is why he rarely finds out about a problem until it is too late to correct it. When John discussed this matter with a supervisor from another department, the supervisor suggested that John's supervisory controls might be inadequate.

The major purpose of supervisory controls is to ensure that things are progressing according to the supervisor's plans. Thus, controls should be designed to alert the supervisor to problems or potential problems before they become critical. Supervisors should use the controlling process to ensure success by detecting deviations early and therefore allowing time to take corrective actions. Controlling is similar to planning in many ways. The major difference between controlling and planning is that controlling usually takes place *after* the fact, whereas planning takes place *before* the fact.

Steps in the Controlling Process

LEARNING OBJECTIVES

Control is accomplished by comparing actual performance with predetermined standards or objectives and then taking action to correct any deviations from the standard. Thus, the control process has three basic requirements: (1) establishing performance standards, (2) monitoring performance and comparing it with standards, and (3) taking necessary corrective action. Establishing performance standards is part of the planning process. Monitoring performance and comparing it with standards and taking necessary corrective action are unique to the control process.

Establishing Performance Standards

When objectives have been set as part of the planning process, they are used as standards. A standard outlines what is expected. Standards are used to set performance levels for machines, tasks, individuals, groups of individuals, or even the organization as a whole. Departmental objectives are types of standards. Usually, standards are expressed in terms of quantity, quality, or time limitations. For example, standards may deal with sales over a given time period, production output per hour, or quality as reflected by customer satisfaction.

Performance standards attempt to answer the question "What is a fair day's work?" or "How good is good enough?" Although designed to reflect normal output, output standards take into account more than just work. Such standards include allowances for rest, delays that occur as part of the job, time for personal needs, time for equipment maintenance, and allowances for physical fatigue. Figure 18.1 lists several types of standards.

Many methods for setting standards are available. Which method is most appropriate depends on the type of standard in question. A common approach is to use the judgment of the supervisor or other recognized experts. A limitation of this approach is that it is very subjective. A variation of this method is for the supervisor and the person or persons performing the job to jointly set the standard. With this method, the individuals actually performing the job provide input. The analysis of historical data, such as production data, is another approach. A potential problem here is that things may have changed since the data were collected. The most objective approach is the employment of industrial engineering methods. These methods usually involve a detailed and scientific analysis of the situation. Motion studies and time

FIGURE 18.1
Major Categories and Examples of Standards

> *Revenue standards*—designed to reflect the level of sales activity.
> Examples: dollar sales, average revenue per customer, per capita sales.
>
> *Cost standards*—designed to reflect the level of costs.
> Examples: dollar cost of operation, cost per unit produced, cost per unit sold.
>
> *Productivity standards*—designed to reflect output per unit of time.
> Examples: number of units produced per work hour, number of units produced over a given time period.
>
> *Material standards*—designed to reflect efficiency of material usage.
> Examples: amount of raw material per unit, average amount of scrap per unit produced.
>
> *Resource usage standards*—designed to reflect how efficiently organizational resources are being used.
> Examples: return on investment, percent of capacity, asset usage.

studies (discussed in the next chapter) are examples of this approach. Whatever method is used, the setting of objectives or standards is an integral part of the planning process.

Monitoring Performance

The overriding purpose of monitoring performance is to provide information on what is actually happening. The major problem in monitoring performance is deciding when, where, and how often to monitor. Monitoring must be done often enough to provide adequate information. If it is overdone, however, it can become expensive and can result in adverse reactions from employees. The key is to view monitoring as a means of providing needed information, not as a means of checking up on employees. Thus, monitoring should be preventive and not punitive. In this light, the reasons for monitoring should always be fully explained to employees.

Timing is also important when monitoring performance. For example, raw materials must be reordered before they run out so as to allow for delivery time.

Most control tools and techniques are primarily concerned with monitoring performance. Reports, audits, budgets, and personal observations are methods commonly used for this purpose. These and other methods of monitoring performance are discussed later in this chapter.

Taking Corrective Action

Only after the actual performance has been determined and compared with the standard can proper corrective action be determined. All too often, however, managers set standards and monitor performance but do not follow up with appropriate actions. If standards are not being met satisfactorily, the supervisor must find the cause of the deviation and correct it. A major problem in this step is determining when standards are not being met satisfactorily. How many mistakes should be allowed? Have the standards been set correctly? Is the poor performance due to the employee or some other factor? The key here is the supervisor's timely intervention. A supervisor should not allow an unacceptable situation to exist for long but should promptly determine the cause and take action.

The type of corrective action depends on the situation. If the performance meets or exceeds the standards, a supervisor might provide positive reinforcement such as commending an employee for a job well done or praising the work group as a whole. When performance is below standards, an approach that works well in most situations is for the supervisor to take increasingly harsh actions. For example, if an employee's productivity is unacceptable, the supervisor might first merely advise the employee of the problem. If the problem continues, the supervisor might take the more direct action of offering to work with the employee to identify difficulties. Once the problem has been clearly identified, the supervisor and the employee should agree on the actions necessary to make the employee's productivity acceptable. Then, if the employee's productivity is still unacceptable, the supervisor may have to take more dramatic action, such as transferring or terminating the employee. In almost all situations, the supervisor should help the employee overcome the deficiency before taking dramatic action. The style, finesse, and method used to take corrective action can greatly affect the results achieved. Supervisors should avoid talking down to employees when taking such action. Supervisors should also fully explain why the action is necessary. All too often, supervisors take corrective action without giving an adequate explanation. It is only natural for employees to resist something that they know very little about.

Preliminary, Concurrent, or Postaction Control

In general, methods for exercising control can be described as either preliminary, concurrent, or postaction. **Preliminary control** methods, sometimes called **steering controls**, attempt to prevent a problem from occurring. Requiring prior approval for purchases of all items over a certain dollar value is an example. **Concurrent controls**, also called **screening controls**, focus on things that happen as inputs are being transformed into outputs. They are designed to detect a problem as it occurs. Personal observation of customers being serviced is an example of a concurrent control. **Postaction control** methods are designed to detect existing problems after they occur but before they reach crisis proportions. Written or periodic reports represent postaction control methods. Most controls are based on postaction methods.

Tools for Supervisory Control

2 LEARNING OBJECTIVES

Many tools and techniques are available to help the supervisor exercise control. Among the tools and techniques most frequently used by supervisors are budgets, written reports, personal observation, electronic monitors, and management by objectives.

Budgets

As defined in Chapter 7, a **budget** is a statement of expected results or requirements expressed in financial or numerical terms. Budgets express plans, objectives, and programs of the organization in numerical terms. While preparation of the budget is primarily a planning function, its administration is a controlling function.

Many different types of budgets are in use (Figure 18.2 outlines some of the most common). Although the dollar is usually the common denominator, budgets may be expressed in other terms. Equipment budgets may be expressed in numbers of machines. Material budgets may be expressed in pounds, pieces, gallons, and so on. Budgets not expressed in dollars can usually be translated into dollars for incorporation into an overall budget. Figure 18.3 presents an example of a simplified expense budget.

FIGURE 18.2
Types and Purposes of Budgets

Type of Budget	Brief Description or Purpose
Revenue and expense budget	Provides details for revenue and expense plans
Cash budget	Forecasts cash receipts and disbursements
Capital expenditure budget	Outlines specific expenditures for plant, equipment, machinery, inventories, and other capital items
Production, material, or time budget	Expresses physical requirements of production, or material, or the time requirements for the budget period
Balance sheet budgets	Forecasts the status of assets, liabilities, and net worth at the end of the budget period

FIGURE 18.3
Simplified Expense Budget

Product Cost	$10,000
Advertising cost	5,000
Shipping cost	5,000
Sales commissions	2,500
Budgeted expenses	$22,500

While budgets are useful for planning and control, they are not without their dangers. Perhaps the greatest danger is inflexibility. Inflexibility is a special threat to organizations operating in an industry characterized by rapid change and high competition. Rigidity in the budget can also lead to a subordination of organizational goals to budgetary goals. The financial manager who won't go $5 over the budget in order to make $500 is a classic example. Another danger is that budgets can hide inefficiencies. Certain expenditures made in the past often become justification for continuing these expenditures when in fact the situation has changed considerably. Budgets can also become inflationary and inaccurate when supervisors pad their budgets because they know they will be cut by their bosses. Since the supervisor is never sure how severe the cut will be, the result is often an inaccurate if not unrealistic budget. The key to the successful use of budgets is to keep things in perspective. The budget should be used as a standard for comparison. However, it should not be inflexible. Cost budgets are described at length in the next chapter.

Zero-Base Budgeting

Zero-base budgeting was designed to stop basing this year's budget on last year's budget. **Zero-base budgeting** requires each supervisor to justify an entire budget request in detail. Every year or budgeting cycle the budget goes back to zero and any expenditures must be re-justified. The burden of proof is on each supervisor to justify why any money should be spent. Under zero-base budgeting, each activity under a supervisor's discretion is identified, evaluated, and ranked by importance. Then each year every activity in the budget is on trial for its life and is matched against all the other claimants for an organization's resources.

Written Reports

Almost all reports are designed to provide information for control. The supervisor may be a preparer or recipient of reports. Supervisors often prepare reports for use by upper management, and employees often prepare reports for use by supervisors. In both cases, the reports are designed to provide information on what is happening.

Written reports can be prepared on a periodic or as-necessary basis. There are two basic types of written reports. **Analytical reports** interpret the facts they present. **Informational reports** only present the facts.

The need for or the use of particular reports should be periodically evaluated. Reports have a way of continuing long past their usefulness. Unnecessary reports can represent a substantial waste of resources.

Personal Observation

Personal observation is sometimes the only way for a supervisor to get an accurate picture of what is really happening. Most supervisors regularly make personal observations. Besides providing information, such observations can communicate the supervisor's interest in the employees. Supervisors seldom seen by employees are often accused of spending too much time in their ivory towers. But supervisors may also be criticized for continually looking over the employees' shoulders. A potential inaccuracy of personal observation is that an employee's behavior may change while he or she is being watched. Another potential inaccuracy lies in the interpretation of the observation. The observer must be careful not to read into the situation

SUPERVISION ILLUSTRATION 18–1

UNILEVER USES TIGHT CONTROLS IN ITS CHINESE PLANT

The ancient Chinese city of Hefei is today a stronghold for manufacturing. Unilever, Coca-Cola, Chinese white-goods and electronics giant Haier Group, Taiwanese food conglomerate Uni-President Enterprises Corporation, and Anhui Jianghuai Automobile Company are just some of the companies that have a major presence in Hefei.

Given the continuing drumbeat of scandalous news of tainted Chinese-produced milk, pet food, cough syrup and toothpaste, manufacturers in the entire city have been under close scrutiny.

Because Unilever's Hefei plant is wholly owned and operated by Unilever, the company is able to keep tight control over almost every phase of the manufacturing process, even in areas that it outsources. The company is extremely serious about hygiene throughout the plant. Just to get inside the plant,

visitors are required to wear protective clothing, a hair net, a hard hat and goggles. Hands must be washed before entering each building. A representative from *Advertising Age,* when touring the plant facilities, was required to wash his hands twice, change clothes, and step into an air-blowing chamber to be sanitized before entering the Lipton tea production area. The plant's water purification system meets Unilever's global standards, which are higher than required by the local government.

In spite of all the tight controls, in October 2008, Unilever recalled four batches of Lipton 3-in-1 milk-tea powder on sale in Hong Kong and Macau. Tests detected melamine, which is an industrial chemical that can make one sick, in only one lot. Even though the level of melamine was at an acceptable level, Unilever chose to recall the affected batches.

Source: Normandy Madden, "Behind the Scenes in a Chinese Factory," *Advertising Age,* October 27, 2008, p. 14.

events that did not actually occur. When observing the work of others, supervisors should concentrate on objective facts such as productivity, not on subjective opinions.

Management by walking around is a type of control based on personal observation. This type of control was popularized by managers at the Hewlett-Packard Company. When this method is used, supervisors are encouraged to walk around and mingle with one another and with the employees. Management by walking around is basically a hands-on approach to control.

Electronic Monitors

Today a number of different types of electronic devices can be used to monitor a work environment. Examples include electronic cash registers that keep a record of what items are sold and when; video cameras that record employee and customer movements; phones that record how long each customer was engaged; Internet programs that track where and how long an employee or customer is at certain Internet sites; and other forms of automated reports.

Management by Objectives

Management by objectives (MBO) was discussed in Chapter 7 as an effective means for setting objectives. The development of an MBO system is part of the planning function. However, once such a system has been developed, it can be used for control purposes. Supervision Illustration 18–1 describes some of the tight controls used by Unilever in one of its Chinese plants.

Supervisory Control in Practice

Supervisors practice control in a number of the areas connected with their jobs. Which specific types of control supervisors practice depends on their areas of responsibility. However, quality assurance and inventory control are two types of control with which almost all supervisors are concerned. Quality assurance includes everything that an organization does to ensure the quality of its products and services, such as the steps taken to prevent quality problems and to monitor the quality of products and services. Inventory control is concerned with monitoring inventory so as to maintain a supply of inventory adequate to meet customer demand but not greater than is necessary for that purpose.

Quality and the Supervisor

3 LEARNING OBJECTIVES

Quality is a relative term. To a space engineer, it represents a million parts that have been carefully made, tested, and assembled so that they will function flawlessly. To the U.S. Department of Agriculture, it means uniformity and an absence of contamination in food. To a fancy restaurant, it may mean lobster flown in daily from Maine. Quality may not mean the same thing to the consumer and the supervisor. The consumer is concerned with service, reliability, performance, and appearance. The supervisor is concerned with the achievement of product or service specifications. The supervisor evaluates quality in relation to the specifications or standards that are set when the product or service is designed.

Why Insist on Quality?

What has caused all the recent concern about quality? Quality has always been important, but never more so than today. Everything from tainted beef and peanut products, from lead-painted toys to poisoned pet food and blood thinners, to exploding laptop batteries has raised the public's awareness for quality. Rising labor and material costs, consumer lawsuits, combined with the need to satisfy more demanding customers, have motivated organizations to become more quality conscious. When labor and materials were less expensive, remaking or scrapping an item wasn't nearly so costly. Also, America's leadership in quality has been eroding for years. In many instances, the quality of foreign products is viewed as better than that of American products. In the service fields, the public now demands higher quality at a lower cost. Historically, many other reasons have existed for maintaining quality. Figure 18.4 lists some of these.

Who Is Responsible for Quality?

In the final analysis, who is responsible for maintaining quality? Who causes quality problems? Most supervisors defend their positions on quality by saying, "If the material we get is good, then we'll send it on good." The obvious implication is that the material they get is often of poor quality. Taking this thought one step further, the supervisor might argue, "How can you expect me to produce quality products or services when I get such bad materials?" Any number of people can be blamed for a supervisor's quality problems. Purchasing, engineering, quality control people, and the human resources department are prime candidates. It is a natural tendency to blame someone else.

The supervisor should be one of the first to know what is going on! In other words, if *all* supervisors provided up-to-standard materials, there would be no quality problems. Every supervisor should first worry about his or her own area of responsibility. If all supervisors

FIGURE 18.4
Reasons for Maintaining Quality

1. Maintain certain standards, such as with interchangeable replacement parts or with service levels.
2. Meet customer specifications.
3. Meet legal requirements.
4. Find defective products that can be reworked.
5. Identify inferior services.
6. Find problems in the production process.
7. Grade products or services (such as lumber, eggs, or restaurants).
8. Provide performance information on individual workers and departments.

assumed responsibility for quality in their respective areas, quality would not be a problem. In the final analysis, accountability for quality is spread across the entire organization.

Types of Quality Control

Organizations usually have some method for monitoring the on-going quality of their products or services. This aspect of quality is referred to as *quality control.* While supervisors are usually not responsible for designing a quality control system, they are frequently responsible for implementing the system. They should therefore have a basic understanding of how quality control works.

Quality control relating to things (products, services, raw materials, etc.) is referred to as **product quality control.** Product quality control is used when quality is being evaluated with respect to a batch of products or services that already exist, such as incoming raw materials or outgoing finished goods. Product quality control lends itself to acceptance sampling procedures. With acceptance sampling, some portion of outgoing items (or incoming materials) is inspected in an attempt to ensure that the items meet specifications with regard to the percentage of defective units that will be tolerated. Under acceptance sampling procedures, the decision to accept or reject an entire batch of items is based on a sample or group of samples. Statistical sampling techniques are often used with product quality control.

Quality control relating to the control of a machine or an operation during the production process is called **process quality control.** Under process quality control, machines and/or processes are periodically checked to ensure that they are operating within certain preestablished tolerances. Adjustments are made as necessary to prevent the machines or processes from getting out of control and producing unacceptable items. Process control is used to prevent the production of defects, whereas product control is used to identify defects after they have been produced.

Today considerable attention is also devoted to controlling the quality of *services* that are offered. Examples include supervisors calling customers to see how they would rate the quality of a service or asking customers to fill out a brief evaluation form regarding a service received.

Quality Assurance

For years the focus of industry was to practice quality control through the inspection process. As discussed in the previous section, the general approach was to produce a product or service and then inspect to ensure that the quality standards were being met. While this approach is still widely used, there has been a shift in philosophy toward placing the operator in charge of his or her own quality—while the product or service is being produced. Thus, *today* the emphasis is on the *prevention* of defects and mistakes rather than on finding and correcting them. The idea of "building in" quality as opposed to "inspecting it in" is known as **quality assurance.** With this approach, quality is viewed as the responsibility of all organization members rather than the exclusive domain of a quality control department. The following quote from Ron Atkinson, chairman of the American Society for Quality, summarizes how the quality trend has unfolded:

"When I started in manufacturing 35 years ago, there was a policeman installed at the end of the line who looked at the parts and said, 'that one is OK, that can be shipped and that one can't.' Gradually, it got to, 'Let's find better ways to do the checking,' and then to, 'Let's find a way to predict what the parts are going to look like when they hit the end of the line,' so we started doing defect prevention. Now where we're at is that quality is expanding to cover everything, including outside of the actual manufacturing process, to 'how do we improve the quality of our HR services and support services? How do we improve the quality of the decisions that are made?'"[1]

Supervision Illustration 18–2 describes one company's attitude toward involving all organization members in the quest for quality.

SUPERVISION ILLUSTRATION 18–2

INVOLVING EVERYONE IN THE QUEST FOR QUALITY

Larry Coburn is vice president of operations at high-tech audio equipment manufacturer Crown Audio. In recent years Larry was experiencing quality problems resulting from the market demands to develop more complex products at a cheaper price. The results were that Crown's first-pass yields through quality inspections had gotten so bad that their rework inventory piled up to the point of becoming a major line item on the balance sheet.

The short-term fix was to stop production, analyze and test the defective inventory, and identify potential process improvement and defect reduction strategies. At the conclusion of this process, Coburn and his team realized that the recommended improvements were only part of the necessary long-term solution. It became evident that "employee engagement" was a necessary part of the long-term solution. Following up on this conclusion, Coburn and his management team looked for and implemented ways to empower their employees and get them invested in the quality of their products.

Today Crown's management team is in the enviable situation of having different production lines and shifts bragging about their first-pass yields to each other. Coburn stresses the point of employee involvement in quality in no uncertain terms. "Morale is everything in quality," he says. "People want to do a good job, and we have to enable that."

Source: Brad Kenney, "Whatever Happened to Quality?," *Industry Week*, April 2008, pp. 42–46.

While there have been many individuals who have championed the prevention approach to quality, W. Edwards Deming is perhaps most responsible. Deming was a statistics professor at New York University in the 1940s who went to Japan after World War II to assist in improving quality and productivity. While he became very much revered in Japan, Deming remained almost unknown to U.S. business leaders until the 1980s when Japan's quality and productivity attracted the attention of the world.

Total Quality Management

6 LEARNING OBJECTIVES

A major question facing today's supervisors is how to build quality into employee performance. How can supervisors get their employees to be concerned about the quality of their everyday work? Most successful attempts to improve quality have focused on the prevention of quality problems through employee involvement. **Total quality management (TQM)** is a management philosophy that emphasizes managing the entire organization so that it excels in all dimensions of products and services that are important to the customer.[2] TQM, in essence, is an organizationwide emphasis on quality as defined by the customer. Under TQM everyone from the CEO on down to the lowest level employee must be involved. TQM can be summarized by the following actions:[3]

1. Find out what customers want. This might involve the use of surveys, focus groups, interviews, or some other technique that integrates the customer's voice in the decision-making process.

2. Design a product or service that will meet (or exceed) what customers want. Make it easy to use and easy to produce.

3. Design a production process that facilitates doing the job right the first time. Determine where mistakes are likely to occur and try to prevent them. When mistakes do occur, find out why so that they are less likely to occur again. Strive to "mistake-proof" the process.

4. Keep track of results and use them to guide improvement in the system. Never stop trying to improve.

5. Extend these concepts to suppliers and to distribution.

Continuous improvement, quality at the source, six sigma, and lean manufacturing are terms that have particular relevance to TQM. **Continuous improvement,** in general, refers to an ongoing effort to make improvements in every part of the organization relative to all of its products and services. With regard to TQM, it means focusing on steady improvement in the quality of the processes by which work is accomplished. The idea here is that the quest for better quality and better service is never ending. **Quality at the source** refers to the philosophy of making each employee responsible for the quality of his or her work. In effect, this approach views every employee as a quality inspector for his or her own work. A major advantage of this approach is that it removes the adversarial relationship that often exists between quality control inspectors and production employees. It also encourages employees to take pride in their work.

Six sigma is both a precise art of statistical tools and a rallying cry for continuous improvement.[4] Six sigma was pioneered by Motorola during the 1980s and literally means, in statistical terms, six standard deviations from the mean. The philosophy of six sigma is that in order to realize the very high level of quality demanded by six sigma (most processes traditionally have used three sigma), the entire production or service system must be examined and improved. **Lean manufacturing** is a systematic approach to identifying and eliminating waste and non-value-added activities.[5] The essence of lean manufacturing is to look at the entire production or service process to eliminate waste or unnecessary activities wherever possible.

All four of the above terms (continuous improvement, quality at the source, six sigma, and lean manufacturing) are approaches for improving quality of the product or service offered. These approaches are not mutually exclusive but rather are complementary; the differences are that each offers a different emphasis. It should be pointed out that each of these approaches, while often associated with manufacturing type environments, can be applied in nonmanufacturing environments such as service, education, and government.

As stated earlier, TQM is an organizationwide emphasis on quality as defined by the customer. It is not a collection of techniques but a philosophy or way of thinking about how people view their jobs and quality throughout the organization.

Some people confuse the concept of reengineering with TQM. **Reengineering,** also called business process engineering, is "the search for and implementation of radical change in business processes to achieve breakthrough results in cost, speed, productivity, and service."[6] Unlike TQM, reengineering is not a program for making marginal improvements in existing procedures. Reengineering is rather a one-time concerted effort, initiated from the top of the organization, to make major improvements in processes used to produce products or services. The essence of reengineering is to start with a clean slate and redesign the organization's processes to better serve its customers.

While TQM has produced positive value for many companies, its success is often dependent on the support and commitment of all levels of management. Naturally supervisors play a critical role in this process. The role of supervisors under TQM is to first understand the concept and then to demonstrate their support of the concept.

While TQM is a highly effective, organizationwide philosophy about quality, there are other techniques and approaches that organizations may adopt to encourage quality. Most of these can be used alone or in conjunction with TQM. Three of these approaches are discussed below.

Other Quality Standards

ISO 9000/ISO 9001

ISO 9000 is a set of quality standards created in 1987 by the International Organization for Standardization (ISO), in Geneva, Switzerland. ISO is currently composed of the national

8 LEARNING OBJECTIVES

standards bodies of 160 countries with the major objective of promoting the development of standardization and facilitating the international exchange of goods and services. The American National Standards Institute (ANSI) is the member body representing the United States in the ISO.

Originally the ISO published five international standards designed to guide internal quality management programs and to facilitate external quality assurance endeavors. The original 1987 standards were slightly revised in 1994. In essence, ISO 9000:1994 outlined the quality system requirements necessary to meet quality requirements in varying situations. ISO 9000:1994 required extensive documentation in order to demonstrate the consistency and reliability of the processes being used. In summary, ISO 9000:1994 certification did not relate to the quality of the actual end product or service, but it guaranteed that the company had fully documented its quality control procedures. While ISO issues the standards, it does not regulate the program internally; regulation is left to national accreditation organizations such as the U.S. Register Accreditation Board (RAB). RAB and other such boards then authorize registrars to issue ISO 9000 certificates.

Revised ISO 9000 standards were implemented beginning fall of 2000. The revised standards emphasized international organization and in-house performance, rather than engineering, as the best way to deliver a product or service. In essence the revised ISO 9000:2000 focused more on continuous improvement and customer satisfaction. ISO 9000:2000, like its predecessor, is really a series of interrelated standards. In ISO 9000:2000 there are three interrelated standards: ISO 9000:2000 deals with fundamentals and vocabulary; ISO 9001:2000 states the requirements for the new system; and ISO 9004:2000 provides guidance for implementation. Because ISO 9001:2000 represents the heart of the new standards, this entire set of standards is often referred to as ISO 9001:2000 as opposed to ISO 9000:2000. As of December 31, 2007, 951,486 organizations in 175 countries had been certified in ISO 9001:2000.[7]

On November 14, 2008, ISO published the fourth edition, ISO 9001:2008, of its quality management systems. ISO 9001:2008 introduced no new requirements compared to the 2000 edition. However, the new edition does provide clarification to the existing requirements of ISO 9001:2000.

Supervision Illustration 18–3 illustrates how one company believes that ISO 9001 has been of great benefit.

ISO 14000

Sparked by the success of ISO 9000, ISO developed a similar series of international standards for environmental management. **ISO 14000** is a series of voluntary international standards covering environmental management tools and systems.[8] While many countries have developed environmental management system standards, these standards are often not compatible. The goal of ISO 14000 is to provide international environmental standards that are compatible. Similar to ISO 9000, which does not prescribe methods to integrate quality processes into an organization, ISO 14000 does not prescribe environmental policies. ISO 14000 does provide an international standard for environmental management systems so that organizations will have a systematic framework for their environmental activities. ISO 14000 focuses heavily on strategic issues such as setting goals and developing policies. ISO 14000 certification requires compliance in four organizational areas:[9] (1) implementation of an environmental management system, (2) assurance that procedures are in place to maintain compliance with laws and regulations, (3) commitment to continual improvement, and (4) commitment to waste minimization and prevention of pollution.

SUPERVISION ILLUSTRATION   18-3

THE BENEFITS OF ISO 9001

Sparrow Adult Outpatient Rehabilitation Services (SAORS), part of the Sparrow Health System in Lansing, Michigan, offers physical, occupational, and speech therapy and industrial rehabilitation services at eight locations. SAORS has 100 employees and treats about 11,000 patients per year, handling approximately 100,000 patient visits. SAORS, which already held state mandated accreditations from the Joint Commission on Accreditation of Health Care Organizations (JCAHO) and the American Osteopathic Association (AOA), achieved certification for ISO 9001:2000 on December 1, 2002.

"JCAHO and AOA tell us how to meet their sets of standards, whereas ISO 9001 creates an environment of creativity and allows us to establish our own set of rules," says Brigette Kieft, quality control and process improvement specialist at SAORS. "ISO 9001 looks deeper into the continual improvement concept . . . ISO 9001 creates an ongoing continual improvement process, which bridges over to other departments and breaks down the silo mentality that afflicts many large organizations, including those in healthcare," explains Kieft.

Because ISO 9001:2000 is relatively new, SAORS has not yet been able to measure the cost savings, but Kieft is confident that Sparrow is saving money as a result of the certification. "Since time is money, I have no doubt ISO 9001 does help with cost saving measures."

Source: Jim Mroz, "Beyond Standards," *Quality Progress,* March 2004, pp. 46–49.

Although the ISO 14000 series will ultimately include 20 separate standards covering everything from environmental auditing to environmental labeling to assessing life cycles of products, ISO 14001 is the first standard released. ISO 14001, Environmental Management Systems—Specifications with Guidance for Use, is the standard companies will use to establish their own environmental management systems. On November 15, 2004, ISO published a revised and improved version of its ISO 14001 standards. The new version is referred to as ISO 14001:2004. As of December 31, 2007, 154,572 companies in 148 countries had been certified for ISO 14001.[10]

9 LEARNING OBJECTIVES

Zero-Defects Approach

The name *zero-defects* is somewhat misleading in that this approach doesn't literally try to cut defects or defective service to zero. This would obviously be very cost ineffective in many situations. A **zero-defects program** attempts to create a positive attitude toward the prevention of low quality. The objective of a zero-defects program is to heighten awareness of quality by making everyone aware of his or her potential impact on quality. Naturally, this should lead to more attention to detail and concern for accuracy.

Most successful zero-defects programs have the following characteristics:

1. Extensive communication regarding the importance of quality—signs, posters, contests, and so on.
2. Organizationwide recognition—publicly granting rewards, certificates, and plaques for high-quality work.
3. Problem identification by employees—employees point out areas where they think quality can be improved.
4. Employee goal setting—employees participate in setting quality goals.[11]

10 LEARNING OBJECTIVES

Quality Circles Approach

This approach, which originated in Japan, has been transplanted to America. A **quality circle** consists of a supervisor and a group of employees who work together under that supervisor.

SUPERVISION ILLUSTRATION 18–4

QUALITY CIRCLES PRODUCE RESULTS FOR QATAR STEEL

Qatar Steel Company, a wholly owned subsidiary of Industries Qatar, was the first integrated steel plant in the Arabian Gulf. The company was established in 1974 with the first steel production coming in 1978. The company employs approximately 1,250 people.

Qatar Steel uses quality circles composed of teams up to 12 people who usually work together and meet regularly on a voluntary basis of identify, investigate and solve work-related problems. The overriding purpose of these meetings is to promote customer satisfaction through on-going quality improvement.

Since there are inherent dangers and employee safety issues associated with the manufacture of steel, a quality circle was asked to identify specific safety problems and then make recommendations for reducing or eliminating each of the identified problems.

The company believes that the actions of the quality circle not only made the plant much safer but that it also resulted in substantial financial savings. Other benefits included: (1) the increased ability of managers and employees to identify future safety issues; (2) improved self confidence among employees; (3) improved technical skills of employees in identifying problems: (4) expansion of the workforce capacity to contribute positively to collaborative decision making and managing their own work processes and (5) a narrowing of the gap between employees and all levels of management.

Source: "Qatar Steel Company Improves Safety for Staff; Quality-Control Circles Also Save Costs," *Human Resource Management International Digest*, 2007, Vol. 15, Issue 6, p. 37.

Membership in a quality circle is almost always voluntary, and the basic purpose is to meet periodically to solve quality problems and identify ways of improving quality. These meetings are normally held once or twice a month and last for one to two hours. Usually, a quality circle begins by receiving specialized training relating to quality. It then proceeds to discuss specific quality problems, which can be brought up by management representatives or by the circle members. Staff experts may be called upon by the circle as needed. As with zero-defects programs, the primary emphasis of quality circles is to get the employees actively involved. Research has shown that a key to quality circle effectiveness is properly training members to function in a quality circle.[12] While quality circles were most popular in the 1980s and 1990s, they are still in use today as evidenced in Supervision Illustration 18–4.

Quality Guidelines

As discussed earlier, the key to the prevention of quality problems is employee involvement. The following 11 guidelines are offered as aids for building quality job habits among employees:

11 LEARNING OBJECTIVES

Guideline 1: Make sure employees have received proper training. Employees can only do quality work if they have been properly trained. Create an environment where employees are not afraid to ask what they don't know.

Guideline 2: Start new employees off right. Make sure the new employee understands that high quality is expected. Set the quality standards high, and make sure they are clearly communicated.

Guideline 3: Keep employee relations on an individual basis. Talk with the employees individually. Tell them what they are doing that is good and what they are doing that is not so good with regard to quality.

Guideline 4: Don't settle for less than desired. Don't accept inferior work or reward an employee for it. Find the cause of inferior work and take the necessary corrective action.

Guideline 5: Communicate the value of top quality. Explain why high quality is necessary. Get down to dollars and cents. Explain the potential costs of inferior quality.

SUPERVISION ILLUSTRATION   18–5

BALDRIGE RECIPIENTS FOR 2008

On November 25, 2008, President Georgia W. Bush and Commerce Secretary Carlos M. Gutierrez announced three organizations as recipients of the 2008 Malcolm Baldrige National Quality Award. The 2008 Baldrige winners were: Cargill Corn Milling North America, Wayzata, Minnesota (manufacturing category); Poudre Valley Health System, Fort Collins, Colorado (health care category); and Iredell-Statesville Schools, Statesville, North Carolina (education category).

Secretary Gutierrez described the recipients: "Each of the recipients we honor today serves as a role model embodying the values of excellence, principled leadership and commitment to employees, customers, partners and community."

The 2008 Baldrige Award recipients were selected from 85 applicants and were evaluated rigorously by an independent board of examiners in seven areas: leadership; strategic planning; customer and market focus; measurement, analysis and knowledge management; workforce focus; process management; and results.

Source: National Institute of Standards and Technology (NIST), news release, November 25, 2008; http://www.nist.gov/public_affairs/releases/2008baldrigerecipients.htm

Guideline 6: Perform thorough inspections. Careful inspections help ensure high quality. This is another way for the supervisor to set the example. A careful inspection should not only find quality problems but also locate their causes.

Guideline 7: Encourage suggestions. Actively solicit suggestions from employees. Implement and give credit for good suggestions.

Guideline 8: Learn from the past. Investigate the areas that have historically caused quality problems. How could these problems have been prevented? What can be done to prevent these problems from recurring?

Guideline 9: Solicit the help of other departments and supervisors. Use individual accountability. Implement systems that make clear the quality responsibilities of each individual employee.

Guideline 10: Assign individual responsibility wherever possible. Use individual accountability. Implement systems that make clear the quality responsibilities of each employee.

Guideline 11: Set the example. If the supervisor strives for high quality in everything that he or she does, so will the employees. On the other hand, if a supervisor performs certain activities sloppily, so will the employees.[13]

The Malcolm Baldrige National Quality Award

12 LEARNING OBJECTIVES

In 1987, the U.S. Congress passed the Malcolm Baldrige National Quality Improvement Act.[14] The purpose of this legislation was to inspire increased efforts by U.S. businesses to improve the quality of their products and services. The **Malcolm Baldrige Award** is named after the late Malcolm Baldrige who was a successful businessman and a former U.S. secretary of commerce. The award is administered by the National Institute of Standards and Technology and can only be awarded to businesses located in the United States. The purpose of this award is to encourage efforts to improve quality and to recognize the quality achievements of U.S. companies. A maximum of two awards are given each year in each of six categories: manufacturing, service, small business (500 or less employees), education, health care, and nonprofits, including government. Education and health care were added in as categories in 1999 and nonprofits were added in 2004.

To apply for the Baldrige award, organizations must submit details showing their achievements and improvements in seven key areas: leadership; strategic planning; customer

From the material presented in this chapter, it appears that John has not given adequate attention to the basic steps in the control function. There is no evidence that he has clearly communicated what standards he expects in each of his problem areas (p. 345). Even if his standards were clear, it is obvious that he does not do an adequate job of monitoring performance (p. 346). John needs to set up systems to alert him and/or his subordinates to problems before they get out of hand. Once problems have been identified, he should take swift and deliberate corrective action (pp. 346–347).

To avoid missed deadlines, mishandling of claims, and basic processing errors, John might set up daily reporting systems to help monitor what is going on. These systems should not be complex or time-consuming; they should simply report the production and quality status of claims. John might also consider implementing some type of quality assurance program as a means of "building in" quality.

and market focus; measurement, analysis, and knowledge management; workforce focus; process management; and results. Applicants receive 300 to 1,000 hours of review and a detailed report on the organization's strengths and opportunities for improvement by an independent board of examiners. "The application and review process for the award is the best, most cost-effective, and comprehensive business health audit you can get," said Arnold Weimerskirch, former Baldrige Award judge and vice president of quality, Honeywell, Inc.

Since the first awards were presented in 1988, the Baldrige National Quality Program has grown in stature and impact. Today, the Baldrige program, the award's criteria for performance excellence, and the Baldrige award recipients are imitated and admired worldwide. The award is viewed as America's highest honor for innovation and performance excellence.

In particular, the Baldrige criteria for performance excellence have played a valuable role in helping U.S. organizations improve. The criteria are designed to help organizations improve their performance by focusing on two goals: delivering ever improving value to customers and improving the organization's overall performance. Several million copies of the criteria have been distributed since 1988, and wide-scale reproduction by organizations and electronic access add to that number significantly. Supervision Illustration 18–5 describes the Baldrige Award recipients for 2008.

Summary

This chapter discusses the controlling function as it affects most supervisors. The chapter begins by defining the controlling function and its components. It then examines specific supervisory control techniques. Quality assurance and inventory control receive special attention.

1. *Outline the three basic steps in the control process.* Control is accomplished by comparing actual performance with predetermined standards or objectives and then taking corrective action to correct any deviations from the standard. Thus, the control process has three basic steps: (1) establishing performance standards, (2) monitoring performance and comparing it with standards, and (3) taking necessary action.

2. *Identify tools and techniques most frequently used by supervisors to exercise control.* Among the tools and techniques most frequently used by supervisors to exercise control are budgets, written reports, personal observation, electronic monitors, and management by objectives.

3. *Define what quality means to a supervisor, and list several reasons for maintaining quality.* Quality is a relative term that means different things to different people. A supervisor's primary concern with quality is that the product or service specifications be achieved to (1) maintain certain standards, (2) meet customer specifications, (3) meet legal requirements, (4) locate defective products, (5) identify inferior services, (6) find problems in

the production process, (7) grade products or services, and (8) provide performance information on employees and/or departments.

4. *Differentiate between product quality control and process quality control.* Quality control relating to things (products, services, raw materials, etc.) is referred to as product quality control. Quality control relating to the control of a machine or an operation during the production process is called process quality control.

5. *Define the concept of quality assurance.* Quality assurance refers to the idea of "building in" quality as opposed to "inspecting it in."

6. *Discuss total quality management.* Total quality management (TQM) is a management philosophy that emphasizes "managing the entire organization so that it excels in all dimensions of products and services that are important to the customer." TQM, in essence, is an organization-wide emphasis on quality as defined by the customer.

7. *Define the following terms: continuous improvement, quality at the source, six sigma, and lean manufacturing.* Continuous improvement refers to an ongoing effort to make improvements in every part of the organization relative to all of its products and services. Quality at the source refers to the philosophy of making each employee responsible for the quality of his or her work. Six sigma is both a precise set of statistical tools and a rallying cry for continuous improvement. Lean manufacturing is a systematic approach to identifying and eliminating waste and non-value-added activities. These approaches to improving quality are not mutually exclusive but rather are complementary; the differences are that each offers a different emphasis.

8. *Summarize the focus of ISO 9000/ISO 9001 and ISO 14000.* ISO 9000 is a set of quality standards established in 1987 by the International Organization for Standardization (ISO). ISO 9000 focuses on the design and operations processes and not on the end product or service. ISO 9000 requires extensive documentation in order to demonstrate the consistency and reliability of the processes being used. The fourth edition (ISO 9001:2008) was published in November of 2008. ISO 14000 is a series of voluntary international standards covering environmental management tools and systems. The goal of ISO 14000 is to provide international environmental standards that are compatible. ISO 14000 does not prescribe environmental policies; it does provide an international standard for environmental management systems so that organizations will have a systematic framework for their environmental activities.

9. *Explain the purpose of a zero-defects program.* A zero-defects program attempts to create a positive attitude toward the prevention of low quality.

10. *Define a quality circle.* A quality circle consists of a supervisor and a group of employees who work together under that supervisor. Its primary purpose is to meet periodically to solve quality problems and identify ways of improving quality.

11. *Cite several guidelines that supervisors can follow to help build quality job habits among employees.* The following guidelines can be used by supervisors to build quality job habits: Start new employees off right, keep employee relations on an individual basis, don't settle for less than desired, communicate the value of top quality, perform thorough inspections, encourage suggestions, learn from the past, solicit the help of other departments and supervisors, assign individual responsibility wherever possible, and set the example.

12. *Relate the overriding purpose of the Malcolm Baldrige National Quality Award.* The overriding purpose of the Malcolm Baldrige National Quality Award is to encourage efforts to improve quality and to recognize the quality achievements of U.S. companies.

Key Terms

Review Questions

1. What is the major purpose of all supervisory controls?

2. Differentiate among preliminary, concurrent, and postaction controls.

3. Name and briefly discuss at least three tools used in supervisory control.

4. What determines the desired level of quality for the supervisor?

5. Define the following terms and explain what they have in common: continuous improvement, quality at the source, six sigma, and lean manufacturing.

6. What is quality assurance?

7. What is the basic philosophy underlying total quality management (TQM)?

8. Differentiate between ISO 9000/ISO 9001 and ISO 14000.

9. Describe the zero-defects and quality circles approaches to quality.

10. What is the difference between product quality control and process quality control?

11. What is the Malcolm Baldrige National Quality Award?

Skill-Building Questions

1. Why do you think that many supervisors are reluctant to take corrective actions when people are involved?

2. Since quality is a relative concept, how does a supervisor ever know if the quality level is optimum?

3. What do you think are the advantages of "building in" quality as opposed to "inspecting in" quality?

4. Many people believe that ISO 14000 will have a larger impact on organizations than ISO 9000. Why do you think that might be true?

5. It has often been said that supervisory planning and supervisory control go hand in hand. Elaborate on this statement.

References

1. Brad Kenney, "Whatever Happened to Quality?" *Industry Week,* April 2008, pp. 42–46.

2. Richard B. Chase, Nicholas J. Aquilano, and F. Robert Jacobs, *Production and Operations Management: A Life Cycle Approach,* 9th ed. (Homewood, IL: Richard D. Irwin, 2001), p. 260.

3. William J. Stephenson, *Production/Operations Management,* 5th ed. (Homewood, IL: Richard D. Irwin, 1996), p. 102.

4. Erik Einset and Julie Marzano, "Six Sigma Demystified," *Tooling and Production,* April 2002, p. 43.

5. Esther Durkalski, "Lean Times Call for Lean Concepts," *Official Board Markets,* October 26, 2002, p. 38.

6. Thomas B. Clark, "Business Process Reengineering," Working Paper, Georgia State University, November 1997, p. 1.

7. http://www.iso.org/iso/pressrelease.htm?refid= Ref1178, accessed on April 8, 2009.

8. Much of this section is drawn from Suzan L. Jackson, "ISO 14000: What You Need to Know," *Occupational Hazards,* October 1997, pp. 127–32; and Cecily A. Raiborn, Brenda E. Joyner, and James W. Logan, "ISO 14000 and the Bottom Line," *Quality Progress,* November 1999, pp. 89–93.

9. Katherine M. Pratt, "Environmental Standards Could Govern Trade," *Transportation and Distribution,* February 1997, p. 68.

10. http://www.iso.org/iso/pressrelease.htm? refid=Ref1178, accessed on April 8, 2009.

11. Richard B. Chase and Nicholas J. Aquilano, *Production and Operations Management,* 3rd ed. (Homewood, IL: Richard D. Irwin, 1981), pp. 654–55.

12. Alan Honeycutt, "The Key to Effective Quality Circles," *Training and Development Journal,* May 1989, pp. 81–84.

13. These guidelines are adapted from Robert M. Sardell, "Building Quality into Employee Performance," *Supervision,* October 1979, pp. 13–14.

14. Much of this section is drawn from "Malcolm Baldrige National Quality Award," http://www.nist.gov/public_affairs/factsheet/mbnqa.htm, accessed on April 9, 2009.

Additional Readings

Cooney, Richard, and Amrik Sohal, "Teamwork and Total Quality Management: A Durable Partnership," *Total Quality Management and Business Excellence,* October 2004, p. 1131.

Kenney, Brad, "Whatever Happened to Quality?" *Industry Week,* April 2008, pp. 42–46.

McManus, Kevin, "So Long Six Sigma?" *Industrial Engineer,* October 2008, p. 19.

Pope, Byron, "Toyota Says Quality Circles Still Paying Dividends," *Ward's Auto World,* June 2008, p. 20.

Weiss, W. H., "High-Quality Employee Output," *Supervision,* June 2004, pp. 13–15.

SKILL-BUILDING APPLICATIONS

Incident 18–1

The Assuming Supervisor

Nancy Keene is a supervisor of the children's clothing department for the Model Dress Company. Model Dress sells women's and children's casual fashions in the low-to-middle price ranges. Because of control problems related to many facets of the business, management decided to implement a management-by-objectives (MBO) system about 10 months ago. Shortly thereafter, Nancy, along with the company's 14 other supervisors, attended a company-sponsored seminar on MBO. After the seminar, Nancy's boss, Joan Chung, outlined what she thought should be Nancy's annual objectives in terms of sales, returns, and personnel turnover. Joan further suggested how these objectives might be passed down to Nancy's subordinates. All of Joan's suggestions seemed perfectly reasonable to Nancy, and she accepted them to the letter. A few days later, Nancy distributed a memo announcing just what the departmental objectives were and how they affected each member of her department. Much to her surprise, several of her subordinates reacted quite negatively and accused her of being "too bossy." After several meetings, Nancy was able to calm down these subordinates and assure them that she was not attempting to force anything on them. Things seemed to move along on an even keel for the next several months.

Then Joan called Nancy into her office, where the following dialogue took place:

Joan: Nancy, we're nine months into our MBO year, and you're running way behind on our agreed-upon objectives.

Nancy: What do you mean?

Joan: According to my records, your department's sales have averaged well below your goal, your returns have been running well over your goal, and your department has already exceeded your turnover goal for the entire year.

Nancy: I had no idea! Are you sure your records are correct? Since I hadn't heard anything from you, I just assumed everything was on target.

Joan: Haven't you been comparing your weekly figures with your goals?

Nancy: No, not really. Like I said, I just assumed everything was OK. And I've been extremely busy, as you know.

Questions

1. Who is most at fault for having allowed this situation to develop, Joan or Nancy? Why?
2. What do you think about Nancy's understanding of MBO?
3. What changes would you suggest to both Joan and Nancy?

Incident 18–2

High-Quality Toys

The Cutee Toy Company of Crossroads City makes all types of metal toys. Cutee has built a good reputation on the quality of its toys, which hold up much better than comparable toys made of plastic. Also, many parents are attracted to metal toys because they grew up with such toys. At the same time, because of the dangers inherent in metal toys, Cutee has to maintain very tight quality standards. Great care must be taken to ensure that no toys are shipped with sharp edges, protruding tabs, or any other hazards. The high price charged by Cutee also requires that the quality standards be kept high.

The basic production process is the same for all of Cutee's products. The parts for a particular toy are stamped out of sheet metal. The parts for the toy are then assembled by fitting small metal tabs on one piece through small slots on the matching piece and bending the tabs over (see Exhibit 18.1). To avoid scratches during the assembly process, the toy is painted after it has been assembled. A silk-screening process is often used to add details after the basic painting process. All finished toys are carefully wrapped in kraft paper and put into boxes to be shipped or stored in inventory.

Questions

1. Assume you are the supervisor of the painting department. What do you think your responsibilities should be regarding the quality of the final product?

EXHIBIT 18.1
Assembly of a Toy Christmas Tree

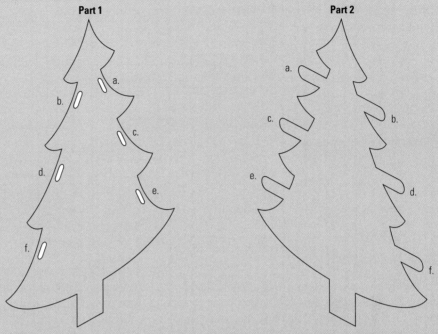

Part 1

Part 2

To assemble, put Tab a. on Part 2 into Slot a. on Part 1 and bend it over; put Tab b. on Part 2 into Slot b. on Part 1 and bend it over, etc.

2. If you were a supervisor charged with inspecting the final products, what general type of inspection system would you set up? Support your answer with justifications.

3. If you were supervisor of the production department, what concerns might you have relating to raw material inventory?

Exercise 18–1

Controlling Production

The Gantt chart was introduced in Chapter 6 as a tool to help supervisors plan. Gantt charts are also frequently used for control purposes. The Cutee Toy Company, described in Incident 18–2, uses the Gantt chart in Exhibit 18.2 to plan and control the production of toy Christmas trees.

1. Assuming that the vertical arrows indicate actual progress made to date, how would you describe Cutee Toy Company's present production situation? Is it ahead of or behind schedule?

2. Assuming that the following events take place, what actions would you take?

   a. The purchasing agent of the Top Mill Company calls and tells you that her order is not wanted until day 25.

   b. No work is done on the Carter Company order during the next two days.

   c. An order change from Keller, Inc., doubles its original order (thus requiring that each operation take twice the scheduled time).

3. If you were the production manager for the Cutee Toy Company, what additional information would you like for control purposes? Make specific recommendations for getting this information.

Exercise 18–2

Assessing Quality

Visit a local fast-food establishment and observe the service from the quality viewpoint. Make notes of the following specific things:

1. Were the facility and parking lot clean?

2. Were you greeted pleasantly and cheerfully by the person taking your order?

3. How long did you wait from the time you entered the facility until you received your order?

4. Was your order correct?

5. How would you rate the taste of the food?

6. Was the rest room clean?

EXHIBIT 18.2
Gantt Chart

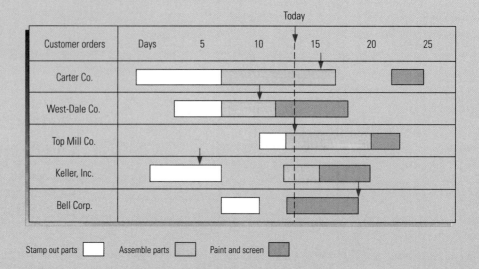

Customer orders	Days	5	10		15	20	25

Today

Carter Co.

West-Dale Co.

Top Mill Co.

Keller, Inc.

Bell Corp.

Stamp out parts ☐   Assemble parts ☐   Paint and screen ■

After you have completed your visit and analyzed your notes, what suggestions do you have for improving quality? Can you think of anything that management might do to increase its employees' concern for quality?

Exercise 18–3

How Important Is Quality?

Think of the last product or service that you purchased that cost at least $500. What role did quality play in making your decision to purchase the item or service? Now that you have used the product or service, are you satisfied with its quality? If you could go through the selection process again, would you make the same choice? What, if anything, would you do differently?

CHAPTER NINETEEN

Improving Productivity

Learning objectives

After studying this chapter, you will be able to:

1. Explain the three major components of organizational productivity.
2. Discuss the benefits of work-methods improvement.
3. Distinguish between motion study and time study.
4. Present a systematic approach for improving work methods.
5. Describe the Kaizen philosophy for improvement.
6. Describe the supervisor's role in improving productivity through cost reduction and control.
7. Summarize several cost-reduction strategies that can be helpful to supervisors.
8. Identify several areas of concern to supervisors that tend to be especially susceptible to cost overruns.
9. Discuss the major types of inventories and explain the purposes for carrying inventories.
10. Explain the just-in-time approach to inventory control.

Supervision Dilemma

Jane Harris returned from the accounting department. She was really impressed with the efficiency of those people! Everything always seemed to be in such perfect order over there. Nothing ever seemed to be out of place. The employees seemed to follow precise methods. Jane was sure that the accounting department had to be the most efficient in the company. All of this made her wonder why her department couldn't be just as efficient. After all, what had impressed her was not the efficiency of the equipment but the efficiency of the people. Jane had heard a lot of talk about productivity, work-methods improvement, cost control, and inventory control. Jane didn't really know a lot about any of these topics, though ever since she had taken over as supervisor of the claims section, she had felt that improvements could be made in the way things were done. Since her costs have steadily risen from day one, maybe now was the time to learn about these ideas.

Productivity may be defined as units of output per employee hour. Historically, the United States has enjoyed very high productivity relative to other countries. However, in the past several decades, this nation's previously unchallenged lead in productivity has been diminishing when compared to many other nations. Because increasing productivity is a key to competing at the local, national, and international levels, both management and labor leaders publicly urge high productivity in the workforce. Unfortunately, many employees interpret this urging only as a plea to work harder.

As shown in Figure 19.1, productivity is the result of three separate major components—efficiency of technology, efficiency of labor, and the effectiveness of management. **Technology** as defined here includes new and improved methods, new ideas, inventions, and innovations, as well as new and improved materials. Efficiency of labor is a function of the labor available and the motivation to work. Given high efficiencies of technology and labor, these inputs must be effectively combined by *management* if high productivity is to result. Thus, productivity is not simply a matter of making employees work longer and harder. The desire to work, which is often referred to as the work ethic, must not be absent; however, it represents only one of several requirements for high productivity.

It has been said that the real meaning of productivity is "to produce more with the same amount of human effort."[1] This statement is based on the fact that, over the long run, far greater gains in productivity have come from efficiency of technology and effective management than from efficiency of labor. For example, by the early 1970s the average factory employee in the United States produced more than six times as much in an hour as that employee's grandfather produced around 1900, and with less effort in most cases.[2] Today the figure is probably more than 10 times as much as in 1900.

Supervisors, as the first level of management, can have a significant impact on all three major components of productivity. Chapter 2 discussed ways that supervisors might encourage innovative and creative ideas. Chapter 4 discussed what supervisors can do to

FIGURE 19.1 Determinants of Productivity

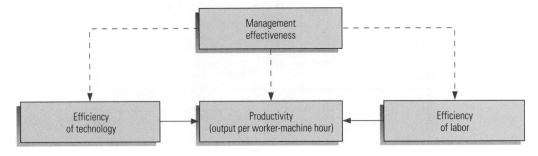

motivate their employees. This chapter focuses on what supervisors can do in the areas of work-methods improvement, cost control, and inventory control.

Methods Improvement and the Supervisor

The best method for performing a task is a combination of how the human body is used, the arrangement of the workplace, and the design of the tools and equipment. **Work-methods improvement** is used to find the most efficient way to accomplish a given task. **Methods engineering** and **work simplification** are other terms referring to the same process. An old saying, "Work smarter, not harder," sums up the objective of work-methods improvement.

A methods improvement program should be concerned with finding the best ways of performing a task or a group of tasks. Although this involves eliminating *unnecessary* work, it need not mean that the scope of the task or job should be restructured. The objective is not to make the task or job as simple as possible, but to increase efficiency by eliminating unnecessary work and by optimally structuring necessary work.

Benefits of Methods Improvement

2 LEARNING OBJECTIVES

The benefits of methods improvement can be significant. Among the potential benefits are reduced costs, higher productivity, reduced delays, higher quality, reduced waste, improved safety, and satisfied employees. The magnitude of the benefits can be quite large even for very simple tasks. For example, management pioneer Frederick W. Taylor increased the productivity of a man manually unloading pig iron from a railcar by almost 300 percent (from 12 tons per day to almost 48 tons per day). Taylor achieved equally impressive improvements in the simple task of shoveling coal. By closely studying the methods involved and designing a special shovel to fit the shoveler's physical characteristics, Taylor significantly increased the shoveler's productivity.

The benefits of methods improvement today are not limited to industrial or manufacturing organizations. Service organizations can apply the principles of methods improvement as effectively as industrial organizations can. For example, methods improvements can be made in the processing of customers through a cafeteria or of patients through a doctor's office. Efficiency of operations that results from work-methods improvement is one of the factors most responsible for McDonald's success as the world's largest fast-food chain (see Supervision Illustration 19–1). Methods improvement can glean substantial benefits for almost any organization.

Supervisors, other managers, employees, consumers, owners, and society in general all benefit from methods improvement (see Figure 19.2). Methods improvement can make jobs more satisfying to employees, especially if the employees have participated in working out the changes. It can also increase employee safety. The increased productivity and lower costs resulting from methods improvement reflect positively on the various levels of management. Consumers and society in general benefit from the cost savings achieved by methods improvement, which may be passed on in the form of lower prices or more goods and services. Owners and investors benefit from the increased profits resulting from methods improvement.

Systematic Methods Improvement

Regrettably, many supervisors look on methods improvement as something that occurs naturally. They base this belief on the assumption that any tasks warranting methods improvement are generally obvious. However, this is often not the case. With methods improvement,

SUPERVISION ILLUSTRATION 19–1

METHODS PLANNING AT MCDONALD'S

The main function of each McDonald's store is the fastest delivery of a consistent high-quality product in a clean facility. One of the keys to McDonald's phenomenal success is the detailed facility layout and the well-planned methods that have been used since the start of the company. All products are prepackaged and premeasured to ensure uniformity. Food is cooked on equipment designed to make an optimum amount without waste. McDonald's even uses a special wide-mouthed scoop to fill a bag with exactly the right amount of french fries. The scoop prevents costly overfilling but creates an impression of abundance (a few fries always end up in the bottom of your bag). The facilities and methods are planned in such detail that employee discretion is virtually eliminated and everything is positioned for a reason. For example, the french fries are situated not only to be accessible to the employees but also to catch the attention of customers and, it is hoped, entice them to order some. The size of the fryer used to cook the french fries is neither too large to cook too many at once (which would allow them to become soggy) nor so small as to require frequent and costly frying. Every other item and area in a McDonald's is equally well thought out.

Source: Theodore Levitt, "Production-Line Approach to Service," *Harvard Business Review,* September–October 1972, p. 41. For more information about McDonald's, visit its web site at: *www.mcdonalds.com.*

3 LEARNING OBJECTIVES

as with almost any other endeavor, a systematic approach produces the best results. The next two sections cover motion study and time study, which are often used as part of an overall methods improvement program.

Motion Study

Motion or **methods study** is concerned with determining how a task is being performed and if it can be performed in a more efficient manner. Thus, the first step in motion study is to identify precisely the steps of the task as it is currently being done. Once these steps have been identified, they need to be evaluated. The necessity of each step should be questioned. Why is it necessary? What would be the cost of eliminating it? Each of the questions in Figure 19.3 should be addressed for each job step. Remember, the overriding purpose here is to identify inefficient work and wasted motions.

As a result of the questioning in each job step, many possibilities for improving the work methods may have surfaced. Each of these possibilities must be examined to determine which possibilities should be pursued. Improvements generally emerge from the questions asked in Figure 19.3. Others become apparent when the completed flowchart is studied.

FIGURE 19.2
Benefits of Methods Improvements Shared by the Supervisor, Management, Employees, Consumers, Society, and Owners

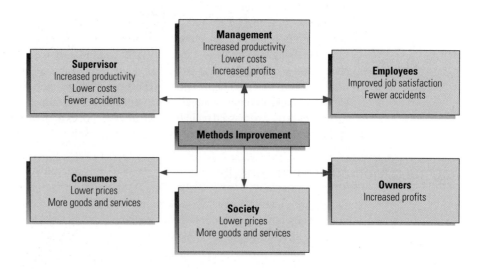

FIGURE 19.3
Questions to Be Addressed at Each Step of the Procedure Being Flowcharted

Overall Question

WHY is this step necessary? Can it be eliminated?

Specific Questions

WHAT is being done? Have all of the steps been included? Does this step serve a purpose? Does this step contribute to the end result?

WHERE is the step being done? Should it be done at some other place?

WHEN should this step be done? Is the best sequence being used? Should this step be moved ahead or back?

WHO should do this step? Who can do it most easily? Is the right person doing it?

HOW is this step being done? Is there an easier way? Can it be done better with other equipment? Can it be simplified?

Recall that the best method for performing a task is a function of (1) the use of the human body, (2) the arrangement of the workplace, and (3) the design of the tools and equipment. It is often possible to make improvements in one or more of these components and in the manner in which they are put together. Improvements can usually be made by eliminating, combining, rearranging, and simplifying the stages of the task. Logically, only some of the improvements that emerge can be used; the objective is to determine which of the suggested improvements are the best. At this point, it is wise to seek the ideas and opinions of the employees currently performing the task, and to keep them apprised of what is happening. This later facilitates implementing the changes selected.

Time Study

Time study is the analysis of a task to determine the elements of work required to perform it, the order in which these elements occur, and the times required to perform them effectively. The objective of a time study is to determine how long it should take an average person to perform the task in question. Time study is not the same as motion study. As discussed in the previous section, motion study is concerned with determining the most efficient way of doing a task or job. Time study is concerned with *how long* it should take to do the task or job under ordinary conditions. The time necessary to perform a task or a group of tasks is called the **standard time.** A time study makes allowances for employee fatigue and rest breaks when establishing a standard. Therefore, a standard time represents the average time, including allowances for rest and fatigue, required to produce one unit of output. The primary use of time study is to provide standards to which employee performance can be compared. Most employee incentive programs use standard times for determining expected output. For example, the time-study method might be used to determine how many units a machine operator should be able to produce in an hour or how many clients a customer service representative should be able to service in a day.

Although the exact method may vary with the practitioner, time study without a preceding motion study involves six basic steps:

1. Breaking the task down into its elemental steps, each of which is then timed. (For example, what motions does a computer operator go through?)
2. Determining which elements are essential for completion of the task. (Which motions are essential and which motions, if any, can be eliminated?)
3. Determining the operating time actually required for each essential element. (How much time does it take to do each of the essential motions? A stopwatch may be used to determine the time requirements of the various motions.)

4. Determining the operation time for the total task by adding the operating times of all the essential elements. (Add up the times arrived at in step 3.)

5. Determining the extra time allowances necessary for rest and fatigue. (Naturally, this depends on the operating time arrived at in step 4.)

6. Determining the standard time for the task by adding the required operating time and the extra time allowances. (Add the results of steps 4 and 5.)

If a methods study has already been completed, a time study would involve only steps 3 through 6 because the methods study would already have determined the essential elements required to do the task.

It should be noted that all work standards should be periodically monitored and evaluated. Changes in technology, equipment, materials, and methods can all require that standards be reevaluated.

The PDCA Cycle

4 LEARNING OBJECTIVES

The PDCA Cycle, also referred to as the Shewhart Cycle or the Deming Circle, is an approach to methods improvement that has enjoyed considerable success. PDCA stands for the four stages that the cycle comprises: *plan, do, check,* and *act.* Each of these stages is discussed below.

Stage 1: Plan—Where and How to Make Improvements

The first step is to plan where and how to make improvements. As discussed previously, most work methods can be improved. Still, it makes good sense to direct your methods improvement efforts to those areas that have the highest likelihood of producing the greatest results. Determining those areas is not always easy. First, talk to other supervisors and to your employees. Find out where they think that improvements can be made. There are certain other indicators that supervisors should look for and recognize. The key is to consciously look for them. Usually fruitful areas for methods improvement are tasks involving a lot of people, where waste or scrap is high, materials are expensive, and labor costs are high. Tasks with repetitive operations also usually have a potential for substantial methods improvement. Other indicators of such a potential include production or customer bottlenecks, extensive overtime, excessive delays, and employee boredom.

Ergonomics **Ergonomics** is the study of the interface between people and the equipment and machines with which they work. A primary concern of ergonomics is that the equipment and the workplace be designed to make jobs as easy as possible. Ergonomics should normally be considered and evaluated as part of Stage 1 to ensure that any improvements being made are ergonomically sound, that is, that the methods and equipment being used interface well with the humans actually performing the task. Supervision Illustration 19–2 discusses an ergonomically designed device for reducing carpal tunnel syndrome of office workers.

Stage 2: Do—Try Out the Improvements

Stage 2 involves trying out the improvements developed in Stage 1. This may require obtaining approval from the boss. Even when approval is not required, it is usually wise to keep the boss informed as a new method or procedure is being developed. Care must be taken in presenting and justifying a proposal. An acceptable proposal includes a brief description of what the proposal will accomplish, how it will work, how much it will save, what it will cost, and what effect it will have on employees.

The improvement must then be put into operation. Acceptance of the improvement and cooperation of the affected employees are mandatory. As discussed in Chapter 5, employees tend to resist change if they have not been involved in the change process. Therefore,

SUPERVISION ILLUSTRATION   19–2

ERGONOMICS IN PRACTICE

Repetitive strain injury, RSI, is a medical catchall category that includes everything from tennis elbow and Blackberry thumb to carpal tunnel syndrome. The disorder involves a swelling or compression of a nerve near a specific joint and it can be very painful. Carpel tunnel syndrome in the wrist is the biggest threat to the millions of desk employees who spend hours everyday in front of a keyboard and mouse. In fact, the National Institutes of Health reports that more than five in 100 office employees suffer from carpal tunnel syndrome, many chronically and some to the point of being unable to work.

The ErgoRest is a forearm support developed by a private company in Finland. The function of the ErgoRest is to support the arm and wrist in the correct position for typing and other related tasks. Currently some twenty models are available for various uses at different work stations. The ErgoRest is easily clamped to your desk and costs about $99. Many users of the ErgoRest use one for each arm.

Sources: Jay Palmer, "Our Gadget of the Week: Wrist Watcher," *Barron's,* March 30, 2009, p. 32 and *www.ergorest.com.* Accessed on April 14, 2009.

employees should be involved as much as possible in any methods improvement program. Any proposed changes should be carefully explained, along with the reasons for them. Ideas for implementing a change should be actively solicited from the employees. The affected employees must receive thorough training in the improved method and on any new equipment.

Stage 3: Check—Evaluate the Results

This stage involves evaluating the results of the "do" stage. Did the changes result in significant improvements? What worked and what did not work? Where appropriate, statistical analysis is used to evaluate the effectiveness of the change.

Stage 4: Act—Take Action and Fine-Tune

The final stage requires action on the conclusions from Stage 3. Appropriate fine-tuning and corrective actions are taken. Once the fine-tuning has been accomplished, the entire cycle is repeated.

Successful implementation of the PDCA Cycle depends on a balanced emphasis on each of the four stages. Such emphasis requires that the methods improvement person or team plan only as much as they can do, do only as much as they can check, check only as much as they can act upon, and act upon only as much as can be planned. The cycle then repeats itself.

Kaizen Philosophy for Improvement

Because of intensified world competition, there has been increased emphasis placed on improvements of all types within today's organizations. **Kaizen** is a philosophy for improvement that originated in Japan and that has recently enjoyed widespread adoption throughout the world. The word *Kaizen* comes from two Japanese words: *Kai,* meaning "change," and *zen,* meaning "good."[3] Hence, Kaizen literally means "good change," and in today's context it describes a process of continuous and relentless improvement. Kaizen is not based on large technical leaps but on the incremental refining of existing processes. Kaizen is basically a system of taking small steps to improve the workplace. Kaizen is based on the belief that the system should be customer driven and involve all employees through systematic and open communication. Under Kaizen, employees are viewed as the organization's most valued asset. This philosophy is put into practice through teamwork and extensive employee participation. In summary, Kaizen applies the principles of participatory management toward incremental improvement of the current methods and processes. Kaizen does not focus on obtaining new and faster machines but rather on improving the methods and procedures used in the existing situation.

The single biggest waste in many companies is overproduction or producing more than needed.[4] Kaizen emphasizes direct communication with customers to clearly ascertain their order and scheduling needs and, thus, to keep inventories to a minimum. This requires open communication among many levels of employees.

A **Kaizen blitz** occurs when an organization undertakes an intense Kaizen effort concentrated in a two- to five-day time period. Most Kaizen blitzes spend the first half day or so discussing the basic Kaizen philosophy and the next two to four days developing and implementing ideas for improvement.

The Supervisor's Role in Cost Reduction and Control

6 LEARNING OBJECTIVES

The supervisor is a key person in most cost reduction and control programs because he or she is often in a position to do something about costs. The supervisor can suggest means of cost reduction and control as well as oversee the implementation and measurement of cost reduction and control ideas. The supervisor also has a direct influence over many costs. Raw material, equipment, and labor costs can be significantly influenced by the supervisor. While many staff specialists such as cost accountants, budget analysts, and cost engineers devise plans to cut costs, they depend on inputs from supervisors; and it is usually the supervisor who implements these plans.

Establishing the Proper Environment

The concept of continuous improvement, which was discussed in Chapter 18, is directly applicable to cost reduction and control. Supervisors should establish a work environment in which employees are continuously looking for ways to reduce costs.

As is true for so many areas of supervision, the attitude of the supervisor toward costs sets the tone for the entire department. If the supervisor is constantly cost conscious, this usually rubs off on employees. The reverse is also true: If the supervisor has little or only periodic concern for costs, employees will seldom be concerned about costs. Additional guidelines for establishing an environment conducive to continuous cost control and reduction are presented next.

7 LEARNING OBJECTIVES

Cost Reduction Should Be Part of the Normal Routine

It should be viewed by supervisors and employees alike as a regular and continual, not a once-a-year, effort. The goal is to develop a constant awareness of costs. All too often, a brief, intensive campaign achieves some cost reduction. But once the campaign ends, costs again begin to increase.

Cost Reduction Should Cover All Areas

The idea is for cost control and reduction to be pervasive throughout the entire organization! It is both ineffective and unfair to permit costs to run wild in one area while rigorously controlling them in another.

A Climate and Format for Encouraging Employee Suggestions Should Be Provided

Employees often represent an organization's greatest potential for cost-reduction ideas. Usually, merely asking employees for cost-reduction ideas is not enough. Employees must feel that their ideas are genuinely desired and that they will be earnestly considered. Furthermore, far more cost-reduction suggestions are likely to be offered if a specific format for the submission of suggestions is provided. Suggestion boxes are used successfully by many companies. Another workable approach is to hold periodic staff meetings for the specific purpose of generating cost-reduction ideas. Electronic media and e-mail also provide means for employees to offer suggestions.

Cost Objectives Should Be Established and Communicated

Knowing what costs to try to control means knowing what are and are not acceptable cost ranges. Employees who are held responsible for certain costs should also understand how those costs are calculated.

Individual Responsibility for Cost Reduction Should Be Made Clear

One general problem with cost reduction is that when it's considered *everybody's* problem, it ends up being *nobody's* problem. Employees should be held responsible for the costs under their control. At the same time, they should be rewarded for controlling and reducing costs.

Incentives for Cost Reduction Should Be Offered

Incentives are often the biggest factor in the success of a cost-reduction program. If employees believe that cost reduction is in their best interest, they are much more likely to participate actively in a cost-reduction program. Some organizations allow employees to share in the cost savings realized. Others give cash awards or time off to employees responsible for efforts that result in cost savings.

Why Do Employees Sometimes Fear Cost Reduction?

Often, the idea of cost reduction represents change to employees, and, therefore, as discussed in Chapter 5, their first reaction is resistance. In addition, employees often see cost reduction only in negative terms and as something that management is doing "to them." Loss of overtime, reduction of regular working hours, and the loss of jobs are some of the more obvious fears that employees might harbor.

On the other hand, when an environment of continual cost control and reduction has been established, employees not only expect but even promote initiatives in this area. These employees understand that continual cost control and reduction is a philosophy and not merely a technique. Unfortunately, cost reduction has gotten a bad name in many instances because supervisors have presented cost control and reduction in a punitive manner and not as a philosophy of managing.

Figuring Costs

Before a supervisor can reduce costs, he or she must know how to figure them. Costs can be thought of as everything expended to produce and/or provide the product or service. Generally, they can be broken down into several categories:

1. **Direct labor costs.** These are expenditures for labor that are *directly applied* in the creation or delivery of the product or service. (The more product or service that is provided, the more direct labor used.) Examples include expenditures for machine operators, claims processors, bank tellers, assembly-line workers, and salespeople.
2. **Raw material costs.** These are expenditures for raw material that are directly applied to the creation of the product or service. (The more product or service that is provided, the more raw material used.)

3. **Indirect labor costs.** These are expenditures for labor that are *not directly applied* to the creation or delivery of the product or service. Examples include human resource specialists, quality-control personnel, housekeeping personnel, and public relations specialists.

4. **Operating supplies costs.** These are expenditures for necessary items that do not become a part of the product or service (items in addition to the product/service raw materials). Examples include brochures explaining a service, cleaning compounds, safety clothing, and office supplies.

5. **Maintenance costs.** These include labor and material costs incurred to repair and maintain equipment and facilities. Examples include expenditures for replacement parts, maintenance personnel, and repairs.

6. **Scrap or waste costs.** These include expenditures for products, parts, or services that cannot be reworked or reused and that do not meet quality standards. Examples include items damaged during manufacture, unusable scrap, and unused services.

7. **Energy costs.** These are charges for electricity, gas, steam, and any other sources of power.

8. **Overhead costs.** These include expenditures for physical space, staff services, research, advertising, and legal services. Generally, overhead costs are shared by several departments; an attempt is usually made to allocate them to each department on some equitable basis.

Depending on the degree of detail needed, each of the above major cost categories may be broken down further. For example, direct labor costs may be broken down by shift or by section within the department. However, this can be overdone; as a rule, cost information should be no more detailed than is necessary for making good decisions.

Supervisors may be provided with weekly or monthly cost reports for their department, based on the above cost categories (see Figure 19.4 for an example). Such reports are usually prepared by the accounting department, based on information provided by the supervisors. Naturally, the reports are no more accurate than the information provided. Therefore, supervisors should be sure they understand what information is being sought. Also, if a supervisor does not understand any of the information on the report, he or she should seek clarification from the accounting department.

FIGURE 19.4 **Sample Cost Report**

Weekly Cost Report Department No. 33
Week ending: March 10, 20 – – Supervisor: Janice Arnold

			Variance				
		For This Week			**Year to Date**		
Account	**Budget**	**Actual**	**Over**	**Under**	**Over**	**Under**	**Comments**
Direct labor	$2,900	$3,140	$240		$1,780		
Raw materials	2,100	2,000		$100		$650	
Indirect labor	750	725		25		120	
Overtime	450	200		250		290	Made
Scrap	400	390		10		70	improvements
Supplies	500	405		95	220		this week but
Utilities	450	505	55		75		still over annual
Overhead	3,750	4,240	500		3,890		budget.

Cost-Reduction Strategies

Where should cost-reduction efforts be focused? Logically, cost reduction should begin in the areas where the greatest savings can be realized. These areas are not always obvious. Locating them may require considerable effort, but that effort usually pays off. At the same time, small cost reductions are also important. This is especially true if they can be repeated frequently, thus adding up to sizable reductions. With this in mind, several general strategies may be used to cut costs.

Increase Output

Output may be increased by utilizing the same or fewer resources. This reduces the cost per item of product or service. The supervisor should always try to operate at the output level that results in the greatest efficiency.

Improve Methods

As discussed earlier in this chapter, efficiency can be improved by eliminating any unnecessary activities or by introducing new methods.

Regulate or Level the Work Flow

A regular, steady work flow with no bottlenecks and no equipment breakdowns is desirable. Work flows with many peaks and valleys are usually inefficient and often require costly overtime.

Minimize Waste

The creation of unnecessary services and the scrapping of partially processed or unused materials can be very expensive. Any effort to reduce such waste can pay big dividends. For example, the supervisor of a cafeteria should carefully plan the quantities of the different foods to prepare so as to minimize the amount of leftovers. Other types of waste include idle personnel, work on projects of little value, and the use of equipment at less than full capacity.

Reduce Overhead

While some overhead costs are not within the supervisor's control, certain items are. Seemingly small things such as lights burning in unused areas, increased janitorial costs due to poor housekeeping, and misuse of office supplies can add up to significant overhead costs.

Analyze All Control Points

Adequate control is necessary. However, excessive control can interfere with the work and can run up costs. For instance, quality checks should be properly spaced to ensure the desired quality, but they should not be overdone to the point of interfering with accomplishment of the work.

Ensure Adequate Storage Space

Inadequate storage space can be very costly. This situation can cause unnecessary materials-handling and production delays. In a service-oriented organization, storage space would include such things as adequate waiting rooms and adequate space for storing supplies.

Minimize Downtime

Obsolete and worn-out equipment is one of the largest causes of downtime. Such equipment should be replaced. This not only increases the efficiency of the equipment used, but also has a positive effect on the operator. For example, one has only to look at the gains achieved by replacing a manually operated machine with a computer controlled machine. Another major cause of downtime is running out of materials. Proper inventory control can keep this from becoming a problem. Inventory control is discussed later in this chapter.

Invest in Employee Training

Employees who properly understand how to do their jobs are more efficient than those who don't. Usually, any front-end investments in training are made up through increased job efficiency.

Deal with Troubled and Problem Employees

As discussed in Chapter 13, both troubled and problem employees can hurt a department's productivity. This can especially be a problem when they are part of a team; team morale can be adversely affected. Troubled or problem employees should be confronted and handled following the guidelines discussed in Chapter 13.

Work Closely with Suppliers

Suppliers can be a good source for cost-saving ideas. Involve suppliers in the design process and keep communication lines open throughout the entire design process.

Cost-Reduction Resources

Supervisors seeking to cut costs will invariably spot some possibilities. The key is to look for them. At the same time, however, supervisors should not fail to enlist the aid of all available resources. Staff specialists can be very helpful: cost analysts, industrial engineers, and others in the staff can offer expertise in certain areas. As mentioned earlier, employees often represent the greatest potential for cost-reduction ideas. The person who does the job every day generally has some good ideas about how it can be improved. The key is to listen to and evaluate all suggestions. It is also important to implement worthwhile suggestions and to give recognition to the employees who make them. Yet another resource is a cost-reduction committee. A cost-reduction committee offers the benefits of group thinking. It also heightens its members' interest in cost reduction.

Cost Areas That Frequently Cause Problems

 8 LEARNING OBJECTIVES

Certain areas that tend to be more susceptible to cost overruns than others have historically caused problems for supervisors. Overtime, absenteeism, tardiness, turnover, employee theft, materials handling, job methods, quality maintenance, and inventory control are potential contributors to cost overruns. Methods improvement was discussed earlier in this chapter and quality was discussed in Chapter 18. Overtime, absenteeism, tardiness, turnover, employee theft, and materials handling are discussed in the following paragraphs.

Overtime

Overtime is a curious phenomenon. Some employees refuse to work overtime; others regard it as a gift from heaven. The attraction of overtime is, of course, that overtime pay rates are higher than normal pay rates. The federal law states that all hours over 40 worked in one week must be paid at least at the rate of time and a half. Some organizations pay double or even triple time for certain overtime. In addition to the obvious cost of higher wages, overtime often has other hidden costs. These include decreased employee efficiency, higher reject rates, and more absenteeism (all due to employee fatigue). In spite of these costs, there is a great temptation to resort to overtime whenever things get behind schedule. Certainly, there are times when the use of overtime is justified. But overtime should not be resorted to at the drop of a hat. Excessive overtime sometimes indicates poor supervision. The old saying "Something is wrong if you can't do your job in eight hours a day" has some validity. Furthermore, overtime can create other problems. Deciding who should work overtime can be difficult. Also, if overtime becomes habitual, employees tend to expect it as a part of regular wages. If it is discontinued, some employees become unhappy because they are "making less pay." Yet another problem is that some employees will pace themselves in order to create overtime.

If overtime looks like it might be necessary, a supervisor should do certain things:

1. Determine the cause of the overtime. Is it poor planning, inappropriate organization, faulty equipment, or what? Can anything be done to avoid or minimize the necessity of overtime in the future?

2. Consider the alternatives. One alternative to overtime is to use the services of a temporary agency. Temporary agencies today can even provide part-time professional employees. The major advantage to using people from temporary agencies is that they do not have to be paid at overtime rates (assuming they work 40 hours or less) and that they usually do not receive benefits.

3. Explain why overtime may be necessary. All the facts should be made available as soon as possible. Tell the employees why and how they were selected for overtime and how long it will last.

4. Have sufficient raw materials and supplies on hand. Overtime is certain to be wasted if this is not done.

5. Include work breaks when overtime is utilized. Remember, employees have already worked a full day. Adequate breaks are essential.

6. Be alert as a supervisor. Because of the increased costs associated with overtime, make sure it is used wisely. Be available to answer employee questions and provide needed guidance.

Absenteeism

The costs associated with absenteeism can be large. Machines may be idle, schedules may slip, and temporary help may have to be hired. One study reported the per employee cost of unscheduled absenteeism to be $660 per year.[5] A second study found that employee absences cost organizations the equivalent of 36 percent of their base payroll on average. The total includes both planned absences (27 percent) such as vacations and holidays, as well as unplanned absences (9 percent).[6] When someone fails to show up for work, it is usually the supervisor who must decide what to do. Should temporary help be hired? Should regular work assignments be altered? What other adjustments should be made? The first survey mentioned in this section reported the following as the five major reasons for unscheduled employee absenteeism: personal illness—35 percent; family issues—21 percent; personal needs—18 percent; entitlement mentality—14 percent; and stress—12 percent.[7]

Unfortunately, unscheduled absenteeism cannot be completely avoided. Employees get sick, relatives die, accidents occur, and certain personal business must be tended to during normal work hours. However, there is an avoidable type of absenteeism—that of the employee who could come to work but stays out instead. Looking at the five major reasons for unscheduled absenteeism, the categories of family issues, personal needs and entitlement mentality certainly involve many situations in which employees could come to work if they really wanted to come. Research has shown that employees tend to come to work when they (1) are satisfied with their jobs and (2) are loyal to the organization. Both of these factors can be significantly affected by the supervisor.

SUPERVISION ILLUSTRATION 19–3

LOYALTY AT PURDY CHOCOLATES

R.C. Purdy Chocolates Ltd. is Western Canada's largest chocolate retailer. Every year its stores in Alberta, British Columbia, and more recently Ontario, sell more than two million pounds of chocolates. Employee loyalty has played a huge role in achieving Purdy's success. The loyalty of Purdy's employees is not luck but rather the end product of sound people practices.

Purdy does several things that foster loyalty among employees. Some of these include: hiring people that have a passion for the company; placing a premium on training, much of which is done through mentoring; communicating performance expectations and measuring results; paying people above the industry average; and sharing information with employees.

"We've worked hard to listen to people, respond to people, to treat people with respect—a lot of the things that are the history of the business and that my father did," says Karen Flavelle, whose father purchased the company in 1963. "Companies often think their employees have to show they're trustworthy. But, really, the trust needs to start with the employer, and then the employees react and respond to that," says Flavelle, now president and owner.

Since Karen took over from her father in 1997, she has opened 10 new stores including four in the tough Ontario market. She has also doubled the annual revenues. Purdy Chocolates celebrated its 100th anniversary in 2007.

Sources: Susanne Baillie-Ruder, "Sweet Devotion," *Profit*, December 2004, pp. 44–48, and Kara Aaserud, "Karen Flavelle," *Profit*, May 2007, p. 21.

Employees may stay out because they find their jobs boring. The jobs may be repetitive, may not use the employees' skills, or may have little responsibility. The challenge for the supervisor is to determine whether these conditions exist and, if so, what to do about them. The boredom in some jobs can be lessened through alternative work designs. Some employees want and seek responsibility; others do not. It is the supervisor's job to determine who does and who does not. Those desiring responsibility should be given it whenever possible. Those wishing to avoid responsibility should not be given any more than necessary. An employee who doesn't get along with his or her peers may also stay out. When this occurs, the supervisor should confront the problem directly and try to help resolve the differences. If this doesn't work, the supervisor may be forced to terminate the employee.

Loyalty to the organization occurs naturally if the employee feels good about the organization. Of course, the reverse is also true. Employees who harbor ill feelings about the organization or the supervisor are rarely loyal. An American at Work study found that of all the things a company can do to inspire loyalty, recognizing the importance of personal and family life has the most impact on employees.[8] Many organizations are implementing programs that address work/life issues to increase loyalty and decrease the cost of absenteeism. These programs include such things as flexible scheduling (flextime), child care, elder care, and part-time employment. Supervision Illustration 19–3 describes the actions of one company to foster loyalty among its employees.

Many organizations have decreased absenteeism by replacing traditional designated benefits programs with paid time-off plans. Designated benefits programs define sick time, holidays, and vacation time as separate times away from work. Paid time-off plans (PTOs) combine all time off into a pool employees can use as they wish. Some organizations offer incentives to encourage employees to take fewer sick days. Some employers, however, believe that such programs can encourage genuinely sick employees to attend work. Many also struggle with the notion of rewarding employees for doing what is expected of them. Supervision Illustration 19–4 discusses some new software designed to help organizations manage employee attendance.

SUPERVISION ILLUSTRATION 19–4

SOFTWARE TO HELP MANAGE ATTENDANCE

InfoTronics, a developer of employee time and attendance software systems, recently released Attendance Enterprise 2.0, which was designed to improve employee time tracking, scheduling, and reporting. Attendance Enterprise transforms employee labor data into information to help companies control overtime, improve employee attendance, and reduce overall labor expenses. The basic package of Attendance Enterprise provides managers and supervisors with real-time essential labor information; identifies attendance exceptions such as tardiness and absenteeism; automates time off requests and approvals; and cuts payroll costs by automating complex payroll policies. Another plus to the system is that it ensures compliance with labor regulations such as the Fair Labor Standards Act (FLSA) and the Family and Medical Leave Act (FMLA).

Optional modules include leave management and benefit accruals. In addition, a custom report writer offers 50 other standard real-time workforce management reports with options for modifying both content and format. "These enhanced time tracking features meet the needs of organizations of all sizes and in a range of industries looking to manage labor costs," said Chris Ciapala, President, InfoTronics. "Plus, the system is cost-effective. Attendance Enterprise 2.0 scales to accommodate the size of the workforce."

Source: "InfoTronics Rolls Out Attendance Enterprise 2.0," *Wireless News*, October 20, 2008.

The general style of supervision employed by supervisors affects employees' feelings about the organization. If employees feel that supervisors are fair, open-minded, and concerned, they are likely to develop good feelings and loyalty toward the organization.

Tardiness

An employee who reports late can run up costs in many of the same ways as the absentee. Tardiness also indicates a lack of job satisfaction and loyalty. In most situations, a small group of chronic offenders account for most tardiness. As with absenteeism, some tardiness is controllable and some is not. Accidental tardiness occurs because of flat tires, severe weather, or personal emergencies. Controllable tardiness relates to the habitual offender—the employee who is late on a regular basis.

Habitual tardiness should be dealt with directly. First, the habitual offender should be identified and verified through the attendance records. Second, the reasons for his or her tardiness should be determined, if possible. Third, a private conference should be held with the offender. During this conference, the seriousness of the situation should be discussed and a plan for eliminating the problems should be agreed upon. If the reason pertains to a condition of the job, steps should be taken to correct it. Fourth, if the tardiness continues, talk to the offender again. Emphasize that the tardiness must stop or disciplinary action will be taken. Fifth, if the tardiness continues, follow the formal disciplinary procedure and discipline the offender. It is essential that matters of this type be dealt with directly and consistently so that all employees receive the same message.

Turnover

Turnover is very expensive for almost any organization.[9] According to the U.S. Department of Labor, it costs a company one-third of a new hire's annual salary to replace an employee.[10] For example, it would cost approximately $18,000 to replace an employee whose annual salary is $54,000. Direct costs of replacing an employee include advertising expenses, headhunter fees, and management's time involved in recruitment, selection, and training. Indirect costs include overtime expenses, decreased productivity until the new employee gets up to speed, other employees' time spent helping a new employee, and training expenses for the new employee.

Given the very high costs associated with turnover, organizations should do whatever possible to minimize turnover. Below are five strategies that will keep turnover low:

1. *Build strong relationships with every employee.* Everyone likes to be made to feel important and to be treated with respect. Go out of your way, as the supervisor, to make people feel important.

2. *Offer praise freely.* People never get tired hearing about a job done well. Take every opportunity to recognize and praise employees, especially in public.

3. *Truly listen to employee feedback.* Employees are almost always willing to tell you their needs and job-related issues—especially if they think you are genuinely interested. Listen carefully and follow up on what is said. If an action isn't possible or desirable, clearly explain why.

4. *Keep the mood light.* Create a fun work environment. Having fun in the workplace goes a long way toward making people feel a part of things. Get employees to laugh with you.

5. *Continually strengthen your team.* Select the best people possible and then provide the necessary experience and training to make them better. Encourage employees to let you know their training needs and desires.

Employee Theft

Employees helping themselves to company funds cost U.S. businesses about $660 billion per year, according to a 2006 report by the Association of Certified Fraud Examiners. This same report found that over 46 percent of all workplace fraud happens to businesses with fewer than 100 employees.[11] Another survey conducted by PricewaterhouseCoopers in 2007 reported that 62 percent of companies with over 5,000 employees experienced fraud. That number dropped to 52 percent of companies with 1001 to 5000 employees and to 32 percent for companies with less than 200 employees.[12] In retail more inventory shrinkage is due to employee theft than to shoplifting. Although many factors may be at the source of employee theft, major contributors are lax selection and hiring policies, readily accessible money and products, and managers and supervisors who project a callous and uncaring attitude. While specific steps can be taken to reduce each of these contributors to theft, building a corporate culture that supports an honest workforce is the most effective approach. The following guidelines should be followed to establish such a culture.

1. Establish a clear, explicit policy on corporate theft.
2. Set a good example in terms of not taking liberties at the expense of the company.
3. Watch for warning signs of abuse.
4. Be consistent in dealing with those employees who violate theft policies.
5. Do not become overly aggressive; conduct a thorough investigation before accusing an employee.
6. Do not police the workplace; be trustful of employees.[13]

Materials Handling

Materials handling involves the movement of materials. These include raw materials, supplies, in-process materials, finished goods, and equipment. In a service organization, materials handling includes the handling of any materials and supplies that are used in creating and providing the service. The average cost of materials handling has been estimated to be as high as 35 to 40 percent in a manufacturing setting. Materials-handling costs are undoubtedly equally high in some service organizations, such as a post office. Associated with materials handling are not only the costs of physically moving things but also the costs of *not* moving them in a timely manner. Idle employees and machines waiting for materials, supplies, or customers can be extremely costly. The questions listed in

FIGURE 19.5
Questions to Help Reduce Materials-Handling Problems

1. Is the travel distance the absolute minimum?
2. Are storage areas convenient and of adequate size?
3. What alternative arrangement might be better?
4. Are components and partial assemblies often damaged in transit?
5. Are materials moved manually from one area to another?
6. Is materials handling performed by any of your skilled employees?
7. Do any loading or unloading operations take considerable time?
8. Are materials moved several times within the department before actually being used?

Figure 19.5 suggest specific ways that materials-handling problems might be reduced. Many of the work methods presented earlier in this chapter can be applied to solving materials-handling problems.

Inventory Control

Inventory control is primarily concerned with monitoring and maintaining a supply of inventory adequate to meet customer demand but not greater than is necessary for that purpose. The costs of poorly managed inventories can be extremely high. If excessive inventory is carried, money is needlessly tied up and unnecessary storage costs are incurred. If too little inventory is carried, customers may be lost, production may be slowed, and employees may be laid off. In addition to determining what levels of inventory to maintain, inventory control systems determine when stock should be replaced and how large orders should be. Inventory management is one of the biggest responsibilities of many supervisors.

9   LEARNING OBJECTIVES

Inventories serve as a buffer between different rates of usage in the production system. Inventories can generally be classified as (1) raw material inventories, (2) in-process inventories, or (3) finished goods inventories. *Raw material inventories* serve as a buffer between purchasing and operations. *In-process inventories* are used to buffer differences in the rates of flow through the various production processes. *Finished goods inventories* act as a buffer between the final stage of production and shipping or delivery of the product. Figure 19.6 illustrates the relationships of the three inventories.

FIGURE 19.6
Inventories as Buffers

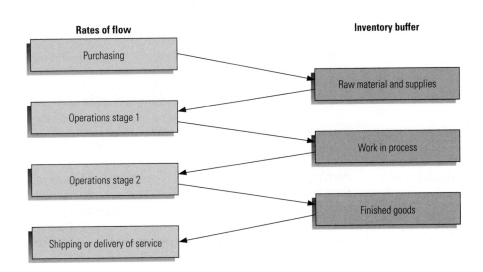

After studying this chapter, Jane should understand how to implement a structured methods improvement program as well as a cost-reduction plan and inventory controls. Also, after studying this chapter, Jane should understand the Kaizen philosophy and implement the PCDA approach to methods improvement (p. 370–371). Following this approach, Jane should first identify the tasks to be improved.

She might also ask her employees for their ideas as to where methods improvement might be made. Once she has selected those tasks that have the greatest potential for methods improvement, she should pick two or three for analysis. Following the analysis, Jane should try out the suggested improvements, evaluate the results, and then make and fine-tune adjustments.

Assuming that Jane understands basic cost categories and the budget within which she must work, she should design and implement a basic cost-reduction plan. In designing her plan, Jane should remember that her employees represent her greatest source of cost-reduction ideas. Keeping this in mind, she should build some incentives for her employees into her program. To emphasize her commitment to cost reduction, she should take advantage of every opportunity to set an example—even such small matters as turning out lights and not wasting supplies (pp. 375–376).

A final action that Jane might take is to take a close look at the different inventories in her section and to determine if she is carrying too much or too little of anything (pp. 381–383).

Inventories provide added flexibility and efficiency to the production system by allowing the organization to:

1. Purchase, produce, and ship in economic batch sizes rather than in small lots.
2. Produce on a smooth, continuous basis even though the demand for the finished product or raw material may fluctuate.
3. Prevent major problems when forecasts of demand are in error or when there are unforeseen slowdowns or stoppages in supply or production.

When making inventory decisions, three basic questions must be answered: (1) what items to carry in inventory, (2) how much of the selected items to order and carry, and (3) when to order the items. Depending on the particular situation, supervisors may or may not be responsible for answering these questions. Even in situations in which supervisors are not responsible for making inventory related decisions, they should understand the basics of what is going on.

If it were not costly, every organization would attempt to maintain very large inventories to facilitate purchasing, production scheduling, and distribution. However, as noted earlier, the cost of carrying excess inventory can be high. Potential inventory costs include such factors as insurance and taxes on the inventory, storage costs, obsolescence costs, spoilage, and the opportunity cost of the money invested in the inventory. The relative importance of these costs depends on the specific inventory being held. For example, when dealing with women's fashions, the obsolescence costs are potentially very high. Spoilage costs are potentially high in the food business. Similarly, storage costs might be very high for dangerous chemicals. Thus, when making inventory decisions, the costs of carrying inventory must be weighed against the costs of running short of raw materials, in-process goods, or finished goods.

Just-in-Time Inventory Control

10 LEARNING OBJECTIVES

Just-in-time inventory control (JIT) was pioneered in Japan but has become popular in the United States. JIT systems are sometimes referred to as zero-inventory systems, stockless systems, or Kanban systems. JIT is actually a philosophy for production so that the right items arrive and leave as they are needed. Traditionally, incoming raw materials are ordered in relatively few large shipments and stored in warehouses until needed for production or for providing a service. Under JIT, organizations make smaller and more frequent orders of raw materials. JIT depends on the elimination of setup time between the production of different batches of different products. JIT can be viewed as an operating philosophy which has as its basic objective the elimination of waste.[14] In this light, waste is "anything other than the minimum amount of equipment, materials, parts, space, and employees' time that are absolutely essential to add value to the product or service."

The JIT philosophy applies not only to inventories of incoming raw materials but also to the production of subassemblies or final products. The idea is to not produce an item or subassembly until it is needed for shipment. JIT is called a demand pull system because items are produced or ordered only when they are needed (or pulled) by the next stage in the production process.

Summary

This chapter begins with a basic discussion of the major factors that affect an organization's productivity. The chapter then discusses the supervisor's role in a work-methods improvement program, a cost reduction program, and in controlling inventory. The benefits of each of these programs are also discussed.

1. *Explain the three major components of organizational productivity.* The three major components of organizational productivity are (1) efficiency of technology, (2) efficiency of labor, and (3) effectiveness of management.

2. *Discuss the benefits of work-methods improvement.* Reduced costs, higher productivity, reduced delays, higher quality, reduced waste, improved safety, and more satisfied employees are among the potential benefits of methods improvement.

3. *Distinguish between motion study and time study.* Motion study is concerned with determining the most efficient set of motions required to do a given task. Time study is the analysis of a task to determine the elements of work required to perform it, the order in which the elements occur, and the time required to perform them effectively.

4. *Present a systematic approach for improving work methods.* The PDCA Cycle presents a systematic approach for improving work methods. The PDCA Cycle consists of four major stages: (1) plan, (2) do, (3) check, and (4) act. Successful implementation of the PDCA Cycle requires a balanced emphasis on each of the four stages.

5. *Describe the Kaizen philosophy for improvement.* Kaizen literally means "good change." In today's context, Kaizen describes a process of continuous and relentless improvement. Kaizen is not based on large technical leaps of innovations but on the incremental refining of existing processes.

6. *Describe the supervisor's role in improving productivity through cost reduction and control.* The supervisor is a key person in any cost reduction and control program because he or she is in an ideal position to do something about costs. The supervisor also sets the tone for the entire department and largely influences the attitudes of the employees with regard to cost reduction and control.

7. *Summarize several cost-reduction strategies that can be helpful to supervisors.* Cost-reduction strategies that can be helpful to supervisors include the following: Increase output, improve methods, regulate or level the work flow, minimize waste, reduce overhead, analyze all control points, ensure adequate storage space, minimize downtime, and invest in employee training.

8. *Identify several areas of concern to supervisors that tend to be especially susceptible to cost overruns.* Areas that tend to be especially susceptible to cost overruns are overtime, absenteeism, tardiness, turnover, employee theft, materials handling, job methods, quality maintenance, and inventory control.

9. *Discuss the major types of inventories and explain the purposes for carrying inventories.* Inventories can generally be classified according to three categories: (1) raw materials, (2) in-process, or (3) finished goods. Inventories provide added flexibility to the production system and allow the organization to purchase, produce, and ship in economic batch sizes; to produce on a smooth, continuous basis even though the demand for the finished product or raw material may fluctuate; and to prevent major problems when forecasts of demand are in error or when there are unforeseen slowdowns or stoppages in supply or production.

10. *Explain the just-in-time approach to inventory control.* The just-in-time (JIT) approach to inventory schedules materials to arrive and leave as they are needed. JIT can be viewed as an operating philosophy which has as its basic objective the elimination of waste.

Key Terms

Direct labor costs, 373
Energy costs, 374
Ergonomics, 370
Indirect labor costs, 374
Inventory control, 381
Just-in-time inventory
   control (J.I.T.), 382
Kaizen, 371

Kaizen blitz, 372
Maintenance costs, 374
Materials handling, 380
Methods engineering, 367
Motion or methods study, 368
Operating supplies costs, 374
Overhead costs, 374
PDCA cycle, 370

Productivity, 366
Raw material costs, 373
Scrap or waste costs, 374
Standard time, 369
Technology, 366
Time study, 369
Work-methods improvement, 367
Work simplification, 367

Review Questions

1. Define *productivity* and describe three major components of productivity.

2. What is the objective of work-methods improvement?

3. Name at least six potential benefits of improved work methods.

4. What is the difference between time study and motion study?

5. Briefly describe the PDCA Cycle.

6. Explain the concept of *kaizen.*

7. What is a Kaizen blitz?

8. Name six major guidelines that should be followed when making attempts to reduce costs.

9. What are the general cost categories with which most supervisors come into contact?

10. Name 11 general strategies for reducing costs.

11. List several areas that tend to be more susceptible to cost overruns than others.

12. What are the three major types of inventories?

13. List several reasons that inventories are carried by organizations.

14. List several other terms that are used to describe just-in-time (JIT) systems.

Skill-Building Questions

1. If your boss asked your opinion of methods improvement, what would you say?

2. Some people argue that methods improvement is too old-fashioned for today's work environment. How would you respond to this argument?

3. Why do you think most employees are not enthusiastic about cost control? What can the supervisor do about this problem?

4. Why do you think overtime is abused in so many organizations?

5. In light of today's high standard of living, why do you think that employee theft is such a widespread problem in industry?

References

1. Richard C. Gertenberg, "Productivity: Its Meaning for America," *Michigan Business Review,* July 1972, p. 2.

2. Ibid., p. 5.

3. Vivienne Walker, "Kaizen—The Art of Continual Improvement," *Personnel Management,* August 1993, pp. 36–38.

4. Gary S. Vasilash, "Walking the Talk of Kaizen at Freudenberg-NOK," *Production,* December 1993, pp. 66–71.

5. Chris Navarro and Cara Bass, "The Cost of Employee Absenteeism," *Compensation and Benefits Review,* November/December 2006, pp. 26–31.

6. "Full Cost of Employee Absence Equals 36 Percent of Payroll, According to New Mercer Study Sponsored by Kronos®," *Business Wire,* October 21, 2008.

7. Chris Navarro and Cara Bass, op. cit.

8. "Employee Loyalty Hangs on Company Recognition That There is Life Beyond Work," *HR Focus,* August 1999, p. 5.

9. Much of this section is drawn from Laura Michaud, "Turning the Tables on Employee Turnover—Five Keys to Maximize Employee Retention," *Midwest Construction,* December 20, 2000, p. 69.

10. Dan Charney, "Top 10 Reasons Good Employees Quit," *Materials Handling Management,* October 2008, pp. 48–49.

11. Patsy R. Brumfield, "Tough Economy Spurs Warnings About Embezzlement," *McClatchy-Tribune Business News,* December 26, 2008.

12. "Fraud Major Threat to Companies Worldwide," *CMA Management,* December 2007/January 2008, p. 13.

13. "Employee Theft: Prevention, Recommendations, Policy Making," *Supervisory Management,* July 2000, pp. 89–100.

14. Nicholas J. Aquilano and Richard B. Chase, *Fundamentals of Operations Management,* (Homewood, IL: Richard D. Irwin, 1991), p. 586.

Additional Readings

Domeyer, Diane, "Doing More With Less: Managing Workflow with Fewer Resources," *Women in Business,* July/August 2004, p. 7.

Drizin, Marc and A. J. Schneider, "Understanding the Connection Between Loyalty and Profit," *Employment Relations Today,* Winter 2004, pp. 43–54.

Hart, Kevin M., "Not Wanted: Thieves," *HR Magazine,* April 2008, pp. 119–124.

Jeppsson, Jessica, "Workspace Comfort," *Industrial Engineer,* March 2009, pp. 58–59.

Toland, Bill, "Employees Waste Time, Study Says," *McClatchy-Tribune Business News,* November 1, 2007.

SKILL-BUILDING APPLICATIONS

Incident 19–1

The Lines at Sam's

Sam Baker owns and manages a cafeteria on Main Street in Dawsonville. Sam has been in business for almost two years. During his two years of operation, Sam has identified several problems that he has not been able to solve. One major problem is that a line always seems to develop at the checkout register during the rush hour. Another problem is that customers are constantly complaining that the employees take too much time to serve the customers as they go down the line. A third problem that has been disturbing Sam is the frequency with which the cafeteria runs out of "choice dishes." The final problem perplexing him is that every Sunday at noon, when a large crowd arrives after church, Sam's invariably runs short of seating space.

Sam had worked at other food establishments for 15 years before he opened his cafeteria, and most of them experienced similar problems. In fact, these and other related problems have come to be expected and are therefore accepted practice for the industry. After all, Sam's former boss used to say, "You can't please everybody all the time." Sam is wondering if he should take the industry's position and just accept these problems as an inherent part of the business.

Questions

1. From a methods improvement viewpoint, what suggestions would you make to Sam?
2. How might Sam implement Kaizen at his cafeteria?

Incident 19–2

Here We Go Again

Word of a drastic cost-reduction program had just come down from top management. The memo read, "If Transistors, Inc., is to survive, it must trim costs significantly. The Japanese have already forced many electronics firms out of business, and there is no reason why Transistors, Inc., will be spared unless we take action."

Emory Sparks, supervisor of one of the assembly areas, responded by talking to all of the people on his line. He explained the dire circumstances and asked them "to get with it." Specific requests made by Emory to his employees included taking shorter coffee breaks, starting on time, and not quitting 15 minutes early. Emory stated that the plant's goal was to keep all machines and lines operating at near capacity. He cautioned that increased productivity did not mean reduced quality, as had been the case on some occasions in the past. All of his employees stated that they would fully cooperate with the cost-reduction program.

Cost-reduction programs were nothing new to Emory. He had seen a multitude of them come and go during his nine years as a supervisor. Although his employees had all agreed to cooperate in the latest cost-reduction program, Emory couldn't help wondering if Transistors, Inc., hadn't tried this approach once too often. As the old saying goes, "You can go to the well only so many times." Another thing that bothered Emory was the inevitable assault of the cost experts. Every time a cost-reduction program was implemented, management sent in a team of accountants to monitor costs. These cost experts rarely knew what they were talking about. They undoubtedly knew accounting, but they didn't understand the production process.

Emory felt that in the final analysis, his department's costs were not out of line. The real problem, in his opinion, was the marketing department. In Emory's words, "The marketing department couldn't sell a coat to an Eskimo."

Questions

1. Can costs always be reduced? Discuss.
2. How successful do you think Emory will be in reducing his departmental costs?
3. What provisions of a cost-reduction program do you feel are warranted in this situation?

Exercise 19–1

Improving Your Exam Performance

The purpose of this exercise is to apply the PDCA Cycle to how you prepare for your class exams. Using anticipated and actual exam scores as a measure of quality, apply the PDCA Cycle to improving your performance on future exams. After analyzing each exam that you have taken so far this term, plan how you might improve your performance. Implement your planned improvements in preparing for your next exam. After you get the results of your exam, evaluate how well your planned improvements worked. Based on these results, make adjustments wherever needed and repeat the cycle for the next exam.

1. Do you think the PDCA Cycle helped improve your performance? Why or why not?
2. Can you think of any other applications for the PDCA Cycle in your role as a student?

Exercise 19–2

Processing Customers

Almost everyone has visited both a McDonald's and a Wendy's restaurant. McDonald's restaurants have a number of different lines and cash registers across the counter. Wendy's restaurants, on the other hand, have one line and one cash register and the line moves down the counter from the cash register to pick up the food and drinks. Both of these customer-processing systems appear to work for their respective companies, yet they are substantially different.

1. Which customer processing system do you like best? Why?
2. From a methods improvement viewpoint, what advantages and disadvantages can you identify for each system?
3. From a methods improvement viewpoint, can you think of any improvement that could be made to either system? If so, explain it.

Exercise 19–3

Preparing a Cost Report

Assume that your boss has asked you to prepare a cost report based on the information presented in Figure 19.4 on page 374. The boss has also requested that your report include recommendations that you would make as a result of your analysis. In two pages or less, prepare the requested report and be prepared to discuss it with the class.

Exercise 19–4

Cost Overruns

Assume that you are the supervisor in charge of running a small branch bank in the suburb of a major metropolitan area. Your branch has three tellers, a customer service representative, and a loan officer. The tellers handle normal transactions that occur at the teller windows. The customer service representative opens new accounts, approves credit card applications, and renders other customer-related services. The loan officer processes loan applications. Recently, your branch has been running over its cost budget in several areas, including overtime, supplies, and utilities. You have mentioned these problems rather casually to your employees, with no apparent results or even concern.

This morning one teller called in sick and your customer service representative reported in an hour late. Normal procedure when an employee is absent is to report the problem to bank headquarters. Usually, headquarters then directs a "travel team" member to substitute for the day and charges the branch a fee for the use of that person. In the 10 A.M. interoffice mail delivery, you received a memo from your district manager expressing her concern about your cost overruns. The memo asked that you submit a written cost-reduction plan to her by the end of the next week.

1. Working by yourself, outline the different cost categories in which you think costs might be reduced. What cost-reduction guidelines should you implement? Formulate a plan for carrying out your ideas.
2. Get together with three or four of your fellow students and compare the ideas that each of you developed in question 1. As a group, design a cost-reduction plan for this situation. Be as detailed as time permits.

Exercise 19–5

Comparing Costs

The Que Company prints personal checks and is located in New York. The company has two options for serving its Washington customers. These options are outlined below:

Option 1. Maintain a sales and customer service office in Washington. Under this arrangement a clerk in the Washington office would receive orders through the mail and telephone them to the New York plant where the order would be produced and shipped directly to the customer. The following costs have been estimated for this arrangement.

Rent for office space	$1,600 per month
Salary for office person	$3,840 per month
Furniture and equipment	$1,600 per month
Telephone expense	$800 per month

Production cost in New York plant	$7.50 per order
Capacity of this method	2,000 orders per month
Price	$13.00 per order

Option 2. Open a small plant in Washington. Under this arrangement, the following costs have been estimated.

Rent on plant space	$4,800 per month
Manager's salary	$6,400 per month
Materials cost	$1.60 per order
Depreciation on equipment	$800 per month
Labor cost:	
1 office clerk	$3,200 per month
1 typesetter/computer person	$4,000 per month
1 binding worker	$3,600 per month
Capacity of this method	3,000 orders per month
Price	$13.00 per order

A. For each of the options listed, classify all of the costs according to the categories described on pages 373–374. Which of these costs are fixed (do not vary with the level of production) and which vary according to the level of production?

B. If Que expects approximately 1,500 orders per month from its Washington customers, should it implement Option 1 or Option 2? Which option should it implement if it expects to average 3,000 orders per month?

Providing a Safe and Healthy Work Environment

Learning objectives

After studying this chapter, you will be able to:

1. Discuss the supervisor's responsibility for safety.
2. Appreciate the costs associated with work-related accidents and illnesses.
3. Discuss the major causes of work-related accidents.
4. Measure safety in the workplace.
5. Explain the basic purposes of a safety program.
6. Outline several organizational strategies for promoting safety.
7. Outline several specific things that the supervisor can do to prevent accidents.
8. Identify several warning signs that can help supervisors learn to recognize potentially violent employees.
9. Understand the purpose of the Occupational Safety and Health Act (OSHA).
10. Explain the basic purpose of the Hazard Communications Standard.

Supervision Dilemma

Jane Harris has just filled out an OSHA accident report concerning the second major injury in her department this year. Both of these injuries occurred when an employee was trying to reach something on a high shelf. In the first instance, Beth Harrison was trying to reach a box of claim forms on a storage shelf when the chair she was standing on slipped and she fell to the floor. She broke an arm and missed five days of work. In the second instance, Joe Evans was standing on the top step of a stepladder in the storage room when he lost his balance and fell. He was out for two weeks with a strained back. If Jane has talked to her employees once about being careful, she has talked to them a dozen times! Jane simply can't believe the stupid things her employees do. Only yesterday, she herself tripped over a Coke bottle someone had left on the floor. Fortunately, she was able to catch herself in time. What can she do to prevent more "useless" accidents?

Safety is an important concern of today's organizations. It has been estimated that approximately 8 out of every 100 American employees in the private sector suffer an injury or illness caused by exposure to hazards in the work environment. Although fewer than half of all instances of injury and illness result in lost workdays, approximately 3.7 million employees suffered disabling injuries in 2006.[1] In the same year, approximately 4,988 work-related deaths occurred in American industry.[2] The associated total work accident cost was estimated to be $164.7 billion.[3]

The Supervisor's Responsibility for Safety

1 LEARNING OBJECTIVES

A successful safety program starts at the very top of the organization. The owners, top executives, and middle managers must all be committed to safety. However, because the supervisor is the one representative of management who has daily contact with the employees, the supervisor is the key person in the program. Even in organizations that have a safety engineer or a safety director, the supervisor is responsible for seeing that the safety directives are carried out. It is from the supervisor that the employees take their cues as to what is important. It is the supervisor who shapes the employees' attitude toward safety.

Because supervisors are responsible for the safety of their employees, they should listen attentively to employee complaints and suggestions relating to safety. Complaints should always be checked out and corrective action taken when necessary. The supervisor should also strive to develop a good working relationship with the safety engineer or safety director (if there is one). The supervisor should consult the safety engineer or safety director on any safety-related problems that come up. These actions can help to head off many accidents before they occur. When a safety committee (safety committees are discussed later in this chapter) exists, the supervisor should work to develop good relations with the committee.

Because safety committees often act in only an advisory capacity, the supervisor is responsible for carrying out its recommendations. Thus, supervisors and safety committees are dependent on each other.

Safety instruction should be an integral part of orienting and training employees. Employees cannot be expected to use safe methods if they don't know what those methods are. Clear instructions regarding safety methods and procedures should be a part of every orientation program.

In addition to the general responsibilities described above, supervisors may also be responsible for such things as accident investigation, first aid, maintenance of proper safety records, and the dissemination of changes in safety regulations and methods.

SUPERVISION ILLUSTRATION   20-1

COMPANY INDICTED AND CONVICTED FOR SAFETY VIOLATIONS

For the first time on record, a construction contractor was charged and convicted for violating job safety regulations. The L.E. Myers Company, one of the nation's oldest electrical contractors, was charged in the death of an apprentice lineman and a journeyman lineman who died in incidents that happened within three months of each other. The indictment alleged that the company willfully violated numerous federal workplace safety regulations. Both of the lineman were working on high-voltage transmission towers when the accidents occurred. At least 35 employees of L.E. Myers have died on the job since 1972.

Lawyers for the company argued that the company began a major safety initiative in the 1990's to improve and expand its training and safety programs. Because of this initiative, the company claimed that the indictment was a surprise.

A jury of nine women and three men found the company guilty in the death of the apprentice lineman and acquitted the company in the other case. The company faces a maximum of 5 years probation and a $500,000 fine. Both of the families of the deceased lineman have civil litigation pending against the L.E. Myers Company.

Sources: Katie Rotella, "Criminal Charges Filed for Violating Safety Regulations," *Plumbing and Mechanical,* January 2004, p. 9, and Tom Rybarczyk, "Firm Guilty in '99 Death," *Knight Ridder Tribune Business News,* May 20, 2005, p. 1.

The Cost of Accidents

2 LEARNING OBJECTIVES

As indicated in the introduction to this chapter, the costs of work-related accidents are high. The factors that contribute to these costs are many and varied. A major category of costs is directly related to lost production. This category includes costs incurred as a result of work slowdowns, damaged equipment, damaged or ruined products, idle equipment, excessive waste, and the profit forgone due to lost sales. A closely related cost is the cost incurred for training new or temporary replacements.

Insurance and medical costs are increasing due to large claims and other costs that are incurred as a result of work-related accidents. This category includes the costs of workers' compensation insurance, health insurance, accident insurance, and disability insurance.

Recently, criminal charges have become a real possibility for companies with a long-standing poor safety record. Supervision Illustration 20–1 discusses one such situation.

Workers' compensation is a form of protection for the employee from loss of income and extra expenses associated with work-related injuries. Some form of workers' compensation is available in all 50 states. Although the specific requirements, payments, and procedures vary among states, the features outlined in Figure 20.1 are common to virtually all programs.

Before any workers' compensation claim is recognized, the disability must be shown to be work-related. This usually involves an evaluation of the claimant by an occupational physician. One major criticism of workers' compensation concerns the variation in coverage provided by different states. The amounts paid, the ease of collecting, and the likelihood of collecting vary significantly from state to state. Figure 20.2 summarizes the types of work-related injuries covered by workers' compensation. Since as early as 1955, several states have allowed workers' compensation payments for job-related cases of anxiety, depression, and certain mental disorders.

Health insurance covers such things as normal hospitalization and outpatient doctor bills. Some health insurance plans also cover prescription drugs and dental, eye, and mental health

FIGURE 20.1

Features Common to Most Workers' Compensation Programs

Source: From *Federal Regulations of Personnel and Human Resource Management*, 2nd ed., by J. Ledvinka © 1982, pages 144–45. Reprinted with permission of South-Western College Publishing, a division of Thomson Learning. Fax 800-730-2215.

1. The laws generally provide for replacement of lost income, medical expense payments, rehabilitation of some sort, death benefits to survivors, and lump-sum disability payments.
2. The employee does not have to sue the employer to get compensation; in fact, covered employers are exempt from such lawsuits.
3. The compensation is normally paid through an insurance program financed through premiums paid by employers.
4. Workers' compensation insurance premiums are based on the accident and illness record of the organization. A large number of paid claims results in higher premiums.
5. An element of coinsurance exists in the workers' compensation coverage. Coinsurance is insurance under which the beneficiary of the coverage absorbs part of the loss. In automobile collision coverage, for example, there is often coinsurance in the amount of $100 deductible for each accident. In workers' compensation coverage, there is coinsurance because the workers' loss is usually not fully covered by the insurance program. For example, most states provide for a maximum payment of only two-thirds of the wages lost due to accident or illness.
6. Medical expenses, on the other hand, are usually covered in full under workers' compensation laws.
7. It is a no-fault system; all job-related injuries and illnesses are covered regardless of where the fault for the disability is placed.

care. Most accident insurance provides funds for a limited period of time to the injured party. Usually, the amount of the benefit is some percentage of the victim's wages or salary.

Disability insurance protects the employee during a long-term or permanent disability. Normally, a one- to six-month waiting period is required following the disability before the employee becomes eligible for benefits. Like accident insurance benefits, disability insurance benefits are usually calculated as a percentage of wages or salary. The rates paid by the organization for each of these insurance coverages are almost always a function of the organization's safety and health record. Organizations with a good safety and health record usually pay rates considerably lower than those paid by organizations with a poor record.

Less obvious costs are those associated with employee morale, employee relations, and community relations. It is only natural that employee morale will suffer in an unsafe environment. Employee reactions to a perceived unsafe environment can range from refusal to work to an unconscious slowdown. For example, a manufacturing company had failed for years to effectively guard a flywheel on a particular machine. On the few occasions when it broke, no one was hurt. However, the possibility of being hurt caused the operators to flinch at any suspicious sound. The result was a considerable loss in operator efficiency.[4] If word gets around that a certain organization is unsafe, prospective employees will often shy away from working there. This can result in having to pay higher wages.

FIGURE 20.2

Work-Related Injuries Covered by Workers' Compensation

Source: Reprinted by permission from *Personnel Administration and the Law*, 2nd ed., by Russell L. Greenman and Eric J. Schmertz, pp. 190–91. Copyright © 1979 by The Bureau of National Affairs, Inc., Washington, DC 20037. For BNA publications call toll free 1-800-960-1220.

1. Accidents in which the employee does not lose time from work.
2. Accidents in which the employee loses time from work.
3. Temporary partial disability.
4. Permanent partial or total disability.
5. Death.
6. Occupational diseases.
7. Noncrippling physical impairments such as deafness.
8. Impairments suffered at employer-sanctioned events such as social events or during travel related to organizational business.
9. Injuries or disabilities attributable to an employer's gross negligence.

The morale of a group may be damaged considerably if a member of the group is injured, and the harmony of the group may be impaired by the absence of the injured employee. It is not unusual for a bad safety record to be a major reason for poor employee relations with management. If employees perceive that management is unconcerned about their physical welfare, employee-management relations can deteriorate. In fact, safety is often a primary reason given for unionizing.

The Causes of Accidents

Accidents don't just happen! They are generally the result of a combination of circumstances and events. The circumstances and events causing accidents are usually unsafe personal acts or an unsafe physical environment, or both.

Personal Acts

Most experts believe that unsafe personal acts cause the bulk of workplace accidents. Such acts have been estimated to cause 80 percent of all such accidents. Acts of this kind include taking unnecessary chances, engaging in horseplay, failing to wear or use protective equipment, using improper tools and equipment, taking unsafe shortcuts, operating equipment too fast, and throwing materials.

It is difficult to determine why employees commit unsafe personal acts. There probably is no single reason. A desire to impress others or project a certain image, fatigue, haste, boredom, stress, poor eyesight, daydreaming, and physical limitations are all potential reasons. However, these reasons do not explain why employees intentionally neglect to wear prescribed safety equipment or don't follow procedures. Most employees think of accidents as always happening to someone else. This attitude can easily lead to carelessness or a lack of respect for what can happen. It is also true that some people get a kick out of taking chances and showing off.

An earlier section of this chapter pointed out that a poor safety record can adversely affect employee morale. Research studies have shown that employees with low morale tend to have more accidents than employees with high morale. This is not surprising when one considers that low morale is likely to be related to employee carelessness.

Physical Environment

Accidents can and do happen in all types of environments. They can happen in offices and retail stores, and they can happen in factories and lumberyards. However, they occur most frequently in certain kinds of situations. Listed in order of decreasing frequency, these locations are:

1. *Wherever heavy, awkward material is handled, using hand trucks, forklifts, cranes, and hoists.* About one-third of workplace accidents are caused by handling and lifting material. Improper lifting is also a frequent cause of accidents.

2. *Around any type of machinery that is used to produce something else.* Among the more hazardous are metalworking and woodworking machines, power saws, and machines with exposed gears, belts, chains, and the like. Even a paper cutter or an electric pencil sharpener has a high accident potential.

3. *Wherever people walk or climb, including ladders, scaffolds, and narrow walkways.* Falls are a major source of accidents.

4. *Wherever people use hand tools, including chisels, screwdrivers, pliers, hammers, and axes.* Hand tools also account for a good many household accidents.

5. *Wherever electricity is used other than for usual lighting purposes.* Among the places where electrical accidents occur are near extension cords, loose wiring, and portable hand tools. Outdoor power lines also have a high accident potential.[5]

FIGURE 20.3
Some Specific Safety Hazards

1. Slippery floors
2. Loose tile, linoleum, or carpeting.
3. Small, loose objects left lying on the floor.
4. Bottles, cans, and books on the floor or stacked on top of filing cabinets or windowsills.
5. Sharp burrs on edges of material.
6. Cluttered aisles and stairs.
7. Reading while walking.
8. Power and extension cords.
9. Computer wires and cords.

Unsafe Physical Conditions

Just as there are certain situations in which accidents occur more frequently, certain physical conditions also seem to result in more accidents. Some of these unsafe physical conditions are:

1. Serious understaffing or not having enough people to do the job safely.
2. Unguarded or improperly guarded machines (such as an unguarded belt).
3. Poor housekeeping (such as congested aisles, dirty or wet floors, and improper stacking of materials).
4. Defective equipment and tools.
5. Poor lighting.
6. Poor or improper ventilation.
7. Improper dress (such as clothing with loose and floppy sleeves worn when working on a lathe).

Figure 20.3 lists some specific safety hazards that also frequently result in accidents.

Accident-Proneness

A reason often given for accidents is that certain people are accident-prone. There is little doubt that due to their physical and mental makeup, some employees are more susceptible to accidents than are others. Accident-proneness may result from inborn traits, but it often develops as a result of the individual's environment. However, this tendency should not be used to justify an accident. Employees who appear to be accident-prone should be identified and receive special attention. Given the right set of circumstances, anyone can be accident-prone. For example, a "normal" employee who was up all night with a sick child might very well be accident-prone the next day.

How to Measure Safety

4 LEARNING OBJECTIVES

Frequency and severity are the two most widely accepted measures of an organization's safety record. A **frequency rate** indicates the frequency with which disabling injuries occur. A **severity rate** indicates how severe the accidents were and how long the injured parties were out of work. Only disabling injuries are used in determining frequency and severity rates. **Disabling injuries** are injuries that cause the employee to miss one or more days of work following an accident. Disabling injuries are also known as **lost-time injuries**. Figure 20.4 gives the formulas for calculating the frequency rate and the severity rate.

Neither the frequency rate nor the severity rate means much unless it is compared with similar figures. Useful comparisons can be made with other departments or divisions within the organization, with the rates of the previous years, or with the rates of other organizations. It is through such comparisons that an organization's safety record can be objectively evaluated.

FIGURE 20.4
Formulas for Computing the Accident Frequency Rate and the Accident Severity Rate

$$\text{Frequency rate} = \frac{\text{Number of disabling injuries} \times 1 \text{ million}}{\text{Total number of labor-hours worked each year}}$$

$$\text{Severity rate} = \frac{\text{Days lost* due to injury} \times 1 \text{ million}}{\text{Total number of labor-hours worked each year}}$$

*The American National Standards Institute has developed tables for determining the number of lost days for different types of accidents. To illustrate, an accident resulting in death or permanent total disability is charged with 6,000 days (about 25 working years).

The Safety Program

5   LEARNING OBJECTIVES

The heart of any safety program is accident prevention. It is obviously much better to prevent accidents than to react to them. A major objective of any safety program is to get the employees to "think safety"—to keep safety and accident prevention on their minds. Many approaches are used to make employees more safety conscious. However, four basic elements are present in most successful safety programs.

1. A safety program that has the support of top and middle management. That support must be genuine, not casual. If upper management takes an unenthusiastic approach to safety, employees will be quick to realize it.

2. A safety program that clearly establishes safety as a line organization responsibility. All line managers should consider safety an integral part of their job. Furthermore, operative employees also have a responsibility for working safely.

3. A positive attitude toward safety exists and is maintained throughout the organization. The employees must believe that the safety program is worthwhile and that it produces results.

4. One person is in charge of the safety program and is responsible for its operation. Typically, this is the safety engineer or the safety director, but it may also be a high-level manager or the human resources manager.

Organizational Strategies for Promoting Safety

6   LEARNING OBJECTIVES

Many strategies are available for promoting safety within an organization. Some suggestions are provided below.

Make the Work Interesting

Uninteresting work often leads to boredom, fatigue, and stress, all of which can cause accidents. In many instances, job enrichment (discussed in Chapter 4) can be used to make the work more interesting. Simple changes can often make the work more meaningful to the employee. Job enrichment attempts are usually successful if they add responsibility, challenge, and similar qualities that contribute to the employee's positive inner feelings about the job.

Incorporate Ergonomics

As discussed in the previous chapter, **ergonomics** is the study of the interface between people and the equipment and machines with which they work. Also called human engineering, ergonomics is concerned with improving productivity and safety by designing workplaces, tools, instruments, and so on, that take into account the physical abilities of people.[6] Major objectives of ergonomics are to reduce fatigue and accidents due to human error. Designing comfortable chairs for computer operators and designing scissors that are easier for left-handed people to use are examples of ergonomics (see Supervision

FIGURE 20.5
Typical Safety
Committee Activities

1. Make regular inspections of the work areas.
2. Sponsor accident-prevention contests.
3. Help prepare safety rules.
4. Promote safety awareness.
5. Review safety suggestions from employees.
6. Supervise the preparation and distribution of safety materials.
7. Make fire-prevention inspections.
8. Supervise the maintenance of first-aid equipment.

Illustration 19–2, page 371, for an in-depth example of ergonomics in practice). Thus, whenever possible, supervisors should encourage the use of equipment and facilities that have been ergonomically designed.

Establish a Safety Committee

Include operative employees and representatives of management. The **safety committee** is a way to get employees directly involved in the operation of the safety program. A rotating membership of 5 to 12 members is usually desirable. Normal duties of a safety committee include inspecting, observing work practices, investigating accidents, and making recommendations. Figure 20.5 outlines typical safety committee activities. The safety committee should hold a meeting at least once a month, and attendance should be mandatory.

Feature Employee Safety Contests

Give prizes to the work group or employee having the best safety record for a given period. Contests can also be held to test safety knowledge. Prizes might be awarded periodically to employees who submit good accident-prevention ideas.

Publicize Safety Statistics

Monthly reports of accidents can be posted and/or distributed by e-mail. Solicit ideas on how such accidents could be avoided in the future.

Periodically Hold Safety Training Sessions

Have employees participate in these sessions as role players or instructors. Use such themes as "Get the shock (electric) out of your life." Audiovisual aids such as videos, slides, PowerPoint presentations and simulations might be used. Supervision Illustration 20–2 describes how immersive simulation tools can be helpful for safety training.

Use Bulletin Boards

Make use of bulletin boards throughout the organization. Pictures, sketches, and cartoons can be effective if they are properly used and frequently changed.

Use E-Mail

Make use of e-mail to periodically remind employees of safety issues and to present new safety information.

Reward Employee Participation

Provide some type of reward or recognition for people who are actively and positively involved in the safety program. One possibility is to recognize one employee each month or quarter as "Safety Employee of the Month."

SUPERVISION ILLUSTRATION 20–2

MAKING SAFETY SECOND NATURE

Human beings are naturally creatures of habit. At best, humans' cognitive capacity allows them to focus consciously on only a few things at the same time. The remaining actions happen on a subconscious habitual level. Realizing this, safety-minded companies can make good use of people's natural habit-forming abilities by building effective learning practices into their safety program.

With an estimated $170 billion annually in direct and indirect costs related to industrial safety problems, game-based immersive simulation tools are emerging to bridge the gap between the workplace and conventional classroom, as well as between video and online safety training. By using immersive simulation tools, employees can practice safe job performance with a safety net. A hallmark of an effective safety training tool is user engagement where employees are active participants in the learning process. With an effective immersive simulation, employees act out step-by-step scenarios and, most importantly, experience the positive or negative results of those actions. This interaction requires significantly more cognitive involvement than other forms of training and, over time, helps ingrain good safety habits.

Source: Jessica Trybus, "Making Safety Second Nature," *Professional Safety,* December 2008, pp. 54–55.

How the Supervisor Can Prevent Accidents

7 LEARNING OBJECTIVES

Because supervisors are the link between management and the operative employees, they are in the best position to promote safety. As previously discussed, the supervisor's attitude toward safety often sets the tone for how employees view safety. In addition to fostering a healthy attitude toward safety, the supervisor can do several specific things to prevent accidents:

1. Be familiar with organizational policies that relate to safety. Make sure that the appropriate policies are conveyed to employees.

2. Be familiar with the proper procedures for safely accomplishing the work. See that each employee knows the proper method for doing the job (this is applicable to long-term employees as well as to new hires).

3. Know what safety devices and personal protective equipment should be used on each job. Ensure that the respective jobholders use the proper safety devices and wear the proper protective equipment.

4. Know what safety-related reports and records are required (such as accident reports and investigation reports). Be sure that these reports are completed and processed on a timely basis.

5. Get to know the employees. Learn to identify both the permanently and the temporarily accident-prone employees. Once these employees have been identified, be sure that they receive proper safety training.

6. Know when and where to make safety inspections. It is generally wise to develop a schedule for making safety inspections. This ensures that they won't be neglected.

7. Learn to take the advice of the safety director and the safety committee. Look at both of these groups as resources. Learn to work closely with these resources.

8. Know what to do in case of an accident. Be familiar with basic first aid. Know how to contact the doctor, emergency services, and the hospital.

9. Know the proper procedures for investigating an accident and determining how it could have been prevented. Know the proper procedures to follow during an investigation.

10. Always set a good example with regard to safety. Remember, employees are always watching the supervisor.

Figure 20.6 summarizes the accident process and the supervisor's role in that process.

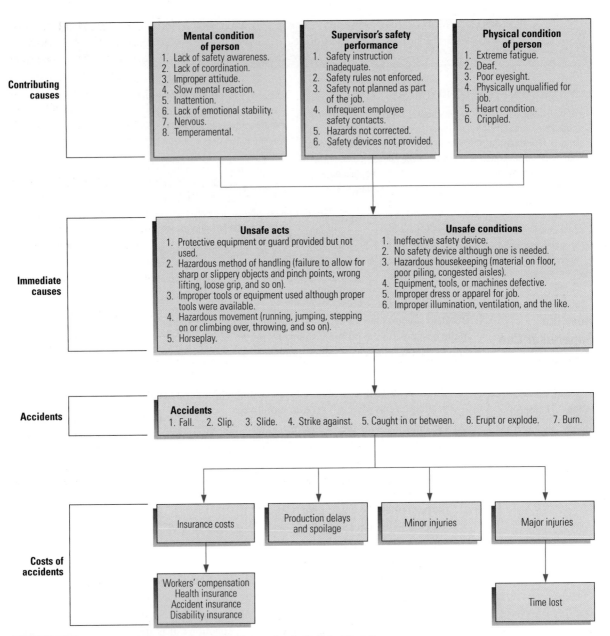

Contributing causes

Mental condition of person
1. Lack of safety awareness.
2. Lack of coordination.
3. Improper attitude.
4. Slow mental reaction.
5. Inattention.
6. Lack of emotional stability.
7. Nervous.
8. Temperamental.

Supervisor's safety performance
1. Safety instruction inadequate.
2. Safety rules not enforced.
3. Safety not planned as part of the job.
4. Infrequent employee safety contacts.
5. Hazards not corrected.
6. Safety devices not provided.

Physical condition of person
1. Extreme fatigue.
2. Deaf.
3. Poor eyesight.
4. Physically unqualified for job.
5. Heart condition.
6. Crippled.

Immediate causes

Unsafe acts
1. Protective equipment or guard provided but not used.
2. Hazardous method of handling (failure to allow for sharp or slippery objects and pinch points, wrong lifting, loose grip, and so on).
3. Improper tools or equipment used although proper tools were available.
4. Hazardous movement (running, jumping, stepping on or climbing over, throwing, and so on).
5. Horseplay.

Unsafe conditions
1. Ineffective safety device.
2. No safety device although one is needed.
3. Hazardous housekeeping (material on floor, poor piling, congested aisles).
4. Equipment, tools, or machines defective.
5. Improper dress or apparel for job.
6. Improper illumination, ventilation, and the like.

Accidents

Accidents
1. Fall. 2. Slip. 3. Slide. 4. Strike against. 5. Caught in or between. 6. Erupt or explode. 7. Burn.

Costs of accidents

Insurance costs

Production delays and spoilage

Minor injuries

Major injuries

Workers' compensation
Health insurance
Accident insurance
Disability insurance

Time lost

FIGURE 20.6 **The Accident Process and the Supervisor's Role in That Process**

Source: Robert W. Eckles, Ronald L. Carmichael, and Bernard R. Sarchet, *Essentials of Management for First-Line Supervisors* (New York: John Wiley & Sons, Inc., 1974), p. 560. © 1974 John Wiley & Sons, Inc. Reprinted by permission of John Wiley & Sons, Inc.

Violence in the Workplace

8 LEARNING OBJECTIVES

Historically, safety prevention has focused on the prevention of accidents in the workplace. Recently, however, violence in the workplace has become an increasing concern. Consider the following: The National Institute for Occupational Safety and Health estimates that, in an average week, 20 workers are murdered and another 18,000 are assaulted at U.S. work-places; homicide is the second leading cause of death on the job, second only to motor vehicle crashes; approximately five percent of all private U.S. businesses experience some form of workplace violence every year.[7] Also, since the events of September 11, 2001, the threat of terrorism in the workplace has become a reality. Recognizing there is no way to guarantee that an organization will not be victimized, a violence-prevention program can greatly reduce the probabilities of a problem. While most violence-prevention programs contain many elements, the following suggestions are things that organizations can do to deter workplace violence:[8]

- *Hire carefully, but realistically.* Screen out potential employees whose histories show a propensity to violence. A full background check can be done in many states for $100 or less.
- *Draw up a plan and involve employees in it.* Develop a plan for preventing violence and for dealing with it if it does occur. Reporting requirements for both violence and threats of violence should be an integral part of the plan. The plan should also be shaped by employee participation.
- *As part of the plan, adopt a "zero tolerance" policy.* "Zero tolerance" does not necessarily mean dismissal; but rather, it means the perpetrator of the violence will face consequences of some kind. When discipline is called for, its purpose should be to teach, not to punish.
- *Enlist the aid of professionals—with an eye on the cost.* Go to external resources when necessary to get help as a problem or a potential problem reveals itself. A few hours with a psychologist or a legal professional can defuse a simmering situation. It might even be necessary to hire a security firm temporarily in some instances.

As is often the case, supervisors always play a key role in making a program successful. All too frequently supervisors and other employees ignore the signs of a potentially violent situation. The tendency is often to do nothing and assume nothing will happen. Because most violent acts are not spontaneous, supervisors must learn to identify potentially violent situations. Specifically, supervisors should learn to spot the following warning signs:

- Employees making threats or being threatened.
- Employees who are suddenly terminated or anticipate being laid off.
- Employees with serious problems at home.
- Employees with a chemical dependency.
- Employees showing signs of paranoia.
- Employees fascinated by weapons.
- Employees who get into fights and/or demonstrate open conflict.
- Employees who demonstrate a loner mentality.
- Employees who make fatalistic statements.

Supervisors should also learn the proper organizational procedures for reporting and dealing with these different types of potentially violent situations.

Occupational Safety and Health Act (OSHA)

9   LEARNING OBJECTIVES

In 1970, Congress passed the Occupational Safety and Health Act (OSHA), which became effective on April 28, 1971. Its original stated purpose was "to assure so far as possible every working man and woman in the nation safe and healthful working conditions and to preserve our human resources."

The Occupational Safety and Health Administration of the U.S. Department of Labor enforces OSHA, which covers nearly all businesses with one or more employees. (There are certain exceptions, such as businesses employing only family members.) Figure 20.7 shows a government poster explaining the basics of OSHA. Under OSHA, the Occupational Safety and Health Administration does the following:

- Encourages employers and employees to reduce workplace hazards and to implement new safety and health management systems or improve existing programs.
- Develops mandatory job safety and health standards and enforces them through work-site inspections, and, sometimes, by imposing citations, penalties, or both.
- Promotes safe and healthful work environments through cooperative programs including the Voluntary Protection Programs, OSHA Strategic Partnerships, and Alliances.
- Establishes responsibilities and rights for employers and employees to achieve better safety and health conditions.
- Supports the development of innovative ways of dealing with workplace hazards.
- Establishes requirements for injury and illness recordkeeping by employers, and for employer monitoring of certain occupational illnesses.
- Establishes training programs to increase the competence of occupational safety and health personnel.
- Provides technical and compliance assistance, and training and education to help employers reduce worker accidents and injuries.
- Works in partnership with states that operate their own occupational safety and health programs.
- Supports the Consultation Programs offered by all 50 states, the District of Columbia, Puerto Rico, the Virgin Islands, Guam and the Northern Mariana Islands.[9]

Few laws have evoked as much initial negative reaction as OSHA. While few people would question the intent of OSHA, many have criticized the manner in which it has been implemented. The sheer volume of regulations has been staggering. Many have also criticized the vague wording of many OSHA regulations. For example, the Occupational Safety and Health Administration developed the following 39-word single-sentence definition of the word *exit:*

> That portion of a means of egress which is separated from all other spaces of the building or structure by construction or equipment as required in this subject to provide a protected way of travel to the exit discharge.[10]

In addition, many OSHA regulations have been criticized as excessively petty. For example, one regulation states: "Where working clothes are provided by the employer and become wet or are washed between shifts, provision shall be made to ensure that such clothing is dry before reuse."

Because of definitions and regulations similar to the above examples, many organizations developed a negative attitude toward OSHA. As a result, legislation was enacted to soften some OSHA requirements. Also, many of the original OSHA standards have been subsequently revoked by the Occupational Safety and Health Administration itself.

It should be emphasized that OSHA has been effective in making the workplace a safer environment. Since 1970, when OSHA was established, occupational fatality rates have been cut by more than 60 percent and the number of cases of occupational injuries has fallen by 40 percent.[11] While OSHA cannot claim all the credit for these impressive

FIGURE 20.7   **Basic Requirements of OSHA**

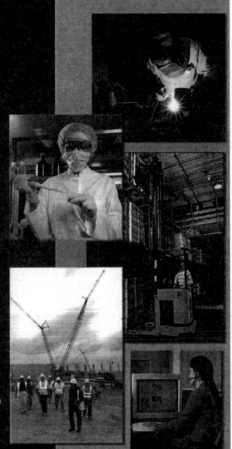

Job Safety and Health

It's the law!

OSHA

**Occupational Safety
and Health Administration
U.S. Department of Labor**

EMPLOYEES:

- You have the right to notify your employer or OSHA about workplace hazards. You may ask OSHA to keep your name confidential.

- You have the right to request an OSHA inspection if you believe that there are unsafe and unhealthful conditions in your workplace. You or your representative may participate in that inspection.

- You can file a complaint with OSHA within 30 days of retaliation or discrimination by your employer for making safety and health complaints or for exercising your rights under the *OSH Act*.
- You have the right to see OSHA citations issued to your employer. Your employer must post the citations at or near the place of the alleged violations.

- Your employer must correct workplace hazards by the date indicated on the citation and must certify that these hazards have been reduced or eliminated.

- You have the right to copies of your medical records and records of your exposures to toxic and harmful substances or conditions.

- Your employer must post this notice in your workplace.

- You must comply with all occupational safety and health standards issued under the *OSH Act* that apply to your own actions and conduct on the job.

EMPLOYERS:

- You must furnish your employees a place of employment free from recognized hazards.

- You must comply with the occupational safety and health standards issued under the *OSH Act*.

This free poster available from OSHA –
The Best Resource for Safety and Health

Free assistance in identifying and correcting hazards or complying with standards is available to employers, without citation or penalty, through OSHA-supported consultation programs in each state.

1-800-321-OSHA
www.osha.gov

OSHA 3165-12-06R

SUPERVISION ILLUSTRATION 20-3

BEYOND NORMAL OSHA STANDARDS

Even though its six U.S. manufacturing plants are receiving accolades for safety and health standards, L'Oreal USA is not satisfied. "When it comes to safety, there is no finish line," says Eric Fox, assistant vice president of plant management in Florence, Kentucky. "You're not satisfied until you're at zero (hazards) forever."

No one can say L'Oreal isn't trying to achieve that goal. Since 1995, all of L'Oreal's six U.S. plants have been recognized for implementing safety and health procedures through the Occupational Safety and Health Administration's Voluntary Protection Program (VPP).

Created in 1982, VPP partners with businesses that show a commitment to effective employee protection beyond the requirements of OSHA standards. VPP participants develop and implement systems to identify, evaluate, prevent, and control workplace hazards to prevent employee injuries and illnesses. L'Oreal USA already had been maintaining health and safety guidelines under an internal plan called Safety Hazard Assessment Process (SHAP). While SHAP worked well, L'Oreal USA was looking for even more and, hence, implemented VPP. L'Oreal USA's participation in VPP has helped the company reduce its rates of lost-time and restricted duty accidents by over 70 percent over the past six years. L'Oreal USA credits employee involvement with much of the success of its safety programs.

Source: David Brandt, "L'Oreal Factories Play it Safe," *Industrial Engineer,* July 2007, pp. 50–51.

reductions, it has certainly had a major positive impact. Supervision Illustration 20–3 discusses how some companies voluntarily go beyond regular OSHA standards to insure a safe working environment.

The Supervisor and OSHA

It should be pointed out that individual states are encouraged to develop and operate their own job safety and health plans. State plans are OSHA-approved job safety and health programs operated by individual states instead of Federal OSHA. Currently 22 states and territories operate complete plans and four operate plans that cover only the public sector.

Under OSHA, employers of 11 or more persons must maintain records of occupational injuries and illnesses as they occur. Businesses classified in a specific low-hazard retail, service, finance, insurance or real estate industry do not normally have to keep injury and illness records. Employers are required to record work-related injuries or illnesses if they result in one of the following: death; days away from work; restricted work or transfer to another job; medical treatment beyond first aid; loss of consciousness; or diagnosis of a significant injury/illness by a physician or other licensed health care professional. Much of this record-keeping responsibility falls directly on the supervisor.

Many OSHA standards have special record-keeping and reporting requirements, but all employers covered by the act must maintain certain forms. Originally, OSHA required that Form 200, Log and Summary of Occupational Injuries and Illnesses, be maintained. This form required that each occupational injury and illness be recorded within six working days from the time the employer learned of the accident or illness. As of January 2002, three new record-keeping forms were required: OSHA Form 300, Log of Work-Related Injuries and Illnesses; OSHA Form 300A, Summary of Work-Related Injuries and Illnesses; and OSHA Form 301, Injury and Illness Incident Report. Forms 300 and 300A replace Form 200. Form 301 replaces Form 201. All three forms are maintained on a calendar-year basis. These forms must be retained for five years by the organization and must be available for inspection. Form 300A must be posted each year from February 1 to April 30.

SUPERVISION ILLUSTRATION 20-4

OSHA LOSES AN HCS APPEAL

A food processing facility that produces frozen meat products uses dry ice in its freezing process. When the dry ice melts, it gives off CO_2 gas, which can cause headaches, nausea, vomiting and even asphyxiation. Following an asphyxiation fatality at the plant, federal OSHA conducted an investigation and cited the employer for several violations of the Hazard Communications Standard (HCS). One citation alleged that the employer violated one standard which required employers to "provide employees with effective information and training on hazardous chemicals in their work area at the time of their initial assignment, and whenever a new physical or health hazard the employees have not previously been trained about is introduced into their work area." "Information and training may be designed to cover categories of hazards (e.g. flammability, carcinogenicity) or specific chemicals. Chemical specific information must always be available through labels and material safety data sheets."

The employer appealed the citation, arguing that it had complied with the applicable standard when it provided hazard category-based (as opposed to chemical-based) training to its employees. The Occupational Safety and Health Review Commission (OSHRC) unanimously rejected OSHA's contention and concluded that "an employer complies with the HazCom standard's requirements by informing employees of the dangers posed by chemicals falling into the relevant 'categories of hazards', identifying their location in the plant or the process in which they are used and training employees on those hazard categories." This was a landmark decision by OSHRC because it invalidated and reversed OSHA's longstanding enforcement policy and affirmed instead the language of the standard itself.

Source: "Does Training Have to be Chemical Specific?", *Safety Compliance Letter,* August 2007, p. 8.

Supervisors are often asked to accompany OSHA officials while these officials inspect an organization's physical facilities. Because many organizations and supervisors feel threatened by OSHA officials, they may tend to behave antagonistically to these officials. However, it is in the best interests of the supervisor and the host organization for the supervisor to cooperate with visiting OSHA officials. An uncooperative supervisor could cause these officials to be more hard-nosed than usual. The end result could be stiffer penalties than would have been imposed otherwise.

Supervisors should be familiar with the OSHA regulations affecting their departments. They should constantly be on the lookout for safety violations. As previously discussed, it is the supervisor's responsibility to see that the employees follow all safety rules. Naturally, these include all OSHA rules and regulations.

Hazard Communications Standard

 **10** LEARNING OBJECTIVES

Over 30 million U.S. employees are potentially exposed to one or more chemical hazards in the workplace. To further emphasize the size of the potential problem, consider the fact that OSHA issued over 7,000 citations for violations of the Hazard Communications Standard in fiscal year 2003.[12] These violations cost U.S. businesses over $1.3 million in fines alone. Because of the threats posed by chemicals in the workplace, OSHA has established a Hazard Communications Standard. This standard is also known as the "right to know" rule. The basic purpose of the rule is to ensure that employers and employees know what chemical hazards exist in the workplace and how to protect themselves against those hazards. The goal of the rule is to reduce the incidence of illness and injuries caused by chemicals.

The **Hazard Communications Standard (HCS)** establishes uniform requirements to ensure that the hazards of all chemicals imported into, produced at, or used in the workplace are evaluated and that the results of these evaluations are transmitted to affected employers and exposed employees. Basically the HCS includes three requirements: hazard determination,

Jane's impromptu talks with her employees have had little effect on reducing accidents. She should attempt to implement a safety program in her department. Such a program has the best chance for success if it has the enthusiastic support of top and middle management. Jane could assume the responsibility for implementing the program, or she could assign the responsibility to one of her subordinates; the important thing is that somebody must be responsible for the program (p. 395). Whoever is charged with responsibility for the safety program should remember that the main purpose of any safety program is to get the employees to "think safety." The safety program might incorporate such things as the establishment of a safety committee, a safety contest, the posting of safety statistics, and periodic safety meetings (pp. 395–396). Every effort should be made to seek and encourage employee input and participation in the program.

hazard communication, and employee training. The responsibility for identifying hazards posed by a specific chemical rests with the manufacturer of the product or the importer that brings it into the United States if it is manufactured abroad. Employers using these chemicals, however, are responsible for meeting hazard communications requirements and for training employees on the proper procedures for dealing with the chemicals.

The HCS specifically requires that employers maintain complete and updated Material Safety Data Sheets (MSDSs). MSDSs provide information on the nature of hazards, including appropriate handling and remedies for unexpected exposure. Employers, manufacturers, or importers of the hazardous material may prepare MSDSs. Many employers now maintain MSDSs electronically, which makes it much easier to keep them current.

OSHA has developed a variety of materials to help employers and employees implement effective hazard communication programs. Supervisors play a role in these programs. In its 25 years of existence, there is little doubt that the HCS has greatly increased the amount of information available on chemicals in the workplace. Supervision Illustration 20–4 discusses an interesting case involving HCS and OSHA.

Summary

This chapter is designed to heighten a supervisor's awareness of the costs of workplace accidents and illnesses and to suggest things that can be done to reduce the occurrence of such accidents and illnesses. The chapter also discusses the Occupational Safety and Health Act (OSHA).

1. *Discuss the supervisor's responsibility for safety.* Supervisors' primary responsibility toward safety is to establish an environment where safety is emphasized. Supervisors also have responsibilities to listen to employee complaints and suggestions, work closely with the safety engineer or director (if there is one), work closely with the safety committee (if there is one), and provide safety instruction. In addition to these general responsibilities, supervisors may be responsible for such things as accident investigations, first aid, maintenance of proper safety records, and the dissemination of changes in safety regulations and methods.

2. *Appreciate the costs associated with work-related accidents and illnesses.* The costs associated with workplace accidents and illnesses are many and varied, but they can usually be classified into three major categories: (1) costs directly related to lost production, (2) insurance and medical costs, and (3) costs resulting from the negative effects of workplace accidents and illnesses on employee morale, employee relations, and community relations. It should also be pointed out that criminal charges have recently become a possibility for companies with a long-standing poor safety record.

3. *Discuss the major causes of work-related accidents.* The circumstances and events causing accidents are usually unsafe personal acts or an unsafe physical environment, or both.

4. *Measure safety in the workplace.* Frequency and severity are the two most widely accepted measures of an organization's safety record. A frequency rate indicates the frequency

with which disabling injuries occur. A severity rate indicates how severe the accidents were and how long the injured parties were out of work.

5. *Explain the basic purposes of a safety program.* The basic purpose of any safety program is to prevent accidents. Since getting employees to "think safety" is one of the more effective ways to prevent accidents, this is a major objective of most safety programs.

6. *Outline several organizational strategies for promoting safety.* Many strategies are available for promoting safety within an organization. These include making the work interesting, incorporating ergonomics, establishing a safety committee, featuring employee safety contests, publicizing safety statistics, periodically holding safety training sessions, using bulletin boards, and rewarding employee participation.

7. *Outline several things that the supervisor can do to prevent accidents.* In addition to fostering a healthy attitude toward safety, the supervisor can do these things to prevent accidents: Make the work interesting; be familiar with organizational policies that relate to safety; be familiar with the proper procedures for safely accomplishing the work; know what safety devices and personal protective equipment should be used; know what safety-related reports and records are required; know the employees; know when and where to make safety inspections; learn to take the advice of the safety director and the safety committee; know what to do in case of an accident; know the proper procedures for investigating an accident and determining how it could have been prevented; and always set a good example with regard to safety.

8. *Identify several warning signs that can help supervisors learn to recognize potentially violent employees.* Supervisors should learn to recognize the following warning signs of potentially violent employees: employees making threats or being threatened, employees who are suddenly terminated or anticipate being laid off, employees with serious problems at home, employees with a chemical dependency, employees showing signs of paranoia, or employees fascinated by weapons.

9. *Understand the purpose of the Occupational Safety and Health Act (OSHA).* The stated purpose of OSHA is to assure so far as possible every working man and woman in the nation safe and healthful working conditions and to preserve our human resources.

10. *Explain the basic purpose of the Hazard Communications Standard.* The basic purpose of the Hazard Communications Standard is to ensure that employers and employees know what chemical hazards exist in the workplace and how to protect themselves against those hazards.

Key Terms

Disability insurance, 392
Disabling injuries, 394
Ergonomics, 395
Frequency rate, 394
Hazard Communications Standard (HCS), 403

Health insurance, 391
Lost-time injuries, 394
Occupational Safety and Health Act (OSHA), 399
Safety committee, 396
Severity rate, 394

Workers' compensation, 391
Workplace violence, 398

Review Questions

1. Name three major categories of accident costs to the organization.

2. What are the differences between workers' compensation and disability insurance?

3. What are the major causes of accidents? Which cause accounts for the majority of work-related accidents?

4. Name several unsafe physical conditions that frequently cause accidents.

5. What is accident-proneness?

6. What are the most widely accepted methods for measuring an organization's safety record?

7. List several things that a supervisor can do to promote safety.

8. State several specific things that a supervisor can do to prevent accidents.

9. What is the stated purpose of OSHA?

10. What does OSHA specifically require of the supervisor?

11. What are Material Safety Data Sheets (MSDSs)?

Skill-Building Questions

1. How would you answer this question: "How can I improve safety in my department since I don't have the authority to significantly alter the physical environment?"

2. Susan Baker has just been appointed the Que Company's director of safety, a newly created job. What are some of the more important safety thoughts that she should keep in mind?

3. Suppose many of your employees circumvent the safety regulations whenever possible because they feel that these regulations slow them down unnecessarily and keep them from making more money. What might you do in this situation?

4. Do you think that the overall benefit of OSHA has been positive or negative? Support your answer.

References

1. "Report on Injuries in America," Highlights from *Injury Facts, 2009 edition,* http://www.nsc.org/lrs/injuriesinamerica.08.aspx. Accessed on April 15, 2009.

2. Ibid.

3. Ibid.

4. Rollin H. Simonds and John V. Grimaldi, *Safety Management,* rev. ed. (Homewood, IL: Richard D. Irwin, 1963), p. 30.

5. Gary Dressler, *Personnel Management: Modern Concepts and Techniques,* 3rd ed., 1984, p. 627. Reprinted with permission of Reston Publishing Company, a Prentice Hall Company, 11480 Sunset Hills Road, Reston, VA 22090.

6. James R. Evans, *Production/Operations Management: Quality, Performance, and Value,* 5th ed. (Minneapolis: West Publishing, 1997), p. 405.

7. "Understanding and Preventing Violence in the Workplace," *Safety Now,* March 2009, pp. 1–3 and Evan Goodenow, "Violence at Work Takes Worker Toll: Violent Crime Has Occurred at 5.3% of Private Companies, Survey Says," *McClatchy— Tribune Business News,* February 2, 2009.

8. Michael Barrier, "The Enemy Within," *Nation's Business,* February 1995, pp. 18–21.

9. *All About OSHA* (Washington, DC: U.S. Department of Labor, 2006), pp. 5–6.

10. *Code of Federal Regulations* (Washington, DC: U.S. Government Printing Office, 1988), p. 126.

11. *All About OSHA* (Washington, DC: U.S. Department of Labor, 2006), p. 4.

12. Jacki Burns and Michael Beckel, "Saving Cash with Compliance," *Occupational Health and Safety,* September 2001, pp. 180–82.

Additional Readings

Bingham, Michael E., "Safety Dummies," *Occupational Health and Safety,* January 2009, p. 49.

Hoek, Christine, "Influx of Summer Workers Makes Now Ideal Time to Review Workplace Safety," *Supervision,* August 2006, pp. 9–10.

Jusko, Jill, "Partner in Accident Prevention," *Industry Week,* June 2004, p. 91.

Kalbaugh, Michael, "5 Steps to a World-Class Safety System," *Occupational Health and Safety,* September 2004, pp. 184–187.

Sinovic, Steve, "Workplace Violence on Minds of Employers," *McClatchy—Tribune Business News,* March 27, 2009.

SKILL-BUILDING APPLICATIONS

Incident 20–1

The Safety Inspection

Because of the risks associated with handling dangerous chemicals, Judith Armanetti was confident that her company would be inspected by the Occupational Safety and Health Administration in the near future. Judith's company, Star Compound and Chemical, processes and packages all types of industrial cleaning compounds and chemicals.

Judith decided to call a meeting of all her supervisors as the first step in preparing for the anticipated OSHA inspection. During the meeting, Judith stressed the importance of safety and the potential costs to the company if Star received a bad OSHA report. Judith handed out a new *OSHA General Standards Manual* (OSHA 2206) to the supervisors and announced that she was going to conduct a surprise mock OSHA inspection in about four weeks.

Joe Brooks is supervisor of the mixing department. His department is responsible for mixing all of Star's liquid compounds and chemicals. Joe, a conscientious supervisor, is committed to seeing that his department is completely up to OSHA standards. Shortly after the meeting with Judith, Joe outlined a three-week program for eliminating safety hazards. Among the actions taken were painting yellow lines to clearly mark the aisles, cleaning the filters on all the exhaust fans, ensuring that all chemicals were stored in their proper places, checking the groundings on all the electrical mixing motors, installing additional lights in the storage areas, and adding rails around the mixing drums.

By the end of three weeks, Joe felt ready for the inspection. In fact, he welcomed the opportunity to show Judith what had been done. Judith appeared for the inspection about a week later. The inspection was going great until the last few mixing drums were reached. No employee in this area was wearing the required safety glasses, two employees were seen smoking in an unauthorized part of the area, and several employees were not wearing the required protective gowns. Joe couldn't believe his eyes! After all of the work that had been done to eliminate safety hazards, his employees were demonstrating almost no concern for the safety rules. Joe was naturally embarrassed.

As soon as Judith left, Joe went over and asked the employees why they had violated the safety rules. The explanations were basically all the same: the safety glasses, gloves, gowns, and so forth, were bulky, and it was much easier to work without them.

Questions

1. Do you think that Joe's problem is unique?
2. Why do you think that employees are often lax with regard to safety rules that have been established for their own safety?
3. What would you do if you were Joe?

Incident 20–2

No One Listens

Several severe accidents have recently occurred in the 12-employee boiler room of City Hospital. Jackson Ward, the boiler room supervisor, is quite upset about the situation. Just yesterday, the hospital administrator called:

Administrator: Jackson, what in the world is going on down there? Are you trying to fill all of our empty beds with your employees?

Jackson: If I've lectured these people about safety once, I've done it 50 times. They just don't seem to listen.

Administrator: Accidents cost us money for repairs, lost time, and medical expenses, not to mention the human suffering involved. Your department's record is awful, and something must be done about it! Maybe you should try something new.

Jackson: I'm not sure what it will be, but I'll come up with something.

Administrator: Good. Please report back to me when you come up with something.

Jackson decided to discuss his problem with several other supervisors in the hospital to see what ideas they might have. One suggestion was that Jackson schedule a weekly 10-minute safety talk by one of his employees. These talks could be on such topics as "Good

Housekeeping," "Using Proper Safety Guards on Equipment," "Following Procedures," and "Health Hazards." Another suggestion was that Jackson review his department periodically and that any unsafe act discovered during his review be punished by an immediate two-day suspension for the offender. The person making this suggestion obviously believed that what Jackson needed was to get tough. A third suggestion was that Jackson talk personally to each employee about the department's safety problems and let the employees know that he was personally interested in each of them. A final suggestion was that Jackson give the employee with the best safety record for the past four months a day off with pay.

Questions

1. Why do you think Jackson has been having safety problems?
2. Which of the suggestions given to Jackson would you attempt to implement?
3. What additional ideas might you try if you were Jackson?

Exercise 20–1

Potential Safety Problems

In groups of three to five students, examine the building in which your class is held and its immediate surrounding areas for potential safety problems and hazards. Pay special attention to the items listed in Figure 20.3 (page 394). For each potential hazard identified, address the following questions:

1. How long do you suspect the hazard has existed?
2. How would you correct the problem or remove the hazard?

3. Why do you think each of the identified problems or hazards has not been addressed?

Also identify any specific steps that appear to have been taken to make the building and its immediate area more safe.

Be prepared to report your findings to the class.

Exercise 20–2

National Safety

Almost everyone has an opinion about the Occupational Safety and Health Act (OSHA). Your opinion may be based on firsthand experience, on what others have told you, or on what you have read. The arguments in favor of OSHA center on the belief that most organizations, when left to their own volition, will not take adequate employee safety and health measures and that OSHA has in fact had a positive impact in reducing occupational injuries and illness. The arguments against OSHA include the belief that it has cost the country a large number of jobs (by causing certain companies to close down rather than comply with expensive OSHA rules), that it is an infringement on personal freedoms, and that it is being implemented by another poorly administered government bureaucracy.

1. All things considered, what is your opinion of OSHA? Without doing any additional research, prepare an outline of the points that you would use to support your position.
2. The instructor will divide the class into two teams. One team will take a pro position regarding OSHA and one will take a con position. Each team will be given equal time to prepare arguments supporting its position. The instructor may ask each team to orally present its arguments.

A

ability   A person's capability.

achievement-power-affiliation approach   This approach holds that all people have three needs: (1) a need for achievement, (2) a need for power, and (3) a need for affiliation.

action planning   The phase of the planning process after the objective has been set, in which the supervisor must decide how the objective can be achieved.

active listening   Absorbing what another person is saying and responding to the person's concerns.

activity   The work necessary to complete a particular event (usually consuming time).

administrative skills   Knowledge about the organization and how it works—the planning, organizing, and controlling functions of supervision.

affirmative action   Refers to an employer's attempt to balance its workforce in all job categories with respect to sex and race in order to reflect the same proportions as those of its general labor market in response to government requirements.

AFL-CIO   American Federation of Labor–Congress of Industrial Organizations; a federation of local, national, and international unions that represent a majority of all union members in the United States.

Age Discrimination in Employment Act of 1968   Prohibits discrimination against individuals over 40 years of age.

agency shop   A type of union requiring employees who are not members of that union to pay a fee instead of union dues.

alternation ranking   Method in which a supervisor's employees are listed down the left side of a sheet of paper. The supervisor then chooses the most valuable employee, crosses this name off the list, and places it at the top of the column on the right side. The supervisor then selects and crosses off the name of the least valuable employee and places it at the bottom of the right-hand column. The supervisor then repeats this process for all the names on the left side. The listing of names on the right side gives the supervisor a ranking of his or her employees from most valuable to least valuable.

Americans with Disabilities Act (ADA)   Gives the disabled sharply increased access to services and jobs.

analytical report   A report that interprets the facts it presents.

apprenticeship training   Supervised training and testing for a minimum time period and until a minimum skill level has been reached.

aptitude tests   Measure a person's capacity or potential ability to learn and perform a job.

arbitration   A process by which both the union and management agree to abide by the decision of an outside party regarding a grievance.

authority   The right to issue directives and expend resources.

autocratic leader   Leader who centralizes power and enjoys giving orders. Followers contribute little to the decision-making process.

avoidance   Giving a person the opportunity to avoid a negative consequence by exhibiting a desired behavior. Also called *negative reinforcement.*

B

balanced scorecard (BSC)   A relatively new performance measurement system, through which organizations define strategic objectives at every level in the organization, combining financial results with measurements of tasks that an organization must perform well to meet its objectives at all levels within an organization.

brainstorming   Presenting a problem and then allowing the group to develop ideas for solutions.

brainwriting   Group members are presented with a problem situation and then asked to jot down their ideas on paper without any discussion.

budget   A statement of expected results or requirements expressed in financial or numerical terms.

burnout   A potential result of excessive job-related stress over a long period of time.

C

career counseling   Supervisory assistance to the employee in evaluating his or her options regarding career development.

centralization and decentralization These refer to the degree of authority delegated by top management.

central tendency The rating of all or most employees in the middle of the scale.

chain of command The principle that authority flows one link at a time from the top of the organization to the bottom.

changes internal to the organization Changes that result from decisions made by the organization's management.

checklist A performance appraisal method in which the supervisor does not actually evaluate, but merely records performance.

Civil Rights Act of 1991 Designed to reverse several Supreme Court decisions of 1989 and 1990 which had been viewed as limiting equal employment and affirmative action opportunity.

classroom training The most familiar type of training, which involves lectures, movies, and exercises.

closed shops Require that a person be a member of the union before he or she could be hired by an employer.

code of ethics A written statement of principles to be followed in the conduct of business.

collective bargaining Process by which a contract or an agreement is negotiated, written, administered, and interpreted.

communication The process by which information is transferred from one source to another and is made meaningful to the involved sources.

compensation Composed of the extrinsic rewards offered by the organization and consists of the base wage or salary, any incentives or bonuses, and any benefits employees receive in exchange for their work.

compressed workweek Number of hours worked per day is increased and the number of days in the workweek is decreased.

computer-assisted instruction (CAI) A computer displays the material and processes the student's answers.

concurrent control Method for exercising control, also called screening control, that focuses on things that happen as inputs are being transformed into outputs.

conciliator A neutral person to help resolve the disputed issues during the bargaining process for a contract.

conflict A condition that results when one party feels that some concern of that party has been frustrated or is about to be frustrated by a second party.

conflict aftermath After the conflict is stopped, new conditions are established, which either lead to a new conflict or to more effective cooperation between the involved parties.

contingency plan A plan made for what to do if something goes wrong.

continuous improvement Refers to an ongoing effort to make improvements in every part of the organization relative to all of its products and services.

control/controlling Comparing actual performance with predetermined standards or objectives and then taking action to correct any deviations from the standard.

corporate culture The overreaching tone and methods proscribing how to do things in a particular company.

creativity Thinking process involved in producing an idea or concept that is new, original, useful, or satisfying to its creator or to someone else.

critical-incident appraisals The supervisor keeps a written record of unusual incidents that show both positive and negative actions by an employee.

cross-training An employee learns several jobs and performs each job for a specific length of time. Also called *job rotation*.

D

decision making The process of choosing from among various alternatives.

decision-making skills The ability to analyze information and objectively reach a decision by choosing among various alternatives.

delegation Refers to the assigning of authority.

democratic leader Leader who wants the followers to share in making decisions, although the leader has the final say.

departmentalization The grouping of activities into related work units.

departmentalization by customer Occurs when a company might have one department for retail customers and one for wholesale or industrial customers.

departmentalization by process or equipment Occurs when organizational units are defined by the specific process of types of equipment being used.

departmentalization by product or service All the activities necessary to produce or market a product or service under a single manager.

departmentalization by time or shift May be used by organizations that work more than one shift.

dependent demand items Typically subassemblies or component parts that will be used in making finished products.

direction How well the person understands what is expected on the job.

directive counseling The supervisor takes the initiative and asks the employee pointed questions about a problem. When the supervisor feels that he or she has a good grasp of what is causing the problem, the supervisor suggests several steps that the employee might take to overcome it.

directive leaders Leaders who focus primarily on successfully performing the work.

direct labor costs Expenditures for labor that is directly applied in the creation or delivery of the product or service.

disability insurance Insurance that protects the employee during a long-term or permanent disability.

disabling injuries Injuries that cause the employee to miss one or more days of work following an accident. Also known as *lost-time injuries*.

discipline The conditions within an organization whereby employees know what is expected of them in terms of the organization's rules, standards, or policies.

diversity Inclusion in the workplace of people with varied physical skills, sexual orientations, ages, religions, nationalities, ethnic groups, races, gender, and socioeconomic backgrounds.

dummies Dashed arrows that show the dependent relationships among activities.

E

economic order quantity (EOQ) The optimum number of units to order.

Education Amendments Act Prohibits discrimination because of sex against employees or students of any educational institution receiving financial aid from the federal government.

effort How hard a person works.

e-mail Electronic mail systems provided by networked and online systems.

employee assistance programs (EAPs) Programs developed by companies to help troubled employees. These may be of varied type and scope, ranging from the organization directly providing care to referring the employee to care providers.

employment agencies State and private services used in hiring certain skilled personnel for organizations; advantageous because the applicants may be already prescreened for the hiring organization.

employment arbitration An agreement that companies may require employees to sign that requires them to resolve any disputes by final and binding arbitration.

employment at will When employees are hired for an indefinite time period and do not have a contract limiting the circumstances under which they can be discharged, the employer can terminate the employees at any time for any or no reason at all.

employment parity When the proportion of protected employees employed by an organization equals the proportion in the organization's relevant labor market.

employment tests Common tools used in medium and large organizations to aid in the employee selection process, which may include aptitude, psychomotor, job knowledge, proficiency, interest, and psychological tests.

empowerment Gives subordinates substantial authority to make decisions.

energy costs Charges for electricity, gas, steam, and any other source of power.

entrepreneur A person who launches and runs their own business.

environmental change Includes all of the nontechnological changes that occur external to the organization.

Equal Employment Opportunity Commission (EEOC) One of two major federal enforcement agencies for equal employment opportunity. The other one is the Office of Federal Contract Compliance (OFCC).

Equal Pay Act This requires that all employers covered by the Fair Labor Standards Act (and others included in the 1972 extension) provide equal pay to men and women who perform work that is similar in skill, effort, and responsibility.

ergonomics Human engineering, concerned with improving productivity and safety by designing workplaces, tools, instruments, and so on, that take into account the physical abilities of people.

essay appraisals Requires the supervisor to write a series of statements about an employee's past performance, potential for promotion, strengths, and weaknesses.

esteem needs These needs include both self-esteem and the esteem of others.

ethics Standards or principles of conduct that govern the behavior of an individual or a group of individuals.

event   Denotes a point in time. The occurrence of an event signifies the completion of all activities leading up to it.

expected decisions   Decisions which can be anticipated, such as salary and promotion recommendations, or the purchase of a new piece of equipment.

exception principle   States that supervisors should concentrate their efforts on matters that deviate from the normal and let their employees handle routine matters.

Executive Order 11246   Issued in 1965 and amended by Executive Order 11375, requires federal contractors and subcontractors to meet certain affirmative action requirements.

extinction   Provides no positive consequences or removes previously provided positive consequences as a result of undesired behavior.

extrinsic rewards   Rewards that are directly controlled and distributed by the organization.

F

Family and Medical Leave Act   Enacted in 1993 to enable qualified employees to take prolonged unpaid leave in order to care for their family or their personal health without fear of losing their jobs.

feedback   The flow of information from the receiver to the sender.

felt conflict   Internal tensions between involved parties, in a conflict situation when the conflict is not yet out in the open.

five W's and an H   Expression relating to the change process, representing the following: what the change is, why the change is needed, whom the change will affect, when the change will take place, where the change will occur, and how the change will take place.

flextime   Flexible working hours allowing employees to choose, within limits, when they start and end their workday.

forced-choice rating   An evaluation method that requires the supervisor to choose which of two statements is either most (or least) applicable to the employee being reviewed.

forced-distribution ranking   The rater compares the performance of employees and places a certain percentage of employees at various performance levels.

formal plan   Written documented plan developed through a process that describes the organization's plans.

formal work groups   These result primarily from the organizing function of government.

frequency rate   The number of times that disabling injuries occur.

frustration   One form of intrapersonal conflict that occurs when people feel that something is stopping them from achieving goals that they would like to achieve.

functional departmentalization   When organization units are defined by the nature or function of the work.

functional plans   Derived from the plans of higher levels of management.

functions of management and supervision   The functions are planning, organizing, staffing, motivating, and controlling.

G

Gantt chart   A diagram on which the activities to be performed are usually shown vertically and the time required to perform them is usually shown horizontally.

gap analysis   Identifying where current situation falls short of a desired state.

geographic departmentalization   Occurs most frequently in organizations with operations or offices that are physically separated from each other.

glass ceiling   Refers to a level within the managerial hierarchy beyond which very few women or minorities advance.

goal   Similar to an objective, but broader in scope and usually longer range in its approach.

goal conflict   Occurs when an individual's goal has both positive and negative aspects or when competing or conflicting goals exist.

grapevine   The informal communication system resulting from casual contacts between friends or acquaintances in various organization units.

graphic rating scale appraisal   The supervisor is asked to evaluate an individual on such factors as initiative, dependability, cooperativeness, and quality of work.

grievance   A formal dispute between management and an employee or employees over some condition of employment.

grievant   Employee that formally complains about some condition of employment.

group cohesiveness   The degree of attraction or stick-togetherness of the group.

group conformity   The degree to which the members of the group accept and abide by the norms of the group.

group norm   An understanding among group members concerning how those members should behave.

groupthink   When the drive to achieve consensus among group members becomes so powerful that it overrides independent, realistic appraisals of alternative actions.

H

halo effect   Occurs when the supervisor allows a single, prominent characteristic of the interviewee/employee to dominate judgment of all other characteristics.

handicapped individual   Individual with a physical or mental impairment that substantially limits one or more major life activities.

Hawthorne effect   States that giving special attention to a group of employees (such as involving them in an experiment) changes their behavior.

Hazard Communications Standard   Establishes uniform requirements to ensure that the hazards of all chemicals imported into, produced, or used in the workplace are evaluated and that the results of these evaluations are transmitted to affected employers and exposed employees.

health insurance   Insurance which covers such things as normal hospitalization and outpatient doctor bills.

hot-stove rule   Discipline should be directed against the act rather than the person. Other key features of the rule are immediacy, advance warning, consistency, and impersonality.

human relations skills   Knowledge about human behavior and the ability to work well with people.

human resource forecasting   Process that attempts to determine the future human resource needs of the organization in light of the organization's objectives.

human resource planning (HRP)   Process of "getting the right number of qualified people into the right job at the right time." Also called *personnel planning.*

hygiene or **maintenance factors**   According to Herzberg, those factors that tend to demotivate or turn off employees, such as job status, interpersonal relations with supervisors and peers, the style of supervision that the person receives, company policy and administration, job security, working conditions, pay, and aspects of personal life that affect the work situation.

I

idiosyncrasy credit   Phenomenon that occurs when certain members who have made or are making significant contributions to the group's goals are allowed to take some liberties within the group.

incorporate ergonomics   Concerned with improving productivity and safety by designing workplaces tools, instruments, etc. that take into account the physical abilities of employees.

independent demand items   Finished goods or other end items.

indirect labor costs   Expenditures for labor that are not directly applied to the creation or delivery of the product or service.

informal work groups   Not defined by the organizing function.

informational reports   A report that presents only the facts.

injunction   A court order to prohibit certain actions.

innovation   Implementing a new idea into a way of doing things.

in-process inventories   Used to buffer differences in the rates of flow through the various operational processes.

input-output scheme   A technique developed by General Electric for use in solving energy-related problems. The first step under this method is to describe the desired output; the next step is to list all possible combinations of inputs that could lead to the desired output.

interest tests   Determine how a person's interests compare with the interests of successful people in a specific job.

internal changes   Changes internal to the organization, such as budget adjustments, methods changes, policy changes, reorganizations, and the hiring of new employees.

Internet   A global collection of independently operating yet interconnected computers.

interpersonal communication   Communication between individuals.

interpersonal conflict   Conflict that is external to the individual.

intranet   A private computer network that uses Internet products and technologies to provide multimedia applications to users within the organization.

intrapersonal conflict   Conflict that is internal to the individual.

intrapreneurship   Entrepreneurship practiced within a large or medium sized company.

intrinsic rewards   Rewards internal to the individual and normally derived from involvement in work activities.

inventory control   The process of monitoring and maintaining a supply of inventory adequate to meet customer demand but not greater than is necessary for that purpose.

ISO 9000   A set of quality standards created in 1987 by the International Organization for Standardization in Geneva, Switzerland.

ISO 14000   Similar in format to ISO 9000, ISO 14000 provides international environmental management standards for voluntary compliance.

J

job analysis   Determines the pertinent information related to the performance of a specific job.

job bidding   Employees bid on a job based on seniority, job skills, or other qualifications.

job description   A written portrayal of a job and the types of work performed in it.

job enlargement   Involves giving an employee more of a similar type of operation to perform.

job enrichment   An approach that involves upgrading the job by adding motivating factors.

job knowledge tests   Measure the applicant's job-related knowledge.

job posting   The posting of notices of available jobs in central locations throughout the organization.

job rotation   An employee learns several jobs and performs each job for a specific length of time. Also called *cross-training*.

job satisfaction   An individual's general attitude toward his or her job.

job specification   The qualifications necessary to perform the job.

just-in-time inventory control (JIT)   Pioneered in Japan but popular in the United States, a philosophy for production so that the right items arrive and leave as they are needed.

K

Kaizen   Means "good change" in Japanese.

Kaizen blitz   Occurs when an organization undertakes an intense Kaizen effort concentrated in a two- to five-day period.

L

Labor-Management Reporting and Disclosure (Landrum-Griffin) Act (1959)   The act is primarily concerned with the protection of the rights of individual union members. For example, it permits union members to sue their unions and it requires that any increase in union dues be approved by a majority of the members (on a secret ballot).

laissez-faire leader   Leader who allows the group members to do as they please, thus allowing them to make all the decisions.

latent conflict   When basic conditions for conflict exist but have not been recognized by the involved parties.

layout chart   A sketch of a facility that shows the physical arrangement of the facility and the major flow of work through it.

leader   Obtains followers and influences them in setting and achieving objectives.

leadership   The ability to influence people to willingly follow one's guidance or adhere to one's decisions.

leading   Involves directing and channeling employee behavior toward the accomplishment of work objectives and providing a workplace where people can be motivated to accomplish the work objectives.

lean manufacturing   A systematic approach to identifying and eliminating waste and non-value-added activities.

learning organization   An organization skilled at creating, acquiring, and transferring knowledge, and in modifying behavior to reflect the new knowledge.

leniency   The grouping of employee ratings at the positive end instead of spreading them throughout the performance scale.

Lewin's force field analysis   Theory that there are two natural sets of forces that impact on any change—those forces that resist the change and those forces that encourage the change.

line authority   Based on the superior-subordinate relationship. With line authority, there is a direct line of authority from the top to the bottom of the organization structure.

linking-pin concept   Because managers are members of overlapping groups, they link formal work groups to the total organization.

lost-time injuries   Injuries that cause the employee to miss one or more days of work following an accident. Also known as *disabling injuries*.

M

maintenance cost Labor and material costs incurred to repair and maintain equipment and facilities.

Malcolm Baldrige Award Administered by National Institute of Standards and Technology and can only be awarded to businesses located in the United States.

management by objectives (MBO) A style of supervising that has its roots in the planning function.

Managerial Grid® Two-dimensional grid used to identify and relate different styles of leadership.

manifest conflict Conflict that is out in the open and is obvious to the uninvolved parties.

materials handling The movement of materials, including raw materials, supplies, in-process materials, finished goods, and equipment.

matrix structure Forming horizontal project teams within two vertical line structure of the organization.

merit pay Employee pay raise based on his or her performance.

methods engineering The process of finding the most efficient way to accomplish a given task, also called work-methods improvement or work simplification.

motion or methods study Concerned with determining the most efficient way of doing a task or job.

motivating/motivation Getting employees to put forth maximum effort while doing their job.

motivation-maintenance approach (or dual factor approach or motivator-hygiene approach) Belief that factors which demotivate employees are usually associated with the work environment, such as job status, relations with peers, etc.

motivator factors Work-related motivating factors, such as achievement, recognition, responsibility, advancement, and the challenges of the job.

multi-rater assessment Questionnaire on the performance of the employee being evaluated that is filled out by managers, peers, customers, suppliers, or colleagues.

N

National Labor Relations Board (NLRB) Determines what the bargaining unit is (which employees the union will represent) and whether the authorization requirement has been fulfilled.

need hierarchy approach Based on the assumption that employees are motivated to satisfy a number of needs and that money can satisfy, directly or indirectly, only some of those needs.

noise Anything introduced into a message that is not included in the message.

nondirective counseling The employee assumes most of the initiative and the supervisor serves primarily as a listener. The employee is encouraged to discuss what he or she thinks is causing the problem and to develop solutions to it.

Nonprogrammed decisions Type of decision-making that is generally unstructured and involves a creative approach by the decision maker.

Nonverbal communication A form of interpersonal communication that does not involve speech.

O

objective A statement of a desired result or what is to be achieved.

occupational parity When the portion of protected employees employed in various occupations in the organization is equal to their proportion in the organization's relevant labor market.

Occupational Safety and Health Act (OSHA) Its purpose is "to assure so far as possible every working man and woman in the nation safe and healthful working conditions and to preserve our human resources."

Office of Federal Contract Compliance (OFCC) One of two major federal enforcement agencies for equal employment opportunity. The other one is the Equal Employment Opportunity Commission (EEOC).

on-the-job training (OJT) Instruction given by the supervisor or a senior employee in which a new employee is shown how the job is performed and then actually does it under the trainer's supervision.

operating supplies costs Expenditures for necessary items that do not become a part of the product or service.

organization chart Chart comprising a series of boxes connected with one or more lines to graphically represent the structure of an organization.

organization structure The result of grouping together work activities and the assignment of each grouping to a manager.

organizational conflict Conflict between employees and the organization.

organizational politics The practice of using means other than merit or good performance for bettering your position or gaining favor in the organization.

organizational rewards All types of rewards, both intrinsic and extrinsic, received as a result of employment by the organization.

organizing   Distributing the work among employees in the work group and arranging the work so that it flows smoothly.

orientation/orienting   The process of introducing new employees to the organization and to the work unit and the job.

overhead costs   Expenditures for physical space, staff services, research, advertising, and legal services.

P

paired-comparison ranking   Method in which the supervisor lists employee names down the left side of a sheet of paper. The supervisor then evaluates the performance of the first employee on the list against the performance of the second employee on the list. If the supervisor feels that the performance of the first employee is better than that of the second employee, he places a check mark by the first employee's name. The first employee is then compared to each of the other employees. In this way, he or she is compared with all the other employees on the list. The process is repeated for each of the other employees. The employee with the most check marks is evaluated to be the most valuable employee, and the employee with the least check marks is evaluated to be the least valuable.

paralanguage   A form of nonverbal communication that includes the pitch, tempo, loudness, and hesitations in the verbal communication.

parity principle   States that authority and responsibility must coincide.

PDCA cycle   An approach to methods improvement; the letters stand for plan/do/check/act.

perceived conflict   The basic conditions for conflict are recognized by one or both of the parties in a conflict situation.

perception   How people view situations.

performance   How well an employee is fulfilling the requirements of the job.

performance appraisal   A process that involves communicating to an employee how well the employee is performing the job and also, ideally, involves establishing a plan for improvement.

performance standards   Standards that set performance levels for machines, tasks, individuals, groups of individuals, or even the organization as a whole.

personal information manager   Software programs designed to provide digital time organizing and planning features to users.

peter principle   Tendency of individuals in a hierarchy to rise to their levels of incompetence.

physical needs   The basic needs for the human body that must be satisfied to sustain life. These needs include food, sleep, water, exercise, clothing, shelter, and so forth.

PIMs (personal information managers)   Software programs specifically designed to help manage individual time priorities and personal business.

planning   Determining the most effective means for achieving the work of the unit.

policies   Broad, general guidelines to action.

political conflicts   Conflicts that are planned and often intentionally started. They result from the promotion of self-interest on the part of an individual or a group.

polygraph   Also known as the lie detector, this device records physical changes in the body as the test subject answers a series of questions.

positive reinforcement   Providing a positive consequence as a result of desired behavior.

postaction control   A method for exercising control that focuses on detecting existing problems after they occur but before they reach crisis proportions.

power   The ability to get others to respond favorably to instructions and orders.

preference-expectancy approach   A theory based on the belief that people attempt to increase pleasure and decrease displeasure. According to this theory, which Victor Vroom pioneered, people are motivated to work if (1) they believe that their efforts will be rewarded and (2) they value the rewards that are being offered.

preliminary control   Method for exercising control, also sometimes called steering control, which focuses on attempting to prevent a problem from occurring.

problem employee   An employee whose behaviors repeatedly disrupt normal operations.

problem solving   The process of determining the appropriate responses or actions necessary to alleviate a problem.

problem-solving skills   The ability to analyze information and objectively reach a decision in order to solve a problem.

procedure   A series of related steps or tasks performed in sequential order to achieve a specific purpose.

process quality control   Quality control that relates to the control of a machine or an operation during the production process.

productivity   Units of output per employee hour.

product quality control   Quality control that relates to things (products, services, raw materials, etc.).

professional manager   Senior, middle, and supervisory managers, paid to perform management functions within a company.

proficiency tests   These measure how well the applicant can do a sample of the work that is to be performed.

programmed decisions   Decisions reached by an established or systematic procedure.

programmed instruction   Training method in which, after the material is presented in text form, the trainee is required to read and answer questions relating to the text.

protected groups   Classes of people identified by race, color, sex, age, religion, national origin, and mental and physical handicaps.

psychological tests   These measure personality characteristics.

psychomotor tests   These measure a person's strength, dexterity, and coordination.

punishment   Provides a negative consequence as a result of undesired behavior.

Pygmalion effect   This concept refers to the tendency of an employee to live up to the supervisor's expectations.

Q

quality   From a supervisor's perspective, quality refers to the degree to which the product or service design specifications are met.

quality assurance   The idea of "building in" quality as opposed to "inspecting it in."

quality at the source   Refers to the philosophy of making each employee responsible for the quality of his or her work.

quality circle   A voluntary group of employees that meets periodically for the sole purpose of solving quality problems and identifying ways of improving quality.

R

ranking methods   Types of performance appraisal that use some method for ranking employees against each other.

Raw materials costs   Expenditures for raw material that are directly applied to the creation of the product or service.

recruiting/recruitment   Involves seeking and attracting qualified candidates for job vacancies.

reengineering   A one-time concerted effort, initiated from the top of the organization, to make major improvements in processes used to produce products or services.

reference checks   Checks that may be performed on a potential employee's personal and academic background, and his or her past employment.

Rehabilitation Act of 1973   Protects handicapped people by ensuring that people are not refused a job merely because of their handicap if the handicap does not affect their ability to do the job.

reinforcement approach   Reinforced behavior is more likely to be repeated.

reliability   Results of a test are reproducible.

resource allocation   The efficient allocation of people, materials, and equipment so as to successfully meet the objectives that have been established.

responsibilities   The things that make up the supervisor's job.

responsibility   Accountability for reaching objectives, using resources properly, and adhering to organizational policy.

right-to-work laws   A law passed by individual states prohibiting union shops.

routing   Determining the best sequence of operations.

rule   Requires that specific and definite actions be taken or not taken.

S

safety committee   Employees directly involved in the operation of a safety program; may include inspecting, observing work practices, investigating accidents, and making recommendations.

safety needs   Needs concerned with protection against danger, threat, or deprivation.

Sarbanes-Oxley Act (SOX)   The Public Company Accounting Reform and Investor Protection Act, an important piece of corporate governance legislation passed in 2002.

satisfaction   An employee's general attitude toward the job, resulting from several specific factors.

scalar principle   States that authority flows one link at a time from the top of the organization to the bottom.

scheduling   The precise timetable that is to be followed in producing products or services.

scrap or waste costs   Expenditures for products, parts, or services that cannot be reworked or reused and that do not meet quality standards.

screening control   A method for exercising control, also called concurrent control, that focuses on things that happen as inputs are being transformed into outputs.

selection   To choose the best person for the job from the candidates.

self-actualization/self-fulfillment   The needs of people to reach their full potential in terms of their abilities and interests.

self-directed work teams (SDWT)   Teams in which members are empowered to control the work they do without a formal supervisor.

semantics   The study of the meaning of words and symbols.

servant leadership   Philosophy of leadership based on the belief that the leader exists to meet the needs of the people whom he or she nominally leads.

severity rate   Indicates how severe the accidents were and how long the injured parties were out of work. Only disabling injuries are used in determining frequency and severity rates.

sexual harassment   Unwelcome sexual advances, requests for sexual favors, and other verbal or physical conduct of a sexual nature are considered sexual harassment.

Sherman Antitrust Act of 1890   A law making it illegal to restrain trade.

sit-down strike   When employees stay on the job but refuse to work.

situational approach to leadership   This leadership approach attempts to identify the particular styles of leadership that are appropriate for particular situations.

six sigma   A precise art of statistical tools, meaning six standard deviations from the mean. The philosophy of six sigma entails realizing this very high level of quality by examining and improving the entire production and/or service system.

skills inventory   Consolidates information about the organization's current human resources.

small business   A company that is independently owned and operated, generally has fewer than 500 employees.

SMART characteristics   SMART stands for the following criteria for attaining objectives: specific, measurable, achievable, relevant, and time-based.

smartphones   Telephone computer devices converged with full-blown embedded computer operating devices. Smartphones function as "mini laptops" with cell phone capabilities.

social needs   Needs that include love, affection, and belonging.

social responsibility   Following through on the obligations individuals and businesses have to help solve social problems.

span of control principle   The number of employees a supervisor can effectively manage.

staff authority   Used to support and advise line authority.

staffing function   Supervision function concerned with obtaining and developing qualified people.

standard operating procedures (SOPs)   Well-established and formalized procedures.

standards   Used to set performance levels.

standard time   Amount of time necessary to perform a specific task or group of tasks.

steering control   Method for exercising control, also sometimes called preliminary control, which focuses on attempting to prevent a problem from occurring.

strategic management   The process of developing strategic plans and keeping them current as changes occur.

strategic or corporate plan   A plan developed by the top management of an organization.

stress   An arousal of mind and body in response to real or perceived demands or threats.

strike   An action that occurs when employees leave their job and refuse to come back to work until a contract has been signed.

structural or intergroup conflict   Conflict that results from the nature of the organization structure and is independent of the personalities involved.

structured interview   Supervisor knows the questions to be asked and records results.

supervision   The first level of management in the organization, concerned with encouraging the members of a work unit to contribute positively toward accomplishing the organization's goals and objectives.

supervisory plans   Derived from the plans of higher levels of management.

supportive leaders   Leaders who are genuinely interested in the well-being of group members and are sensitive to the employees as human beings.

synectics   Use of metaphorical thinking to make the "familiar strange and the strange familiar" in order to creatively solve problems.

systemic discrimination   Large differences in either occupational or employment parity.

T

Taft-Hartley Act of 1947   Spelled out rights of and restrictions on unions.

team building Process by which the formal work group develops an awareness of those conditions that keep it from functioning effectively and then requires the group to eliminate those conditions.

technical skills Knowledge about such things as machines, processes, and methods of production.

technological change Includes such things as new equipment, machinery, and processes.

technology New and improved methods, new ideas, inventions, innovations, new and improved materials.

telecommuting The practice of periodically or regularly working from home, from another remote location, or while traveling.

Theory X Maintains that the average employee dislikes work.

Theory Y States that people like to work, and it comes as naturally as rest and play.

time caddy Chart used to prepare a time inventory.

time inventory Analysis of the work day to see how time is actually spent.

time study The analysis of a task to determine the elements of work required to perform it, the order in which these elements occur, and the times required to perform them effectively. The objective of a time study is to determine how long it should take an average person to perform the task in question.

Title VI of the Civil Rights Act of 1964 Prohibits discrimination based on race, color, or national origin in all programs or activities that receive federal financial aid in order to provide employment.

Title VII of the Civil Rights Act of 1964 Amendments to this act make it illegal to hire, fire, pay, or take other management actions on the basis of race, color, religion, national origin, or sex.

"to do" list Itemized list of tasks to be accomplished in the immediate future.

total quality management (TQM) A management philosophy that emphasizes managing the entire organization so that it excels in all dimensions of products and services that are important to the customer.

traditional approach Based on the assumption that money is the primary motivator of people.

training The acquisition by employees of the skills, information, and attitudes necessary for improving their effectiveness.

transactional leadership The approach that leaders engage in a bargaining relationship with their followers.

transformational leadership The approach that leaders engage in changing the dynamic of the relationship with their followers.

troubled employee Employee whose job performance is affected by personal problems that normal counseling or disciplinary measures cannot correct.

U

unexpected decisions Unanticipated decisions such as an employee requesting a transfer, or equipment malfunctions affecting production.

union organization drive Started by the employees of the organization when, for one or more reasons, a group of employees determines that a union is desirable.

union shop The union can require an employee who has been working for a specified period of time to become a member.

union steward An operative employee whom the union members elect to work with them on handling their grievances.

unity of command principle States that an employee should have one and only one immediate boss.

unstructured interviews These have no definite checklist of questions or preplanned strategy.

V

validation Test results are proven to be a significant predictor of an applicant's ability to perform job-related tasks.

vestibule training The individual uses procedures and equipment similar to those of the actual job, but which are located in a special area called a vestibule.

Veterans Readjustment Act Requires federal government contractors and subcontractors to take affirmative action to hire and promote Vietnam War and disabled veterans.

virtual work team A group of team members working together across geographical or organizational boundaries by means of information technology.

W

wellness or work/life program Company-implemented program designed to prevent illness and enhance employee wellness.

whistle blowing   Disclosing what an employee believes to be wrong doings within the organization, usually undertaken after determining that employee's manager does not support such claims.

wildcat strike   A strike in which employees leave their job and refuse to work during the contract period.

workaholism   Working to the exclusion of everything else in one's life.

workers' compensation   Protection for the worker from loss of income and extra expenses associated with work-related injuries.

work-methods improvement   Used to find the most efficient way to accomplish a given task.

workplace violence   Any form of violence that occurs in the workplace.

work simplification   The process of finding the most efficient way to accomplish a given task, also called methods engineering or work-methods improvement.

work-standards approach   Attempts are made to establish objective measures of an employee's work performance.

Y

yellow-dog contract   An agreement between an employee and management that, as a condition of employment, the employee will not join a labor union.

Z

zero-base budgeting   Requires a supervisor to justify in detail an entire budget request.

zero-defects program   A program which tries to create a positive attitude toward the prevention of low quality.

COMPANY INDEX

Quality circles, 185, 189, 355–356, 359
Quality control, 351
Quality of work life, 9

R

Ranking methods, 295, 298–299, 307
Raw material costs, 373
Raw-materials inventories, 381
Reading material, 146–147
Recommended referral, 242
Recruiting, 195, 211
Recruitment, 199–201
Reengineering, 353
Reference checks, 204
Rehabilitation Act of 1973, 218, 221
Reinforcement approach, to motivation, 69, 73
Reliability, 225
Religion, employment discrimination and, 228–229
Report writing, 146
Resource allocation, 127
Resource usage standards, 346
Responding, 46
Responsibility, 104
    delegating, 165–171
    supervisor and, 162–163, 171
Revenue standards, 346
Right-to-work laws (RTW), 329
Role stress, 278
Routing, 127
Rules, 126

S

Safety
    causes of accidents, 393–394, 404
    cost of accidents, 391–393, 404
    measuring, 394–395, 404–405
    Occupational Safety and Health Act (OSHA), 399–404, 405
    program, 395–398, 405
    promoting, 395–396, 405
    specific hazards, 394
    supervisor's responsibility for, 390, 404
    violence in the workplace, 398–399, 405
Safety committee, 396
Safety needs, and motivation, 64, 65
Sarbanes-Oxley Act, 101, 107
    major points of, 102
Satisfaction, 72
Scalar principle, 164–165
Scheduling, 127
Scrap costs, 374
Screening controls, 347
Selection, 195, 211

Self-actualization, and motivation, 65–66
Self-directed work team (SDWT), 186, 189
Self-fulfilling prophecy, 63, 259
Self-fulfillment, and motivation, 65–66
Self-Help (Smiles), 141
Self-referral, 242
Semantics, 43–44, 53
Servant leadership, 258, 263
Severity rate, 394–395, 404–405
Sexual harassment, preventing, 227–228, 230
Sexual orientation, employment discrimination and, 220, 230
Sherman Antitrust Act of 1890, 328, 330, 335
Shewhart Cycle; *See* PDCA Cycle
Situational leadership, 261
Six sigma, 353, 359
Skills inventory, 196–198
Small business, 12, 13
Small Business Administration (SBA), 12
Smart characteristics, 121–122
Smartphones, 144
Socializing, within the organization, 106–107, 108
Social needs, and motivation, 65
Social responsibility, 103–104, 108
Social stress, 278
Society for Human Resource Management (SHRM), 151, 241
Sole proprietors, 11
Span of control principle, 165
Span of management; *See* Span of control principle
Staff authority, 161, 171
Staffing, 6–7, 13
    internal and external sources, 198–199
Staffing function, 195
Standard operating procedures (SOPs), 125
Standards, categories and examples of, 346
Standard time, 369
Steering controls, 347
Strategic management, 118
Strategic plan, 117, 118
Stress management, 277–281
    guidelines for, 280, 281
Structural conflict, 273–275, 281
Structured interviews, 205
Substance Abuse and Mental Health Services Administration (SAMHSA), 238
Supervision
    defined, 3, 13
    functions of, 5–8
    job titles, 5
    keys to success, 7–8, 13
    need for, 3–5
    progression of jobs into, 5, 6

Supervision, 19
Supervisors
    antidiscrimination laws and, 224–226
    authority and, 160–162
    change and, 79–90
    ethical conduct by, 100, 107
    informal work groups and, 187–189
    leadership today and, 262
    motivation and, 69–71, 73
    objectives and, 123
    OSHA and, 402–403
    power and, 163
    preventing accidents, 397–398, 405
    responsibilities and unions, 332, 333–334
    responsibility and, 162–163, 171
    role in accident process, 398
    role in cost reduction and control, 372–373, 383
    role in planning, 119, 120, 130–131
    safety and, 390, 404
    skills of, 7–9, 13
    strategic planning and, 118
    typical responsibilities of, 163
Supervisory control
    in practice, 349–350
    tools for, 347–349, 358
Supervisory Management, 19
Supervisory plans, 119, 120
Supportive leaders, 256
Symbolic analogies, 32
Synectics, 31–32
Systemic discrimination, 223, 230

T

Taft-Hartley Act, 4–5, 329, 330, 335
Tardiness, 379, 383
Task stress, 278
Task structure, 261
Team building, 182–183, 184, 189
Teams
    importance of, 182–186
    phases in the life of, 185, 189
    steps for building, 184
Technical skills, 7–9, 13
Technological change, 80
Technology, 366
Telecommuting, 150
Telephone, time management and, 148
Theory X, 259, 260, 263
Theory Y, 259, 263
360-degree feedback, 295, 299, 307
Thriving on Chaos (Peters), 79
Time, alternative work schedules and, 149–151, 152
Time caddy, 142, 143
Time inventory, 142